The Philosophy of Social Science Reader

The Philosophy of Social Science Reader is an outstanding and comprehensive collection of key readings in the philosophy of social science, covering all the essential issues, problems, and debates in the field. Each section is carefully introduced by the editors and the readings placed in context.

The anthology is organized into seven clear parts:

- Values and Social Science
- Causal Inference and Explanation
- Interpretation
- Rationality and Choice
- Individualism
- Norms
- Cultural Evolution.

Readings from key philosophers and social scientists are included, such as Ernest Nagel, Ian Hacking, John Searle, Clifford Geertz, Daniel Kahneman, Steven Lukes and Richard Dawkins.

Daniel Steel is Associate Professor of Philosophy at Michigan State University, USA. His research on causal inference and explanation in social science and biology has appeared in *Philosophy of the Social Sciences*, *The British Journal of the Philosophy of Science*, and in his book, *Across the Boundaries: Extrapolation in Biology and Social Science* (2008).

Francesco Guala is Associate Professor in the Department of Economics at the University of Milan, Italy. He is the author of *The Methodology of Experimental Economics* (2005) and of many articles published in philosophical and scientific journals. He won the *2001 Prize of the International Network of Economic Method* and the *2001 History of Economic Analysis Award*. He is currently book review editor of the journal *Economics and Philosophy*.

The Philosophy of
Social Science Reader

Edited by

Daniel Steel and Francesco Guala

Routledge
Taylor & Francis Group

LONDON AND NEW YORK

This edition published 2011
by Routledge
2 Park Square, Milton Park, Abingdon, Oxon, OX14 4RN

Simultaneously published in the USA and Canada
by Routledge
270 Madison Ave, New York, NY 10016

Routledge is an imprint of the Taylor & Francis Group, an informa business

© 2011 Daniel Steel and Francesco Guala for selection and editorial matter;
individual contributors for their contributions.

Typeset in Perpetua and Bell Gothic by
Florence Production Ltd, Stoodleigh, Devon
Printed and bound in Great Britain by
CPI Antony Rowe, Chippenham, Wiltshire

British Library Cataloguing in Publication Data
A catalogue record for this book is available from the British Library

Library of Congress Cataloging in Publication Data
The philosophy of social science reader/edited by Daniel Steel &
Francesco Guala.
     p. cm.
   Includes bibliographical references and index.
  1. Social sciences—Philosophy.   I. Steel, Daniel, 1970–.
  II. Guala, Francesco, 1970–.
  H61.15.P484 2010
  300.1—dc22   2010015196

ISBN13: 978–0–415–77968–5 (hbk)
ISBN13: 978–0–415–77969–2 (pbk)

Contents

Figures

Acknowledgments

We were helped in this project by a number of people who have kindly shared their expertise (and, in several cases, their syllabi) in the philosophy of social science: Anna Alexandrova, Natalie Gold, Till Grüne, Harold Kincaid, Martin Kusch, Daniel Little, Robert Northcott, Wendy Parker, Nigel Pleasants, Thomas Uebel, and the late Susan Hurley deserve a big "thank you" from both of us. Comments from four anonymous reviewers of the original proposal were extremely helpful and resulted in a number of changes, including the insertion of an anchoring classic chapter at the head of each section. We are also grateful to the authors of the selections for allowing their work to be reprinted here. Finally, we would like to thank the two editors at Routledge, Katy Hamilton and Adam Johnson, who suggested a new philosophy of social science reader and who worked diligently to ferry the manuscript through the various stages of preparation for publication.

Permissions

To comply with limits of space most chapters have been abridged. The publisher and the editors wish to thank the following for permission to reprint material under copyright:

Part I: Social values and social science

Nagel, E. (1961) "The Value-Oriented Bias of Social Inquiry", Section V of Ch. 14 of *The Structure of Science*, Harcourt, Brace & World, Inc., pp. 185–190. © 1961 E. Nagel. Reprinted by permission of Hackett Publishing Company, Inc. All rights reserved.

Hacking, I. (1995) "The Looping Effects of Human Kinds", in D. Sperber, D. Premack, and A. Premack (eds.), *Causal Cognition: A Multidisciplinary Debate*, Clarendon Press, pp. 351–383. © 1995 I Hacking. Oxford University Press. Reproduced by kind permission.

Fricker, M. (2006) "Powerlessness and Social Interpretation", *Episteme* 3, Edinburgh University Press, pp. 96–108. Reproduced by kind permission.

Wylie, A. (2007) "The Feminism Question in Science: What Does it Mean to 'Do Social Science as a Feminist'?", in S. N. Hesse-Biber (ed.), *Handbook of Feminist Research: Theory and Praxis*, SAGE, pp. 567–577. © 2007 SAGE Publications Inc. Reprinted by Permission of SAGE Publications Inc.

Part II: Causal inference and explanation

Hempel, C. (1942) "The Function of General Laws in History", *Journal of Philosophy* XXXIX, 2 (January 15, 1942), pp. 35–48. Reproduced by kind permission.

Kincaid, H. (1996) "Causes, Confirmation, and Explanation", Ch. 3 of *Philosophical Foundations of the Social Sciences*, Cambridge University Press, pp. 58–100 [Abridged]. © 1996 Cambridge University Press, reproduced with permission.

Woodward, J. (2000) "Explanation and Invariance in the Special Sciences", *British Journal of the Philosophy of Science* 51, Oxford University Press, pp. 197–254. © 2000 Oxford University Press. Reproduced by kind permission.

Steel, D. (2004) "Social Mechanisms and Causal Inference", *Philosophy of the Social Sciences* 34, SAGE, pp. 55–78. © 2004 SAGE Publications. Reprinted by Permission of SAGE Publications.

Part III: Interpretation

Part IV: Rationality and choice

Part V: Methodological individualism

Part VI: Norms, conventions, and institutions

Lewis, D. (1969) "Coordination and Convention" and "Common Knowledge", selections from Ch. 1 and Ch. 2 of *Convention: A Philosophical Study*, 1969 Harvard University Press. (Reprinted 2002 by Blackwell, Oxford). Reproduced by kind permission of John Wiley and Sons.

Gilbert, M. (2008) "Social Convention Revisited", *Topoi* 27, Springer, pp. 5–16. 2008 Springer Netherlands. Reproduced by kind permission.

Searle, J. (2005) "What Is An Institution?", *Journal of Institutional Economics* 1, Cambridge University Press, pp. 1–22. © 2005 The JOIE Foundation, published by Cambridge University Press, reproduced with permission.

Bicchieri, C. (2006) "The Rules We Live By", Ch. 1 of *The Grammar of Society*, Cambridge University Press. © Cristina Bicchieri 2006, published by Cambridge University Press, reproduced with permission.

Part VII: Cultural evolution

Dawkins, R. (1976) "Memes: The New Replicators", Ch. 11 of *The Selfish Gene*, Oxford University Press, pp. 189–201. © 1976 Oxford University Press. Reproduced by kind permission.

Sperber, D. (1996) "Selection and Attraction in Cultural Evolution", Ch. 5 of *Explaining Culture: A Naturalistic Approach*, Blackwell, pp. 98–118. Reproduced by kind permission of the author and John Wiley and Sons.

Alexander, J. and B. Skyrms (1999) "Bargaining with Neighbors: Is Justice Contagious?", *Journal of Philosophy* 96: 588–598. Reproduced by kind permission.

Richerson, P. and R. Boyd (2005) "Culture Evolves", Ch. 3 of *Not by Genes Alone: How Culture Transformed Human Evolution,* University of Chicago Press, pp. 58–98. © 2005 University of Chicago Press. Reproduced by kind permission.

DANIEL STEEL AND FRANCESCO GUALA

INTRODUCTION

PUBLISHING A BOOK LIKE THIS implicitly raises two interconnected questions: Why study the philosophy of social science and why publish a new anthology on the topic? Luckily the answers are pretty obvious in our case. The answer to the first question is that social science studies topics—such as economic growth, employment, crime, social inequality, cultural conflicts, and so on—that matter enormously to almost everyone, and philosophy is important to social science. For example, there is little consensus across the social sciences as to basic methods, aims, and fundamental assumptions about human beings, and disputes on such topics are inevitably linked to long-standing discussions in philosophy. The answer to the second question is that the philosophy of social science has changed quite dramatically over the last two decades. So a new anthology is required to keep track of the best research, and to map the moving boundaries of this important subfield of philosophy. In this introductory section, we group these changes under four headings: Disunity, Interdisciplinarity, Naturalism, and Values. As we shall see, some of these themes are truly revolutionary with respect to the discipline as it was configured until the 1980s, while others modulate or build on approaches that have been there all along in the history of philosophy and social science. In any case, collectively they have led to a radical restructuring of the debates and even the styles of research of philosophers of social science. To appreciate the significance of these recent developments it is necessary to reconstruct briefly the trajectory of the discipline over the last half century, focusing in particular on its relation to the philosophy of natural science. This brief survey also serves to illustrate some of the ways in which philosophical questions are relevant to social science theory and practice.

Disunity

The philosophy of social science has been for a long time the Cinderella of philosophy. For much of the twentieth century philosophers' views of science were inspired mainly by physics, which was taken as a point of reference both in epistemology (its methods of inquiry were considered *the* methods of science) and in ontological matters (the scientific worldview was fundamentally the point of view of physics). In the 1950s and 1960s the logical empiricists shaped the debates on the so-called "special sciences" by advocating for biology, psychology, economics, sociology (etc.), standards that were inspired by physics.

For example, one group of issues dealt with the applicability of Carl Hempel's (1965) deductive-nomological model of explanation to the social sciences. This discussion proceeded on the assumption that, if social science is to provide genuinely scientific explanations, it must possess laws that resemble those of physics (Winch 1958, Rosenberg 1988). However, the "can-social-science-be-squeezed-into-the-logical-empiricist-model" debate entered a state of crisis in the 1980s, for several reasons. First, philosophers questioned the adequacy of the logical empiricist account even for the "core" case of physics (e.g. Cartwright 1983, Hacking 1983, Salmon 1984). As a consequence Hempel's model of explanation and the related "Standard View" of theories (Suppe 1974) were abandoned, and there are now a number of proposals about scientific explanation that are not premised on universal laws of nature. Secondly, and simultaneously, philosophers working on biology, economics, neuroscience, and so forth, demonstrated convincingly that each scientific discipline uses methods of inquiry and explanation that are suited to their particular domain of investigation. The success or failure of each method depends both on the goals to be achieved by scientists, and on contingent matters of fact that ought to be investigated empirically.

This new "disunity of science" movement (Galison and Stump eds. 1996) had a liberating effect in the philosophy of social science too. Many philosophers had argued since the nineteenth century that the study of human behavior requires different tools from those of natural science. The distinction between *Natür* and *Humanwissenschaften*, explanation and interpretation, was central in the *Methodenstreit* that agitated European intellectual life from 1870 until the 1930s, and re-emerged powerfully in the 1960s and 1970s with the diffusion of the Continental hermeneutic tradition in Anglo-American philosophy (e.g. Taylor 1971, Rorty 1979). By framing the debate in terms of "natural" vs. "human" science, however, even anti-positivist philosophers tended to rely on a priori arguments (on human freedom and determinism, or the nature of intentional action) that were detached from actual scientific practice. Moreover, anti-positivists bought a view of natural science – the logical positivist picture – that we now consider largely incorrect (see Geertz 1994 for an insightful discussion). Finally, their arguments clash with the fact that social scientists sometimes do use methods (models, styles of reasoning) borrowed from natural science, and profitably so. Whether these methods work or not, then, has probably less to do with general truths about "the" appropriate methodology for social science, than with scientists' detailed knowledge of the contexts and objectives of their research.

Interdisciplinarity

It is somewhat ironic that while the reductionistic model of science was gradually losing its philosophical appeal, the special sciences themselves were busy constructing bridges between their various branches. Recognition of the disunity of science, therefore, does not imply – and has not fostered – an insulation of the social sciences from neighbour disciplines. On the contrary, there is now increasing collaboration between anthropology, economics, and political science (*internal* contamination), as well as between each of these disciplines and psychology, biology, and neuroscience (*external* contamination). This cross-fertilization has produced a *proliferation* of research subfields and the birth of several hybrid styles of theorizing, instead of the progressive reduction forecasted by the logical empiricist model of science (e.g. Oppenheim and Putnam 1958). When social scientists speak of unity, these days, they mean a unity of purpose and language, but within a plurality of methods and styles of research (Gintis 2009).

The greatest source of influence from outside the social sciences has probably come from cognitive science. The cognitive sciences are themselves a striking example of successful eclecticism, covering diverse fields such as linguistics, psychology, and computer science. Since coming to maturity in the 1980s they have provided social scientists with a wealth of empirical data and a range of theoretical techniques for modelling human cognitive processes—from decision making to causal inference, learning, and imitation. These models have filled important holes in some social science disciplines, and complemented existing models (like those of rational choice theory) in those areas, like economics, that had already reached a high level of theoretical sophistication (e.g. Turner 2001, Ross 2005).

Philosophy, meanwhile, has not been immune from the cognitive revolution. Indeed, the best naturalistic work in epistemology, ethics, and the philosophy of mind makes heavy use of the data and theories of contemporary cognitive science. A fraction of this work has substantial implications for the social sciences and the direction they will take over the next decade. In some cases—like the fast progress of brain-imaging technology—it is still too early to say what the future will bring us, but it is safe to predict that these cross-contaminations will raise important questions about explanation, modelling, prediction, and epistemic weight, which will call for philosophical analysis and resolution.

Naturalism

It is useful to distinguish between two "*naturalisms,*" and the way they have influenced the philosophy of social science. Naturalism, broadly speaking, is a family of views stressing the centrality of science in philosophy (De Caro and MacArthur eds. 2004). In the philosophy of social science, unfortunately, it has been indentified for a long time with the thesis that social scientists should endorse the methods and standards of natural science (especially physics) (Bhaskar 1979). While this monistic sort of naturalism has by and large been rejected, another naturalistic thesis has become increasingly popular: the claim that philosophy is contiguous with science—or that science and philosophy enjoy a fruitful relation of mutual support, rather than one being somehow superior or subordinated to the other (Guala 2007).

Having oscillated between extreme arrogance ("philosophy as the queen of science") and modesty ("philosophy as the under-labourer of science"), many philosophers now endorse a middle ground position, according to which the distinction between scientific and philosophical questions is at best fuzzy and partly conventional. Philosophers address questions that are similar to those of science, albeit perhaps at a higher level of abstraction, and cannot afford to ignore scientific results and methodologies. At the same time, because scientists often ask philosophical questions (or make philosophical assumptions in their work) they can benefit from the expertise and skills that philosophers have developed over 2000 years of struggle with such issues.

This contamination has made the philosophy of social science an exciting arena for philosophers and scientists alike. It has also reinforced its reputation as an area of philosophy that actually matters. Unlike the philosophy of physics—which has had marginal or no impact on scientific research—the philosophy of social science has always been an important force of change within the social sciences. Hempel's first defence of the deductive-nomological model for example occurs in a paper (Hempel 1942) devoted to *history*. This is no accident, and indeed was part of a project of reform intended to lead the social sciences onto the same path followed by progressive sciences like physics. Philosophers, to put it differently, thought they had a lot to *learn* from physics, and something to *teach* social science. Most of the gains of philosophical research were to be had in the relatively underdeveloped areas of science, rather than at its most advanced frontier.

Although they have overcome their physics' envy, philosophers luckily have not abandoned their old ambition of informing social science. On the contrary, some of the best work done in recent years has taken place at the borders between philosophy and science, and is aimed explicitly at improving the quality of scientific research. This is important, not only because it invites a sane and adult collaboration between philosophers and scientists—free of inferiority or superiority complexes—but also because it contributes to making progress in an area that is immensely important for our everyday lives and aspirations. Although the magnificent technologies inspired by physics and biology (computers, lasers, medical treatments, genetically modified food) provoke reactions of admiration and awe in the media, we often forget that the social sciences and their technologies also have enormous effects on our lives. A bad social policy can kill thousands of children, a misguided political reform can cause the collapse of whole nations, and bad reforms are often the consequences of bad scientific ideas or our incapacity to put good ideas into practice.

Values

Policies must be judged by their success relative to certain goals, and which goals are to be achieved depends to a large extent on the values shared by the members of a community. The importance of social science for policy, therefore, results in a complex relationship with normative, moral and political issues (Kincaid et al., eds. 2007). This is not only unavoidable, but in many ways it is also a desirable feature of social science research. Social science is value-laden because it matters, not because of the alleged unscientific attitude of its practitioners. The main reason why values affect the social sciences more than, for example, astronomy is simply that the former deal with issues (such as poverty, population growth, or democracy) that are quite literally vital for us. Whether the universe is expanding or not, in contrast, is an intellectual curiosity most people do not really care about once they have finished reading the Sunday literary supplement.

This approach marks another major departure from the philosophical views that have dominated the twentieth century. While supporters of the positive/normative divide castigated social scientists for not respecting the "value-neutrality" of scientific research (e.g. Friedman 1953), their opponents often took the diametrically opposite view that social scientists should be openly activist and support specific political projects (Habermas 1971). An emerging strand of the philosophy of science literature attempts to develop a third path between these two extremes by recognizing the inevitable role of values in the course of social science research while at the same time taking seriously the need to maintain scientific objectivity and integrity. With respect to the philosophy of social science in particular, this "third way" involves an analysis of the ways in which social science shapes and is shaped by the social phenomena it studies and of how ethical and political values are enmeshed in that reciprocal process. The section on values features discussions of the value-laden dimensions of the interplay between social science and social reality, as well as chapters exploring the question of what an activist social science would be and how it could be done without compromising scientific standards.

Plan

The contents of the volume have been chosen to reflect the themes outlined above. The choice of topics and chapters has been guided mainly by an interest in *new* developments in the philosophy of social science. Most of the chapters reprinted here were originally published between 1990 and 2009. To provide a historical perspective, however, each section opens with a classic chapter that has shaped the field and still exerts some influence on current debates. Even then, we haven't gone back too much in time, and we have mainly selected contributions from the 1960s and 1970s. Like all intellectual enterprises, philosophy thrives when the participants share a conceptual background and a terminology that allows fruitful communication and mutual criticism. Since background assumptions and vocabulary tend to change over time, older contributions now have mostly an antiquarian interest. Of course reading the classics can shed light on important matters, and even lead to rediscovering unjustly neglected ideas. But since other anthologies do include older classics (e.g. Martin and MacIntyre, eds. 1994, Delanty and Strydom, eds. 2003) it would have made little sense to reproduce them here, either *in toto* or in part.

We modified the traditional sequence of topics by placing the issue of values upfront, rather than leaving as an afterthought at the end. This departure from tradition strikes us as desirable for two reasons. First, big questions about the relationships between social science and the broader political and moral currents of society are an inherently interesting topic, and hence a good lead in for students. Second, it is important to think about the overarching aims and goals of any enterprise before diving into the minutiae of disagreements among the particular approaches. The sequence of ensuing topics attempts to follow a logical thread in which the subsequent section addresses questions and issues that would naturally arise from the prior one. The section after the initial one on values deals with causation and explanation, and devotes a large amount of space to the work on causation and causal mechanisms that has loomed large in the debate of the last two decades. The material naturally follows the values section, since causation is directly related to policy questions: any perspective about how society should be changed inevitably rests on causal claims about the explanation of its current problems. Interpretation is a good follow-up to causation, because it is traditionally treated as an alternative non-causal mode of explaining social phenomena. But interpretation presumes some account of how humans reason and make decisions, which is the topic of the subsequent section on rationality. The section on methodological individualism follows naturally on the discussion of rationality, since the central question in that debate is whether models of individual decision making provide a general basis for explanation in social science. The section on norms highlights the central issues of the previous two sections, as the primary issue in that debate is whether, and if so how, models of individual reasoning and decision making can account for social norms. Finally, the discussions about norms and rationality are a good preparation for the literature on cultural evolution. Not only does the literature on cultural evolution utilize many of the same game-theoretic concepts and models, but the evolution of social norms is one of the central issues for students of cultural evolution.

As can be seen from this list, there are some traditional philosophy of social science topics—such as functional explanation—that we have not included, and some less traditional topics—such as cultural evolution—that we have. The reasons for these choices are a combination of space availability and a sense of what the most thriving topics are in the literature. For example, while we regard functional explanation as a worthy topic for philosophers of social science, that topic has received far less attention in recent years than issues relating to social norms and cultural evolution. Since this volume aims to provide an introduction to the current literature on the philosophy of social science, we have endeavored to select topics and readings that represent the contemporary state of the field.

References

Bhaskar, R. (1979) *The Possibility of Naturalism*. London: Routledge.

Cartwright, N. (1983) *How the Laws of Physics Lie*. Oxford: Clarendon Press.

De Caro, M. and MacArthur, D. (eds.) (2004) *Naturalism in Question*. Cambridge, MA: Harvard University Press.

Delanty, G. and Strydom, P. (eds.) (2003) *Philosophies of Social Science: The Classic and Contemporary Readings*. Maidenhead: Open University Press.

Friedman, M. (1953) "The Methodology of Positive Economics," in *Essays in Positive Economics*. Chicago, IL: University of Chicago Press.

Galison, P. and Stump, D. (eds.) (1996) *The Disunity of Science: Boundaries, Contexts, and Power*. Stanford, CA: Stanford University Press.

Geertz, C. (1994) "The Strange Estrangement: Taylor and the Natural Sciences," in *Available Light: Anthropological Reflections on Philosophical Topics*. Princeton, NJ: Princeton University Press.

Gintis, H. (2009) *The Bounds of Reason: Game Theory and the Unification of Behavioral Science*. Princeton, NJ: Princeton University Press.

Guala, F. (2007) "The Philosophy of Social Science: Metaphysical *and* Empirical," *Philosophy Compass* 2: 954–80.

Habermas, J. (1971) *Knowledge and Human Interests*. Boston, MA: Beacon.

Hacking, I. (1983) *Representing and Intervening*. Cambridge: Cambridge University Press.

Hempel, C.G. (1942) "The Function of General Laws in History," *Journal of Philosophy* 39: 35–48. (Reprinted as Chapter 5 in this anthology.)

Hempel, C.G. (1965) *Aspects of Scientific Explanation*. New York: Free Press.

Kincaid, H., Dupré, J., and Wylie, A. (eds.) (2007) *Value-Free Science? Ideals and Illusions*. Oxford: Oxford University Press.

Martin, M. and McIntyre, L. (eds.) (1994) *Readings in the Philosophy of Social Science*, Cambridge, MA: MIT Press.

Oppenheim, P. and Putnam, H. (1958) "Unity of Science as a Working Hypothesis," in Feigl, H., Scriven, M., and Maxwell, G. (eds.) *Minnesota Studies in the Philosophy of Science*. Minneapolis, MN: University of Minnesota Press.

Rorty, R. (1979) *Philosophy and the Mirror of Nature*. Princeton, NJ: Princeton University Press.

Rosenberg, A. (1988) *The Philosophy of Social Science*. Boulder, CO: Westview.

Ross, D. (2005) *Economic Theory and Cognitive Science: Microexplanation*. Cambridge, MA: MIT Press.

Salmon, W. (1984) *Scientific Explanation and the Causal Structure of the World*. Princeton, NJ: Princeton University Press.

Suppe, F. (1974) *The Structure of Scientific Theories*. Urbana, IL: University of Illinois Press.

Turner, M. (2001) *Cognitive Dimensions of Social Science*. Oxford: Oxford University Press.

Taylor, C. (1971) "Interpretation and the Sciences of Man," *Review of Metaphysics* 1: 3–51; reprinted in *Philosophy and the Human Sciences: Philosophical Papers II*. Cambridge: Cambridge University Press, pp. 15–57.

Winch, P. (1958) *The Idea of a Social Science and its Relation to Philosophy*. London: Routledge.

PART I

Values and social science

THE POPULAR IMAGE OF A scientist is a person who reasons logically and impartially from the results of esoteric experiments to important discoveries about the inner workings of nature. Part of what this popular image excludes is the possibility that such things as political beliefs, ethical commitments, or personal tastes—often lumped together under the umbrella term "values"—should play any role in deciding what scientific conclusions to draw from the data. In philosophy, this view of science is known as the *value-free ideal*. The extent to which the value-free ideal is a feasible or even desirable aspiration for science in general remains the topic of continued philosophical discussion (cf. Douglas 2009; Kincaid et al. 2007; Lacey 1999; Longino 2002; Machamer and Wolters 2004). But whatever one thinks of the value-free ideal in relation to "hard" sciences like physics or molecular biology, the ideal seems especially precarious in the social sciences. While the finer details of subatomic particles and DNA seem far removed from political and moral hot-button issues, the same cannot be said of the subject matter of the social sciences. In general, political and moral perspectives typically rely on beliefs about the workings of the social world—about the causes of prosperity, crime, or educational achievement—and such matters are central foci of the social sciences.

Some conceptual distinctions of the several ways in which values could influence science will be helpful for clarifying the issues at stake. Hugh Lacey (1999) distinguishes three senses in which science might be thought to be value free. The first, called *autonomy*, insists that scientists' choice of research projects should be entirely driven by their own intellectual curiosity, and not by judgments of non-scientists about which lines of research have the potential to be the most useful or beneficial to society. In contrast, *impartiality* is the idea that values should have no influence on the processes by which scientists draw inferences from the data. For example, impartiality would prohibit a scientist from taking feminism as a reason for thinking that differences in average scores between boys and girls on standardized mathematics tests are due to cultural rather than genetic factors. Finally, *neutrality* is the claim that the results of scientific research do not have direct implications for what is good or bad, right or wrong. According to neutrality, social science might be able to tell us what the effects of a particular policy are, but moral and political values would be needed in addition to decide whether that policy should be supported.

Few would today defend the idea that science should be value-free in the sense of being autonomous. Almost everyone accepts, for instance, that considerations about a scientific project's potential value to society can be legitimate factors influencing decisions about whether to provide funding for it. And sources of funding can, of course, influence which projects scientists choose to pursue. The real debates about the value-free ideal, therefore, focus on impartiality and neutrality. The classic account of the value-free ideal in social science was provided by Max Weber in his work, *The Methodology of the Social Sciences*, originally published in 1880. Weber recognized that value judgments inevitably guide a social scientist's assessments of which topics are important and worthy of study. Indeed, Weber went a step further than this by claiming that the concepts employed by social scientists are also influenced by pervasive values of the society. For example, the unemployment rate in economics is normally defined as the percentage of the working-age population that is searching for work but unable to find it. Excluding people not searching for work from the lists of the unemployed can be viewed as a reflection of the value judgment that making people want to work is not a responsibility of the government when it comes to economic policy. Instead, the government's chief interest in the employment market would be that there are sufficient opportunities for those who are interested in working.

But although he granted that social science could not be autonomous, Weber nevertheless insisted that it must be impartial and neutral, and his view has influenced many subsequent defenses of the value-free ideal of social science. The first chapter in Part I, by Ernest Nagel, is a classic example: Nagel's argumentative strategy is to assume that the ideal works as a reasonable approximation for the natural sciences and then to attempt to show that there is no fundamental difference between natural and social science that would prevent it from working there, too. Like Weber, Nagel accepts that social science cannot be autonomous but insists that it should still strive for impartiality and neutrality. Nagel recognizes that there are a number of practical reasons why the ideal is more difficult to achieve in social than in natural science, but claims nevertheless that social scientists should attempt to approximate the ideal as best they can.

A pragmatic argument for impartiality stresses that science is widely regarded as an authoritative source of knowledge only insofar as it is thought to draw conclusions from evidence in an even-handed manner. A similar pragmatic reason for neutrality is that being partisan would risk alienating social institutions, such as universities and the government, upon which science depends for support. For example, if social science was perceived as politically partisan, then it would be placed in jeopardy if the government came to be controlled by members of an opposing political party. Such concerns became even more pressing for science by the mid-twentieth century, when government funding for scientific research became common and obtaining grants became a necessary component of a successful scientific career. In the United States, for instance, the social sciences were not originally included among the sciences that would be supported by the National Science Foundation, created after World War II. In Congressional hearings on the topic, one member of the House of Representatives expressed the opinion that providing funding for social science research would lead to "a lot of short-haired women and long-haired men messing into everybody's personal affairs" (Greenberg 1967, p.109). Thus, social science needed to avoid being perceived as pushing some radical political agenda if it was to obtain the federal funding for research that other scientific disciplines had begun to enjoy.

The value-free ideal remains prevalent in mainstream social science. For example, in a controversial essay, John Donohue and Steven Levitt (2001) argue that legalized abortion in the United States in 1973 was the most important factor behind the nationwide decline in crime rates that occurred in the 1990s. Their central theme is that children born from unwanted pregnancies are at much greater risk of engaging in criminal activity when they become adults. But they insist that their hypothesis is neutral with respect to political and moral disputes about abortion. They suggest that the crime-reducing effects of legalized abortion might also be attained through increased access to birth control or by social programs aimed at assisting at-risk youth (2001, p.415). However, critics of the value-free ideal charge that it is unfeasible and often a cover for values that tend to maintain a status quo involving inequalities drawn along gender, racial, and economic lines. Michael Root (1994) argues that the results of social science research often will have real-world implications for political and moral issues, and hence that neutrality is not possible. Root's argument is nicely illustrated by Donohue and Levitt's hypothesis that legalizing abortion in 1973 resulted in a drop in crime rates a generation later. Although it is conceivable that one might oppose abortion while advocating greater access to contraception and more social programs for at-risk youth, that is not the position typically taken by opponents of abortion in the United States. The claim that the value-free ideal can serve to conceal value assumptions that favor prevailing social inequalities is illustrated by critiques of the use of cost-benefit analysis as an economic tool for assessing social policies (Anderson 1993; Hausman and McPherson 2006).

The next two selections contrast with Nagel's chapter by focusing on an aspect of social science that differentiates it from most natural sciences and which is relevant to the question of values in science. The chapter by Ian Hacking elaborates a distinction between *indifferent* and *interactive kinds*. As an example of an indifferent kind, consider the concept of an isotope, which is an atom whose number of neutrons differs from its number of protons. The existence of isotopes and their behavior are entirely indifferent to whether human beings have the concept of "isotope" and whether that concept is widely disseminated in popular culture. Isotopes don't care what we say or think about them. By contrast, many conceptual categories developed in social science are interactive kinds: the existence and widespread use of the concept has a direct impact on those individuals to whom the concept applies. For instance, the emergence of the concept of child abuse has had a profound effect on how corporal punishment of children is perceived, and thereby on the behaviors of parents and children. Moreover, changes in the behaviors of individuals following the introduction of the concept can in turn lead to subsequent modifications of the concept itself, which can lead to further changes in the behaviors of those classified by the concept, and so on. Hacking calls this interactive process the *looping effect*.

Looping effects can have oppressive as well as liberating consequences, and for this reason constitute a politically charged topic. The work of Michel Foucault (1961, 1979), in particular, provided a generation of scholars with exemplary explorations of how the reconceptualization of a field of discourse can be functional to new techniques of social control (as in the case of madness) or lead to the discovery of new personal and political identities (as in the case of the gay rights movement). The third chapter, by Miranda Fricker, directly tackles the epistemic aspects of these effects through exploring the concept of *epistemic injustice*. Epistemic injustices occur when a particular person or group is unfairly denied opportunities to acquire or communicate knowledge. Treating the testimony of women or members of a racial minority as inherently less credible would be an example of an epistemic injustice. In the chapter included here, Fricker is concerned with a particular type of epistemic injustice that she calls *hermeneutic injustice*. A hermeneutic injustice occurs when a broader pattern of social injustice, such as sexism, constrains available conceptual categories in such a way that important aspects of the experience of individuals subject to injustice are difficult, if not impossible, to understand or communicate. Fricker's central example of this phenomenon is the invention of the concept of sexual harassment in the 1970s. Prior to the articulation and uptake of this idea, women subjected to unwanted sexual advances in the workplace lacked concepts both for adequately understanding their own experiences and for communicating them to others. Thus, an important part of the struggle for fair treatment of women in the workplace was the development of new social concepts that could subsequently be assumed in social science research.

There is a straightforward connection between Hacking's discussion of interactive kinds and Fricker's account of hermeneutic injustice. According to Hacking, concepts employed by social scientists not merely describe social reality but also play an interactive role in shaping it. The interactive nature of many social categories is an underlying premise of Fricker's account of hermeneutic injustice, which transforms Hacking's insight into a proposal about how social science concepts can be purposefully devised to promote valuable social aims, such as gender equality. Thus, these two chapters aim to identify a role for values in social science research that would be less relevant to the natural sciences.

The final chapter in this section, by Alison Wylie, provides an example of a proposal from a feminist perspective of what social science might look like if it rejected the value-free ideal. Since the value-free ideal functioned in part to explain how the integrity and objectivity of science could be maintained despite the inevitable biases and passions of real human beings, proposals that reject the ideal often emphasize an alternative account of scientific integrity and objectivity. Wylie reviews suggestions made by several prominent feminist philosophers of science on this topic, and develops her own proposal based on an account of situated knowledge. This approach emphasizes how a person's social location can make a difference to what he or she can know about the social world. For example, a man is less likely than a woman to notice sexism in the workplace. Wylie aims to explain how this common theme of feminist epistemology can avoid assuming that all women share some uniquely female perspective while still being sufficiently robust to have significant implications for the methods and practices of the social sciences.

Further reading

For a classic critique of the value-free ideal in social science see Taylor (1967), and for a more recent defense of the ideal along the lines of Nagel's chapter see Kincaid (1996). There are good philosophical discussions on the topic of values in connection to several specific social sciences. For economics, good places to start would be Sen (1987), Anderson (1993), and Hausman and McPherson (2006). For more on Fricker's concept of economic injustice, see Fricker (2007). For philosophical work on values in anthropology, see Wylie (2007), Risjord (2007), and for a fascinating case study in anthropology that illustrates many of these issues see Borofsky (2005). For a recent discussion of Hacking's indifferent/interactive kind distinction see Martínez (2009).

References

Anderson, E. (1993) *Values and Ethics in Economics*. Cambridge, MA: Harvard University Press.
Borofsky, R. (2005) *Yanomami: The Fierce Controversy and What We Can Learn from It*. Berkeley, CA: University of California Press.

Donohue, J. and S. Levitt (2001) "The Impact of Legalized Abortion on Crime," *Quarterly Journal of Economics* 116: 379–418.

Douglas, H. (2009) *Science, Policy and the Value-Free Ideal*. Pittsburgh, PA: University of Pittsburgh Press.

Foucault, M. (1961) *Madness and Civilization*. New York: Vintage.

Foucault, M. (1979) *History of Sexuality, Vol. 1*. London: Allen & Lane.

Fricker, M. (2007) *Epistemic Injustice: Power and the Ethics of Knowing*. Oxford: Oxford University Press.

Greenberg, D. (1967) *The Politics of Pure Science*. Chicago, IL: University of Chicago Press.

Hausman, D. and M. McPherson (2006) *Economic Analysis, Moral Philosophy, and Public Policy*. Second edition. Cambridge: Cambridge University Press.

Kincaid, H. (1996) *The Philosophical Foundations of the Social Sciences*. Cambridge: Cambridge University Press.

Kincaid, H., J. Dupré, and A. Wylie (eds.) (2007) *Value-Free Science?*. Oxford: Oxford University Press.

Lacey, H. (1999) *Is Science Value Free?*. London: Routledge.

Longino, H. (2002) *The Fate of Knowledge*. Princeton, NJ: Princeton University Press.

Machamer, P. and G. Wolters (eds.) (2004) *Science, Values and Objectivity*. Pittsburgh, PA: University of Pittsburgh Press.

Martínez, M. (2009) "Ian Hacking's Proposal for the Distinction between the Natural and Social Sciences," *Philosophy of the Social Sciences* 39: 212–34.

Risjord, M. (2007) "Scientific Change as Political Action: Franz Boas and the Anthropology of Race," *Philosophy of the Social Sciences* 37: 24–45.

Root, M. (2004) *Philosophy of Social Science*. Cambridge: Blackwell.

Sen, A. (1987) *On Ethics and Economics*. Oxford: Oxford University Press.

Taylor, C. (1967) "Neutrality in Political Science," in P. Laslett and W. G. Runciman (eds.), *Philosophy, Politics and Society*. Oxford: Blackwell, pp. 25–57.

Weber, M. (1949 [1880]) *The Methodology of the Social Sciences*. New York: Free Press.

Wylie, A. (2007) "Doing Archeology as a Feminist: Introduction," *Journal of Archeological Method and Theory* 14: 209–16.

Chapter 1

ERNEST NAGEL

THE VALUE-ORIENTED BIAS OF SOCIAL INQUIRY

WE TURN, FINALLY, TO THE difficulties said to confront the social sciences because the social values to which students of social phenomena are committed not only color the contents of their findings but also control their assessment of the evidence on which they base their conclusions. Since social scientists generally differ in their value commitments, the "value neutrality" that seems to be so pervasive in the natural sciences is therefore often held to be impossible in social inquiry. In the judgment of many thinkers, it is accordingly absurd to expect the social sciences to exhibit the unanimity so common among natural scientists concerning what are the established facts and satisfactory explanations for them. Let us examine some of the reasons that have been advanced for these contentions. It will be convenient to distinguish four groups of such reasons, so that our discussion will deal in turn with the alleged role of value judgments in (1) the selection of problems, (2) the determination of the contents of conclusions, (3) the identification of fact, and (4) the assessment of evidence.

1. The reasons perhaps most frequently cited make much of the fact that the things a social scientist selects for study are determined by his conception of what are the socially important values. According to one influential view, for example, the student of human affairs deals only with materials to which he attributes "cultural significance," so that a "value orientation" is inherent in his choice of material for investigation. Thus, although Max Weber was a vigorous proponent of a "value-free" social science—i.e., he maintained that social scientists must appreciate (or "understand") the values involved in the actions or institutions they are discussing but that it is not their business as objective scientists to approve or disapprove either those values or those actions and institutions—he nevertheless argued that:

> The concept of culture is a *value-concept*. Empirical reality becomes "culture" to us because and insofar as we relate it to value ideas. It includes those segments and only those segments of reality which have become significant to us because of this value-relevance. Only a small portion of existing concrete reality is colored by our value-conditioned interest and it alone is significant to us. It is significant because it reveals relationships which are important to us due to their connection with our values. Only because and to the extent that this is the case is it worthwhile for us to know it in its individual features. We cannot discover, however, what is meaningful to us

by means of a "presuppositionless" investigation of empirical data. Rather perception of its meaningfulness to us is the presupposition of its becoming an *object* of investigation.[1]

It is well-nigh truistic to say that students of human affairs, like students in any other area of inquiry, do not investigate everything, but direct their attention to certain selected portions of the inexhaustible content of concrete reality. Moreover, let us accept the claim, if only for the sake of the argument, that a social scientist addresses himself exclusively to matters which he believes are important because of their assumed relevance to his cultural values. It is not clear, however, why the fact that an investigator selects the materials he studies in the light of problems which interest him and which seem to him to bear on matters he regards as important, is of greater moment for the logic of social inquiry than it is for the logic of any other branch of inquiry. For example, a social scientist may believe that a free economic market embodies a cardinal human value, and he may produce evidence to show that certain kinds of human activities are indispensable to the perpetuation of a free market. If he is concerned with processes which maintain this type of economy rather than some other type, how is this fact more pertinent to the question whether he has adequately evaluated the evidence for his conclusion, than is the bearing upon the analogous question of the fact that a physiologist may be concerned with processes which maintain a constant internal temperature in the human body rather than with something else? The things a social scientist *selects for study* with a view to determining the conditions or consequences of their existence may indeed be dependent on the indisputable fact that he is a "cultural being." But similarly, were we not human beings though still capable of conducting scientific inquiry, we might conceivably have an interest neither in the conditions that maintain a free market, nor in the processes involved in the homeostasis of the internal temperature in human bodies, nor for that matter in the mechanisms that regulate the height of tides, the succession of seasons, or the motions of the planets.

In short, there is no difference between any of the sciences with respect to the fact that the interests of the scientist determine what he selects for investigation. But this fact, by itself, represents no obstacle to the successful pursuit of objectively controlled inquiry in any branch of study.

2. A more substantial reason commonly given for the value-oriented character of social inquiry is that, since the social scientist is himself affected by considerations of right and wrong, his own notions of what constitutes a satisfactory social order and his own standards of personal and social justice do enter, in point of fact, into his analyses of social phenomena. For example, according to one version of this argument, anthropologists must frequently judge whether the means adopted by some society achieves the intended aim (e.g., whether a religious ritual does produce the increased fertility for the sake of which the ritual is performed); and in many cases the adequacy of the means must be judged by admittedly "relative" standards, i.e., in terms of the ends sought or the standards employed by that society, rather than in terms of the anthropologist's own criteria. Nevertheless, so the argument proceeds, there are also situations in which

we must apply absolute standards of adequacy, that is evaluate the end results of behavior in terms of purposes we believe in or postulate. This occurs, first, when we speak of the satisfaction of psycho-physical 'needs' offered by any culture; secondly, when we assess the bearing of social facts upon survival; and thirdly, when we pronounce upon social integration and stability. In each case our statements imply judgments as to the worth-whileness of actions, as to 'good' or 'bad' cultural solutions of the problems of life, and as to 'normal' and 'abnormal' states of affairs. These are basic judgments which we cannot do without in social enquiry and which clearly do not express a purely personal philosophy of the enquirer or values arbitrarily assumed. Rather do they grow out of the history of human thought, from which the anthropologist can seclude himself as little as can anyone else. Yet as the history of human thought has led not to one philosophy but to several, so the value attitudes implicit in our ways of thinking will differ and sometimes conflict.[2]

It has often been noted, moreover, that the study of social phenomena receives much of its impetus from a strong moral and reforming zeal, so that many ostensibly "objective" analyses in the social sciences are in fact disguised recommendations of social policy. As one typical but moderately expressed statement of the point puts it, a social scientist

cannot wholly detach the unifying social structure that, as a scientist's theory, guides his detailed, investigations of human behavior, from the unifying structure which, as a citizen's ideal, he thinks ought to prevail in human affairs and hopes may sometimes be more fully realized. His social theory is thus essentially a program of action along two lines which are kept in some measure of harmony with each other by that theory-action in assimilating social facts for purposes of systematic understanding, and action aiming at progressively molding the social pattern, so far as he can influence it, into what he thinks it ought to be.[3]

It is surely beyond serious dispute that social scientists do in fact often import their own values into their analyses of social phenomena. It is also undoubtedly true that even thinkers who believe human affairs can be studied with the ethical neutrality characterizing modern inquiries into geometrical or physical relations, and who often pride themselves on the absence of value judgments from their own analyses of social phenomena, do in fact sometimes make such judgments in their social inquiries. Nor is it less evident that students of human affairs often hold conflicting values; that their disagreements on value questions are often the source of disagreements concerning ostensibly factual issues; and that, even if value predications are assumed to be inherently capable of proof or disproof by, objective evidence, at least some of the differences between social scientists involving value judgments are not in fact resolved by the procedures of controlled inquiry

In any event, it is not easy in most areas of inquiry to prevent our likes, aversions, hopes, and fears from coloring our conclusions. It has taken centuries of effort to develop habits and techniques of investigation which help safeguard inquiries in the natural sciences against the intrusion of irrelevant personal factors; and even in these disciplines the protection those procedures give is neither infallible nor complete. The problem is undoubtedly more acute in the study of human affairs, and the difficulties it creates for achieving reliable knowledge in the social sciences must be admitted.

However, the problem is intelligible only on the assumption that there is a relatively clear distinction between factual and value judgments, and that however difficult it may sometimes be to decide whether a given statement has a purely factual content, it is in principle possible to do so. Thus, the claim that social scientists are pursuing the twofold program mentioned in the above quotation makes sense, only if it is possible to distinguish between, on the one hand, contributions to theoretical understanding (whose factual validity presumably does not depend on the social ideal to which a social scientist may subscribe), and on the other hand contributions to the dissemination or realization of some social ideal (which may not be accepted by all social scientists). Accordingly, the undeniable difficulties that stand in the way of obtaining reliable knowledge of human affairs because of the fact that social scientists differ in their value orientations are practical difficulties. The difficulties are not necessarily insuperable, for since by hypothesis it is not impossible to distinguish between fact and value, steps can be taken to identify a value bias when it occurs, and to minimize if not to eliminate completely its perturbing effects.

One such countermeasure frequently recommended is that social scientists abandon the pretence that they are free from all bias, and that instead they state their value assumptions as explicitly and fully as they can.[4] The recommendation does not assume that social scientists will come to agree on their social ideals once these ideals are explicitly postulated, or that disagreements over values can be settled by scientific inquiry. Its point is that the question of how a given ideal is to be realized, or the question whether a certain institutional arrangement is an effective way of achieving the ideal, is on the face of it not a value question, but a factual problem—to be resolved by the objective methods of scientific inquiry—concerning the adequacy of proposed means for attaining stipulated ends. Thus, economists may permanently disagree on the desirability of a society in which its members have a guaranteed security against economic want, since the disagreement may have its source in inarbitrable preferences for different social values. But when sufficient evidence is made available by economic inquiry, economists do presumably agree on the factual proposition that, *if* such a society is to be achieved then a purely competitive economic system will not suffice.

Although the recommendation that social scientists make fully explicit their value commitments is undoubtedly salutary, and can produce excellent fruit, it verges on being a counsel of perfection. For the most part we are unaware of many assumptions that enter into our analyses and actions, so that despite resolute efforts to make our preconceptions explicit some decisive ones may not even occur to us. But in any event, the difficulties generated for scientific inquiry by unconscious bias and tacit value orientations are rarely overcome by devout resolutions to eliminate bias. They are usually overcome, often only gradually, through the selfcorrective mechanisms of science as a social enterprise. For modern science encourages the invention, the mutual exchange, and the free but responsible criticisms of ideas; it welcomes competition in the quest for knowledge between independent investigators, even when their intellectual orientations are different; and it progressively diminishes the effects of bias by retaining only those proposed conclusions of its inquiries that survive critical examination by an indefinitely large community of students, whatever be their value preferences or doctrinal commitments. It would be absurd to claim that this institutionalized mechanism for sifting warranted beliefs has operated or is likely to operate in social inquiry as effectively as it has in the natural sciences. But it would be no less absurd to conclude that reliable knowledge of human affairs is unattainable merely because social inquiry is frequently value-oriented.

3. There is a more sophisticated argument for the view that the social sciences cannot be value-free. It maintains that the distinction between fact and value assumed in the preceding discussion is untenable when purposive human behavior is being analyzed, since in this context value judgments enter inextricably into what appear to be "purely descriptive" (or factual) statements. Accordingly, those who subscribe to this thesis claim that an ethically neutral social science is in principle impossible, and not simply that it is difficult to attain. For if fact and value are indeed so fused that they cannot even be distinguished, value judgments cannot be eliminated from the social sciences unless all predications are also eliminated from them, and therefore unless these sciences completely disappear.

For example, it has been argued that the student of human affairs must distinguish between valuable and undesirable forms of social activity, on pain of failing in his "plain duty" to present social phenomena truthfully and faithfully:

> Would one not laugh out of court a man who claimed to have written a sociology of art but who actually had written a sociology of trash? The sociologist of religion must distinguish between phenomena which have a religious character and phenomena which are a-religious. To be able to do this, he must understand what religion is. . . . Such understanding enables and forces him to distinguish between genuine and spurious religion, between higher and lower religions; these religions are higher in which the specifically religious motivations are effective to a higher degree. . . . The sociologist of religion cannot help noting the difference between those who try to gain it by a change of heart. Can he see this difference without seeing at the same time the difference between a mercenary and nonmercenary attitude? . . . The prohibition against value-judgments in social science would lead to the consequence that we are permitted to give a strictly factual description of the overt acts that can be observed in concentration camps, and perhaps an equally factual analysis of the motivations of the actors concerned: we would not be permitted to speak of cruelty. Every reader of such a description who is not completely stupid would, of course, see that the actions described are cruel. The factual description would in truth, be a bitter satire. What claimed to be a straightforward report would be an unusually circumlocutory report . . ., Can one say anything relevant on public opinion polls . . . without realizing the fact that many answers to the questionnaires are given by uninitelligent, uninformed, deceitful, and irrational people, and that not a few questions are formulated by people of the same caliber—can one say anything relevant about public opinion polls without committing one value-judgment after another?[5]

Moreover, the assumption implicit in the recommendation discussed above for achieving ethical neutrality is often rejected as hopelessly naive—this is the assumption, it will be recalled, that relations of means to ends can be established without commitment to these ends, so that the conclusions of social inquiry concerning such relations are objective statements which make *conditional* rather than categorical assertions about values. This assumption is said by its critics to rest on the supposition that men attach value only to the ends they seek, and not to the means for realizing their aims. However, the supposition is alleged to be grossly mistaken. For the character of the means one employs to secure some goal affects the nature of the total outcome; and the choice men make between alternative means for obtaining a given end depends on the values they ascribe to those alternatives. In consequence, commitments to specific valuations are said to be involved even in what appear to be purely factual statements about means-ends relations.

We shall not attempt a detailed assessment of this complex argument, for a discussion of the numerous issues it raises would take us far afield. However three claims made in the course of the argument will be admitted without further comment as indisputably correct: that a large number of characterizations sometimes assumed to be purely factual descriptions of social phenomena do indeed formulate a type of value judgment; that it is often difficult, and in any case usually inconvenient in practice, to distinguish between the purely factual and the "evaluative" contents of many terms employed in the social sciences; and that values are commonly attached to means and not only to ends. However, these admissions do not entail the conclusion that, in a manner unique to the study of purposive human behavior, fact and value are fused beyond the possibility of distinguishing between them. On the contrary, as we shall try to show, the claim that there is such a fusion and that a value-free social science is therefore inherently absurd, confounds two quite different senses of the term "value judgment": the sense in which a value judgment expresses *approval or disapproval* either of some moral (or social) ideal or of some action (or institution) because of a commitment to such an ideal; and the sense in which a value judgment expresses *an estimate* of the degree to which some commonly recognized (and more or less clearly defined) type of action, object, or institution is embodied in a given instance.

It will be helpful to illustrate these two senses of "value judgment" first with an example from biology. Animals with blood streams sometimes exhibit the condition known as "anemia." An anemic animal has a reduced number of red blood corpuscles, so that, among other things, it is less able to maintain a constant internal temperature than are members of its species with a "normal" supply of such blood cells. However, although the meaning of the term "anemia" can be made quite clear, it is not in fact defined with complete precision; for example, the notion of a "normal" number of red corpuscles that enters into the definition of the term is itself somewhat vague, since this number varies with the individual members of a species as well as with the state of a given individual at different times (such as its age or the altitude of its habitat). But in any case, to decide whether a given animal is anemic, an investigator must judge whether the available evidence *warrants* the conclusion that the specimen is anemic."[6] He may perhaps think of anemia as being of several distinct kinds (as is done in actual medical practice), or he may think of anemia as a condition that is realizable with greater or lesser completeness (just as certain plane curves are sometimes described as better or worse approximations to a circle as defined in geometry); and, depending on which of these conceptions he adopts, he may decide either that his specimen has a certain kind of anemia or that it is anemic only to a certain degree. When the investigator reaches a conclusion, he can therefore be said to be making a "value judgment," in the sense that he has in mind some standardized type of physiological condition designated as "anemia" and that he *assesses* what he knows about his specimen with the measure provided by this assumed standard. For the sake of easy reference, let us call such evaluations of the evidence, which conclude that a given characteristic is in some degree present (or absent) in a given instance, "characterizing value judgments."

On the other hand, the student may also make a quite different sort of value judgment, which asserts that, since an anemic animal has diminished powers of maintaining itself, anemia is an undesirable condition. Moreover, he may apply this general judgment to a particular case, and so come to deplore the fact that a given animal is anemic. Let us label such evaluations, which conclude that some envisaged or actual state of affairs is worthy of approval or disapproval, "appraising value judgments." It is clear, however, that an investigator making a characterizing value judgment is not thereby logically bound to affirm or deny a corresponding appraising evaluation. It is no less evident that he cannot consistently make an appraising value judgment about a given instance (e.g., that it is undesirable for a given animal to continue being anemic), unless he can affirm a characterizing judgment about that instance independently of the appraising one (e.g., that the animal is anemic). Accordingly, although characterizing judgments are necessarily entailed by many appraising judgments, making appraising judgments is not a necessary condition for making characterizing ones.

Let us now apply these distinctions to some of the contentions advanced in the argument quoted above. Consider first the claim that the sociologist of religion must recognize the difference between mercenary and nonmercenary attitudes, and that in consequence he is inevitably committing himself to certain values. It is certainly beyond dispute that these attitudes are commonly distinguished; and it can also be granted that a sociologist of religion needs to understand the difference between them. But the sociologist's obligation is in this respect quite like that of the student of animal physiology, who must also acquaint himself with certain distinctions—even though the physiologist's distinction between, say, anemic and nonanemic may be less familiar to the ordinary layman and is in any case much more precise than is the distinction between mercenary and nonmercenary attitudes. Indeed, because of the vagueness of these latter terms, the scrupulous sociologist may find it extremely difficult to decide whether or not the attitude of some community toward its acknowledged gods is to be characterized as mercenary; and if he should finally decide, he may base his conclusion on some inarticulated "total impression" of that community's manifest behavior, without being able to state exactly the detailed grounds for his decision. But however this may be, the sociologist who claims that a certain attitude manifested by a given religious group is mercenary, just as the physiologist who claims that a certain individual is anemic, is making what is primarily a characterizing value judgment. In making these judgments, neither the sociologist nor the physiologist is necessarily committing himself to any values other than the values of scientific probity; and in this respect, therefore, there appears to be no difference between social and biological (or for that matter, physical) inquiry.

On the other hand, it would be absurd to deny that in characterizing various actions as mercenary, cruel, or deceitful, sociologists are frequently (although perhaps not always wittingly) asserting appraising as well as characterizing value judgments. Terms like 'mercenary,' 'cruel,' or 'deceitful' as commonly used have a widely recognized pejorative overtone. Accordingly, anyone who employs such terms to characterize human behavior can normally be assumed to be stating his disapprobation of that behavior (or his approbation, should he use terms like 'nonmercenary,' 'kindly,' or 'truthful'), and not simply characterizing it.

However, although many (but certainly not all) ostensibly characterizing statements asserted by social scientists undoubtedly express commitments to various (not always compatible) values, a number of "purely descriptive" terms as used by natural scientists in certain contexts sometimes also have an unmistakably appraising value connotation. Thus, the claim that a social scientist is making appraising value judgments when he characterizes respondents to questionnaires as uninformed, deceitful, or irrational can be matched by the equally sound claim that a physicist is also making such judgments when he describes a particular chronometer as inaccurate, a pump as inefficient, or a supporting platform as unstable. Like the social scientist in this example, the physicist is characterizing certain objects in his field of research; but, also like the social scientist, he is in addition expressing his disapproval of the characteristics he is ascribing to those objects.

Nevertheless—and this is the main burden of the present discussion—there are no good reasons for thinking that it is inherently impossible to *distinguish* between the characterizing and the appraising judgments implicit in many statements, whether the statements are asserted by students of human affairs or by natural scientists. To be sure, it is not always easy to make the distinction formally explicit in the social sciences—in part because much of the language employed in them is very vague, in part because appraising judgments that may be implicit in a statement tend to be overlooked by us when they are judgments to which we are actually committed though without being aware of our commitments. Nor is it always useful or convenient to perform this task. For many statements implicitly containing both characterizing and appraising evaluations are sometimes sufficiently clear without being reformulated in the manner required by the task; and the reformulations would frequently be too unwieldy for effective communication between members of a large and unequally prepared group of students. But these are essentially practical rather than theoretical problems. The difficulties they raise provide no compelling reasons for the claim that an ethically neutral social science is inherently impossible.

Nor is there any force in the argument that, since values are commonly attached to means and not only to ends, statements about means–ends relations are not value-free. Let us test the argument with a simple example. Suppose that a man with an urgent need for a car but without sufficient funds to buy one can achieve his aim by borrowing a sum either from a commercial bank or from friends who waive payment of any interest. Suppose further that he dislikes becoming beholden to his friends for financial favors, and prefers the impersonality of a commercial loan. Accordingly, the comparative values this individual places upon the alternative means available to him for realizing his aim obviously control the choice he makes between them. Now the *total* outcome that would result from his adoption of one of the alternatives is admittedly different from the *total* outcome that would result from his adoption of the other alternative. Nevertheless, irrespective of the values he may attach to these alternative means, each of them would achieve a result—namely, his purchase of the needed car—that is common to both the total outcomes. In consequence, the validity of the statement that he could buy the car by borrowing money from a bank, as well as of the statement that he could realize this aim by borrowing from friends, is unaffected by the valuations placed upon the means, so that neither statement involves any special appraising evaluations. In short, the statements about means–ends relations are value-free.

4. There remains for consideration the claim that a value-free social science is impossible, because value commitments enter into the very *assessment of evidence* by social scientists, and not simply into the content of the conclusions they advance. This version of the claim itself has a large number of variant forms, but we shall examine only three of them.

The least radical form of the claim maintains that the conceptions held by a social scientist of what constitute cogent evidence or sound intellectual workmanship are the products of his education and his place in society, and are affected by the social values transmitted by this training and associated with this social position; accordingly, the values to which the social scientist is thereby committed determine which statements he *accepts* as well-grounded conclusions about human affairs. In this form, the claim is a *factual* thesis, and must be supported by detailed empirical evidence concerning the influences exerted by a man's moral and social values upon what he is ready to acknowledge as sound social analysis. In many instances such evidence is indeed available; and differences between social scientists in respect to what they accept as credible can sometimes be attributed to the influence of national, religious, economic, and other kinds of bias. However, this variant of the claim excludes neither the possibility of recognizing assessments of evidence that are prejudiced by special value commitments, nor the possibility of correcting for such prejudice. It therefore raises no issue that has not already been discussed when we examined the second reason for the alleged value oriented character of social inquiry (pages 13–15).

Another but different form of the claim is based on recent work in theoretical statistics dealing with the assessment of evidence for so-called "statistical hypotheses"—hypotheses concerning the probabilities of random events, such as the hypothesis that the probability of a male human birth is one-half. The central idea relevant to the present question that underlies these developments can be sketched in terms of an example. Suppose that, before a fresh batch of medicine is put on sale, tests are performed on experimental animals for its possible toxic effects because of impurities that have not been eliminated in its manufacture, for example, by introducing small quantities of the drug into the diet of one hundred guinea pigs. If no more than a few of the animals show serious aftereffects, the medicine is to be regarded as safe, and will be marketed; but if a contrary result is obtained the drug will be destroyed. Suppose now that three of the animals do in fact become gravely ill. Is this outcome significant (i.e., does it indicate that the drug has toxic effects), or is it perhaps an "accident" that happened because of some peculiarity in the affected animals? To answer the question, the experimenter must *decide* on the basis of the evidence between the hypothesis H_1: the drug is toxic, and the hypothesis H_2: the drug is not toxic. But how is he to decide, if he aims to be "reasonable" rather than arbitrary? Current statistical theory offers him a rule for making a reasonable decision, and bases the rule on the following analysis.

Whatever decision the experimenter may make, he runs the risk of committing either one of two types of errors: he may reject a hypothesis though in fact it is true (i.e., despite the fact that H_1 is actually true, he mistakenly decides against it in the light of the evidence available to him); or he may accept a hypothesis though in fact it is false. His decision would therefore be eminently reasonable, were it based on a rule guaranteeing that no decision ever made in accordance with the rule would commit either type of error. Unhappily, there are no rules of this sort. The next suggestion is to find a rule such that, when decisions are made in accordance with it, the relative frequency of each type of error is quite small. But unfortunately, the risks of committing each type of error are not independent; for example, it is in general logically impossible to find a rule so that decisions based on it will commit each type of error with a relative frequency not greater than one in a thousand. In consequence, before a reasonable rule can be proposed, the experimenter must compare the relative importance to himself of the two types of error, and state what risk he is willing to take of committing the type of error he judges to be the more important one. Thus, were he to reject H_1 though it is true (i.e., were he to commit an error of the first type), all the medicine under consideration would be put on sale, and the lives of those using it would be endangered; on the other hand, were he to commit an error of the second type with respect to H_1, the entire batch of medicine would be scrapped, and the manufacturer would incur a financial loss. However, the preservation of human life may be of greater moment to the experimenter than financial gain; and he may perhaps stipulate that he is unwilling to base his decision on a rule for which the risk of committing an error of the first type is greater than one such error in a hundred decisions. If this is assumed, statistical theory can specify a rule satisfying the experimenter's requirement, though how this is done, and how the risk of committing an error of the second type is calculated, are technical questions of no concern to us. The main point to be noted in this analysis is that the rule presupposes certain appraising judgments of value. In short, if this result is generalized, statistical theory appears to support the thesis that value commitments enter decisively into the rules for assessing evidence for statistical hypotheses.[7]

However, the theoretical analysis upon which this thesis rests does not entail the conclusion that the rules actually employed in every social inquiry for assessing evidence necessarily involve some *special* commitments, i.e., commitments such as those mentioned in the above example, as distinct from those generally implicit in science as an enterprise aiming to achieve reliable knowledge. Indeed, the above example illustrating the reasoning in current statistical theory can be misleading, insofar as it suggests that alternative decisions between statistical hypotheses must invariably lead to alternative actions having immediate practical consequences upon which different special values are placed. For example, a theoretical physicist may have to decide between two statistical hypotheses concerning the probability of certain energy exchanges in atoms; and a theoretical sociologist may similarly have to choose between two statistical hypotheses concerning the relative frequency of childless marriages under certain social arrangements. But neither of these men may have any *special* values at stake associated with the alternatives between which he must decide, other than the values, to which he is committed as a member of a scientific community, to conduct his inquiries with probity and responsibility. Accordingly, the question whether any special value commitments enter into assessments of evidence in either the natural or social sciences is not settled one way or the other by theoretical statistics; and the question can be answered only by examining actual inquiries in the various scientific disciplines.

Moreover, nothing in the reasoning of theoretical statistics depends on what particular subject matter is under discussion when a decision between alternative statistical hypotheses is to be made. For the reasoning is entirely general; and reference to some special subject matter becomes relevant only when a definite numerical value is to be assigned to the risk some investigator is prepared to take of making an erroneous decision concerning a given hypothesis. Accordingly, if current statistical theory is used to support the claim that value commitments enter into the assessment of evidence for statistical hypotheses in social inquiry, statistical theory can be used with equal justification to support analogous claims for all other inquiries as well. In short, the claim we have been discussing establishes no difficulty that supposedly occurs in the search for reliable knowledge in the study of human affairs which is not also encountered in the natural sciences.

A third form of this claim is the most radical of all. It differs from the first variant mentioned above in maintaining that there is a necessary *logical* connection, and not merely a contingent or causal one, between the "social perspective" of a student of human affairs and his standards of competent social inquiry, and in consequence the influence of the special values to which he is committed because of his own social involvements is not eliminable. This version of the claim is implicit in Hegel's account of the "dialectical" nature of human history and is integral to much Marxist as well as non-Marxist philosophy that stresses the "historically relative" character of social thought. In any event, it is commonly based on the assumption that, since social institutions and their cultural products are constantly changing, the intellectual apparatus required for understanding them must also change; and every idea employed for this purpose is therefore adequate only for some particular stage in the development of human affairs. Accordingly, neither the substantive concepts adopted for classifying and interpreting social phenomena, nor the logical canons used for estimating the worth of such concepts, have a "'timeless validity"; there is no analysis of social phenomena which is not the expression of some special social standpoint, or which does not reflect the interests and values dominant in some sector of the human scene at a certain stage of its history. In consequence, although a sound distinction can be made in the natural sciences between the origin of a man's views and their factual validity, such a distinction allegedly cannot be made in social inquiry; and prominent exponents of "historical relativism" have therefore challenged the universal adequacy of the thesis that "the genesis of a proposition is under all circumstances irrelevant to its truth." As one influential proponent of this position puts the matter:

The historical and social genesis of an idea would only be irrelevant to its ultimate validity if the temporal and social conditions of its emergence had no effect on its content and form. If this were the case, any two periods in the history of human knowledge would only be distinguished from one another by the fact that in the earlier period certain things were still unknown and certain errors still existed which, through later knowledge were completely corrected. This simple relationship between an earlier incomplete and a later complete period of knowledge may to a large extent be appropriate for the exact sciences. . . . For the history of the cultural sciences, however, the earlier stages are not quite so simply superseded by the later stages, and it is not so easily demonstrable that early errors have subsequently been corrected. Every epoch has its fundamentally new approach and its characteristic point of view, and consequently sees the "same" object from a new perspective. . . . The very principles, in the light of which knowledge is to be criticized, are themselves found to be socially and historically conditioned. Hence their application appears to be limited to given historical periods and the particular types of knowledge then prevalent.[8]

Historical research into the influence of society upon the beliefs men hold is of undoubted importance for understanding the complex nature of the scientific enterprise; and the sociology of knowledge—as such investigations have come to be called—has produced many clarifying contributions to such an understanding. However, these admittedly valuable services of the sociology of knowledge do not establish the radical claim we have been stating. In the first place, there is no competent evidence to show that the principles employed in social inquiry for assessing the intellectual products are *necessarily* determined by the social perspective of the inquirer. On the contrary, the "facts" usually cited in support of this contention establish at best only a contingent causal relation between a man's social commitments and his canons of cognitive validity. For example, the once fashionable view that the "mentality" or logical operations of primitive societies differ from those typical in Western civilization—a discrepancy that was attributed to differences in the institutions of the societies under comparison—is now generally recognized to be erroneous, because it seriously misinterprets the intellectual processes of primitive peoples. Moreover, even extreme exponents of the sociology of knowledge admit that most conclusions asserted in mathematics and natural science are neutral to differences in social perspective of those asserting them, so that the genesis of these propositions is irrelevant to their validity. Why cannot propositions about human affairs exhibit a similar neutrality, at least in some cases? Sociologists of knowledge do not appear to doubt that the truth of the statement that two horses can in general pull a heavier load than can either horse alone, is logically independent of the social status of the individual who happens to affirm the statement. But they have not made clear just what are the inescapable considerations that allegedly make such independence inherently impossible for the analogous statement about human behavior, that two laborers can in general dig a ditch of given dimensions more quickly than can either laborer working alone.

In the second place, the claim faces a serious and frequently noted dialectical difficulty— a difficulty that proponents of the claim have succeeded in meeting only by abandoning the substance of the claim. For let us ask what is the cognitive status of the thesis that a social perspective enters essentially into the content as well as the validation of every assertion about human affairs. Is this thesis meaningful and valid only for those who maintain it and who thus subscribe to certain values because of their distinctive social commitments? If so, no one with a different social perspective can properly understand it; its acceptance as valid is strictly limited to those who can do so, and social scientists who subscribe to a different set of social values ought therefore dismiss it as empty talk. Or is the thesis singularly exempt from the class of assertions to which it applies, so that its meaning and truth are not inherently related to the social perspectives of those who assert it? If so, it is not evident why the thesis is so exempt; but in any case, the thesis is then a conclusion of inquiry into human affairs that is presumably "objectively valid" in the usual sense of this phrase—and, if there is one such conclusion, it is not clear why there cannot be others as well.

To meet this difficulty, and to escape the self-defeating skeptical relativism to which the thesis is thus shown to lead, the thesis is sometimes interpreted to say that, though "absolutely objective" knowledge of human affairs is unattainable, a "relational" form of objectivity called "relationism" can nevertheless be achieved. On this interpretation, a social scientist can discover just what his social perspective is; and if he then formulates the conclusions of his inquiries "relationally," so as to indicate that his findings conform to the canons of validity implicit in his perspective, his conclusions will have achieved a "relational" objectivity. Social scientists sharing the same perspective can be expected to agree in their answers to a given problem when the canons of validity characteristic of their common perspective are correctly applied. On the other hand, students of social phenomena who operate within different but incongruous social perspectives can also achieve objectivity, if in no other way than by a "relational" formulation of what must otherwise be incompatible results obtained in their several inquiries. However, they can also achieve it in "a more roundabout fashion," by undertaking "to find a formula for translating the results of one into those of the other and to discover a common denominator for these varying perspectivistic insights."[9]

But it is difficult to see in what way "relational objectivity" differs from "objectivity" without the qualifying adjective and in the customary sense of the word. For example, a physicist who terminates an investigation with the conclusion that the velocity of light in water has a certain numerical value when measured in terms of a stated system of units, by a stated procedure, and under stated experimental conditions, is formulating his conclusion in a manner that is "relational" in the sense intended; and his conclusion is marked by "objectivity," presumably because it mentions the "relational" factors upon which the assigned numerical value of the velocity depends. However, it is fairly standard practice in the natural sciences to formulate certain types of conclusions in this fashion. Accordingly, the proposal that the social sciences formulate their findings in an analogous manner carries with it the admission that it is not in principle impossible for these disciplines to establish conclusions having the objectivity of conclusions reached in other domains of inquiry. Moreover, if the difficulty we are considering is to be resolved by the suggested translation formulas for rendering the "common denominators" of conclusions stemming from divergent social perspectives, those formulas cannot in turn be "situationally determined" in the sense of this phrase under discussion. For if those formulas were so determined, the same difficulty would crop up anew in connection with them. On the other hand, a search for such formulas is a phase in the search for invariant relations in a subject matter, so that formulations of these relations are valid irrespective of the particular perspective one may select from some class of perspectives on that subject matter. In consequence, in acknowledging that the search for such invariants in the social sciences is not inherently bound to fail, proponents of the claim we have been considering abandon what at the outset was its most radical thesis.

In brief, the various reasons we have been examining for the intrinsic impossibility of securing objective (i.e., value-free and unbiased) conclusions in the social sciences do not establish what they purport to establish, even though in some instances they direct attention to undoubtedly important practical difficulties frequently encountered in these disciplines.

Notes

1   Max Weber, *The Methodology of the Social Sciences*, Glencoe, Ill., 1947, p. 76.

2   S.F. Nadel, *The Foundations of Social Anthropology*, Glencoe, Ill., 1951, pp. 53–54.

3   Edwin A. Burtt, *Right Thinking*, New York, 1946, p. 522.

4   See, e.g., S.F. Nadel, *op. cit.*, p. 54; also Gunnar Myrdal, *op. cit.*, p. 120, as well as his *Political Element in the Development of Economic Theory*, Cambridge, Mass., 1954, esp. Chap. 8.

5   Leo Strauss, "The Social Science of Max Weber," *Measure*, volume 2 (1951), pp. 211–14.

6   The evidence is usually a count of red cells in a sample from the animal's blood. However, it should be noted that "The red cell count gives only an estimate of the *number of cells per unit quantity of blood*," and does not indicate whether the body's total supply of red cells is increased or diminished. Charles H. Best and Norman B. Taylor, *The Physiological Basis Of Medical Practice*, 6th ed., Baltimore, 1955, pp. 11, 17.

7   The above example is borrowed from the discussion in J. Neymann, *First Course in Probability and Statistics*, New York, 1950, Chap. 5, where an elementary technical account of recent developments in statistical theory is presented.

8   Karl Mannheim, *Ideology and Utopia*, New York, 1959, pp. 271, 288, 292.

9   Karl Mannheim, *op. cit.*, pp. 300–01.

Chapter 2

IAN HACKING

THE LOOPING EFFECTS OF HUMAN KINDS

What are human kinds?

'**H**UMAN KINDS' IS SUCH AN ugly turn of phrase that, as Auguste Comte said of *sociologie*, no one else would ever want to use it. I do not intend to pick out a definite and clearly bounded class of classifications. I mean to indicate kinds of people, their behaviour, their condition, kinds of action, kinds of temperament or tendency, kinds of emotion, and kinds of experience. I use the term 'human kinds' to emphasize kinds – the systems of classification – rather than people and their feelings. Although I intend human kinds to include kinds of behaviour, act, or temperament, it is kinds of people that concern me. That is, kinds of behaviour, act, or temperament are what I call human kinds if we take them to characterize kinds of people.

However, I do not mean any kinds of people. I choose the label 'human kinds' for its inhumane ring, and mean the kinds that are studied in the marginal, insecure, but enormously powerful human and social sciences. An operational definition of an insecure science is: a science whose leaders say they are in quest of a paradigm, or have just found a paradigm. Insecurity is consistent with immense power. Thus, to turn to a natural science, Walter Gilbert, tsar of the best-funded non-military research programme in the world, the $300 million human genome project, responded to criticism with an article entitled 'Towards a paradigm shift in biology' (Gilbert 1991).

By human kinds I mean kinds about which we would like to have systematic, general, and accurate knowledge; classifications that could be used to formulate general truths about people; generalizations sufficiently strong that they seem like laws about people, their actions, or their sentiments. We want laws precise enough to predict what individuals will do, or how they will respond to attempts to help them or to modify their behaviour. The model is that of the natural sciences. Only one kind of causality is deemed relevant: efficient causation. One event brings about another, although the causal laws may be only probabilistic laws of tendency.

The term 'human kind' is patterned after the philosopher's 'natural kind', and so I have to make some disclaimers. It is hard to believe that a philosopher could be so mealy-mouthed about natural kinds. I have no doubt that nature has kinds which we distinguish. Some seem fairly cosmic: quarks, probably genes, possibly cystic fibrosis. Others are mundane: mud, the common cold, headlands, sunsets. The common cold is as real as cystic fibrosis, and sunsets are as real as quarks. More law-like regularities are known about mud than quarks – known to youths who play football, parents who do the family laundry, and to mud engineers on oil rig sites. The regularities about mud do not have profound consequences for theoreticians. That does not make mud any the less a natural kind of stuff. In the domain of living things, Atran's speciemes – trees, vines, grasses – are kinds that we find in nature; so are the species of today's systematics.

Nelson Goodman has used the happy phrase 'relevant kinds' in which he includes 'such artificial kinds as musical works, psychological experiments and types of machinery'. As far as I am concerned, natural kinds are relevant kinds that we find in nature. Are the varieties of plants and animals that we owe to horticulturalists and stock breeders 'natural' by now? For me, plutonium is a natural kind, even though humans made it. There are many distinctions to be made among the natural kinds, including historical ones. Psycholinguists debate whether children innately distinguish the artefactual from the natural, or the mechanical from the living. On a quite different level there is undoubtedly a sense in which some kinds are more cosmic (the word is Quine's) than others. Perhaps nature and its laws are such that some kinds are more truly fundamental than others. Graceless philosophers repeat Plato's words out of context and talk of carving nature at her joints. Does nature have ultimate joints? For present purposes I am indifferent to all such questions – metaphysical, psycholinguistic, or historical. This is because they do not matter to the distinctions that I do wish to notice between human kinds and natural kinds.

Since I am so tolerant about natural kinds, should I not count human kinds among the natural kinds? For a certain convenience I shall restrict human kinds to kinds that are, at least at first sight, peculiar to people in a social setting. I do not deny that people are natural or that human societies are part of nature. For convenience, I follow the custom of calling something natural only when it is not peculiar to people in their communities. A great many types of attributes of people apply in the world at large or at least to other living beings: mass, longevity, distribution of digestive organs, the pancreatic enzymes such as amylopsin, trypsin, and steapsin, or the structure of the genome. Many items that occur in the scientific study of human beings present no significant contrast with other kinds that we find in nature. There is a proper tension here, because one thrust of research into human kinds is to biologize them. Drunkards form a human kind; according to one school of thought, apparently favoured by the editor of *Science*, alcoholism is carried by a gene. Five years ago I copied from a doctor's office the statement 'We have learned more about this illness in the past five years than in the past five hundred years and it is now evident that alcoholism and other drug additions are truly psychosocial biogenetic diseases'. Suicide is a kind of human behaviour; it was proposed late in 1990 that it too has a genetic component. These are instances not so much of what Imre Lakatos called research programmes as of what Gerald Holton called themata. Holton gives atomism in its successive manifestations (Leucippus, Lucretius, Boyle, Dalton, and onwards) as an example of a thema. Equally old and powerful is the idea that we acquire knowledge of humanity by replacing human kinds by physiological or mechanical or neuroelectrical or biochemical ones. This is not just a tradition of research, but also represents a metaphysics.

There are many more tensions – some in the philosophy of the natural and some in the methodology of the biological. Yet I think that there is little difficulty in picking out characteristic human kinds. When I speak of human kinds, I mean (i) kinds that are relevant to some of us, (ii) kinds that primarily sort people, their actions, and behaviour, and (iii) kinds that are studied in the human and social sciences, i.e. kinds about which we hope to have knowledge. I add (iv) that kinds of people are paramount; I want to include kinds of human behaviour, action, tendency, etc. only when they are projected to form the idea of a kind of person. Homosexuality provides us with a perhaps all too familiar example. It is quite widely asserted that, although same-sex acts are common in most human societies, the idea of 'the homosexual' as a kind of person came into being only late in the nineteenth century as homosexual behaviour became an object of scientific scrutiny. If this were correct, then homosexual behaviour would be what I am calling here a 'human kind' only late in the nineteenth century, even though there has been plenty of pederasty, for example, at all times and places, for only at that time was this kind of behaviour taken as an indication of a kind of person.

In important personal relationships we seldom think or feel directly in terms of human kinds. In friendship, love, and animosity we care about all that is particular, unusual, intimate, and circumstantial, all that is glimpsed or shared or felt glancingly – in short, all that is caught in the nuance of the novel rather than the classifications of the scientist. One person is trusting, another gentle, a third selfish and arrogant. One, who although forgetful is responsive and enthusiastic, has a friend who is an insensitive busybody. We know a great deal about such kinds of people, but we do not profess scientific knowledge about them. We neither make surveys that count their proportions in a given population, nor subject them to factor analysis. Yet these are the kinds that matter to us – the kinds we use to organize our thoughts about our companions, friends, and loved ones, not to mention those whom we try to avoid. Since they also matter to employers, teachers, and the military, psychologists devise tests that use questions often recalling these familiar traits. The results are tabulated or summarized to form 'profiles' or 'personal inventories' that then become human kinds. They are digests of what matters in intimacy, but they acquire the abstraction of the sciences or impersonal management.

Yet human kinds are not so irrelevant to us as people. Straightforward and well-established human kinds studied in the social sciences *do* affect intensely personal concerns. If you see someone whom you love (or see yourself) as of a kind, that may change your entire set of perceptions. Human kinds usually present themselves as scientific and hence as value-free, but they have often been brought into being by judgements of good and evil. Sociology of the numerical sort began by measuring the incidence of behaviour such as suicide. Durkheim's classic and originating work *Suicide* could draw upon 80 years of studies. Suicide was tabulated because it was a Bad Act, perhaps the very worst, beyond the possibility of repentance and even forgiveness. A body of knowledge about suicide changed beliefs about what kind of deed it was, and hence its moral evaluation: 'an attempted suicide is a cry for help'. Your attitude to a friend who attempts suicide will be different from that which your great-grandparents would have had. Suicides in novels today are not what they were at the time of young Werther or Heinrich Kleist, partly because science has made suicide into a human kind.

Human kinds are of many categories. I use the word 'category' in an old fashioned way, which is also the colloquial way. A category is a tree of classifications, or else the most general classification at the top of such a tree. Many authorities, ranging from cognitive scientists to psycholinguists, now use 'category' as a synonym for 'class' as in George Lakoff's title, *Women, fire and dangerous things: What categories show about the human mind*. Women-fire-and-dangerous-things is a class, or kind, distinguished by an Australian people, but Lakoff calls it a category. I do not. Race, gender, native language, nationality, type of employment, and age cohort are all what I call categories. The experts most versed in these categories work out of census bureaux, institutions whose modern form is coeval with quantitative social science. Indeed I willingly extend my grouping, human kinds, to include any of the kinds enumerated by the census, or at least those kinds when endowed with their social connotations. Say, to abbreviate too much, that gender is the social meaning of sex – the category of sex not being peculiar to human beings, but the category of gender being peculiar to humans in a society. I follow tradition surprisingly closely in all this. Philosophers took 'natural kind' as a term of art after J.S. Mill. As soon as he had introduced his idea of a *real Kind*, he asked whether the sexes and races were real Kinds. (He hoped not. His programme was anti-sexist and anti-racist.) These two human categories, race and gender, have been obsessively discussed of late. Our thoughts about them are so redolent of ideology that I shall leave them on one side. Conclusions about human kinds are indeed relevant to those categories, but we would be misled about human kinds if we followed Mill and used race and gender as our core examples. The very relationship between science, and race or gender, is unclear. I have defined human kinds as the objects of the insecure sciences, as the kinds about which we would like to have knowledge. I took for granted that those sciences are modelled on natural science, particularly in their conception of causality. That was what Mill was talking about. However, there is a strong present prejudice against making race the object of science. A few forthright spokesmen like Michael Dummett make plain that we do not want the knowledge that we might find out. The more familiar pusillanimous complaint is that race science is bad science. In the case of gender, many outspoken feminists claim knowledge, but reject a knowledge patterned on causal natural science. These important issues would take us aside from my main topic.

I have mentioned kinds 'with their social meaning' – an obscure phrase. To illustrate, take teen-age pregnancy. That is as determinate a classification as could be. You are teen-aged, female, pregnant, and (unwritten premise) unmarried. There is a regorous definition, then, with succinct chronological, physiological and legal clauses. If we make 'teen-age' precise and adapt 'unmarried', then this concept can be applied in many cultures unlike our own. However, it became a relevant kind only at a certain moment in American history. After 1967 it was the subject of interminable sociological study and debate. Recently the cultural meaning of the term has switched sufficiently that a euphemism has been introduced by sociologists: early parenting. Teen-age pregnancy – the word, and also the idea with a certain set of implications – reared its ugly head in the white American suburbs of the 1960s. Early parenting connotes black urban ghettos of the 1990s. Thus far we have an idea and no knowledge, but once the idea was in motion experts arrived to determine a knowledge and to transform it. The classification 'teen-age pregnancy' or 'early parenting' is completely grounded in nature, but is a human kind – and is the subject of social science – only in a certain social context. There is a similarity to and a difference from another human kind of person – the adolescent. Adolescence cannot be fully grounded in nature. Even if we define it as beginning with first menarche/ejaculation, there is nothing in nature beyond a social context that signals its end. Anna Freud said that we owe the discovery of adolescence to psychoanalysis. Historians of developmental psychology locate its discovery elsewhere. Nevertheless there is a remarkable agreement that whatever grander social changes made adolescence possible, the adolescent exists as a kind of person thanks to the social sciences. The first major work on adolescence was the two volume treatise by G. Stanley Hall (1904), the man who is commonly called the founder of American experimental psychology. He called it *Adolescence: its psychology and its relations to physiology, anthropology, sociology, sex, crime, religion and education.* You might think that this title is exhaustive, but it is not quite. After over 1200 pages we reach a long final chapter, 'Ethnic psychology and pedagogy, or adolescent races and their treatment'. We find that one third of the human race are 'adolescents of adult size'. Even lineages which are by now regarded as 'decadent', 'often exemplify the symptom of *dementia praecox* magnified to macrobiotic proportions' (Hall 1904, Vol. II, p. 649).

Those were the bad old days, of course. To fix ideas further, I shall take two up-to-date human kinds and a recently proposed causal law that connects them. Child abuse is a kind of human behaviour. It breaks up into several kinds, including sexual abuse, physical abuse, neglect, and, a current topic of fierce controversy in North America, sadistic cult abuse (read Satanic rituals). Child abuse is a kind that has been remarkably malleable. It has connections with cruelty to children, a classic kind of behaviour brought to the fore in Europe and America about 120 years ago. But the present classification, child abuse, began exactly 30 years ago with battered baby syndrome, took incest and sexual abuse under its wing 18 years ago, and picked up cruel ritual cult abuse 5 years ago. The recent trajectory is primarily American with European classifications following loosely in step (Hacking 1991, 1992c).

Child abuse certainly fits my rough and ready criteria for being a human kind.

1. In many quarters today, it is a highly relevant kind.
2. It is peculiar to people, even when we draw some analogies to some sorts of primate behaviour.
3. It is a kind of behaviour about which we would like to have knowledge, for example to prevent child abuse and to help abused children.
4. We have an inclination to project the kind of behaviour to the person, i.e., we think that there are child abusers, that abusive parents may be a type of parent.

We can make an even stronger statement about child abuse. The Center for Advanced Study in the Behavioral Sciences at Stanford University liked, and perhaps still likes, to use the epithet 'cutting edge' for work conducted under its auspices. An operational definition of a cutting-edge human kind would be: there is at least one professional society of experts dedicated to studying it; there are regular conferences, one of which is major and a number of which are more specialized; there is at least one recently established professional journal to which the authorities contribute (and which helps define who the authorities are). We have the International Society for the Prevention of Child Abuse and Neglect, a great many conferences, and the journal *Child Abuse and Neglect*, among others. Child abuse is a cutting-edge human kind.

Child abusers are all too common. A much rarer kind of person is the one suffering from what is now called multiple personality disorder (Hacking 1992b). These people used to be very rare indeed, and they usually suffered from two, or perhaps three or four, alternative personalities; one personality was usually amnesic for another. There has been an epidemic of multiple personalities in North America, starting in the early 1970s; the 9th International Conference on the topic was attended by 800 professionals (psychiatrists, psychologists, social workers), many of whom have case loads of over 40 multiples a year. The face of multiplicity has changed a great deal in the past 20 years. It is now commonplace for clinicians to have patients with 25 alter personalities. This whole discourse takes place under a larger rubric of 'dissociative behaviour'. Dissociation was first named by Pierre Janet during the French wave of multiples that started in Bordeaux in 1875, but has been retrieved only recently. In the inner circles of dissociation experts, Janet is revered while Freud is cast out.

Many psychiatrists, particularly those with a medical/biochemical/neurological approach to mental illness, are dubious or even cynical about multiple personality. They argue that multiples are a cultural artefact. Now, if I had said (as so many philosophers do say) that human kinds must in some sense be indubitably 'real', and perhaps even cross-culturally cosmic, I should have been obliged to discuss this opposition. Instead, I made some disclaimers not only about the human but also about the natural. I do believe that some psychiatrists, the media, a wing of the women's movement, concern about sexual abuse of children, and much else have brought about the present prevalence of multiple personality disorder. That does not make the malady any less real. It is a condition with associated behaviour that afflicts a significant number of people who at present are crying out for help. It is a human kind, and a cutting-edge human kind to boot. There is the International Society for the Study of Multiple Personality and Dissociation. There is an annual international conference and many regional conferences. The journal *Dissociation* is about to enter its fifth year of publication.

I stated that we want knowledge about human kinds. There has been a remarkable break-through in thinking about multiple personality. The cause of this disorder is now known to people who work in the field. Multiple personality is the consequence of repeated trauma early in childhood, almost always involving sexual abuse. This fact is so accepted among workers in the field that many regard it as almost definitional. This causal knowledge is deeply incorporated into theories of the disorder. The various alters represent dissociated ways of coping with particular experienced trauma. This in turn has had a great impact on methods of treatment, which now focus on abreaction of the trauma through the voices of the various alters which may in time become co-conscious, collaborative, and finally integrated. Thanks to media exposure, particularly on afternoon television talk shows that appeal to lower-class women who empathize with the oppressed and the bizarre, this scientific knowledge is very widely disseminated in the USA. The details are the property of experts, but the general structure is remarkably common knowledge.

My example is sensational but serves to fix ideas. Despite its role in social rhetoric and politics of numerous stripes, child abuse was first presented and is still intended to be a 'scientific' concept. Of course, there are demarcation disputes. Which science? Medicine, psychiatry, sociology, psychology, social work, jurisprudence, or self-help? Whatever the standpoint, there are plenty of authorities firmly convinced that there are important truths about child abuse, for example 'most abusers were abused as children'. Research and experiment should reveal them. We hope that cause and effect are relevant, that we can find predictors of future abuse, that we can explain it, that we can prevent it, and that we can determine its consequences and counteract them. For example, it is held that abusive mothers have often not bonded adequately to their children, and that premature babies in incubators are at risk of inadequate bonding. This causal hypothesis leads authorities to establish elaborate bonding rituals in maternity hospitals.

It might be thought that child abuse is such a complex concept that questions of developmental psychology or the theory of cognition could not arise. We are considering how a social organization makes and moulds an idea, not about concept acquisition in children. Quite the contrary. Lawrence Hirschfeld (1995) discusses the early stage at which American children acquire concepts of race. A parallel issue has been debated, with very practical consequences, in connection with child abuse. Many American jurisdictions introduced early training to enable children to recognize and report incipient abuse. Two years ago California rescinded these laws, on the basis of declarations by expert witnesses, based on Piagetian grounds, that children could not understand these ideas. There is now a back-backlash contesting this cognitive claim.

On the score of being scientific, a different type of issue emerges. Perhaps we fail to help children (some say) because all our endeavours assume that we are dealing with a scientific kind? This worry has been expressed in terms of the 'medicalization' of child abuse. Child abuse is not for the doctors, even if paediatricians did first sound the alert with battered baby syndrome. Thus far, the complaint is only about the type of expert, not about the very possibility of expertise. In general, the anti-experts usually claim that they are the true experts: the social workers defy the police, the psychologists confront the judiciary, etc. Multiple personality is a case of yet another type of concern about scientism. Some critics contend that there is no such thing as multiple personality disorder (I have heard it called 'the UFO of psychiatry') and that multiple behaviour results from interaction with doctors or, more recently, from sensationalist reports in the media. Nevertheless the debate is left to experts. This or that group claims to have knowledge about what really ails the troubled patients and how they could be treated better.

Thus what I call human kinds begin in the hands of scientists of various stripes. Human kinds live there for a while. A while? My example of the homosexual foreshadows something to be discussed later. People of the kind may rise up against the experts. The known may overpower the knowers.

I have stated that *we* want laws precise enough to predict what individuals will do. Or *we* want to know how people of a kind will respond to attempts to help them or to modify their behaviour. I have stated 'we' would like all this, typically in order to help 'them'. I made these statements because that is what the social sciences have been up to since their inception. The search for human kinds that conform to psychological or social laws is inextricably intertwined with prediction and reform. These aims can be perverted, but they have generally been well-intentioned when seen from the vantage point of the reformers. Groups of experts now collaborate and say that together they are members of the 'helping professions': social workers, therapists, parole officers, policemen, judges, psychiatrists, teachers, 'Ph.D. psychologists', paediatricians. They try to distinguish kinds of people or behaviour that are deviant. They invite more theoretical and foundational studies on which to base their practical work. Sociologists and statisticians form and test law-like conjectures about people of those kinds. Such knowledge enables the front line to interfere and intervene so as to help more effectively and predictably. Or so the sciences present themselves: cynics suspect that there is no knowledge to be had, and that these forms of knowledge legitimate the use of power.

Why are my examples so unattractive? I seem to have in mind a rather shady bunch of kinds, marginal human kinds, kinds about which we claim or hope to have systematic knowledge, kinds that are, loosely, topics for actual or prospective sciences. But not real social science! I could develop the argument that what I call human kinds are at the historical root of sociology – the science of normality and deviance. Even if I am correct, should not 'human kinds' by now serve as the generic name for the classifications used in the social sciences – the *sciences humaines*, or perhaps even *Geisteswissenschaften*? What then of the classifications made in anthropology, linguistics, economics, and history? Why lay such emphasis on the sciences of deviancy, social pathology, healing, and control?

I shall evade the question (and the historical or archaeological response) by saying that I am choosing my own type of causal understanding to think about. I fix on a certain type of practical causality. By human kinds I mean kinds of people and their behaviour which (it is hoped) can enter into practical laws – laws that if we knew them we would use to change present conditions, and predict what would ensue. We want the right classification – the correct sorting of child abuse or teen-age pregnancy – so that confronted by abusive parents or pregnant teenagers we can embark on a course of action that will change them for the better and will prevent others from joining their ranks. We do not want to know the 'structure' of teen-age pregnancy in the fascinating but abstract way in which we want to know the structure of kinship among a certain people, or the structure of the modal auxiliaries in their language. We want principles according to which we can interfere, intervene, help, and improve. The closest comparison within the social sciences would be with economics. The applied economists say that they want to make things better, but their kinds are not usually what I call human kinds. Most of them are at least one remove from individual people and their actions. The bank rate and the money supply depend upon what some people do, but they are not kinds of people.

I have been trying to make vivid the concept of a human kind. There is one last general point to make. Which comes first, the classification or the causal connections between kinds? There are two coarse pictures of concept formation. In one, people first make certain distinctions and then learn the properties and causal relationships between distinguished classes. In another, causal relationships are recognized between individuals, and these relationships are used to distinguish classes. I believe that my fellow philosophers are the chief sinners in cleaving to one or other of these extreme pictures. Whatever conclusion be urged about infant cognition, it is plain that in later life recognition and expectation are of a piece. Or, to put it linguistically, to acquire and use a name for any kind is, among other things, to be willing to make generalizations and form expectations about things of that kind. We should take for granted that guessing at causes goes hand in hand with increasingly precise definition.

To take two examples which are unfavourable to this theme, suicide and teen-age pregnancy have been with us always, and with many another society. Hence one might have the picture of first there being the kind of human behaviour or condition, and then the knowledge. That is not the case. The kind and the knowledge grow together. At the beginning of the nineteenth century people were still debating the noble suicide of Cato the Elder, but soon suicide was to be defined as 'a kind of madness' with numerous subkinds, all tended over by the right sort of medical man. Suicides were sorted by their conjectured causes. When we turn to child abuse, it sounds as if it were a classification of behaviour preceding any knowledge. But this is not the case. It emerged in 1961–1962 in company with a quite specific body of knowledge – paediatric X-rays (which showed unexpected healed fractures of babies' arms and legs). The technology of the rapidly declining profession of infant radiology was revived to define 'battered baby syndrome', and doctors asserted in powerful public statements that they were in control of the treatment and prevention of abusive behaviour. Cause, classification, and intervention were of a piece.

What's so special about human kinds?

My phrase 'human kind' is patterned after 'natural kind'. Evidently I think that human kinds are importantly different from natural kinds. In this section I shall do three things.

1. I shall sympathetically state the idea to which I am opposed: that human kinds are, at worst, messy natural kinds.
2. I shall make plain that I am not arguing anything remotely like *either* a *Verstehen or* a constructionist position. Yes, I think that the human differs from the natural, but not because what I call human kinds are to be understood hermeneutically rather than explained by causal principles. Yes, I think that the human differs from the natural, but not because human kinds are social constructions while natural kinds are discovered in nature.
3. I shall state the difference between natural and human kinds that interests me. I do not argue that it is the only difference. Perhaps the *Verstehen* and the construction distinctions are both right, but they are not mine. They are deep. Mine is shallow.

Natural and human

The modern phrase 'natural kind' resonates with antique controversies. Does nature have kinds, or are they of our making? If nature has kinds, do those kinds themselves have natures (essences)? Whatever stance we take on these issues, another arises. Given the aspirations of those sciences that investigate human kinds, will not something be a 'real', or at any rate a useful human kind, only if it is a natural kind?

The positivist version of this idea proceeds roughly as follows. If we want to obtain knowledge about people and their behaviour, we have to make correct distinctions. Only if we sort correctly will we be able to formulate descriptive law-like statements. But that fact is not peculiar to the human sciences. In any science we must discover what the natural kinds are. That involves rigorous exploration, experimentation, conjecture, and refutation. As we hone our causal hypotheses, we sharpen our classifications, and approach closer and closer to the kinds that are found in nature. The chief difference between natural and human kinds is that the human kinds often make sense only within a certain social context. But even there we constantly strive to go behind the phenomena. Where once we had descriptive criminology, now we have genes for violence and we are working on the genetic component of suicide.

The positivist supposes that the idea of a natural kind is clear and timeless. Here is a historicist version of the view that the human must be the natural. The idea of a natural kind (it is proposed) is not timeless but has evolved during the history of Western science. Long before the advent of the natural sciences, kinds played a major role in the development of early technological civilizations. Sowing and reaping, breeding and baking, mining and melting, have all needed an ability to pick out the right kinds. The kinds of animals, vegetables, and minerals that came to be named, cultivated, and created are the very kinds that philosophers came to call natural kinds. Some features of them have been invaluable as we have learned how to alter, improve, control, or guard against nature. The different theories about these kinds, whether in Aristotle, Locke, Mill, or Hilary Putnam, are owl-of-Minerva state of the art. That is, they effectively correspond to the level of technological expertise and scientific mastery current at the time that they were proposed. Each author thought that he was giving a timeless account of universals, or sorts (Locke), or real Kinds (Mill), or kind terms (Putnam). But each obediently represented a particular state of mastery of the non-human world, so that when we read these authors, we read a précis that could have been headed 'natural kinds as we know them today'. The chief source of the differences among these canonical writings is that they represent different stages in the growth of Western knowledge. The concept 'natural kind' (by whatever name) is not impugned. We are reminded only that this idea is (like everything else) historical and evolving.

The history of human kinds will prove (continues the historicist) to be similar and indeed part of the story. We find attention to suicide, incest, cruelty to children, and even teen-age pregnancy in many places and times. Some scholars urge that demonic possession, trance states, and shamanism are 'the same kind of condition' as multiple personality disorder, perhaps even deploying distinct sites in the brain. Human kinds require a fairly specific social organization for their existence. Teen-age pregnancy cannot exist until unmarried teen-age girls form a distinct group who are not supposed to be pregnant. The idea of juvenile delinquency depends partly on the family, on views of dependency, and on how age cohorts are structured. Nevertheless, there may be some human kinds that are of more general application than others.

We have (the historicist concludes) slowly come to a correct understanding of the idea of a law of nature – we have passed from Aristotelian essences through positivist instrumentalism, and to some extent back again to universal laws of causation and symmetry. In much the same way we will come to a correct understanding of laws of human beings. We could only do so, perhaps, when our idea of law had passed from the deterministic to the probabilistic, when we had created a new type of science geared to normalcy and deviation from the norm, when (just as essences gave way to law-like natural kinds) the idea of human nature had been displaced by the idea of normal people (Hacking 1990). The right laws about human beings have been slow in coming, and we have only just begun to come to grips with human kinds that will prove to be useful. But human kinds will in the end be a subclass of natural kinds. That will not leave things the same. The inclusion of human kinds within natural kinds will be one further step in the evolution of our causal understanding of nature.

You will have expected, from my early profession of indifference to any particular theory about natural kinds, that I do not want to conduct a stale argument with the positivist view, that all good human science is natural science, and that all good human kinds will be made into natural kinds. I take issue with the far more sensitive historicist view. It is the right view about philosophies of natural kinds, but it is wrong about the end of the story.

Understanding, construction

I am liable to be misunderstood. I shall be thought to be arguing for old theses, not for a new one. I have to make plain that whatever cleavage may result from my analysis, it is not one that has been much discussed. I do not argue for or imply either of two extremely important-sounding theses. I do not contend that the natural sciences want explanation while the human sciences demand understanding. I do not urge that human kinds are constructed while natural kinds are not.

The *Verstehen* dispute has partly to do with methodology, a subject that I abhor. There is an immense body of argument to the effect that quite distinct methods befit the natural and the human sciences, the one aiming at explanation and the other at understanding. I believe that there are some deep insights on the *Verstehen* side of the argument, but here they are irrelevant. That is because I have defined human kinds as finding their place in bodies of knowledge patterned after the efficient causation of the natural sciences. I am not about to say that human kinds are a horrible mistake – the error of striving for control rather than understanding.

We do not have the choice not to use human kinds, and human kinds (as I have defined the idea) are causal and instrumental. We are stuck with human kinds that demand causal analysis rather than *Verstehen* or meanings. They are part of what we mean by knowledge about people. It may be a pleasant romantic fantasy to think of abandoning or replacing the instrumental human sciences, but that is not possible. They are not just part of our system of knowledge; they are part of what we take knowledge to be. They are also our system of government, our way of organizing ourselves; they have become the great stabilizers of the Western post-manufacturing welfare state that thrives on service industries. The methodology of making 'studies' to detect law-like regularities and tendencies is not just our way of finding out what's what; 'studies' generate consensus, acceptance, and intervention. The one great argument for Durkheimian functionalism is weirdly self-reflexive: although the conscious aims of the social sciences are knowledge and helping, the function served is that of preserving and adapting the status quo. This fits Douglas's (1986) 'feedback' gloss on functionalism in her lectures *How institutions think*. The more the status quo is dissatisfied with itself, the more social science studies are in demand, and the greater the reliance on their results as definitive. As questioning is put aside, stability tends to ensue.

I now turn to the other way in which I might be understood. I do not claim that human kinds are somehow constructed while natural kinds are somehow given. Here I try to take absolutely no view on the constructionist controversies that swirl around us. I cannot exactly take no notice, because I have found that the anti-constructionist ('realist', for short) says that all good human kinds are (real) natural kinds, while the social constructionist says that everything is social and so the natural is social. (In a discussion some years ago of an article of mine on child abuse, James Bogen said the former and Bruno Latour said the latter.)

I take courage from the fact that the most compelling social constructionist arguments about kinds are about high class 'high tech' natural kinds. I think of Latour's first book (with

Steven Woolgar), *Laboratory life: the (social) construction of a scientific fact* – the word 'social' was in the 1979 edition but deleted from the 1986 edition on the ground that everything is social. The book is about the discovery of the chemical structure of a tripeptide important to the hypothalamus, to metabolism, and to maturation. Or I think of Andy Pickering's *Constructing quarks*. These authors contend, among many other things, that it is misleading to talk of scientific discoveries. The facts in question were constructed by a microsociological process, and in an important sense did not exist before the incidents described.

My strategy is willingly to swerve to the left and side with the constructionists. Yes, facts are socially constructed, and so are the kinds about which there are facts. But within the domain of social constructions, I can still claim that there is an important difference between quarks and tripeptides on the one hand, and what I call human kinds on the other. Hearing an uproar to my right I then turn to the realists and willingly agree that multiple personality disorder and adolescence are just as real as electricity and sulphuric acid; Anna Freud claims the discovery of adolescence for psychoanalysis, and the discovery of the phenomenon of dissociation is claimed for Pierre Janet. Who am I to resist such claims to fame, except on petty points that perhaps somebody else made the discovery?

Hence for present purposes I operate as if there were no vital contradiction between realism and constructionism. Teen-age pregnancy is as 'real' as could be, with rigorous defining characteristics. It is also aptly described as socially constructed as a human kind at a certain point in American history. Likewise, children were abused before 'child abuse'. The history of the concept in the past three decades displays social making and moulding if anything could. This example has the fortuitous advantage that some of the more vociferous social constructionists, who urge that almost anything is a social construction, say (without noticing the switch) exactly the opposite about child abuse. It is, they rightly say, a real evil that the family and the state covered up. Our discovery of the prevalence of child abuse is a powerful step forward in Western awareness, they say. I agree. Child abuse is a real evil, and it was so before being socially constructed as a human kind. Neither reality nor construction should be in question.

I do not mean to imply that no construction–realism issues are important for human kinds. They do matter, but only in a specific context. Their significance is independent of inflated all-purpose general philosophical themes. The most carefully worked-out example, i.e. what has been called the social constructionist controversy about homosexuality, has mattered deeply to the people who were classified. It was important to one party to maintain that 'the homosexual' as a 'kind of person' is a social construct, chiefly of psychiatry and jurisprudence. It was important for others to insist that some people in every era have been sexually and emotionally attracted chiefly to people of their own sex. There are endless variants on these themes. Stein (1992) (in an essay in his collection *Forms of desire*) has made the appropriate conceptual distinctions, and thereby established several ways in which essentialist and constructionist attitudes are not only compatible but also mutually supporting.

Looping

How then may natural kinds differ from what I call human kinds? I do accept, but wish to downplay, one fundamental difference. Human kinds are laden with values. Caked mud and polarized electrons may be good or bad depending on what you want to do with them, but child abuse is bad and multiple personality is a disorder to be healed.

It is the shibboleth of science that it is value-neutral. Throughout the history of the social sciences there has been a strident insistence on the distinction between fact and value. That is a give-away, for the natural sciences have seldom had to insist upon this distinction. On the contrary, elderly natural scientists regularly regret that there are not more values to be found in the natural sciences. Should we not argue that we are moving closer to the mind of God, and therefore to the Good? In social science things go differently. There is the clarion call for facts, facts, and more facts. Only with facts, and generalizations inferred therefrom, can the social scientist serve the apparatus of our civilization. The social sciences deliver the raw facts and we, the people, are then able to make rational choices depending on the facts and our values.

There has been much cynical backbiting about the valiant claim to value neutrality. It is said that the professed knowledge serves certain interests, and so is value-laden. That is controversial, and I have little use for what has been called interest theory – the sweeping attribution of interests to all sorts of knowledge. Instead, I dwell on the less controversial observation that the classes I call human kinds are themselves laden with value. In sociology they have typically been classes of deviants, to which have been opposed normal children, normal behaviour, normal development, normal reactions, and normal feelings, and the deviations are usually bad. Of course, normal distributions in statistics have two tails, idiots on one side of normal intelligence, and geniuses on the other, with (as Francis Galton put it) mediocrity in between. Value-free? I am not implying that there need be evaluation in the causal laws about characteristic human kinds. The discoveries need serve no interest and the facts discovered may be value-free. I am drawing attention to the presuppositions of enquiries: we investigate human kinds that are loaded with values.

There is a regular attempt to strip human kinds of their moral content by biologizing or medicalizing them. Child abusers are not bad; they are sick and need help! Their crimes are not their fault. They were abused as children, and that is why they abuse their own children. We must not make pregnant teen-age girls feel guilty. The world would be a better place if there were no single parents / child abusers / suicides / multiple personalities / vagrants / prostitutes / juvenile delinquents / recidivists / bulimics / alcoholics / homosexuals / pae-dophiles / chronic unemployed / homeless / runaways, etc. But let us not blame them, let us medicalize them. This fits well with the metaphysical thrust that I mentioned earlier, that somehow causal connections between kinds are more intelligible if they operate at a biological rather than a psychological or social level.

I do not propose to discuss the intense moral content of human kinds. I am not interested in the moral overtones of human kinds as a way of challenging the fact-value distinction, or as a way of challenging sociology's claim to be above (or underneath) the level of evaluation. I mention it because it is relevant to another difference between the human and the natural. Human kinds are kinds that people may want to be or not to be, not in order to attain some end but because the human kinds have intrinsic moral value.

If N is a natural kind and Z is N, it makes no direct difference to Z, if it is called N. It makes no direct difference to either mud or a mud puddle to call it 'mud'. It makes no direct difference to thyrotropin-releasing hormone or to a bottle of TRH to call it TRH. Of course seeing that the Z is N, we may do something to it in order to melt it or mould it, cook it or drown it, breed it or barter it. If there is mud on my child's T-shirt I use ordinary detergent to remove it, not the enzyme-activated product that I would use for a grass stain or blood. Because a particular liquid is a thyrotropin-releasing factor, an experimenter may see what happens if it is injected into sex-starved frogs or sleeping alligators, or given in megadoses to suicidal women (true stories all). But calling Z N, or seeing that Z is N, does not, in itself, make any difference to Z.

If H is a human kind and A is a person, then calling A H may make us treat A differently, just as calling Z N may make us do something to Z. We may reward or jail, instruct or abduct.

But it also makes a difference to A to know that A is an H, precisely because there is so often a moral connotation to a human kind. Perhaps A does not want to be H! Thinking of me as an H changes how I think of me. Well, perhaps I could do things a little differently from now on. Not just to escape opprobrium (I have survived unscathed so far) but because I do not want to be that kind of person. Even if it does not make a difference to A it makes a difference to how people feel about A – how they relate to A – so that A's social ambience changes.

It is a common theme in the theory of human action that to perform an intentional act is to do something 'under a description'. As human kinds are made and moulded, the field of descriptions changes and so do the actions that I can perform, i.e. the field of human kinds affects the field of possible intentional actions. Yet intentional action falls short of the mark. There are more possible ways to see oneself, more roles to adopt. I do not believe that multiple personalities intentionally choose their disorder, or that they are trained by their therapists. However, if this way of being were not available at the moment, hardly anyone would be that way. It is a way for troubled people to express their difficulties; the role is one of many that awaits, and some are chosen for it, often by a new way of describing their own past.

Human kinds have (what could be presented as) an even more amazing power than that of opening possibilities for future action. They enable us to redescribe our past to the extent that people can come to experience *new* pasts. A striking number of adults come to see themselves as having been abused as children. There has recently been a fashion of saying that we define ourselves by our biographies, by our personal narratives. Well, if there are new story lines, there can be new stories. To take an extreme example, some people come to see themselves as incest survivors, which in turn changes their lives and their relationships to their families. This is no mere matter of recovering forgotten trauma; it is a matter of there being new descriptions available, connected in law-like ways to other new descriptions, explanations, and expectations. One of the more powerful words in this group of examples is 'trauma' itself, naming a relatively new kind of human experience. The word used to denote physical wounds, injuries, or lesions, but now it denotes a kind of mental event in the lives of people – the psychic wound, forgotten but ever active. We did not know that we had them until recently – or, more paradoxical but more true, they were not a possible kind of experience to have had. But surely trauma, in its present sense of psychic wound, has been a permanent fixture in human life? Only in the past century has it been a human kind, i.e. a kind of experience about which scientific knowledge is claimed. Only recently has it become a self-evident link between rape, infant seduction, shell-shock, and being held hostage by terrorists, as in Judith Herman's powerful study, *Trauma and recovery* (1992).

Thus one way in which some human kinds differ from some kinds of thing is that classifying people works on people, changes them, and can even change their past. The process does not stop there. The people of a kind themselves are changed. Hence 'we', the experts, are forced to rethink our classifications. Moreover, causal relationships between kinds are changed. Sometimes they are confirmed to the point of becoming essential definitional connections. It becomes part of the *essence* of multiple personality that it is caused by repeated childhood trauma. This is not because we have found out more about the natural disorder, but because people who see themselves as having this human disorder now find in themselves memories of trauma, often traumas of a kind that they could not even have conceptualized 20 years ago. (This can be illustrated by astonishing empirical facts, for example hundreds of people with memories of grotesque sadistic ritual cult abuse appeared in American clinics 6 years ago; much of what they remember under these descriptions they could not have thought of 12 years ago.)

To create new ways of classifying people is also to change how we can think of ourselves, to change our sense of self-worth, even how we remember our own past. This in turn generates a looping effect, because people of the kind behave differently and so are different. That is to say the kind changes, and so there is new causal knowledge to be gained and perhaps, old causal knowledge to be jettisoned.

Here I should both acknowledge labelling theory and distance myself from it. It was once argued that calling a person a juvenile delinquent (etc.), and institutionally confirming that label, made the person adopt certain stereotypical patterns of behaviour. When a youth was labelled as J, he assumed more and more of the characteristic features of J. That is a claim about labelling *individuals*. I am sure that there is some truth in it for some individuals. I go two steps further. I assert that there are changes in individuals of that kind, which means that the kind itself becomes different (possibly confirmed in its stereotype but, as I go on to urge, quite the opposite may happen). Next, because the kind changes, there is new knowledge to be had about the kind. But that new knowledge in turn becomes part of what is to be known about members of the kind, who change again. This is what I call the looping effect for human kinds.

The greater the moral connotations of a human kind, the greater the potential for the looping effect. Although I shall not develop the theme here, we find similar effects in the relatively value-neutral kinds counted by the national census and similar government agencies. These effects have been investigated with remarkable results by a number of researchers such as Desrosières (1993). That is a piece of self-reflection in itself – the bureau that includes the French census looking at what past censuses have done to the very people who have been enumerated. Each decade the census draws up a new classification of the population, a classification that then becomes experienced as the structure of the society for the next decade or more. Similarly, Americans know that 'Hispanic' is an ethnic kind invented by the Bureau of the Census, with some effect on many people who now think of themselves as Hispanic and with rather more effect on their non-Hispanic neighbours. I have myself asserted, with too little argument, that the endless reports and tabulations prepared by countless British government functionaries, and so carefully scrutinized by Karl Marx, had more to do than Marx himself with the formation of class consciousness.

Responses of people to attempts to be understood or altered are different from the responses of things. This trite fact is at the core of one difference between the natural and human sciences, and it works at the level of kinds. There is a looping or feedback effect involving the introduction of classifications of people. New sorting and theorizing induces changes in self-conception and in behaviour of the people classified. Those changes demand revisions of the classification and theories, the causal connections, and the expectations. Kinds are modified, revised classifications are formed, and the classified change again, loop upon loop.

References

Desrosières, A. (1993). *La Politique des grands nombres*. Découverte, Paris.

Douglas, M. (1986). *How institutions think*. Syracuse University Press.

Gilbert, W. (1991). Towards a paradigm shift in biology. *Nature* **349**, 99.

Hacking, I. (1986). Making up people. In *Reconstructing individualism* (ed. P. Heller, M. Sosna, and D. Wellberry), pp. 222–36. Stanford University Press.

Hacking, I. (1990). The normal state. *The taming of chance*, Chapter 19, pp. 160–9, see also pp. 178 ff. Cambridge University Press.

Hacking, I. (1991). The making and molding of child abuse, *Critical Inquiry* **17**, 235–58.

Hacking, I. (1992*a*). 'Style' for historians and philosophers. *Studies in the History and Philosophy of Science* **22**, 1–20.

Hacking, I. (1992*b*). Multiple personality disorder and its hosts. *History of the Human Sciences* **5**(2), 3–31.

Hacking, I. (1992*c*). World-making by kind-making: child abuse for example. In *How classification works* (ed. M. Douglas and D. Hull), pp. 180–238. Edinburgh University Press.

Hall, G. (1904). *Adolescence. Its psychology and its relation to physiology, anthropology, sociology, sex, crime, religion and education*. Appleton, New York.

Herman, J. L. (1992). *Trauma and recovery*. Basic Books, New York.

Hirschfield, L. (1995). Anthropology, psychology, and the meanings of social causality. In *Causal cognition: a multidisciplinary debate* (ed. D. Sperber, D. Premack, and A. Premack), pp. 313–44. Clarendon Press, Oxford.

Stein, E. (1992). The essentials of constructionism and the construction of essentialism. In *Forms of desire* (ed. E. Stein), pp. 295–325. Routledge, Chapman and Hall, Inc.

Chapter 3

MIRANDA FRICKER

POWERLESSNESS AND SOCIAL INTERPRETATION

I WANT TO EXPLORE THE IDEA THAT social understanding—in particular our understanding of our own social experiences—is a sphere of epistemic activity in which relations of identity and power can create a particular kind of epistemic injustice, with the upshot that some social groups are unable to dissent from distorted understandings of their social experiences. To see better what the contours of such an injustice might be, let us begin with a historical example drawn from Susan Brownmiller's memoir of the U.S. Women's Liberation Movement, which concerns the experience of what we are these days in a position to name sexual harassment:

> Carmita Wood, age forty-four, born and raised in the apple orchard region of Lake Cayuga, and the sole support of two of her children, had worked for eight years in Cornell's department of nuclear physics, advancing from lab assistant to a desk job handling administrative chores. Wood did not know why she had been singled out, or indeed if she had been singled out, but a distinguished professor seemed unable to keep his hands off her.
>
> As Wood told the story, the eminent man would jiggle his crotch when he stood near her desk and looked at his mail, or he'd deliberately brush against her breasts while reaching for some papers. One night as the lab workers were leaving their annual Christmas party, he cornered her in the elevator and planted some unwanted kisses on her mouth. After the Christmas party incident, Carmita Wood went out of her way to use the stairs in the lab building in order to avoid a repeat encounter, but the stress of the furtive molestations and her efforts to keep the scientist at a distance while maintaining cordial relations with his wife, whom she liked, brought on a host of physical symptoms. Wood developed chronic back and neck pains. Her right thumb tingled and grew numb. She requested a transfer to another department, and when it didn't come through, she quit. She walked out the door and went to Florida for some rest and recuperation. Upon her return she applied for unemployment insurance. When the claims investigator asked why she had left her job after eight years, Wood was at a loss to describe the hateful episodes. She was ashamed and embarrassed. Under prodding—the blank on the form needed to be filled in—she answered that her reasons had been personal. Her claim for unemployment benefits was denied.

'Lin's students had been talking in her seminar about the unwanted sexual advances they'd encountered on their summer jobs,' Sauvigne relates. 'And then Carmita Wood comes in and tells Lin *her* story. We realized that to a person, every one of us—the women on staff, Carmita, the students—had had an experience like this at some point, you know? And none of us had ever told anyone before. It was one of those *click, aha!* moments, a profound revelation.'

... Meyer located two feminist lawyers in Syracuse, Susan Horn and Maurie Heins, to take on Carmita Wood's unemployment insurance appeal. 'And then . . .' Sauvigne reports 'we decided that we also had to hold a speak-out in order to break the silence about this.'

The 'this' they were going to break the silence about had no name. 'Eight of us were sitting in an office of Human Affairs,' Sauvigne remembers, 'brainstorming about what we were going to write on the posters for our speak-out. We were referring to it as 'sexual intimidation,' 'sexual coercion,' 'sexual exploitation on the job.' None of those names seemed quite right. We wanted something that embraced a whole range of subtle and unsubtle persistent behaviors. Somebody came up with 'harassment.' *Sexual harassment!* Instantly we agreed. That's what it was.'

(Brownmiller 1990, 280–1)

Here is a story about how extant collective heremeneutical resources can have a lacuna where the name of a distinctive social experience should be. So described, we can see that women such as Carmita Wood suffered (among other things) an acute cognitive disadvantage from a gap in the collective hermeneutical resource. But this description does not quite capture it, for if the epistemic wrong done to Carmita Wood were construed simply as a matter of plain cognitive disadvantage, then it is unclear why the epistemic wrong is suffered only by her and not also by her harasser. For the lack of proper understanding of women's experience of sexual harassment was a collective disadvantage more or less shared by all. Prior to the collective appreciation of sexual harassment as such, the absence of a proper understanding of what men were doing to women when they treated them like that was *ex hypothesi* quite general. Different groups can be hermeneutically disadvantaged for all sorts of reasons, as the changing social world frequently generates new sorts of experience of which our understanding may dawn only gradually, but only some of these cognitive disadvantages will strike one as unjust. For something to be an injustice it must be harmful but also wrongful, whether because discriminatory or otherwise unfair. In the present example, harasser and harassee alike are cognitively handicapped by the heremeneutical lacuna—neither has a proper understanding of how he is treating her—but the harasser's cognitive disablement is not a significant disadvantage to him. Indeed there is an obvious sense in which it suits his purpose. (Or at least it suits his immediate purpose in that it leaves his conduct unchallenged. This is not to deny that if he is a decent person underneath, so that a better understanding of the seriousness of his bad behaviour would have led him to refrain, then the hermeneutical lacuna is for him a source of epistemic and moral bad luck.) By contrast, the harassee's cognitive disablement is seriously disadvantageous to her. The cognitive disablement prevents her from understanding an important patch of her own experience; that is, a patch of experience which it is strongly in her interests to understand, for without that understanding she is left deeply troubled, confused, and isolated, not to mention vulnerable to continued harassment. Her hermeneutical disadvantage renders her unable to make sense of her ongoing mistreatment, and this in turn prevents her from protesting it, let alone securing effective measures to stop it.

The fact that the hermeneutical lacuna creates such an asymmetrical disadvantage for the harassee already fuels the idea that there is something wrongful about her cognitive disadvantage in particular. We would not describe her as suffering an injustice if it were not significantly disadvantageous for *her in particular*. But there is more than this to be said about the wrong that she sustains. We need to find the deeper source of the intuition that she incurs an injustice. We can easily imagine, after all, similarly serious hermeneutical disadvantages that do not inflict any epistemic injustice. If, for instance, someone has a certain medical condition affecting their behaviour at a historical moment at which that condition is still misunderstood and largely undiagnosed, then they may suffer a hermeneutical disadvantage that is, while collective, especially damaging to them in particular. They are unable to render their experiences intelligible by reference to the idea that they have a disorder, and so they are personally in the dark, and may also suffer seriously negative consequences from others' non-comprehension of their condition. But they are not subject to hermeneutical injustice; rather, theirs is a poignant case of circumstantial epistemic bad luck. In order to find the deeper source of the intuition that there is an epistemic injustice at stake in our example from Brownmiller we should focus on the background social conditions that were conducive to the relevant hermeneutical lacuna. Women's position at the time of second wave feminism was still one of marked social power-lessness in relation to men; and, specifically, the unequal relations of power prevented women from participating on equal terms with men in those practices by which collective social meanings are generated. Most obvious among such practices are those sustained by professions such as journalism, politics, academia, and law—it is no accident that Brownmiller's memoir recounts so much pioneering feminist activity in and around these professional spheres and their institu-tions. Women's powerlessness meant that their social position was one of unequal hermeneutical participation, and something like this sort of inequality provides the crucial background condition for the epistemic injustice affecting Carmita Wood.

Hermeneutical marginalization and hermeneutical injustice

Hermeneutical inequality is an epistemic inequality that arises from social inequality, and it is inevitably hard to detect. Our interpretive efforts are naturally geared to interests, as we try hardest to understand those things it serves us to understand. Consequently, a group's unequal hermeneutical participation will tend to show up in a localised manner in hermeneutical hotspots—locations in social life where the powerful have no interest in achieving a proper interpretation, perhaps indeed where they have a positive interest in sustaining the extant misinterpretation (such as that repeated sexual propositions in the workplace are necessarily just a way of 'flirting', and their uneasy rejection by the recipient a matter of her 'lacking a sense of humour'). But then in such a hotspot as this, the unequal hermeneutical participation remains positively disguised by the existing meaning attributed to the behaviour ('flirting' ...), and so it is all the more difficult to detect. No wonder that moments of its revelation can come as a life-changing flash of enlightenment. Unlike our example of a person with a condition for which medical science does not yet have the proper diagnosis, what women like Carmita Wood had to contend with at work was no plain epistemic bad luck, for it was no accident that their experience had been falling down the hermeneutical cracks. As they struggled in isolation to make proper sense of their various experiences of harassment, the whole engine of collective social meaning was effectively geared to keeping these obscured experiences out of sight. Her unequal hermeneutical participation is the deeper reason why Carmita Wood's cognitive disablement constitutes an injustice.

Let us say that when there is unequal hermeneutical participation with respect to some significant area(s) of social experience, members of the disadvantaged group are *hermeneutically marginalized*. The notion of marginalization is a moral-political one indicating subordination and exclusion from some practice that would have value for the participant. Obviously there can be more and less persistent and/or wide-ranging cases of hermeneutical marginalization. Although the term will be most at home in cases where the subject is persistently denied full hermeneutical participation in respect of a wide range of social experiences, nonetheless we can apply the term in slighter cases. Thus someone might be hermeneutically marginalized only fleetingly, and/or only in respect of a highly localized patch of their social experience. But hermeneutical marginalization is always socially coerced. If you simply opt out of full participation in hermeneutical practices as a matter of choice (perhaps, fed up with it all, you become a modern hermit) then you do not count as hermeneutically marginalized—you've opted out but you could have opted in. Hermeneutical marginalization is always a form of powerlessness, whether structural or one-off.

Social subjects of course have more or less complex social identities, and so one might be marginalized in a context where one aspect of one's identity is to the fore ('woman') but not in other contexts where other aspects of one's identity are determining one's level of participation ('middle-class'). The net result is that while a hermeneutically marginalized subject is prevented from generating meanings pertaining to some areas of the social world, she might well maintain a fuller participation as regards others. If she has a well-paid job in a large corporation with a macho work ethic she may be entirely unable to frame meanings, even to herself, relating to the need for family-friendly working conditions (such sentiments can only signal a lack of professionalism, a failure of ambition, a half-hearted commitment to the job), and yet she may be in a hermeneutically luxurious position as regards her ability to make sense of other, less gendered, areas of her work experience. Thus the complexity of social identity means that hermeneutical marginalization afflicts individuals in a differentiated manner; that is, it may afflict them *qua* one social type, but not another.

We can now define hermeneutical injustice of the sort suffered by women like Carmita Wood. It is: *the injustice of having some significant area of one's social experience obscured from collective understanding owing to persistent and wide-ranging hermeneutical marginalization*. But the latter notion is cumbersome, and we would do well to make our definition slightly more explicit in terms of what is bad about hermeneutical marginalization of the persistent and wide-ranging sort. From the epistemic point of view, what is bad about this sort of hermeneutical marginalization is that it renders the collective hermeneutical resource *structurally prejudiced*, for it will tend to issue interpretations of that group's social experiences that are biased because insufficiently influenced by the subject group and therefore unduly influenced by more hermeneutically powerful groups (thus, for instance, sexual harassment as flirting, rape in marriage as non-rape, post-natal depression as hysteria, reluctance to work family-unfriendly hours as unprofessionalism, and so on). We can now colour our definition slightly differently, without altering its substance, so that it better conveys the discriminatory nature of hermeneutical injustice. Hermeneutical injustice is: *the injustice of having some significant area of one's social experience obscured from collective understanding owing to a structural prejudice in the collective hermeneutical resource*.

Our definition has grown out of the effort to identify the sort of hermeneutical injustice suffered by Carmita Wood, and as a result the definition is not generic. Rather it specifically captures what we might call the *systematic* case of hermeneutical injustice. Now what exactly does 'systematic' mean here? The thought is that some groups may suffer marginalization in respect of only one localized area of their social life, whereas others—those perhaps like Carmita Wood—are also marginalized economically, and/or politically, educationally, professionally, and so on. (Indeed, in cases of systematic hermeneutical injustice, the hermeneutical marginalization *entails* marginalization of at least a socio-economic sort, since it entails non-participation in professions that make for significant hermeneutical participation such as journalism, politics, law, and so on.) Let us say, then, that if marginalization pursues the subject through a range of different dimensions of social activity besides the hermeneutical, then any hermeneutical injustices to which it gives rise are systematic. Systematic hermeneutical injustices are part of the broad pattern of a social group's general susceptibility to different sorts of injustice. We should think of systematic hermeneutical injustice as the central case—it is central from the point of view of an interest in how epistemic injustice is woven into the fabric of social injustice more generally.

By contrast, there can be cases of hermeneutical injustice that are not part of the general pattern of social power, and are more of a one-off. They are not systematic but *incidental*. Whereas systematic cases will tend to involve persistent and wide-ranging hermeneutical marginalization, incidental cases will tend to involve hermeneutical marginalization only fleetingly and/or in respect of a highly localized patch of the subject's experience. Incidental hermeneutical injustices, then, stem not from any structural inequality of power but rather from a more one-off moment of powerlessness. What might an incidental case of hermeneutical injustice look like? In Ian McEwan's novel *Enduring Love* the main protagonist, Joe, is stalked by a young man called Jed Parry, a religious fanatic with delusions of love between him and Joe. When Joe tells his partner, Clarissa, about it he meets first affectionate derision and then, later—although she accepts the basics of what he is telling her—her reaction is more one of concerned reserve about his state of mind. When, subsequently, he calls the police, Joe finds that the form of stalking he is enduring does not make the legal grade and is represented as trivial:

> 'Are you the person being harassed?'
> 'Yes. I've been . . .'
> And is the person causing the nuisance with you now?'
> 'He's standing outside my place this very minute.'
> 'Has he inflicted any physical harm on you?'
> 'No, but he . . .'
> 'Has he threatened you with harm?'
> 'No.' I understood that my grievance would have to be poured into the available bureaucratic mould. There was no facility refined enough to process every private narrative. Denied the release of complaint, I tried to take comfort in having my story assimilated into a recognisable public form. Parry's behaviour had to be generalised into a crime.
> 'Has he made threats against your property?'
> 'No.'
> 'Or against third parties?'
> 'No.'
> 'Is he trying to blackmail you?'
> 'No.'
> 'Do you think you could prove that he intends to cause you distress?'
> 'Er, no.'
> . . . 'Can you tell me what he's doing then?'

'He phones me at all hours. He talks to me in the . . .'

The voice was quick to move back to his default position, the interrogative flow chart. 'Is he using obscene or insulting behaviour?'

'No. Look, officer. Why don't you let me explain. He's a crank. He won't let me alone.'

'Are you aware of what he actually wants?' . . .

'He wants to save me.'

'Save you?'

'You know, convert me. He's obsessed. He simply won't leave me alone.'

The voice cut in, impatience taking hold at last. 'I'm sorry caller. This is not a police matter. Unless he harms you, or your property, or threatens the same he's committing no offence. Trying to convert you is not against the law.' Then he terminated our emergency conversation with his own little stricture. 'We do have religious freedom in this country.'

(McEwan 1998, 73–74)

Joe's own understanding of his experience of being stalked is only slightly hindered by the lack of hermeneutical reciprocation by partner and police, but still a collective hermeneutical lacuna is preventing him from rendering his experience communicatively intelligible. It is very much in his interests to share his experience with certain others from the off; but he cannot, for the true nature of his experience of being stalked by Jed Parry is obscured by two misfit interpretations that trivialize it in different ways. According to one he seems to be failing to see the funny side and becoming worryingly obsessed; according to another he is exaggerating the level of threat and even cramping someone else's religious freedom into the bargain. But if the obscurity of Joe's experience constitutes a kind of hermeneutical injustice, this has nothing to do with any general social powerlessness or any general subordination as a generator of social meaning, for his social identity is that of the proverbial white, educated, straight man. Still he is none the less up against a one-off moment of hermeneutical marginalization. The competing and trivializing interpretations coming from Clarissa and the police respectively mean that Joe's hermeneutical participation is hindered in respect of a significant, if highly localized, patch of his social experience, and for this reason his case qualifies as a hermeneutical injustice. The injustice does not stem from any structural prejudice in hermeneutical resources— on the contrary, he suffers the injustice not because of but rather in spite of the hermeneutical ease he normally enjoys, indeed in spite of his general position of social power. Clearly Joe's hermeneutical injustice is not a systematic case; it is incidental.

Awareness of such cases motivates a more generic definition of hermeneutical injustice than those so far given, which were designed to capture what we can now more clearly see to be the distinctively systematic case. The generic definition now called for captures hermeneutical injustice *per se* as: *the injustice of having some significant area of one's social experience obscured from collective understanding owing to hermeneutical marginalization*. This definition simply omits what is special to the systematic case, namely that the hermeneutical marginalization is 'persistent and wide-ranging', or, equivalently, that there is a 'structural prejudice in the collective hermeneutical resource.' This generic definition, then, covers both the systematic case and the incidental case. As ever, the systematic case is central from our point of view. The non-centrality of incidental cases does not entail ethical triviality. Indeed it is life-shattering for Joe that his experience is not better understood from the start, since this allows Jed Parry's stalking to escalate to ultimately mortally threatening levels, and it contributes too to the eventual collapse of his long relationship with Clarissa. Incidental hermeneutical injustices can be every bit as harmful as systematic ones.

We have encountered, then, two sorts of hermeneutical injustice: systematic and incidental. If someone is disadvantaged, as for instance Joe is, from having their experience left obscure owing to a lacuna in the collective hermeneutical resource, then that is broadly sufficient for a claim of incidental hermeneutical injustice, even though the hermeneutical marginalization is localized and one-off. By contrast, if someone is disadvantaged, as for instance Carmita Wood is, by having their experience left obscure owing to a lacuna in the collective hermeneutical resource, where the lacuna is caused and maintained by a wide-ranging and persistent hermeneutical marginalization, then the hermeneutical injustice is systematic. For in such cases the hermeneutical marginalization is part of a more general susceptibility to different forms of social marginalization, so that any given hermeneutical injustice incurred is likewise part of a more general susceptibility to different kinds of injustice. Whether the injustice is of the systematic or the incidental kind, it involves no perpetrator, no culprit. Hermeneutical injustice is a structural notion, for it is a form of inequality—it is an epistemic inequality. The background condition for hermeneutical injustice is the subject's hermeneutical marginalization. And the actual moment of hermeneutical injustice comes when the background condition expresses itself in a more or less doomed attempt on the part of the subject to render an experience intelligible, either to herself or to an interlocutor. The hermeneutical inequality that exists, dormant, in a situation of hermeneutical marginalization erupts in injustice only when some actual attempt at intelligibility is handicapped by it.

Now that we have a clear idea of what defines hermeneutical injustice, in its systematic and incidental forms, let us try to probe the nature of the wrong it does to the subject whose interpretive efforts at social understanding are hampered by it.

The wrong of hermeneutical injustice

I have talked in terms of hermeneutical injustice involving an asymmetrical cognitive disadvantage. The general point here is that collective hermeneutical impoverishment impacts on members of different groups in different ways. It did not harm the interests of Carmita Wood's harasser that he (as the example goes) did not have a proper grasp of the nature of his treatment of her; but it harmed Carmita Wood a great deal that she could not make adequate sense of it to herself, let alone to others. The asymmetry arises from the concrete social and practical context in which the collective hermeneutical impoverishment impinges. It is only when the collective impoverishment is concretely situated in specific social situations that it comes to be especially and unjustly disadvantageous to some groups and not others. Hermeneutical lacunas are like holes in the ozone—it's the people who live under them that get burned. Fundamentally, then, hermeneutical injustice is a kind of structural discrimination. Compare a society that has a welfare state providing free healthcare at the point of delivery, but where there is a gap in state provision: no free dental care. Formally speaking, there is nothing intrinsically unjust about there being a general lack of free dental care, for it is the same for everyone—there is, so to speak, a collective lacuna in the welfare system. There is a formal equality, then; but as soon as one looks to how this formal equality plays out in practice in the lived social world, a *situated* inequality quickly reveals itself: people who cannot afford private dental care suffer from the lack of general provision, and people who can do not. In such cases of formal equality but lived inequality, the injustice is a matter of some group(s) being asymmetrically disadvantaged by a blanket collective lack, and so it is, I suggest, in the case of hermeneutical injustice.

A hermeneutical injustice is done when a collective hermeneutical gap impinges so as to significantly disadvantage some group(s) and not others, so that the way the collective impoverishment plays out in practice is effectively discriminatory. Let us say, then, that the primary harm of hermeneutical injustice consists in a *situated hermeneutical inequality*: the concrete situation is such that the subject is rendered unable to make communicatively intelligible something which it is particularly in his or her interests to be able to render intelligible.

Such is the primary harm. But there are also secondary harms, caused by the primary one, that may be usefully distinguished. The primary harm of situated hermeneutical inequality must, by definition, issue in further practical harms—those harms which render the collective hermeneutical impoverishment asymmetrically disadvantageous to the wronged party. To illustrate, let us simply remind ourselves of Carmita Wood's story. The primary epistemic harm done to her was that a patch of her social experience which it was very much in her interests to understand was not collectively understood and so remained barely intelligible even to her. From the story we can see that among the secondary harms caused by this were that she developed physical symptoms of stress, could not apply successfully for a transfer owing to the fact that she had no nameable reason to cite, and eventually simply had to quit her job. Further, when she came to apply for unemployment benefits, the lack of a name for the cause of all this again guaranteed that she lost out—she was refused the benefits. A little imagination allows one to see how far-reaching the ramifications of such a case of hermeneutical injustice could be. If Carmita Wood, and other women like her, had never gone to consciousness-raising, the experience of sexual harassment would have remained under wraps for much longer and would have done more to ruin the professional advancement, the personal self-confidence and, most relevantly here, the general epistemic confidence of women than it was in fact allowed to do, thanks to second wave feminism. When you find yourself in a situation where you seem to be the only one to feel the dissonance between received understanding and your own intimated sense of a given experience it tends to knock your faith in your own ability to make sense of the world, or at least the relevant region of the world. We can see, then, that not only does hermeneutical injustice have knock-on practical disadvantages for the subject, it also has epistemic disadvantages associated with it.

The sorts of epistemic disadvantages at stake stem most basically from the subject's loss of epistemic confidence. Many conceptions of knowledge implicitly or explicitly cast some sort of epistemic confidence as a condition of knowledge, whether it comes in as part of the belief condition, or as part of a justification condition. If we are to name one seminal epistemological view in this connection, then it must surely be Descartes's idea that a state of absolute confidence in one's belief—a state of certainty—is requisite for knowledge, for the some such internalist assumption has made itself felt in so many conceptions of knowledge subsequently. The significance for the present discussion is that, on any confidence-including conception of knowledge, the implications for someone whose epistemic performance is affected by hermeneutical injustice are grim: not only is he repeatedly subject to the primary harm, but where this causes him to lose confidence in his beliefs and/or his justification for them, he literally *loses knowledge*. Perhaps some piece of knowledge he possesses is washed away in a one-off wave of under-confidence. Or perhaps he suffers a prolonged erosion of epistemic confidence so that he is ongoingly disadvantaged, repeatedly failing to gain items of knowledge he would otherwise have been able to gain.

A less direct way in which someone's general loss of epistemic confidence might result in an ongoing failure to gain knowledge is by preventing him from developing certain intellectual virtues. Most notably, for instance, loss of epistemic confidence is likely to inhibit the development of intellectual courage, the virtue of not backing down in one's convictions too quickly in response to challenge. This is an important feature of epistemic function. James Montmarquet categorizes the epistemic virtues into those of 'impartiality', 'intellectual sobriety', and 'intellectual courage', where this last category includes 'most prominently the willingness to conceive and examine alternatives to popularly held beliefs, perseverance in the face of opposition from others (until one is convinced one is mistaken), and the determination required to see such a project through to completion' (Montmarquet 1993, 23). These different virtues relating to intellectual courage require epistemic confidence and are obviously susceptible to erosion by hermeneutical injustice. So if a history of such injustices gnaws away at a person's intellectual confidence, or never lets it develop in the first place, this damages his epistemic function quite generally. The under-confident subject will tend to back down too soon in the face of challenge, or even at the very prospect of it, and this tendency may well deprive him of knowledge he would otherwise have gained. In such a case there will be a series of specific deprivations of knowledge—beliefs or hypotheses that are given up too quickly—where some of these epistemic deprivations may constitute significant losses. More generally, and quite apart from the obvious fact that feelings of under-confidence are generally unpleasant in themselves, there is also an epistemic loss to the subject in terms of his intellectual character. The value of an intellectual virtue is not reducible to the value of those particular items of knowledge it might bring, but derives also from its place in the harmony of a person's intellectual character taken as a whole. Whatever the consequences may or may not be for the subject in terms of knowledge loss, an enduring loss of intellectual confidence entails a certain regrettable malformation of epistemic character.

Unjust social constructions

With the primary and secondary aspects of the wrong of hermeneutical injustice set out, perhaps we can now dig a little deeper into the nature of the primary aspect—the situated hermeneutical inequality—to see whether it might sometimes affect not only one's understanding of one's experiences but one's very social identity. Can hermeneutical injustice impact on the very development of self? Consider a new example. In Edmund White's autobiographical novel, *A Boy's Own Story*, which tells the story of his growing up in nineteen-fifties America, we are presented with many different ways in which the hermeneutical resources of the day burden his sexual experience with layers of falsifying meaning. As he grows up he has to contend with various powerful bogeymen constructions of what it is to be a Homosexual. None of them fits, but these collective understandings are so powerful, and the personal experiential promise of an alternative understanding so lonely and inarticulate, that they have some significant power to construct not only the subject's experience (his desire becomes shameful and so on) but also his very social being. Not without a fight, for sure, and this autobiographical story presents us above all with a young person who wrestles these bullying would-be selves with courage and wit, now giving in to their bid to claim his identity, now resisting. This is explicit in a passage that recounts a visit to a psychoanalyst, Dr O'Reilly. Here we see how one version of the unnatural homosexual—as a vampire-like version of a man—leads our adolescent subject to fear the name, and to experience his own nascent identity as a homosexual as a terrifying prospect, something to be pre-empted at all costs and, in so far as it already exists, disguised:

> Just as years before, when I was seven, I had presented myself to a minister and had sought for his understanding, in the same way now I was turning to a psychoanalyst for help. I wanted to overcome this thing I was becoming and was in danger soon of being, the homosexual, as though that designation were the mold in which the water

was freezing, the first crystals already forming a fragile membrane. The confusion and fear and pain that beset me . . . had translated me into a code no one could read, I least of all, a code perhaps designed to defeat even the best cryptographer . . .

I see now that what I wanted was to be loved by men and to love them back but not to be a homosexual. For I was possessed with a yearning for the company of men, for their look, touch and smell, and nothing transfixed me more than the sight of a man shaving and dressing, sumptuous rites. It was men, not women, who struck me as foreign and desirable and I disguised myself as a child or a man or whatever was necessary in order to enter their hushed, hieratic company, my disguise so perfect I never stopped to question my identity. Nor did I want to study the face beneath my mask, lest it turn out to have the pursed lips, dead pallor and shaped eyebrows by which one can always recognize the Homosexual. What I required was a sleight of hand, an alibi or a convincing act of bad faith to persuade myself I was not that vampire.

(White 1983, 169–70)

At some level his personal sexual experience was of a simple love of men, and yet this aspect of his experience being inarticulable, the only psychological rebellion he could hope to pull off against what this meant about his identity was denial. Denial is the first stage of the double-think (the sleight of hand, the act of bad faith) that is required in order to rebel against internalized yet falsifying hermeneutical constructions of one's social identity. For authoritative social constructions can effect a *constitutive* construction of one's identity, so that one comes to count socially as a vampire-like creature, even while it remains the case that one is not. Constitutive construction falls short of *causal* construction, for while the former is a matter of what one counts as socially, the latter is a matter of actually coming to be what one is constructed as being. White's autobiographical story gives us no particular evidence to think of him as subject to causal construction, though it is entirely plausible that being constitutively constructed as an unnatural vampire-like creature with shameful desires might encourage one to live out a familiar motif of inverted rebellion by behaving more and more like such a creature in defiant embrace of one's sins. One may be able to pull this off ironically, but then again one may not. In any case, it is enough to notice that so much of what the younger narrator is grappling with as he grows up and his social identity congeals around him can be thought of as authoritative—collectively endorsed meanings attaching to homosexuality that have the power not just to haunt him with bogeyman would-be selves but actually to constitute his social being. His sometimes playful resistance to these constructions of his identity is, as regards his social being, a matter of life and death.

To the extent that resistance is possible, part of what makes it possible is historical contingency. Our narrator had history on his side in as much as the sixties were on the horizon when all sorts of sexual liberations were to be articulated, indeed demanded. But something else that allows for resistance is that other aspects of one's identity (being educated and middle-class, perhaps) might equip one with resources for rebellion, as will certain personal characteristics (our narrator was surely fiercely intelligent, psychologically tough, and socially resourceful). Authoritative constructions in the shared hermeneutical resource, then, impinge on us collectively but not uniformly, and the non-uniformity of their hold over us can create a sense of dissonance between an experience and the various constructions that are ganging up to overpower its proper nascent meaning. As individuals, some authoritative voices have special power over us while others, for whatever reason, do not. Our narrator, for instance, is wholly untroubled by negative Christian constructions of homosexuality, for he simply does not believe in the ropes and pulleys of heaven above and eternal damnation below, and his plain anti-authoritarian impulse renders him gloriously immune to whatever remaining visceral hold religious censure might have had over him. When he spends Thanksgiving with the Scotts—the housemaster Latin teacher and his wife, both fervent Christians ambitious to convert him (and equally ambitious to seduce him, their fear of being bourgeois outstripping their fear of being sinners)—they introduce him to Father Burke, 'their "confessor" and spiritual guardian' (White 1983, 199):

> 'Well, yes,' I said, 'I am seeing a psychiatrist because I have conflicts over certain homosexual tendencies I'm feeling.'
>
> At these words Father Burke's face lurched up out of his hands. Not the nervous little confession he had expected. He recovered his poise and decided to laugh boisterously, the laugh of Catholic centuries. '*Conflicts?*' he whooped, in tears of laughter by now. Then, sobering for a second, the priest added in a low, casual voice, 'But you see, my son, homosexuality isn't just a *conflict* that needs to be *resolved*'—his voice picked up these words as though they were nasty bits of refuse—'homosexuality is also a sin.'
>
> I think he had no notion how little an effect the word *sin* had on me. He might just as well have said, 'Homosexuality is bad *juju*.'
>
> (White 1983, 204)

By contrast, however, this immunity to the idea of sin is no enduring defence, for it takes almost nothing from the priest—only his identity as a priest, or perhaps simply as a straight male confessor—to conjure up a conspiracy of truly mortifying stereotypes. The passage continues:

> 'But I feel very drawn to other men,' I said. Although something defiant in me forced these words out, I felt myself becoming a freak the moment I spoke. My hair went bleach-blond, my wrist went limp, my rep tie became a lace jabot: I was the simpering queen at the grand piano playing concert versions of last year's pop tunes for his mother and her bridge club. There was no way to defend what I was. All I could fight for was my right to choose my exile, my destruction.
>
> (204)

A person's bold sense of dissonance, then, is a fragile thing, for a construction that one is able simply to find absurd may swiftly be followed by one that holds sway over one's psyche. But at least a sense of dissonance is possible. What makes it possible is that if one finds one or more of the common constructions of one's sexuality as shameful to be manifestly false, even ridiculous, then this raises the question whether other discourses in league with it are suspect too. Finding something potentially authoritative to be absurd gives one critical courage; one hermeneutical rebellion inspires another. The sense of dissonance, then, is the starting point for both the critical thinking and the moral-intellectual courage that rebellion requires. That, I take it, is part of the mechanism of consciousness raising. Put a number of people together who have felt a certain dissonance about an area of social experience, and factor in that each of them will have a different profile of immunity and susceptibility to different authoritative discourses, and it is not surprising that the sense of dissonance can find strength in numbers and become critically emboldened.

The primary harm of hermeneutical injustice, then, is to be understood not only in terms of the subject's being unfairly disadvantaged by some collective hermeneutical lacuna, but also in terms of the very construction (constitutive and/or causal) of social identity. In certain social contexts, hermeneutical injustice can mean that someone is socially constituted as, and perhaps even caused to be, something they are not, and which it is against their interests to be seen to be. Thus we can say, without essentializing, that they are prevented from becoming who they really are. Hermeneutical injustice is an epistemic injustice with social constructive power. It is an epistemic inequality that can bring real injury to the insult of hermeneutical marginalization. If all epistemic injustice undermines the subject specifically in his capacity as a knower, then we can identify the distinctive manner in which hermeneutical injustice does this by saying that it undermines the subject in his capacity as an interpreter of his own social experience, in his capacity, that is, for social self-knowledge.

References

Brownmiller, S. (1990). *In Our Time. Memoir of a Revolution*. New York: The Dial Press.
McEwan, Ian (1998) *Enduring Love*. New York: Anchor Books.
Montmarquet, J. A. (1993). *Epistemic Virtue and Doxastic Responsibility*. Maryland: Rowman and Littlefield.
White, E. (1983). *A Boy's Own Story*. London: Picador.

Chapter 4

ALISON WYLIE

THE FEMINISM QUESTION IN SCIENCE
What does it mean to "do social science as a feminist"?

FROM THE TIME FEMINISTS TURNED A critical eye on conventional practice in the social sciences, they have asked what it would mean to do better, more inclusive research. For many, initially the challenge was to counteract sexist, androcentric erasure and bias in conventional research. Practical guidelines and handbooks proliferated, like Eichler's (1988) *Nonsexist Research Methods*, codifying principles many of which are now widely accepted. But for others the challenge was to think beyond conventional practice: What forms of social science do we need to develop to be effective in addressing questions that have largely been left out of account, questions that particularly matter for understanding, with precision and explanatory force, the systems of social differentiation and conditions of life, the forms of experience and identity, that are, to varying degrees and in diverse ways, oppressive for those categorized as women or as sex/gender variant? It was this question that became the focus of sustained discussion through the 1980s and early 1990s in the context of the feminist method debate: the "feminism question in science," as I will refer to it, inverting the question Harding (1986) poses in *The Science Question in Feminism*.

I focus here on two broad strategies of response: Longino's discussion of what it means to "do science as a feminist," and a distillation of the guidelines for practice proposed by feminist social scientists. I then consider examples of feminist research that both exemplify and put epistemically consequential pressure on these principles. The anxiety that haunts these discussions is that if research is guided by explicitly feminist values, its epistemic credibility is irrevocably compromised. The methodological principles I will consider illustrate how this worry is countered in practice; I conclude with an argument for a reformulation of feminist standpoint theory that captures the wisdom implicit in this practice.

Methodological essentialism and the value(s) of science

One family of answers to my central question has long been highly contentious: that feminists must seek a distinctive form of practice, a uniquely "feminist science," because conventional strategies of research practice in the social sciences are inherently patriarchal and cannot be recuperated. Those who might be interpreted as holding such a position, a view more often attributed to feminists than exemplified by their practice, include feminist critics of the social sciences who saw these disciplines as one node in a network of "ruling practices" that operate by "eclipsing" women's roles and contributions, marginalizing their experience, and trivializing their self-understanding (Smith, 1978)—as an enterprise animated by interests that are systematically obscured by a positivist rhetoric of objectivity and value neutrality (Mies, 1983; Stanley & Wise, 1983b). As one example of a more general antipathy for the sciences, such a stance, and its presumed implication for practice—that feminists must seek a distinctively feminist form of practice—has been sharply criticized by epistemic conservatives, who reject the very idea of feminist science on the ground that it is a contradiction in terms. To take one prominent example, Haack (1993) objects that any intrusion of gender-specific interests into the sciences can only compromise their integrity; to advocate a feminist methodology or a feminist science is to abandon "honest inquiry"—inquiry inspired by a "genuine desire to find out how things are"—in favor of a dogmatic commitment to "make a case for a foregone conclusion" ("sham" research). Moreover, Haack argues, the quest for feminist forms of practice presupposes an untenable gender essentialism: that women *qua* women must share a distinctively female or feminine "way of knowing" and that women scientists must rely on feminine forms of intuition and (non)reason that have been (in Haack's view, rightly) ignored by traditional theories of knowledge and marginalized within mainstream science.

In fact, feminists were among the earliest and most uncompromising critics of gender essentialism, and some of the sharpest challenges to the quest for a distinctively feminist method came from advocates of feminist practice in the social sciences. One catalyst for the feminist method debate was the question, why limit feminist initiatives to one particular set of methods or research strategy (Jayaratne, 1983)? By the early 1990s, Reinharz (1992a) could identify feminist uses of virtually every research method and methodology available in the social sciences; and by the end of the 1990s, Gottfried (1996) concluded that feminist practitioners had made a decisive "move from singularity to plurality" (p. 12). Parallel arguments had been made a decade earlier by Harding (1987) and by Longino (1987), who argued that there is no brief for positing "a distinctive female way of knowing"; why should feminists allow methodological commitments to define in advance the scope of their research agenda? Was this not simply to re-entrench at the core of feminist research programs the mystification of method that feminists found so debilitating in the sciences they hoped to reform (Harding, 1987. p. 19)? Longino (1987) urged that questions about the nature and direction of feminist research be reframed: We should ask not what it means to build or to do "feminist science" but what is involved in "doing science as a feminist" (p. 53). By extension, we should be prepared to recognize that what "doing research as a feminist" means in practice will be as diverse as what it means to be a feminist and as situationally specific as the fields in which feminists have undertaken to "do science."

While Haack and like-minded critics might be reassured by this repudiation of essentialism, they would no doubt find just as worrisome the endorsement of pluralism, predicated as it is on the conviction that scientific inquiry is always *relative to* context, if not *relativist* (Hesse, 1980, p. 181). But *contra* Haack, far from being a marginal extreme, the arguments for a pragmatic, contextualist turn in thinking about the sciences—for recognizing that the sciences are historically contingent and deeply structured by context-specific interests and values—are by now generic to the philosophy of science (Lloyd, 1995). Arguments from such canonical philosophical theses as Quine-Duhem holism, the theory ladenness of evidence, and the underdetermination of theory by evidence establish that cognitive, evidential, and logical factors rarely, if ever, determine theory choice: "whatever grounds for knowledge we have, they are not sufficient to warrant the assertion of claims beyond doubt" (Longino, 1994, p. 472). Crucially, this is not just a matter of the underdetermination of content, such that contextual factors must take up the slack in determining the significance of empirical data as evidence. It is, in addition, a matter of meta-underdetermination: The cognitive and epistemic values presumed to be constitutive of well-functioning (unbiased, objective) science are themselves underdetermined as guidelines for practice. Such widely cited principles as a commitment to maximize the empirical adequacy, predictive and explanatory power, intertheoretic consistency, and internal coherence of scientific theories, as well as quasi-aesthetic values such as simplicity or formal elegance, are by no means transparent; they require interpretation and typically cannot be simultaneously maximized (Doppelt, 1988; Kuhn, 1977, p. 322; Longino, 1995; Wylie, 1995). What counts as meeting a requirement of empirical adequacy, for example, is by no means given by the facts themselves or by abstract ideals of rationality. Standards of empirical adequacy are context specific and evolve within distinct research traditions, in response to goals and interests that are external to inquiry as well as to internal theoretical and technical considerations. And when epistemic values come into conflict, as when a commitment to formal idealization (e.g., to expand explanatory and predictive scope) requires a trade-off of localized empirical adequacy, the question of which constitutive value should take precedence must generally be settled by appeal to the noncognitive goals and values that inform the research program.

Doing (social) science as a feminist is a matter, then, of insisting that we be accountable for the values and interests that shape not just our choice of research questions but also the whole range of decisions and conventions that constitute our research practice. Far from seeing this pragmatism as grounds for despair, or for outrage (in the case of Haack), I join a growing contingent of science studies theorists who argue that we should regard contextual values as a crucial condition for the success of the sciences, not only (or always) as a source of compromising contamination (Wylie & Nelson, in press).

The feminist question in (social) science

Consider, then, two ways in which feminists have articulated a mandate for "doing research as a feminist": Longino's philosophical account of the community values that inform the research undertaken by feminists in the sciences generally and the methodological guidelines developed by feminist social scientists.

Longino has identified six community values—or "theoretical virtues"—as characteristic of the work of feminist scientists (1987, 1990, 1994; Wylie, 1995). There is some ambiguity about the status of these virtues: whether they describe what feminist practitioners actually do (in an unspecified range of sciences) or are intended to capture what feminists could or should do. And they are strikingly free of any explicit feminist content. They cluster around three focal concerns:

1. *Epistemic values*: Longino finds feminists committed, first and foremost, to a fundamental requirement of empirical adequacy and to a preference for novel hypotheses (Longino, 1994, p. 476, 1995, p. 386).
2. *Ontological*: She identifies, as well, a preference for hypotheses that take full account of diversity in the objects of study—that allow "equal standing for different types"—and that treat "complex interaction as a fundamental principle of explanation" (Longino, 1994, pp. 477–478; see also Longino, 1995, pp. 387–388).
3. *Normative and pragmatic values*: She finds feminist research animated by a commitment to use the tools of scientific inquiry to generate knowledge that is "applicab[le] to current human needs" (Longino, 1994, p. 476, 1995, p. 389) and to democratize the production of knowledge in ways that foster an "equality of intellectual authority" (Longino, 1990, pp. 78–81, 1993a, 1993b, 1995, p. 389).

Even this last, most explicitly normative, commitment is warranted not because it makes scientific practice a site for institutional change along lines advocated by feminists in other contexts, but because it provides for a redistribution of power and resources within the sciences that Longino (1990, pp. 76–80) believes will enhance the epistemic integrity of inquiry. It counteracts the reification of epistemic authority, expanding the range of perspectives brought to bear on conventional assumptions; it reinforces a recognition that knowledge production is a pluralistic enterprise that serves divergent goals ("cognitive needs"), engaging dissent seriously and fostering if not an idealized "view from everywhere," at least "views from many wheres" (Longino, 1993b, p. 113; see the elaboration of these epistemic norms in Longino, 2002, pp. 128–135).

The sense in which these community values are *feminist* is that they embody what Longino (1994) describes as a "bottom line" feminist commitment. They have the effect of "prevent[ing] gender from being disappeared," and in this they are evaluative standards that "mak[e] gender a relevant axis of investigation" (p. 481). So, for example, the preference for novelty counteracts the conservative, gender-disappearing effects that can be expected to follow from the more typical directive to maximize consistency with other well-established theories (given that these are likely to be predicated on just the kinds of gender-conventional wisdom feminists are intent on challenging). The preference for ontological and causal complexity likewise counters conventions of practice that privilege the sorts of simplifying idealization Smith (1978) found responsible for the sociological "eclipsing" of women's experience. And a commitment to democratize scientific practice, while justified on gender-neutral epistemic grounds, puts the onus on the scientific community to ensure that marginal voices are not systematically silenced, including the voices of women. Longino (1994) adds to these principles and the "bottom line" maxim one further metaprinciple: *epistemic provisionalism*. Each of the other community values must be held open to revision in light of what feminists learn from practice (p. 483).

In the context of feminist social science, Longino's community values find their clearest articulation in the guidelines for nonsexist research mentioned at the outset, where the goal is to improve research by conventional standards. Feminist interests and values figure as a resource; they draw attention to gaps and distortions in conventional research and to aspects of the subject domain and explanatory possibilities that have been overlooked. In practice, however, feminist research has been animated by much more explicitly feminist goals than these; the principles articulated in the context of the method debate are broadly consistent with Longino's community values but go well beyond them. I identify four widely shared commitments around which the overlapping systems of general principles, ideals, maxims, and guidelines for feminist research have coalesced since the early 1980s.

The principle to which feminist social scientists typically give first priority is a specification of explicitly *feminist goals*: The "human needs" that feminist researchers should be concerned to address when they practice as feminists are those of women and, more generally, those oppressed by gender-structured systems of inequality. Sometimes these feminist goals have been articulated as a requirement that feminist research should be "movement-generated"; not only should it expose the sexism inherent in extant institutions—"muckraking research" (Ehrlich, 1975, p. 10)—it should also generate strategies for changing these institutions (p. 13). The other orienting principles are articulations of how best to realize feminist goals however these are defined.

The second is a directive to *ground feminist research in women's experience*: to take "as our starting point" women's experience and everyday lives (Smith, 1974, 1987, p. 85). In effect, Longino's (1994, p. 481, 1995, p. 391) "bottom line maxim" is reframed as a commitment, not just to ensure that gender is "not disappeared," but also to treat gendered experience and self-understanding as a crucial resource in developing a systematic understanding of the gendered dimensions of community life and institutions, systems of belief, social differentiation, and inequality. Sometimes this principle counters the second, ontological cluster of values Longino (1994, pp. 477–478, 1995, pp. 387–388) identifies. Rather than advocate ontological heterogeneity and multidirectional causality as desirable in themselves, it suggests that feminists should build into their theories whatever degree of complexity (or simplification) is necessary to do justice to women's experience and the sex/gender systems that structure their lives.

A third cluster of principles specify ethical commitments that give further content to Longino's (1994, p. 478, 1995, p. 389) normative and pragmatic values. They require that feminists hold themselves *accountable to research subjects*, broadly construed. At the very least the research process should not oppress or exploit research subjects; ideally, it should empower them, particularly when they are themselves oppressed by sex/gender systems. Feminist practitioners often insist, more ambitiously, that they should make research practice a site for instituting feminist social and political values: They should deliberately counteract the hierarchical structures that make social science a "ruling practice" and implement egalitarian, participatory forms of knowledge production. Here, a general argument for democratizing research practice is specified as a commitment to break down the (gendered) hierarchies of power and authority that operate in much conventional research; in the ideal, research subjects and those affected by research should play an active, collaborative role at all stages of research design, data collection, analysis, and authorship.

Fourth, virtually every set of published guidelines for feminist research in the social sciences emphasizes the importance of cultivating a stance of sustained and critical *reflexivity*. As Narayan (1988) puts it, "One of the most attractive features of feminist thinking is its commitment to contextualizing its claims" (p. 32). At the very least, this requires feminist social scientists to "state their premises rather than hide them" (Reinharz, 1992b, p. 426). On stronger formulations, it requires that feminists, *qua* feminists, take into account the various ways in which their own social locations, their interests and values, are constitutive of the research process and of the understanding it produces (e.g., Cook & Fonow, 1986; Fonow & Cook, 1991; Mies, 1983). Standpoint theorists specify what this involves in terms of a requirement for "strong objectivity": The tools of jointly empirical and conceptual inquiry should be applied (reflexively) to the research process itself (Harding, 1993). With this, Longino's (1994, p. 483) principle of "methodological provisionalism" is reframed as a requirement, not just that feminists should be willing to revise orienting principles but that they should subject them, actively and continuously, to conceptual, empirical scrutiny.

Doing social science as a feminist, in practice

The research projects that most straightforwardly realize these principles and that stood as an ideal for much early feminist social science were various forms of community self-study: *research undertaken by women, on women, for women* (Gorelick, 1991, p. 459; e.g., Jacobson, 1977). Here, women's experience gives rise directly to the questions asked; inquiry is motivated by explicitly activist objectives and designed with the aim of leveling the hierarchy of authority inherent in traditional "expert" forms of social scientific research. The use of qualitative, participatory methods of inquiry (e.g., oral history, ethnography, discourse analysis) serves not only to engage research subjects directly in the research process but also to resituate the particularities of women's experience and self-understanding at the center of inquiry, counteracting the "eclipsing" of this experience and its assimilation to gender-conventional categories of description and analysis (Smith, 1974, 1978). In some cases, these projects were directly inspired by consciousness-raising practice conceived as a matter of "grasp[ing] the collective reality of women's condition from within the perspective of that experience" (MacKinnon, 1982, p. 536), bearing witness to the particularities of women's lives and critically situating these in the frame of broader patterns of gender politics and gendered institutions (Wylie, 1992, p. 237). A classic example is the grassroots research on workplace environment issues—the "chilly climate" that women encounter in academia and other traditionally male-dominated professions—that proliferated in the late 1970s and 1980s (Chilly Collective, 1995). In these projects the four methodological principles I have identified are given a literal interpretation and are mutually reinforcing.

At the same time, however, feminists were exploring a range of questions and research strategies that pointed up ambiguities inherent in the interpretation of these principles and showed how they might come into conflict with one another. Consider, specifically, some examples that put pressure on a literal reading of the directive to ground feminist research in women's experience—the most contentious of the four principles where worries about epistemic integrity and objectivity are concerned.

The subject of research

First, and perhaps most obviously, if the goal of feminist research is to address questions that are relevant for understanding and ultimately changing gendered systems of oppression, it does not follow that women must always be the primary subject of feminist inquiry. Stanley and Wise (1979, 1983a, 1983b) argued, in this connection, that if feminists are to understand the hostility to women that underpins patriarchal culture, it will be necessary to study the attitudes and behaviors of sexist and misogynist men; this was the rationale for their early work on obscene telephone calls. The course of development of "chilly climate" research makes it clear how important comparison with male peers is in discerning conditions that reproduce inequality, some of which are effective precisely because they are opaque to women (Wylie, 2004).

But beyond changing the subject, feminist practitioners often draw on women's experience as a source of research questions and interpretive insight rather than taking it as a direct subject of inquiry. This opens up space for feminist research in fields where women themselves, and the experiential dimensions of social life, are often inaccessible, as in archaeology (Wylie, 2001), or where the subject of inquiry is projectively gendered, as in primatology (Strum & Fedigan, 2000). It also throws into relief the potentially radical implications of a thoroughgoing commitment to epistemic provisionalism. Those who undertake research as feminists routinely discover that what they most need to understand, to address a problem initially identified in gender terms, are the dynamics of class formation and the emergence and maintenance of systemic racism, along with myriad other forms of social differentiation that are mutually constitutive of contemporary sex/gender systems. The lessons from queer theory and transnational feminisms make it especially clear that a sophisticated understanding of gender inequality cannot be expected to arise from research that focuses narrowly on gendered institutions, symbolic economies, roles, and identities. Far from dogmatically recapitulating foregone conclusions, the substantive results of feminist research frequently destabilize—even "disappear"—the categories that originally gave it direction.

Critiques of experientialism

Even when women and gender are the primary subject of analysis, there are two further reasons to resist a literal reading of the directive to ground research in women's experience. One targets an early construal of the "grounding" requirement that took it to be a proscription against questioning women's experience, as when Stanley and Wise (1983a, 1983b) insisted that in countering sexist assumptions about the credibility and significance of women's self-reports—in treating women as authorities about their own experience—feminist researchers must never "go beyond" women's experience. The pitfalls of such "experientialism" became an immediate focus of attention in the feminist method debate (e.g., Brunsdon, 1978; Grant, 1987). In her classic article, "The Evidence of Experience," Scott (1991) objects that "when experience is taken as the origin of knowledge, the vision of the individual subject becomes the bedrock on which explanation is built," foreclosing questions about the "constructed nature of experience, about how subjects are constituted different in the first place, about how one's vision is structured" (p. 776). "Giving voice is not enough" (Gorelick, 1991, pp. 463, 477), even when the goal of research is to bear witness to forms of community life and experience that have been systematically marginalized in a sexist, heteronormative society.

The practical implications of this critique are evident, for example, in the care with which Kennedy and Davis (1993) scrutinize their subjects' recollections of a working-class lesbian community that grew up in Buffalo in the 1940s and 1950s. They worry about the vagaries of memory, where interviewees were asked to recall events and conditions of life from 30 or 40 years earlier, and about the impact on these memories of fundamental changes in social and cultural conceptions of what it means to be a lesbian that had emerged in the intervening years. They employ a strategy of triangulation, systematically cross-checking interviewees' accounts to ensure the factual accuracy of the historical ethnography they constructed. It is precisely because they respect their subjects and the larger community they represent that Kennedy and Davis insist on the need to treat these experiential accounts judiciously, not disrespectfully but with critical caution.

Similar principles are operative in the context of feminist research that is explicitly designed as a form of therapeutic and activist intervention. The staff of the Battered Women's Advocacy Center (BWAC) in London (Ontario, Canada) developed a standardized intake form, which made it possible to collect information about the demography, family histories, experiences of violence, and strategies of response of the women making use of BWAC's services. While this form provided crucial support for the research mandate of the agency, the front-line advocates and counselors reported that it also served an important counseling function (Greaves, Wylie, & the staff of the BWAC, 1995). Sometimes questions about particular aspects of a recent violent episode or about long-term patterns of physical and collateral forms of abuse (economic control, social isolation, psychological abuse) would elicit an overall picture that was starkly at odds with an interviewee's initial self-report. The shock of recognition, when a standardized question draws attention to some hitherto unacknowledged or unspoken aspect of a woman's experience, does more than any general assurance could to make it clear that however unique a woman might think her own experience of violence, it is often by no means idiosyncratic. In short, "going beyond" our experience—questioning it, rethinking it, putting it in perspective, asking how and why it arises—is a crucial part of coming to terms with the sex/gender oppression of a heteronormative society.

A second, related concern often raised about strong experientialist readings of the second principle is that any directive to "ground feminist research in women's experience" must be articulated with some care if it is not to prove perniciously parochial, reproducing and reifying precisely the conditions of oppression that feminists ought to challenge. In *White Women, Race Matters*, Frankenberg (1993) reads her subjects' testimony against the grain with an eye to discerning the contours of race privilege, including the privileges of ignorance, that define the lives of white women. She focuses on contradictions inherent in first-person accounts that reveal the unacknowledged "racial geography" of her interviewees' lives. Critiques of the early 1990s generalize the methodological point implicit here, drawing attention to the inherent elitism of inquiry grounded in the experience of those relatively privileged women who are most likely to be in a position to undertake systematic empirical research (Mohanty, 1991) or to be recruited as research subjects (Cannon, Higginbotham, & Leung, 1991). Women's experience may offer a crucial corrective to the systems of common sense and scientific knowledge that render it invisible and inauthoritative, but it is always intersectionally partial, and in this, it offers, at most, a point of departure, not an end point for feminist inquiry (Bannerji, 1991, p. 67; Smith, 1974, pp. 12–13).

The upshot is that the liberatory goals of feminist research—articulated as the first principle—put considerable pressure on any literal or essentialist reading of the second principle (the requirement for experiential grounding). Effective activism depends on understanding accurately and in detail how "specific form[s] of oppression originated, how [they have] been maintained and all the systemic purposes [they] serve" (Narayan, 1988, p. 36), and this routinely requires that feminists go substantially beyond women's experience and self-understanding in a number of senses. They must expand the range of experience on which they ground social research, on the principle that all experience reflects the partiality of location. They must be prepared to critically interrogate this experience, on the principle that it is often the opacity of social institutions and practices that makes them effective in conditioning our self-understanding. And they must contextualize it, on the principle that we need to grasp "how [the world of everyday experience] is put together," to posit the socio-economic order that lies "in back" of and that makes possible and organizes immediate experience (Gorelick, 1991, pp. 463–466; Smith, 1974, pp. 12–13).

Crucially, it is not only the subjects' gendered experience that must be situated, read against the grain, treated as a point of departure and not a destination; it is also the researcher's own experience and self-understanding that require scrutiny in all these ways. What practitioners rely on when they do social science are, therefore, the resources of a feminist standpoint, not just a gendered social location.

Conclusion

Two epistemic implications follow from these observations about feminist practice in the social sciences. First, far from illustrating a sad decline into cynical dogmatism—a state in which, Haack (1993) feared, "foregone conclusions" would dictate not only the goals but also the outcomes of research—the dominant effect of feminist community values has been to mobilize transformative critique (Longino, 1990, pp. 73–76). Feminist commitments have catalyzed much more searching critical scrutiny of the presuppositions of research—including those that inform feminists' practice as well as the conventions they challenge—than conventional epistemic virtues had done or faith in the self-correcting capacity of scientific method seems likely to do.

Second, the feminist standpoint that, as I have suggested, is pivotal to this enterprise need not be construed in essentialist terms or be accorded any automatic epistemic privilege—the key features that worry critics like Haack (1993). Central to this conception of a feminist standpoint is a situated knowledge thesis: what we experience and understand, the differential strengths and liabilities we develop as epistemic agents, are systematically shaped by our location in hierarchically structured systems of power relations, the material conditions of our lives, the relations of production and reproduction that shape our social interactions, and the conceptual resources we rely on to interpret and represent these relations. Gender is one dimension along which our lives are structured in epistemically consequential ways. What feminist standpoint theory adds to this account of situated knowledge is an inversion thesis. Those who are subject to structures of domination that systematically marginalize and oppress them may in fact have substantial (contingent) epistemic advantage relative to those who are comparatively privileged (and who enjoy a presumption of epistemic authority on this basis); they may have access to an expanded range of evidence and interpretive heuristics, as well as a critical perspective on otherwise unacknowledged framework assumptions, by virtue of what they typically experience and how they understand their experience (Wylie, 2004, pp. 32–39).

Two points follow where the specifics of "doing social science as a feminist" are concerned. First, the directive to ground feminist research in women's experience should be construed, in standpoint terms, as a recommendation to treat the situated knowledge of gendered subjects as a resource (not a foundation) for understanding the form and dynamics of the sex/gender systems that shape their lives. Second, Longino's (1994, 1995) commitment to epistemic provisionality should be framed as a substantive requirement that feminists develop an explicitly feminist standpoint on knowledge production; they should build into their research enterprise a critical consciousness of our social location(s) and the difference it makes epistemically. Far from signaling an abdication of epistemic responsibility, these guidelines for doing research as a feminist effectively raise the epistemic bar (see Harding, 1993, on "strong objectivity"); they direct feminists to make discerning use of contingent epistemic advantages that may accrue to them by virtue of their gendered social locations and hard-won feminist standpoint.

References

Bannerji, Himani. (1991). But who speaks for us? Experience and agency in conventional feminist paradigms. In Himani Bannerji, Linda Carty, Kari Dehli, Susan Heald, & Kate McKenna (Eds.), *Unsettling relations: The university as a site of feminist struggle* (pp. 67–108). Toronto, Ontario, Canada: Women's Press.

Brunsdon, Charlotte. (1978). It is well known that by nature women are inclined to be rather personal. In Women's Studies Group, Centre for Cultural Studies, University of Birmingham (Eds.), *Women take issue: Aspects of women's subordination* (pp. 18–34). London: Hutchinson.

Cannon, Lynn Weber, Higginbotham, Elizabeth, & Leung, Marianne L. A. (1991). Race and class bias in qualitative research on women. In Mary Margaret Fonow & Judith A. Cook (Eds.), *Beyond methodology: Feminist scholarship as lived research* (pp. 107–118). Bloomington: Indiana University Press.

Chilly Collective. (Eds.). (1995). *Breaking anonymity: Anonymity: The Chilly Climate for Women Faculty*. Waterloo, Ontario, Canada: Wilfrid Laurier Press.

Cook, Judith A., & Fonow, Mary Margaret. (1986). Knowledge and women's interests: Issues of epistemology and methodology in feminist sociological research. *Sociological Inquiry*, 56, 2–29.

Doppelt, Gerald D. (1988). The philosophical requirements for an adequate conception of scientific rationality. *Philosophy of Science*, 55(1), 104–133.

Ehrlich, Carol. (1975). *The conditions of feminist research* (Research Group One Report No. 21). Baltimore: Vacant Lots Press.

Eichler, Margrit. (1988). *Nonsexist research methods: A practical guide*. Boston: Allen & Unwin.

Fonow, Mary Margaret, & Cook, Judith A. (Eds.). (1991). Back to the future: A look at the second wave of feminist epistemology and methodology. In *Beyond methodology: Feminist scholarship as lived research* (pp. 1–15). Bloomington: Indiana University Press.

Frankenberg, Ruth. (1993). *White women, race matters: The social construction of whiteness*. Minneapolis: University of Minnesota Press.

Gorelick, Sherry. (1991). Contradictions of feminist methodology. *Gender & Society*, 5, 459–477.

Gottfried, Heidi. (Ed.). (1996). *Feminism and social change: Bridging theory and practice*. Urbana: University of Illinois Press.

Grant, Judith. (1987). I feel therefore I am: A critique of female experience as the basis for a feminist epistemology. *Women and Politics*, 7(3), 99–114.

Greaves, Lorraine, Wylie, Alison, & the staff of the Battered Women's Advocacy Clinic. (1995). Women and violence: Feminist practice and quantitative method. In Sandra D. Burt & Lorraine Code (Eds.), *Changing methods: Feminists transforming practice* (pp. 301–326). Peterborough, ON: Broadview Press.

Haack, Susan. (1993). Knowledge and propaganda: Reflections of an old feminist. *Partisan Review*, *60*, 556–565. (Reprinted in *Scrutinizing feminist epistemology: An examination of gender in science*, by Cassandra Pinnick, Noretta Koertge, & Robert Almeder (Eds), 2003, New Brunswick, NJ: Rutgers University Press)

Harding, Sandra. (1986). *The science question in feminism*. Ithaca, NY: Cornell University Press.

Harding, Sandra. (1987). The method question. *Hypatia*, *2*, 19–36.

Harding, Sandra. (1993). *Whose science? Whose knowledge? Thinking from women's lives*. Ithaca, NY: Cornell University Press.

Hesse, Mary. (1980). In defense of objectivity. In *Revolutions and reconstructions in the philosophy of science* (pp. 167–186). New York: Harvester Press.

Jacobson, Helga E. (1977). *How to study your own community: Research from the perspective of women*. Vancouver, British Columbia, Canada: Vancouver Women's Research Centre.

Jayaratne, Toby Epstein. (1983). The value of quantitative methodology in feminist research. In Gloria Bowles & Renate Duelli Klein (Eds.), *Theories of women's studies* (pp. 140–162). London: Routledge & Kegan Paul.

Kennedy, Elizabeth Lapovsky, & Davis, Madeline D. (1993). *Boots of leather, slippers of gold: The history of a lesbian community*. New York: Penguin Books.

Kuhn, Thomas. (1977). Objectivity, value judgment, and theory choice. In *The essential tension: Selected studies in scientific tradition and change* (pp. 320–339). Chicago: University of Chicago Press.

Lloyd, Elisabeth. (1995). Objectivity and the double standard for feminist epistemologies. *Synthese*, *104*(3), 351–381.

Longino, Helen. (1987). Can there be a feminist science? *Hypatia*, *2*(3), 51–64.

Longino, Helen. (1990). *Science as social knowledge: Values and objectivity in scientific inquiry*. Princeton, NJ: Princeton University Press.

Longino, Helen. (1993a). Feminist standpoint theory and the problems of knowledge. *Signs*, *19*, 201–212.

Longino, Helen. (1993b). Subjects, power and knowledge: Description and prescription in feminist philosophies of science. In Linda Alcoff & Elizabeth Potter (Eds.), *Feminist epistemologies* (pp. 101–120). New York: Routledge.

Longino, Helen. (1994). In search of feminist epistemology. *The Monist*, *77*(4), 472–485.

Longino, Helen. (1995). Gender, politics, and the theoretical virtues. *Synthese*, *104*, 383–397.

Longino, Helen. (2002). *The fate of knowledge*. Princeton, NJ: Princeton University Press.

MacKinnon, Catherine. (1982). Feminism, Marxism, method and the State: An agenda for theory. *Signs*, *7*, 515–544.

Mies, Maria. (1983). Towards a methodology for feminist research. In Gloria Bowles & Renate Duelli Klein (Eds.), *Theories of women's studies* (pp. 117–139). London: Routledge & Kegan Paul.

Mies, Maria. (1991). Women's research or feminist research? The debate surrounding feminist science and methodology. In Mary Margaret Fonow & Judith A. Cook (Eds.), *Beyond methodology: Feminist scholarship and lived research* (pp. 60–84). Bloomington: Indiana University Press.

Mohanty, Chandra Talpade. (Ed.). (1991). Under Western eyes: Feminist scholarship and colonial discourses. In Chandra Talpade Mohanty, Ann Russo, & Lourdes Torres (Eds.), *Third world women and the politics of feminism* (pp. 51–80). Bloomington: Indiana University Press.

Narayan, Uma. (1988). Working together across difference: Some considerations on emotions and political practice. *Hypatia*, *3*(2), 31–48.

Reinharz, Shulamit. (1992a). *Feminist methods in social research*. New York: Oxford University Press.

Reinharz, Shulamit. (1992b). The principles of feminist research: A matter of debate. In Cheris Kramarae & Dale Spender (Eds.), *The knowledge explosion: Generations of feminist scholarship* (pp. 423–437). New York: Teachers College Press.

Scott, Joan W. (1991). The evidence of experience. *Critical Inquiry*, *17*, 773–797.

Smith, Dorothy E. (1974). Women's perspective as a radical critique of sociology. *Sociological Inquiry*, *44*, 7–13.

Smith, Dorothy E. (1978). A peculiar eclipsing: Women's exclusion from man's culture. *Women's Studies International Quarterly*, *1*, 281–295. (Reprinted in Smith, 1987)

Smith, Dorothy E. (1987). *The everyday world as problematic: A feminist sociology*. Toronto, Ontario, Canada: University of Toronto Press.

Stanley, Liz, & Wise, Sue. (1979). Feminist research, feminist consciousness and experiences of sexism. *Women's Studies International Quarterly*, *2*, 359–374.

Stanley, Liz, & Wise, Sue. (1983a). "Back into the personal" or: Our attempt to construct "feminist research." In Gloria Bowles & Renate D. Klein (Eds.), *Theories of women's studies* (pp. 192–209). London: Routledge & Kegan Paul.

Stanley, Liz, & Wise, Sue. (1983b). *Breaking out: Feminist consciousness and feminist research*. London: Routledge & Kegan Paul.

Strum, Shirley C., & Fedigan, Linda M. (Eds.). (2000). *Primate encounters: Models of science, gender, and society*. Chicago: Chicago University Press.

Wylie, Alison. (1992). Reasoning about ourselves; feminist methodology in the social sciences. In Elizabeth Harvey & Kathleen Okruhlik (Eds.), *Women and reason* (pp. 225–244). Ann Arbor: University of Michigan Press.

Wylie, Alison. (1995). Doing philosophy as a feminist: Longino on the search for a feminist epistemology. *Philosophical Topics, 23*(2), 345–358.

Wylie, Alison. (2001). Doing social science as a feminist: The engendering of archaeology. In Angela Creager, Elizabeth Lunbeck, & Londa Schiebinger (Eds.), *Feminism in twentieth century science, technology, and medicine* (pp. 23–45). Chicago: Chicago University Press.

Wylie, Alison. (2004, February). *The gender of science: Chilly climate issues for women in science*. Lecture presented to the Barnard Center for Research on Women (BCRW) and summarized in the description of the BCRW conference, Women, Work and the Academy, December 2004. (Available at www.barnard.edu/bcrw/womenandwork)

Wylie, Alison, & Nelson, Lynn Hankinson. (2007). Coming to terms with the values of science: Insights from feminist science scholarship. In Harold Kincaid, John Dupre, & Alison Wylie (Eds.), *Value free science: Ideal or illusion?* Oxford, UK: Oxford University Press.

PART II

Causal inference and explanation

THE DESIRE TO KNOW NOT ONLY what happened but *why* is a fundamental driving force of research in every realm of science. The interest in such questions is, moreover, not solely a matter of pure intellectual curiosity. For example, knowing the explanation of an adverse event—like a plane crash or a disease—can be essential for efforts to prevent future occurrences of it. Likewise, knowing the causes of desirable things, such as health or economic prosperity, is necessary for being able to take effective steps to promote them. An interest in explanation, then, has a strong practical component, and that is especially true of the social sciences. Even the most casual glance at the broader social world reveals many things that we would be better off without—poverty, inequality, corruption, crime, wars, inter-ethnic strife, to name just a few. Although no one expects social science to create a utopia, better understandings of social processes might be hoped to inform improved policies and institutions that address such issues.

Explanations are answers to "why" questions and exactly what a proper scientific explanation consists of is a longstanding question in the philosophy of science. The classic view on this topic, crystallized by Carl Hempel (1965), asserts that a scientific explanation of an occurrence shows how it followed from laws of nature together with the particulars of the situation. In discussions of Hempel's model of scientific explanation, the paradigm examples of laws of nature are typically drawn from physical sciences. For example, it is a law of physics that nothing can travel faster than the speed of light. Or consider Isaac Newton's law of universal gravitation, which says that every two objects exert a force of mutual attraction that is directly proportional to the product of their masses and inversely proportional to the square of the distance between them. An astronomer might explain why Mars aligned with Saturn on a particular date by pointing out how this event is a consequence of Newton's laws together with facts such as the masses of the two planets and their positions and velocities at an earlier time. This conception of scientific explanation is often referred to as the "covering law" model. According to this perspective, then, explanations in social science are genuinely scientific only if they too are grounded in laws of nature. That is precisely the position that Hempel defends in the first chapter in this section.

But it is questionable whether there are laws of social science in anything like the sense that there are laws of physics. In fact, it is rare that generalizations in social science are referred to as "laws," the laws of supply and demand being one of the few exceptions. Moreover, such "laws" as there are in social science do not hold everywhere and always as laws of physics are often presumed to do. For example, the law of supply depends upon a market mechanism in which manufacturers respond to rising prices for their goods with increased production and to lower prices with decreased production. When this mechanism is disrupted or absent—for instance, in an economy in which production and prices are fixed by decree from a centralized government as was the case in the Soviet Union—the laws of supply and demand can be false. Physical laws, by contrast, are often assumed to be universal and without exception: if the law says nothing travels faster than the speed of light, then that's how it is everywhere and always.

Hempel's answer to this difficulty is to suggest that laws of nature can be statistical, making claims about what happens for the most part rather than about what invariably occurs. For instance, it might be a law of social science that democratic nations rarely go to war with one another, although there are a few cases in history when this has happened (cf. Rasler and Thompson 2004). Hempel also suggests that many explanations in social science are really what he calls *explanation sketches.* An explanation sketch is a partial or incomplete covering law explanation. For example, one might have some idea of what the relevant law is but be unable to state it in any precise form. Hempel suggested that explanation sketches can play a legitimate role in the scientific process by functioning as a step towards a more complete covering law explanation.

A variation on Hempel's proposal suggests that explanations in social science depend on what are known as "ceteris paribus" laws. The phrase "ceteris paribus" is Latin for "other things being equal," although in discussions of ceteris paribus laws it is often interpreted to mean something along the lines of "so long as nothing interferes." The idea, then, is that laws in social science come with a ceteris paribus qualification attached to them. The law of supply could be interpreted to assert that, other things being equal, the higher the price of an item, the more of it manufacturers will produce. The ceteris paribus clause in this case refers to other causes that might affect supply as well as to factors that might disrupt the functioning of the market mechanism (Hausman 1990). Thus, an increase in demand might drive up the price yet not be followed by an increase in supply if the quantities of raw materials needed for increased production are unavailable or prohibitively expensive. Ceteris paribus laws differ from statistical laws as described by Hempel, because a ceteris paribus law need not assert that the generalization holds true for the most part. Indeed, a ceteris paribus law need not specify any number for how frequently the generalization is correct and how frequently it isn't. Rather than assert that the law of supply is true 90 percent, 75 percent, 50 percent or any other percentage of the time, a typical presentation would say that the law holds "other things being equal," and follow up with some examples of how other things might fail to be equal. In the second chapter in this section, Harold Kincaid defends the idea that explanations in social science rely on ceteris paribus laws.

There is a good deal of controversy in the philosophy of science literature on the topic of ceteris paribus laws. The standard objection to ceteris paribus laws is that they are vacuous, because to say a law holds "other things being equal" boils down to no more than saying that the law is true unless something makes it false. Such a generalization could never be overturned by data, since whenever its predictions failed one could just say, "Well, other things must not have been equal." But it is often thought that scientific hypotheses must be testable, that is, it is possible that experiments or observations could provide evidence that the hypothesis should be rejected. Thus, a common criticism of ceteris paribus laws is that they are untestable and consequently not really scientific. In his chapter, Kincaid responds to such objections by suggesting ways that ceteris paribus laws could be subject to genuine scientific tests and explaining how they could be confirmed by data. According to Kincaid, ceteris paribus laws should be interpreted as describing causal tendencies that can be promoted or overridden by other causes that may or may not be present. Kincaid suggests that such claims can be scientifically tested by experimental and statistical techniques that enable factoring out other relevant causes.

Defenders of ceteris paribus laws share the central idea of the covering law model that genuine scientific explanation must be based on laws of nature. This perspective can be viewed as stemming from what Sandra Mitchell (2000) calls a paradigmatic approach to laws. This approach begins with a few examples of paradigm scientific explanations—that is, explanations that are widely regarding as attaining a very high scientific standard—and evaluates other explanations in terms of how closely they approximate the paradigms. Thus, Hempel's covering law model takes explanation in physical science as the paradigm, while the ceteris paribus approach to laws attempts show that explanation in social science can, despite first appearances, be squeezed into the same format. However, this approach to understanding scientific explanation has been questioned on a number of grounds. One line of criticism arises from studies suggesting that *mechanisms* rather than laws are the central basis for explanation in the biological sciences (Machamer, Darden, and Craver 2000; Craver 2007). Hence, if biological explanation is usually grounded in mechanisms rather than laws, there seems no reason to insist that laws are required for explanation in social science. A second and related line of criticism approaches scientific explanation from a pragmatic perspective by focusing on what distinctive functions scientific explanations are supposed to serve (Mitchell 2000). The chapter by Jim Woodward pursues this pragmatic approach.

The central idea in Woodward's approach is that the fundamental motivation underlying an interest in explanation is the desire to manipulate or change our surroundings. This "manipulationist" conception of explanation differs from Hempel's covering law model, wherein scientific explanation is a matter of showing how something could have been *predicted*. To see how these two things are different, consider the question of the relationship between playing violent video games and engaging in aggressive behavior. Not surprisingly, children who spend more time playing violent video games are more likely to behave aggressively (Weber, Ritterfield and Mathiak 2006). Thus, if presented with two groups, one composed of children who frequently play violent video games and the other composed of children who rarely do so, we could predict that the rate of aggressive behavior would be higher in the first group than in the second. But it does not necessarily follow from this that restricting access to violent video games in a group of children would reduce their proclivity for aggression. Perhaps the correlation is due to the fact that children who are predisposed to engage in aggressive behavior find violent video games more appealing. In this case, those children would still behave aggressively even if deprived of their video games. Woodward's question, then, is what is the distinguishing feature of generalizations that can serve as the basis for effective strategies for changing the world around us in ways we want? His answer is that such generalizations are invariant under interventions. Consider what this would mean in the violent video game example. An intervention in this case would consist of some action to directly control the amount of time the children spend playing the games. One way to do this would be by a randomized experiment in which some children are assigned to spend a certain amount of time per day playing violent video games, while others are required to play a non-violent video game. If the association is invariant, then it continues to hold true under these circumstances. If the association between violent video games and aggressive behavior is not invariant, then it "breaks down" when the intervention is implemented. In the chapter included here, Woodward suggests that invariance is a better framework than the tradition conception of law of nature for understanding explanation in the "special" (which includes social) sciences.

Causal inference is the process of using data to discover what causes what. This is often a significant challenge in social science, where there are typically multiple possible interpretations and explanations of a given set of data. That point is illustrated by the example about video games and aggressive behavior. The correlation in that case might result from violent video games causing aggressive behavior, or the reverse, or from a common cause of both. Perhaps parental neglect makes children more likely behave aggressively while also making them more inclined to play violent video games. Since there are typically many (often difficult to measure) variables that might be reasonably supposed to be relevant to any cause and effect relationship in social science, there are often many possible alternative explanations of any set of data, which can make it very difficult to draw firm conclusions about what is causing what. Mechanisms are sometimes put forward as a solution to this problem. The thought is that a focus on mechanisms can help to distinguish among alternative causal hypotheses in social science and thereby assist causal inference. In his chapter included here, Daniel Steel argues that proponents of this idea have not provided an adequate account of how mechanisms could perform this function. After all, learning mechanisms from the data is also a form of causal inference, so it needs to be explained how mechanisms could be discovered despite the challenges just described. Steel attempts to improve the mechanisms proposal by developing the notion of *process tracing*, in which social scientists attempt to piece together mechanisms from interpretations of social practices.

One of the things that makes causal inference in social science difficult is that it is usually not possible to directly experiment with social systems. For example, you can't randomly assign nations to be democracies or dictatorships and then measure the effects on warfare. But there is a long history of collecting social statistics on such things as employment, income, education, suicides, among many others. One question, then, is whether it is possible answer questions about cause and effect in social science through a careful examination of such data. In the final chapter in this section, Richard Scheines presents the central concepts of a theory—founded on something known as Bayesian networks—that is designed to do just this. Scheines's main theme in the chapter included here is that causal inference in both experimental and non-experimental contexts depends on finding what he calls a *detectible instrumental variable*. He explains how detectible instrumental variables can, in fortuitous circumstances, be discovered from social statistics, and concludes that it is a mistake to suppose that causal conclusions can only be properly drawn from randomized experiments.

Further reading

There is a very extensive (both in terms of size and historical duration) literature dealing with objections to and refinements of Hempel's covering law model. For an excellent survey see Salmon (2006). See Cartwright (1983) for a classic argument that the laws of physics, to the extent that they are interpreted as regularities, are also qualified by ceteris paribus clauses. Cartwright's claim is disputed by Earman and Roberts (1999) who argue that no interpretation of ceteris paribus laws succeeds in avoiding vacuity. The edited volume by Earman, Glymour, and Mitchell (2003), originally published as an issue of the journal *Erkenntnis* in 2002, includes a representative sample of the leading approaches to the topic of ceteris paribus laws. Woodward gives the fullest elaboration of his approach to causal explanation in his (2003) book. See Reiss (2005) for a critical discussion of the usefulness of Woodward's proposal for social science. See Hedström and Swedberg (1998) and Mayntz (2004) for discussions of the concept of a social mechanism. See Weber (2007, 2008) and Steel (2007, 2008) for further discussion of the Steel chapter on mechanisms and causal inference included in this volume. For further debates about the importance, or lack of importance, of mechanisms in social science see Reiss (2007) and Brante (2008). For a good introduction to Bayesian networks approaches to causation, see Pearl (2001) and Neopolitan (2004). For further discussion of Bayes nets to approaches to causal inference with a philosophy of social science angle see Hoover (2001) and Cartwright (2007).

References

Brante, T. (2008) "Explanatory and Non-Explanatory Goals in the Social Sciences: A Reply to Reiss," *Philosophy of the Social Sciences* 38: 271–78.

Cartwright, N. (1983) *How the Laws of Physics Lie.* Oxford: Oxford University Press.

—— (2007) *Hunting Causes and Using Them: Approaches in Philosophy and Economics.* Cambridge: Cambridge University Press.

Craver, C. (2007) *Explaining the Brain: The Mosaic Unity of Neuroscience.* Oxford: Oxford University Press.

Earman, J., Glymour, C. and Mitchell, S. (2003) *Ceteris Paribus Laws.* New York: Springer.

Earman, J. and Roberts, J. (1999) "Ceteris Paribus, There is No Problem of Provisos," *Synthese* 118: 439–78.

Hausman, D. (1990) "Supply and Demand Explanations and Their Ceteris Paribus Clauses," *Review of Political Economy* 2: 168–87; reprinted in *Essays on Philosophy and Economic Methodology.* New York: Cambridge University Press, 1992.

Hedström, P. and Swedberg, R. (eds.) (1998) *Social Mechanisms: An Analytical Approach to Social Theory.* Cambridge: Cambridge University Press.

Hempel, C.G. (1965) *Aspects of Scientific Explanation.* New York: Free Press.

Hoover, K. (2001) *Causality in Macroeconomics.* Cambridge: Cambridge University Press.

Machamer, P., Darden, L. and Craver, C. (2000) "Thinking about Mechanisms," *Philosophy of Science* 67: 1–25.

Mayntz, R. (2004) "Mechanisms in the Analysis of Social Macro-Phenomena," *Philosophy of the Social Sciences* 34: 237–259.

Mitchell, S. (2000) "Dimensions of Scientific Law," *Philosophy of Science* 67: 242–6.

Neopolitan, R. (2004) *Learning Bayesian Networks.* Upper Saddle River, NJ: Prentice Hall.

Pearl, J. (2001) *Causality.* Cambridge: Cambridge University Press.

Rasler, K. and Thompson, W. (2004) "The Democratic Peace and a Sequential, Reciprocal Causal Arrow Hypothesis," *Comparative Political Studies* 37: 879–908.

Reiss, J. (2005) "Causal Instrumental Variables and Interventions," *Philosophy of Science* 72: 964–76.

—— (2007) "Do We Need Mechanisms in the Social Sciences?," *Philosophy of the Social Sciences* 37: 163–84.

Salmon, W. (2006) *Four Decades of Scientific Explanation.* Pittsburgh: University of Pittsburgh Press.

Steel, D. (2007) "With or Without Mechanisms: A Reply to Weber," *Philosophy of the Social Sciences* 37: 360–65.

—— (2008) *Across the Boundaries: Extrapolation in Biology and Social Science.* Oxford: Oxford University Press.

Weber, E. (2007) "Social Mechanisms, Causal Inference, and the Policy Relevance of Social Science," *Philosophy of the Social Sciences* 37: 348–59.

—— (2008) "Reply to Daniel Steel's 'With or Without Mechanisms'," *Philosophy of the Social Sciences* 38: 267–70.

Weber, R., Ritterfield, U. and Mathiak, K. (2006) "Does Playing Violent Video Games Induce Aggression? Empirical Evidence of a Functional Magnetic Resonance Imaging Study," *Media Psychology* 8: 39–60.

Woodward, J. (2003) *Making Things Happen: A Causal Theory of Explanation.* Oxford, UK: Oxford University Press.

Chapter 5

CARL HEMPEL

THE FUNCTION OF GENERAL LAWS
IN HISTORY

1. **IT IS A RATHER WIDELY HELD** opinion that history, in contradistinction to the so-called physical sciences, is concerned with the description of particular events of the past rather than with the search for general laws which might govern those events. As a characterization of the type of problem in which some historians are mainly interested, this view probably can not be denied; as a statement of the theoretical function of general laws in scientific historical research, it is certainly unacceptable. The following considerations are an attempt to substantiate this point by showing in some detail that general laws have quite analogous functions in history and in the natural sciences, that they form an indispensable instrument of historical research, and that they even constitute the common basis of various procedures which are often considered as characteristic of the social in contradistinction to the natural sciences.

By a general law, we shall here understand a statement of universal conditional form which is capable of being confirmed or disconfirmed by suitable empirical findings. The term 'law' suggests the idea that the statement in question is actually well confirmed by the relevant evidence available; as this qualification is, in many cases, irrelevant for our purpose, we shall frequently use the term 'hypothesis of universal form' or briefly 'universal hypothesis' instead of 'general law', and state the condition of satisfactory confirmation separately, if necessary. In the context of this paper, a universal hypothesis may be assumed to assert a regularity of the following type: In every case where an event of a specified kind C occurs at a certain place and time, an event of a specified kind E will occur at a place and time which is related in a specified manner to the place and time of the occurrence of the first event. (The symbols 'C' and 'E' have been chosen to suggest the terms 'cause' and 'effect', which are often, though by no means always, applied to events related by a law of the above kind.)

2.1 The main function of general laws in the natural sciences is to connect events in patterns which are usually referred to as *explanation* and *prediction*.

The explanation of the occurrence of an event of some specific kind E at a certain place and time consists, as it is usually expressed, in indicating the causes or determining factors of E. Now the assertion that a set of events—say, of the kinds $C_1, C_2, \ldots, C_n$—have caused the event to be explained, amounts to the statement that, according to certain general laws, a set of events of the kinds mentioned is regularly accompanied by an event of kind E. Thus, the scientific explanation of the event in question consists of

(1) a set of statements asserting the occurrence of certain events $C_1, \ldots C_n$ at certain times and places,
(2) a set of universal hypotheses, such that
    (a) the statements of both groups are reasonably well confirmed by empirical evidence,
    (b) from the two groups of statements the sentence asserting the occurrence of event E can be logically deduced.

In a physical explanation, group (1) would describe the initial and boundary conditions for the occurrence of the final event; generally, we shall say that group (1) states the *determining conditions* for the event to be explained, while group (2) contains the general laws on which the explanation is based; they imply the statement that whenever events of the kind described in the first group occur, an event of the kind to be explained will take place.

2.2 It is important to bear in mind that the symbols 'E', 'C', 'C_1', 'C_2', etc., which were used above, stand for kinds or properties of events, not for what is sometimes called individual events. For the object of description and explanation in every branch of empirical science is always the occurrence of an event of a certain *kind* (such as a drop in temperature by 14°F., an eclipse of the moon, a cell-division, an earthquake, an increase in employment, a political assassination) at a given place and time, or in a given empirical object (such as the radiator of a certain car, the planetary system, a specified historical personality, etc.) at a certain time.

What is sometimes called the *complete description* of an individual event (such as the earthquake of San Francisco in 1906 or the assassination of Julius Caesar) would require a statement of all the properties exhibited by the spatial region or the individual object involved, for the period of time occupied by the event in question. Such a task can never be completely accomplished.

A fortiori, it is impossible to give a *complete explanation* of an individual event in the sense of accounting for *all* its characteristics by means of universal hypotheses, although the explanation of what happened at a specified place and time may gradually be made more and more specific and comprehensive.

But there is no difference, in this respect, between history and the natural sciences: both can give an account of their subject-matter only in terms of general concepts, and history can "grasp the unique individuality" of its objects of study no more and no less than can physics or chemistry.

3. The following points result more or less directly from the above study of scientific explanation and are of special importance for the questions here to be discussed.

3.1 A set of events can be said to have caused the event to be explained only if general laws can be indicated which connect "causes" and "effect" in the manner characterized above.

3.2 No matter whether the cause-effect terminology is used or not, a scientific explanation has been achieved only if empirical laws of the kind mentioned under (2) in 2.1 have been applied.[1]

3.3 The use of universal empirical hypotheses as explanatory principles distinguishes genuine from pseudo-explanation, such as, say, the attempt to account for certain features of organic behavior by reference to an entelechy, for whose functioning no laws are offered, or the explanation of the achievements of a given person in terms of his "mission in history," his "predestined fate," or similar notions. Accounts of this type are based on metaphors rather than laws; they convey pictorial and emotional appeals instead of insight into factual connections; they substitute vague analogies and intuitive "plausibility" for deduction from testable statements and are therefore unacceptable as scientific explanations.

Any explanation of scientific character is amenable to objective checks; these include

(*a*) an empirical test of the sentences which state the determining conditions;
(*b*) an empirical test of the universal hypotheses on which the explanation rests;
(*c*) an investigation of whether the explanation is logically conclusive in the sense that the sentence describing the events to be explained follows from the statements of groups (1) and (2).

4. The function of general laws in *scientific prediction* can now be stated very briefly. Quite generally, prediction in empirical science consists in deriving a statement about a certain future event (for example, the relative position of the planets to the sun, at a future date) from (1) statements describing certain known (past or present) conditions (for example, the positions and momenta of the planets at a past or present moment), and (2) suitable general laws (for example, the laws of celestial mechanics). Thus, the logical structure of a scientific prediction is the same as that of a scientific explanation, which has been described in 2.1. In particular, prediction no less than explanation throughout empirical science involves reference to universal empirical hypotheses.

The customary distinction between explanation and prediction rests mainly on a pragmatic difference between the two: While in the case of an explanation, the final event is known to have happened, and its determining conditions have to be sought, the situation is reversed in the case of a prediction: here, the initial conditions are given, and their "effect"—which, in the typical case, has not yet taken place—is to be determined.

In view of the structural equality of explanation and prediction, it may be said that an explanation as characterized in 2.1 is not complete unless it might as well have functioned as a prediction: If the final event can be derived from the initial conditions and universal hypotheses stated in the explanation, then it might as well have been predicted, before it actually happened, on the basis of a knowledge of the initial conditions and the general laws. Thus, e.g., those initial conditions and general laws which the astronomer would adduce in explanation of a certain eclipse of the sun are such that they might also have served as a sufficient basis for a forecast of the eclipse before it took place.

However, only rarely, if ever, are explanations stated so completely as to exhibit this predictive character (which the test referred to under (*c*) in 3.3 would serve to reveal). Quite commonly, the explanation offered for the occurrence of an event is incomplete. Thus, we may hear the explanation that a barn burnt down "because" a burning cigarette was dropped in the hay, or that a certain political movement has spectacular success "because" it takes advantage of widespread racial prejudices. Similarly, in the case of the broken radiator, the customary way of formulating an explanation would be restricted to pointing out that the car was left in the cold, and the radiator was filled with water. In explanatory statements like these, the general laws which confer upon the stated conditions the character of "causes" or "determining factors" are completely omitted (sometimes, perhaps, as a "matter of course"), and, furthermore, the enumeration of the determining conditions of group (1) is incomplete; this is illustrated by the preceding examples, but also by the earlier analysis of the broken radiator case: as a closer examination would reveal, even that much more detailed statement of determining conditions and universal hypotheses would require amplification in order to serve as a sufficient basis for the deduction of the conclusion that the radiator broke during the night.

In some instances, the incompleteness of a given explanation may be considered as inessential. Thus, e.g., we may feel that the explanation referred to in the last example could be made complete if we so desired; for we have reasons to assume that we know the kind of determining conditions and of general laws which are relevant in this context.

Very frequently, however, we encounter "explanations" whose incompleteness can not simply be dismissed as inessential. The methodological consequences of this situation will be discussed later (especially in 5.3 and 5.4).

5.1 The preceding considerations apply to *explanation in history* as well as in any other branch of empirical science. Historical explanation, too, aims at showing that the event in question was not "a matter of chance," but was to be expected in view of certain antecedent or simultaneous conditions. The expectation referred to is not prophecy or divination, but rational scientific anticipation which rests on the assumption of general laws.

If this view is correct, it would seem strange that while most historians do suggest explanations of historical events, many of them deny the possibility of resorting to any general laws in history. It is possible, however, to account for this situation by a closer study of explanation in history, as may become clear in the course of the following analysis.

5.2 In some cases, the universal hypotheses underlying a historical explanation are rather explicitly stated, as is illustrated by the italicized passages in the following attempt to explain the tendency of government agencies to perpetuate themselves and to expand:

> As the activities of the government are enlarged, more people develop a vested interest in the continuation and expansion of governmental functions. *People who have jobs do not like to lose them; those who are habituated to certain skills do not welcome change; those who have become accustomed to the exercise of a certain kind of power do not like to relinquish their control—if anything, they want to develop greater power and correspondingly greater prestige.* . . .
>
> Thus, government offices and bureaus, once created, in turn institute drives, not only to fortify themselves against assault, but to enlarge the scope of their operations.[2]

Most explanations offered in history or sociology, however, fail to include an explicit statement of the general regularities they presuppose; and there seem to be at least two reasons which account for this:

First, the universal hypotheses in question frequently relate to individual or social psychology, which somehow is supposed to be familiar to everybody through his everyday experience; thus, they are tacitly taken for granted. This is a situation quite similar to that characterized in section 4.

Second, it would often be very difficult to formulate the underlying assumptions explicitly with sufficient precision and at the same time in such a way that they are in agreement with all the relevant empirical evidence available. It is highly instructive, in examining the adequacy of a suggested explanation, to attempt a reconstruction of the universal hypotheses on which it rests. Particularly, such terms as "hence," "therefore," "consequently," "because," "naturally," "obviously," etc., are often indicative of the tacit presupposition of some general law: they are used to tie up the initial conditions with the event to be explained; but that the latter was "naturally" to be expected as a "consequence" of the stated conditions follows only if suitable general laws are presupposed. Consider, for example, the statement that the Dust Bowl farmers migrated to California "because" continual drought and sandstorms made their existence increasingly precarious, and because California seemed to them to offer so much better living conditions. This explanation rests on some such universal hypothesis as that populations will tend to migrate to regions which offer better living conditions. But it would obviously be difficult accurately to state this hypothesis in the form of a general law which is reasonably well confirmed by all the relevant evidence available. Similarly, if a particular revolution is explained by reference to the growing discontent, on the part of a large part of the population, with certain prevailing conditions, it is clear that a general regularity is assumed in this explanation, but we are hardly in a position to state just what extent and what specific form the discontent has to assume, and what the environmental conditions have to be, to bring about a revolution. Analogous remarks apply to all historical explanations in terms of class struggle, economic or geographic conditions, vested interests of certain groups, tendency to conspicuous consumption, etc.: all of them rest on the assumption of universal hypotheses[3] which connect certain characteristics of individual or group life with others; but in many cases, the content of the hypotheses which are tacitly assumed in a given explanation can be reconstructed only quite approximately.

5.3 It might be argued that the phenomena covered by the type of explanation just mentioned are of a statistical character, and that therefore only probability hypotheses need to be assumed in their explanation, so that the question as to the "underlying general laws" would be based on a false premise. And indeed, it seems possible and justifiable to construe certain explanations offered in history as based on the assumption of probability hypotheses rather than of general "deterministic" laws, i.e., laws in the form of universal conditionals. This claim may be extended to many of the explanations offered in other fields of empirical science as well. Thus, e.g., if Tommy comes down with the measles two weeks after his brother, and if he has not been in the company of other persons having the measles, we accept the explanation that he caught the disease from his brother. Now, there is a general hypothesis underlying this explanation; but it can hardly be said to be a general law to the effect that any person who has not had the measles before will get it without fail if he stays in the company of somebody else who has the measles; that contagion will occur can be asserted only with high probability.

Many an explanation offered in history seems to admit of an analysis of this kind: if fully and explicitly formulated, it would state certain initial conditions, and certain probability hypotheses,[4] such that the occurrence of the event to be explained is made highly probable by the initial conditions in view of the probability hypotheses. But no matter whether explanations in history be construed as causal or as probabilistic, it remains true that in general the initial conditions and especially the universal hypotheses involved are not clearly indicated, and can not unambiguously be supplemented. (In the case of probability hypotheses, for example, the probability values involved will at best be known quite roughly.)

5.4 What the explanatory analyses of historical events offer is, then, in most cases not an explanation in one of the senses indicated above, but something that might be called an *explanation sketch*. Such a sketch consists of a more or less vague indication of the laws and initial conditions considered as relevant, and it needs "filling out" in order to turn into a full-fledged explanation. This filling-out requires further empirical research, for which the sketch suggests the direction. (Explanation sketches are common also outside of history; many explanations in psychoanalysis, for instance, illustrate this point.)

Obviously, an explanation sketch does not admit of an empirical test to the same extent as does a complete explanation; and yet, there is a difference between a scientifically acceptable explanation sketch and a pseudo-explanation (or a pseudo-explanation sketch). A scientifically acceptable explanation sketch needs to be filled out by more specific statements; but it points into the direction where these statements are to be found; and concrete research may tend to confirm or to infirm those indications; i.e., it may show that the kind of initial conditions suggested are actually relevant; or it may reveal that factors of a quite different nature have to be taken into account in order to arrive at a satisfactory explanation.

The filling-out process required by an explanation sketch will in general effect a gradual increase in the precision of the formulations involved; but at any stage of this process, those formulations will have some empirical import: it will be possible to indicate, at least roughly, what kind of evidence would be relevant in testing them, and what findings would tend to confirm them. In the case of nonempirical explanations or explanation sketches, on the other hand—say, by reference to the historical destiny of a certain race, or to a principle of historical justice—the use of empirically meaningless terms makes it impossible even roughly to indicate the type of investigation that would have a bearing upon those formulations, and that might lead to evidence either confirming or infirming the suggested explanation.

5.5 In trying to appraise the soundness of a given explanation, one will first have to attempt to reconstruct as completely as possible the argument constituting the explanation or the explanation sketch. In particular, it is important to realize what the underlying explanatory hypotheses are, and to appraise their scope and empirical foundation. A resuscitation of the assumptions buried under the gravestones 'hence', 'therefore', 'because', and the like will often reveal that the explanation offered is poorly founded or downright unacceptable. In many cases, this procedure will bring to light the fallacy of claiming that a large number of details of an event have been explained when, even on a very liberal interpretation, only some broad characteristics of it have been accounted for. Thus, for example, the geographic or economic conditions under which a group lives may account for certain general features of, say, its art or its moral codes; but to grant this does not mean that the artistic achievements of the group or its system of morals has thus been explained in detail; for this would imply that from a description of the prevalent geographic or economic conditions alone, a detailed account of certain aspects of the cultural life of the group can be deduced by means of specifiable general laws.

A related error consists in singling out one of several important groups of factors which would have to be stated in the initial conditions, and then claiming that the phenomenon in question is "determined" by that one group of factors and thus can be explained in terms of it.

Occasionally, the adherents of some particular school of explanation or interpretation in history will adduce, as evidence in favor of their approach, a successful historical prediction which was made by a representative of their school. But though the predictive success of a theory is certainly relevant evidence of its soundness, it is important to make sure that the successful prediction is in fact obtainable by means of the theory in question. It happens sometimes that the prediction is actually an ingenious guess which may have been influenced by the theoretical outlook of its author, but which can not be arrived at by means of his theory alone. Thus, an adherent of a quite metaphysical "theory" of history may have a sound feeling for historical developments and may be able to make correct predictions, which he will even couch in the terminology of his theory, though they could not have been attained by means of it. To guard against such pseudo-confirming cases would be one of the functions of test (c) in 3.3.

6. We have tried to show that in history no less than in any other branch of empirical inquiry, scientific explanation can be achieved only by means of suitable general hypotheses, or by theories, which are bodies of systematically related hypotheses. This thesis is clearly in contrast with the familiar view that genuine explanation in history is obtained by a method which characteristically distinguishes the social from the natural sciences, namely, *the method of empathic understanding:* The historian, we are told, imagines himself in the place of the persons involved in the events which he wants to explain; he tries to realize as completely as possible the circumstances under which they acted and the motives which influenced their actions; and by this imaginary self-identification with his heroes, he arrives at an understanding and thus at an adequate explanation of the events with which he is concerned.

This method of empathy is, no doubt, frequently applied by laymen and by experts in history. But it does not in itself constitute an explanation; it rather is essentially a heuristic device; its function is to suggest psychological hypotheses which might serve as explanatory principles in the case under consideration. Stated in crude terms, the idea underlying this function is the following: The historian tries to realize how he himself would act under the given conditions, and under the particular motivations of his heroes; he tentatively generalizes his findings into a general rule and uses the latter as an explanatory principle in accounting for the actions of the persons involved. Now, this procedure may sometimes prove heuristically helpful; but it does not guarantee the soundness of the historical explanation to which it leads. The latter rather depends upon the factual correctness of the generalizations which the method of understanding may have suggested.

Nor is the use of this method indispensable for historical explanation. A historian may, for example, be incapable of feeling himself into the role of a paranoiac historic personality, and yet he may well be able to explain certain of his actions by reference to the principles of abnormal psychology. Thus, whether the historian is or is not in a position to identify himself with his historical hero is irrelevant for the correctness of his explanation; what counts is the soundness of the general hypotheses involved, no matter whether they were suggested by empathy or by a strictly behavioristic procedure. Much of the appeal of the "method of understanding" seems to be due to the fact that it tends to present the phenomena in question as somehow "plausible" or "natural" to us;[5] this is often done by means of persuasive metaphors. But the kind of "understanding" thus conveyed must clearly be separated from scientific understanding. In history as anywhere else in empirical science, the explanation of a phenomenon consists in subsuming it under general empirical laws; and the criterion of its soundness is not whether it appeals to our imagination, whether it is presented in terms of suggestive analogies or is otherwise made to appear plausible—all this may occur in pseudo-explanations as well— but exclusively whether it rests on empirically well confirmed assumptions concerning initial conditions and general laws.

7.1 So far, we have discussed the importance of general laws for explanation and prediction, and for so-called understanding in history. Let us now survey more briefly some other procedures in historical research which involve the assumption of universal hypotheses.

Closely related to explanation and understanding is the so-called *interpretation of historical phenomena* in terms of some particular approach or theory. The interpretations which are actually offered in history consist either in subsuming the phenomena in question under a scientific explanation or explanation sketch; or in an attempt to subsume them under some general idea which is not amenable to any empirical test. In the former case, interpretation clearly is explanation by means of universal hypotheses; in the latter, it amounts to a pseudo-explanation which may have emotive appeal and evoke vivid pictorial associations, but which does not further our theoretical understanding of the phenomena under consideration.

7.2 Analogous remarks apply to the procedure of ascertaining the "*meaning*" of given historical events; its scientific import consists in determining what other events are relevantly connected with the event in question, be it as "causes," or as "effects"; and the statement of the relevant connections assumes, again, the form of explanations or explanation sketches which involve universal hypotheses; this will be seen more clearly in the next subsection.

7.3 In the historical explanation of some social institutions great emphasis is laid upon an analysis of the *development* of the institution up to the stage under consideration. Critics of this approach have objected that a mere description of this kind is not a genuine explanation. This argument may be given a slightly different form in terms of the preceding reflections: An account of the development of an institution is obviously not simply a description of all the events which temporally preceded it; only those events are meant to be included which are "*relevant*" to the formation of that institution. And whether an event is relevant to that development is not a matter of evaluative opinion, but an objective question depending upon what is sometimes called a causal analysis of the rise of that institution.[6] Now, the causal analysis of an event establishes an explanation for it, and since this requires reference to general hypotheses, so do assumptions about relevance, and, consequently, so does the adequate analysis of the historical development of an institution.

7.4 Similarly, the use of the notions of *determination* and of *dependence* in the empirical sciences, including history, involves reference to general laws.[7] Thus, e.g., we may say that the pressure of a gas depends upon its temperature and volume, or that temperature and volume determine the pressure, in virtue of Boyle's law. But unless the underlying laws are stated explicitly, the assertion of a relation of dependence or of determination between certain magnitudes or characteristics amounts at best to claiming that they are connected by some unspecified empirical law; and that is a very meager assertion indeed: If, for example, we know only that there is some empirical law connecting two metrical magnitudes (such as length and temperature of a metal bar), we can not even be sure that a change of one of the two will be accompanied by a change of the other (for the law may connect the same value of the "dependent" or "determined" magnitude with different values of the other), but only that with any specific value of one of the variables, there will always be associated one and the same value of the other; and this is obviously much less than most authors mean to assert when they speak of determination or dependence in historical analysis.

Therefore, the sweeping assertion that economic (or geographic, or any other kind of) conditions "determine" the development and change of all other aspects of human society, has explanatory value only in so far as it can be substantiated by explicit laws which state just what kind of change in human culture will regularly follow upon specific changes in the economic (geographic, etc.) conditions. Only the establishment of specific laws can fill the general thesis with scientific content, make it amenable to empirical tests, and confer upon it an explanatory function. The elaboration of such laws with as much precision as possible seems clearly to be the direction in which progress in scientific explanation and understanding has to be sought.

8. The considerations developed in this paper are entirely neutral with respect to the problem of "*specifically historical laws*": they do not presuppose a particular way of distinguishing historical from sociological and other laws, nor do they imply or deny the assumption that empirical laws can be found which are historical in some specific sense, and which are well confirmed by empirical evidence.

But it may be worth mentioning here that those universal hypotheses to which historians explicitly or tacitly refer in offering explanations, predictions, interpretations, judgments of relevance, etc., are taken from *various* fields of scientific research, in so far as they are not pre-scientific generalizations of everyday experiences. Many of the universal hypotheses underlying historical explanation, for instance, would commonly be classified as psychological, economical, sociological, and partly perhaps as historical laws; in addition, historical research has frequently to resort to general laws established in physics, chemistry, and biology. Thus, e.g., the explanation of the defeat of an army by reference to lack of food, adverse weather conditions, disease, and the like, is based on a—usually tacit—assumption of such laws. The use of tree rings in dating events in history rests on the application of certain biological regularities. Various methods of testing the authenticity of documents, paintings, coins, etc., make use of physical and chemical theories.

The last two examples illustrate another point which is relevant in this context: Even if a historian should propose to restrict his research to a "pure description" of the past, without any attempt at offering explanations or statements about relevance and determination, he would continually have to make use of general laws. For the object of his studies would be the past— forever inaccessible to his direct examination. He would have to establish his knowledge by indirect methods: by the use of universal hypotheses which connect his present data with those past events. This fact has been obscured partly because some of the regularities involved are so familiar that they are not considered worth mentioning at all; and partly because of the habit of relegating the various hypotheses and theories which are used to ascertain knowledge about past events, to the "auxiliary sciences" of history. Quite probably, some of the historians who tend to minimize, if not to deny, the importance of general laws for history, are prompted by the feeling that only "genuinely historical laws" would be of interest for history. But once it is realized that the discovery of historical laws (in some specified sense of this very vague notion) would not make history methodologically autonomous and independent of the other branches of scientific research, it would seem that the problem of the existence of historical laws ought to lose some of its importance.

The remarks made in this section are but special illustrations of two broader principles of the theory of science: first, the separation of "pure description" and "hypothetical generalization and theory-construction" in empirical science is unwarranted; in the building of scientific knowledge the two are inseparably linked. And, second, it is similarly unwarranted and futile to attempt the demarcation of sharp boundary lines between the different fields of scientific research, and an autonomous development of each of the fields. The necessity, in historical inquiry, to make extensive use of universal hypotheses of which at least the overwhelming majority come from fields of research traditionally distinguished from history is just one of the aspects of what may be called the methodological unity of empirical science.

> Illustration: Let the event to be explained consist in the cracking of an automobile radiator during a cold night. The sentences of group (1) may state the following initial and boundary conditions: The car was left in the street all night. Its radiator, which consists of iron, was completely filled with water, and the lid was screwed on tightly. The temperature during the night dropped from 39°F. in the evening to 25°F. in the morning; the air pressure was normal. The bursting pressure of the radiator material is so and so much. Group (2) would contain empirical laws such as the following: Below 32°F., under normal atmospheric pressure, water freezes. Below 39.2°F., the pressure of a mass of water increases with decreasing temperature, if the volume remains constant or decreases; when the water freezes, the pressure again increases. Finally, this group would have to include a quantitative law concerning the change of pressure of water as a function of its temperature and volume.
>
> From statements of these two kinds, the conclusion that the radiator cracked during the night can be deduced by logical reasoning; an explanation of the considered event has been established.

Notes

1   Maurice Mandelbaum, in his generally very clarifying analysis of relevance and causation in history (*The Problem of Historical Knowledge*, New York, 1938, Chapters 7, 8) seems to hold that there is a difference between the "causal analysis" or "causal explanation" of an event and the establishment of scientific laws governing it in the sense stated above. He argues that "scientific laws can only be formulated on the basis of causal analysis," but that "they are not substitutes for full causal explanations" (*l.c.*, p. 238). For the reasons outlined above, this distinction does not appear to be justifiable: every "causal explanation" is an "explanation by scientific laws"; for in no other way than by reference to empirical laws can the assertion of a causal connection between events be scientifically substantiated.

2   Donald W. McConnell *et al.*, *Economic Behavior*; New York, 1939; pp. 894–95. (Italics supplied.)

3   What is sometimes misleadingly called an explanation by means of a certain *concept* is, in empirical science, actually an explanation in terms of *universal hypotheses* containing that concept. "Explanations"

involving concepts which do not function in empirically testable hypotheses—such as "entelechy" in biology, "historic destination of a race" or "self-unfolding of absolute reason" in history—are mere metaphors without cognitive content.

4   E. Zilsel, in a stimulating paper on "Physics and the Problem of Historico-Sociological Laws" (*Philosophy of Science*, Vol. 8, 1941, pp. 567–79), suggests that all specifically historical laws are of a statistical character similar to that of the "macro-laws" of physics. The above remarks, however, are not restricted to specifically historical laws since explanation in history rests to a large extent on nonhistorical laws (cf. section 8 of this paper).

5   For a criticism of this kind of plausibility, cf. Zilsel, *l.c.*, pp. 577–78, and Sections 7 and 8 in the same author's "Problems of Empiricism," in *International Encyclopedia of Unified Science*, Vol. II, 8 (Chicago: University of Chicago Press, 1941).

6   See the detailed and clear exposition of this point in M. Mandelbaum's book, Chapters 6–8.

7   According to Mandelbaum, history, in contradistinction to the physical sciences, consists "not in the formulation of laws of which the particular case is an instance, but in the description of the events in their actual determining relationships to each other; in seeing events as the products and producers of change" (*l.c.*, pp. 13–14). This is, in effect, a conception whose untenability has been pointed out already by Home, namely, that a careful examination of two specific events alone, without any reference to similar cases and to general regularities, can reveal that one of the events produces or determines the other. This thesis does not only run counter to the scientific meaning of the concept of determination which clearly rests on that of general law, but it even fails to provide any objective criteria which would be indicative of the intended relationship of determination or production. Thus, to speak of empirical determination independently of any reference to general laws is to use a metaphor without cognitive content.

Chapter 6

HAROLD KINCAID

CAUSES, CONFIRMATION, AND EXPLANATION

THIS CHAPTER BEGINS THE argument for a *science* of society. I argue that the social sciences can produce well-confirmed causal explanations and laws. No inherent conceptual obstacles prevent the social sciences from providing good causal explanations. Nor are there any insurmountable practical obstacles either. Complications abound, of course, but some good social research manages to overcome those difficulties as well as good work in the natural sciences.

My major concern shall be to defend causal explanations rather than laws. Although I think laws play a secondary role in good science, it is important for my overall argument to defend laws as well. Not all philosophers share my skepticism about unificationist accounts of explanation; they will think laws important because they unify. Furthermore, though the exact role of laws in confirmation is also controversial, prima facie laws seem to play an important role in testing. Finally, I shall argue later that in practice there is no very important difference between laws on the one hand and generalizations on the other. So defending causal explanations and defending causal laws naturally shade into each other.

The chapter is organized as follows: Section 3.1 takes on conceptual arguments coming from Searle, Davidson, Taylor and others. After disposing of those objections, Section 3.2 examines a much more serious and practical obstacle to causal laws – the fact that most alleged social laws are qualified *ceteris paribus*. Generalizations with open-ended escape clauses look unfalsifiable and unexplanatory. Section 3.2 argues that these qualifications are ubiquitous to all science and outlines the various ways good natural science deals with such problems. I then look at some recent social research – namely, Paige's work on agrarian political movements – and argue that his research handles the *ceteris paribus* problem as well as some of our best work in biology. [. . .]

3.1 Some *a priori* objections

Philosophers have given numerous reasons for thinking social laws impossible. Some point to the alleged fact that the basic kinds or predicates of the social sciences have no determinate physical definition. Others think that the social sciences will never produce real laws because they cannot describe all the causes operative in their domain. Still others argue that humans are "self-defining" and that this fact precludes causal explanations. In this section I sketch these arguments and argue that all fail.

John Searle (1984) has recently argued that social laws are impossible because social kinds or categories have multiple realizations. According to Searle, "the defining principle of . . . social phenomena set no physical limits on what can count as the physical realization" (p. 78). "Money," for example, is through and through social in nature – its definition refers to its social function, not its physical attributes. As a result, nearly anything can serve as money. Most or all social kinds are in the same boat: they have indefinitely many diverse physical realizations. This "means that there can't be any systematic connections between the physical and the social . . . therefore there can't be any matching . . . of the sort that would be necessary to make strict laws of the social sciences possible" (p. 79). Other philosophers (Churchland 1979, Rosenberg 1980, p. 107) have offered similar arguments to show that "folk" psychology – explanation in terms of beliefs and desires – is bereft of laws.

Let's tighten up Searle's argument a bit. He seems to be saying something like this:

(1) Social kinds have indefinitely many physical realizations.
(2) When a kind has indefinitely many physical realizations, it has no systematic connection to the physical.
(3) If a kind is not systematically connected to the physical, it cannot support genuine laws.
(4) Thus social kinds cannot support genuine laws.

This argument is, so far as I can see, either invalid or unsound, depending on how we read "systematic connection." If a systematic connection requires a law-like relation between social and physical predicates, then premise (3) makes a highly implausible claim: that the social sciences cannot produce laws unless they are reducible to physics.

If reduction to physics is required for laws, then large parts of the natural sciences cannot produce laws either. The fundamental predicate in population genetics and evolutionary theory, namely fitness, clearly has no unique physical definition, for an organism can be fit in indefinitely many physical ways (Rosenberg 1978). So there is no single or even complex physical characteristic which we can use to define "fit." The same problem surfaces in molecular biology for terms such as "antibody," "signals," or "receptors," which all have open-ended physical realizations. Even "planetary body" in Kepler's laws seemingly has no unique definition in quantum mechanical terms. So if we read "systematic connection" as the type-type connection of reduction, much natural science cannot produce laws. Searle's argument shows too much.

Perhaps we should read "systematic connection" as a looser relation, namely, supervenience. One set of facts A "supervenes" on a set B roughly if fixing the B facts also fixes the A facts. Premise (3) becomes more plausible on this construal, since *reduction* to physics is no longer required for laws (reduction requires more than supervenience). However, premise (2) is now false, for supervenience does not rule out multiple realizations. For example, physically identical organisms will have the same fitness, but there are indefinitely many physical ways to be fit. Thus either premise (2) or premise (3) is false, depending on how we understand "systematic connection." Equivocating on the term would, of course, render the argument invalid.

Another common argument (Davidson 1970; Taylor 1971) turns on the fact that the social realm is not "closed." Laws by nature must be universal. But if the social world constitutes an open realm subject to outside forces – physical or biological events for example – then social theory will remain forever incomplete and forever without true laws. Laws seem precluded.

We can take this argument in two ways: as arguing (1) from a fact about social systems as objects in the world or (2) from an alleged fact about social theories, namely, that they do not cover all the forces or causes in their domain. Neither rendering produces a sound argument.

Social systems – a given institution, society, or even world system – are obviously not closed systems. They depend on both physical and biological factors. However, every physical system short of the entire universe is also influenced by outside causes. So merely describing open systems cannot preclude laws. If it does, then the only laws in physics are those that describe the totality of the universe, another unacceptable conclusion, I assume.

Perhaps the crucial issue concerns not the open or closed nature of actual systems but instead a theory's ability to handle those outside factors. A closed theory is complete: it can describe and explain *in its own terms* all the forces acting in its domain. So, the argument runs, forces affecting open physical systems can be fully handled within physics itself. In the social sciences, however, outside factors are not social in nature and thus social theory cannot handle them. Consequently, alleged social laws are bound to be incomplete.

This argument again threatens to prove too much, namely, that no physical laws are possible either. Biological, psychological, and social events influence the physical universe, thus creating apparent exceptions to physical laws. If, however, our biological, psychological and social theories are even in part irreducible to physics, then we cannot handle these exceptions in entirely physical terms. Physics will be incomplete as well – and thus, if this argument is right, without laws. I again assume that conclusion is unacceptable.

The open nature of social science carries little weight for another reason. Why does a real or strict law have to invoke language only from one theory? The above argument assumes it must, but that assumption seems quite unwarranted. Cellular biology invokes chemical facts, and evolutionary theory does the same with physical facts about the environment. Why should that undercut laws if the law identifies kinds and relates them in whatever manner laws require? This problem is particularly acute because each physical law invokes only a subset of the total physical language. When other *physical* forces interfere, that subset obviously will not have the vocabulary to handle this more complicated situation. Are those laws only apparent because they are not refinable in their own terms? Here it just seems silly to make lawfulness turn on some prior notion of the "right" vocabulary. The real issue is whether potential exceptions can be handled in a systematic way. Thus there might well be social laws even if they are not refinable in a purely social vocabulary.

A final influential argument turns on the idea that humans are "self-defining." Taylor (1971), Fay (1984), and numerous others have advanced versions of this argument. The basic idea is that how we categorize our behavior determines in part what that behavior is. As autonomous agents, humans change their self-conception. As a result, any causal generalizations about the social world are bound to be flawed and without real nomic force. Only by completely ignoring social context and treating human behavior as brute motion could we ever develop such laws. So the reasoning goes.

We can take this argument in several different ways. In particular, these doubts might be about applying natural science *methods* to human behavior or about *laws* in the social sciences. [. . .] Here I want to focus on this reasoning as a more direct objection to laws.

Two different arguments seem to be lurking here. One builds on the contextual nature of human behavior. Bare bodily motion is not the object of the social sciences. Rather, it is behavior in a social context. Since social context is intertwined with our self-conceptions, and since self-conceptions vary enormously through history and across cultures, then we should expect no social laws. Laws are universal, but human social behavior is contextual.

Once spelled out, this reasoning is uncompelling. Assume human behavior is contextual. That prevents laws only if no science produces laws. When gases become fluids, the gas laws no longer apply and we need different laws for the new situation, thus the gas laws are specific to context. So are innumerable other generalizations in the natural sciences. If appeal to context prevents laws, then the natural sciences have few or no laws either. Thus reference to contexts does not rule out laws.

A second version of this argument appeals to free will. One problem with the previous argument is that even if humans define themselves, those definitions might change in predictable ways. So appeal to context alone must be inconclusive. This suggests that critics are really focusing on the idea that humans are free. Certainly Popper's (1982) attack on laws of history had some such motivation. So this revised argument says that human behavior depends on self-definition and self-definition is a free human product. Thus human behavior cannot be law governed.

There are obvious replies to such an argument, replies so familiar in the philosophical tradition that I shall just mention them: (1) at least some conceptions of freedom, for example freedom as lack of compulsion, are entirely compatible with laws of human behavior; (2) the idea that humans are free in some other sense is notoriously hard to clarify, since uncaused events sound like random events which fit no one's notion of freedom; and (3) even if humans are free in the sense of uncaused, it might still be the case that large-scale human behavior is patterned, just as indeterminacy might hold at the subatomic level and Newton's laws at the level of medium-sized objects. Thus this version of Taylor's argument also fails.

No doubt there are numerous other arguments alleging that social laws are impossible. Some of those arguments will come up in later chapters on interpretation and functionalism. At this point I want to turn to a much more serious obstacle to social laws – namely, the fact that most alleged social laws are qualified *ceteris paribus*.

3.2 Confirmation and qualifications

Eliminating conceptual objections is, of course, only a first step. While a science of society might be possible, it might be only that. In reality social research might never achieve even minimum standards of scientific adequacy. Having answered *a priori* objections, I now begin a more fundamental task: showing that the social sciences *in practice* can and sometimes do produce well-confirmed causal explanations. This section begins that argument by focusing on one serious practical obstacle. Almost every candidate for social laws is qualified *ceteris paribus* – "other things being equal." For critics, however, *ceteris paribus* clauses look like open-ended escape clauses, making the social sciences seem unfalsifiable and non-explanatory. That appearance is deceptive, or so I shall argue. In the process we shall make a prima facie case that some research actually does produce well-confirmed causal explanations.

3.2.1 How can ceteris paribus laws be confirmed and how can they explain?

Nearly every purported causal explanation in the social sciences is implicitly qualified with "other things being equal" or "assuming nothing else interferes." These escape clauses raise doubts about whether social generalizations can be confirmed or can explain. The problems about confirmation are obvious. We may never observe a case where other things really are equal. The weather, for example, influences the economy by numerous routes and the economy in turn influences every aspect of society. Nonetheless, almost no social research makes weather a variable; it falls under the implicit *ceteris paribus* clauses. If, however, we never observe social factors without such disturbing influences, how can we have compelling evidence for any social explanation? It looks like no social generalization could ever be disproven. After all, disconfirming evidence might show only that other things were not equal. And when we do find evidence for a social law, we apparently do not know how to distribute credit. Our law might be predictively accurate only because other things were not equal. *Ceteris paribus* general-izations seem unconfirmable.

There are also puzzles about how *ceteris paribus* laws *explain*. Since in the real world other things generally are not equal, explanations qualified seem irrelevant. They describe how things would behave, not how they do. But, we want to explain this world, not some other possible world. More concretely, if there are interfering factors, then how do we know that the causes our law picks out are the operative ones rather than the interfering factors? How do we tell the genuinely explanatory laws from the irrelevant ones – since strictly speaking no *ceteris paribus* law literally applies? Since *ceteris paribus* qualifications are rife in the social sciences, these questions are pressing.

Ceteris paribus qualifications surely do plague the social sciences. That, however, does not separate them from the natural sciences, for *ceteris paribus* clauses are endemic even in our best physics. Fundamental physical laws describe single forces in isolation. When we explain, however, we are usually faced with a complex physical process where several forces are at work. Only rarely can physics completely flesh out the needed *ceteris paribus* clauses in a systematic, theoretic way. Instead, physicists employ numerous ad hoc principles and rules of thumb to tie *ceteris paribus* clauses down to reality.

A similar point can be made for other "hard" sciences, for example, molecular biology. Molecular biology produces numerous causal generalizations about cells – among them, that cellular processes are produced by the DNA-to-mRNA-to-protein process and that internal cell functioning is stimulated by external tissue through signals bound at the membrane that are amplified by a second messenger carrying the signal to its destination. Yet, these generalizations are really simplifications of more complex processes. Explaining actual cellular events requires factoring in cell type, the kind of organelles involved, the source of the external signal, and so on. Most causal generalizations in molecular biology are qualified *ceteris paribus*.

Ceteris paribus clauses are therefore no *inherent* obstacle to well-confirmed causal explanations in the social sciences. However, defending science in the social sciences still requires answering three questions about *ceteris paribus* laws: (1) How can they explain at all? (2) How does good work in the natural sciences deal with the *ceteris paribus* problem? and (3) Can the social sciences employ similar strategies? I begin with the first, more philosophical question and then turn to look at these problems in practice.

Ceteris paribus generalizations cause problems because things are seldom equal, yet we use those laws to explain. If other things are not equal, then our explanation is strictly speaking false. So how can a *ceteris paribus* law explain? We cannot answer this fundamental question without some picture of explanation. In the last chapter I sketched approaches to explanation: those emphasizing causation and those emphasizing unification. The causal approach, I shall argue, has a natural account of how and when *ceteris paribus* laws explain. [. . .]

If explanation depends on causation, then *ceteris paribus* laws can explain if they cite causes. Obviously when the *ceteris paribus* clause is satisfied, *ceteris paribus* laws explain because they cite the real causes at work. However, the hard question is how can *ceteris paribus* laws cite operative causes when other things are not equal? They can do so by picking out *tendencies*. When a *ceteris paribus* law really helps explain, it does so because it identifies one factor in a complex situation. So while other things may not be equal, we can still make sense of the idea that a *ceteris paribus* law is relevant. It covers the phenomena to be explained because it picks out a real aspect or tendency.

Tendencies, in the sense I am using the term, are partial causes, single aspects or factors in a complex causal network. The law of gravity, for example, holds only *ceteris paribus*. Yet it can explain the behavior of sub-atomic particles even where other factors do interfere. The law of gravity explains in this case because it picks out a component force or cause from the complex causal structure. In my terminology, it picks out a tendency. Defined as "partial causal factors," tendencies are no more mysterious than causation in general. Admittedly, tendencies are frequently associated with much more metaphysical and controversial notions. As I employ them, however, tendencies need not involve those large commitments.

We can clarify tendencies as partial causal factors by looking at what they do *not* require. The law "*A* causes *B*, *ceteris paribus*" can pick out tendencies without it being the case that *A* is frequently seen to bring about *B*. In other words, a causal law can pick out a tendency – a partial causal factor or influence – even if the tendency itself is never dominant. For example, gravity partly explains the behavior of a body with an electrical charge. Yet if electrical forces were always greater than gravitational forces, we would never see the body follow the law of gravity. Thus there can be a tendency for *A* to cause *B* without it being the case that *B* happens frequently or at all.

Similarly, tendencies as understood here do not require some notion of approximate truth. The law that *A* causes *B*, *ceteris paribus*, may pick out a real tendency even though it is not even approximately true (whatever that means) that when *A* occurs, *B* does so as well. If other forces always outweigh gravity in some domain, then objects will not even approximately follow the law of gravity. Of course, some *ceteris paribus* laws – sometimes labelled idealizations – are meant to pick out approximate or rough truths. But there is no requirement that they must. Many *ceteris paribus* claims are *abstractions:* they describe particular components from a complex with no claim that the component is dominant.

Tendencies are also not to be equated with counterfactual claims. No doubt *ceteris paribus* laws do entail counterfactual claims – most obviously, that if other things were equal, *A* would result in *B*. But not every counterfactual claim must identify an explanatory tendency. For example, *if* markets were perfect, then economic forces would cause firms to choose the output where marginal cost, marginal revenue and price are equal. However, that counterfactual assertion does not ensure that such a tendency exists in real, imperfect markets. Because other things are not equal, there may be no such tendency at all. In short, true counterfactual claims do not entail true, explanatory tendency claims.

Finally, not every type of *ceteris paribus* law must be analyzed via tendencies. Science produces laws or law-like statements that are apparently not about causes at all. Such laws simply describe behavior. It does not make much sense to think of these as about tendencies. A body moving along a vector may be composed mathematically from two simpler notions. But a behavioral law describing one of those component motions apparently does not describe real tendencies as defended here. If it did, we would be forced to conclude that the planets actually do move in a straight line and fall to the center, not that we can usefully describe their behavior as if they did. Similarly, consider Marx's alleged law that the profit rate tends to fall. If we never observe a decline in profit rates, can we still explain the actual profit trends as resulting from a real tendency of profits to fall? Insofar as Marx's law is a behavioral law rather than a causal one, we cannot. So tendencies may not make much sense for behavioral laws qualified *ceteris paribus*.

Is this a problem for taking *ceteris paribus* explanations as being about tendencies? I do not think so. Recall what motivated us to posit tendencies in the first place. It was a desire to show that *ceteris paribus* laws can explain. Yet if we focus on explanation as the citing of causes, then we are not forced to posit tendencies for behavioral laws. Behavioral laws do not cite causes and thus need not explain, whatever their other scientific virtues. Thus tendencies need not lead us to the mysterious conclusion that the planets both move in a straight line and fall to the center.

We can understand how *ceteris paribus* laws explain on the causal approach. It is not so obvious we can do so if we emphasize unification. Laws explain on the unification approach because they take many diverse phenomena and reduce them to an instance of one basic principle. Without an appeal to tendencies, *ceteris paribus* laws are apparently false when other things are not equal. But false statements arguably do not give us real – as opposed to merely possible – explanations. So however much *ceteris paribus* laws unify, they still cannot explain because they are false. *Ceteris paribus* laws remain a mystery on the unification view.

Defenders of the unification approach can either bite the bullet and allow that false statements explain or find their own surrogate for tendencies. The former tack threatens to make explanation a largely psychological, subjective matter. The latter move is not impossible, but proposed notions like "approximate truth" are both hard to clarify and will not suffice for abstractions that are not even close to the truth. Thus I shall not try to defend *ceteris paribus* laws as explaining via unification. Fortunately, we can understand many of them, causally construed.

Given that we can at least make sense of how causal *ceteris paribus* laws explain, we have next to (1) say how we can confirm *ceteris paribus* laws and (2) give criteria for telling when they are irrelevant. The two questions are intimately related. The key issue in both cases is whether data indicates our laws pick out the real causes at work.

Standard scientific methods – especially those designed to separate real causes from spurious ones – will help confirm *ceteris paribus* laws and tell us when those laws explain. Among the testing practices that lend credence to *ceteris paribus* laws are the following:

(1) We can sometimes show that in some narrow range of cases the *ceteris paribus* conditions are satisfied. Rational economic man is an idealization, but sometimes consumers do act on well-ordered preferences and maximize. Or, we can *make* other things equal through controlled experiments. We can then confirm the law directly.

(2) We can sometimes show that although other things are not equal, it makes little difference: the law holds for the large part. Such tests are of course not decisive, since the law might still hold precisely because other things are not equal. However, if we already have independent reason for thinking that interfering factors have a small influence, then showing our law holds approximately is evidence for its truth.

(3) We can look for evidence that the unspecified factors have no systematic influence. Signs of systematic influence raise the prospect that our law holds for spurious reasons; finding only random deviations suggests that we have identified the causes at work. This general strategy is of course one rationale for randomized experimental design and for the requirement in statistical testing that error terms be randomly distributed.

(4) When a *ceteris paribus* law fails to hold in reality, we can nonetheless explain away its failure. Sometimes the counteracting factors can be cited and relevant laws invoked, giving us at least an approximate prediction of their combined effect. Other times the interfering factors may be unique and fall under no known law, yet we can reasonably explain away their influence. Of course, explaining away can become mere ad hoc curve fitting, but it need not; such explanations can and should have independent evidence.

(5) Sometimes we can provide inductive evidence for a *ceteris paribus* law by showing that as conditions approach those required by the *ceteris paribus* clause, the law becomes more predictively accurate – and vice versa. This gives us evidence that our law does not hold accidentally and that the postulated causal process is really producing our data.

(6) We can try to show that our *ceteris paribus* law is what Leamer (1983) calls "sturdy." A *ceteris paribus* law is sturdy if we can add in possible counteracting influences and show that the law still holds. Doing so is an indication that the law describes real factors.

In statistical testing, this method involves adding in variables and showing that the alleged relation still holds. Similarly, simulations can give the same result by using background information to see if possible interfering factors might undercut the law being tested.

(7) We can provide evidence that there exists some mechanism connecting the variables in our purported law. Evidence for a mechanism is evidence that a real causal tendency is at work, even if it is not dominant.

(8) We can sometimes have domain-specific generalizations telling us that specific *ceteris paribus* clauses are no problem. For example, when a biologist uses natural selection to explain traits, he or she makes a *ceteris paribus* assumption that other factors are absent. Over time, biologists have learned when and where that assumption is reasonable. In short, once we use the above methods to confirm *ceteris paribus* claims, we may then infer that other similar *ceteris paribus* clauses are reasonable.

(9) Finally, we can show that a *ceteris paribus* law has other important scientific virtues: for example, that it holds up against diverse kinds of data, that the *ceteris paribus* law, when combined with other well-confirmed generalizations, yields successful predictions, and so on.

When these methods are applied to causal laws, they both help confirm and show that a real tendency is at work. Each increases our confidence that a *ceteris paribus* law fits the facts because it describes a real relation and not because of spurious factors not described.

Method (6) – looking for sturdiness – provides both cross tests and fair tests. By seeing if the law holds up when other possible factors are added in, we are testing our law against different background assumptions; if we use the variables of competing theories, then searching for sturdiness is likewise providing a fair test. Looking for more realistic predictions from more realistic qualifications (method [5]) also provides a cross test against different assumptions. Using information from successful tests to infer which qualifications are reliable – method (8) – gives us a cross test of those other results, as does method (9) for assumptions about mechanisms. Methods (3), (4), and (6), which all involve factoring in or out other variables, give independent tests, if those variables are supported by other evidence and not simply motivated by the need to save the generalization at issue.

So the methods listed above for dealing with *ceteris paribus* generalizations flesh out the symptoms of good science described earlier. And, these methods in turn become much more concrete and precise when embodied, for example, in specific statistical techniques. As I argued earlier, broad scientific virtues are abstractions; doing and evaluating science requires successfully realizing these virtues and methods in concrete, domain-specific practices. Of course, there is no fully *mechanical* procedure for applying these methods. Nonetheless, they are powerful tools for establishing causal laws and showing that those laws describe tendencies which explain the phenomena. Exactly when *ceteris paribus* laws are supported and explanatory is a judgment call. But that is the nature of science.

3.2.2 Ceteris paribus *in practice*

So *ceteris paribus* qualifications need not prevent good science. Do they prevent good *social* science? To answer that question, we must ask if the social sciences can and do successfully employ methods like those just sketched. To defend naturalism I obviously must argue that they can. I begin that argument here and extend it in later chapters. This section discusses some good social research in detail, looking at how it deals with the *ceteris paribus* problem.

To show that this research not only confirms its *ceteris paribus* generalizations but does so "successfully," I shall compare it to some of the best work in ecology and evolutionary biology. The comparison is favorable – some social research handles the *ceteris paribus* problem as well as some of our best biology.

Jeffrey Paige, in *Agrarian Revolution* (1975), has produced an exemplary piece of social science research. Building on the Marxist sociological tradition, Paige sets out to determine the primary causes of agrarian political behavior, particularly in developing countries. His work, however, is not doctrinaire Marxism, for he modifies the Marxian view at many places. Not content with anecdotal evidence, Paige produces a sophisticated statistical, cross-national study of agrarian revolutions, revolts and reform movements. Detailed case studies further confirm those results. Paige's results are not beyond criticism. Nonetheless, they are rigorous and careful; they provide compelling evidence that social research can be scientifically respectable. Moreover, Paige explains in terms of large-scale social processes and as a result his work will later be used to defend holism as well. So I want to discuss Paige's results in some detail.

Paige's primary hypothesis is that class structure largely determines agrarian political behavior in developing countries. The social classes in agrarian systems are of two basic kinds, depending on whether they are composed of cultivators or non-cultivators. Cultivators include sharecroppers, resident wage laborers, peasants with small holdings, and usufructuaries; non-cultivators are the landed aristocracy and agricultural corporations. These cultivators and non-cultivators in turn fall into different social classes depending on the source of their income, in particular on whether their income comes primarily from land, capital, or wages.

Four basic agrarian class systems are thus possible (see Figure 6.1). In the first type of system, both cultivators and non-cultivators draw their income primarily from rights to the

Source of Income

Agrarian class system	Noncultivators	Cultivators
Commercial hacienda	Land	Land (right to cultivate small plots)
Large estate	Land	Wages
Corporation-owned plantation	Capital investment	Wages
Small holding	Capital investment	Land

Figure 6.1 Paige's four basic agrarian class systems; with the source of income and non-cultivators in each system.

land rather than from capital or wages. The most common system of this type is the commercial hacienda or manor. It is an individually owned enterprise which does not depend essentially on power-driven processing machinery or other similar capital investments; its workers typically receive compensation by rights to cultivate small plots of land. In the second type of system, non-cultivators draw their income from the land and workers are paid in wages. Usually these systems involve large estates with little or no power-driven machinery and workers who are either sharecroppers or migratory wage laborers. In the third type, non-cultivators draw their income in large part from capital investments and workers are paid in wages. Plantations owned by a commercial corporation typify this sort of system. Crops are processed on site by power-driven machinery and workers are more or less permanent residents who are paid in money wages. In the fourth type, non-cultivators depend primarily on capital and the cultivators depend primarily on land. Prime examples include small family farms or small-holding peasants producing a cash crop sold to a large agricultural corporation.

Paige predicts that these different economic systems will produce different types of political behavior. To derive specific hypotheses, Paige looks first at how income source affects cultivators and non-cultivators separately. Using those hypotheses he then predicts what happens when those separate behaviors are combined in the four basic class systems. For non-cultivators, Paige proposes the following hypotheses (see Figure 6.2):

(1) Dependence on land versus capital for income determines the economic strength of non-cultivating classes. Large agricultural estates relying solely on labor and land are less efficient than other forms of agriculture, especially the small holding. In particular, they are unable to increase productivity by increasing investments in capital. The historical trend shows

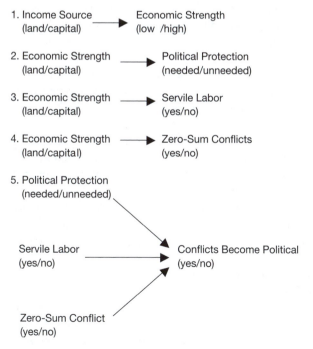

Figure 6.2 Paige's hypothesis about the influence of income source of non-cultivators on their political behavior.

that the large estate without capital investment loses out in free market competition to other forms.

(2) The economic strength of a non-cultivating class determines whether it will depend on political means to ensure its control of the land. Classes dependent on land are economically pressed; increases in income depend on increases in land holdings. As a result, this agricultural class seeks help from the state to protect its economic position against competition from other forms and encroachments from lower classes wanting land. Classes dependent on capital have much less need for direct political protection since they are economically stronger.

(3) The economic strength of a non-cultivating class also influences the labor it employs. Economically pressed landed estates compete poorly against more efficient forms in free labor markets. This leads the cultivating classes to seek servile labor, and servile labor usually means labor with few political rights as well. Hereditary serfdom and compulsory agricultural labor enforced by colonial regimes are probably the most common forms.

(4) The economic strength of the non-cultivating class also determines whether conflicts with cultivators are zero-sum conflicts. Since classes drawing their income solely from land find productivity increases hard to come by, any dispute with cultivators tends to be a zero-sum game. Upper classes dependent on capital are in a different situation, since they have an increasing pie to divide.

(5) The income source of the upper classes will also determine whether conflicts with other classes tend to be over political authority and property rights or over economic issues and income levels. This hypothesis follows from the earlier ones. The weak economic position of those drawing income from the land makes them dependent on political protection and on servile labor without political rights; any conflict with the cultivating classes is a zero-sum conflict. Thus conflicts over economic issues quickly become conflicts over political control. Those conflicts are (a) not easily resolved and (b) generally outside legal channels, given the servile nature of the cultivators.

Income source also makes an important difference to cultivator behavior. Income from small holdings or from rights to the land lead to quite distinct incentives and circumstances than does income from wages. Paige (see Figure 6.3) proposes that:

(6) Income from rights to land means competitive relations with other cultivators, who are fellow competitors in the market for the crop being produced. Market competition also leads to stratification of cultivators into the relatively rich and poor. As a result of competition and stratification, collective action is diminished.

(7) Income from land makes cultivators risk averse, especially when it comes to political action. Since the cultivators' land is the only source of income, they have a great deal to lose, and typically begging is the fate of the landless in developing countries. Thus radical political movements will be avoided.

(8) Income from land means cultivators generally work in isolation and have few inherent ties to other cultivators, leading to weak social ties.

(9) Income from wages generally indicates cooperative labor by a relatively homogeneous work force who have no property to lose. As a result, collective action, including action over political issues, will be more likely than among those who derive their income from the land.

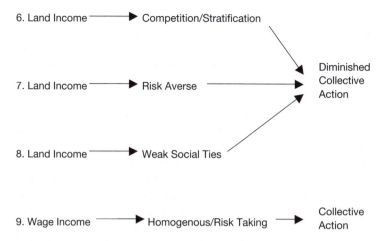

Figure 6.3 Paige's hypothesis about the influence of income source of cultivators on their political behavior.

So, in short, income from land generally undermines collective action, income from wages encourages it.

From these hypotheses Paige is able to predict how different class systems affect agrarian political behavior (see Figure 6.4). When owners depend upon capital and cultivators on wages (as in large plantations), Paige predicts that cultivators will engage in collective action, but action limited to economic issues such as wages and working conditions and action that ends in compromise settlements. Because of their laboring conditions, cultivators will act collectively over economic issues. Owners, however, are economically strong and generally have an increasing pie to divide; moreover, owners are not seriously dependent on political protection by the state, and their workers can legally act collectively over economic issues. Disputes over economic issues will thus not be naturally transformed into disputes over political power, and compromise will be the name of the game. (Paige thus argues against Marx here.)

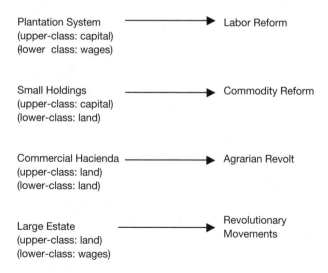

Figure 6.4 Paige's hypothesis about the influence of agrarian class systems on political behavior.

The small holding system will likewise produce limited challenges to political authority. Cultivators will draw income from the land and sell products in the market. They will thus be risk averse and divided between rich and poor, reducing the prospects for collective action. If collective action over economic issues occurs, it will not involve challenges to political authority nor be long-lived. The commercial class, which owns the factories processing the products from small holders, does not depend on political protection and is not involved in a zero-sum game. Moreover, the market mediates its relation to small holders, thus minimizing conflict. So small holding systems should result in limited protests over credit, market prices, and the like – what Paige calls a reform commodity movement.

When both cultivators and non-cultivators get their income from the land, we can expect a more severe conflict. Owners are economically weak, dependent upon the state for protection, and unable to compromise by sharing gains in productivity with cultivators. Cultivators are typically without political rights. This combination of factors means economic disputes cannot be easily settled and will naturally spread to issues about land ownership and property redistribution. However, the cultivators are subject to all the factors that undercut collective action. So cultivator movements should not become revolutionary movements, unless other forces like urban political parties intervene to introduce organization from the outside. So, in Paige's terminology, "revolts" may occur, but sustained support for thoroughgoing political revolution should be rare.

Finally, upper-class land income and cultivator income in wages make for the most explosive situation. The upper class is economically pressed, weak, unable to compromise through sharing productivity gains, and dependent on state protection. Cultivators typically are not divided along income lines and have no property to lose in collective action. So economic disputes should be frequent and should quickly become disputes over political authority, since the upper class depends upon political force to maintain itself. Revolutionary movements should thus be most frequent when this class system predominates.

Such are Paige's hypotheses. Are they true? Paige does a meticulous job of arguing that they are. His evidence falls into three basic categories: previous research, mostly case studies, supporting the hypothesized mechanisms linking class structure and political behavior (hypotheses [1]–[9] above); a world study looking primarily for correlations between economic systems and political behavior; and case studies of Peru, Angola and Vietnam. It is the world study which is most original and impressive; since it is also most easily summarized in a short space, I shall concentrate on it here.

Paige divides the developing world into 135 export sectors. He categorizes each sector by the dominant class system and measures agrarian political behavior in each sector. If Paige's hypotheses are right, the data should show that political behavior varies across sectors according to the dominant form of agrarian production. An export sector is a region that is the main producer for a specific export crop within a specific country. Paige picks export sectors as the unit of analysis for several reasons: (a) export sectors, unlike nations, are relatively homogeneous and thus help avoid the problem of spurious correlation facing aggregate data; (b) export sectors tend to dominate the economy of developing nations; (c) it is in export sectors where the landed upper classes are under the most pressure from market forces and thus where Paige's proposed processes should be most visible; and (d) it is mostly in the export sector where several of the class systems – sharecropping and the industrial plantation – are present. Paige does not think that export sectors present the whole story about agrarian political behavior, but he believes focusing on them provides the best test of his hypotheses.

Paige places each of the 135 export sectors into four different categories: (1) the hacienda and (2) the sharecropped or migratory labor estate, both of which involve upper-class income from the land but differ on payment systems for cultivators, and (3) the plantation and (4) the small family holding, both of which involve income from capital. Over the period Paige studied – 1948 to 1970 – nearly all of the 135 sectors fell into one of these categories and nearly all remained in the same category for the entire time data were collected.

The other key component of Paige's data comes from measuring rural political movements in each export sector. Paige does so by counting newspaper reports of agrarian political events – such as land seizures, demonstrations, and so on. For an event to count for the study, it must be collective, outside of established political institutions, involve some sense of shared identity, and be performed by agricultural cultivators. This means panics, mass migrations, and the like were excluded as were events involving primarily students, workers, or urban-based guerrillas. Nonetheless, Paige's data base contained 1,603 events. The coding of these events was checked for reliability by using outside coders; coding was 99 percent reliable.

Paige's theory predicts that events should fall into roughly four different categories. Revolutionary political events were those that involved demands for unconstitutional political change or radical change in rural class structure. Events involving a demand for expropriation and redistribution of land but not unconstitutional political change Paige classifies as instances of agrarian revolt. Labor events are actions around wages, working conditions, and so on but not involving constitutional change or land redistribution. Commodity reform events are protests about the way the market works for agricultural commodities – for example, demands for controls on credit or price supports.

With the data classified into event types and sector types, the test of Paige's hypotheses is obvious: export sectors dominated by commercial hacienda systems should show agrarian revolt; sectors involving share-cropping or migratory labor will show revolutionary activity; in sectors where small holding systems predominate, commodity reform actions will be most common; and where plantations predominate, labor reform events will be found. Using both tests of correlation and path analysis, the data support all of Paige's hypotheses: political behavior is associated with class relations in just the way Paige's theory predicts.

Are Paige's hypotheses qualified *ceteris paribus?* Of course they are. However, he provides relatively good evidence that the *ceteris paribus* qualification is no fatal flaw. For starters, we know that Paige's results do hold for the most part regardless of disturbing influences, because he finds a strong positive correlation between the proposed event types and sector types. Paige also shows that his results can be refined; adding in complicating factors does not undermine his results and in fact generally strengthens them. For example, Paige considers the following complicating variables:

(1) *contagion effects:* The probability of an event occurring at one period may be considerably increased simply by the fact that such an event occurred in the previous period. We can imagine numerous mechanisms that might make contagion effects likely – success at one time makes recruitment to a movement easier at subsequent times, publicity from one event increases support for similar events thereafter, and so on. To be sure he is measuring the influence of class structure rather than contagion effects, Paige uses an exponential function to describe the number of events. Since contagion effects are likely to mimic an exponential growth function, using the latter is a way of controlling for contagion effects.

(2) *centralized versus decentralized production:* We can break sharecropping systems into two kinds, depending on how directly the landowner controls work. Centralized systems, which typically are cotton estates, actually have much in common with the commercial hacienda or manor. Plots in centralized sharecropping are often inherited; workers are frequently deeply in debt to a company store owned by the landlord; and long-term tenure is common.

These characteristics make sharecroppers in the centralized system dependent on the landlord and risk averse, much like cultivators in the commercial hacienda. Paige controls for this complication by subdividing the sharecropping sectors into decentralized and centralized production. He finds that doing so increases the strength of the predicted relationship.

(3) *the presence of urban parties:* Paige predicted that peasants working on commercial haciendas would be involved in agrarian revolts over land, but that those revolts were likely to be short-lived and unsuccessful because the peasants' economic circumstances undermined collective action. However, if organization is introduced from the outside in the form of urban political parties, then we would expect the odds of agrarian revolts to increase. So Paige adds in a variable for the presence of urban revolutionary parties to his tests and finds that (a) the predicted correlation increases in strength and (b) the correlation between agrarian revolt and the commercial hacienda system is not due simply to the presence of urban parties.

(4) *extent of the market:* Small family holdings differ considerably. Some are only minimally involved in producing for a market and involve primarily subsistence farming. Thus Paige's prediction that the small family holding system will lead to commodity reform movements should get more accurate if we factor in the degree of market participation. Paige uses a measure of market participation for each sector to test this refined hypothesis; he finds that the original correlation increases in strength as predicted.

So Paige identifies numerous factors falling under the *ceteris paribus* clause and shows that his causal claims hold up and are strengthened when these factors are included.

Paige also explains away the most obvious exceptions to his hypothesis. For example, Malayan agricultural wage earners were involved in revolutionary movements, yet they should not have been on Paige's theory. Paige explains away this apparent exception without invoking ad hoc devices. The Malayan cultivators in question worked on rubber estates. Rubber production involves conditions very different from the typical industrial plantation. It does not require large quantities of capital; economies of scale are minimal compared to other crops. As a result, owners are in an economic situation much closer to that of the typical landed estate, where income is derived from land, not capital. Improvements in productivity are limited. Thus the Malayan rubber plantations are similar to the landed estates which do tend to produce revolutionary movements. So the Malayan case, once the details are filled in, fits the predictions of the theory rather than contradicting them.

Finally, we noted in the last section that identifying reasonable mechanisms can help support *ceteris paribus* claims. Paige has also done that. Hypotheses (1)–(9) are the mechanisms tying class relations to political behavior. Those mechanisms had much prior plausibility from previous studies, and Paige himself also provides some new evidence for them as well. In particular, he provides indirect evidence that commercial haciendas are inefficient, a key postulated mechanism.

So Paige's theory of agrarian movements certainly seems to have the traits of good science. It exhibits the *evidential* virtues summarized by independent, fair, and cross tests. Though its laws are qualified *ceteris paribus*, it confirms those claims by applying testing methods common in the natural sciences. Paige's theory also seems to have explanatory virtues: it explains by providing relevant *causal generalizations*. Those causal generalizations, of course, describe tendencies or partial causal factors. Yet Paige's testing procedures provide good evidence that those tendencies are actually operative. Paige's work thus gives us a prima facie case that good science in the social sciences is not only possible but sometimes actual.

Skeptics may grant my claims so far but remain unconvinced. Even if Paige's work does embody basic scientific virtues, it may not do so *well enough*. To assuage such doubts, I want to argue next that Paige's work compares favorably with much good work in the natural sciences. I do so by looking at evolutionary theory and ecology and arguing that they face roughly the same problems with the same success as does Paige. The end result will be a yet stronger case for naturalism.

I start with ecology. Modern ecology roughly divides into two domains: community ecology and population ecology. Community ecology describes the overarching structure and function of concrete ecosystems; population ecology searches for the general principles that determine the rise and fall of individual populations. Obviously the two domains are interrelated.

Ecologists have made continual, albeit slow, progress in identifying the main factors determining population dynamics. In the broadest terms, population dynamics depend upon the relative rates of emigration and immigration and birth and death. Behind these factors lie numerous complex determinants. Each organism has reproductive potential. Each environment has carrying capacity. Environment and reproductive potential interact to determine population size. These two factors can again be broken down. Understanding how a specific population develops requires understanding exactly what in the environment causes organisms to die. It also requires knowing at what part of the life cycle those factors operate and how they depend upon the traits of individual organisms. Population ecology is thus naturally led to consider species interaction – for example, predator–prey interactions. These are in turn explained in part by the search strategies of predators and avoidance strategies of prey. Obviously things get complex very fast. But population ecologists have nonetheless developed general models that describe how these factors interact and that allow them to identify, at least for some specific populations, the factors determining population dynamics.

Despite these successes, population ecology has much to learn. While they can identify major causes or limiting factors, ecologists can neither cite all the variables nor determine with precision how known variables interact. The influence of ecological variables is often context sensitive: effects differ as population density differs and as time lags change. Understanding how predation and disease affect population in one concrete eco-system at one population density does not guarantee we understand how those factors work elsewhere. Density dependence and time lags are not of course the only complexities. Variable environments and patchy habitats may make important differences as well.

Thus population ecology really looks much like the best work in the social sciences. We can cite with some certainty major mechanisms and dynamics. Some phenomena are understood in detail. But most studies make simplifying assumptions and leave variables uncontrolled. Even when we know the variables, we often have no general, automatic way to combine them or describe their interaction: putting causal factors together is often a piecemeal and ad hoc process. We can make generalizations, but they are bound to have exceptions and to assume that other variables, known and unknown, do not interfere. Also, most generalizations hold only for specific kinds of populations.

Community ecology is in much the same boat. It describes, for example, laws of succession. Such laws are known to have exceptions; among the counteracting factors is radical environmental change, though other unknown factors may be involved. Similarly, another prime law from community ecology – namely, that organisms with the same ecologies cannot coexist in the same environment – may fail to hold when the environment is sufficiently variable, when population sizes at equilibrium are equal, and when selective forces are weak. The complexities of real competitive situations make it unlikely that these are the only possible counteracting factors.

Ecology is no exception. Evolutionary theory, which is the heart of biology, the theory that ties all of biology together, looks much the same. The basic components of evolutionary theory are of course well developed. The Hardy-Weinberg law describes gene frequencies in a population when no forces are present. Natural selection acting on variation causes changes from equilibrium. Theoretically, selective forces can be quantified and resulting trajectories of populations determined for particular situations. For simple selective forces acting on individuals of known fitness, the results are known with mathematical precision.

However, selection is not the only force acting on real populations. Under certain conditions – for example, small population size or weak selection – gene frequencies may change due to random factors. The result is called genetic drift, and it too can be factored in by population genetics. Selection also involves more than the mortalities and fecundity of individuals. Individuals low on both measures may nonetheless be well represented in the population, due to what is generally called kin selection. An organism may spread its genes by ways other than ensuring its own survival or that of its own offspring. Siblings and others may also carry an organism's genes. Helping them survive is thus an indirect contribution to fitness. So effects on kin also have to be incorporated into the basic theory. Finally, organisms may survive long and have great reproductive potential – and yet be relatively unfit. Mates must be attracted. So some traits may be selected for sexual reasons, not because they contribute to adaptedness in the normal sense. Thus "sexual selection" must also be added to any complete model.

These additional factors suggest that evolutionary explanations will be qualified *ceteris paribus* and that adding in interfering factors will be a complex process much like that in ecology. However, drift, sexual selection, and kin selection are just the beginning. Numerous other factors influence real populations. Selection is standardly taken to operate on individuals. Yet selection can operate at both higher and lower levels – on genes and chromosomes and on trait groups, populations and perhaps even species or species groups. Thus selection at multiple levels may be a complicating factor. Models exist to incorporate some multi-level forces, but even on the theoretical level biologists are not sure how exactly to combine them with more ordinary determinants of evolution.

Similar complexity arises from other known influences on evolution. Basic population genetic models treat genes like beads on a string – they are independent and separable. The real world is far more complex. Genes interact to produce a given trait or produce multiple traits. Such "gene linkage" throws off predictions made from simpler models. Furthermore, basic evolutionary theory often assumes that natural selection will produce those traits best promoting fitness. Again, the real world is more complex. Developmental constraints may influence evolution in important ways. We have at best only a rough idea how developmental constraints are to be factored in; usually, we are limited to citing their qualitative effects in particular cases.

The complexities do not stop here. Talk of a selective "force" is misleading and metaphorical. In reality, organisms face a complex environment influencing their survival in numerous complex ways. Environments are often "patchy," and there is no automatic, theoretical way to factor in such variability. Furthermore, any real account of selective forces inherits ecology's complexity as well, for it is ecological factors that make up the environment. Finally, not all selection has to be genetically based. Organisms do learn. Those that learn well and pass that learning on will survive more frequently. Explaining behavior thus may require including the effects of cultural selection.

Evolutionary theory thus paints a familiar picture: We know the major factors and how they interact. We can control for some interfering factors, but we must ignore or abstract from others. Some factors we know how to incorporate in a theoretical way, others we do not. Causal generalizations are bound to be exception prone and to hold only for restricted domains.

These complications confront even the most careful evolutionary research, as we can see by considering a paradigmatic piece of good evolutionary research. Peter Grant's *Ecology and*

Evolution of Darwin's Finches (1986) is the definitive research to date on finch evolution on the Galápagos Islands. It is widely recognized as a paradigm of evolutionary research. Nonetheless, Grant's work runs into all the complications discussed above. I want to discuss Grant's results in some detail, for they nicely illustrate just how similar Paige's work is to good work in the natural sciences.

Grant's task is to describe the evolutionary forces that produced the remarkable diversity of finches in the Galápagos. From more than ten years of study in the islands plus a mass of previous work, Grant develops a detailed evolutionary picture. Finch beaks are adapted to different seed sizes. Seed availability is a strong constraint on population size. Selection is currently occurring among some populations, favoring large body and beak size. Current species apparently originated under gradual directional selection. Speciation was driven by both allopatry (separation with subsequent adaptation to different food sources) and competitive exclusion.

Grant recognizes the many possible complicating factors and attempts to rule them out. Drift seems not to be important, since finches flock and populations are usually relatively large. Internal constraints appear minimal, since beak and body size involve small, accumulative genetic changes. Nonetheless, Grant's work faces numerous complications. His predictions are qualitative – he can argue for the direction of selection, but not its strength. Mutation rates and gene flow are complicating factors, but their relative importance is unknown. Sexual selection has played some role, but it is not clear how much nor how exactly (1986, p. 103). Rain, large seed production, timing of seed production, and other food sources may influence to what extent seed actually serves as a population limit and selective force; at best, Grant gives reasons to think these factors are less important. Predation and disease are additional selective forces that are not included in his model; again, field experience indicates they are seldom important. Competition and habitat diversity play an unclear role in speciation. Hybridization does occur, but the simplest explanation is one that gives it small place. While selection clearly picks out beak size, it is not clear *how* it does so – the precise mechanism is uncertain. Finally, Grant's major findings have exceptions in the Galápagos themselves, exceptions that must be explained away by appeal to unusual circumstances.

My point is not to challenge the quality of Grant's work. Far from it. The correct inference is rather that good work in the social sciences faces problems very much like those confronting the best work in biology and handles them with the same approximate success. *Ceteris paribus* generalizations and the ensuing complexities do not separate the social sciences from the natural sciences.

[. . .]

References

Churchland, P. (1979) *Scientific Realism and the Placiticity of Mind*. Cambridge: Cambridge University Press.
Davidson, D. (1970) "Mental Events." In L. Foster and J. Swanson (eds.), *Experience and Theory*. Amherst: University of Massachusetts Press, pp. 79–101.
Fay, B. (1984) "Naturalism as a Philosophy of Social Science," *Philosophy of the Social Sciences* 14: 529–542.
Grant, P. (1986) *Ecology and Evolution of Darwin's Finches*. Princeton: Princeton University Press.
Leamer, Edward. (1983) "Let's take the Con out of Econometrics." *American Economic Review* 73: 31–43.
Paige, J. (1975) *Agrarian Revolution*. New York: The Free Press.
Popper, K. (1982) *The Open Society and Its Enemies*. London: Routledge and Kegan Paul.
Rosenberg, A. (1978) "The Supervenience of Biological Concepts," *Philosophy of Science* 45: 368–386.
——— (1980) *Sociobiology and the Preemption of Social Science*. Baltimore: Johns Hopkins University Press.
Searle, J. (1984) *Minds, Brains and Science*. Cambridge, MA: Harvard University Press.
Taylor, C. (1971) "Interpretation and the Sciences of Man," *Review of Metaphysics* 25: 3–51.
Brit. J. Phil. Sci. 51 (2000), 197–254.

Chapter 7

JAMES WOODWARD

EXPLANATION AND INVARIANCE IN THE SPECIAL SCIENCES

1 Introduction

A **CENTRAL PROBLEM IN THE PHILOSOPHY** of the special sciences concerns the nature and status of explanatory generalizations in those disciplines. Many philosophers are committed to a *nomothetic* conception of explanation according to which all successful explanations must appeal to laws. The standard assumption about laws is that they are exceptionless generalizations meeting various other familiar conditions—they must contain only qualitative predicates, support counterfactuals, and so on. Together these assumptions generate a dilemma. On the one hand, most of us believe that the special sciences sometimes succeed in providing explanations. On the other, it looks as though most generalizations in the special sciences fail to conform to the standard criteria for lawhood—for example, they are not exceptionless and hold at best over limited domains or spatio-temporal intervals. The usual strategy for resolving this difficulty is to argue, despite all appearances to the contrary, that explanatory generalizations in the special sciences do meet, or somehow serve as stand-ins for generalizations that meet, the standard conditions for lawhood. The appeal of this strategy lies not in its inherent plausibility but rather in the difficulty of formulating a defensible alternative to the nomothetic conception of explanation.

This paper explores a new way out of this dilemma. It will argue that we need to rethink both the nomothetic conception of explanation and the standard conditions for lawhood, at least in so far as these are taken to provide criteria for distinguishing explanatory from unexplanatory generalizations. The standard framework suggests that there are just two, mutually exclusive possibilities: either a generalization is a law or else it is purely accidental. Most explanatory generalizations in the special sciences do not fit comfortably into either of these two categories. What we need is a new way of thinking about generalizations and the role that they play in explanation that allows us to recognize intermediate possibilities besides laws and accidents and to distinguish among these with respect to their degree or kind of contingency. This account should also allow us to understand how a generalization can play an explanatory role even though it holds only within a certain domain or over a limited spatio-temporal interval and has exceptions outside of these.

The alternative account I will propose rests on several key ideas. The first is a claim about explanation: explanatory relationships are relationships that *in principle* can be used for manipulation and control in the sense that they tell us how certain (explanandum) variables would change if other (explanans) variables were to be changed or manipulated. The qualification 'in principle' means that what matters for the purposes of explanation is not whether the manipulation in question can actually be carried out but rather whether the putative explanatory relationship correctly describes what would happen on the (possibly counterfactual) supposition that the manipulation is carried out.

Second, given this conception of explanation, it follows that whether or not a generalization can be used to explain has to do with whether it is *invariant* rather than with whether it is lawful. A generalization is invariant if (i) it is, in a sense I will try to make more precise below, change-relating and (ii) it is stable or robust in the sense that it would continue to hold under a special sort of change called an *intervention*. When invariance is so characterized, some laws turn out not to be invariant because they are not change-relating. Hence some laws are not explanatory. More importantly, there are many examples of invariant relationships that are not laws. Appeal to laws is thus neither sufficient nor necessary for successful explanation. In contrast to the standard notion of lawfulness, the notion of invariance is well suited to capturing the distinctive characteristics of explanatory generalizations in the special sciences. A generalization can be invariant within a certain domain even though it has exceptions outside that domain. Moreover, unlike lawfulness, invariance comes in gradations or degrees.

As remarked above, to characterize invariance we need the notion of an intervention which we can think of as an idealized experimental manipulation. An intervention is an exogenous causal process that changes some variable of interest X in such a way that any change in some second variable Y occurs entirely as the result of the change in X. On the conception I will be defending, we may think of explanation as having to do not with subsumption under laws but rather with the exhibition of patterns of counterfactual dependence of a special sort, involving *active* counterfactuals—counterfactuals the antecedents of which are made true by interventions. Only invariant generalizations will support active counterfactuals—hence the connection between explanation and invariance.

[. . .]

2 Interventions

I begin with the notion of an intervention. Heuristically, one may think of an intervention as an idealization of an experimental manipulation carried out on some variable X for the purpose of ascertaining whether changes in X are causally or nomologically related to changes in some other variable Y. However, as we shall see shortly, any process, whether or not it involves human beings or their activities, will qualify as an intervention as long as it has the right causal characteristics. The idea we want to capture is roughly this: an intervention on some variable X with respect to some second variable Y is a causal process that changes X in an appropriately exogenous way, so that if a change in Y occurs, it occurs only in virtue of the change in X and not as a result of some other set of causal factors.

Suppose that one wants to know whether treatment with some drug is effective in producing recovery from a disease. We may represent the treatment received by an individual subject i by means of a binary variable T that takes one of two values 0 and 1 depending on whether i does or does not receive the drug. Similarly, recovery may be represented by means of a variable R taking values 0 and 1, depending on whether or not individuals with the disease recover. Intuitively what one wants to know is whether if some subject i who has not received the treatment and who suffers from the disease (for whom $T(i) = 0$ and $R(i) = 0$) were to be given the drug (i.e. if $T(i)$ were to be changed to 1), i would recover or would be more likely to recover (whether $R(i)$ would be changed to 1). Obviously, one cannot investigate this question by both giving the treatment to and withholding it from the same subject. However, one may employ a more indirect method: divide the subjects with the disease into a treatment and control group, intervene by giving the drug to the former and not the latter, and then observe the incidence of recovery in the two groups. The experimenter's interventions (which we may represent by means of an intervention variable I) will thus consist in the assignment of values of T to individual subjects. Obviously, these interventions must meet various further conditions if the experiment is to tell us anything about the efficacy of T. First, if the experimenter's interventions I are correlated with some other cause of recovery besides T, this may undermine the reliability of the experiment. This would happen, for example, if the patients in the treatment group were much healthier than those in the control group. However, it would be too strong to require that I (or T) be uncorrelated with all other causes of R. As long as T is efficacious, I and T will be correlated with other causes of R that are themselves caused by I or by T. For example, if treatment by the drug does cause recovery and does so by killing (K) a certain sort of bacterium, then it will be no threat to the validity of the experiment if the experimenters' interventions I are correlated K, even though K causally affects R. What we need to rule out is the possibility that there are causes of R that are correlated with I or caused by I, and that affect R independently of the $I \rightarrow T \rightarrow K \rightarrow R$ causal chain.

A third condition is that I should not directly affect recovery independently of T but only, if at all, through it. This means, among other things, that I must not be a common cause of both T and R. This condition would be violated if, for example, the subjects learn whether or not they have been assigned to the treatment group and the control group and this has a placebo effect—an effect on R that is independent of any effect of T itself on R. (Perhaps those in the treatment group are made more hopeful by the fact that they are in this group and those in the control group are discouraged.) In this case I directly affects R independently of T and we will not be able to reach reliable conclusions about the effect of T on R.

Assembling these requirements together, we are led to the following characterization: Suppose that I is an intervention on (or manipulation of) the variable X, where X is some property possessed by the unit i, the intent being to assess some postulated relationship (G) according to which changes in X cause or explain changes in some other variable Y by observing whether the intervention on X produces the change in Y predicted by (G). Call the value of X possessed by i prior to the intervention x_0 and the value after the intervention x_1. Then I should have the following conjunction of features (M):

M1) I changes the value of X possessed by i from what it would have been in the absence of the intervention (i.e. $x_1 \neq x_0$) and this change in X is entirely due to I.

M2) The change in X produced by I is claimed by (G) to change the value of Y. That is, according to (G), the value, y_0, that Y takes when $X = x_0$, is different from the value, y_1, that Y takes when $X = x_1$.

M3) I changes Y, if at all, only through X and not directly or through some other route. That is, I does not directly cause Y and does not change any causes of Y that are distinct from X except, of course, for those causes of Y, if any, that are built into the I–X–Y connection itself; that is, except for (a) any causes of Y that are effects of X (i.e. variables that are causally between X and Y) and (b) any causes of Y that are between I and X and have no effect on Y independently of X. In addition, I does not change the causal relationships between Y and its other causes besides X. Moreover, a similar point holds for any cause Z of I itself—i.e. Z must change Y, if at all, only through X and not through some other route.

M4) I is not correlated with other causes of Y besides X (either *via* a common cause of I and Y or for some other reason) except for those falling under (M3a) and (M3b) above.

There are several features of this characterization that are worth noting. First, as advertised above, the characterization makes no essential reference to human activities or to what human beings can or can't do. A causal process that does not involve human beings at any point will qualify as an intervention as long as it meets conditions M1–4. Indeed, it is precisely this sort of possibility one has in mind when one talks about a 'natural experiment'.

A second issue concerns circularity. The characterization (M) employs causal language at a number of points—not only must the intervention I cause a change in the variable X, but I must not itself directly cause Y, must not be correlated with other causes of Y that are independent of the putative $I{\rightarrow}X{\rightarrow}Y$ chain, and so on. Because the notion of an intervention is already a causal notion, it follows that one cannot appeal to it to explain what it is for a relationship to be causal or nomological (or invariant) in terms of concepts that are themselves entirely non-causal or non-nomological. Nonetheless, it is important to understand that the characterization is not viciously circular in the sense that the characterization of an intervention on X with respect to Y itself makes reference to the presence or absence of a causal relationship between X and Y. Instead the characterization makes reference to *other* causal relationships—to the existence of a causal relationship between I and X and to the distribution of other possible causes of Y besides X. The characterization (M) thus fits with a non-reductive account of causal and nomological relationships and of how we infer to the existence of such relationships. The fundamental idea is that we can explain what it is for a relationship between X and Y to be causal or nomological (or invariant) by appealing to facts about *other* causal or nomological relationships involving X and Y and to non-causal correlational facts involving X and Y. That there is a coherent notion of an intervention to be captured, and that some explication of this notion that is not viciously circular must be possible, is strongly suggested by the fact that we do seem to sometimes find out whether a causal or nomological relationship exists between X and Y by manipulating X in an appropriate way and determining whether there is a correlated change in Y. This fact by itself seems to show that we must have some notion of a manipulation of X that would be suitable for finding out whether X is causally or nomological linked to Y, and that this notion can be characterized without presupposing that there is a causal or nomological relationship between X and Y. It is just this notion that (M) attempts to capture.

A third issue concerns clause (M1). This says that carrying out an intervention on X requires that there be a well-defined notion of changing the value of X possessed by some individual in such a way that the very same individual is caused by the intervention to possess a different value of X. One consequence of (M1) is that there is no well-defined notion of an intervention with respect to properties or magnitudes that, for logical or conceptual reasons, can only take one value. For example, if everything that exists is necessarily a physical object there is no well-defined notion of intervening to change whether something is a physical object. Even with respect to variables that can take more than one value, the notion of an intervention will not be well defined, if there is no well-defined notion of changing the values of that variable for a particular individual. For example, we might introduce a variable 'animal' which takes the values {trout, kitten, raven} but if, as I suspect, we have no coherent idea of what it is to change a raven into trout or kitten, there will be no well-defined notion of an intervention for this variable. This restriction on the notion of an intervention to variables for which there is a well-defined notion of change is both implicit in the notion of an intervention itself and also follows from our guiding idea that explanatory relations are relations that can be used for manipulation and control. If there is no well-defined notion of changing the value of X, we cannot, even in principle, manipulate some other variable by changing X. Similarly, unless as (M2) requires, the contemplated intervention on X is, according to the generalization we are assessing, associated with a change in Y, this generalization will not tell us how intervening on

X can be used to manipulate Y. As we will see below, both (M1) and (M2) have important consequences for the sorts of generalizations that can figure in explanations.

It will help to clarify the notion of an intervention if we consider an additional example. Suppose that, in a certain region, changes in atmospheric pressure (A) are a common cause and the only cause of the occurrence of storms (S) and of the reading (B) of a particular barometer and that there is no direct causal relationship between B and S. Imagine that we are ignorant of the causal structure of this system and wish to find out whether B directly causes S by changing B and ascertaining whether there is a corresponding change in S. It is clear that certain ways of changing B are inappropriate for this purpose. If we change B by changing A, or by means of some causal process that is perfectly correlated with changes in A, then S will also change, but this will not establish that there is a causal relationship between B and S. Similarly, if we change B via some process that directly affects S. None of these ways of changing B will qualify as interventions on B for the purpose of ascertaining whether there is a causal relationship between B and S— they run afoul, respectively, of clauses (M3) and (M2) in (M).

By contrast, suppose that we employ a random number generator which is causally indepen- dent of A and, depending just on the output of this device, repeatedly physically fix the barometer reading at different values by moving the dial to either a high or low reading and driving a nail through it. Suppose that this procedure results in repeated settings of the dial that are uncorrelated with A. If—as it seem reasonable to believe—this procedure satisfies the other conditions in (M), repetitions of it will count as interventions on B with respect to S. This illustrates the sense in which interventions involve *exogenous* changes—such changes in the A-B-S system are exogenous in the sense that they do not operate through A or through processes correlated with A. Such changes break or disrupt the previously existing endogenous causal relationship between A and B since the state of B is now set by the intervention, independently of A. When the barometer reading is changed in this way, what we expect of course is that the previous association or correlation between B and S will break down or disappear (that it will be non-invariant) and hence that the relationship between B and S will fail to qualify as a causal or nomological.

[. . .]

3 Invariance

Once we have the notion of an intervention, we can use it to characterize more precisely the notion of invariance under interventions, which I take to be the key feature that a generalization must possess if it is to play an explanatory role or to describe a causal or nomological relationship. The general idea of invariance is this: a generalization describing a relationship between two or more variables is invariant if it would continue to hold—would remain stable or unchanged— as various other conditions change. The set or range of changes over which a relationship or generalization is invariant is its *domain* of invariance. As we will see in more detail below, invariance is a relative matter—typically a relationship will be invariant with respect to a certain range of changes but not with respect to other changes.

It is useful to distinguish two sorts of changes that are relevant to the assessment of invariance. First, there are changes in what we would intuitively regard as the background conditions to some generalization—changes that affect other variables besides those that figure in the generalization itself. For example, in the case of a system of masses conforming to the gravitational inverse square law (1) $F = Gm_1 m_2/r^2$, changes in the position or velocity of the system as a whole which do not change the relative positions of the masses will count as a changes in background conditions, as will a change in the color of the masses or their electrical charge, or the Dow–Jones Industrial average. The inverse square law is invariant under changes in all these background conditions.

Second, there are changes in those variables that figure explicitly in the generalization itself—for example, in the case of (1), mass and distance. An important subclass of such changes are changes that result from an intervention (in the sense specified in section 1) on the variables figuring in the generalization. The gravitational inverse square law is invariant not just under changes in background conditions but also under a wide range of interventions that change the distances between gravitating masses or the magnitudes of the masses themselves. We will see later that this is crucial to its explanatory status. I will say that a generalization is invariant *simpliciter* if and only if (i) the notion of an intervention is applicable to or well-defined in connection with the variables figuring in the generalization (see below) and (ii) the generalization is invariant under at least some interventions on such variables. In other words, for a generalization to count as invariant there must exist some interventions (satisfying the conditions (M1)–(M4)) for variables figuring in the relationship under which it is invariant. To count as invariant it is *not* required that a generalization be invariant under all interventions. For brevity, I will often speak of a generalization as 'invariant under interventions' as shorthand for 'invariant under some interventions on variables explicitly figuring in the generalization'.

The generalization (1) is naturally regarded as a generalization that relates changes—it describes how changing the magnitudes of two masses or the distance between them will change the gravitational force they exert on each other. Other generalizations, including some we may regard as laws, are not naturally interpreted as true descriptions of relationships between changes. Such generalizations fall into several categories. First, there are generalizations that, to put it loosely, do not tell us how to produce certain changes but rather that they are impossible. Consider the generalization (2) 'No material object can be accelerated from a velocity less than that of light to a velocity greater than that of light'. This generalization does not tell us, as (1) does, how changes in one set of variables will produce changes in another set of variables. Instead, it rather tells us, in effect, that there are no physically possible changes that will produce a change from subluminal to superluminal velocities.

[. . .]

A second possibility is illustrated by the generalization (3) 'All men who take birth control pills regularly fail to get pregnant' (*cf.* Salmon [1971]). There are at least two possible ways of understanding this generalization. First, it may be understood as a generalization that does not even purport to be change-relating. Interpreted in this way, (3) does not claim that changes in whether or not men take birth control pills are correlated with changes in whether or not they become pregnant but only that male pill-takers do not get pregnant. It says nothing about whether males who do not take birth control pills will get pregnant. Under this interpretation, (3) is true but there is no well-defined notion of an intervention associated with it and it fails to be invariant for this reason. Second, (3) may be interpreted as claiming that the correlation described above does hold. Under this interpretation, while there is a well-defined notion of intervention associated with (3) (one can intervene to change men who are pill-takers to non-pill-takers and *vice versa*), (3) is false, since the claimed correlation fails to hold: whether or not a male takes birth control pills is not correlated with whether he becomes pregnant. Intuitively, (3) cannot be used to explain why some particular man fails to get pregnant, because taking birth control pills is irrelevant to whether a man becomes pregnant. We will see in Section 4 how the fact that (3) is not an invariant change-relating generalization underlies this judgment of irrelevance.

When a generalization like (1) that relates changes is invariant under interventions on variables figuring in the relationship, it describes a relationship that is hypothetically exploitable for purposes of manipulation and control—hypothetically exploitable in the sense that although it may not always be possible, as a practical matter, to intervene to change the values of the quantities described by the variables that figure in the generalization, we can nonetheless think of the generalization as telling us that *if* it were possible to change those values, one could use them to change others. Thus, for example, because the gravitational inverse square law is invariant under a range of interventions that change mass and distance, it tells us how, if we or some natural process were to manipulate these quantities in some system of gravitating masses, the gravitational force they exert would change in a systematic way. Similarly, because (4), the ideal gas law $PV = nRT$, is invariant under a range of interventions that change temperature, it correctly describes how, by manipulating the temperature of a gas and holding its volume constant, one could change its pressure.

Why does it matter whether a generalization is invariant under (at least some) interventions on the variables figuring in the relationship as opposed to merely being invariant under some changes in background conditions? The reason is that any generalization, no matter how 'accidental', non-lawful, non-causal or unexplanatory, will be stable or will continue to hold under some changes in background conditions—for example, under changes in conditions that are causally independent of the factors related by the generalization. Thus, special circumstances aside, a paradigmatic accidental generalization like

(5) All the coins in Bill Clinton's pocket on January 8, 1999 are dimes.

will continue to describe correctly the contents of Clinton's pockets on this date under many possible changes in background conditions. For example, presumably (5) will be stable under changes in the position of Mars, the leadership of China, or the barometric pressure in Paris, and so on. Similarly, the generalization (6), describing the relationship between the barometer reading B and the onset of a storm S considered in Section 2, will be stable under many changes in background conditions.

The feature that distinguishes generalizations like (5) and (6) from generalizations like (1) and (4) is that (5) and (6) are not invariant under interventions on the variables that explicitly figure in them and do not describe relationships that tell us how by manipulating one variable we may change or manipulate another—they do not describe relationships that are hypothetically exploitable for purposes of manipulation and control. To see this consider what an intervention would involve in the case of (5). To apply the characterization (M) to (5) we must interpret (5) as a change-relating generalization—i.e. as claiming that changing whether or not a coin is located in Clinton's pocket changes whether or not it is a dime. More specifically, think of X as a variable that measures whether or not a coin is located within Clinton's pocket and Y as a variable that measures whether or not it is a dime. According to clause (M2) in (M) for the introduction of a coin into Clinton's pocket to qualify as intervention, the coin must be such that (G) claims that its value would change if its location were changed from being outside Clinton's pocket to being inside. The introduction of a dime into Clinton's pocket will not meet this condition but the introduction of a penny would. However, (5) is plainly not invariant under such interventions—the introduction of non-dimes into Clinton's pocket will not transform them into dimes. More generally, (5) is not invariant under any interventions on the variable X. A similar point holds for (6). As observed in Section 2, (6) is not invariant under interventions that consist in manipulating the barometer dial. While (4), the ideal gas law, tells us how we can make the pressure or volume of a gas change by changing its temperature, we cannot change non-dimes into dimes by introducing them into Clinton's pocket. And we cannot alter whether or not storms occur by fiddling with barometer dials.

I will suggest below that this difference between (5) and (6), on the one hand, and (1) and (4), on the other, is crucial to their explanatory status.

4 Explanation

I suggested above that explanation requires appeal to invariant generalizations. In this section I want to sketch an account of explanation that supports this suggestion.

Consider a gas enclosed in a rigid container of volume V^* which under goes a temperature increase to T^* in virtue of being connected to a heat source. If we want to provide a simple but nonetheless genuine explanation of (7), why the pressure of the gas increases to P^*, it seems relevant to cite the new temperature T^*, the constant volume V^* and the ideal gas law (4). According to an account of explanation which I have defended in more detail elsewhere (Woodward [1979], [1984], [1997]), this information is explanatory because it can be used to answer a range of counterfactual or what-if-things-had-been-different questions about the explanandum (7). What I mean by this is that the generalization (4) can be used, in conjunction with information about the 'initial conditions' of the gas (the fact that it has temperature T^* and volume V^*) to show how the explanandum (7) would change, if these initial conditions were to change in various ways. That is, not only can (4) be used, in conjunction with information about the initial conditions of the gas to show that the explanandum (7) 'was to be expected', as the traditional DN model demands, but (4) can also be used to tells us how the pressure of the gas would *change*—how the pressure would have been different—if the temperature had instead increased or decreased to a different value T^{**} or if the volume of the container had changed to a different value V^{**}. In this way the explanation in terms of (4) locates the explanandum (7) within a space of alternative possibilities (other possible values for the pressure that might have occurred) and shows us how which of these alternative possibilities is realized systematically depends on the initial temperature and volume of the gas. In seeing how the actual pressure P^* would have been different, had the actual temperature T^* and volume V^* of the gas been different, we see in detail how the pressure depends on these factors and how they are explanatory relevant to the pressure. In short, we can think of the explanation that appeals to (4) as exhibiting a systematic pattern of counterfactual dependence of the pressure of the gas on its temperature and volume. The exhibition of such a pattern is at the heart of successful explanation.

Consider another example. The gravitational inverse square law allows us to see how the gravitational force between two or more objects would have been different had the distances between these objects or their masses had been different in various ways. In combination with the Newtonian laws of motion, this information allows us to see that, given an object with a certain mass, initial position and velocity, it will follow a certain trajectory under the gravitational influence of a second object. However, these laws also enable us to see how this trajectory would change given changes in these initial conditions or in the mass of the attracting object. For example, we can use the inverse square law and the equations of motion to see how under certain conditions the first object will follow an elliptical orbit about the second, how under other conditions it will spiral into the second and so on. In this way we see how the actual trajectory depends on these factors and in seeing this we come to understand why the actual trajectory took the form it did.

The intuitive attractiveness of the idea that explanation has to do with the exhibition of systematic patterns of counterfactual dependence is further reinforced by the fact that we usually think of explanation as having to do with the exhibition of causal relationships and it seems undeniable that there is a close connection between causal relationships and counterfactuals.

If explanations cite causes, it seems very plausible that some form of counterfactual theory of explanation must be correct.

However, familiar difficulties with counterfactual theories of causation also remind us that there is an obvious objection to such a proposal: there are relationships of counterfactual dependence which are not causal or explanatory. For example, assuming that the barometer-storm-atmospheric pressure system of Section 2 operates deterministically and that A is the only cause of B and S, it looks as though there is a perfectly good sense in which it is true that

(8) If the reading B of the barometer were falling, a storm would occur and also true that

(9) If the reading B were rising, there would be no storm

However, despite the fact that S counterfactually depends on B, B doesn't cause S and one can't appeal to B to explain S.

We can deal with this difficulty by appealing to the ideas introduced in Section 2. As explained earlier, the correlation between B and S is not invariant under interventions on B. While there is (arguably) an interpretation of the counterfactuals (8) and (9) according to which they are true, there is also natural interpretation of the counterfactual

(10) If an intervention were to occur which lowers (increases) B, then the storm would occur (not occur)

according to which it is false. This is the interpretation we adopt when we take (10) to be claiming that an intervention on B would be a way of controlling or manipulating or changing whether or not a storm occurs and that the previously obtaining correlation between B and S would be invariant under such interventions. Let us say that when (10) is interpreted in this way, it is an *active* counterfactual. This reading contrasts with the *passive* interpretation of the counterfactuals (8) and (9) appealed to above which carries with it no such claim about would happen to S under interventions on B. My claim is that the kind of counterfactual dependence that matters for successful explanation is active counterfactual dependence. Put differently, a successful explanation should appeal to factors or variables such that interventions on those factors will be systematically associated with corresponding changes in its explanandum. An explanation of the pressure of a gas in terms of its pressure and volume meets this requirement—it supports or is associated with active counterfactuals while a purported explanation of the occurrence of a storm that appeals to the correlation between B and S does not.

On this understanding of what an explanation does, the connection between explanation and invariance should be transparent. It is only if a generalization is invariant under some range of interventions and changes that we can appeal to it to answer what-if-things-had-been-different questions about what would happen under these interventions and changes. For example, if the ideal gas law systematically broke down under interventions that change temperature and volume, then we could not appeal to it to answer questions about how the pressure of a gas would change under such changes. Similarly it is because the gravitational inverse square law is invariant under interventions that change the distances between various objects and their masses that we can use this generalization to show how the gravitational forces exerted by those objects would change if their masses and the distances between them would change.

I can further clarify this account of explanation by means of an additional comparison with the most familiar rival account—the DN model defended in Hempel ([1965]). In the examples described above, we are shown, just as the DN model demands, that an explanandum (e.g.

(7)) is deducible from a law (e.g. (4)) and a statement of initial conditions. However, we are also shown something in addition to this—namely how (4) can be used to answer a set of what-if-things-had-been-different questions about (7). This represents an independent condition or constraint, that has no counterpart in the DN model and does not follow just from the DN requirement that (7) be derivable from a law and a statement of initial conditions. One way of bringing this out is to remind ourselves of a familiar counter-example to the DN model, drawn from Salmon ([1971]). Consider the derivation:

(Ex. 11)
(L_{11}) All men who take birth control pills regularly fail to get pregnant
(C_{11}) Mr. Jones is a man who takes birth control pills regularly.
(E_{11}) Mr. Jones fails to get pregnant.

If we agree that (L_{11}) is a law, (Ex. 11) meets the conditions for successful DN explanation. None the less it is a defective explanation. The theory I have proposed explains why in a natural way: the condition cited in the explanans of (Ex. 11) is not such that changes in it produced by interventions would lead to changes in the outcome being explained. A change in whether Jones takes birth control pills will lead to no change in whether or not he gets pregnant. In consequence, (Ex. 11) fails to satisfactorily answer a what-if-things-had-been-different question about its explanandum: it fails to correctly identify the conditions under which an outcome different from (E_{11}) would occur and, indeed, wrongly suggests that the condition cited (taking birth control pills) is a condition such that changes in it would lead to changes in whether Jones gets pregnant when in fact this is not true. This failure is reflected in our judgment that taking birth control pills is explanatorily irrelevant to whether Jones gets pregnant. Put differently, what (Ex. 11) shows is that a derivation can cite a nomologically sufficient condition for an explanandum and yet fail to answer a what-if-things-had-been-different question about it and hence fail to explain it. Hence it shows how the account that I have provided differs from accounts that take explanation to be just a matter of derivation from a law.

Consider, by way of contrast (Ex. 12):

(L_{12}) All women who meet condition K (K has to do with whether the woman is fertile, has been having intercourse regularly and so forth) and who take birth control pills regularly will not get pregnant and furthermore all women who meet condition K and do not take birth control pills regularly will get pregnant.
(C_{12}) Ms. Jones is a woman who meets condition K and has been having intercourse regularly.
(M_{12}) Ms. Jones does not get pregnant.

Here, of course, we have considerably more inclination to say that at least a crude explanation of (M_{12}) has been provided. On the account that I advocate this difference between (Ex. 11) and (Ex. 12) is a reflection of the fact that the latter, but not the former, satisfies the what-if-things-had-been-different condition on explanation. The condition K cited in (Ex. 12) is such that changes in it would lead to changes in the outcome being explained—if Ms. Jones stops taking birth control pills, is fertile and has intercourse, she will or at least may get pregnant; if she fails to take the pills but also doesn't have intercourse she will not get pregnant and so on. (Ex. 12) thus draws our attention to a systematic pattern of active counterfactual dependency of changes in its explanandum (E_{12}) on changes in its explanans. Unlike (Ex. 11), (Ex. 12) does locate its explanandum within a range of possible alternatives and shows, at least in a crude way, the range of conditions under which this explanandum would hold and what sorts of changes in those conditions would instead lead to one of these alternatives. In doing this (Ex. 12) shows us as how the conditions cited in its explanans make a difference for, or are explanatorily relevant to its explanandum. To put the point a bit differently, the contrast between (Ex. 11) and (Ex. 12) shows that explanatory relevance—the key feature that is lacking in (Ex. 11) but present in (Ex. 12)—is just a matter of the holding of the right sort of pattern of active counterfactual dependence between explanans and explanandum: to a first approximation, S is explanatorily irrelevant to M if M would hold both if S were to hold and if S were not to hold when these counterfactuals are interpreted actively.

There is a second respect in which the account I am recommending differs from the traditional DN account. The DN model requires that every explanation must appeal to at least one law. Since laws (or more precisely laws that connect changes and do not contain irrelevancies in the sense specified in Section 3), in virtue of their invariance characteristics and the support they provide for active counterfactuals, provide information relevant to answering what-if-things-had-been-different questions, my account agrees with the DN model in holding that laws play a crucial role in (at least) some explanations. That is, one way, illustrated by the examples described above, in which an explanation can satisfy the requirement that it provide answers to a range of what-if-things-had-been-different questions is by appealing to a law. However, in taking invariance and support for active counterfactuals rather than lawfulness *per se* to be crucial to successful explanation we open up an intriguing possibility that is not available within the DN or other purely nomothetic frameworks: the possibility that there are generalizations that are invariant and that can be used to answer a range of what-if-things-had-been-different questions and that hence are explanatory, even though we may not wish to regard them as laws and even though they lack many of the features traditionally assigned to laws by philosophers. In Sections 12 and 13, I will argue that many explanatory generalizations in the special sciences have exactly this character—they are invariant generalizations that are not naturally regarded as laws. To put the point a bit differently, the account provided above allows us to reject the assumption, accepted by many if not most philosophical commentators, that if the generalizations of the special sciences are genuinely explanatory, they must either be or be closely associated in some way with laws of nature. It thus allows us to avoid the various puzzles and difficulties that nomothetic conceptions of explanation encounter when we attempt to apply them to the special sciences.

5 Degrees of invariance

My argument so far has been that generalizations like (2) and (3), in contrast to (1) and (4) are not invariant under (any) interventions (that is, on the variables that explicitly figure in those generalizations) at all—they are, as I shall say, non-invariant and hence non-explanatory. However, as already intimated, invariance is not an all or nothing matter. Most generalizations that are invariant under some interventions and changes are not invariant under others. As we shall see shortly, we may legitimately speak of some generalizations as more invariant than others—more invariant in the sense that they are invariant under a larger or more important set of changes and interventions than other generalizations. Moreover, there is a connection between range of invariance and explanatory depth—generalizations that are invariant under a larger and more important set of changes often can be used to provide better explanations and are valued in science for just this reason. The picture that I will be defending is thus one in which there is both a threshold—some generalizations fail to qualify as invariant or explanatory at all because they are not invariant under any interventions on the variables that explicitly figure in the generalization—

and above this threshold a notion of invariance that admits distinctions or gradations of various sorts. This picture corresponds to how, intuitively, we seem to think about explanatory (or causal or nomological) relationships. Some relationships—e.g. the relationship described by (3)—are not causal or explanatory at all, but among those that are, some may be used to provide deeper or more perspicuous explanations than others. This represents just one of many points at which the invariance based account that I will be defending contrasts with more traditional frameworks for thinking about laws and their role in explanation. The traditional frameworks suggest a dichotomy: that either a generalization is a law or else it is purely accidental. Moreover, it is assumed that the boundary between laws and non-laws coincides with the boundary between those generalizations that can be used to explain and those that cannot. The invariance-based account rejects both of these ideas.

The ideas introduced in the previous paragraph—that generalizations may differ in the range of changes or interventions over which they are invariant and that these differences are connected to differences in their explanatory status—are familiar themes in the econometrics literature. They are illustrated and endorsed by Tygre Haavelmo, one of the founding figures of econometrics, in a well-known passage from his monograph 'The Probability Approach in Econometrics' ([1944]). In this passage, Haavelmo introduces a notion which he calls autonomy but is really just another name for what we have been calling invariance. He writes:

> If we should make a series of speed tests with an automobile, driving on a flat, dry road, we might be able to establish a very accurate functional relationship between the pressure on the gas throttle (or the distance of the gas pedal from the bottom of the car) and the corresponding maximum speed of the car. And the knowledge of this relationship might be sufficient to operate the car at a prescribed speed. But if a man did not know anything about automobiles, and he wanted to understand how they work, we should not advise him to spend time and effort in measuring a relationship like that. Why? Because (1) such a relation leaves the whole inner mechanism of a car in complete mystery, and (2) such a relation might break down at any time, as soon as there is some disorder or change in any working part of the car. We say that such a relation has very little autonomy, because its existence depends upon the simultaneous fulfillment of a great many other relations, some of which are of a transitory nature. On the other hand, the general laws of thermodynamics, the dynamics of function, etc., etc., are highly autonomous relations with respect to the automobile mechanism, because these relations describe the functioning of some parts of the mechanism *irrespective* of what happens in some other parts ([1944], pp. 27–8).

Haavelmo then suggests the following, more formal characterization of autonomy:

> Suppose that it would be possible to define a *class S, of structures*, such that *one member or another* of this class would, approximately, describe economic reality in *any practically conceivable situation*. And suppose that we define some non-negative measure of the 'size' (or the 'importance' or 'credibility') of any subclass, W in S including itself, such that, if a subclass contains completely another subclass, the measure of the former is greater than, or at least equal to, that of the latter, and such that the measure of S is positive. Now consider a particular subclass (of S), containing all those—and only those—structures that satisfy a particular relation 'A' is autonomous with respect to the subclass of structures W_A. And we say 'A' has a degree of autonomy which is the greater the larger the 'size' of W_A as compared with that of S ([1944], pp. 28–9).

Although this characterization is far from completely transparent (among other things, Haavelmo does not tell us how to go about determining the 'size' or 'importance' of W—matters which we will address below), the underlying idea is perhaps clear enough. In the most general sense the degree of autonomy of a relationship has to do with whether it would remain stable or invariant under various possible changes. (As we have argued, if, like Haavelmo, we wish to use this idea to distinguish between those relationships to which we can appeal to explain and those that cannot be so used, we need to include, among the changes over which we demand that a relationship be autonomous, those that correspond to interventions on the variables figuring in the relationship.) The larger the class of changes under which the relation would remain invariant—the more structures in W compatible with relation—the greater its degree of autonomy. Haavelmo suggests that physical laws such as the laws of thermodynamics and fundamental engineering principles such as those governing the internal mechanism of the car will be highly autonomous in this sense. By contrast, the relationship (call it (13)) between the pressure on the gas pedal and the speed of the car will be far less autonomous. We may imagine that (13) holds stably for some particular car if we intervene repeatedly to depress the pedal under sufficiently similar conditions. (13) will thus be invariant under some interventions. Nonetheless, (13) will be disrupted by all sort of changes—by variations in the incline along which the car travels, by changes in the head wind which the car faces, by changes in the fuel mixture that the car consumes, by changes in the internal structure of the car engine (e.g. by cleaning the spark plugs and adjusting the carburetor) and so on. (13) will also be disrupted by extreme interventions on the gas pedal—for example, those that are sufficiently forceful that they destroy the pedal mechanism. (13) is thus relatively fragile or non robust in the sense that it holds only in certain very specific background conditions and for a restricted range of interventions. Intuitively, although (13) is invariant under some interventions and changes, it is invariant under a 'smaller' set of interventions and changes than fundamental physical laws.

According to the account of explanation defended in Section 4 if (13) holds invariantly for some range of interventions that depress the gas pedal by various amounts, for some type of car in a kind of environment, then we may appeal to (13) and to the depression of the pedal to explain the speed of the car, provided that the car is within the domain of invariance of (13). Within its domain of invariance (13) describes a relationship that can be exploited for purposes of manipulation and control—it describes how we can change the speed of the car by changing the depression of the gas pedal. This is a feature which (13) shares with paradigmatic laws like the gravitational inverse square law and which distinguishes both from purely accidental generalizations like (5) and (6). Because (13) is not completely lacking invariance, an explanation that appeals to (13) will exhibit, albeit in a very limited way, the pattern of active counterfactual dependence that I claimed in Section 4 was at the heart of successful explanation. We can appeal to (13) to explain even if, because of its relative fragility or for other reasons, we are unwilling to regard it as a law of nature. We can thus think of this example as illustrating my claim that it is invariance and not lawfulness *per se* that is crucial in explanation.

However, like Haavelmo I also take it to be obvious that an explanation of the speed of the car that appeals just to (13) is shallow and unilluminating. I follow Haavelmo in tracing this to the fact that the relation (13) is relatively fragile—it is invariant only over a very limited range of interventions and changes in background conditions and can be used to answer only a very limited range of what-if-things-had-been-different questions. A deeper explanation for the behavior of the car would need to appeal to laws and engineering principles (14)—like those mentioned by Haavelmo—that are invariant under a much wider range of changes and interventions. Not coincidentally such a deeper explanation is such that it could be used to answer a much wider range of what-if-things-has-been-different questions. For example, unlike (13) the generalization (14) appealed to in this deeper explanation are such that they could be used to explain why the car moves with speed that it does over a variety of different kinds of terrain and road conditions, under a variety of different kinds of mechanical changes in the internal structure of the car and so on. The what-if-things-had-been-different account of explanation thus seems to capture the relevant features of Haavelmo's example in a very natural way.

What might it mean to say, as Haavelmo does, that one generalization, is invariant under a 'larger' set of changes or interventions than another? In Haavelmo's example, this question has a straightforward answer. To a very good degree of approximation, the range of changes and interventions over which (13) is invariant is a proper subset of the range of changes and interventions over which the generalizations (14) of the deeper engineering theory of the behavior of the car are invariant. That is, any change that will disrupt the latter will also disrupt (13) but not *vice versa*. Thus any properly behaved measure will assign a larger size to the domain of invariance of the latter.

A similar basis for comparison exists in the case of many other pairs of generalizations. Compare the ideal gas law (4) with the van der Waals force law

$$[P + a/V^2][V - b] = RT \qquad (15)$$

Here a and b are constants characteristic of each gas, with b depending on the diameter of the gas molecules and a on the long range attractive forces operating between them. For any given gas, the generalization (15) holds invariantly in circumstances in which the ideal gas law (4) holds, but it also holds invariantly in at least some circumstances—roughly those in which intermolecular attractive forces are important and in which the volume of the constituent molecules of gas are large in comparison with the volume of the gas—in which (4) breaks down. The range of changes or interventions over which (15) is invariant is again 'larger' than the range of changes over which (4) is invariant in the straightforward sense that the latter set of changes is a proper subset of the former. Moreover, just as in Haavelmo's example, this larger range of invariance means that we can use (15) to answer a larger set of what-if-things-had-been-different questions than (4). Thus we can use (15) to answer questions not just about what would happen to the values of one of the variables P, V and T given changes in the others in circumstances in which intermolecular forces are unimportant and intermolecular distances large in comparison with molecular volumes, but also what would happen to P, V or T when these conditions no longer hold. We can also use the van der Waals equation to explain various phenomena having to do with phase transitions—again circumstances in which the simpler (4) breaks down. A similar relationship holds between many other pairs of generalizations—for example, between the laws of General Relativity and those of Newtonian gravitational theory.

It is important to understand that the claim that the range of changes and interventions over which a generalization (G_1) is invariant is a proper subset of the claim that a second generalization (G_2) is invariant is *not* merely a restatement of the claim that (G_1) and (G_2) are both true and that (G_1) is derivable from (G_2) but not *vice versa*. For one thing (G_1) may be derivable from (G_2) but not *vice versa* even if neither generalization is invariant at all. For example, the true generalization (G_1) that the all spatiotemporal regions of 1 meter radius within 10 light years of the earth contain cosmic background radiation at 2.7 degrees K is derivable from the generalization (G_2) that all spatiotemporal regions in the universe contain such background radiation but neither generalization is invariant—neither is change—relating and both apparently depend in an extremely sensitive way on the initial conditions obtaining in the early universe. As another illustration, Mendel's law of segregation is derivable from and not equivalent to the conjunction of Mendel's law and Galileo's law of freely falling bodies but the conjunctive law is not invariant under a wider range of interventions than Mendel's law. When we compare generalizations with respect to range of invariance, we compare generalizations along a very specific dimension of generality. Such comparisons are very different from the comparisons that we make when we simply ask whether one generalization is derivable from another.

Although we may compare the range over which two generalizations are invariant when the proper subset relation just described holds, this obviously yields only a partial ordering. For many pairs of generalizations neither will have a range of invariance that is a proper subset of the other. Moreover, the proper subset relation provides at best a basis for ordinal comparisons. We can say that one generalization is invariant under a larger set of changes than another, but we have no basis for claiming that this set is large or 'important' (to use Haavelmo's word) in some more absolute sense. Is there some other basis on which we can make such claims? I believe that there is. This basic idea is more easily illustrated than precisely characterized, but the underlying intuition is this: for different sorts of generalizations, applicable to different sets of phenomena or subject matters, there often will be specific sorts of changes that are privileged or particularly important or significant from the point of view of the assessment of invariance—privileged in the sense that it is thought to be especially desirable to construct generalizations that are invariant under such changes and that generalizations that are invariant under such changes are regarded as having a fundamental explanatory status in comparison with generalizations that are not so invariant. The privileged changes in question will be subject matter or domain specific—one set of changes will be important in fundamental physics, another in evolutionary biology and yet another in microeconomics. Thus expectations about the sorts of changes over which fundamental relationships will be invariant help to set the explanatory agenda for different scientific disciplines. These expectations will in turn be grounded in very general empirical discoveries about the sorts of relationships in the domains of these disciplines have been found to be invariant in the past and under what sorts of changes.

As an illustration consider that in physics fundamental laws are expected to satisfy certain symmetry requirements. It is widely recognized that such symmetry requirements, especially when interpreted 'actively', are invariance requirements. They amount to the demand that fundamental laws remain invariant under certain kinds of changes—for example under spatial or temporal translation of a system of interest or under spatial rotations or under translation from one inertial frame to another (Lorentz-invariance). These demands are rooted in very general empirical facts about the natural world: that relationships can be found that are invariant under these changes and not others is an empirical discovery. These empirical discoveries in turn generate expectations about the kinds of symmetries physical laws should exhibit. At least at present, generalizations that fail to satisfy such symmetry requirements are unlikely to be regarded as candidates for fundamental laws or explanatory principles, regardless of whatever other features they possess. The requirements thus have a special or privileged status—from the point of view of the assessment of invariance in physics they are more important than invariance under other sorts of changes. Unlike traditional accounts of laws, which leave it opaque why fundamental laws are expected to satisfy symmetry requirements, an invariance-based account makes these requirements intelligible.

For purposes of comparison, consider what counts as an important kind of change for the purposes of assessing invariance in contemporary microeconomics. In microeconomics, individual economic agents are often assumed to conform to the behavioral generalizations comprising rational choice theory (RCT). For the purposes of this paper I will take these generalizations to include the principles of expected utility theory, as described, for example, in Luce and Raiffa ([1957]), together with the assumption that choices are self-interested in the sense that agents act so as to maximize some quantity which is directly related to their material interests, such as income or wealth. Even if we assume, for the sake of argument, that these generalizations are roughly accurate descriptions of the behavior of many participants in markets, it is clear that there are many changes and interventions over which these generalizations will fail to be invariant. For example, there are many pharmaceutical interventions and surgically produced changes in brain structure that will lead (and in some cases have led) previously selfish agents to act in non-self-interested ways or to violate such principles of RCT as preference transitivity. However, economists have not generally regarded these sorts of failures of invariance as interesting or important, at least if, as is often the case, they occur relatively rarely in the populations with which they deal.

By contrast, failures of invariance under other sorts of changes are regarded as much more important. For example, microeconomists often require that fundamental explanatory generalizations such as the principles of RCT be invariant under changes in information available to economic agents or under changes in their beliefs and under changes in the incentives or relative prices they face. Indeed, a standard assumption among many microeconomists—one might take it to be constitutive of a certain sort of methodological individualism—is that the generalizations that will be invariant under such changes in information and prices all describe the behavior of individual economic agents rather than the relations between macroeconomic or aggregate-level variables like 'inflation', 'unemployment', and 'gross domestic product'. That is, the idea is that there are no purely macroeconomic relationships that are invariant under changes in information and incentives and hence that their are no fundamental explanatory relationships between macroeconomic variables.

As an illustration, consider the macroeconomic relationship known as the Phillips curve. This describes the historically observed inverse relationship or trade-off between unemployment and inflation in many Western countries from the mid-nineteenth to mid-twentieth centuries. A crucial question is whether this relationship is (or was) invariant under policy interventions on these variables. According to some Keynesian models, the Philips curve does describe a relationship which is invariant under at least some governmental interventions that change the inflation rate. If so, governments would be able by increasing the inflation rate to decrease the unemployment rate—a highly desirable result. The burden of an influential criticism of these models developed by Lucas ([1983]) (the so-called Lucas critique) is that the relationship discovered by Philips is not invariant under such interventions—that the result of interventions that increase the inflation rate will not be to lower the unemployment rate but rather simply to produce changes in the Philips curve itself. Very roughly, according to this critique, increasing inflation will reduce unemployment only if employers or employees mistake an absolute increase in prices for a favorable shift in relative prices and (given the assumption that these agents are 'rational') this is not a mistake they will make systematically or for any length of time. As soon as these agents realize that a general increase in the price level has occurred or come to expect that such an increase will occur, unemployment will return to its original level. To put the point abstractly, the Philips curve is not invariant under changes in the information available to economic agents or under changes in their expectations of a sort that almost certainly will occur once the government begins to intervene to change the inflation rate. A similar point will hold for many other macroeconomic relationships.

This example illustrates how issues about invariance arise naturally in economics. The interesting question for economists is not whether the Philips curve is a law of nature or completely exceptionless but rather whether it is invariant under certain specific kinds of changes and interventions. If the Philips curve is not invariant under the relevant sorts of interventions, it will not be regarded as a fundamental economic relationship or as a relationship which it would be satisfactory to take as primitive in a deep economic explanation. (For example, if the Lucas critique is correct, it would be unsatisfactory to appeal to the inflation rate and the Philips curve to explain the unemployment rate.) This is not because it fails to be invariant under all possible changes and interventions (including all-out nuclear war or radical psycho-surgery performed on the entire US population) but because it (allegedly) fails to be invariant under a specific set of possible changes that are thought to be particularly important—changes in the information that economic agents receive.

My suggestion, then, is that both of the considerations described in this section—comparisons of invariance based on the proper subset relation and judgments about the significance or importance of the intervention over which a generalization is invariant—play an important role in the construction and assessment of explanatory generalizations. Together they provide a basis for distinguishing among invariant generalizations with respect to degree and kind of invariance and for judging that although a generalization is invariant under some interventions, it is nonetheless relatively fragile or unrobust in the sense that it is stable only under an unimportant set of interventions or under a set of changes that is relatively small in comparison with some rival generalization. As remarked above, the idea that generalizations can differ from one another in the range or importance of the interventions over which they are invariant is one of a number of respects in which the invariance-based framework that I am recommending departs from the traditional framework for thinking about laws of nature and their role in explanation. In contrast to the traditional framework, which admits just two mutually exclusive possibilities (a generalization is either a law or else it is 'accidental'), the notion of invariance allows us to make a much richer set of distinctions among invariant generalizations. As we shall see, this makes the invariance-based framework much better suited for capturing the characteristics of explanatory generalizations in the special sciences.

[. . .]

11 Are all invariant generalizations laws?

I suggested above that there are invariant generalizations that are not naturally regarded as laws, if one has even a modestly demanding conception of what a law is. Section 13 will discuss some examples in more detail. Nevertheless, it will be useful at this point to introduce a simple physical example that illustrates the contrast I have in mind. My object in doing so is not to legislate regarding the proper use of the word 'law' but rather to draw attention to some differences between paradigmatic laws and other sorts of invariant generalizations.

Consider again a particular sort of spring S which, over a certain range of extensions, conforms to Hooke's law (17) $F = -K_s X$, where X is the extension of S, F the restoring force it exerts, and K_s a constant characterizing S. Suppose that (17) is invariant under some interventions that change the extension of S, but breaks down for extensions that are too large and for other sorts of changes in background conditions as well. As we have seen, this fact by itself does not distinguish (17) from paradigmatic laws of nature, such as Maxwell's equations. Nonetheless, there appear to be several respects in which (17) does differ from paradigmatic laws. First, as already discussed, (17) is much narrower in scope. A second difference, which is perhaps more significant from the point of view of explanation is this: not only will there be a range of 'extreme' extensions for which (17) breaks down but even if we confine our attention to extensions of S that are not in this range—i.e. extensions for which (17) sometimes holds—there will be a large number of possible changes in background conditions that do not explicitly figure in (17), for which (17) will be violated. For example, even if it is true that in 'normal' circumstances S will conform invariantly to (17) under small extensions, it will not do so if it is heated to a high temperature or cut with shears. Similarly, (17) will break down if we intervene to produce even a small extension in the wrong way—for, example, if the intervention physically deforms the spring. How we produce a given value of X in (17) and not just what that value is matter for whether (17) is invariant under that change. The set of possible 'interfering conditions' for (17) is very large and heterogeneous and will resist any simple, informative characterization. Because we don't know how to characterize all the items in this set in a way that is non-circular and illuminating, we find ourselves saying things like the following: (17) holds, if 'other things are equal' or in the absence of 'disturbing factors' where no very precise independent specification of the quoted phrases is available.

By way of contrast, although paradigmatic laws like Maxwell's equations do break down under certain extreme values of the variables that figure in those equations, whether the equations hold or not depends just on the values of those variables and not on how those values are brought about. That is, in contrast to (17), within the classical regime for which Maxwell's equations hold, it does not matter how we change the distances between point charges, or the intensities of electromagnetic fields and so on—Maxwell's equations will continue to hold under such changes. Moreover, changes in background conditions play a different role in connection with the invariance characteristics of paradigmatic laws than in connection with generalizations like (17). When the circumstances under which paradigmatic laws fail to be invariant are known, they typically can be given a relatively simple, unified characterization. Such circumstances seem to fall into one of two categories: laws break down either for extreme values of variables that explicitly figure in the them (e.g. high temperatures and pressures in the case of the ideal gas law) or when some very small set of variables that have been omitted from the law diverge from a limiting value—the pattern being that the law holds when the variables take this limiting value but not otherwise. For example, according to a well-known textbook on General Relativity, the Newtonian inverse square law 'is an excellent approximation in the limiting case of low velocity in a weak gravitational field' (Ohanian [1976], p. 2). That is, the law breaks down both when gravitational fields are strong (an extreme value of an included variable) and also when an omitted variable (velocity) is not small in comparison with the speed of light.

On this way of looking at matters, the differences between (17), on the one hand, and paradigmatic laws like Maxwell's equations, on the other, although real, look very much like differences in degree (of scope and of range of interventions and changes in background conditions over which these generalizations are invariant) rather than of kind. Paradigmatic laws are simply generalizations with wide scope that are invariant under a large and important set of changes that can be given a theoretically perspicuous characterization. We are willing to regard other invariant generalizations as laws to the extent that we judge that they resemble these paradigms in these respects. It is thus not surprising that the boundary between those invariant generalizations we regard as laws and those that we do not regard as laws is fuzzy and contentious—an additional reason for resisting models of explanation that require a sharp law/non-law boundary.

These considerations raise in turn an obvious question: given that the difference between Maxwell's equations and (17) is one of degree, why not reflect this continuity by extending the notion of a law to cover all generalizations that are invariant under some interventions and changes in background conditions, so that generalizations like (17) count as laws as well, albeit local or qualified or ceteris paribus laws? In fact, many writers have proposed that we do just this (Hausman [1992]; Fodor [1991]; Kincaid [1989]).

In thinking about this proposal, it is important to separate issues that are largely terminological in the sense that they reflect decisions about how to use the word 'law' from more substantive issues. To the extent that the proposal under discussion accepts what I have say about the importance of invariance and its role in explanation and simply extends the word 'law' to cover all invariant generalizations, it differs only verbally from my own position. In fact, however, few if any philosophers who have wanted to extend the notion of law have had in mind only such a terminological proposal. Instead, philosophers who have thought of generalizations like (17) (or the various generalizations of the special sciences) as laws have usually been motivated by a very different account from the one I have been defending of the features of such generalizations which make them explanatory. They have tried to show that such generalizations are explanatory in virtue of satisfying (or to the extent they satisfy) various of the traditional criteria for lawfulness rather than in virtue of being invariant or figuring in the answers to a range of what-if-things-had-been-different questions. For example, the treatments of so-called *ceteris paribus* laws, which are discussed in Section 13, are all motivated by the idea that if a generalization is to be a law and hence explanatory it must be or be backed by an exceptionless generalization. The philosophers who advocate such treatments are not merely proposing that we extend the word 'law' to cover the explanatory generalizations of the special sciences but are instead adopting a distinctive substantive position about the features (*viz.* exceptionlessness) which such generalizations must possess if they are to figure in explanations.

It is in part for this reason—that in practice, the project of extending the notion of law to cover the generalizations of the special sciences is closely bound up with the (in my view thoroughly misguided) project of showing that, despite appearances to the contrary, these generalizations are explanatory because they satisfy (at least many of) the traditional criteria for lawfulness—that I think that clarity is best served by adopting a more restricted notion of law. Moreover, there are additional reasons for such a restricted notion. First, while there are, as I have argued, important continuities between generalizations like Maxwell's and (17), there are also very real differences. While these may be matters of degree, they are not for that reason unimportant. The features possessed by generalizations, like Maxwell's equations— greater scope and invariance under larger, more clearly defined, and important classes of interventions and changes—represent just the sort of generality and unconditionality standardly associated with laws of nature. Their relative absence from generalizations like (17) and from many of the explanatory generalizations of the special sciences makes it misleading to assimilate these to paradigmatic laws. Second, and perhaps more importantly, if the argument of this paper about invariance and explanation is correct, there is no real motivation for such an assimilation. The claim that the explanatory generalizations of the special sciences are laws would have an obvious motivation if there was some independent reason for supposing that all explanation requires laws, understood along the traditional lines. It would also have an obvious motivation if there were some independent reason to suppose that all generalizations must fall into one of two mutually exclusive categories—the lawful or the purely accidental. However, I have argued that we should reject these assumptions. Both are gratuitous—we don't need to accept them once we have the notion of invariance and the account of explanation sketched above. Once we accept this alternative account of explanation, we don't need to argue that the generalizations of the special sciences are laws (thereby incurring the burden of claiming that they do not differ in important respects from Maxwell's equations or that, appearances to the contrary, they satisfy such traditional criteria as exceptionlessness) to vindicate their explanatory status. Finally, as will became clear in Section 12, the more restricted usage that I favor also has the advantage that it captures what seems to be at stake when philosophers and scientists deny, as they frequently do, that the explanatory generalizations of the special sciences are laws. Writers who take this position typically are not merely making a proposal about terminology; instead they think that there are important differences between generalizations like Maxwell's equations and many of the explanatory generalizations of the special sciences which a descriptively adequate account of explanatory practice in different areas of science should to aim to capture. The framework I have proposed allows us to do this.

[. . .]

13 Invariance and *ceteris paribus* laws

It will help to bring out what is distinctive about the ideas about invariance and explanation that I have been defending if we contrast them with a standard alternative account of the conditions that explanatory generalizations in the special sciences must meet. I will call this the *completer* account—versions can be found in many writers, from Hempel ([1965]), to more recently Fodor ([1991]), Hausman ([1992]) and Pietroski and Rey ([1995]). Each of these writers adds refinements and complications, but in what follows I will focus on the core idea. I shall argue that this is sufficiently mistaken that the embellishments will not help. The completer account adopts the assumptions with which we began this paper—that all explanation requires 'subsumption' under laws and that a necessary condition for a generalization to count as a 'strict' or unproblematic law is that it be exceptionless. [. . .] We then face the familiar problem of reconciling these assumptions with the apparent paucity of exceptionless generalizations in the special sciences. In schematic form, the solution proposed by the completer account is this: suppose one begins with a generalization of form (37) 'All Fs are Gs' which has exceptions. (37) will be a legitimate kind of law—a so-called *ceteris paribus* law—and will have explanatory import if and only if there is some further condition C such that (38) 'All Fs in C are Gs' is a strict or exceptionless law (that is, F and C is nomologically sufficient for G) and neither F by itself nor C by itself is nomologically sufficient for G. Adopting (and somewhat modifying) some terminology due to Fodor ([1991]), let us call such a condition C a 'completer' for (37). The simplest version of the completer account then says that a ceteris paribus generalization is genuine law and hence explanatory if and only if it has a completer. It is crucial to the structure of this account that we *not* impose the requirement that someone who appeals to (37) to explain must be able to actually describe its completer C in a non-trivial way or to state or produce the exceptionless generalization (38). As we have repeatedly noted, it is rarely possible to do this in the special sciences. Instead, it is enough that the completer exists or, alternatively, perhaps that we know or have some reason to think that it exists, even if we are unable to provide a non-trivial description of it.

The apparent attraction of the completer strategy is that it allows one to retain the idea that there is a sense in which explanation requires laws and that laws must be exceptionless while at the same time according an explanatory role to generalizations that have exceptions—this is accomplished by requiring that (37) be 'backed' or associated with the exceptioness, law (38). The idea is that somehow (38), in virtue of its exceptionlessness, endows (37) with explanatory import and gives it a status as a legitimate (*ceteris paribus*) law that it would not possess if it did not have a completer. We can also think of this strategy as illustrating a general point made in Section 11—that the claim that a generalization like (37) is a 'law' (albeit a *ceteris paribus* law) becomes a substantive claim and not merely a recommendation about terminology when it is embedded in a more general set of ideas about the features a generalization must possess (in this case, completability into an exceptionless generalization) if it is to be explanatory. The claim that (37) is explanatory when and only when it has a completer is a substantive claim, not a bit of verbal stipulation.

Despite its apparent naturalness, I believe that the completer strategy is fundamentally flawed and that an appreciation of these flaws will bring out the superiority of the invariance based account that I favor. To begin with, the underlying motivation for the account is problematic. This motivation depends on the idea that there is an invidious contrast between *ceteris paribus* laws like (37), which have exceptions, and genuine or strict laws which are exceptionless, and that, because of this, to vindicate the former we must show that they are backed in an appropriate way by the latter. However, as we have already observed and as defenders of the completer account readily acknowledge, there are few examples of exceptionless laws to be found anywhere in science, even in fundamental physics. (Indeed, both Fodor ([1991]) and Pietroski and Rey ([1995]) explicitly say that there may be *no* known examples of exceptionless laws.) Surely, the natural conclusion to draw from this observation is that the whole idea that genuine laws must be exceptionless and that explanation requires exceptionless laws needs rethinking. It is just this conclusion that I have advocated in this essay.

In fact, as I shall now argue, the fundamental intuition underlying the completer strategy is wrong—the distinction between those generalizations that have completers and those that do not does not coincide with the distinction between those generalizations that are lawful (or invariant or explanatory) and those that are not. Under the assumption of macrodeterminism, which virtually all defenders of the completer strategy endorse, there are many generalizations that have completers that no one would regard as explanatory or as ceteris paribus laws. Consider the generalization

(39) All human beings with normal neurophysiological equipment speak English with a southern U.S. accent.

This generalization is of course false—it has exceptions—but under the assumption of determinism there will be a very complicated set of conditions K that are nomologically sufficient in conjunction with being a human being with a normal neurophysiology for speaking English with a southern accent and which satisfy the other conditions for being a completer, such as those described in Pietroski and Rey ([1995]). Indeed, we even have a general sense of what those conditions are—they include some very complex set of environmental conditions including appropriate early exposure to English spoken with a southern accent. These together with being a human being with the appropriate neurological structures are nomologically sufficient to insure that one will learn to speak English with a southern accent. So (39) has a completer—(40) 'All human beings with normal neurophysiology in K speak English with a Southern accent' is not just exceptionless but arguably satisfies many of the other standard conditions for lawfulness such as support for counterfactuals. Nonetheless, (39) is surely not the kind of generalization that anyone would regard as a *ceteris paribus* law—and not just because it has many exceptions. Even if we imagine that (39) is exceptionless—that, as the result of political and economic changes, all living humans were to come to speak English with a southern accent and even if past history had been different in such a way that throughout all history, all human beings spoke English with a southern accent—(39) would not be a plausible candidate for a law of any sort, *ceteris paribus* or otherwise. Nor can we appeal to (39) to provide an explanation of why some particular person speaks English with a southern accent. (We can, of course, appeal to (40) to explain this but (40) is not (39).)

By contrast, the invariance-based account does explain in a natural way why (39) is a poor candidate for an explanatory generalization—it is either non-invariant or invariant only under a very narrow range of interventions. Even if as a result of political changes it becomes true at some future date that everyone in the world speaks English with a southern accent and even if, because the past history of the human race was very different, it was true that all human beings in the past had spoken southern English, (39) would still be highly fragile. Its truth would depend upon a great many very specific contingencies and if these were to change, (39) would be disrupted. Only in a very special and rare kind of environments (rare in comparison with the full range of environments in which human beings learn to speak some language or other) do human beings learn to speak English with a southern accent.

We can further bring out the difference between the completer account and the invariance based account by considering what the former has to say about the contrast between, on the one hand, the 'shallow' generalization (13) linking the position of the gas-pedal and the speed of a car and, on the other, the deeper engineering style theory (14) described in Haavelmo's example (Section 5). (13) has exceptions but, according to the completer strategy, will qualify as a *ceteris paribus* law because there exists some complicated condition K (specifying the details of the functioning of the car engine and the environmental conditions in which it is operated) such that the generalization 'In K, (13) holds' is an exceptionless law. For similar reasons, (14) will also qualify as a non-strict, *ceteris paribus* law—there will be circumstances in which it breaks down but it will also have a completer. However, the invariance-based approach allows us to say that (14) furnishes a deeper explanation of the behavior of the car because (14) is invariant under a wider range of interventions than (13) and can be used to answer a wider range of what-if-things-had-been-different questions. By contrast, the complete strategy provides no basis for such a discrimination—all that it says about (13) and (14) is that they are both *ceteris paribus* laws. Again, I take this to illustrate how the invariance-based account focuses on a very different set of considerations in assessing the explanatory credentials of a generalization than the completer strategy. Simply asking whether a generalization has a completer gives us no insight into the range of changes over which it is invariant and the range of what-if-things-had-been-different questions it can be used to answer. Yet it is just these questions that are crucial to explanatory assessment.

Both of these examples illustrate the more general point that when we ask whether a generalization has a completer and when we ask whether it is invariant we are asking very different questions. The invariance of a *ceteris paribus* generalization like (37) 'All Fs are Gs' depends not just on whether it has a completer C but on the details of the way in which the holding of (37) depends on both on C and on the various alternatives to C—on whether, for example, C represents a special case with (37) holding only when C does or whether, on the other hand, C is a more generic case and (37) would continue to hold under some range of alternatives to C. Again, the relevance of these sorts of considerations to explanatory assessment are lost if we focus only on the question of whether (37) has a completer.

14 Conclusion

In this paper I have argued for a number of general claims. First, explanations involve the exhibition of patterns of active or non-backtracking counterfactual dependence rather than nomic subsumption. Second, explanatory generalizations describe how changes in a set of explanans variables produce changes in a set of explanandum variables and must be invariant under some range of interventions on the explanans variables. Third, the requirement that explanatory generalizations must be invariant is very different from the traditional demand that explanatory generalizations must be laws. Unlike lawfulness, invariance admits of degrees. Moreover, the traditional criteria for lawfulness are neither necessary nor sufficient for a generalization to be invariant or explanatory. In particular, a generalization can be explanatory even if it is not exceptionless and is very restricted in scope. A focus on invariance leads to a more illuminating account of the nature of explanatory generalizations in the special sciences than alternatives such as the completer account.

References

Fodor, J. [1991]: 'You Can Fool Some of the People All of the Time, Everything Else Being Equal: Hedged Laws and Psychological Explanation', *Mind*, **100**, pp. 19–34.

Haavelmo, T. [1944]: 'The Probability Approach in Econometrics', *Econometrica*, **12** (Supplement), pp. 1–118.

Hausman, D. [1992]: *The Inexact and Separate Science of Economics*, Cambridge: Cambridge University Press.

Hempel, C. [1965]: *Aspects of Scientific Explanation and Other Essays in the Philosophy of Science*, New York: Free Press.

Kincaid, H. [1989]: 'Confirmation, Complexity and Social Laws', in A. Fine and J. Leplin (eds), *PSA 1988.*, East Lansing, MI: Philosophy of Science Association.

Lucas, R. [1983]: 'Econometric Policy Evaluation: A Critique', in K. Brunner and A. Meltzer (eds), *Carnegie–Rochester Conference on Public Policy, Supplementary Series to the Journal of Monetary Economics*, **1**, Amsterdam: North Holland, pp. 257–84.

Luce, R. D. and Raiffa, H. [1957]: *Games and Decisions*, New York: John Wiley & Sons.

Ohanian, H. [1976]: *Gravitation and Spacetime*, New York: W. W. Norton & Company.

Pietroski, P. and Rey, G. [1995]: 'When Other Things Aren't Equal: Saving Ceteris Paribus Laws from Vacuity', *British Journal for the Philosophy of Science*, **46**, pp. 81–110.

Salmon, W. [1971]: 'Statistical Explanation', in W. Salmon (ed.), *Statistical Explanation and Statistical Relevance*, Pittsburgh: University of Pittsburgh Press, pp. 29–87.

Woodward, J. [1979]: 'Scientific Explanation', *British Journal for the Philosophy of Science*, **30**, pp. 41–67.

Woodward, J. [1984]: 'A Theory of Singular Causal Explanation', *Erkenntnis*, **21**, pp. 231–62. Reprinted in D. Reuben (ed.), *Explanation*, Oxford: Oxford University Press [1993], pp. 246–74.

Woodward, J. [1997]: 'Explanation, Invariance and Intervention', in *PSA 1996*, **2**, pp. 26–41.

Chapter 8

DANIEL STEEL

SOCIAL MECHANISMS AND CAUSAL INFERENCE

A CENTRAL PROBLEM CONFRONTING social research is that an association between two variables can often be explained by the hypothesis that one is a cause of the other or that both are effects of a common cause. Given the general impossibility of performing experiments and the difficulty of knowing whether all possible common causes have been taken into account, one is faced with a serious challenge to the possibility of making reliable inferences about the causes of social phenomena. It is sometimes claimed that the consideration of social mechanisms can significantly ameliorate this problem (Elster 1983, 47–48; Little 1991, 24–25; Hedström and Swedberg 1999, 9). In this article, I inquire into whether mechanisms can indeed perform this service and, if so, how.

The case on behalf of mechanisms is sometimes posed in terms of the claim that reliable causal inference in social science is *impossible* without knowledge of mechanisms, a proposition that Harold Kincaid (1996, chap. 5) has disputed. Although I agree with Kincaid in rejecting the claim that mechanisms are always necessary for causal inference in social science, I also maintain that the proposal can be made independently of that proposition. On the interpretation I suggest, the account of how mechanisms assist causal inference in social science has a positive and a negative aspect. On the positive side, we can infer that X is a cause of Y if we know that there is a mechanism through which X influences Y. The negative flip side is that if no plausible mechanisms running from X to Y can be conceived of, then it is safe to conclude that X does not cause Y, even if the two variables are probabilistically dependent. As I explain, neither of these lines of reasoning entails that mechanisms are necessary for causal inference in social science, and consequently they are not undermined by the criticisms raised by Kincaid.

Nevertheless, I argue that this account of how mechanisms significantly assist causal inference in social science is not successful as it stands. The positive account is not helpful unless some explanation is given of how it is possible to learn about social mechanisms without running afoul of the problem of unmeasured common causes. Yet to the best of my knowledge, no such explanation has hitherto been provided. On the other hand, the effectiveness of the negative side is undermined by the ease of imagining mechanisms connecting nearly any two variables representing aspects of social phenomena.

However, I propose that the positive side of the account can be shored up, thereby generating a better explanation of the value of mechanisms to causal inference in social science. I argue that knowledge of social norms and practices can be attained in a manner that is independent of the problem of unmeasured common causes. Furthermore, by examining how several social practices are linked together, one can sometimes make a persuasive argument for a qualitative causal hypothesis to the effect that one variable is a cause of another. I illustrate this argument with several examples drawn from social science, particularly from anthropology.

What are social mechanisms?

One of the earliest explicit uses of the term *mechanisms* in the context of social science occurred in Robert Merton's (1968) essay, "On Sociological Theories of the Middle Range," first published in 1949. In that essay, Merton advocated a social theory that refrains from grand systems that attempt to encompass all aspects of human society. Instead, he proposed that social theory should focus on hypotheses concerning the dynamics of specific types of social interactions. Middle-range theories, in Merton's account, relied heavily on mechanisms (p. 43). One of Merton's most well-known mechanisms is the self-fulfilling prophecy, which he illustrated by means of the example of a run on a bank and, more interestingly, through the self-reinforcing aspects of racial discrimination (chap. 13).

In spite of Merton's prominence, the idea that mechanisms should occupy a central place in social theory did not catch on in sociology, and little effort was dedicated to clarifying the notion (Hedström and Swedberg 1999, 6). Consequently, the philosophical literature on social mechanisms is not very extensive, being mostly due to a handful of authors (Elster 1983, 1985, 1989; Stinchcombe 1991; Little 1991, 1998). However, there has been some revival of interest in the topic as of late (Hedström and Swedberg 1996, 1999), and the renewed interest in social mechanisms has had some influence on actual research (Brochmann and Hammar 1999, 19–20). One of the main motivations for interest in social mechanisms is the conviction that adequate explanations in general, and of social phenomena in particular, require an explication of underlying causal processes in addition to a recognition of patterns of correlation and dependence among aggregate-level variables (Harré and Secord 1979; Elster 1989; Little 1998; Hedström and Swedberg 1999). This aspect of the social mechanisms literature, however, is not the focus of the present article, which examines the proposal that social mechanisms provide an effective basis for ameliorating the problem of confounders.

But before launching into the argument, some initial clarification of the notion of a social mechanisms is in order. Mechanisms in general can be roughly characterized as sets of entities and activities organized so as to produce a regular series of changes from a beginning state to an ending one (Machamer, Darden, and Craver 2000). Social mechanisms in particular are usually thought of as complexes of interactions among individuals that underlie and account for aggregate social regularities (Little 1991, 13; Stinchcombe 1991, 367; Schelling 1999, 33; Gambetta 1999, 102). But there is more to social mechanisms than just individual interactions: typically, the individuals are categorized into relevantly similar groups defined by a salient position their members occupy vis-à-vis other members of the society (Hernes 1999). In the description of the mechanism, the relevant behavior of an individual is often assumed to be a function of the group into which he or she is classified. For example, consider the anthropologist Bronislaw Malinowski's (1935) account of how having more wives was a cause of increased wealth among Trobriand chiefs. Among the Trobrianders, men were required to make substantial annual contributions of yams to the households of their married sisters. Hence, the more wives a man had, the more yams he would receive. Yams, meanwhile, were the primary form of wealth in Trobriand society and served to finance such chiefly endeavors as canoe building and warfare. Although individuals play a prominent role in this account, they do so as representatives of social categories: brothers-in-law, wives, and chiefs.

The categorization of component entities into functionally defined types is not unique to social mechanisms. Biological mechanisms (e.g., that of HIV replication) are often described using such terms as *enzyme* and *coreceptor*. The terms *enzyme* and *coreceptor* resemble *chief* and *brother-in-law* in virtue of being functional: all of these terms provide some information about what role the designated thing plays in the larger system of which it is a part. The existence of social categories into which the individuals composing the mechanism are important insofar as the social roles will usually persist far longer than the particular individuals who occupy them, as is illustrated by the Trobriand example. Stable social roles, therefore, are a source of constancy for the mechanisms in which they are involved and for the higher level causal generalizations that depend on these mechanisms.

Social mechanisms are sometimes tied to the assumption that the individuals composing them are rational, say in the sense of being utility maximizers. For instance, Tyler Cowen (1999) writes, "I interpret social mechanisms . . . as rational-choice accounts of how a specified combination of preferences and constraints can give rise to more complex social outcomes" (p. 125). I shall not adopt this perspective. Hypotheses about social mechanisms will not be restricted to ones in which the individuals in question are represented as rational agents.

In sum, social mechanisms can be characterized as follows. Social mechanisms are complexes of interacting individuals, usually classified into specific social categories, that generate causal relationships between aggregate-level variables. A mechanism will be said to be *from* the variable *X* to the variable *Y* if it is a mechanism through which *X* influences *Y*.

Mechanisms and the problem of confounders

A great deal of social science involves collecting aggregate data relevant to some phenomena of interest (e.g., through government records or surveys) and performing statistical tests to decide whether pairs of variables are probabilistically dependent conditional on sets of other variables. In some cases, the purpose of such inquiries might be solely to identify factors that can serve as useful forecasting tools, but often the goal is to discover what variables cause which others. In the social sciences, this leads directly to the thorny problem making causal inferences without the aid of experiment. The classic obstacle to such inferences is that a probabilistic dependence between two variables might be explained either by one variable being a cause of the other or by the existence of a common cause of both. We can call this the *problem of confounders*, where the term *confounders* refers to common causes, often unmeasured, that might explain an observed correlation. The challenge that the problem of confounders poses for social science is expressed nicely by Elster (1983):

> By the latter [spurious explanations] one usually refers to a correlation between two variables that does not stem from a causal relation between them, but from their common relation to some third variable. . . . The danger of confusing correlation and causation is a constant problem in this mode of statistical explanation.
>
> (p. 47)

Though progress has been made in recent years on the topic of causal inference from observational data (Glymour and Cooper 1999; Pearl 2000; Spirtes, Glymour, and Scheines 2000), the problem of confounders remains both extremely difficult and of central importance to the social sciences.

Mechanisms are sometimes proposed as the basis of a partial solution to the problem of confounders. For example, according to Little (1991):

We can best exclude the possibility of a spurious correlation between variables by forming a hypothesis about the mechanisms at work in the circumstances. If we conclude that there is no plausible mechanism linking nicotine stains to lung cancer, then we can also conclude that the observed correlation is spurious.

(pp. 24–25)

The general principle concerning mechanisms and causation on which the argument in this passage rests is the following:

(M) X is a cause of Y if and only if there is a mechanism from X to Y.

Clearly, (M) is not intended as a universally true principle regarding causality, since there is presumably some "rock bottom" level of physical causation below which no mechanisms lie. Thus, (M) should be understood as being restricted to complex systems composed of multiple, interacting components, for instance, an organism or a society.

Given (M), it follows that if we know that there is a mechanism from X to Y, then we can conclude that X is a cause of Y. Conversely, if we have good reason to believe that there is no mechanism from X to Y, then we can conclude that X is not a cause of Y. The latter of these two corollaries of (M) is illustrated by Little's example about nicotine stains and lung cancer. Hedström and Swedberg (1999) make the same point with a different example:

Some epidemiological studies have found an empirical association between exposure to electromagnetic fields and childhood leukemia. However, the weight of these empirical results is severely reduced by the fact that there exists no known biological mechanism that can explain how low-frequency magnetic fields could possibly induce cancer. . . . The lack of a plausible mechanism increases the likelihood that the weak and rather unsystematic empirical evidence reported in this epidemiological literature, simply reflects unmeasured confounding factors rather than a genuine cause relationship.

(p. 9)

Elster (1983, 47–48) provides a similar example, though with a slight twist, that we will consider below.

Thus, the argument for the importance of mechanisms to causal inference in the social sciences is that knowledge of what mechanisms are present, or absent, can rule out alternatives that are consistent with statistical data. In this way, inquiries into mechanisms are asserted to significantly ameliorate the problem of confounders in social science.

Kincaid's objections

Although the proposal described in the foregoing section maintained that inquiries into social mechanisms can significantly ameliorate the problem of confounders, no claim was made to the effect that they are *necessary* for resolving this problem. However, that claim is sometimes made in close association with the proposal described above. For example, according to Little (1995), "it is *only* on the basis of hypotheses about underlying causal mechanisms that social scientists will be able to use empirical evidence to establish causal connections" (pp. 53–54, italics added). Kincaid (1996, 179–82) raises two objections to the claim that social mechanisms are necessary for causal inference in the social sciences, the first of which takes the form of a *reductio ad absurdum*.

In Kincaid's (1996) discussion, the proposition at issue is that "we need to identify individualist mechanisms to confirm causal relations between social variables" (p. 179). Let us formulate this proposition in the following way:

(M*) One knows that X is a cause of Y only if one can identify at least one mechanism from X to Y.

Kincaid's *reductio ad absurdum* then proceeds as follows. Suppose that a mechanism relating two aggregate-level social variables is demanded to support the claim that one of the variables is a cause of the other.

Do we need it at the small-group level or the individual level? If the latter, why stop there? We can, for example, always ask what mechanism brings about individual behavior. So we are off to find neurological mechanisms, then biochemical, and so on.

(p. 179)

Given (M*), therefore, demands for mechanisms can be pressed all the way down to fundamental physics, yielding the absurd result that no causal claim can be established unless such impossible amounts of detail are provided.

One might try to defend (M*) from such objections by maintaining that it is only intended to apply to fields in which experiment is not possible and not all common causes can be measured (Little 1998, 10–12). Since controlled experiments are routine in such fields as neuroscience and molecular biology, this would nip Kincaid's reductio ad absurdum in the bud. However, I think that a simpler line of response is to agree with Kincaid that (M*) is false but to point out that it is not required for the proposal described in the foregoing section. That proposal rested on the proposition (M), which stated that X is a cause of Y if and only if there is a mechanism from X to Y. The target of Kincaid's reductio ad absurdum, meanwhile, is (M*). But does (M) entail (M*)? Defenders of mechanisms in social science sometimes seem to presume that it does. For example, consider the following statement of Little's (1995):

I maintain that the central idea of causal ascription is the idea of a causal mechanism: to assert that A causes B is to assert that A in the context of typical causal fields brings about B through a specific mechanism (or increases the probability of the occurrence of B). This may be called "causal realism," since it rests on the assumption that there are real causal powers underlying causal relations. This approach places central focus on the idea of a causal mechanism: *to identify a causal relation between two kinds of events or conditions, we need to identify the typical causal mechanisms through which the first kind brings about the second.*

(p. 34, italics added)

Notice that the first sentence in this quotation is a clear statement of (M): there is a causal relationship just in case there is an underlying mechanism. In contrast, one interpretation of the italicized sentence is as a statement of (M*): mechanisms must be identified before we can claim to know that one variable is a cause of another. However, (M) does *not* entail (M*).

To see the point, imagine a person who accepts (M) but who also regards randomized controlled experiments as a reliable means of learning about cause and effect. Suppose that a randomized controlled experiment establishes that X is a cause of Y. Then the person concludes from (M) that there is a mechanism from X to Y. Nevertheless, the person may not be able

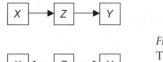

Figure 8.1
Two statistically indistinguishable
causal graphs

to identify any mechanism from X to Y; in short, she knows *that* there is a mechanism but not necessarily *what* this mechanism is. Therefore, such a person would not be committed to taking the stance that serves as the basis of Kincaid's reductio ad absurdum; that is, she would not be committed to (M*). Her inability to identify a mechanism is compatible with her knowledge that there is a mechanism and, hence, with her knowledge of a causal relationship. In general, one can consistently accept (M) while rejecting (M*) by holding, reasonably enough, that the identification of mechanisms is not the only possible way to learn about cause and effect.

Kincaid's (1996) second objection to (M*) is that there are ways of distinguishing between cause and mere correlation available to social scientists that have nothing to do with mechanisms, particularly, by conditioning on potential confounders (pp. 179–80). I agree that there are cases in which one can draw reasonable conclusions about what causes what without the aid of experiment or substantial knowledge of underlying mechanisms. However, the usefulness of conditioning on potential common causes does not undermine the proposal that mechanisms significantly aid causal inference in the social sciences, since social scientists are rarely able to measure all potential common causes. Indeed, the inability to exhaustively consider all potential common causes is a basic element of the problem of confounders, to which mechanisms are being considered as a partial solution.

In addition, evidence regarding conditional dependencies and independencies may fail to unambiguously identify causal structure even when all potential common causes have been measured. For example, consider Figure 8.1. Both graphs in this figure predict that X and Y are probabilistically dependent. Moreover, both predict that X and Y are independent conditional on Z. So, measuring Z would not enable us to decide whether X is a cause of Y, even if there were no other confounders.

Elster's (1983, 48) argument for the importance of mechanisms to causal inference in social science is motivated by an example that illustrates the same point. In Elster's example, the variable X represents "the percentage of female employees who are married" and Y represents "the average number of absences per week per employee" (p. 48). Elster supposes that X and Y are positively correlated but that they are independent conditional on a third variable Z, "the amount of housework performed per week per employee" (p. 48). Both causal graphs in Figure 8.1 can explain this imagined statistical evidence; hence, we are unable to decide from that evidence alone whether X is a cause of Y. However, Elster suggests, since there is no plausible mechanism through which Z could influence X, we can conclude that Z is not a cause of X and, hence, not a common cause of X and Y. The only remaining alternative, therefore, is that X is a cause of Z, which in turn is a cause of Y. Thus, this example illustrates how (M) might be used to establish a positive causal conclusion that could not have been reached through the examination of statistical data alone.

In sum, Kincaid has effectively criticized (M*), the proposition that one can know that X is a cause of Y only if one can identify a mechanism from X to Y. However, (M*) is not required for the account presented in the foregoing section of how inquiries into mechanisms play a central role in causal inference in the social sciences. Nevertheless, that proposal leaves much to be desired.

No plausible mechanism

There is, as was noted above, a positive and a negative side of the account of the importance of mechanisms to causal inference in the social sciences. The positive side rests on the premise that we can show that X is a cause of Y if we can discover a mechanism from X to Y. The negative side relies on the premise that we can infer that X is not a cause of Y if we know that there is no plausible mechanism from X to Y. It was the negative side that was illustrated by Little's nicotine stains and lung cancer example, Hedström and Swedberg's example concerning electromagnetic fields and child leukemia, and Elster's example about the proportion of female employees and number of missed workdays. In this section, I argue that the negative side of the account of the importance of mechanisms to causal inference in social science is unsuccessful.

The problem lies in the ease of imagining social mechanisms through which nearly any aggregate-level social variable can influence another. Thus, it is rarely the case that no plausible mechanism can be imagined that could connect two variables representing aspects of social phenomena. Consider, for instance, a well-known example from the sociological literature discussed by one of the contributors to Hedström and Swedberg's (1999) volume, Diego Gambetta. The example is the association—reported in Samuel Stouffer's (1949) *The American Soldier*—between satisfaction and opportunity for advancement among military personnel.

Surprisingly, soldiers in branches of the military offering little opportunity, such as the military police, were on average more satisfied with their positions than those in branches with greater chances for advancement, such as the army air corps. Gambetta (1999) describes five mechanisms proposed by sociologists over the years to account for how greater opportunity could cause less satisfaction (pp. 114–19). However, he does not consider the alternative possibility that opportunity has little or no negative influence on happiness and that the association found by Stouffer is due to an unmeasured common cause. For example, it is possible that extremely ambitious people are much more likely to embark on career paths that promise greater opportunities for advancement and that their lofty aspirations are also more likely to make them dissatisfied with their current stations in life. Listing possible mechanisms through which opportunity could produce unhappiness does nothing to rule out this plausible alternative. Indeed, this case illustrates how an overabundance of plausible mechanisms is a major source of difficulty for causal inference in the social sciences.

No doubt there are some pairs of variables X and Y representing aggregate aspects of social phenomena such that no plausible mechanism through which X causes Y can be imagined. However, I suspect that such cases are too few and far between for the no-plausible-mechanism strategy to be of much use in distinguishing cause from mere correlation in social science. Although Elster, Little, as well as Hedström and Swedberg illustrate their arguments with an example, only Elster's—a toy example not based on actual research—has any relation to social science. Despite their interest in doing so, these authors apparently found it difficult to produce a serious example of actual social research in which the inability to imagine a plausible mechanism from one social variable to another significantly aided causal inference.

Process tracing and interpretation

As we saw, (M) can be used to generate a positive as well as a negative account of the value of mechanisms to causal inference in social science. Having found the negative proposal wanting, let us turn to the positive one. From (M) it follows that if we know that there is a mechanism from X to Y, we can infer that X is a cause of Y. The difficulty is that it is unclear how we are to learn about mechanisms in a way that does not run directly into the problem of confounders, which was the problem that mechanisms were supposed to help us overcome. For example, consider Little's (1991) discussion of how one acquires knowledge of mechanisms:

> To credibly identify causal mechanisms we must employ one of two forms of inference. First, we may use a deductive approach, establishing causal connections between social factors based on a theory of the underlying process. . . . Second, we may use a broadly inductive approach, justifying the claim that a caused b on the ground that events of type A are commonly associated with event of type B. . . . But in either case the strength of the causal assertion depends on the discovery of a regular association between event types.
>
> (p. 30)

Thus, according to Little, the identification of causal mechanisms depends on prior knowledge of probabilistic dependencies among variables. But the problem of confounders immediately rears its ugly head at this juncture, since the probabilistic dependence might result from a common cause rather than from A being a cause of B. The procedure that Little describes for identifying mechanisms, therefore, presupposes that some means already exist for resolving the problem of confounders, which has the consequence that it is unable to shed any light on how the problem of confounders might be alleviated by the identification of mechanisms.

Hence, to make the positive side succeed, it is necessary to explain how one might learn about social mechanisms in a way that does not presuppose a prior solution to the problem of confounders. That is the task that I undertake in what follows. My proposal is nicely illustrated by Malinowski's (1935) hypothesis that the possession of many wives was a cause of wealth and influence among Trobriand chiefs. Malinowski's evidence for this hypothesis is primarily nonstatistical; it consists of descriptions of social processes in Trobriand society that any reasonably skilled ethnographer could produce. First, there is a custom whereby brothers contribute substantial gifts of yams to the households of their married sisters—gifts that are larger than usual when the sister is married to a chief. Second, political endeavors and public projects undertaken by chiefs are financed primarily with yams. If we grant that Malinowski was right about these two points, it is difficult to avoid the obvious conclusion that the number of wives had an influence on wealth among Trobriand chiefs.

Malinowski's reasoning is an example of what I shall call *process tracing*. Process tracing consists in presenting evidence for the existence of several prevalent social practices that, when linked together, produce a chain of causation from one variable to another. A successful instance of process tracing, then, demonstrates the existence of a social mechanism connecting the variables of interest. For instance, in the case just described, the social practices are (1) that brothers are required to contribute a substantial store of yams to the households of their sisters and (2) that yams are the primary means used by chiefs to finance their various endeavors. Supposing that Malinowski was right about (1) and (2), the conclusion that the number of wives had an influence on wealth among Trobriand chiefs is unavoidable. The most difficult part of arguing for a causal hypothesis via process tracing, therefore, usually is constructing a convincing case that the posited social processes actually exist. Once the relevant social practices are given, the logical implications of their joint operation often follow straightforwardly.

Malinowski's argument is not an isolated anomaly. Arguments employing process tracing are often found in regions of social science in which one is interested in questions about what causes what but in which good statistical data are unavailable. For example, consider Brian

Ferguson's (1995) account of the effect of the introduction of such manufactured items as steels tools on indigenous warfare in the context of colonial expansion and in the political consolidation of postcolonial states, particularly among the Yanomami. Ferguson (1990) has long argued that European colonial expansion profoundly reshaped indigenous warfare in the Americas and elsewhere. One of the ways in which European contact influenced warfare was through introduction of manufactured valuables, particularly such steel tools as machetes, axes, and knives. These items were often quick to become necessities of life, but they differed significantly from their indigenous analogues in that they could not be manufactured locally. Moreover, in more than a few cases, these precious items were available only from a limited number of peripheral source points. Ferguson (1984, 1995) argues that in such circumstances, groups close to the source often attempt to establish a local monopoly on the flow of manufactured goods so as to be able to trade on advantageous terms with their neighbors. Naturally, such monopolizing efforts were apt to generate resentment among more remote groups, which might attempt to circumvent the monopolists or dislodge them by force. Likewise, the would-be monopolists might resort to violence to maintain their privileged position.

[. . .]

I regard process tracing as a procedure *both* for developing, or formulating, causal hypotheses and for providing evidence for them. Process tracing is not intended merely as a means of inventing intriguing new hypotheses, and it is clear that it must be more than this if it is to ameliorate the problem of confounders. For if the *only* evidence for hypotheses generated through process tracing consisted of statistical tests concerning aggregate-level variables, the problem of confounders would be confronted anew with no progress having been made toward its resolution. After all, the difficulty lies not in imagining hypotheses concerning the causes of social phenomena but in deciding which among the large number of such conceivable hypotheses is correct. Therefore, it is important to address concerns that a skeptic might have concerning the capacity of process tracing to provide evidence for causal claims.

A striking feature of Malinowski's (1935) argument is that it is compelling yet utterly lacking in statistical sophistication of any kind. No large sample of data is produced to demonstrate a positive correlation between wealth and number of wives among Trobriand chiefs. Nor is any thought given to possible confounding common causes that could generate such a probabilistic dependence if it existed. And potential common causes are easily conceived of. For instance, one could imagine that establishing alliances with other chiefs results both in having more wives (used as a means of cementing political bonds) and in greater wealth. As if by magic, Malinowski seems to have established that one variable is the cause of another without the aid of any experimental or statistical technique for dealing with the possibility of unmeasured common causes.

A skeptic might wonder whether applications of process tracing are in fact little more than tricks of smoke and mirrors masquerading as science. How does process tracing differ from mere storytelling? Surely, the problem of alternative hypotheses capable of accounting for the available evidence is not made to disappear through a description of salient social processes. To the extent that process tracing can provide a compelling argument for a causal generalization, the skeptic might continue, it relies on implicit causal generalizations already established by other means. Hence, the skeptic might conclude, if process tracing works at all, it does so only by presupposing a solution to the problem of confounders; consequently, an adequate explanation of how attention to mechanisms can ameliorate this problem has yet to be provided.

Let us consider these objections in turn. The first thing to be emphasized is that making an argument for a causal conclusion via process tracing requires marshalling evidence for claims concerning the social processes at work in the society in question. For instance, Malinowski has to convince us that the custom of brothers making significant contributions of yams to the households of their sisters is indeed a pervasive feature of Trobriand social life. Malinowski's argument rises above the level of mere storytelling only to the extent that he succeeds in making this case.

It is also important to recognize how modest the accomplishments claimed by process tracing actually are. Without the aid of statistical data, the best one can hope to establish by means of process tracing is purely qualitative causal claims. For instance, in Malinowski's example, all we can conclude is that there is at least one path through which the number of wives exerts a positive influence on wealth among Trobriand chiefs. Not only does this conclusion fail to specify anything about the strength of the influence generated by this mechanism, it does not even entail that the overall effect of the number of wives on wealth is positive. One would naturally presume that having more wives would mean having more members of the household to provide for, which would be expected to exert a downward influence on wealth. Clearly, statistical data concerning the average cost-benefit ratio in yams of acquiring additional wives would be needed to decide which of these two conflicting influences was predominant, and no such data are provided by Malinowski.

It is not difficult to find cases in which process tracing is used in tandem with statistical analysis. Justin Lin and Dennis Yang's (2000) analysis of the Chinese famine of 1959–61 provides an excellent illustration of this point. Inspired by Amartya Sen's (1981) entitlement approach to famines, they argue that the stage was set for the famine by a combination of a heavy-handed grain procurement regime and an urban-biased rationing system. The famine was then triggered by a decline in agricultural production apparently resulting from the disastrous policies of the Great Leap Forward. A central part of their argument, therefore, is a matter of linking together aspects of the Chinese food distribution system of the period and noting their joint implications. In addition, Lin and Yang use aggregate data to estimate quantitative effects of the decline in food production and the urban-biased redistribution system on mortality rates. This example illustrates an important way in which arguments by process tracing and statistical analysis work together: process tracing is used to establish qualitative claims about causal structure, and statistical analysis is called on to estimate the strengths of these relationships.

Yet the points that establishing a causal conclusion by means of process tracing involves producing a considerable body of evidence and that process tracing, on its own, is only intended to establish qualitative causal conclusions do not fully answer the skeptic's concerns. In particular, it has not been shown how knowledge of social practices and norms can be acquired in a way that does require a solution to the problem of confounders. The answer to this concern, I suggest, lies in the observation that what one has here are two *distinct* underdetermination problems; thus, one might be able to resolve one without necessarily having resolved the other.

The problem of underdetermination arises in the context of arguments by means of process tracing but in a different way than when one is attempting to make causal inferences from statistical associations and independencies among variables. In the context of process tracing, the chief difficulty is that of interpreting a social practice. For example, Malinowski (1935) faced the challenge of making an inference about a social practice of which he had no initial inkling from beginning observations of large quantities of yams being moved to and fro. No doubt, multiple possible explanations occurred to Malinowski at the start of this process. Evidence relevant to distinguishing between these alternatives would typically consist of observing people's behavior and asking them about what they are doing and why, as well as what would happen to someone who behaved differently. Thus, Malinowski makes observations about the quantity of yams produced by several apparently typical men, and he makes observations about the quantity that is contributed to the households of sisters. In addition, he questions native informants about the process, relying in part on what-would-happen-if questions, such as, "What would people say if so-and-so did not contribute a significant portion of his crop to the households of his sisters?" Of course, evidence of this sort might fail to unambiguously single out a particular interpretation of the practice in question. Nevertheless, it would be hard to deny that skilled investigators can sometimes reliably acquire knowledge of important social practices by such means.

In the context of making a causal inference from data concerning statistical associations and independencies among variables, in contrast, the primary challenge arises from the possibility that there are unmeasured common causes that can account for an observed association between the putative cause and effect. Since the two underdetermination problems are distinct, it is possible that there are situations in which one of them is resolved while the other is not. Thus, the fact that Malinowski had no solution to the problem of unmeasured common causes does not entail that he could not have successfully used process tracing to argue for the existence of a social mechanism through which the number of wives exerted a positive influence on wealth among Trobriand chiefs.

However, the skeptic might doubt that the two cases really are so different. For would not inferences concerning which interpretation is best depend, at least implicitly, on substantive causal generalizations about human psychological and cognitive tendencies? And if that is so, then it seems that the problem of confounders has merely been shunted off to a less noticeable location. Although this is a legitimate concern, I think that it is answerable.

Some of the implicit causal generalizations involved in interpretations of social practices fall into the category of folk psychology—for example, statements such as, "If somebody wants A and he or she thinks that B is the best way to get it, then he or she is more likely to do B." Such generalizations can be plausibly regarded as a part of one's background knowledge, thus requiring no special justification. Investigations into matters of what causes what never commence from a position of Cartesian doubt; some background knowledge is always presupposed. Moreover, unlike the presumption that all potential common causes of a given social phenomena have been taken into account, simple generalizations like the one above are plausible and generally unproblematic.

I suspect that simple folk psychological generalizations often suffice for relatively straightforward interpretations of social practices such as that in the Malinowski example. But I agree with Todd Jones (1999, 356–58) that there are interpretations in which less obvious and more precise psychological assumptions would be called for. In such cases, Jones's proposal is that one should turn to modern cognitive psychology for assistance. Now, the problem of confounders can certainly be expected to arise in research regarding causal generalizations concerning human cognitive capacities. However, here the situation is different from that in social science, since controlled experiments are much more frequently a practical possibility in cognitive psychology than in social science. Consequently, in cognitive psychology the problem of confounders, though real, is less severe.

Having discussed and defended process tracing, let us return to the question of the importance of mechanisms to causal inference in the social sciences. Process tracing does not rely on the premise that causal inference is only possible provided knowledge of underlying mechanisms, which was the assumption that generated Kincaid's reductio ad absurdum. Hence, in advocating the usefulness of process tracing for causal inference in the social sciences, I do not claim that reliable causal inference in social science would never be possible without mechanisms. Nevertheless, there is a plausible argument that process tracing has a very important role to play in learning the causes of social phenomena.

It is generally not possible to perform experiments to test causal claims that are of interest in social science; moreover, it is rarely the case that all plausible common causes can be measured. As a result, making causal inferences from statistical data with no substantive knowledge of the underlying social processes in question is an extremely difficult—though I would not say impossible—task. Process tracing, to the extent that it provides qualitative information about relevant social mechanisms, can significantly ameliorate this situation. Beginning with substantive knowledge of the qualitative causal relationships facilitates the process of using statistical data to make causal inferences insofar as it rules out entire classes of alternatives from the start. Moreover, qualitative knowledge about some of the relevant mechanisms can serve an important heuristic purpose in that it directs attention toward causally meaningful statistics. For example, Malinowski's hypothesis suggests that among the Trobriand islanders, the cost-benefit ratio in yams of acquiring more wives is a worthwhile object of attention. What we have, then, is not an argument that mechanisms are absolutely essential to causal inference in social science. Rather, we have a variety of reasons for thinking that without process tracing, causal inference in social science would be significantly more difficult than it actually is. This conclusion is strong enough to vindicate the intuitive idea that mechanisms are of central importance to learning about cause and effect in the social sciences, while not leading to claim that reliable causal inference in social science is impossible without mechanisms.

Conclusion

This article has aimed to clarify the ways in which inquiries into mechanisms are helpful in dealing with one of the most significant challenges to causal inference in the social sciences, the problem of confounders. I proposed that accounts hitherto provided for the usefulness of mechanisms in ameliorating this problem can be interpreted so as to be independent of the proposition that mechanisms are *necessary* for causal inference, a proposition critiqued by Kincaid. Nevertheless, I argued that even given this more charitable interpretation, the proposal still does not withstand critical scrutiny. The negative side of the argument is undermined by the ease of imagining plausible mechanisms that could link nearly any two aggregate-level social variables. The positive side of the argument is ineffective unless some explanation is provided of how knowledge of mechanisms is to be acquired without a prior solution to the problem of confounders.

Consequently, I developed an account concerning how the positive side of the argument could be improved, which was based on what I called process tracing. Norms or practices present in a society can often be linked together to shed considerable light on mechanisms, knowledge that in turn significantly facilitates efforts to draw causal inferences from statistical data. Moreover, I argued that knowledge of such norms and practices can be obtained even in circumstances in which not all potential common causes have been taken into account. This account, I hope, helps to elucidate the manner in which mechanisms play an important role in causal inference in the social sciences.

References

Brochmann, G. and T. Hammar, eds. 1999. *Mechanisms of immigration control: A comparative analysis of European regulation policies.* Oxford, UK: Blackwell.

Cowen, T. 1999. Do economists use social mechanisms to explain? In *Social mechanisms: An analytical approach to social theory,* edited by P. Hedström and R. Swedberg, 125–46. Cambridge, UK: Cambridge University Press.

Elster, J. 1983. *Explaining technological change: A case study in the philosophy of science.* Cambridge, UK: Cambridge University Press.

——. 1985. *Making sense of Marx.* Cambridge, UK: Cambridge University Press.

——. 1989. *Nuts and bolts for the social sciences.* Cambridge, UK: Cambridge University Press.

Ferguson, R. B. 1984. A reexamination of the causes of northwest coast warfare. In *Warfare, culture, and environment*, edited by R. B. Ferguson, 267–328. Orlando, FL: Academic Press.

——. 1990. Blood of the Leviathan: Western contact and warfare in Amazonia. *American Ethnologist* 17:237–57.

——. 1995. *Yanomami warfare: A political history.* Santa Fe, NM: School of American Research Press.

Gambetta, D. 1999. Concatenations of mechanisms. In *Social mechanisms: An analytical approach to social theory*, edited by P.Hedström and R. Swedberg, 102–24. Cambridge, UK: Cambridge University Press.

Glymour, C. and G. Cooper. 1999. *Computation, causation, and discovery.* Menlo Park, CA: American Association for Artificial Intelligence.

Harré, R. and P.F. Secord. 1979. *The explanation of social behavior.* Totowa, NJ: Littlefield and Adams.

Hedström, P. and R. Swedberg. 1996. Social mechanisms. *Acta Sociologica* 39:281–308.

——, eds. 1999. *Social mechanisms: An analytical approach to social theory.* Cambridge, UK: Cambridge University Press.

Hernes, G. 1999. Real virtuality. In *Social mechanisms: An analytical approach to social theory*, edited by P. Hedström and R. Swedberg, 74–101. Cambridge, UK: Cambridge University Press.

Jones, T. 1999. FIC descriptions and interpretive social science: Should philosophers roll their eyes? *Journal for the Theory of Social Behavior* 29:337–69.

Kincaid, H. 1996. *Philosophical foundations of the social sciences.* Cambridge, UK: Cambridge University Press.

Lin, J. and Dennis Yang. 2000. Food availability, entitlements and the Chinese famine of 1956–61. *Economic Journal* 110:136–58.

Little, D. 1991. *Varieties of social explanation: An introduction to the philosophy of social science.* Boulder, CO: Westview.

——. 1995. Causal explanation in the social sciences. *Southern Journal of Philosophy* 34 (suppl.): 31–56.

——. 1998. *Microfoundation, method, and causation.* New Brunswick, NJ: Transaction Publishers.

Machamer, P., L. Darden, and C. Craver. 2000. Thinking about mechanisms. *Philosophy of Science* 67:1–25.

Malinowski, B. 1935. *Coral gardens and their magic.* New York: American Book Co.

Merton, R. 1968. *Social theory and social structure.* New York: Free Press.

Pearl, J. 2000. *Causality: Models, reasoning, and inference.* Cambridge, UK: Cambridge University Press.

Schelling, T. 1999. Social mechanisms and social dynamics. In *Social mechanisms: An analytical approach to social theory*, edited by P. Hedström and R. Swedberg, 32–44. Cambridge, UK: Cambridge University Press.

Sen, A. 1981. *Poverty and famines: An essay on entitlement and deprivation.* Oxford, UK: Clarendon.

Spirtes, P., C. Glymour, and R. Scheines. 2000. *Causation, prediction, and search.* 2nd ed. Cambridge, MA: MIT Press.

Stinchcombe, A. 1991. The conditions of fruitfulness of theorizing about mechanisms in social science. *Philosophy of the Social Sciences* 21:367–88.

Stouffer, S. 1949. *The American soldier.* New York: John Wiley.

Chapter 9

RICHARD SCHEINES

THE SIMILARITY OF CAUSAL INFERENCE IN EXPERIMENTAL AND NON-EXPERIMENTAL STUDIES

1. Introduction

PHILOSOPHERS, STATISTICIANS, AND computer scientists, at least those who have abandoned the goal of producing a reductive account of causation, have come to largely agree on how to represent qualitative causal claims and how to connect such claims to statistical evidence through probabilistic independence and dependence (Glymour and Cooper 1999; Pearl 2000; Spirtes et al. 2000; Woodward 2003). Included in this scheme is a method for representing experimental interventions, and for clarifying what sorts of assumptions we must make about interventions in order to consider them 'ideal'. With this apparatus, it is easy to show that if we have ideally intervened experimentally upon (X), then an association between X and Y entails that X is a cause of Y. Inferring that one variable is a cause of another is what I call 'causal inference'.

With this apparatus, Spirtes et al. (2000), Pearl (1988, 2000) and others have developed algorithms for determining the *set* of causal structures that are consistent with the independence relations assumed to hold over a set of measured variables in a non-experimental, or observational study, even causal structures that include latent, or unmeasured variables. In some instances all the causal structures in an equivalence class agree on some subset of the causal relations, and in some cases they all agree that one variable X is a cause or direct cause of another Y. In these cases we can, using basically the same assumptions as are made in experimental studies, infer that X is a cause of Y.

Although we have no general characterization of the conditions under which a causal inference to $X \rightarrow Y$ can be made in observational studies, it turns out that when the inference is possible it is often driven by the existence of what I call a *detectible instrumental variable* that stands in the same relationship to X and Y in the observational study as does the ideal intervention on X in the experimental study. In what follows, I briefly sketch the key ideas behind the representational system, I show how an experimental causal inference works in this system, how the typical observational causal inference works involving detectible instrumental variables, and the parallel between detectible instrumental variables and experimental interventions.

2. Representing causation

2.1. Causal graphs, probability distributions, and the Causal Markov Axiom

Recently from computer science, but as far back as Sewall Wright in the early twentieth century (Wright 1934), the fundamental representational device for causal systems is the directed graph. A directed graph is simply a collection of vertices and directed edges over pairs of these vertices. In a directed graph interpreted as a causal graph, each directed edge (or arrow) from one vertex X to another Y is taken to assert that X is a direct cause of Y relative to the set of vertices in the graph. For example, Figure 9.1 represents a graph G = V, E, with vertices V = {Exposure, Infection, Symptoms}, and edges E = {Exposure, Infection, Infection, Symptoms}. We further assume that the vertices in such a graph can be interpreted as random variables with some probability distribution P, and that causal processes situated in some definite background context generate probability distributions over these variables.

A causal graph is assumed to be representationally complete in the following sense: if two variables in the graph are effects of a common cause C, then C is included in the graph. This does *not* require us to include all the causes of a variable in the graph, it only requires that we include all the common causes. To be clear, this is a representational assumption, not one concerning which variables we will measure when the goal is inference. The key assumption connecting causal graphs to probability distributions is an axiom that constrains the set of probability distributions that a given causal graph can generate (Spirtes et al. 2000):

> **Causal Markov Axiom**. In any probability distribution **P** generated by a given causal graph **G**, each variable X is probabilistically independent of the set **Y** consisting of all variables that are not effects of X, conditional on the direct causes of X. That is, $\forall$ $X \in$ **G**, **X** $\perp\!\!\!\perp$ **Non-effects of X** | **Direct Causes of X**, in **P**.

This entails, for example, that Exposure is independent of Symptoms conditional on Infection in any probability distribution that the causal graph in Figure 9.1 can generate. In acyclic causal graphs, the Causal Markov Axiom is equivalent to a graphical relation called d-separation (Pearl 1988). If **X** and **Y** are d-separated by **Z**, then the Causal Markov Axiom entails that **X** and **Y** are independent conditional on **Z**.

2.2. Interventions

To model experimental interventions on a causal system, we add a new variable representing the intervention, connect it to the graph in a particular way, and make an assumption about how ideal interventions change the causal graph (Spirtes et al. 2000; Pearl 2000). For simplicity we restrict interventions to act only on one variable at a time. Let an intervention on X be called I_x, and model this by adding I_x to the graph as a direct cause of only X, and the effect of no variable. For example, to model an experimental intervention on Infection in the causal graph in Figure 9.1, we build the graph in Figure 9.2.

Figure 9.1 Causal graph

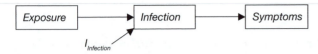

Figure 9.2 Modeling an intervention

Modeling an intervention as a direct cause makes explicit the fact that this account of causation does not attempt to reduce causation to intervention. It goes to the other extreme, it reduces intervention to the idea of a direct cause. Direct cause is left undefined, but connected to probability through the Causal Markov Axiom.

Finally, we say an intervention is 'ideal' if it totally determines the probability distribution of its target. For example, a medical trial assessing the effect of St. John's Wort on depression might assign either of two treatments: St. John's Wort or placebo, by flipping a fair coin to randomly assign subjects to one of these two treatments. This intervention is ideal if the coin flip totally determines the treatment, leaving no influence from the subject's disposition to take alternative medicines, etc.

If I_x is an *ideal* intervention on X, then we eliminate, or 'x-out' any arrows in the original causal graph that point into X (Figure 9.3). This represents the idea that our ideal intervention has taken over X's probability distribution, overriding any influence its direct causes might have had prior to our intervention. In contrast, we do not x-out arrows coming *out of* X. So ideal interventions on X annihilate the relationship between X and its direct causes, but leave intact the relationship between X and its direct effects.

3. Causal inference in experimental studies.

The problem of causal inference from association is under-determination. If two variables X and Y are associated in a non-experimental study, then many different causal graphs can explain the association. In general, three kinds of causal connection (Figure 9.4) can produce an association (probabilistic dependence) between two variables X and Y:

1. A path[1] from X to Y
2. A path from Y to X
3. A pair of paths, one from some third variable C (possibly latent) to X and one from C to Y.

Consider the same problem after an ideal intervention on X, however. The intervention eliminates the influence of all the direct causes of X in the original graph, thus all causal connections save paths from X to Y are destroyed (Figure 9.5).

The result is incredibly simple, but incredibly powerful. If X and Y are associated after an ideal intervention on X, then X is a cause of Y. Further, the quantitative degree of association can be used to estimate the size of the effect of X on Y (Pearl 2000). The key to this type of simple experimental inference is that the intervention is: (i) a direct cause of X, (ii) not adjacent to Y, and (iii) ideal. Consider why it is desirable that it satisfy these conditions. First, if the

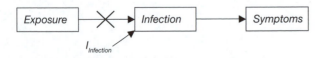

Figure 9.3 Modeling an ideal intervention

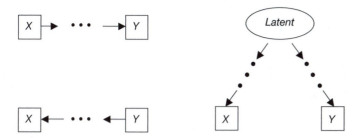

Figure 9.4 Causal connections which explain an association between X and Y

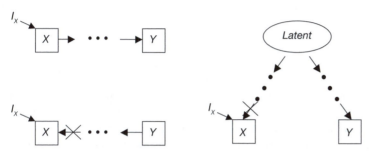

Figure 9.5 Causal connections after an ideal intervention on X

(a)   (b)

Figure 9.6 Fat-hand interventions

intervention is a direct cause of X, but also of Y or some other cause of Y, then X and Y will be associated in virtue of the intervention, not in virtue of the effect of X on Y (Figure 9.6). It is possible to handle the second form of fat-hand intervention (Figure 9.6b) by looking not just at whether X and Y are associated but also at whether X and Y are associated *conditional* on Z. The first type of fat-hand intervention (Figure 9.6a), in which I_x is a direct cause of Y is fatal to causal inference.

Similarly, the intervention must itself not be an effect of any other variable, a problem I will call treatment-bias (Figure 9.7). Again, in such cases X and Y would be associated after an intervention, but not because of an effect of X on Y. Again, we could handle the second form of treatment-bias (Figure 9.7b) by conditioning on Z, but the first form (Figure 9.7a) is fatal.

Generally then, an intervention on X can be fat-hand or treatment-biased without making causal inference impossible, but I_x *cannot be adjacent*[2] *to Y* in the causal graph. Need the intervention be ideal? Is causal inference still possible in cases in which the intervention on X does not fully determine X's probability distribution and thereby x-out the influence of all other direct causes on X? For the argument as I have sketched it above, clearly yes, but in general the answer is no.

(a)   **(b)**

Figure 9.7 Treatment-bias interventions

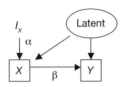

Figure 9.8 Instrumental variable I_x

In cases where we know something about the parametric form of the dependence of effects on their causes, for example linear structural equation models (Bollen 1989), interventions need not be ideal. In linear structural equation models each effect is a linear combination of its direct causes plus Gaussian noise, and in certain such models instrumental variable estimators (Bowden and Turkington 1984) can be used to estimate the strength of causal influence even in the presence of latent common causes. In Figure 9.8, for example, I_x is an instrumental variable for $X \rightarrow Y$, and the quantity $\rho_{IX,Y}/\rho_{IX,X} = \alpha\beta/\alpha = \beta$ is a consistent estimator of the effect of X on Y, even though X and Y are confounded by a latent common cause. If I_x is an intervention, but not an ideal intervention, as in Figure 9.8, and the dependencies are linear, then the instrumental variable estimator can be used to do causal inference; we simply statistically test whether $\beta = 0$. Whether or not the instrumental variable Z is an intervention, (i) Z must be adjacent to X but not an effect of X, and (ii) Z may not be adjacent to Y.

To summarize, in experimental settings causal inferences concerning whether X is a cause of Y are driven by interventions on X which are: (i) direct causes of X, (ii) not adjacent to Y, and (iii) ideal (they totally determine the probability of X).

4. Causal inference in non-experimental studies

In non-experimental studies, we have no intervention variable with known relationships to the variables under study. We have only a set of measured variables governed by some causal structure that we assume satisfies the Causal Markov Axiom, but which might include unmeasured common causes of the variables we have measured. To set aside statistical diffi-culties, we will assume that we can determine which probabilistic independence relations hold over the measured variables with perfect reliability. Finally, we will assume that the probability distribution **P** is Faithful to the causal graph (Spirtes et al. 2000). That is, we assume that all independence relations that hold in **P** are entailed by the Causal Markov Axiom, thereby ruling out independence relations holding in **P** in virtue of particular settings for the probabilities in **P**.

In this setting, the underdetermination of causation can be characterized with an equivalence class of causal graphs, each member of which is a causal graph that entails all and only those independence relations observed to hold in some distribution $\mathbf{P_o}$ over the set of observed variables **O**. As you would expect, when we allow the equivalence class to include graphs that have unobserved common causes, that is, variables not in **O**, then the class is infinite. Spirtes and Richardson (1996) describe a graphical object called a Partial Ancestral Graph or **PAG**, to compactly represent equivalence classes that include latent common causes.

Fortunately, it is sometimes the case that all members of the equivalence class represented by a **PAG** share features of a causal relationship between two variables in **O**. For example, if we have measured three variables, Z_1, Z_2, and X, and find Z_1 and Z_2 to be unconditionally independent, then the **PAG** and some of the members of the equivalence class it represents are pictured in Figure 9.9. Even though X is associated with both Z_1 and Z_2, in no member of this equivalence class is X a cause of either Z_1 or Z_2. We can't, from three variables and no extra background knowledge make a positive causal inference, but we can make two negative ones: X is not a cause of Z_1 nor is it a cause of Z_2. With four variables we can actually make a positive causal inference. Adding Y, and assuming that Y is unconditionally associated with all the other variables but independent of Z_1 and Z_2 conditional on X, the PAG in Figure 9.10 represents the set of causal graphs that entail all and only these independencies. In every member of the equivalence class represented by the PAG in Figure 9.10, X is a cause of Y, and in no member of the equivalence class is there a latent common cause of X and Y, exactly the same conclusion we can reach by finding an association between X and Y in an experimental study in which we have ideally intervened upon X.

The FCI algorithm (Spirtes et al. 2000) computes PAGs from given independencies, assuming the Causal Markov Axiom, Faithfulness, and that there is a graph that generated the independencies given. By examining one set of conditions required by the algorithm in order to determine that (i) X is cause of Y and (ii) there is not latent common cause of X and Y in every member of the equivalence class, I will try to illuminate the similarity between causal inference in experimental and non-experimental settings.

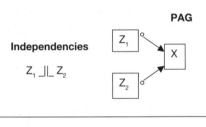

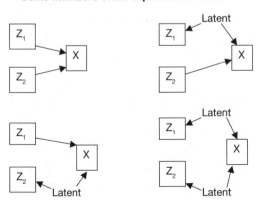

Figure 9.9 Equivalence class

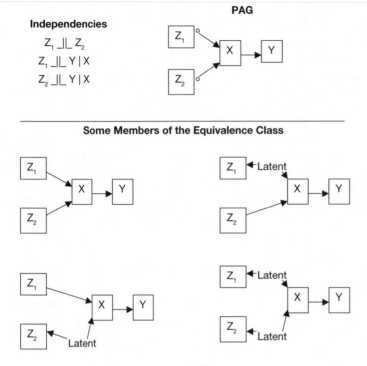

Figure 9.10 PAG that gives a causal inference

The FCI algorithm proceeds in two stages. In the first it identifies the adjacencies in the PAG, and in the second it orients any of these adjacencies it can. Any pair of variables that are not adjacent after the adjacency phase are not adjacent in any causal graph in the final equivalence class (Spirtes et al. 2000). In a PAG, an unoriented adjacency is represented as Ao-oB. The possible orientations and what they represent about the members of the equivalence class are:

- A o→ B means that B is not a cause of A in any member of the class, but either A is a cause of B or they have a latent common cause.
- A ← → B means that A and B have a latent common cause in every member of the class.
- A → B means that A is a cause of B with no latent common cause in every member, and
- A o-$o\underline{B}o$-o C means that either (i) B is a cause of A and there is no latent common cause of A and B, *or* (ii) B a cause of C with no latent common cause.

In the orientation phase, the algorithm looks for triples A, B, C such that A and B are adjacent, B and C are adjacent, but A and C are *not* adjacent, i.e., A o-o B o-o C. If B *is* included in the set that made A and C independent,[3] then we orient this triple as a 'non-collider' at B: A o-$o\underline{B}o$-o C, else we orient the triple as a 'collider' at B: A o→ B ←o C. We call this orientation step the 'collider rule'.

After going through all the triples and orienting them with the collider rule, we go through them again, this time looking for triples in which B was oriented as a non-collider from the triple A, B, C, but as collider from a triple A, B, D, that is Figure 9.11. We can then combine these orientations to fully orient the B o-o C adjacency as B → C, which is the only way to

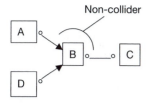

Figure 9.11

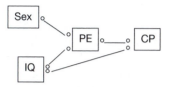

Figure 9.12 After adjacency phase

orient *B* o-o *C* in order to avoid making *B* a collider in the *A*, *B*, *C* triple. We call this the 'away-from-collider rule'.[4]

Consider a concrete empirical case to illustrate. Sewall and Shah (1968) collected data on over 10,000 Wisconsin high school seniors in order to study the relationship between parental encouragement (PE) and college plans (CP). They also measured socio-economic status (SES), Sex, and IQ. For simplicity I omit SES. The independence relations that hold statistically among PE, CP, Sex, and IQ are: Sex $\perp\!\!\!\perp$ IQ, Sex $\perp\!\!\!\perp$ CP | PE. After the adjacency phase of FCI, we have Figure 9.12. There are two triples that satisfy the requirements for orientation: (1) Sex o-o PE o-o IQ, and (2) Sex o-o PE o-o CP. In (1), we can orient PE as a collider,[5] and in (2), we can orient PE as a non-collider.[6] So after applying the collider rule we have the orientation in Figure 9.13. Going back through these two triples, we can apply the away-from-collider rule to the Sex, PE, CP triple, giving us a PAG[7] in which parental encouragement is an unconfounded cause of college plans (Figure 9.14).

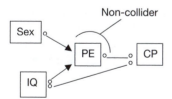

Figure 9.13 After applying the collider rule

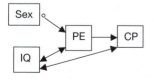

Figure 9.14 PAG for college plans

5. The similarities

Consider the inference to $X \rightarrow Y$ in a non-experimental setting with the away-from-collider rule. We need a triple $Z \; o\!\rightarrow \underline{X}o\text{-}o \; Y$. Besides knowing that X and Y are adjacent,[8] this construction involves a *detectible instrument* Z that is: (i) adjacent to X but not an effect of X, and (ii) not adjacent to Y.

These conditions match precisely with those required of an instrumental variable as used commonly in econometrics (see Section 3 above), and they also match quite closely to the two conditions I specified for experimental studies, which I repeat here. Interventions I_x on X should at a minimum: (i) be direct causes of X, and (ii) not be adjacent to Y.

A variable V that satisfies the first condition will also satisfy the first condition for a detectible instrument Z, but structurally it is not necessary for V to directly cause X. It is enough that the adjacency between V and X be *into* X, that is, either V is a direct cause of X or there is a latent common cause of V and X. By intervening on X with I_x, we ensure that the adjacency between I_x and X is *into* X, but for the causal inference it is not strictly necessary.

I use the word 'detectible' to highlight the fact that, in a non-experimental study, the issue is finding a variable that detectibly satisfies the same basic conditions that we believe are satisfied in an experimental study. For example, in the case study involving college plans and parental encouragement above, we managed to detect that the adjacency between Sex and PE was *into* PE because Sex and IQ are independent, thus giving us a collider oriented triple: Sex $o\!\rightarrow$ PE $\leftarrow\!o$ IQ.

Suppose, however, that Sewall and Shah had not thought to measure IQ. Just measuring Sex, PE, and CP, and finding only that Sex $\perp\!\!\!\perp$ CP | PE, we would have the following PAG: Sex $o\text{-}\underline{o}$ PE $o\text{-}o$ CP, which does not support a causal inference between PE and CP. Why? Because we do not know that the Sex $o\text{-}o$ PE adjacency is *into* PE. If, however, we add the perfectly plausible background knowledge that parental encouragement cannot be a cause of one's gender, then the variable Sex *would* satisfy the conditions for a detectible instrument: Sex is adjacent to PE but not an effect of PE (Sex $o\!\rightarrow$ PE), and Sex is not adjacent to CP. In that case would have a detectible instrument and could, from the Causal Markov Axiom and Faithfulness assumptions, infer that parental encouragement is indeed a cause of college plans with no latent common cause between them.

The parallels between these forms of experimental and non-experimental inference are not complete, nor are they necessary. They do suggest, however, that faced with a causal question that does not permit, for ethical or practical reasons, an experimental intervention, a good causal scientist should not throw up his hands and proclaim that "only experimental studies can support causal conclusions." Rather she should seek to systematically combine background knowledge and statistical analysis to find detectible instruments for causal inference.

Notes

1. A path is just a sequence of arrows all pointing in the same direction.
2. X and Y are adjacent if X is a direct cause of Y or Y a direct cause of X.
3. This was necessary to eliminate the adjacency between A and C.
4. There are other orientation rules that can support a positive causal inference, e.g., the definite-discriminating-path rule, but they are too complicated to explain or characterize in the space I have here.
5. We do *not* need to condition on PE to make Sex and IQ independent.
6. We *do* need to condition on PE to make Sex and CP independent.
7. The orientation of the IQ-CP and IQ-PE adjacencies results from applying another rule I will not explain. It is not relevant to orienting the PE $\rightarrow$ CP adjacency.
8. This means they are associated no matter what set we condition on.

References

Bollen, K. A. (1989), *Structural Equations with Latent Variables*. New York: Wiley.

Bowden, R. and D. Turkington (1984), *Instrumental Variables*. New York: Cambridge University Press.

Cartwright, Nancy (2003), "What Is Wrong with Bayes Nets?", in Henry Kyburg and Mariam Thalos (eds.), *Probability Is the Very Guide of Life*. Peru, IL: Open Court Press, 253–276.

Glymour, C. and G. Cooper (1999), *Computation, Causation, and Discovery*. Menlo Park, CA: AAAI Press.

Hausman, D. (1998), *Causal Asymmetries*. Cambridge: Cambridge University Press.

Pearl, J. (1988), *Probabilistic Reasoning in Intelligent Systems*. San Francisco: Morgan Kaufmann.

—— (2000), *Causality: Models, Reasoning, and Inference*. Cambridge: Cambridge University Press.

Sewall, W. and V. Shah (1968), "Social Class, Parental Encouragement, and Educational Aspirations", *American Journal of Sociology* 73: 559–572.

Spirtes, P. C. Glymour, and R. Scheines (2000), *Causation, Prediction, and Search*. Cambridge, MA: MIT Press.

Spirtes, P. and T. Richardson (1996), "A Polynomial Time Algorithm for Determining DAG Equivalence in the Presence of Latent Variables and Selection Bias", in *Proceedings of the 6th International Workshop on Artificial Intelligence and Statistics*.

Woodward, James (2003), *Making Things Happen: A Theory of Causal Explanation*. Oxford: Oxford University Press.

Wright, S. (1934), "The Method of Path Coefficients", *Annals of Mathematical Statistics* 5: 161–215.

PART III

Interpretation

DOING SOCIAL SCIENCE INEVITABLY involves interpreting people's actions. This is true even for mundane social science tasks such as collecting survey statistics on topics like rates of marriage and divorce, homeownership, and so on. After all, some basic understanding of prevailing social norms and institutions is needed to know whether a particular activity counts as a marriage, a purchase of a house, or what have you. The importance of interpretation to social science is especially obvious when it comes to actions occurring within the context of an unfamiliar culture. In such cases, one might see people's behaviors and perhaps even recognize their words but nevertheless have little idea of what is going on. Interpretations of actions involve "getting inside" the actors' world views: attributing motives, concepts, convictions, and beliefs to the actors in an effort to make sense of what they do. In everyday situations, we do this so effortlessly that we hardly notice it. It is typically only when confronted with actions that strike us as odd and inexplicable that we pay conscious attention to our own practices of interpreting others.

Interpretation seems to mark a difference between social and natural science. We might sometimes metaphorically attribute beliefs and desires to inanimate objects—for instance, if I say that my car just didn't want to start this morning—but we don't think that a proper scientific explanation should do so. In the social sciences, by contrast, interpretation seems unavoidable. In the philosophy of science literature in the second half of the twentieth century, interpretation was the focus of much discussion on the topic of whether the social sciences should emulate the methods of natural science or whether they should adopt humanities-oriented approaches. This debate typically proceeded on the assumption that there is a set of reasonably clear and informative principles that constitute the methods of natural science. Hempel's covering law model is a good example of the sort of thing that the phrase "natural science methods" evoked in this discussion. However, the picture of science as following a single unified method (usually assumed to be exemplified by physics) has been gradually undermined in the philosophy of science within the last several decades. One reason for this has been the growth of interest in the philosophy of biology. Although a number of philosophers have argued that the methods of biology differ from those of physics in some significant respects—for instance, because mechanisms rather than laws are the most common basis for explanations—there is no inclination to conclude that biology is therefore not a genuine science. Likewise, the fact that interpretation is important to social science in ways that it is not in biology or physics or chemistry does not in itself indicate anything about the scientific status of studies of human societies. After all, distinct subjects often call for different methods.

Consequently, the old "is there a fundamental cleavage between social and natural science?" question that was once so prevalent in philosophical debates about interpretation has become increasingly peripheral. Nevertheless, some issues remain interesting and important even if one abandons the assumption that there is a unified method of natural science. Prominent among these are questions about how exactly humans interpret one another. Two approaches to this question figure prominently in the current literature. The first, known as the "theory theory," proposes that humans interpret one another by forming and testing hypotheses in a manner that roughly parallels scientific reasoning (Gopnik and Meltzoff 1998). For example, suppose that Suzy sees Tommy put a toy in a box, and then sees that when Tommy isn't looking the toy is removed from the box and replaced with a cookie. In order to predict that Tommy will act surprised when he opens the box, Suzy might hypothesize that Tommy has beliefs that guide his expectations but which do not always accurately represent the way things really are. (E.g. in this case Tommy believes there is a toy in the box when there is not.) According to the theory theory, then, children postulate hidden mental states such as beliefs and desires in order to explain their observations about human behavior in much the same way as a physicist might hypothesize a new subatomic particle to explain a puzzling experimental result. In contrast, simulation theory proposes a much less intellectualized account of interpretation. According to simulation theory, people have a natural tendency to put themselves in another's shoes by internally simulating what they would experience if they were in the other's position. To see the idea, think about what happens when you watch a scene from a horror movie in which a victim is being stalked by a murderous psychopath: you cringe in your seat and feel afraid. Simulation theory says that interpretation arises from a similar cognitive mechanism. For example, in order to predict how Tommy will react when he opens the box, we effortlessly simulate what we would feel and do if we were Tommy.

The disagreement between these two accounts of interpretation is interesting to the philosophy of social science for at least two reasons. First, since interpretation is an important part of human social dynamics, a good understanding of how humans interpret one another is relevant to social theory. Second, since social scientists interpret the actions of the people they study, an account of interpretation is relevant to discussions of social science methods. For example, a good understanding of interpretation could indicate conditions in which interpretations are more or less likely to be accurate. In addition, the contrast between simulation theory and theory theory also bears a vague resemblance to the old dispute about whether social science can utilize methods drawn from natural sciences. That is, if the theory theory is correct, then interpretation is a type of scientific inference like any other, and hence the important role of interpretation in social science would not distinguish it from natural science in any fundamental way. On the other hand, if simulation theory is correct, then there are cognitive mechanisms we use to understand human behavior that are rarely, if ever, required for natural science explanation. However, this difference does not correspond to some simple division between natural science and humanistic approaches to knowledge. For example, one of the main research projects of advocates of the simulation theory is to discover the neurological mechanisms that support our capacity to simulate the experiences of others (Gallese 2003; Gallese and Goldman 1998). Nor would the truth of the simulation theory preclude social scientists from using methods found in natural science—for instance, methods for using statistical data to test causal claims.

The first chapter in this section is a classic on interpretation and culture by Clifford Geertz. In this chapter, Geertz presents his program of social science centered on interpretation within cultural contexts or what he terms *thick description*. Part of Geertz's project is to defend a theory of culture, according to which culture is not locked up in the heads of individuals but is instead embodied in public performances such as rituals or sporting events and material objects such as buildings or monuments. In Geertz's slogan, "Culture is public because meaning is." Thus, Geertz's ethnography often probes the significance of specific activities or events, which he uses as a source of insights concerning webs of local social norms that imbue behaviors with meaning. Geertz contrasts interpretive social science with "experimental science in search of law" but his statements about the scientific status of his approach are quite ambiguous. For example, he says that he is not at all timid about asserting that anthropology is a science and sketches an analogy between cultural interpretation and medical diagnosis. But he also says that the "canons of appraisal" for ethnographic interpretations are "if not wholly nonexistent, very nearly so."

Geertz's work attracted a great deal of interest, including many critiques by philosophers and social scientists who read him as advocating the abandonment of objective, scientific methods in social science. The next chapter in this section, by Todd Jones, is a good example of this type of reaction to Geertz. Jones begins proposing that interpretive social scientists are best understood as attempting to infer typical mental reactions that members of a culture have in particular kinds of circumstances. For example, according to Jones, a social scientist studying American culture from an interpretivist perspective might ask how the typical African American felt while watching the inauguration of President Barack Obama. Moreover, Jones suggests that interpretivists are especially interested in "hidden" mental states that reflect the deeper symbolic meaning of rituals or other sorts of cultural activities or events. Such hidden meanings are harder to discover since the participants are not consciously aware of them. Jones' main thesis, then, is that hidden mental states of this sort can only be inferred from behavioral and environmental cues given well confirmed scientific theories about human psychology. But if this is what interpretive social science requires, then the supposed contrast between cultural interpretation and science collapses. Notice that Jones' argument illustrates the consequence of the theory theory described above. If the theory theory is right, then interpretation is just a type of scientific inference. It is no coincidence, then, that Jones makes a point of criticizing simulation theory (see footnote 1 in his essay).

The next chapter is a presentation and defense of simulation theory by Alvin Goldman. Goldman argues that one of the chief advantages of simulation theory is that it does a better job of explaining data from cognitive psychology. For example, children begin attributing mental states such as beliefs, hopes, fears, etc at around 3 or 4 years old, yet it seems unlikely that such young children are able to engage in complex chains of scientific reasoning, as the theory theory would require. Even more striking is the fact that people with autism perform much more poorly at interpretation tasks than individuals with Down's Syndrome despite being much better at logical and analytical reasoning. This suggests that interpretation is not, as the theory theory would suggest, the product of general capacities for logical and analytical reasoning. Goldman briefly discusses the connection between simulation theory and interpretivist approaches in social science, while also pointing out that this connection would not support any sharp and fundamental divide between social and natural science. However, Goldman does not discuss the relationship between culture and interpretation from the perspective of simulation theory. But that issue is taken up by Karsten Stueber in the final chapter of this section.

Stueber defends simulation, or reenactment to use his preferred term, as a legitimate component of explanation in social science, while stressing its limitations in cases involving major cultural differences. Stueber's central argument in defense of reenactment is that a full understanding of individual action involves not only being able to predict a person's behavior but also an ability to appreciate how that person's reasons motivated her to act as she did. For example, consider the generalization that people who are subjected to sexual abuse as children are more likely to suffer from substance abuse problems, such as alcoholism, as adults. This generalization might be used as a basis for explanations in the style of (the statistical version of) Hempel's covering law model, but it does not tell us much about the reasons that might motivate a victim of childhood sexual abuse to engage in heavy alcohol consumption. According to Stueber, the only way we can understand how a person's circumstances constituted reasons for her to do as she did is to re-enact how we would have been similarly moved had we been in her place. However, Stueber emphasizes that cultural differences often constitute a strong barrier to such reenactments. The accuracy of simulation as a source of interpretations depends on relevant similarities between the people involved. Some of this similarity results from being members of the same species, but it is also clear that much of it is culturally based. Stueber suggests that overcoming barriers to cross cultural interpretation requires supplementing reenactment with generalizations about human psychology. Thus, while being friendlier to simulation theory than Jones, Stueber ultimately reaches a similar conclusion insofar as claiming that cross-cultural interpretation cannot operate independently of more scientifically minded research in psychology or cognitive science.

Further reading

See Bunzl (1994) and Strauss and Quinn (1997) for discussions of Geertz's thesis that cultural meaning is public. For debates about whether Geertz's approach is a viable alternative to more scientifically oriented social science, see Jones (1998), Martin (1993), Segal (1999), Shankman (1984), and Yoshida (2007). Probably the best known advocate of theory theory is Alison Gopnik (Gopnik 1996, 2003; Gopnik and Meltzoff 1998; Gopnik and Wellman 1992). For critical discussion of the theory theory, see Downes (1999), McDonald (2002), and Stich and Nichols (1998). For defenses of simulation theory, see Gallese (2003), Gallese and Goldman (1998), and Goldman (2006, 2009). For critical discussions of simulation theory, see Borg (2007), Jacob (2008), and Stich and Nichols (1997). For a commentary on Stueber's chapter, see D'oro (2009). For essays that attempt to develop an alternative to both simulation and theory theory, see Andrews (2009), Chenari (2009), Gallagher (2008), and Ohreen (2008).

References

Andrews, K. (2009) "It's in Your Nature: A Pluralistic Folk Psychology," *Synthese* 165: 13–29.
Borg, E. (2007) "If Mirror Neurons are the Answer, What was the Question?" *Journal of Consciousness Studies* 14(8): 5–19.
Bunzl, M. (1994) "Meaning's Reach," *Journal for the Theory of Social Behavior* 24: 267–80.
Chenari, M. (2009) "Hermeneutics and Theory of Mind," *Phenomenology and the Cognitive Sciences* 8: 17–31.
D'oro, G. (2009), "Reclaiming the Ancestors of Simulation Theory," *History and Theory* 48: 129–39.
Downes, S. (1999) "Can Scientific Development and Children's Cognitive Development be the Same Process?" *Philosophy of Science* 66: 565–78.
Gallagher, S. (2008) "Interference or Interaction: Social Cognition without Precursors," *Philosophical Explorations* 11: 163–74.

Gallese, V. (2003) "The Manifold Nature of Interpersonal Relations: The Quest for a Common Mechanism," *Philosophical Transactions of the Royal Society of London* B 358: 517–28.

Gallese, V. and Goldman, A. (1998) "Mirror Neurons and the Simulation Theory of Mind-Reading," *Trends in Cognitive Science* 2(12): 493–501.

Goldman, A. (2006) *Simulating Minds: The Philosophy, Psychology, and Neuroscience of Mind Reading*. New York: Oxford University Press.

Goldman, A. (2009) "Mirroring, Simulating and Mindreading," *Mind and Language* 24: 235–52.

Gopnik, A. (1996) "The Scientist as Child," *Philosophy of Science* 63: 485–514.

Gopnik, A. (2003) "The Theory Theory as an Alternative to the Innateness Hypothesis." In L. Antony and N. Hornstein (eds.) *Chomsky and his Critics*. Oxford: Blackwell, pp. 238–54.

Gopnik, A. and Meltzoff, A. (1998) *Words, Thoughts and Theories*. Cambridge, MA: MIT Press.

Gopnik, A. and Wellman, H. (1992) "Why the Child's Theory of Mind is Really a Theory," *Mind and Language* 7: 145–71.

Jacob, P. (2008) "What do Mirror Neurons Contribute to Human Social Cognition?" *Mind and Language* 23: 190–223.

Jones, T. (1998) "Interpretive Social Science and the 'Native's Point of View': A Closer Look," *Philosophy of the Social Sciences* 28: 32–68.

McDonald, C. (2002) "Theories of Mind and the 'Commonsense View,'" *Mind and Language* 17: 467–88.

Martin, M. (1993) "Geertz and the Interpretive Approach in Anthropology," *Synthese* 97: 269–86.

Ohreen, D. (2008), "A Socio-Linguistic Approach to the Development of Folk Psychology," *Human Affairs* 18: 214–24.

Segal, D. (1999) "A Response to Jones's Critique of Interpretive Social Science," *Philosophy of the Social Sciences* 29: 306–09.

Shankman, P. (1984) "The Thick and the Thin: On the Interpretive Theoretical Program of Clifford Geertz," *Current Anthropology* 24: 261–80.

Stich, S. and Nichols, S. (1997) "Cognitive Penetrability, Rationality and Restricted Simulation," *Mind and Language* 12: 297–326.

Stich, S. and Nichols, S. (1998) "Theory Theory to the Max," *Mind and Language* 13: 421–49.

Strauss, C. and Quinn, N. (1997) *A Cognitive Theory of Cultural Meaning*. Cambridge: Cambridge University Press.

Yoshida, K. (2007) "Defending Scientific Study of the Social: Against Clifford Geertz (and his Critics)," *Philosophy of the Social Sciences* 37: 289–314.

Chapter 10

CLIFFORD GEERTZ

THICK DESCRIPTION: TOWARD AN INTERPRETIVE THEORY OF CULTURE

I

IN HER BOOK, *Philosophy in a New Key*, Susanne Langer remarks that certain ideas burst upon the intellectual landscape with a tremendous force. They resolve so many fundamental problems at once that they seem also to promise that they will resolve all fundamental problems, clarify all obscure issues. Everyone snaps them up as the open sesame of some new positive science, the conceptual center-point around which a comprehensive system of analysis can be built. The sudden vogue of such a *grande idée*, crowding out almost everything else for a while, is due, she says, "to the fact that all sensitive and active minds turn at once to exploiting it. We try it in every connection, for every purpose, experiment with possible stretches of its strict meaning, with generalizations and derivatives."

After we have become familiar with the new idea, however, after it has become part of our general stock of theoretical concepts, our expectations are brought more into balance with its actual uses, and its excessive popularity is ended. A few zealots persist in the old key-to-the-universe view of it; but less driven thinkers settle down after a while to the problems the idea has really generated. They try to apply it and extend it where it applies and where it is capable of extension; and they desist where it does not apply or cannot be extended. It becomes, if it was, in truth, a seminal idea in the first place, a permanent and enduring part of our intellectual armory. But it no longer has the grandiose, all-promising scope, the infinite versatility of apparent application, it once had. The second law of thermodynamics, or the principle of natural selection, or the notion of unconscious motivation, or the organization of the means of production does not explain everything, not even everything human, but it still explains something; and our attention shifts to isolating just what that something is, to disentangling ourselves from a lot of pseudoscience to which, in the first flush of its celebrity, it has also given rise.

Whether or not this is, in fact, the way all centrally important scientific concepts develop, I don't know. But certainly this pattern fits the concept of culture, around which the whole discipline of anthropology arose, and whose domination that discipline has been increasingly concerned to limit, specify, focus, and contain. It is to this cutting of the culture concept down to size, therefore actually insuring its continued importance rather than undermining it, that the essays below are all, in their several ways and from their several directions, dedicated. They all argue, sometimes explicitly, more often merely through the particular analysis they develop, for a narrowed, specialized, and, so I imagine, theoretically more powerful concept of culture to replace E. B. Tylor's famous "most complex whole," which, its originative power not denied, seems to me to have reached the point where it obscures a good deal more than it reveals.

The conceptual morass into which the Tylorean kind of *pot-au-feu* theorizing about culture can lead, is evident in what is still one of the better general introductions to anthropology, Clyde Kluckhohn's *Mirror for Man*. In some twenty-seven pages of his chapter on the concept, Kluckhohn managed to define culture in turn as: (1) "the total way of life of a people"; (2) "the social legacy the individual acquires from his group"; (3) "a way of thinking, feeling, and believing"; (4) "an abstraction from behavior"; (5) a theory on the part of the anthropologist about the way in which a group of people in fact behave; (6) a "store-house of pooled learning"; (7) "a set of standardized orientations to re-current problems"; (8) "learned behavior"; (9) a mechanism for the normative regulation of behavior; (10) "a set of techniques for adjusting both to the external environment and to other men"; (11) "a precipitate of history"; and turning, perhaps in desperation, to similes, as a map, as a sieve, and as a matrix. In the face of this sort of theoretical diffusion, even a somewhat constricted and not entirely standard concept of culture, which is at least internally coherent and, more important, which has a definable argument to make is (as, to be fair, Kluckhohn himself keenly realized) an improvement. Eclecticism is self-defeating not because there is only one direction in which it is useful to move, but because there are so many: it is necessary to choose.

The concept of culture I espouse, and whose utility the essays below attempt to demonstrate, is essentially a semiotic one. Believing, with Max Weber, that man is an animal suspended in webs of significance he himself has spun, I take culture to be those webs, and the analysis of it to be therefore not an experimental science in search of law but an interpretive one in search of meaning. It is explication I am after, construing social expressions on their surface enigmatical. But this pronouncement, a doctrine in a clause, demands itself some explication.

II

Operationalism as a methodological dogma never made much sense so far as the social sciences are concerned, and except for a few rather too well-swept corners—Skinnerian behaviorism, intelligence testing, and so on—it is largely dead now. But it had, for all that, an important point to make, which, however we may feel about trying to define charisma or alienation in terms of operations, retains a certain force: if you want to understand what a science is, you should look in the first instance not at its theories or its findings, and certainly not at what its apologists say about it; you should look at what the practitioners of it do.

In anthropology, or anyway social anthropology, what the practioners do is ethnography. And it is in understanding what ethnography is, or more exactly *what doing ethnography is*, that a start can be made toward grasping what anthropological analysis amounts to as a form of knowledge. This, it must immediately be said, is not a matter of methods. From one point of view, that of the textbook, doing ethnography is establishing rapport, selecting informants, transcribing texts, taking genealogies, mapping fields, keeping a diary, and so on. But it is not these things, techniques and received procedures, that define the enterprise. What defines it is the kind of intellectual effort it is: an elaborate venture in, to borrow a notion from Gilbert Ryle, "thick description."

Ryle's discussion of "thick description" appears in two recent essays of his (now reprinted in the second volume of his *Collected Papers*) addressed to the general question of what, as he puts it, "*Le Penseur*" is doing: "Thinking and Reflecting" and "The Thinking of Thoughts." Consider, he says, two boys rapidly contracting the eyelids of their right eyes. In one, this is an involuntary twitch; in the other, a conspiratorial signal to a friend. The two movements are, as movements, identical; from an I-am-a-camera; "phenomenalistic" observation of them alone, one could not tell which was twitch and which was wink, or indeed whether both or either was twitch or wink. Yet the difference, however unphotographable, between a twitch and a wink is vast; as anyone unfortunate enough to have had the first taken for the second knows. The winker is communicating, and indeed communicating in a quite precise and special way: (1) deliberately, (2) to someone in particular, (3) to impart a particular message, (4) according to a socially established code, and (5) without cognizance of the rest of the company. As Ryle points out, the winker has not done two things, contracted his eyelids and winked, while the twitcher has done only one, contracted his eyelids. Contracting your eyelids on purpose when there exists a public code in which so doing counts as a conspiratorial signal *is* winking. That's all there is to it: a speck of behavior, a fleck of culture, and—*voilà!*—a gesture.

That, however, is just the beginning. Suppose, he continues, there is a third boy, who, "to give malicious amusement to his cronies," parodies the first boy's wink, as amateurish, clumsy, obvious, and so on. He, of course, does this in the same way the second boy winked and the first twitched: by contracting his right eyelids. Only this boy is neither winking nor twitching, he is parodying someone else's, as he takes it, laughable, attempt at winking. Here, too, a socially established code exists (he will "wink" laboriously, overobviously, perhaps adding a grimace—the usual artifices of the clown); and so also does a message. Only now it is not conspiracy but ridicule that is in the air. If the others think he is actually winking, his whole project misfires as completely, though with somewhat different results, as if they think he is twitching. One can go further: uncertain of his mimicking abilities, the would-be satirist may practice at home before the mirror, in which case he is not twitching, winking, or parodying, but rehearsing; though so far as what a camera, a radical behaviorist, or a believer in protocol sentences would record he is just rapidly contracting his right eyelids like all the others. Complexities are possible, if not practically without end, at least logically so. The original winker might, for example, actually have been fake-winking, say, to mislead outsiders into imagining there was a conspiracy afoot when there in fact was not, in which case our descriptions of what the parodist is parodying and the rehearser rehearsing of course shift accordingly. But the point is that between what Ryle calls the "thin description" of what the rehearser (parodist, winker, twitcher . . .) is doing ("rapidly contracting his right eyelids") and the "thick description" of what he is doing ("practicing a burlesque of a friend faking a wink to deceive an innocent into thinking a conspiracy is in motion") lies the object of ethnography: a stratified hierarchy of meaningful structures in terms of which twitches, winks, fake-winks, parodies, rehearsals of parodies are produced, perceived, and interpreted, and without which they would not (not even the zero-form twitches, which, *as a cultural category*, are as much nonwinks as winks are nontwitches) in fact exist, no matter what anyone did or didn't do with his eyelids.

Like so many of the little stories Oxford philosophers like to make up for themselves, all this winking, fake-winking, burlesque-fake-winking, rehearsed-burlesque-fake-winking, may seem a bit artificial. In way of adding a more empirical note, let me give, deliberately unpreceded by any prior explanatory comment at all, a not untypical excerpt from my own field journal to demonstrate that, however evened off for didactic purposes, Ryle's example presents an image only too exact of the sort of piled-up structures of inference and implication through which an ethnographer is continually trying to pick his way:

> The French [the informant said] had only just arrived. They set up twenty or so small forts between here, the town, and the Marmusha area up in the middle of the mountains, placing them on promontories so they could survey the countryside. But for all this

they couldn't guarantee safety, especially at night, so although the *mezrag*, trade-pact, system was supposed to be legally abolished it in fact continued as before.

One night, when Cohen (who speaks fluent Berber), was up there, at Marmusha, two other Jews who were traders to a neighboring tribe came by to purchase some goods from him. Some Berbers, from yet another neighboring tribe, tried to break into Cohen's place, but he fired his rifle in the air. (Traditionally, Jews were not allowed to carry weapons; but at this period things were so unsettled many did so anyway.) This attracted the attention of the French and the marauders fled.

The next night, however, they came back, one of them disguised as a woman who knocked on the door with some sort of a story. Cohen was suspicious and didn't want to let "her" in, but the other Jews said, "oh, it's all right, it's only a woman." So they opened the door and the whole lot came pouring in. They killed the two visiting Jews, but Cohen managed to barricade himself in an adjoining room. He heard the robbers planning to burn him alive in the shop after they removed his goods, and so he opened the door and, laying about him wildly with a club, managed to escape through a window.

He went up to the fort, then, to have his wounds dressed, and complained to the local commandant, one Captain Dumari, saying he wanted his 'ar—i.e., four or five times the value of the merchandise stolen from him. The robbers were from a tribe which had not yet submitted to French authority and were in open rebellion against it, and he wanted authorization to go with his *mezrag*-holder, the Marmusha tribal *sheikh*, to collect the indemnity that, under traditional rules, he had coming to him. Captain Dumari couldn't officially give him permission to do this, because of the French prohibition of the *mezrag* relationship, but he gave him verbal authorization, saying, "If you get killed, it's your problem."

So the *sheikh*, the Jew, and a small company of armed Marmushans went off ten or fifteen kilometers up into the rebellious area, where there were of course no French, and, sneaking up, captured the thief-tribe's shepherd and stole its herds. The other tribe soon came riding out on horses after them, armed with rifles and ready to attack. But when they saw who the "sheep thieves" were, they thought better of it and said, "all right, we'll talk." They couldn't really deny what had happened—that some of their men had robbed Cohen and killed the two visitors—and they weren't prepared to start the serious feud with the Marmusha a scuffle with the invading party would bring on. So the two groups talked, and talked, and talked, there on the plain amid the thousands of sheep, and decided finally on five-hundred-sheep damages. The two armed Berber groups then lined up on their horses at opposite ends of the plain, with the sheep herded between them, and Cohen, in his black gown, pillbox hat, and flapping slippers, went out alone among the sheep, picking out, one by one and at his own good speed, the best ones for his payment.

So Cohen got his sheep and drove them back to Marmusha. The French, up in their fort, heard them coming from some distance ("Ba, ba, ba" said Cohen, happily, recalling the image) and said, "What the hell is that?" And Cohen said, "That is my 'ar." The French couldn't believe he had actually done what he said he had done, and accused him of being a spy for the rebellious Berbers, put him in prison, and took his sheep. In the town, his family, not having heard from him in so long a time, thought he was dead. But after a while the French released him and he came back home, but without his sheep. He then went to the Colonel in the town, the Frenchman in charge of the whole region, to complain. But the Colonel said, "I can't do anything about the matter. It's not my problem."

Quoted raw, a note in a bottle, this passage conveys, as any similar one similarly presented would do, a fair sense of how much goes into ethnographic description of even the most elemental sort—how extraordinarily "thick" it is. In finished anthropological writings, including those collected here, this fact—that what we call our data are really our own constructions of other people's constructions of what they and their compatriots are up to—is obscured because most of what we need to comprehend a particular event, ritual, custom, idea, or whatever is insinuated as background information before the thing itself is directly examined. (Even to reveal that this little drama took place in the highlands of central Morocco in 1912— and was recounted there in 1968—is to determine much of our understanding of it.) There is nothing particularly wrong with this, and it is in any case inevitable. But it does lead to a view of anthropological research as rather more of an observational and rather less of an inter- pretive activity than it really is. Right down at the factual base, the hard rock, insofar as there is any, of the whole enterprise, we are already explicating: and worse, explicating explica- tions. Winks upon winks upon winks.

Analysis, then, is sorting out the structures of signification—what Ryle called established codes, a somewhat misleading expression, for it makes the enterprise sound too much like that of the cipher clerk when it is much more like that of the literary critic—and determining their social ground and import. Here, in our text, such sorting would begin with distinguishing the three unlike frames of interpretation ingredient in the situation, Jewish, Berber, and French, and would then move on to show how (and why) at that time, in that place, their copresence produced a situation in which systematic misunderstanding reduced traditional form to social farce. What tripped Cohen up, and with him the whole, ancient pattern of social and economic relationships within which he functioned, was a confusion of tongues.

I shall come back to this too-compacted aphorism later, as well as to the details of the text itself. The point for now is only that ethnography is thick description. What the ethnog- rapher is in fact faced with—except when (as, of course, he must do) he is pursuing the more automatized routines of data collection—is a multiplicity of complex conceptual structures, many of them superimposed upon or knotted into one another, which are at once strange, irregular, and inexplicit, and which he must contrive somehow first to grasp and then to render. And this is true at the most down-to-earth, jungle field work levels of his activity: interviewing informants, observing rituals, eliciting kin terms, tracing property lines, censusing households . . . writing his journal. Doing ethnography is like trying to read (in the sense of "construct a reading of") a manuscript—foreign, faded, full of ellipses, incoherencies, suspicious emendations, and tendentious commentaries, but written not in conventionalized graphs of sound but in transient examples of shaped behavior.

III

Culture, this acted document, thus is public, like a burlesqued wink or a mock sheep raid. Though ideational, it does not exist in someone's head; though unphysical, it is not an occult entity. The interminable, because unterminable, debate within anthropology as to whether culture is "subjective" or "objective," together with the mutual exchange of intellectual insults ("idealist!"—"materialist!"; "mentalist!"—"behaviorist!"; "impressionist!"—"positivist!") which accompanies it, is wholly misconceived. Once human behavior is seen as (most of the time; there *are* true twitches) symbolic action—action which, like phonation in speech, pigment in painting, line in writing, or sonance in music, signifies—the question as to whether culture is patterned conduct or a frame of mind, or even the two somehow mixed together, loses sense. The thing to ask about a burlesqued wink or a mock sheep raid is not what their

ontological status is. It is the same as that of rocks on the one hand and dreams on the other—
they are things of this world. The thing to ask is what their import is: what it is, ridicule or
challenge, irony or anger, snobbery or pride, that, in their occurrence and through their agency,
is getting said.

This may seem like an obvious truth, but there are a number of ways to obscure it. One
is to imagine that culture is a self-contained "superorganic" reality with forces and purposes
of its own; that is, to reify it. Another is to claim that it consists in the brute pattern of
behavioral events we observe in fact to occur in some identifiable community or other; that
is, to reduce it. But though both these confusions still exist, and doubtless will be always with
us, the main source of theoretical muddlement in contemporary anthropology is a view which
developed in reaction to them and is right now very widely held—namely, that, to quote
Ward Goodenough, perhaps its leading proponent, "culture [is located] in the minds and hearts
of men."

Variously called ethnoscience, componential analysis, or cognitive anthropology (a terminological wavering which reflects a deeper uncertainty), this school of thought holds that culture
is composed of psychological structures by means of which individuals or groups of individuals
guide their behavior. "A society's culture," to quote Goodenough again, this time in a passage
which has become the *locus classicus* of the whole movement, "consists of whatever it is one
has to know or believe in order to operate in a manner acceptable to its members." And from
this view of what culture is follows a view, equally assured, of what describing it is—the
writing out of systematic rules, an ethnographic algorithm, which, if followed, would make
it possible so to operate, to pass (physical appearance aside) for a native. In such a way, extreme
subjectivism is married to extreme formalism, with the expected result: an explosion of debate
as to whether particular analyses (which come in the form of taxonomies, paradigms, tables,
trees, and other ingenuities) reflect what the natives "really" think or are merely clever
simulations, logically equivalent but substantively different, of what they think.

As, on first glance, this approach may look close enough to the one being developed here
to be mistaken for it, it is useful to be explicit as to what divides them. If, leaving our winks
and sheep behind for the moment, we take, say, a Beethoven quartet as an, admittedly rather
special but, for these purposes, nicely illustrative, sample of culture, no one would, I think,
identify it with its score, with the skills and knowledge needed to play it, with the understanding
of it possessed by its performers or auditors, nor, to take care, *en passant*, of the reductionists
and reifiers, with a particular performance of it or with some mysterious entity transcending
material existence. The "no one" is perhaps too strong here, for there are always incorrigibles.
But that a Beethoven quartet is a temporally developed tonal structure, a coherent sequence
of modeled sound—in a word, music—and not anybody's knowledge of or belief about anything,
including how to play it, is a proposition to which most people are, upon reflection, likely to
assent.

To play the violin it is necessary to possess certain habits, skills, knowledge, and talents,
to be in the mood to play, and (as the old joke goes) to have a violin. But violin playing is
neither the habits, skills, knowledge, and so on, nor the mood, nor (the notion believers in
"material culture" apparently embrace) the violin. To make a trade pact in Morocco, you have
to do certain things in certain ways (among others, cut, while chanting Quranic Arabic, the
throat of a lamb before the assembled, undeformed, adult male members of your tribe) and
to be possessed of certain psychological characteristics (among others, a desire for distant
things). But a trade pact is neither the throat cutting nor the desire, though it is real enough,
as seven kinsmen of our Marmusha sheikh discovered when, on an earlier occasion, they were
executed by him following the theft of one mangy, essentially valueless sheepskin from Cohen.

Culture is public because meaning is. You can't wink (or burlesque one) without knowing what counts as winking or how, physically, to contract your eyelids, and you can't conduct a sheep raid (or mimic one) without knowing what it is to steal a sheep and how practically to go about it. But to draw from such truths the conclusion that knowing how to wink is winking and knowing how to steal a sheep is sheep raiding is to betray as deep a confusion as, taking thin descriptions for thick, to identify winking with eyelid contractions or sheep raiding with chasing woolly animals out of pastures. The cognitivist fallacy—that culture consists (to quote another spokesman for the movement, Stephen Tyler) of "mental phenomena which can [he means "should"] be analyzed by formal methods similar to those of mathematics and logic"— is as destructive of an effective use of the concept as are the behaviorist and idealist fallacies to which it is a misdrawn correction. Perhaps, as its errors are more sophisticated and its distortions subtler, it is even more so.

The generalized attack on privacy theories of meaning is, since early Husserl and late Wittgenstein, so much a part of modern thought that it need not be developed once more here. What is necessary is to see to it that the news of it reaches anthropology; and in particular that it is made clear that to say that culture consists of socially established structures of meaning in terms of which people do such things as signal conspiracies and join them or perceive insults and answer them, is no more to say that it is a psychological phenomenon, a characteristic of someone's mind, personality, cognitive structure, or whatever, than to say that Tantrism, genetics, the progressive form of the verb, the classification of wines, the Common Law, or the notion of "a conditional curse" (as Westermarck defined the concept of 'ar in terms of which Cohen pressed his claim to damages) is. What, in a place like Morocco, most prevents those of us who grew up winking other winks or attending other sheep from grasping what people are up to is not ignorance as to how cognition works (though, especially as, one assumes, it works the same among them as it does among us, it would greatly help to have less of that too) as a lack of familiarity with the imaginative universe within which their acts are signs. As Wittgenstein has been invoked, he may as well be quoted:

> We . . . say of some people that they are transparent to us. It is, however, important as regards this observation that one human being can be a complete enigma to another. We learn this when we come into a strange country with entirely strange traditions; and, what is more, even given a mastery of the country's language. We do not *understand* the people. (And not because of not knowing what they are saying to themselves.) We cannot find our feet with them.

IV

Finding our feet, an unnerving business which never more than distantly succeeds, is what ethnographic research consists of as a personal experience; trying to formulate the basis on which one imagines, always excessively, one has found them is what anthropological writing consists of as a scientific endeavor. We are not, or at least I am not, seeking either to become natives (a compromised word in any case) or to mimic them. Only romantics or spies would seem to find point in that. We are seeking, in the widened sense of the term in which it encompasses very much more than talk, to converse with them, a matter a great deal more difficult, and not only with strangers, than is commonly recognized. "If speaking *for* someone else seems to be a mysterious process," Stanley Cavell has remarked, "that may be because speaking *to* someone does not seem mysterious enough."

Looked at in this way, the aim of anthropology is the enlargement of the universe of human discourse. That is not, of course, its only aim—instruction, amusement, practical counsel, moral advance, and the discovery of natural order in human behavior are others; nor is anthropology the only discipline which pursues it. But it is an aim to which a semiotic concept of culture is peculiarly well adapted. As interworked systems of construable signs (what, ignoring provincial usages, I would call symbols), culture is not a power, something to which social events, behaviors, institutions, or processes can be causally attributed; it is a context, something within which they can be intelligibly—that is, thickly—described.

The famous anthropological absorption with the (to us) exotic—Berber horsemen, Jewish peddlers, French Legionnaires—is, thus, essentially a device for displacing the dulling sense of familiarity with which the mysteriousness of our own ability to relate perceptively to one another is concealed from us. Looking at the ordinary in places where it takes unaccustomed forms brings out not, as has so often been claimed, the arbitrariness of human behavior (there is nothing especially arbitrary about taking sheep theft for insolence in Morocco), but the degree to which its meaning varies according to the pattern of life by which it is informed. Understanding a people's culture exposes their normalness without reducing their particularity. (The more I manage to follow what the Moroccans are up to, the more logical, and the more singular, they seem.) It renders them accessible: setting them in the frame of their own banalities, it dissolves their opacity.

It is this maneuver, usually too casually referred to as "seeing things from the actor's point of view," too bookishly as "the *verstehen* approach," or too technically as "emic analysis," that so often leads to the notion that anthropology is a variety of either long-distance mind reading or cannibal-isle fantasizing, and which, for someone anxious to navigate past the wrecks of a dozen sunken philosophies, must therefore be executed with a great deal of care. Nothing is more necessary to comprehending what anthropological interpretation is, and the degree to which it, *is* interpretation, than an exact understanding of what it means—and what it does not mean— to say that our formulations of other peoples' symbol systems must be actor-oriented.

What it means is that descriptions of Berber, Jewish, or French culture must be cast in terms of the constructions we imagine Berbers, Jews, or Frenchmen to place upon what they live through, the formulae they use to define what happens to them. What it does not mean is that such descriptions are themselves Berber, Jewish, or French—that is, part of the reality they are ostensibly describing; they are anthropological—that is, part of a developing system of scientific analysis. They must be cast in terms of the interpretations to which persons of a particular denomination subject their experience, because that is what they profess to be descriptions of; they are anthropological because it is, in fact, anthropologists who profess them. Normally, it is not necessary to point out quite so laboriously that the object of study is one thing and the study of it another. It is clear enough that the physical world is not physics and *A Skeleton Key to Finnegan's Wake* not *Finnegan's Wake*. But, as, in the study of culture, analysis penetrates into the very body of the object—that is, *we begin with our own interpretations of what our informants are up to, or think they are up to, and then systematize those*—the line between (Moroccan) culture as a natural fact and (Moroccan) culture as a theoretical entity tends to get blurred. All the more so, as the latter is presented in the form of an actor's-eye description of (Moroccan) conceptions of everything from violence, honor, divinity, and justice, to tribe, property, patronage, and chiefship.

In short, anthropological writings are themselves interpretations, and second and third order ones to boot. (By definition, only a "native" makes first order ones: it's *his* culture.) They are, thus, fictions; fictions, in the sense that they are "something made," "something fashioned"—the original meaning of *fictiō*—not that they are false, unfactual, or merely "as if" thought experiments. To construct actor-oriented descriptions of the involvements of a Berber chieftain, a Jewish merchant, and a French soldier with one another in 1912 Morocco is clearly an imaginative act, not all that different from constructing similar descriptions of, say, the involvements with one another of a provincial French doctor, his silly, adulterous wife, and her feckless lover in nineteenth century France. In the latter case, the actors are represented as not having existed and the events as not having happened, while in the former they are represented as actual, or as having been so. This is a difference of no mean importance; indeed, precisely the one Madame Bovary had difficulty grasping. But the importance does not lie in the fact that her story was created while Cohen's was only noted. The conditions of their creation, and the point of it (to say nothing of the manner and the quality) differ. But the one is as much a *fictiō*—"a making"—as the other.

Anthropologists have not always been as aware as they might be of this fact: that although culture exists in the trading post, the hill fort, or the sheep run, anthropology exists in the book, the article, the lecture, the museum display, or, sometimes nowadays, the film. To become aware of it is to realize that the line between mode of representation and substantive content is as undrawable in cultural analysis as it is in painting; and that fact in turn seems to threaten the objective status of anthropological knowledge by suggesting that its source is not social reality but scholarly artifice.

It does threaten it, but the threat is hollow. The claim to attention of an ethnographic account does not rest on its author's ability to capture primitive facts in faraway places and carry them home like a mask or a carving, but on the degree to which he is able to clarify what goes on in such places, to reduce the puzzlement—what manner of men are these?—to which unfamiliar acts emerging out of unknown backgrounds naturally give rise. This raises some serious problems of verification, all right—or, if "verification" is too strong a word for so soft a science (I, myself, would prefer "appraisal"), of how you can tell a better account from a worse one. But that is precisely the virtue of it. If ethnography is thick description and ethnographers those who are doing the describing, then the determining question for any given example of it, whether a field journal squib or a Malinowski-sized monograph, is whether it sorts winks from twitches and real winks from mimicked ones. It is not against a body of uninterpreted data, radically thinned descriptions, that we must measure the cogency of our explications, but against the power of the scientific imagination to bring us into touch with the lives of strangers. It is not worth it, as Thoreau said, to go round the world to count the cats in Zanzibar.

V

Now, this proposition, that it is not in our interest to bleach human behavior of the very properties that interest us before we begin to examine it, has sometimes been escalated into a larger claim: namely, that as it is only those properties that interest us, we need not attend, save cursorily, to behavior at all. Culture is most effectively treated, the argument goes, purely as a symbolic system (the catch phrase is, "in its own terms"), by isolating its elements, specifying the internal relationships among those elements, and then characterizing the whole system in some general way—according to the core symbols around which it is organized, the underlying structures of which it is a surface expression, or the ideological principles upon which it is based. Though a distinct improvement over "learned behavior" and "mental phenomena" notions of what culture is, and the source of some of the most powerful theoretical ideas in contemporary anthropology, this hermetical approach to things seems to me to run the danger (and increasingly to have been overtaken by it) of locking cultural analysis away from its proper object, the informal logic of actual life. There is little profit in extricating a concept from the defects of psychologism only to plunge it immediately into those of schematicism.

Behavior must be attended to, and with some exactness, because it is through the flow of behavior—or, more precisely, social action—that cultural forms find articulation. They find it as well, of course, in various sorts of artifacts, and various states of consciousness; but these draw their meaning from the role they play (Wittgenstein would say their "use") in an ongoing pattern of life, not from any intrinsic relationships they bear to one another. It is what Cohen, the sheikh, and "Captain Dumari" were doing when they tripped over one another's purposes—pursuing trade, defending honor, establishing dominance—that created our pastoral drama, and that is what the drama is, therefore, "about." Whatever, or wherever, symbol systems "in their own terms" may be, we gain empirical access to them by inspecting events, not by arranging abstracted entities into unified patterns.

A further implication of this is that coherence cannot be the major test of validity for a cultural description. Cultural systems must have a minimal degree of coherence, else we would not call them systems; and, by observation, they normally have a great deal more. But there is nothing so coherent as a paranoid's delusion or a swindler's story. The force of our interpretations cannot rest, as they are now so often made to do, on the tightness with which they hold together, or the assurance with which they are argued. Nothing has done more, I think, to discredit cultural analysis than the construction of impeccable depictions of formal order in whose actual existence nobody can quite believe.

If anthropological interpretation is constructing a reading of what happens, then to divorce it from what happens—from what, in this time or that place, specific people say, what they do, what is done to them, from the whole vast business of the world—is to divorce it from its applications and render it vacant. A good interpretation of anything—a poem, a person, a history, a ritual, an institution, a society—takes us into the heart of that of which it is the interpretation. When it does not do that, but leads us instead somewhere else—into an admiration of its own elegance, of its author's cleverness, or of the beauties of Euclidean order—it may have its intrinsic charms; but it is something else than what the task at hand—figuring out what all that rigamarole with the sheep is about—calls for.

The rigamarole with the sheep—the sham theft of them, the reparative transfer of them, the political confiscation of them—is (or was) essentially a social discourse, even if, as I suggested earlier, one conducted in multiple tongues and as much in action as in words.

Claiming his 'ar, Cohen invoked the trade pact; recognizing the claim, the sheikh challenged the offenders' tribe; accepting responsibility, the offenders' tribe paid the indemnity; anxious to make clear to sheikhs and peddlers alike who was now in charge here, the French showed the imperial hand. As in any discourse, code does not determine conduct, and what was actually said need not have been. Cohen might not have, given its illegitimacy in Protectorate eyes, chosen to press his claim. The sheikh might, for similar reasons, have rejected it. The offenders' tribe, still resisting French authority, might have decided to regard the raid as "real" and fight rather than negotiate. The French, were they more *habile* and less *dur* (as, under Mareschal Lyautey's seigniorial tutelage, they later in fact became), might have permitted Cohen to keep his sheep, winking—as we say—at the continuance of the trade pattern and its limitation to their authority. And there are other possibilities: the Marmushans might have regarded the French action as too great an insult to bear and gone into dissidence themselves; the French might have attempted not just to clamp down on Cohen but to bring the sheikh himself more closely to heel; and Cohen might have concluded that between renegade Berbers and Beau Geste soldiers, driving trade in the Atlas highlands was no longer worth the candle and retired to the better-governed confines of the town. This, indeed, is more or less what happened, somewhat further along, as the Protectorate moved toward genuine sovereignty. But the point here is not to describe what did or did not take place in Morocco. (From this simple incident one can widen out into enormous complexities of social experience.) It is to demonstrate what a piece of anthropological interpretation consists in: tracing the curve of a social discourse; fixing it into an inspectable form.

The ethnographer "inscribes" social discourse; *he writes it down*. In so doing, he turns it from a passing event, which exists only in its own moment of occurrence, into an account, which exists in its inscriptions and can be reconsulted. The sheikh is long dead, killed in the process of being, as the French called it, "pacified"; "Captain Dumari," his pacifier, lives, retired to his souvenirs, in the south of France; and Cohen went last year, part refugee, part pilgrim, part dying patriarch, "home" to Israel. But what they, in my extended sense, "said" to one another on an Atlas plateau sixty years ago is—very far from perfectly—preserved for study. "What," Paul Ricoeur, from whom this whole idea of the inscription of action is borrowed and somewhat twisted, asks, "what does writing fix?"

> Not the event of speaking, but the "said" of speaking, where we understand by the "said" of speaking that intentional exteriorization constitutive of the aim of discourse thanks to which the *sagen*—the saying—wants to become *Aus-sage*—the enunciation, the enunciated. In short, what we write is the *noema* ["thought," "content," "gist"] of the speaking. It is the meaning of the speech event, not the event as event.

This is not itself so very "said"—if Oxford philosophers run to little stories, phenomeno-logical ones run to large sentences; but it brings us anyway to a more precise answer to our generative question, "What does the ethnographer do?"—he writes. This, too, may seem a less than startling discovery, and to someone familiar with the current "literature," an implausible one. But as the standard answer to our question has been, "He observes, he records, he analyzes"—a kind of *veni, vidi, vici* conception of the matter—it may have more deep-going consequences than are at first apparent, not the least of which is that distinguishing these three phases of knowledge-seeking may not, as a matter of fact, normally be possible; and, indeed, as autonomous "operations" they may not in fact exist.

The situation is even more delicate, because, as already noted, what we inscribe (or try to) is not raw social discourse, to which, because, save very marginally or very specially, we are not actors, we do not have direct access, but only that small part of it which our informants can lead us into understanding. This is not as fatal as it sounds, for, in fact, not all Cretans are liars, and it is not necessary to know everything in order to understand something. But it does make the view of anthropological analysis as the conceptual manipulation of discovered facts, a logical reconstruction of a mere reality, seem rather lame. To set forth symmetrical crystals of significance, purified of the material complexity in which they were located, and then attribute their existence to autogenous principles of order, universal properties of the human mind, or vast, a priori *weltanschauungen*, is to pretend a science that does not exist and imagine a reality that cannot be found. Cultural analysis is (or should be) guessing at meanings, assessing the guesses, and drawing explanatory conclusions from the better guesses, not discovering the Continent of Meaning and mapping out its bodiless landscape.

VI

So, there are three characteristics of ethnographic description: it is interpretive; what it is interpretive of is the flow of social discourse; and the interpreting involved consists in trying to rescue the "said" of such discourse from its perishing occasions and fix it in perusable terms.

The *kula* is gone or altered; but, for better or worse, *The Argonauts of the Western Pacific* remains. But there is, in addition, a fourth characteristic of such description, at least as I practice it: it is microscopic.

This is not to say that there are no large-scale anthropological interpretations of whole societies, civilizations, world events, and so on. Indeed, it is such extension of our analyses to wider contexts that, along with their theoretical implications, recommends them to general attention and justifies our constructing them. No one really cares anymore, not even Cohen (well . . . maybe, Cohen), about those sheep as such. History may have its unobtrusive turning points, "great noises in a little room"; but this little go-round was surely not one of them.

It is merely to say that the anthropologist characteristically approaches such broader interpretations and more abstract analyses from the direction of exceedingly extended acquaintances with extremely small matters. He confronts the same grand realities that others—historians, economists, political scientists, sociologists—confront in more fateful settings: Power, Change, Faith, Oppression, Work, Passion, Authority, Beauty, Violence, Love, Prestige; but he confronts them in contexts obscure enough—places like Marmusha and lives like Cohen's—to take the capital letters off them. These all-too-human constancies, "those big words that make us all afraid," take a homely form in such homely contexts. But that is exactly the advantage. There are enough profundities in the world already.

Yet, the problem of how to get from a collection of ethnographic miniatures on the order of our sheep story—an assortment of remarks and anecdotes—to wall-sized culturescapes of the nation, the epoch, the continent, or the civilization is not so easily passed over with vague allusions to the virtues of concreteness and the down-to-earth mind. For a science born in Indian tribes, Pacific islands, and African lineages and subsequently seized with grander ambitions, this has come to be a major methodological problem, and for the most part a badly handled one. The models that anthropologists have themselves worked out to justify their moving from local truths to general visions have been, in fact, as responsible for undermining the effort as anything their critics—sociologists obsessed with sample sizes, psychologists with measures, or economists with aggregates—have been able to devise against them.

Of these, the two main ones have been: the Jonesville-is-the-USA "microcosmic" model; and the Easter-Island-is-a-testing-case "natural experiment" model. Either heaven in a grain of sand, or the farther shores of possibility.

The Jonesville-is-America writ small (or America-is-Jonesville writ large) fallacy is so obviously one that the only thing that needs explanation is how people have managed to believe it and expected others to believe it. The notion that one can find the essence of national societies, civilizations, great religions, or whatever summed up and simplified in so-called "typical" small towns and villages is palpable nonsense. What one finds in small towns and villages is (alas) small-town or village life. If localized, microscopic studies were really dependent for their greater relevance upon such a premise—that they captured the great world in the little—they wouldn't have any relevance.

But, of course, they are not. The locus of study is not the object of study. Anthropologists don't study villages (tribes, towns, neighborhoods . . .); they study *in* villages. You can study different things in different places, and some things—for example, what colonial domination does to established frames of moral expectation—you can best study in confined localities. But that doesn't make the place what it is you are studying. In the remoter provinces of Morocco and Indonesia I have wrestled with the same questions other social scientists have wrestled with in more central locations—for example, how comes it that men's most importunate claims to humanity are cast in the accents of group pride?—and with about the same conclusiveness. One can add a dimension—one much needed in the present climate of size-up-and-solve social science; but that is all. There is a certain value, if you are going to run on about the exploitation of the masses in having seen a Javanese sharecropper turning earth in a tropical downpour or a Moroccan tailor embroidering kaftans by the light of a twenty-watt bulb. But the notion that this gives you the thing entire (and elevates you to some moral vantage ground from which you can look down upon the ethically less privileged) is an idea which only someone too long in the bush could possibly entertain.

The "natural laboratory" notion has been equally pernicious, not only because the analogy is false—what kind of a laboratory is it where *none* of the parameters are manipulable?—but because it leads to a notion that the data derived from ethnographic studies are purer, or more fundamental, or more solid, or less conditioned (the most favored word is "elementary") than those derived from other sorts of social inquiry. The great natural variation of cultural forms is, of course, not only anthropology's great (and wasting) resource, but the ground of its deepest theoretical dilemma: how is such variation to be squared with the biological unity of the human species? But it is not, even metaphorically, experimental variation, because the context in which it occurs varies along with it, and it is not possible (though there are those who try) to isolate the y's from x's to write a proper function.

The famous studies purporting to show that the Oedipus complex was backwards in the Trobriands, sex roles were upside down in Tchambuli, and the Pueblo Indians lacked aggression (it is characteristic that they were all negative—"but not in the South"), are, whatever their empirical validity may or may not be, not "scientifically tested and approved" hypotheses. They are interpretations, or misinterpretations, like any others, arrived at in the same way as any others, and as inherently inconclusive as any others, and the attempt to invest them with the authority of physical experimentation is but methodological sleight of hand. Ethnographic findings are not privileged, just particular: another country heard from. To regard them as anything more (*or anything less*) than that distorts both them and their implications, which are far profounder than mere primitivity, for social theory.

Another country heard from: the reason that protracted descriptions of distant sheep raids (and a really good ethnographer would have gone into what kind of sheep they were) have general relevance is that they present the sociological mind with bodied stuff on which to feed. The important thing about the anthropologist's findings is their complex specificness, their circumstantiality. It is with the kind of material produced by long-term, mainly (though not exclusively) qualitative, highly participative, and almost obsessively fine-comb field study in confined contexts that the mega-concepts with which contemporary social science is afflicted— legitimacy, modernization, integration, conflict, charisma, structure, . . . meaning—can be given the sort of sensible actuality that makes it possible to think not only realistically and concretely *about* them, but, what is more important, creatively and imaginatively *with* them.

The methodological problem which the microscopic nature of ethnography presents is both real and critical. But it is not to be resolved by regarding a remote locality as the world in a teacup or as the sociological equivalent of a cloud chamber. It is to be resolved—or, anyway, decently kept at bay—by realizing that social actions are comments on more than themselves; that where an interpretation comes from does not determine where it can be impelled to go. Small facts speak to large issues, winks to epistemology, or sheep raids to revolution, because they are made to.

VII

Which brings us, finally, to theory. The besetting sin of interpretive approaches to anything— literature, dreams, symptoms, culture—is that they tend to resist, or to be permitted to resist, conceptual articulation and thus to escape systematic modes of assessment. You either grasp an interpretation or you do not, see the point of it or you do not, accept it or you do not. Imprisoned in the immediacy of its own detail, it is presented as self-validating, or, worse, as validated by the supposedly developed sensitivities of the person who presents it; any attempt to cast what it says in terms other than its own is regarded as a travesty—as, the anthropologist's severest term of moral abuse, ethnocentric.

For a field of study which, however timidly (though I, myself, am not timid about the matter at all), asserts itself to be a science, this just will not do. There is no reason why the conceptual structure of a cultural interpretation should be any less formulable, and thus less susceptible to explicit canons of appraisal, than that of, say, a biological observation or a physical experiment—no reason except that the terms in which such formulations can be cast are, if not wholly nonexistent, very nearly so. We are reduced to insinuating theories because we lack the power to state them.

At the same time, it must be admitted that there are a number of characteristics of cultural interpretation which make the theoretical development of it more than usually difficult. The first is the need for theory to stay rather closer to the ground than tends to be the case in sciences more able to give themselves over to imaginative abstraction. Only short flights of ratiocination tend to be effective in anthropology; longer ones tend to drift off into logical dreams, academic bemusements with formal symmetry. The whole point of a semiotic approach to culture is, as I have said, to aid us in gaining access to the conceptual world in which our subjects live so that we can, in some extended sense of the term, converse with them. The tension between the pull of this need to penetrate an unfamiliar universe of symbolic action and the requirements of technical advance in the theory of culture, between the need to grasp and the need to analyze, is, as a result, both necessarily great and essentially irremovable. Indeed, the further theoretical development goes, the deeper the tension gets. This is the first condition for cultural theory: it is not its own master. As it is unseverable from the immediacies thick description presents, its freedom to shape itself in terms of its internal logic is rather limited. What generality it contrives to achieve grows out of the delicacy of its distinctions, not the sweep of its abstractions.

And from this follows a peculiarity in the way, as a simple matter of empirical fact, our knowledge of culture . . . cultures . . . a culture . . . grows: in spurts. Rather than following a rising curve of cumulative findings, cultural analysis breaks up into a disconnected yet coherent sequence of bolder and bolder sorties. Studies do build on other studies, not in the sense that they take up where the others leave off, but in the sense that, better informed and better conceptualized, they plunge more deeply into the same things. Every serious cultural analysis starts from a sheer beginning and ends where it manages to get before exhausting its intellectual impulse. Previously discovered facts are mobilized, previously developed concepts used, previously formulated hypotheses tried out; but the movement is not from already proven theorems to newly proven ones, it is from an awkward fumbling for the most elementary understanding to a supported claim that one has achieved that and surpassed it. A study is an advance if it is more incisive—whatever that may mean—than those that preceded it; but it less stands on their shoulders than, challenged and challenging, runs by their side.

It is for this reason, among others, that the essay, whether of thirty pages or three hundred, has seemed the natural genre in which to present cultural interpretations and the theories sustaining them, and why, if one looks for systematic treatises in the field, one is so soon disappointed, the more so if one finds any. Even inventory articles are rare here, and anyway of hardly more than bibliographical interest. The major theoretical contributions not only lie in specific studies—that is true in almost any field—but they are very difficult to abstract from such studies and integrate into anything one might call "culture theory" as such. Theoretical formulations hover so low over the interpretations they govern that they don't make much sense or hold much interest apart from them. This is so, not because they are not general (if they are not general, they are not theoretical), but because, stated independently of their applications, they seem either commonplace or vacant. One can, and this in fact is how the field progresses conceptually, take a line of theoretical attack developed in connection with one exercise in ethnographic interpretation and employ it in another, pushing it forward to greater precision and broader relevance; but one cannot write a "General Theory of Cultural Interpretation." Or, rather, one can, but there appears to be little profit in it, because the essential task of theory building here is not to codify abstract regularities but to make thick description possible, not to generalize across cases but to generalize within them.

To generalize within cases is usually called, at least in medicine and depth psychology, clinical inference. Rather than beginning with a set of observations and attempting to subsume them under a governing law, such inference begins with a set of (presumptive) signifiers and attempts to place them within an intelligible frame. Measures are matched to theoretical predictions, but symptoms (even when they are measured) are scanned for theoretical peculiarities—that is, they are diagnosed. In the study of culture the signifiers are not symptoms or clusters of symptoms, but symbolic acts or clusters of symbolic acts, and the aim is not therapy but the analysis of social discourse. But the way in which theory is used—to ferret out the unapparent import of things—is the same.

Thus we are lead to the second condition of cultural theory: it is not, at least in the strict meaning of the term, predictive. The diagnostician doesn't predict measles; he decides that someone has them, or at the very most *anticipates* that someone is rather likely shortly to get them. But this limitation, which is real enough, has commonly been both misunderstood and exaggerated, because it has been taken to mean that cultural interpretation is merely post facto: that, like the peasant in the old story, we first shoot the holes in the fence and then paint the bull's-eyes around them. It is hardly to be denied that there is a good deal of that sort of thing around, some of it in prominent places. It is to be denied, however, that it is the inevitable outcome of a clinical approach to the use of theory.

It is true that in the clinical style of theoretical formulation, conceptualization is directed toward the task of generating interpretations of matters already in hand, not toward projecting outcomes of experimental manipulations or deducing future states of a determined system. But that does not mean that theory has only to fit (or, more carefully, to generate cogent interpretations of) realities past; it has also to survive—intellectually survive—realities to come. Although we formulate our interpretation of an outburst of winking or an instance of sheep-raiding after its occurrence, sometimes long after, the theoretical framework in terms of which such an interpretation is made must be capable of continuing to yield defensible interpretations as new social phenomena swim into view. Although one starts any effort at thick description, beyond the obvious and superficial, from a state of general bewilderment as to what the devil is going on—trying to find one's feet—one does not start (or ought not) intellectually empty-handed. Theoretical ideas are not created wholly anew in each study; as I have said, they are adopted from other, related studies, and, refined in the process, applied to new interpretive problems. If they cease being useful with respect to such problems, they tend to stop being used and are more or less abandoned. If they continue being useful, throwing up new understandings, they are further elaborated and go on being used.

Such a view of how theory functions in an interpretive science suggests that the distinction, relative in any case, that appears in the experimental or observational sciences between "description" and "explanation" appears here as one, even more relative, between "inscription" ("thick description") and "specification" ("diagnosis")—between setting down the meaning particular social actions have for the actors whose actions they are, and stating, as explicitly as we can manage, what the knowledge thus attained demonstrates about the society in which it is found and, beyond that, about social life as such. Our double task is to uncover the conceptual structures that inform our subjects' acts, the "said" of social discourse, and to construct a system of analysis in whose terms what is generic to those structures, what belongs to them because they are what they are, will stand out against the other determinants of human behavior. In ethnography, the office of theory is to provide a vocabulary in which what symbolic action has to say about itself—that is, about the role of culture in human life—can be expressed.

Aside from a couple of orienting pieces concerned with more foundational matters, it is in such a manner that theory operates in the essays collected here. A repertoire of very general, made-in-the-academy concepts and systems of concepts—"integration," "rationalization," "symbol," "ideology," "ethos," "revolution," "identity," "metaphor," "structure," "ritual," "world view," "actor," "function," "sacred," and, of course, "culture" itself—is woven into the body of thick-description ethnography in the hope of rendering mere occurrences scientifically eloquent. The aim is to draw large conclusions from small, but very densely textured facts; to support broad assertions about the role of culture in the construction of collective life by engaging them exactly with complex specifics.

Thus it is not only interpretation that goes all the way down to the most immediate observational level: the theory upon which such interpretation conceptually depends does so also. My interest in Cohen's story, like Ryle's in winks, grew out of some very general notions indeed. The "confusion of tongues" model—the view that social conflict is not something that happens when, out of weakness, indefiniteness, obsolescence, or neglect, cultural forms cease to operate, but rather something which happens when, like burlesqued winks, such forms are pressed by unusual situations or unusual intentions to operate in unusual ways—is not an idea I got from Cohen's story. It is one, instructed by colleagues, students, and predecessors, I brought to it.

Our innocent-looking "note in a bottle" is more than a portrayal of the frames of meaning of Jewish peddlers, Berber warriors, and French proconsuls, or even of their mutual interference. It is an argument that to rework the pattern of social relationships is to rearrange the coordinates of the experienced world. Society's forms are culture's substance.

VIII

There is an Indian story—at least I heard it as an Indian story—about an Englishman who, having been told that the world rested on a platform which rested on the back of an elephant which rested in turn on the back of a turtle, asked (perhaps he was an ethnographer; it is the way they behave), what did the turtle rest on? Another turtle. And that turtle? "Ah, Sahib, after that it is turtles all the way down."

Such, indeed, is the condition of things. I do not know how long it would be profitable to meditate on the encounter of Cohen, the sheikh, and "Dumari" (the period has perhaps already been exceeded); but I do know that however long I did so I would not get anywhere near to the bottom of it. Nor have I ever gotten anywhere near to the bottom of anything I have ever written about, either in the essays below or elsewhere. Cultural analysis is intrinsically incomplete. And, worse than that, the more deeply it goes the less complete it is. It is a strange science whose most telling assertions are its most tremulously based, in which to get somewhere with the matter at hand is to intensify the suspicion, both your own and that of others, that you are not quite getting it right. But that, along with plaguing subtle people with obtuse questions, is what being an ethnographer is like.

There are a number of ways to escape this—turning culture into folklore and collecting it, turning it into traits and counting it, turning it into institutions and classifying it, turning it into structures and toying with it. But they *are* escapes. The fact is that to commit oneself to a semiotic concept of culture and an interpretive approach to the study of it is to commit oneself to a view of ethnographic assertion as, to borrow W. B. Gallie's by now famous phrase, "essentially contestable." Anthropology, or at least interpretive anthropology, is a science whose progress is marked less by a perfection of consensus than by a refinement of debate. What gets better is the precision with which we vex each other.

This is very difficult to see when one's attention is being monopolized by a single party to the argument. Monologues are of little value here, because there are no conclusions to be reported; there is merely a discussion to be sustained. Insofar as the essays here collected have any importance, it is less in what they say than what they are witness to: an enormous increase in interest, not only in anthropology, but in social studies generally, in the role of symbolic forms in human life. Meaning, that elusive and ill-defined pseudoentity we were once more than content to leave philosophers and literary critics to fumble with, has now come back into the heart of our discipline. Even Marxists are quoting Cassirer; even positivists, Kenneth Burke.

My own position in the midst of all this has been to try to resist subjectivism on the one hand and cabbalism on the other, to try to keep the analysis of symbolic forms as closely tied as I could to concrete social events and occasions, the public world of common life, and to organize it in such a way that the connections between theoretical formulations and descriptive interpretations were unobscured by appeals to dark sciences. I have never been impressed by the argument that, as complete objectivity is impossible in these matters (as, of course, it is), one might as well let one's sentiments run loose. As Robert Solow has remarked, that is like saying that as a perfectly aseptic environment is impossible, one might as well conduct surgery in a sewer. Nor, on the other hand, have I been impressed with claims that structural linguistics, computer engineering, or some other advanced form of thought is going to enable us to understand men without knowing them. Nothing will discredit a semiotic approach to culture more quickly than allowing it to drift into a combination of intuitionism and alchemy, no matter how elegantly the intuitions are expressed or how modern the alchemy is made to look.

The danger that cultural analysis, in search of all-too-deep-lying turtles, will lose touch with the hard surfaces of life—with the political, economic, stratificatory realities within which men are everywhere contained—and with the biological and physical necessities on which those surfaces rest, is an ever-present one. The only defense against it, and against, thus, turning cultural analysis into a kind of sociological aestheticism, is to train such analysis on such realities and such necessities in the first place. It is thus that I have written about nationalism, about violence, about identity, about human nature, about legitimacy, about revolution, about ethnicity, about urbanization, about status, about death, about time, and most of all about particular attempts by particular peoples to place these things in some sort of comprehensible, meaningful frame.

To look at the symbolic dimensions of social action—art, religion, ideology, science, law, morality, common sense—is not to turn away from the existential dilemmas of life for some empyrean realm of de-emotionalized forms; it is to plunge into the midst of them. The essential vocation of interpretive anthropology is not to answer our deepest questions, but to make available to us answers that others, guarding other sheep in other valleys, have given, and thus to include them in the consultable record of what man has said.

Chapter 11

TODD JONES

UNCOVERING "CULTURAL MEANING"
Problems and solutions

FROM THE EARLIEST DAYS OF THE social sciences, scholars have fought fierce battles about whether their endeavors should be thought of as being like those of natural scientists or more like those of literary critics. These skirmishes have become very intense over the last three decades, especially in disciplines such as anthropology, sociology, political science, and history, in which members of both camps exist in large numbers. The two sides have used various terms and descriptions to characterize their respective views: scientistic vs. humanistic, positivistic vs. hermeneutic, quantitative vs. qualitative, and *Naturwissenschaften* vs. *Geisteswissenschaften*. One very influential way of characterizing these differing views was put forth in anthropologist Clifford Geertz's *The Interpretation of Cultures*. In this work Geertz argued that the study of culture ought to be "not an experimental science in search of law but an interpretive one in search of meaning" (1973, p. 5). *The Interpretation of Cultures* helped fuel an upsurge of non-naturalistic science "humanistic" movements in numerous social sciences (see Walters, 1980). With Geertz, "interpretivists" in the social sciences held that the central quest of researchers in the social sciences should be uncovering the "meaning" of a society's symbolic actions and artifacts.

The idea that "meaning" should be the central focus of the social sciences continues to have many influential adherents to this day. A central problem with this approach, however, is that the term "meaning" is vague and multifaceted. It is not completely clear what meaning amounts to even when we are talking about verbal utterances—the realm in which it seems least problematic. What, then, are Geertz and those like him looking for in seeking to uncover the meaning of a cockfight, a sheep theft, or an anti-colonial movement? In a number of places I have argued that the interpretivist movement has been beset by conceptual problems (Jones, 1997, 1998, 1999, 2000a, 2000b). In this paper, however, I will assume that the term "meaning" does capture one of the main realms we want to investigate in the social sciences. But what, precisely, are we looking for when we focus on uncovering "the meaning" of an artifact or an event? I will argue that the best conceptualization of the kind of meaning that interpretivists are interested in is not the sort of thing to be found by emulating literary critics, but something better uncovered by familiarizing oneself with findings from psychology. However interpretive social scientists themselves try to explicate the term "meaning," I believe that the best way of making sense of their practice is to see them as looking for the *typical mental reactions* that people in a given culture have to certain acts and artifacts. Meaning-seeking interpretivists tend to see themselves as eschewing science in general and psychology in particular. I will argue, by contrast, that people interested in meaning should look to psychology for help in their endeavors. Indeed, it is precisely by eschewing psychological theories that people interested in uncovering meaning get into the most trouble. I claim that interpretivists and psychology-oriented social scientists can be allies in looking at meaning to understand culture.

What are interpretivists looking for in seeking meaning?

The term "meaning" has quite a variety of uses. We say, for example, "he meant to change that light bulb," "that cloudy sky means rain tomorrow," "'histrionic' means outgoing," and "the meaning of life is serving the Lord." What does "meaning" mean in the context of understanding cultural actions or artifacts? Interpretive social scientists themselves are of remarkably little help in making clear what sense of the term they have in mind. In *The Interpretation of Cultures* alone Geertz seems to endorse a view of meaning that encourages us to focus *externally* on both small scale-behaviors (e.g., those emphasized by psychologists like E. Galanter) and on giant macro-structural entities (e.g., those discussed by sociologist Talcott Parsons). At the same time, his "interpretations" are full of the same familiar *internal* mentalistic terminology we usually take as describing internal mental states. If interpretivists are not very clear about what they mean by meaning, however, there are some things they clearly are not looking for. They are not looking for ultimate purpose as in "the meaning of life" or "the meaning of friendship." They are not looking at Gricean "natural meaning" as in "smoke means fire" or "red spots mean the measles." What they do seem to be continually talking about are native hopes and fears. They often talk about what kinds of images and stories native children grow up hearing. They often describe what items are associated with what other items via resemblance. Interpretivists maintain they are interested in understanding "the native's point of view." In the end, the only way that I can see the phrase "interpreting meaning" as describing what interpretivists do is to view them as trying to uncover the *beliefs and other mental states* typically engendered in individual natives by certain actions and artifacts.

Claiming that interpretivists who say they are interested in meaning are ultimately interested in uncovering mental states helps to clarify what it is that interpretivists are doing, but it raises questions of its own: What is meant by a *mental* state? This question can be divided into several sub-questions. One concerns which features are considered to be prototypical features of mental states in our *ordinary language* usage of mental terms. Another concerns what *particular* implicit or explicit theories of mental states interpretivists use in going about their work. Another concerns which philosophical or psychological theories of the mental are ultimately correct. All of these questions will be touched upon in this essay, but we should start by saying something about the general features of the states we talk about as being "mental" in our ordinary language usage. A mental state, whatever else it is, is a state internal to the brain or mind of an organism. Mental states are typically thought to come to represent states in the external world, during and after the organism's sensory apparatus interacts with features of the external environment. Mental states are also thought to help cause behavior when a mind sends signals to the motor system and causes certain movements to be initiated. Given that mental states are thought to interact with the world in these ways (on almost any view of the mental), scholars interested in attributing mental states to people usually take a history of exposure to certain environmental features as evidence that people have certain beliefs about those features. Scholars interested in attributing mental states also typically look at sets of behavior as evidence telling them something about the internal states that cause this behavior. Just how behavioral and environmental evidence can enable people to uncover mental states is something that will be discussed in the next section.

There are numerous different terms that different theories use for the internal mental states that respond to the world and cause the production of certain movements. Such terms include "representations," "points of view," "assumptions," "structures," "information," "affordances," "goals," "drives," "dispositions," "wants," and "needs." The generic terms most often used in ordinary language for such internal states are "belief" and "desire." For our purposes it is sufficient to discuss interpretivists' attributions of mental states to people by speaking of the beliefs and desires that interpretivists view people as having. In viewing the "meaning" that interpretivists are interested in as consisting in the beliefs typically engendered in individual natives in certain situations, I see them as focused on a type of meaning similar to the sort that psychologist Charles Osgood was interested in his monumental 1957 work.

But there is a twist to the types of beliefs on which interpretivists seem to focus. The mental states that interpretive social scientists seem to have the most interest in are "hidden" ones—ones with a family resemblance to the states Freud sought to uncover (hence the title *The Interpretation of Cultures*). Perhaps this is why they are so fond of the term "meaning." One of the times we are most inclined to use terms like "meaning" in ordinary language is when we can't readily see a person's underlying motivation for an action—"what did he mean by giving me a kiss on the cheek?"—or when we are unclear about what thoughts or associations someone has—"what does Christmas mean to you?" Thus, interpretive anthropologist Ohnuki-Tierney (1984) engages in the project of trying to get us to see the meaning of a Japanese monkey performance by showing us how, when the performances end, the audience "realizes that it was they who were the untamed nature to be culturalized by the monkey" (p. 304). Similarly, Feldman (1994) seeks to explicate the Rodney King police brutality case by showing us how, for Sergeant Stacey Koon:

> The successful confinement of King—the symmetry of a body lying at attention with the face in the dirt—and the acquisition of linguistic reciprocity marked the neutering of the animalized body and its internalization of the will of the state. A "gorilla in the mist," a black "bear" that was insistent on rising on its haunches was turned by violence into a speaking subject.
>
> (p. 410)

In what follows, I'll assume that uncovering hidden mental states is the project that interpretive social scientists are really involved in. Let me describe the central difficulties of such projects.

Methods of interpreting

Informally, the beliefs, desires, and other mental states we can categorize as hidden states are those that tend *not* to be ascribable using whatever methods we typically use to ascribe everyday beliefs. Most of us endowed with functioning perceptual equipment and a basic knowledge of our cultural practices could easily infer that during the beating, Stacey Koon believed Rodney King was trying to get to his feet. But it is clear we have to make a special effort to learn that King was seen by Koon as a gorilla/bear that needed to be neutered and made to speak. What methods do interpretivists use to uncover these sorts of hidden beliefs?

Interpretivists themselves tend to be very unclear about how they know they've really located the hidden beliefs of an agent. Geertz himself once wrote, "You either grasp an interpretation or you do not, see the point of it or you do not, accept it or you do not" (1973, p. 16). Despite this (rather appalling) arrogance, I contend that there actually are systematic methods interpretivists tend to use. Unless interpretivists are just *divining* or *inventing* belief ascriptions, they must be ascribing beliefs based on some sort of *evidence* that those mental states are there. Since one can't observe mental states directly, one has to rely on indirect evidence. Given the types of things that mental states are thought to be, there are two main types of indirect evidence people could use as their starting point for uncovering the existence of hidden mental states. One can start with the idea that certain mental states are *caused* to be there by exposure to certain features of the external environment. Trying to figure out what mental states are there by focusing on features of the environment that likely produce certain mental states can be termed the *environmental* strategy. One could also go in the other direction and reason that certain internal mental states tend to *cause* certain behaviors. When those resulting behaviors are observed, that's taken to be good evidence that those purported mental states are, in fact, there. This method can be called the *behavioral* strategy. Whether or not they explicitly discuss it, the general environmental and behavioral strategies are likely to be the starting points for all interpretive hermeneutic methods aimed at uncovering meaning, for there aren't many other places scholars interested in looking at hidden mental structures *could* start.

However, environmental and behavioral evidence alone can't take one very far. As a point of logic, gathering behavioral or environmental *data* alone cannot enable one to infer a causing or resulting mental state without some kind of psychological *theory*. Before any observation of an environmental feature can count as evidence for the presence of a certain mental state, one has to have a theory about how certain types of mental states are caused by environmental exposure. Before any observation of behavior can count as evidence for the presence of a certain mental state, one has to have a theory about how certain kinds of mental states cause certain types of behavior. Freud, for example, once claimed that his patient's reciting a line from a poem mentioning flowing water counted as evidence that the patient was unconsciously worried about his lover's missed menstruation (Grunbaum, 1984). That piece of observable behavior could only be connected to an unconscious worry by relying on a massive amount of theory specifying just how that sort of external state was connected to that sort of internal state. To connect them, Freud had to have theories about internal mechanisms of concept association, theories about mechanisms of repression, and theories about mechanisms of sublimation. The abstract logic of the situation is that if we want to infer the presence of any unseen cause, C, from an observation, O, we have to also have a theory specifying the laws or processes by which O-effects are the result of C-causes. Similarly, if we want to infer the presence of an unseen effect, E, from some observed O suspected of causing it, we need to have a theory specifying the laws or processes by which E-effects are caused by O-causes. We use theories and models in this manner so routinely that we often *don't notice* that they are there. Still, it's only the combination of the observable evidence and some theory of the nature of the unobservable entities, and how they connect to the observable, that allows us to make these sorts of inferences.

All interpretive methods, then, must use some type of psychological theory to ascribe mental states to the people they study. Interpreters must combine the behavioral and environmental strategies of gathering *observable evidence* with some kinds of *theories* about how the external states observed cause and are caused by certain external states. They must do this if they want to use that observable evidence to infer that certain mental states are present. So which psychological theories do interpretivists tend to use in ascribing hidden mental states to people? Different interpretivists, of course, tend to use different theories. The theorist of the mental most commonly utilized by interpretivists is, of course, Freud himself. From time to time, however, numerous other thinkers in the psychoanalytic tradition (e.g., Jung, Erikson,

Bettelheim, and Lacan) have been leaned on to provide the supplemental psychological theories necessary for enabling behavioral or environmental evidence to lead one to infer the presence of this or that hidden mental state. In the 1960s and 1970s, a major rival to psychoanalytic theories developed in the structuralist theories of Claude Levi-Strauss. These psychological theories would then be combined with basic evidence-gathering strategies to produce a hidden belief ascription.

Interpretivists would use the environmental strategy by seeing what environments their subjects were exposed to and ascribing to their subjects only those mental states that were consistent with this history of exposure. They would utilize the behavioral strategy to posit certain mental structures that were consistent with a large range of observed behavior. They would further narrow down their posits by making sure the ascribed mental structures were also consistent with their favored psychological theories concerning which mental structures tended to be present in which situations. Those with a psychoanalytic orientation would posit that various things were viewed as sexual stand-ins. Structuralists thought people were labeling things in the world as being instances of nature-type things that were opposing culture-type things. A "good interpretation" was one that was consistent with the favored psychological theory and a wide range of environmental and behavioral observations.

By the 1980s and 1990s, however, popular postmodern and deconstructionist literary criticism had made many scholars skeptical of "totalizing narratives" of any kind. All scientific theories, including psychological theories, came to be viewed with increasing suspicion by postmodernists. Scientific theories that made claims about what was true came to be seen as being an impediment to understanding things from multiple perspectives. As a result, in the 1980s and 1990s one found fewer and fewer interpretive social scientists making explicit reference to *any* kind of psychological theory. It got to the point that in the 1990s Brad Shore was able to write of his participation in a cognitive science conference:

> My assignment at the conference was to try to characterize the implicit theory of mind that anthropologists employed in their cultural analyses. In such heady company, it soon became clear to me that most of our work in symbolic anthropology proceeded innocent of any well-formed theory of mind whatsoever.
>
> (1996, p. vii)

I've argued, however, that without *some* type of theory of mental processing, observing behaviors and environments can tell you *nothing whatsoever* about inner mental structures. This means that when interpretivists draw conclusions about what kinds of beliefs are present, they *must be* using some or other theory of how the mental works, whether or not they are aware of *which* ones they are using.[1] Since interpretivists have continued to churn out ascriptions of mental states to people, I contend that they have been operating using (unacknowledged) psychological theories. My guess is that they are relying on what might be called "minimalist" theories of the mental. Minimalist theories are those that make such a small number of assumptions—or have such widely shared assumptions—that it is easy not to notice that one is making them. I suspect that the two minimalist theories that interpretivists make the most use of are associationism and rationality. Interpretivists assume that people behave in a rational manner that will get them what they desire according to the beliefs they have. They assume that when people see things, they are reminded of other things that are associated with them. As with the interpretations of the 1960s and 1970s, the interpretations that are seen as good ones are those mental structure posits that are consistent with the subjects' history of environmental exposure, consistent with their behavior, and consistent with favored psychological theories—here, rationality and association. In the following section I will discuss in more detail how these minimalist theories can be used to ascribe interpretive meanings. I will also say why these theories are *too* minimal to give us ascriptions we should have any confidence in.

Problems with interpretation with minimalist theories of mind

Rationality

One very minimal theory of mind that enables a scholar to make inferences about beliefs on the basis of behavioral observations assumes that the person studied is a (mostly) rational agent.

The rationality assumption consists of positing that when a person has certain desires and certain beliefs about the way the world is, the behaviors he will engage in are the ones that would rationally enable him to meet those desires, if the world is as he believes. The behaviors one observes, then, are assumed to be *caused by* an agent rationally calculating that certain movements are the ones that have to be made in order to achieve his desires in a world he believes to be structured in a certain way. This means that one can reason backwards and use observations of behavior and the assumption of rational processing to make inferences about the belief—desire set that must be causing these behaviors. An interpretivist using the rationality assumption will ask, "which beliefs and desires would the behaviors I observe be the result of, assuming that person is rational?" This behavioral-strategy-plus-rationality approach to ascribing mental states is a species of a general method for uncovering unseen entities called "abductive" or "inference to the best explanation."

An example of someone using abductive inference in this way can be seen in the work of social critic Warren Farrell. In his book *The Myth of Male Power* (1993) one of the things Farrell is interested in is the attitudes that lie behind the way Americans treat women and the way they treat men. In this work Farrell assembles a large set of observations of behavior toward men. Among his observations are:

- The military does not give combat assignments to women.
- Twenty-four of the twenty-five professions rated as most hazardous are virtually all male.
- The more hazardous the job, the higher percentage of men it has.
- Men are twice as likely to be victims of violent crimes than women and three times more likely to be murder victims.
- The suicide rate among men in their early twenties is six times higher than that of women the same age, and the suicide rate of men over age 85 is 1350 times higher.
- Breast cancer receives 600% more funding than prostate cancer, even though death rates from each are equal.

Which rational beliefs and desires could create these sorts of behaviors towards men? For Farrell (rightly or wrongly), the only belief/desire set in which such behaviors are rational is the belief that *women* are actually perceived as the valuable gender (especially in evolutionary terms) who need to be protected and preserved at all cost, while men (a dime a dozen in evolutionary terms) are thought of as essentially disposable. Farrell clearly comes to this conclusion by assuming rationality then trying to infer the presence of certain beliefs and desires by asking *which* beliefs and desires could produce these observable behaviors in beings that were rational.

As many philosophers of science have documented, abductive inference is one of the central strategies used throughout successful sciences. While interpretivist social scientists may not have direct evidence for the belief states they postulate, they seem to be trying to use abductive inference plus assumptions about rationality to uncover the hidden structure of the mind in the same way that theoretical physicists have always used experimental evidence plus physical theories to postulate the underlying atomic structures that would be able to produce the evidence observed.

In interpretive social science, as in other areas of inquiry, one proceeds by accumulating observations, coming up with causal mechanisms that (according to prior theory) could best generate these observations, and inferring that such mechanisms must be present. Observing further behavior that would be predicted by such an inner structure is thought to help confirm that one has "hit upon" the correct view of the inner structure.

But this strategy tends to be problematic when used to try to uncover *beliefs*—even garden-variety ones. It is a point of elementary logic that merely showing that one can confirm a prediction entailed by a hypothesis isn't enough to show that that hypothesis is true. If there are viable alternative hypotheses that could generate the observed prediction, then observing that prediction doesn't give you *any* evidence that the hypothesis in question, rather than its equally well-predicting rivals, is true (see Laudan, 1996 for an articulation of this point). If different beliefs and desires could rationally have produced the same behavior, then observing that behavior provides no evidence for the existence of any particular beliefs or desires. One of the root difficulties of belief ascription is that, unlike the sparse fundamental building blocks of some other sciences, there exist not merely a few dozen—or even a few thousand—different possible beliefs and desires, but an infinite number of them. We must begin, then, by selecting from an unlimited number of potential belief posits. The only beliefs we can properly ascribe using the behavioral strategy and a "minimalist rationality" theory of mind are those that could rationally cause the behavior we observe. This, however, is a very weak restriction. We can think of beliefs as something like maps used for getting around the world. A central problem is that many different sorts of maps could usefully lead you to the same destination. Any given behavior is, thus, consistent with positing numerous different core beliefs and desires. To adapt Quine's example (1960), when Malinowski's Trobrianders initially pointed to an outrigger canoe and said "Kewo'u," he initially had no firm way of telling whether they were thinking "there's a boat," "there's a group of undetached boat parts," or "there's a stage in a boat's existence."

There are still further difficulties. Beliefs do not cause behavior by themselves, but do so in conjunction with desires and, often, with other beliefs. A selection of vanilla over chocolate may be based on the belief that vanilla is tastier and a desire for the tastiest ice cream. It may also, however, stem from the belief that chocolate is tastier but also more fattening, and a desire to lose weight. Selecting vanilla could also stem from a superstitious belief that chocolate should never be eaten on Wednesdays, and a desire not to offend the gods. The vanilla-choosing behavior alone will not tell you which of these beliefs and desires are behind it. If one's task is to find a belief that, along with a string of auxiliary beliefs and desires, would lead to the production of a given behavior—with no prior restrictions on the number and type of such strings—then the task is analogous to guessing a number which, when added to some string of positive or negative numbers, yields the sum of five. If one makes the appropriate adjustment in the strings of added numbers then literally *every* number can qualify. Similarly, with the right adjustments in auxiliary beliefs and desires, it is logically possible for *any* belief to cause *any* behavior. Increasing the numbers of behaviors one observes can help rule out some possible belief/desire sets by showing that some of the predictions of that set are incompatible with the further observed behaviors. But even large sets of behaviors can be shown to be compatible with any given belief/desire set as long as one is willing to postulate the existence of enough additional (perhaps very odd) beliefs and desires that make all those behaviors rational. Simply observing behaviors and assuming that people are rational, then, cannot enable us to say what sorts of hidden beliefs are present in the people observed. What one needs are theories (and experiments) that can go further in constraining which, of the many possible mental structures that *could* generate the behaviors we observe, are likely to be the sets that actually *do* generate these behaviors.

Associationism

A different minimalist theory of mind that could be (and I believe is) used by interpretivists is one best used in conjunction with the environmental strategy. The environmental strategy seeks to infer the existence of mental states by going in the opposite direction of the behavioral strategy. While the behavioral strategy looks at behavioral outputs, the environmental strategy looks at the environmental *inputs* that people in a particular culture tend to have. This strategy must, then, combine knowledge of these inputs with some sort of *theory of mental state formation processes* to infer what sorts of mental states these environmental inputs lead people to have. A family of minimalist theories of mind that has existed at least since Hume's time is that the contents of mind, at any given time, arise due to certain features of environment or of another internal state "calling to mind" other features *associated* with these. For "ordinary" beliefs the clusters of features brought to mind at a given time are the ones that are most commonly perceived to be adjacent in space or time. The sight of a bat, thus, easily brings to mind thoughts of echolocation and night flight.

It might also, however, bring up thoughts of caves, Batman, or Dracula. I suggest that many of the mental states that seem especially "hidden" are thought to be so because they are the results of more peripheral associations that are far too numerous for us to make confident guesses about, merely by seeing what our compatriots see. Besides being numerous, each person's associations are highly idiosyncratic due to his or her unique personal history. If we don't know the details of these life histories (and even if we did know them), there are innumerable associations one might be making, looking at any given thing. The mental states people find themselves in through following chains of association are therefore likely to be quite "hidden" from third parties in a way that ordinary world-mapping beliefs are not. Such thoughts might also be hidden from the conscious view of the cognizer herself. The question, then, is how interpretivists could come to know these hidden associations are there. Observing that certain entities and events are frequently associated with others might tell us, for example, that the Swat of Pakistan believe that leather workers won't discipline their patron's children. But how could we infer, as Lindholm (1981) does, that these leather workers are seen as symbolic male mothers?

One thing interpretivists often do is look extensively at the cultural environments of the people studied to see what kinds of concrete or abstract features tend to be paired together in that culture. In the analysis of the Japanese monkey performance mentioned above, Ohnuki-Tierney (1984) comes to the conclusion that:

> At the end of the performance, (the audience) realizes that it was they who were the untamed nature to be culturalized by the monkey. Put another way, the monkey and the outcast are the small eyes in yin and yang. For this reason, I think, even amidst the laughter at the monkey performance the audience is reminded, albeit vaguely, of their darker side, as represented by the monkey and the outcast trainer.
>
> (pp. 301–304)

Ohnuki-Tierney tries to convince us that this is so by describing in great detail the various ways in which monkeys are depicted in Japanese history and folk tales. Such exposure is supposed to show us the sorts of symbolic associations Japanese people might have with monkeys that we would not initially be able to see.

While it is certainly helpful to be made aware of possible associations that we wouldn't have thought of by learning about other people's history and culture, the degree to which we can rely on such a strategy for accurate hidden belief ascription is acutely limited. After all, even if we knew *all* of a person's environmental inputs, this, by itself, would tell us nothing about where that person's train of thought tended to go at any given time. Any seen feature has millions of other features potentially associated with it. To know which associations are more likely to arise at a given time than others requires additional knowledge of the internal mental mechanisms that specify which items are the ones most frequently called to mind by other items.

Along with looking at common cultural pairings, interpretivists using an associationist theory of mind could also look for associations by looking at which items are connected by resemblance and contiguity. When confronted with items thought to have a deeper symbolic meaning, interpretivist social scientists, much like psychoanalysts and literary critics, often suggest that observed surface features are mentally associated with some other features, in native minds, because of a vague resemblance or contiguity. Thus Wilson (1959) interprets the meaning of eating a banana in a ritual performed by the bride in Nyakyusa culture as a symbol of the sex she will have with her husband. Shells and coral have been said to be symbolically associated with the ocean by Levi-Strauss (1963) because of spatiotemporal contiguity. Interpretivists also posit that something can symbolize something else not merely by being mentally associated with it in some way but just by being associated with something else that is. Hence, something can be symbolically associated with something else through elaborate chains of association. Such a convoluted chain can be seen in Sapir's discussion of the symbolic association of lepers and hyenas among the Kujamaat Diola. Lepers, on Sapir's account, are thought to be burned by a magic fire associated with iron working forges. Leprosy is associated with the forge because the way that leprosy acts on the body is seen to be isomorphic to the way that forge fire works on iron. The forge is thought to send leprosy when someone attacks something that the forge, a source of spiritual power, is thought to protect (primarily cattle or children). If a cow is killed through witchcraft, it is thought likely to have been done by the person in the form of a were-hyena. "Hence," writes Sapir, "if you had leprosy, you were caught stealing something protected by the forge; and if you were stealing, you might have been stealing in the guise of a hyena" (1981, p. 533). Thus the symbolic connection between lepers and hyenas.

The basic problem with using association to find symbolic meaning is that, as Anderson and Bower (1973) demonstrated long ago (and players of the "six degrees of separation" or "Kevin Bacon" games have discovered more recently), virtually anything can be associated with anything else in the right circumstances. Bananas can serve as phallic symbols, but they could also possibly serve as symbols of the tropics, of monkeys, of banana bicycle seats, of the Velvet Underground, or of Bob Dole. Showing an interesting *possible* set of associations by itself does nothing to establish that such a set of remindings is *actually* present among the people studied. It's possible, as Feldman suggests, that Officer Koon saw Rodney King as a wild bear that needed to be socialized by submitting to state authority. So is the idea that King was seen as a symbol of a black revolutionary movement, one that threatened the American government and way of life. But perhaps Koon saw King as a symbolic snake, and believed that it is proper for snakes to be lying on the ground. Maybe, in trying to put King down, Koon remembered a tree that he chopped and chopped at but couldn't fell as a child, and King became the symbol of Koon's continual failings. With only resemblance and contiguity as constraints, there is simply no telling a person's mental state at a given time. A minimalist theory of the mental that says that features in the environment call to mind features "associated" with them is no better at telling us what *specific* mental states are there than the minimalist rationality theory.

Better ascriptions through better theories

Environmental and behavioral strategies, combined with only minimalist theories of mind, then, are able to specify only that a given person *might possibly be* in any of a large number of different hidden mental states. The remedy, however, seems clear: Interpretive belief ascribers need to combine environmental and behavioral strategies with more substantive, less minimal theories of mind. To make it plausible that one hidden belief is active rather than any of an infinite set of alternatives, one needs to make use of *more constraining* theories about which symbols tend to be invoked when.

Now, some interpretivists do try to do just this when, in addition to the environmental and behavioral strategies, they try to make sure their ascriptions of mental states are also consistent with certain substantive (nonminimal) psychological theories. A Freudian theory, for example, will put some constraints on what a symbol means in light of its "sex drive/ hydraulic" posits about which types of thought are the ones most commonly brought to mind. There are several problems, however, with the sorts of substantive psychological theories that interpretivists tend to use. Since coming up with good interpretations requires that our ascriptions be constrained by psychological theories that say which sorts of structures and mechanisms are possible, it's important that these constraining are ones we really have good reasons to believe are there. Unfortunately, the sorts of psychological theories that interpretivists tend to favor when they use psychological theories at all are the very ones whose proponents tend to eschew making systematic attempts to provide evidence for them (see Harris, 1979; Grunbaum, 1984). Worse, when attempts by independent researchers have been made to test the two most prominent theories, Freudian and Levi-Straussian, the results have consistently been stunning failures for both (see Harris, 1979; Erwin, 1993). Even more problematic, however, is that even if such theories were correct, the types of theories interpretivists tend to favor tend not to be constraining enough to narrow the field of plausible interpretations very far. Neither Freudian nor Levi-Straussian (or Jungian, etc.) theories provide enough constraints to keep dozens and dozens of different thoughts and associations as counting as potential states of mind at a given time, even within the constraints of the theory. All of the different possible interpretations of King's attempt to rise to his feet that I suggested for Koon above, for example, are compatible with all of the theories of the unconscious just mentioned.

What interpretivist social scientists clearly need to do is use less minimal, more constraining, more well-supported psychological theories in coming up with the interpretations they do. Our best attributions of what mental states people in a group tend to have will be the ones that fit best with not only all the observations gathered using the environmental and behavioral strategies, but also the ones most consistent with our best psychological theories concerning which mental states appear when. The more an interpretation fits with all of these, the better it will be, and the closer the psychological theories used are to the ultimately correct ones, the more likely it is that we are actually able to see "the native's point of view." Other things equal, the better the psychological theories used, the better the interpretation.

Is there anything general we can say about where better psychological theories can be found? To begin with, interpretivists would certainly be better off using models of mind whose implications have been experimentally tested and refined in recent decades. There is no reason why interpretivists should be relying on the speculative theories of nineteenth- and early twentieth-century savants like Freud and Levi-Strauss. It is true that there have been many good criticisms of observations that are likely to have been artifacts of the artificial laboratory situations (see Agar, 1980), but that doesn't mean that we are better off using models that are never explicitly tested. What we want are theories and models whose implications are tested in as many ways as possible—in natural settings and in refined unnatural settings. Confirmations and failures in laboratory settings do provide a lot of evidence that we can use for refining and redeveloping models. There should be a presumption in favor of models of mind that have been developed and refined through years of clinical testing regardless of whether or not those tests were in laboratory or more naturalistic settings. Interpretivists, then, would make better ascriptions simply by looking at the psychological theories developed by recent researchers. Paying more attention to the work of recent research in psychology is one very straightforward way to get better psychological theories and therefore make better interpretations. Obvious as it is, however, it is a "radical" step that most interpretivists have yet to take.

There are other ways of trying to ensure that good theories of mind are used. The likely reasons that the behavioral and environmental strategies are so heavily relied on in interpretivist social science (and the likely reason that so little attention is paid to focusing on mental structures themselves) are that larger-scale mental structures of mind are not directly observable to us. There is, therefore, an inclination to treat the mind as a "black box" whose inner workings are best revealed by looking at the behaviors it emits—but there are other general ways to build theories about "black boxes" whose inner structure we can't directly observe. For any "black box," one way to come up with a model of its workings is to start with a theory of its *component parts* of which it is constructed and use theories of how such parts link together in space to create more complex constructions (as in atomic theory or chemistry). Alternatively, for any black box mechanism at a given time, one might start with theories about *earlier initial* conditions then use dynamic law theories to talk about how forces from within and without will change this set to produce a resulting construction (as in predicting how a satellite will stabilize into an orbit). If one is lucky enough to have well-supported theories of components, combination rules, initial conditions, and modification rules, one has important additional ways to build models of black box mechanisms besides relying on observations of inputs and outputs. If the black box we are talking about here is the mind or brain, we have at least the skeletons of models constructed along these lines based on decades of research by teams of researchers from neurology, psychology, and computer science. However incomplete these models are, they are far more advanced than the non-experiment-based speculations about the mind made by Freud or Levi-Strauss. The "composite-construction" strategy is pursued by neurologists and connectionist modelers looking at how neurons and neuron clusters are linked together to create specific machines that tend to bring certain sorts of things to mind in certain situations (see, e.g., Clark, 1993; McClelland & Rumelhart, 1986; Morris, 1994; Squire, 1987). At a higher level, numerous cognitive modelers have investigated how various items of knowledge fit together to form mental models and theories (e.g., Bower & Glass, 1976; Johnson-Laird, 1993; Palmer, 1977). Versions of the initial-conditions-and-changes strategy can be looked at across both high and low levels and over large and small time scales. At smaller time scales various researchers have studied how initial mental states are changed by new perceptual information (Biederman, 1987; Marr & Nishihara, 1978), by operant conditioning (Honig & Staddon, 1977), and by learning to relax or tighten conditions under which certain behavioral or informational schemas are invoked (Holyoak & Koh, 1987). Over larger time scales biologists and evolutionary psychologists have studied how the process of natural selection has reshaped earlier mental structures (e.g., Barkow, Cosmides, & Tooby, 1992). Information from these realms promises to tell us much about which sorts of beliefs and desires people are predisposed to have and which they are likely to have developed at a given place and time. If we want to understand what Geertz and others call "the native point of view," I believe it is by borrowing methods from cognitive science—not psychoanalysis or literary theory—that we are most likely to succeed. In general, if we want to know which sorts of associated items are brought to mind in certain situations, a model like John Anderson's ACT* system, supported by decades of clinical research and computer modeling, should surely be preferred to a Freudian's armchair speculations about which associations people are making when. Interpretive belief ascribers could surely improve their ability to narrow down the meanings that an artifact or event has for someone by combining behavioral and environmental observations with improved theories of mind.

Concluding remarks

In the long-running battle between whether the social sciences ought to proceed as though they were social science or humanities disciplines, the idea that the social sciences ought to center around uncovering *meaning* became a central rallying point in the last several decades. One can find much that is laudable in this focus. Such an emphasis encourages researchers to look at things that were ignored during the years when various forms of crude environmental determinism dominated the social sciences.

At the same time there are problems with focusing on "meaning." The term "meaning" is vague and multifaceted and does not, by itself, specify the areas of human activity on which it is profitable to focus. Despite this vagueness I have argued that the bulk of social science researchers who say they are interested in meaning actually tend to focus on uncovering *typical hidden mental states regarding* some cultural action or artifact.

If uncovering the hidden mental states is what social scientists who study meaning are really doing, then the central question becomes one about which sorts of interpretations are going to be the best ones. I have argued that the best mental state ascriptions are ones that satisfy three sorts of constraints: 1) they must be consistent with observed behavior; 2) they must be consistent with the subjects' exposure to certain environments; and 3) they must be consistent with our best psychological theories regarding how mental states cause and are caused by things. The effort many interpretists of various sorts make in trying to ensure that their ascriptions are consistent with observed environmental histories and observed behaviors is certainly laudable, but almost all current interpretivist approaches are deficient in making sure their ascriptions are consistent with the third logical requirement for good ascriptions. The most currently fashionable interpretivists utilize *no explicit* psychological theories, but since *some* psychological theory is required to ascribe mental states at all, they are likely to be implicitly relying on vague general associationist and rationality theories of mind. For interpretivists using such minimal theories of mind, I have argued, almost anything goes. With rationality and associationism as the only internal constraints, *almost any belief ascription one can imagine* can be shown to be consistent with all the behaviors and environments observed. A consequence of using only the most minimal theories of mind is that there is just *no saying* which interpretive belief ascriptions are good ones and which aren't, no matter how much environmental and behavioral evidence one cites. There is no way to tell which ascriptions are close to any *actual* hidden mental states operating and which ones are elaborate works of fiction, since an enormous array of ascriptions are *all* consistent with all the environmental and behavioral observations and the minimalist theories of mind used. There is nothing to keep postmodernist-inspired minimalist-theory-based ascriptions of mental states from being inventive unconstrained speculation. Minimalist hermeneutic approaches will not give those aiming at understanding meaning what they really want.

In some respects older, less currently fashionable interpretivist approaches do a better job of telling us which particular mental states we should infer to be there. This is simply because the psychological theories used to make ascriptions that predominated interpretivism in the 1960s and 1970s were richer. A theory that gives explicit theories about various kinds of inferencing mechanisms is more constraining than one saying merely that inferencing is vaguely "rational." A theory that provides detailed ideas about which kinds of associations are most likely to be called to mind in a given situation is more constraining than a theory that merely views the mind as working in an associationist manner. Psychoanalytic and structuralist theories of mind, with their richer ideas about association and inference, thus enable interpretive approaches using these theories to provide more definitive assertions. Interpretivists using these theories can say more about what hidden mental structures should be there than the theorists using the implicit "minimalist" theories of mind that most interpretivists currently favor.

I have argued, however, that these sorts of psychological theories—which are the ones that interpretivists tend to favor when they use psychological theories at all—are also deficient. While they are more constraining than minimalist theories, they still tend to allow a *large* number of different ascriptions that are all consistent not only with observations but also with these theories' assumptions about which sorts of mental states tend to be present when. It's not "anything goes" but it's "an awful lot goes." Even more damaging, however, is the fact that there is not much independent evidence for (and much evidence against) the existence of the constraining structures and mechanisms that these theories assume are there and are used to make inferences about mental states. The theories that interpretivists who use explicit theories of mind tend to favor (structuralist and psychoanalytic approaches) are the very theories of mind whose assumptions are poorly confirmed. These sorts of approaches, then, can't give us ascriptions that we should feel any certainty about either.

Most current interpretivist approaches, then, are not providing us with ascriptions of mental states that we should have much confidence in. However, that doesn't mean that the task of interpretation itself—of finding the hidden mental states subjects have in their natural settings— is an impossible one. I have argued that intepretivists can go far in getting what they are looking for by using better psychological theories. I have outlined a number of ways that we can identify psychological theories that we can have more confidence in. There is little to be said about which *specific* psychological theories of this sort will be most useful; that is likely to vary depending on which sorts of perception, memory, and behavior are involved and to the particular sorts of hidden beliefs an interpretivist is focusing on. Which specific psychological theories are most useful will also vary from year to year as various theories become better confirmed. What is clear is the *general type* of psychological theories interpretivists should rely on. They should rely on psychological theories and initial-conditions-and-change theories, those supported by composite-construction theories, and those whose assumptions have been carefully examined and tested. They should not rely on minimalist psychological theories or general theories that lack corroborating evidence. Few current interpretive methods are very successful at ascribing hidden beliefs, but interpretive methods that use psychological theories developed in the ways I have been describing have the potential to enable us to ascribe hidden mental states with much greater accuracy.

Many scientifically oriented psychologists, then, need not present themselves as enemies of researchers who say they want to focus on meaning. Though interpretivist researchers may say they are interested in meaning rather than in uncovering laws (as natural scientists do), psychologists can point out that uncovering meaning actually *requires* a systematic understanding of the mechanisms of mental processing. By coming up with theories of mental processing, scientifically-inclined psychologists are in a position to provide important assistance to those who say that they are focused on meaning. Psychologists can point out that their naturalistic work can complement "hermeneutic" work. Research on meaning can thus be an area where those who utilize humanities research methods can make use of the findings of those who utilize scientific research methods. Whatever other disagreements scientists and humanists in the social sciences may have, stating that a central mission of the social sciences should be to uncover meaning need not be a source of contention.

Note

1   An exception to the rule that one needs some sort of theory to understand what others are thinking is the possibility of uncovering others' thoughts by doing some kind of *simulation*. One proposal found in the belief ascription literature is that simulation is our primary way of attributing beliefs. Ascribing beliefs in this way requires very little prior *knowledge* about how people's minds work or about the various primary and surrounding beliefs and desires they hold. All one has to do to see what another believes is to physically put oneself in his or her position—or imagine oneself in the other's position— then check to see what beliefs and desires pop into one's own mind. If others' minds indeed work like ours do and the simulation is a realistic one, this provides a pretty good indication that these thoughts are what appear in their minds in such situations (see Goldman, 1993; Gordon, 1986). However, the view that we use simulation rather than theory to ascribe thoughts to other people is highly contested by many theorists (see Stich & Nichols, 1997). Even if it is correct, it is not likely to be that useful in the kind of situations that interpretive social scientists are most interested in, such as: 1) ascribing beliefs to people from other cultures who are most likely to be *unlike* us, and 2) uncovering *hidden* beliefs that are not likely to be ones that pop into our conscious minds during a simulation.

References

Agar, M. (1980). *The professional stranger*. Orlando, FL: Academic Press.
Anderson, J. & Bower, G. (1973). *Human associative memory*. Washington, DC: Winston and Sons.
Barkow, J., Cosmides, L., & Tooby, J. (1992). *The adapted mind. Evolutionary psychology and the generation of culture*. Oxford: Oxford University Press
Biederman, I. (1987). Recognition by components, a theory of human image understanding. *Psychological Review*, *94*, 115–147.
Bower, G. & Glass, A. L. (1976). Structural units and the reintegrative power of picture framents. *Journal of Experimental Psychology: Human Learning and Memory*, *2*, 456–466.
Cherniak, C. (1986). *Minimal rationality*. Cambridge, MA: MIT Press.
Clark, A. (1993). *Associative engines*. Cambridge, MA: MIT Press.
Erwin, E. (1993). Philosophers on Freudianism. In J. Earman et al. (Eds.), *Philosophical problems of the internal and external. Words: Essays on the philosophy of Adolf Grunbaum* (pp. 409–459). Pittsburgh, PA: University of Pittsburgh Press.
Farrell, W. (1993). *The myth of male power*. New York: Simon and Schuster.
Feldman, A. (1994). On cultural anesthesia: From Desert Storm to Rodney King. *American Ethnologist*, *21*, 404–418.
Geertz, C. (1973). *The interpretation of cultures: Selected essays*. New York: Basic Books.
Goldman A. I. (1993). The psychology of folk psychology. *Behavioral and Brain Sciences*, *16*, 15–28.
Gordon, R. (1986). Folk psychology as simulation. *Mind and Language*, *1*, 158–171.
Grunbaum, A. (1984). *The foundations of psychoanalysis. A philosophical critique*. Berkeley, CA: University of California Press.
Harris, M. (1979). *Cultural materalism*. New York: Random House.
Holyoak, K. & Koh, K. (1987). Surface and structural similarity in analogical transfer. *Memory and Cognition*, *15*, 332–340.
Honig, W. & Staddon, J. (1977). *Handbook of operant conditioning*. Englewood Cliffs, NJ: Prentice-Hall.
Johnson-Laird, P. N. (1993). *Human and machine thinking*. Hillsdale, NJ: Erlbaum.

Jones, T. (1997). Thick description, fat syntax, and alternative conceptual schemes. *Pragmatics and Cognition*, 5, 131–162.

Jones, T. (1998). Interpretive social science and the native's point of view: A closer look. *Philosophy of the Social Sciences*, 28, 32–68.

Jones, T. (1999). FIC descriptions and interpretive social science: Should philosophers roll their eyes? *Journal for the Theory of Social Behavior*, 29, 337–369.

Jones, T. (2000a). Ethnography, belief ascription, and epistemological barriers. *Human Relations*, 53, 117–152.

Jones, T. (2000b). Ethnography and sister sciences: Why refuse assistance? A reply to Weeks. *Human Relations*, 53, 299–310.

Laudan, L. (1996). *Beyond positivism and relativism*. Boulder, CO: Westview Press.

Levi-Strauss, C. (1963). *Structural anthropology*. New York: Basic Books.

Lindholm, C. (1981). Leatherworkers and love potions. *American Ethnologist*, 8(3), 512–525.

Marr, D. & Nishihara, H. (1978). Representation and recognition of the spatial organization of three-dimensional shape. *Proceedings of the Royal Society of London*, 200, 269–294.

McClelland, J. L. & Rumelhart, D. (1986). *Parallel distributed processing: explorations in the microstructures of cognition*. Cambridge, MA: MIT Press.

Morris, T. (1994). The neural basis of learning with particular reference to the role of synaptic plasticity: Where are we a century after Cajal's speculations? In N. J. Mackintosh (Ed.), *Animal learning and cognition* (pp. 135–183). San Diego, CA: Academic Press,

Ohnuki-Tierney, E. (1984). Monkey performances: A multiple structure of meaning and reflexivity in Japanese culture. In E. Bruner (Ed.), *Text, play, and story* (pp. 289–314). Washington, DC: American Ethnological Society.

Osgood, C., Suci, G., & Tannenbaum, M. (1957). *The measurement of meaning*. Urbana, IL: University of Illinois Press.

Palmer, S. (1977). Hierarchical structure in perceptual representation, *Cognitive Psychology*, 9, 441–474.

Quine, W. (1960). *Word and object*. Cambridge, MA: The MIT Press.

Sapir, D. (1981). Leper, hyena, and blacksmith in Kujamaat Diola thought. *American Ethnologist*, 8, 526–543.

Shore, B. (1996). *Culture in mind: Cognition, culture, and the problem of meaning*. New York: Oxford University Press.

Skorupski, J. (1976). *Symbol and theory: a philosophical study of theories of religion in social anthropology*. Cambridge: Cambridge University Press.

Squire, L.R. (1987). *Memory and brain*. Oxford: Oxford University Press.

Stich, S. & Nichols, S. (1997). Cognitive penetrability, rationality, and restricted simulation. *Mind and Language*, 12, 297–326.

Walters, R. (1980). Sign of the times: Clifford Geertz and the historians. *Social Research*, 47, 537–556.

Wilson, M. (1959). *Communal rituals of the Nyakyusa*. Oxford: Oxford University Press.

Chapter 12

ALVIN I. GOLDMAN

INTERPRETATION PSYCHOLOGIZED

I

ACENTRAL PROBLEM OF philosophy of mind is the nature of mental states, or the truth-conditions for the ascription of such states. Especially problematic are the propositional attitudes: beliefs, desires, and so forth. One popular strategy for attacking these problems is to examine the practice of speakers in ascribing these states, especially to others. What principles or procedures guide or underlie the ascriber's activity? In identifying such principles or procedures, one hopes to glean the criteria or satisfaction conditions of the mentalistic predicates (or something like this). Now the ascription of the attitudes involves the assignment of some sort of 'content' or 'meaning' to the mind, which can be seen as a kind of 'interpretation' of the agent or his behavior. (It is also related, on many theories, to the interpretation of the agent's utterances.) Thus, ascription of mental states, especially the attitudes, can be thought of as a matter of interpretation; and the strategy of studying the interpreter, in order to extract the conditions of mentality, or propositional attitudehood, may be called the *interpretation strategy*. I do not assume here that this strategy will or can succeed. Nonetheless, its popularity, if nothing else, makes it worthy of investigation.

The aim of this paper, then, is to study interpretation, specifically, to work toward an account of interpretation that seems descriptively and explanatorily correct. No account of interpretation can be philosophically helpful, I submit, if it is incompatible with a correct account of what people actually do when they interpret others. My question, then, is: how does the (naive) interpreter arrive at his/her judgments about the mental attitudes of others? Philosophers who have addressed this question have not, in my view, been sufficiently psychological, or cognitivist, even those who are otherwise psychologically inclined. I shall defend some proposals about the activity of interpretation that are, I believe, psychologically more realistic than their chief competitors.

In the very posing of my question—how does the interpreter arrive at attributions of propositional attitudes (and other mental states)—I assume that the attributor herself has contentful states, at least beliefs. Since I am not trying to prove (to the skeptic) that there is content, this is not circular or question-begging. I assume as background that the interpreter has beliefs, and I inquire into a distinctive subset of them, *viz.* beliefs concerning mental states. It is conceivable, of course, that a proper theory of interpretation, together with certain ontological assumptions, would undermine the ontological legitimacy of beliefs. This is a prospect to which we should, in principle, stay alert, though it is not one that will actively concern me here. I shall proceed on the premise that the interpreter has beliefs. Indeed, it is hard to see how to investigate the problem without that assumption.

Since I am prepared to explain the interpreter's activity in terms of contentful states, I am obviously not attempting to give a purely 'naturalistic' theory of interpretation, *i.e.* a theory that makes no appeal to semantical notions. Interpretation theorists standardly hope to extract naturalistic truth-conditions for the presence of content. I take it to be an open question, however, whether the interpretation strategy can yield such fruit.

I structure the discussion in terms of three types of interpretation theories. Two of these have tended to dominate the field: (1) rationality, or charity, theories, and (2) folk-theory theories. According to the first approach, an attributor A operates on the assumption that the agent in question, S, is rational, *i.e.* conforms to an ideal or normative model of proper inference and choice. The attributor seeks to assign to S a set of contentful states that fits such a normative model. According to the second approach, the attributor somehow acquires a common-sense or folk psychological theory of the mental, containing nomological generalizations that relate stimulus inputs to certain mental states, mental states to other mental states, and some mental states to behavioral outputs. She then uses this theory to infer, from stimulus inputs and behavioral outputs, what states S is in. The related doctrine of analytical functionalism asserts that our commonsense mentalistic predicates are implicitly *defined* in terms of this common-sense psychological theory. The third approach, which I shall defend, is the simulation theory. This approach has been placed in the field but has not received sustained development, and is not yet sufficiently appreciated.

II

The most widely discussed version of the charity approach is that of Donald Davidson (1980; 1984). Actually, Davidson's approach to interpretation involves three strands. First, there is a compositional postulate for assigning meanings to the agent's whole utterances as a function of the meanings of their parts. Second, there is a charity principle that enjoins the interpreter (*ceteris paribus*) to assign belief states to the agent so as to maximize (or optimize) the proportion of truths in the agent's belief set. Third, there is the rationality principle which enjoins the interpreter (*ceteris paribus*) to assign beliefs and desires so as to maximize the agent's rationality. Another prominent specimen of the rationality approach is that of Daniel Dennett (1971; 1987a). Dennett's 'intentional stance' is a method of attributing intentional states by first postulating ideal rationality on the part of the target system, and then trying to predict and/or explain the system's behavior in terms of such rationality.

I shall say nothing here about Davidson's compositional postulate. But a brief comment on his truthfulness principle is in order before turning to more extended discussion of rationality. Davidson holds that one constraint on interpretation precludes the possibility of ascribing 'massive' or 'preponderant' error (by the interpreter's lights) to the interpretee. In an early essay he writes: 'A theory of interpretation cannot be correct that makes a man assent to very many false sentences: it must generally be the case that a sentence is true when a speaker holds it to be' (Davidson 1984, p. 168). And in a more recent essay he says: 'Once we agree to the general method of interpretation I have sketched, it becomes impossible correctly to hold that anyone could be mostly wrong about how things are' (LePore 1986, p. 317). These contentions, however, are dubious. Along with Colin McGinn (1977), I have presented examples of possible cases in which it seems natural to ascribe to an agent a set of beliefs that are largely, in fact predominantly, false (Goldman 1986, pp. 175–6). Furthermore, if Davidson were right in this matter, one could dismiss the intelligibility of radical skepticism out of hand; but it seems implausible that principles of interpretation should have this result (see McGinn 1986). There are at least two sorts of context in which an attributor, A, will assign beliefs to an agent, S, which are false by A's lights: first, where S is exposed to misleading evidence, and second, where S uses poor inductive methods such as hasty generalization, or inferential maxims such as 'Believe whatever your cult leader tells you.' These points are stressed by David Lewis in his own theory of interpretation (Lewis 1983a).

Let us turn to the rationality component of Davidson's charity approach, a component which is common to many writers. For the rationality principle to have substance, there must be some specification of the norms of rationality. While few writers say precisely how these norms are to be chosen or fixed, there seems to be wide agreement that they are derived from *a priori* models of ideal rationality, models inspired by formal logic, by the calculus of probability, and/or by Bayesian decision theory (or its ilk). Even so, there is room for stronger and weaker norms. Dennett often imputes to the intentional stance the component of deductive closure. Davidson usually illustrates rationality with the weaker norm of logical consistency. Let us test the rationality approach by reference to logical consistency and probabilistic coherence. Do interpreters impose these norms in making interpretations? I shall argue in the negative.

Consider a paradox-of-the-preface example. My friend Hannah has just completed a book manuscript. She says that although she is fully confident of each sentence in her book, taken singly, she is also convinced of her own fallibility, and so believes that at least one of her claims is false. At least this is how she *reports* her beliefs to me. But if these were indeed Hannah's beliefs, she would be guilty of believing each of a logically inconsistent set of propositions. Now if the consistency norm were part of our ordinary interpretation procedure, an interpreter would try, other things equal, to avoid ascribing to Hannah all the beliefs she ostensibly avows. Understood as a description of interpretive practice, the rationality approach 'predicts' that interpreters confronted with Hannah's avowals will try to find a way to assign a slightly different set of beliefs than Hannah seems to endorse. Interpreters will feel some 'pressure', some *prima facie* reason, to revise their belief imputation to be charitable to Hannah. Of course, as Davidson admits, other constraints on interpretation, *e.g.* the compositional meaning constraint, might make a revision too costly. So an interpreter might settle for imputing inconsistency after all. But some vector will be exerted to avoid the imputation.

Does this approach accord with the facts? Speaking as one interpreter, I would feel no temptation to avoid ascribing the inconsistent belief set to Hannah. And I submit that other everyday interpreters would similarly feel no such temptation. Admittedly, if Hannah said that she recognized she was being inconsistent, but still believed all these things anyway, many people might feel something is amiss. Recognition of inconsistency can be expected to breed caution. But let us suppose that Hannah shows no sign of recognizing the inconsistency. Surely, an ordinary interpreter would have no qualms in attributing an inconsistent belief set to her. An analogous example is readily produced for the norm of probabilistic coherence. Suppose my friend Jeremy has just been the subject of a probability experiment by the psychologists Amos Tversky and Daniel Kahneman (see Tversky and Kahneman 1983). In this experiment, Jeremy is given a thumbnail sketch of someone called 'Linda', who is described as having majored in philosophy in college, as having been concerned with issues of social justice, and having participated in an anti-nuclear demonstration. Subjects are then asked to rate the probabilities that Linda is now involved in certain vocations or avocations. Like so many other subjects, Jeremy rates the probability of Linda being both a bank teller and a feminist higher than he rates the probability of Linda being a bank teller. But these comparative probability judgments violate the probability calculus: it is impossible for any conjunctive event A & B to be more probable than either of its conjuncts. So if I accept the coherent probabilities norm of interpretation, my duty is to try to reassign contents so as to avoid the indicated imputations to Jeremy.

Again, as one interpreter, I report feeling no such duty. There seems nothing even *prima facie* wrong about attributing to Jeremy this set of probability assignments, despite their incoherence. I have no reason to seek a revised interpretation. So this norm must not in fact play its alleged role in interpretation.

A defender of the rationality approach may hold out for an alternate formulation more sensitive to differences among inconsistencies. Perhaps only flat out contradictions or 'obvious' inconsistencies are ones the interpreter tries to avoid imputing. But which inconsistencies are 'obvious'? That is a question that logic *per se* cannot answer, for obviousness is a psychological notion. If norms of rationality are to be derived from pure logic, there can be no appeal to (degrees of) obviousness. Perhaps the rationality theorist will choose to abandon the attempt to distill norms of rationality from subjects like logic or probability theory. But how, then, should they be distilled? Are they to be extracted from the actual practices of human agents in inference and choice?

There are two problems with this approach. Experimental findings strongly suggest that human agents think in ways that contravene widely accepted norms. They often commit the so-called gambler's fallacy; in making choices, they commonly flout the 'sure-thing' principle (as Allais' paradox shows); and when it comes to deductive inference, they display a number of failings. It is doubtful, therefore, whether actual practice can establish norms of rationality. Secondly, it is dubious that the naive interpreter has an accurate reflective grasp of actual practice. But it is precisely the interpretive practice of naive agents that we seek to illuminate.

Assuming that correct norms of rationality can somehow be identified, is it psychologically plausible to suppose that ordinary interpreters appeal to such norms in making (or constraining) their interpretations? Untrained adults are not generally acquainted with abstract principles like maximizing expected utility, or the sure-thing principle, or probabilistic coherence. Furthermore, we should bear in mind that children display interpretive skills quite early, at least by age four, five, or six. It stretches credulity to suppose that such children employ any of the abstract precepts that rationality theorists commonly adduce. Thus, if we seek to extract principles of interpretation from the psychological determinants of ordinary interpretive practice, norms of rationality do not look promising.

It may be replied that although children lack any explicitly formulated concept of rationality, or any articulated principles of reasoning, they do have *de facto* patterns of reasoning that govern their own cognitive behavior. Perhaps they simply apply those same tacit patterns in interpreting others. This indeed strikes me as a plausible hypothesis. But it is, in effect, a statement of the simulation approach that I shall be advocating shortly.

III

I turn next to the folk-theory approach to interpretation. Here again one must wonder whether naive interpreters, including children, really possess the sorts of principles or common-sense nomological generalizations that this approach postulates, and whether such principles are indeed applied in (all) their interpretive practice.

The first sort of worry about this claim is that attempts by philosophers to articulate the putative laws or 'platitudes' that comprise our folk-theory have been notably weak. Actual illustrations of such laws are sparse in number; and when examples are adduced, they commonly suffer from one of two defects: vagueness and inaccuracy. Vagueness comes in the form of *ceteris paribus* clauses, with which such laws are typically larded. Inaccuracy is frequently associated with attempts to formulate causal-functional relations between desires, beliefs, and actions, but ignore crucial differences between occurrent desires and beliefs and merely dispositional desires and beliefs. Without systematic distinction between these categories of mental states, one cannot hope to state accurate generalizations about practical reasoning (see Goldman 1970, chapter 4, and Goldman 1986, section 10.1).

The vagueness of the laws is doubtless appealing to the functionalist, since it seems doubtful that ordinary folk have a grasp of any *precise* laws. On the other hand, it is hard to see how an interpreter could draw any reasonably definite interpretive conclusions using laws so vague. Yet interpreters commonly do manage to make fairly definite assignments of desires and beliefs. On the matter of accuracy, it is important for analytical functionalism that the laws be reasonably accurate. For if the names of mental states work like theoretical terms, especially in the Ramsey-sentence account of theoretical terms, they do not name anything unless the theory (the cluster of laws) in which they appear is more or less *true* (see Lewis 1983b and 1972).

Perhaps the functionalist will reply that although the 'folk' do have (more or less) true laws in their possession, philosophers have simply failed to articulate those laws correctly. But why, one wonders, should it be so difficult to articulate laws if we appeal to them all the time in our interpretive practice? Admittedly, they may be merely tacit generalizations, and tacit representations are characteristically difficult to reconstruct. A skeptic is entitled to suspect, however, that what goes on when philosophers proffer mentalistic platitudes is not the extraction of pre-existing representations in the minds of the 'folk', but the fresh creation of laws designed to accommodate philosophical preconceptions about the character of 'theoretical' terms.

Still more grounds for doubt center on the problem of acquisition. Recall the point that children seem to display interpretive skills by the age of four, five, or six. If interpretation is indeed guided by laws of folk psychology, the latter must be known (or believed) by this age. Are such children sophisticated enough to represent such principles? And how, exactly, would they acquire them? One possible mode of acquisition is cultural transmission (*e.g.* being taught them explicitly by their elders). This is clearly out of the question, though, since only philosophers have even tried to articulate the laws, and most children have no exposure to philosophers. Another possible mode of acquisition is private construction. Each child constructs the generalizations for herself, perhaps taking clues from verbal explanations of behavior which she hears. But if this construction is supposed to occur along the lines of familiar modes of scientific theory construction, some anomalous things must take place. For one thing, all children miraculously construct the same nomological principles. This is what the (folk-) theory theory ostensibly implies, since it imputes a single folk psychology to everyone. In normal cases of hypothesis construction, however, different scientists come up with different theories. This is especially natural if they do not communicate their hypotheses, which is what obtains in the present case where the hypotheses are presumed to be tacit and unformulated. It is also surprising that the theory should stay fixed in each cognizer once it is acquired, as functionalism apparently assumes. This too contrasts with normal scientific practice, where theories are commonly amended at least to some degree with the accumulation of new data.

It is open to the functionalist, of course, to postulate *innate* knowledge (or belief) in folk psychological principles. This is the hypothesis that Jerry Fodor currently favors (Fodor 1987, pp. 129–33). In support of this hypothesis, Fodor cites the report of developmental psychologists that a rudimentary awareness of the existence of the mental world seems to be present in toddlers and preschoolers. But such awareness only testifies to their grasp of mentalistic phenomena, not mentalistic *laws*. Fodor goes on to challenge the suggestion that language acquisition is a prime source of learning the apparatus of intentional explanation. Only a child who (already) has an idea of what remembering *is*, he argues, could be expected to learn to use the verb 'remember'. Again, this may suggest that children have an innate propensity to identify mental categories within themselves, just as they apparently have innate propensities to identify and individuate material bodies. But it does not support an innate grasp of laws or generalizations. Fodor is assuming that the apparatus of intentional explanation consists in the possession of laws. But that is precisely what I am challenging.

IV

The account I favor may be introduced by reference to a proposal of Richard Grandy (1973). Grandy proposes to replace charity principles with what he calls the 'humanity principle'. This is the constraint imposed on translations that the imputed pattern of relations among beliefs, desires, and the world be as similar to our own as possible. This conforms, says, Grandy, with our actual practice of predicting people's behavior based on our attitudinal attributions. We do not use mathematical decision theory (*i.e.* expected utility theory) to make predictions; rather, we consider what *we* should do if we had the relevant beliefs and desires. Now I do not think that naive interpreters advert to Grandy's humanity principle as an abstract precept. Rather, they ascribe mental states to others by pretending or imagining themselves to be in the other's shoes, constructing or generating the (further) state that they would then be in, and ascribing that state to the other. In short, we *simulate* the situation of others, and interpret them accordingly. This idea has been explicitly put forward by Robert Gordon (1986; also Gordon 1987, chapter 7), and something like it has been endorsed by Adam Morton (1980). The idea has been a dominant motif in the Verstehen and hermeneutic traditions, and earlier precursors include the 18th century Scottish philosophers.

Several writers on interpretation put forward somewhat analogous views in discussing belief ascriptions. W. V. Quine explains indirect quotation in terms of an 'essentially dramatic act' in which we project ourselves into the speaker's mind (Quine 1960, p. 219). Similarly, drawing on Davidson's paratactic account of indirect discourse, Stephen Stich proposes that when I say 'Andrea believes that lead floats on mercury', I am performing a little skit: I am saying that Andrea is in a belief state content-identical to one that would lead me to assert the sentence which follows the 'that'-clause (Stich 1983, p. 84). However, these writers do not explicitly develop the simulation approach; nor do I mean to endorse the proposed paraphrase of belief-state ascriptions.

The simulation idea has obvious initial attractions. Introspectively, it seems as if we often try to predict others' behavior—or predict their (mental) choices—by imagining ourselves in their shoes and determining what we would choose to do. To use one of Gordon's 1986 examples, if we are playing chess, I may try to anticipate your next move by imagining myself in your situation and deciding what I would choose to do. Similarly, if we agree to meet for lunch tomorrow, I (mentally) 'predict' that you will expect me at roughly the appointed time and place. I ascribe this expectation to you because this is the expectation I would form if I were in your (presumed) situation. The simulation procedure can also be used for explanatory, or 'retrodictive', assignment of mental states. (Indeed, this is the more central type of case for the theme of 'interpretation'.) If you make a surprising chess move, I may infer a new strategy on your part, one that might have led me, if I were in your situation, to the observed move. To assure the plausibility of this being your strategy, I would see whether I could simulate both (a) arriving at this strategy from your presumed antecedent states, and (b) choosing the observed move given this strategy. Ascriptions of intent that lie behind observed behavior would, on the simulation theory, commonly take this second, explanatory form.

In all of these examples, my inference to a new state of yours draws on assumptions about your prior mental states. Does this not threaten a regress? How do I get any initial entree into your mental world? Can that be explained by simulation? Yes. The regress presumably stops at perceptual cases, and at basic likings or cravings. From your perceptual situation, I infer that you have certain perceptual experiences or beliefs, the same ones I would have in your situation. I may also assume (pending information to the contrary) that you have the same basic likings that I have: for food, love, warmth, and so on.

Simulation is also relevant in inferring *actions* from mental states, not just mental states from other mental states. For ordinary 'basic' actions, I expect your 'choice' of an action to issue in its production because my own choice would so issue. In more problematic cases, such as uttering a tongue-twister, simulation might lead me to doubt that you will succeed. Morton (1980) points out that 'analysis-by-synthesis' accounts of speech perception invoke a (tacit) simulation of motor activity. According to this approach, in trying to categorise a speaker's acoustic sequence as one or another phonemic string, the perceiver constrains the choice of interpretation by 'running a model' of how his own vocal apparatus might articulate those sounds.

It would be a mistake, of course, to use the simulation procedure too simplistically, without adequate attention to individual differences. If I am a chess novice and you are a master, or vice versa, it would be foolish to assume that your analysis would match mine. To optimize use of the simulation procedure, I must not only imagine myself in possession of your goals and beliefs about the board configuration, but also in possession of your level of chess sophistication. People may not always take such factors into account; and frequently they lack information to make such adjustments accurately. In any case, there is no assumption here that people are always successful or optimal simulators. What I do conjecture is that simulation—whether explicit or implicit— is the fundamental method used for arriving at mental ascriptions to others. (A more complex variant of the simulation theme will be briefly sketched in Section V.)

I am not saying, it should be emphasized, that simulation is the *only* method used for interpersonal mental ascriptions, or for the prediction of behavior. Clearly, there are regularities about behavior and individual differences that can be learned purely inductively. If Jones always greets people with a smile whereas Brown greets them with a grunt, their acquaintances can form appropriate expectations without deploying simulation. If people who enter a car in the driver's seat regularly proceed to start it, this is the basis for future expectations that need not appeal to simulation. The suggestion, then, is that simulation is an intensively used heuristic, and one on which interpretation fundamentally rests. Inductive or nomological information is not wholly absent, but it is sparser than the folk-theory approach alleges.

Does the simulation approach accommodate the problems confronting the rational norms approach? Very straightforwardly. The mere fact that the 'preface' belief ('at least one of my claims is false') produces inconsistency does not tempt me to withhold attribution of this belief to Hannah. This is just the belief I too would form, especially if I were unaware of the inconsistency (a similar point is made by Stich 1985). Similarly, the mere fact that Jeremy's probability assignments violate the probability calculus does not make me shrink from attributing them; for I too can feel their intuitive pull.

The merits of the simulation approach are further demonstrated by seeing how easily it handles a number of cases that the rival approaches cannot handle, or can handle only with difficulty. In an experiment by Daniel Kahneman and Amos Tversky (1982), subjects were given the following example:

> Mr. Crane and Mr. Tees were scheduled to leave the airport on different flights, at the same time. They traveled from town in the same limousine, were caught in a

traffic jam, and arrived at the airport 30 minutes after the scheduled departure time of their flights. Mr. Crane is told that his flight left on time. Mr. Tees is told that his was delayed, and just left five minutes ago. Who is more upset?

Surely people do not possess a tacit folk psychological *theory* that warrants any particular answer to this question. But 96% of the subjects in the experiment said that Mr. Tees would be more upset. How did they severally arrive at the same answer? Clearly, by simulation. They imagined how *they* would feel in Mr. Crane's and Mr. Tees' shoes, and responded accordingly.

More evidence in a similar vein comes from the domain of verbal communication. Verbal communicators commonly make assumptions—often correct—about the contextual information accessible to their audience and likely to be used in the comprehension process. For example, inspired by the landscape, Mary says to Peter: 'It's the sort of scene that would have made Marianne Dashwood swoon.' This allusion to Austen's *Sense and Sensibility* is based on Mary's expectation that this utterance will act as a prompt, making Peter recall parts of the book that he had previously forgotten, and construct the assumptions needed to understand the allusion. My question is: How does a communicator proceed to estimate what pieces of information will be marshalled, or made salient, in the mind of the audience, in short, which pieces of information are 'calculable'.

Dan Sperber and Deirdre Wilson (1986), from whom the preceding example was borrowed, have an interesting theory of the hearer, which postulates a variety of pertinent cognitive traits. For example, they postulate that cognizers have a number of rules of deductive inference, but these are all *elimination* rules (*e.g.* from 'P & Q' you may infer 'Q') and not *introduction* rules (*e.g.* from 'P' you may infer 'P or Q'). Now assume that this piece of cognitive psychology is correct. Clearly, it is not known or believed by the naive speaker. The speaker cannot appeal to any such *theoretical* knowledge to make predictions of what is likely to be derived or calculated by the hearer. Nonetheless, speakers are evidently pretty good at making such predictions, more precisely, at predicting what kinds of 'implicatures', will be appreciated by an audience. How do they do that? Again, I suggest, by simulation. They can simulate in themselves the states that result from the inference rules, without knowing what those rules are. Hence, they can project, with fairly substantial reliability, what hearers will be able to infer and understand.

A related point concerns people's intuitive grasp of what others will find *funny*. Again it seems far-fetched to suppose that my ability to gauge what will amuse you is based on a theory of humor (of what amuses people). I do not possess any general theory of this sort. More plausibly, I gauge *your* probable reaction to a joke by projecting my own. (There can be adjustments here for factual information about inter-personal differences, but this is just a corrective to the basic tactic of simulation.) There are (arguably) two states of yours that I judge or anticipate through simulation. I estimate by simulation that you will grasp the intended point of the joke: a cognitive state. I also judge by simulation that you will be amused by it: not a purely cognitive state.

Apropos of non-cognitive states, it is worth stressing that a virtue of the simulation theory is its capacity to provide a uniform account of all mental state attributions, not only of propositional attitudes but of non-propositional mental states like pains and tickles. This contrasts with the rationality approach, which has no resources for explaining the latter. No principle of *rationality* dictates when a person should feel pain, or what one should do when in pain. Similarly for tickles. Thus, a rationality (or charity) approach to propositional attitude interpretation would have to be supplemented by an entirely different element to account for attributions of sensations, and perhaps emotions as well. Such bifurcation has less appeal than the unified account offered by the simulation approach.

In a brief discussion of the simulation idea, Dennett (1987b) finds it very puzzling. How can it work, he asks, without being a kind of theorizing? If I make believe I am a suspension bridge and wonder what I will do when the wind blows, what comes to mind depends on how sophisticated my *knowledge* is of the physics and engineering of suspension bridges. Why should making believe that I have your beliefs be any different? Why should it too not require theoretical knowledge?

To answer this question, we need to say more about the general idea of simulation. For a device to simulate a system is for the former to behave in a way that 'models', or maintains some relevant isomorphism to, the behavior of the latter. This is the sense in which a computer might simulate a weather system or an economy. Now if a person seeks to simulate the weather or the economy, in the sense of mentally constructing or anticipating an actual (or genuinely feasible) sequence of its states, she is very unlikely to be accurate unless she has a good theory of the system. A successful simulation of this kind must be *theory-driven*, let us say. This is Dennett's point. But must all mental simulations be theory-driven in order to succeed? I think not. A simulation of some target systems might be accurate even if the agent lacks such a theory. This can happen if (1) the *process* that drives the simulation is the same as (or relevantly similar to) the process that drives the system, and (2) the initial states of the simulating agent are the same as, or relevantly similar to, those of the target system. Thus, if one person simulates a sequence of mental states of another, they will wind up in the same (or isomorphic) final states as long as (A) they began in the same (or isomorphic) initial states, and (B) both sequences were driven by the same cognitive process or routine. It is not necessary that the simulating agent have a theory of what the routine is, or how it works. In short, successful simulation can be *process-driven*.

Now in central cases of interpretation, the interpreter is not actually in the very same initial states as the interpretee. While there may be overlap in beliefs and goals, there are typically relevant differences as well. So how can the interpreter succeed via simulation? The critical move, of course, is that the interpreter tries to imagine, or 'feign', the same initial states as the interpretee. She 'pretends' or 'makes believe' she has the relevant initial states, and then performs reasoning operations (or other cognitive operations) to generate successive states in herself. But are these 'pretend' states—the pseudo-beliefs, pseudo-desires, and so forth—relevantly similar to the genuine beliefs and desires that they model? Is it plausible that imagined beliefs and actual beliefs would yield the same, or analogous, outputs when operated upon by the same cognitive operations?

It *is* plausible, I submit. Consider hypothetical, or subjunctive, reasoning. I ask myself, 'Suppose I did action A—what would be the result?' How do I proceed to answer this question? It seems that what I do is imagine myself believing the proposition 'I do A', and then draw causal inferences from that pseudo-belief together with (certain) antecedent genuine beliefs. Furthermore, it seems that I use the very same inference processes as those I would use on a set of wholly genuine belief inputs. (The output, though, is only a belief in the same hypothetical mood, not a genuine belief.) Similarly, I make contingency plans by executing practical reasoning operations on feigned beliefs in certain contingencies; and these are the same planning operations that I would apply to genuine beliefs in those contingencies. So it seems that 'pretend' belief states *are* relevantly similar to belief states; there are significant isomorphisms. The possibility of isomorphisms between 'genuine' states and imaginatively, or artificially, generated 'copies' is further illustrated in the imagery domain. Roger Shepard, Stephen Kosslyn, and their respective colleagues have produced striking evidence to support the claim that visual images are similar in important respects to genuine visual perceptions (Shepard and Cooper 1982; Kosslyn 1980). To determine the congruence or non-congruence of two shapes, forming a mental image of one being rotated into alignment with the other can be almost as reliable as actually seeing the results of this rotation. This would hardly be possible if imagery were not relevantly similar to genuine perception.

V

Let us explore the psychological defensibility of the simulation approach in more detail. We may first note that several cognitive scientists have recently endorsed the idea of mental simulation as one cognitive heuristic, although these researchers stress its use for knowledge in general, not specifically knowledge of others' mental states. Kahneman and Tversky (1982) propose that people often try to answer questions about the world by an operation that resembles the running of a simulation model. The starting conditions for a 'run', they say, can either be left at realistic default values or modified to assume some special contingency. Similarly, Rumelhart, Smolensky, McClelland, and Hinton (1986) describe the importance of 'mental models' of the world, in particular, models that simulate how the world would respond to one's hypothetical actions. They first apply this idea to actual and imagined conversations, and later describe a PDP (parallel distributed processing) network for playing tic-tac-toe, a network that embodies 'simulations' of the world's (*i.e.* the opponent's) response to the agent's possible moves.

Since part of my argument rests on the superior plausibility of the simulation approach in accounting for children's interpretational ability, let us next look at recent work by developmental psychologists that bear on this point. The most striking findings are those by Heinz Wimmer and Josef Perner, conjoined with a follow-up study by Simon Baron-Cohen, Alan Leslie, and Uta Frith. Various experimental studies had previously shown that as early as $2\frac{1}{2}$ years, children use a substantial vocabulary about perception, volition, major emotions, and knowledge. But experiments by Wimmer and Perner (1983) strongly indicate that around the ages of four to six, an ability to clearly distinguish between someone else's belief state and reality becomes firmly established. In their study, children between three and nine years of age observed a sketch of how a protagonist put an object into a location X and then witnessed that, in the absence of the protagonist, the object was transferred from X to location Y. Since this transfer came as a surprise, they should assume that the protagonist still believed that the object was in X. Subjects were then required to indicate where the protagonist will look for the object on his return. None of the 3–4-year olds, 57% of the 4–6-year olds, and 86% of the 6–9-year olds pointed correctly to location X. In their related study, Baron-Cohen, Leslie and Frith (1985) studied the ability of autistic children to perform this sort of task. Of critical relevance here are two facts about autistic children. First, the main symptom of autism is impairment in verbal and nonverbal communication. Second, autistic children show a striking poverty of pretend play. Baron-Cohen *et al.*'s experiment showed that when the tested children were asked where the doll protagonist would look for her marble, 85% of the normal children answered correctly, but only 20% of the autistic children (with a mean age close to 12 and a relatively high mean IQ of 82) answered correctly. Especially striking was the fact that the test also included a pool of Down's syndrome children, 86% of whom answered the crucial question *correctly*. This suggests that the failure of the autistic children is not due to general mental retardation, a trait shared by Down's syndrome children. Rather it is specific cognitive deficit. Baron-Cohen *et al.* hypothesize that autistic children as a group fail to acquire a 'theory of mind', *i.e.* an ability to impute beliefs to others and therefore predict their behavior correctly. This would account for their social and communicational impairment. It might also be related to their lack of pretend play. Perhaps, as Gordon (1986) suggests, all this points to a prepackaged 'module' for simulation directed at other human beings, a module which is impaired in autism.

One of the co-authors of the autism study, Alan Leslie, has sketched a theory that interrelates pretend play and the representation of mental states (Leslie 1987). He points out that pretending is in some ways an odd practice. From an evolutionary point of view, one might expect a high premium on maintaining an accurate and objective view of the world. A child who acts as if dolls have genuine feelings is scarcely acting upon a veridical picture of the world. Yet pretend play emerges at an early age, and becomes more elaborate during development. It is not implausible to conjecture that pretend play is a preliminary exercise of a mechanism the primary function of which is the simulation of real people's mental states. Roughly this theme is articulated both by Leslie and by Saami and Harris (1989). Such a mechanism, on the present theory, underlies interpersonal interpretation, prediction, and perhaps communication as well.

Whatever the force of these findings and speculations, there is a straightforward challenge to the psychological plausibility of the simulation approach. It is far from obvious, introspectively, that we regularly place ourselves in another person's shoes, and vividly envision what we would do in his circumstances. This is a natural thing to do while watching a tennis match, perhaps, or while listening to someone relating their tragic life story. But the simulation approach ostensibly makes this empathic attitude the standard mode of interpretation. Is that not difficult to accept?

Two replies should be made. First, simulation need not be an introspectively vivid affair. The approach can certainly insist that most simulation is semi-automatic, with relatively little salient phenomenology. It is a psychological commonplace that highly developed skills become automatized, and there is no reason why inter-personal simulation should not share this characteristic. (On the issue of conscious awareness, the simulation theory is no worse off than its competitors. Neither the rationality approach nor the folk-theory theory is at all credible if it claims that appeals to its putative principles are introspectively prominent aspects of interpretation.)

A second point might be that many cases of rapid, effortless interpretation may be devoid of even automatized simulation. When a mature cognizer has constructed, by simulation, many similar instances of certain action-interpretation patterns, she may develop generalizations or other inductively formed representations (schemas, scripts, and so forth) that can trigger analogous interpretations by application of those 'knowledge structures' alone, *sans* simulation. I have, of course, already acknowledged the role of inductively based predictions of behavior, and the need for standard empirical information to make adjustments for individual differences. The present point is a slightly larger concession. It agrees that in many cases the interpreter relies solely (at the time of interpretation) on inductively acquired information. But this information, it suggests, is historically derived from earlier simulations. If this story is right, then simulation remains the fundamental source of interpretation, though not the essence of every act (or even most acts) of interpretation. We might call this the *complex* variant of the simulation approach. It converges somewhat toward the folk-theory theory (though the exact degree of convergence depends on the nature of the inductively based knowledge structures it posits). It still remains distinct, however, (A) because the folk-theory theory makes no allowance for simulation, and (B) because the complex variant postulates simulation as the originating source of (most) interpretation.

Commenting in part on an earlier version of this paper, Paul Churchland (1989) poses two difficulties for the simulation theory. First, he says, simulation is not necessary for understanding others. People who are congenitally deaf, or blind, are quite capable of understanding normal people, and people who have never themselves felt profound grief or rejection can nevertheless provide appropriate interpretations of others who are so afflicted. In general, understanding goes beyond what one has personally experienced. I have already granted, however, that straightforwardly empirical information is required to accommodate individual differences, and these examples are just more extreme illustrations of the point. We must certainly allow for the human capacity to extrapolate from one's own case, to project types of sensory or emotional sensibility that one does not oneself instantiate. This concession does not undermine the point that interpretation primarily starts from the home base of one's own experience.

Churchland further objects that while simulation may account for the prediction of others' behavior, it does not provide for *explanation*. The simulation theory makes the understanding of others depend crucially on having an initial understanding of oneself. But it leaves mysterious, he says, the nature of first person understanding. More specifically, *explanatory* understanding requires appreciation of the *general patterns* that comprehend individual events in both cases. This requires a *theory*, which the simulation approach spurns. In my opinion, however, explanation can consist of telling a story that eliminates various alternative hypotheses about how the event in question came about, or could have come about. This can effectively answer a 'Why'-question, which is the essence of explanation (see van Fraassen 1980, chapter 5). In the case of interpretive explanation this is done by citing a specific set of goals and beliefs, which implicitly rules out the indefinitely many alternative desire-and-belief sets that might have led to the action.

Churchland rejects the deductive nomological theory of explanation on the grounds that it presupposes a sentential, or propositional attitude, account of knowledge representation. He proposes to replace this picture of cognition with a prototype-based picture, especially one that is elaborated within a connectionist framework. He still wishes to count human cognition as significantly *theoretical*, but theory-possession is apparently no longer associated with nomologicality. Churchland is welcome to use the term 'theory' in this neological fashion; but it cannot resuscitate the standard version of the folk-theory approach to interpretation. It is only in the usual, nomological construal of theories that I am addressing (and rejecting) that approach. I am pleased to see Churchland also reject that approach, but it seems to have ramifications for his other views that I shall mention below.

VI

Considering the complexity of the human organism, it may well be considered remarkable that we are able to predict human behavior as well as we do. Is this impressive success fully accounted for by the simulation theory? Only, I think, with an added assumption, *viz.* that the other people, whose behavior we predict, are psychologically very similar to ourselves. Just as the child readily learns a grammar of a natural language because its native grammar-learning structures mirror those of its language-creating mates, so a person can successfully simulate the internal operations of others because they are largely homologous to her own. The fuller picture, then, has strong affinities to Noam Chomsky's emphasis on the role of species-specific traits in mental activity.

Although I view this theme as Chomskyesque, it is also similar to one made by Quine (1969). Quine asks how the language learner manages to learn the law of English verbal behavior connected with 'yellow'. The answer, he says, is that the learner's quality spacing is enough like his neighbor's that such learning is almost a foregone conclusion: he is making his induction in a 'friendly world'. He is playing a game of chance with favorably loaded dice. Similarly, I am suggesting, people's predictions of other people's behavior, based heavily on attributions of content, are so successful because people operate with the same set of fundamental cognitive constraints. (Notice, I need not say that people are successful at assigning correct contents to people's mental states; that would assume that there is an independent fact of the matter about content, prior to the activity of interpretation. Since some interpretation theorists would reject this thesis, I can confine my claim to successful prediction of *behavior*.)

The constraints I have in mind must be constraints on the specific contents assigned to an agent's propositional attitudes. Without positing such constraints, it is hard to account for the definiteness and interpersonal uniformity in content attributions. There would seem to be too much 'play', too much looseness, in the sorts of abstract constraints that a theorist like Davidson, for example, imposes. Assuming the interpretations of the interpreter to be given, we need to explain why she makes those rather than the innumerable other conceivable interpretations.

In a similar (though not identical) context, Lewis worries whether enough constraints on content are imposed by his theory to exclude preposterous and perverse misinterpretations (Lewis 1983c). To exclude perverse interpretations, Lewis says we need *a priori* presumptions about just what sorts of things are apt to be believed or desired. These presumptions should be thought of as built into our interpretation procedures. Adopting a suggestion of Gary Merrill, Lewis proposes that natural kinds are more eligible for content attributions than non-natural kinds. Taking naturalness to be a graded affair, more natural kinds have greater eligibility for content inclusion than less natural kinds. Principles of content possession should therefore impute a bias toward believing that things are green rather than grue, toward having a basic desire for long life rather than for long-life-unless-one-was-born-on-Monday-and-in-that-case-life-for-an-even-number-of-weeks.

I agree with Lewis that to get things right, *i.e.* to conform to our actual content attributions, account must be taken of what is 'natural' and 'unnatural'. But only if this means 'natural for us': congenial to human psychology. This is not what Lewis means. By 'natural' Lewis means properties Nature herself deems natural, those categories that are objectively, independently, non-anthropocentrically natural. This is not very plausible. Granted that the kind 'a mass of molecules' is more of a natural kind than, say, 'table', it is still less plausible to attribute beliefs about masses of molecules to scientifically untutored people than beliefs about tables. Or take the hue yellow. From an objective, non-anthropocentric viewpoint, yellow is less natural than other possible spectral or reflectancy categorizations. Nonetheless, it is more plausible to attribute contents involving yellow than more objective categorizations of light frequency. Clearly, it is concepts that are humanly more natural, *i.e.* psychologically congenial, that are more eligible for content.

What I am suggesting, then, is that uniformity in cross-personal interpretations should be partly explained by psychological preferences for certain modes of categorization and 'entification', or more basically, by operations that generate categorial and entificational preferences. The precise nature of these operations and/or preferences remains to be spelled out by cognitive science. But let me give some examples of what I mean.

Our entification practices include propensities to group together, or unify, certain sets of elements in a perceptual display rather than others. The Gestalt principles of similarity, proximity, closedness, and good continuation, are attempts to systematize the mental operations that underpin these unificational practices. The Gestalt principles apply not only in the visual domain, but in the temporal domain as well. Thus, presented with the opening passage of Mozart's 40th symphony, principles of temporal proximity (and so forth) make it natural to segment the passage into three distinct phrases (I oversimplify here). Other conceivable segmentations are highly unnatural. It is plausible to conjecture that the same Gestalt principles are at work in fixing our conceptual (as opposed to perceptual) intuitions of identity, or unity, of objects through time (see Goldman 1987).

Another set of categorial preferences feature what Eleanor Rosch calls the 'basic level' of categories (Rosch 1975, 1978). Language (and presumably thought) is full of category hierarchies such as *poodle, dog, mammal, animal, physical object*. Experiments show that the categories in the middle of such hierarchies, in the present case *dog* rather than *poodle* or *physical object*, have a definite psychological primacy.

How do entitative and categorial preferences of the interpreter get deployed in the interpretation process? Two slightly different hypotheses are possible. First, the preferences may be registered directly; that is, the interpreter uses her own categorial preferences to assign content to the interpretee. Second, they might be used in conjunction with the simulation heuristic. In assigning reference and meaning, the interpreter imagines what the agent's concept-forming or proposition-forming devices might generate in the present context, and this imaginative act is structured by the interpreter's own concept-forming and judgment-forming operations.

In either case, the hypotheses I am advancing would account for a substantial degree of uniformity in specific content attributions. It would also mesh with Davidson's theme of belief similarity among interpreters and interpretees, but only subject to important qualifications. The simulation hypothesis assumes that the interpreter tends to impute to the interpretee the same fundamental categories as her own, or at least the same basic category-forming (and proposition-forming) operations. She also tends to project the same basic belief-forming processes. But these practices still leave room for wide divergence in belief content. The simulation procedure can take account of differences in the agent's evidential exposures, and in the special inferential habits, algorithms, and heuristics that he has learned or acquired. Differences along these dimensions can ramify into substantial differences in belief sets.

My emphasis on conspecific psychological traits may suggest the possibility that only other *people* are interpretable by us. That is not a claim I endorse. On the contrary, we certainly think of ourselves as interpreting other animals; and although we may partly deceive ourselves with misplaced anthropomorphism, we do have moderate predictive success. Of course, the use of straightforward inductively gathered information is prominent here. But, as indicated earlier, we also use our own psychology as a home base, and make conservative revisions from that starting-point. Perhaps this is why it is more difficult to construct right-seeming interpretations of heterospecifics than conspecifics. Dolphins seem to be highly intelligent and to communicate among themselves, yet no human has constructed a plausible interpretation of their language.

Although my discussion centers on the psychological dimensions involved in content attributions, it by no means precludes an important role for the external world, especially causal relations with the external world, in the choice of semantic assignments to thoughts. In deciding what is the *referent* of an imputed thought, in particular, it seems clear that the interpreter takes into account the thought's causal history. Similarly, it is plausible to suppose that imputation of other semantic dimensions of thought involves mind-world connections. These are plausibly part of the conceptual background with which the interpreter operates. Although I am not addressing these issues, which lie at the heart of much current debate, they are complementary to the themes I am pursuing.

VII

In this final section I briefly address several possible philosophical ramifications of the simulation approach, including the interpretation strategy with which I began.

Does the simulation approach imply a sharp divide between explanations of the mental and the physical? If so, it would vindicate the claim of the hermeneutic tradition, which contrasts understanding of human action with understanding of physical phenomena. No sharp contrast necessarily follows from the simulation theory. For one thing, we have already noted that simulation or mental modelling is sometimes postulated as a cognitive heuristic for representing physical phenomena as well as mental states. Admittedly, this realization of the simulation heuristic would presumably be theory driven rather than process driven. Still, this already admits an important parallel. Furthermore, proponents of interpretational simulation need not maintain that nomological explanation of human phenomena is impossible. They just maintain that *common sense* explanations and predictions of the mental do not (in the main) invoke laws.

A second philosophical issue raised by the simulation theory is the epistemology of other minds. Ostensibly, the theory is a version of the 'analogical' theory of mental state ascription. It seems to impute to interpreters inferences of roughly the following form: 'If he is psychologically like me, he must be in mental state M; he is psychologically like me; therefore, he is in mental state M.' But there is a long-standing suspicion of such arguments from analogy, centering on the second premise. How can the interpreter know (or believe justifiably) that the agent is psychologically like her? Can physical and behavioral similarity support this premise? Is not an analogy based on a single case a thin reed on which to rest?

The best line of reply, I think, is to deny that interpreters must believe the second premise. Many beliefs are formed by mechanisms, or routines, that are built into the cognitive architecture. Although these mechanisms might be described in terms of 'rules' or 'principles', it would be misleading to say that the cognizers believe those rules or principles. For example, it is plausible to say that people form perceptual beliefs (or representations) in accord with Gestalt rules, but implausible to say that they literally believe those rules. They represent certain partly occluded figures as being single, unitary objects when there is sufficient 'continuity' between their perceived parts; but they do not believe the continuity principle itself. In our case, cognizers make interpretations in accordance with a routine that could be formulated by the principle, 'Other people are psychologically like me'. But this is not really a believed 'premise' on which they inferentially base their interpretations.

Could a belief that is produced by such a routine qualify as justified, or as a piece of knowledge, if the rule is not believed? Reliabilism is one species of epistemology that would be congenial to this result. If the routine, or process, is a generally reliable one, then reliabilism (in certain forms) may be prepared to count its output beliefs as justified (see, for example, Goldman 1986). So there is at least one type of epistemology that promises to resolve the epistemic challenge to the simulation theory.

A third noteworthy philosophical point concerns the ramification of abandoning the folk-theory theory. This theory has been a salient premise in the argument for eliminativism about propositional attitudes. Eliminativists standardly begin by emphasizing that the attitudes—and all our common sense mentalistic notions—are part of a folk psychological theory. They then point to the bleak history of past folk scientific theories, suggesting that the same scenario is in store for folk psychology (see Churchland 1981). Since folk psychology will ultimately prove to have poorer predictive value than scientific psychology, its constructs will need to be replaced or eliminated, just like the constructs of, say, alchemy. However, if it turns out that there is no folk theory, in the sense of a set of common-sense generalizations that define the mental terms, then an important premise for eliminativism is no longer available. (This point has been made by Gordon.)

Let me turn now to what is probably the most pressing philosophical issue posed by the simulation theory. What is the relation, it may be asked, between the simulation approach and what it is for mental ascriptions to be *correct*? The simulation theory purports to give an account of the procedure used in ascribing mental states to others. What light does this shed, however, on the conditions that are *constitutive* of mental state possession (especially possession of the attitudes)? The interpretation strategist hopes to extract from the interpretation procedure some criteria of correctness for mentalistic ascriptions. Certainly the rationality and functionalist theories would generate answers to this question. (Whether or not the answers they generate are correct is another matter. Functionalist definitions, for example, have many familiar problems.) But the simulation theory looks distinctly unpromising on this score. Since simulation is such a fallible procedure, there is little hope of treating 'M is ascribed (or ascribable) to S on the basis of simulation' as constitutive of 'S is in M'. Furthermore, simulation assumes a prior understanding of what state it is that the interpreter ascribes to S. This just re-raises the same question: what state is it that the interpreter is imputing to the agent when she ascribes state M? What does her understanding of the M-concept consist in?

As far as the interpretation strategy is concerned, it indeed appears that if the simulation theory is correct, the interpretation strategy is fruitless. One cannot extract criteria of mentalistic ascription from the practice of inter-personal interpretation if that practice rests on a prior and independent understanding of mentalistic notions. As far as the interpretation strategy goes, then, the moral of the simulation theory is essentially a negative one. It should be recalled, however, that I warned from the outset that the hope of the interpretation strategy may not be well-founded.

What does the prior understanding of mentalistic notions consist in? For one thing, we should not assume that it consists in the grasp of some necessary and sufficient conditions. More generally, the psychology and philosophy of concept representation is far too poorly understood to make any definite assumptions here. If the simulation theory is right, however, it looks as if the main elements of the grasp of mental concepts must be located in the first-person sphere. Is this objectionable? We should recall, first, how problematic purely third-person accounts of the mental have turned out to be. Second, we should note that the simulation approach does not confine its attention to purely 'private', 'internal' events. It also invokes relations between mental states, on the one hand, and both perceptual situations and overt actions. Thus, there may well be enough ingredients of the right sort to make sense of a first-person-based grasp of mental concepts. In any case, this is not a topic that can be pursued here.

Whether or not I have mounted a successful defence of the simulation theory, I hope I have at least persuaded the reader of the importance of getting the descriptive story of interpretive activity right. Although I think that the evidence in favor of the simulation account is substantial, I am even more convinced of the thesis that philosophers (as well as cognitive scientists) must pay closer attention to the psychology of the interpreter. Making that point has been the principal aim of this paper.

References

Baron-Cohen, S., Leslie, A. and Frith, U. 1985: Does the Autistic Child Have a 'Theory of Mind'? *Cognition*, 21, 37–46.
Churchland, P. 1981: Eliminative Materialism and the Propositional Attitudes. *Journal of Philosophy*, 78, 67–90.
Churchland, P. 1989: Folk Psychology and the Explanation of Human Behavior. In his *The Neurocomputational Perspective*. Cambridge, Mass.: MIT Press.
Davidson, D. 1980: *Essays on Actions and Events*. Oxford: Oxford University Press.
Davidson, D. 1984: *Inquiries into Truth and Interpretation*. Oxford: Oxford University Press.
Dennett, D. 1971: Intentional Systems. *Journal of Philosophy*, 68, 87–106.
Dennett, D. 1987a: True Believers. In his *The Intentional Stance*. Cambridge, Mass.: MIT Press.
Dennett, D. 1987b: Making Sense of Ourselves. In his *The Intentional Stance*. Cambridge, Mass.: MIT Press.
Fodor, J. 1987: *Psychosemantics: The Problem of Meaning in the Philosophy of Mind*. Cambridge, Mass.: MIT Press.

Goldman, A. 1970: *A Theory of Human Action*. Englewood Cliffs, N.J.: Prentice Hall.

Goldman, A. 1986: *Epistemology and Cognition*. Cambridge, Mass.: Harvard University Press.

Goldman, A. 1987: Cognitive Science and Metaphysics. *Journal of Philosophy*, 84, 537–44.

Gordon, R. 1986: Folk Psychology as Simulation. *Mind and Language*, 1, 158–71.

Gordon, R. 1987: *The Structure of Emotions*. Cambridge: Cambridge University Press.

Grandy, R. 1973: Reference, Meaning, and Belief. *Journal of Philosophy*, 70, 439–52.

Kahneman, D. and Tversky, A. 1982: The Simulation Heuristic. In Kahneman, D., Slovic, P. and Tversky, A. (eds.), *Judgment Under Uncertainty*. Cambridge: Cambridge University Press.

Kosslyn, S. 1980: *Image and Mind*. Cambridge, Mass.: Harvard University Press.

LePore, E. (ed.) 1986: *Truth and Interpretation*. Oxford: Basil Blackwell.

Leslie, A. 1987: Pretense and Representation: The Origins of 'Theory of Mind'. *Psychological Review*, 94, 412–26.

Lewis, D. 1972: Psychophysical and Theoretical Identifications. *Australasian Journal of Philosophy*, 61, 249–58.

Lewis, D. 1983a: Radical Interpretation. In his *Philosophical Papers*, Vol. 1. New York: Oxford University Press.

Lewis, D. 1983b: How to Define Theoretical Terms. In his *Philosophical Papers*, Vol. 1. New York: Oxford University Press.

Lewis, D. 1983c: New Work for a Theory of Universals. *Australasian Journal of Philosophy*, 50, 343–77.

Loar, B. 1987: Subjective Intentionality. *Philosophical Topics*, 15, 89–124.

McGinn, C. 1977: Charity, Interpretation, and Belief. *Journal of Philosophy*, 74, 521–35.

McGinn, C. 1986: Radical Interpretation and Epistemology. In LePore 1986.

Millikan, R. 1984: *Language, Thought, and Other Biological Categories*. Cambridge, Mass.: MIT Press.

Morton, A. 1980: *Frames of Mind*. Oxford: Oxford University Press.

Quine, W. V. 1960: *Word and Object*. Cambridge, MA: MIT Press.

Quine, W. V. 1969: Natural Kinds. In his *Ontological Relativty and Other Essays*. New York: Columbia University Press.

Rosch, E. 1975: Cognitive Representations of Semantic Categories. *Journal of Experimental Psychology*: General, 104, 192-233.

Rosch, E. 1978: Principles of Categorization. In Rosch, E. and Lloyd, B. (eds.), *Cogntion and Categorization*. Hillsdale, N.J.: Lawrence Erlbaum.

Rumelhart, D., Smolensky, P., McClelland, J., and Hinton, G. 1986: Schemata and Sequential Thought Processes in PDP Models. In McClelland, J., Rumelhart, D., and the PDP Research Group, *Paralllel Distributed Processing*, Vol. 2. Cambridge, MA: MIT Press.

Saami, C. and Harris, P. 1989: *Children's Understanding of Emotion*. Cambridge, UK: Cambridge University Press.

Shepard, R. and Cooper, L. 1982: *Mental Images and Their Transformations*. Cambridge, MA: MIT Press.

Sperber, D. and Wilson, D. 1986: *Relevance*. Oxford: Basil Blackwell.

Stich, S. 1983: *From Folk Psychology to Cognitive Science*. Cambridge, MA: MIT Press.

Stich, S. 1985: Could Man Be An Irrational Animal? In Kornblith, H. (ed.): *Naturalizing Epistemology*. Cambridge, MA: MIT Press.

Tversky, A. and Kahneman, D. 1983: Extensional versus Intuitive Reasoning: The Conjunction Fallacy in Probability Judgment. *Psychological Review*, 90, 293-315.

van Fraassen, B. 1980: *The Scientific Image*. New York: Oxford University Press.

Wimmer, H. and Perner, J. 1983: Beliefs about Beliefs: Representation and Constraining Function of Wrong Beliefs in Young Childrens's Understanding of Deception. *Cognition*, 13, 103-29.

Chapter 13

KARSTEN R. STUEBER

THE PSYCHOLOGICAL BASIS OF HISTORICAL EXPLANATION
Reenactment, simulation, and the fusion of horizons

I. Introduction

IN THE PHILOSOPHY OF THE OF the human sciences, empathy has long lost its past glory from the days when it was proposed as the method uniquely suited for the explanation of human action and historical phenomena. With the exception of some adherents of Collingwood's doctrine of reenactment, philosophers from both the analytic and continental-hermeneutic traditions tend to dismiss empathy as a viable principle of explanation or interpretation of human affairs. According to Carl Hempel, a representative of naturalism in the philosophy of social science, empathy can only be understood as a heuristic means within the context of discovery. It does not serve any function within the context of justification. Even if philosophers do not any longer regard Hempel's epistemic model of scientific explanation as an authoritative analysis of our concept of explanation,[1] the demise of Hempel's model did not help to revive the theory of empathy. Naturalists in the philosophy of social science still think of explanation as mediated by an appeal to theory that articulates the underlying causal mechanism of a particular domain of investigation. On the continental-hermeneutic side, on the other hand, Hans-Georg Gadamer's critique made certain that empathy was regarded as an impossible and outdated attempt to make the human sciences scientifically respectable. Gadamer has objected to empathy because of what he perceived to be its indefensible association with a metaphysics of "original authorial intent" conceived of as a realistic standard for the correctness of the interpretation of texts and the past. Instead, he proposed that interpretation be conceived of as a fusion of horizons.

In this article I will challenge this received orthodoxy by arguing that Collingwood was right in claiming that reenactment—albeit somewhat revised—plays an epistemically central role in historical explanations, since it alone allows us to account sufficiently for individual agency. Yet, as should also become clear in the following, I am not committing myself thereby to the Collingwoodian claim[2] that all history is the history of thought and that reenactment is the only method historians should use.

First, I will construct two arguments for the centrality of reenactment, focusing on the explanations of actions in terms of the agent's reasons and on our understanding of the rationally compelling nature of an action given these reasons. I will also show that reenactment is necessary because of what I call the essential indexicality of thought, emphasizing that the psychological efficacy of the first-person pronoun or indexical cannot be replaced by any description of its objective referent. My aim here is not primarily an exegesis of Collingwood. Rather, I will try to systematically strengthen his position by availing myself of insights from contemporary debate in the philosophy of mind and psychology between simulation theory and what has come to be called "theory theory."

Second, I will discuss Gadamer's influential critique of Collingwood's theory of reenactment. Whereas Collingwood's remark about the logic of question and answer in his *Autobiography* was important for Gadamer's own hermeneutic position, Gadamer rejects reenactment because he thinks it does not fully overcome a positivist conception of the human sciences. I will argue that Gadamer's critique of Collingwood is most plausible insofar as works of art are concerned. However, it does not apply to the interpretation and explanation of actions, where we are conceptually committed to treat reasons as causes for actions.

Third, I will expand on the conception of reenactment and simulation discussed so far, by explicating the limitations of the reenactment strategy for understanding individual agency in cases of great cultural differences between agents. *Pace* Collingwood, the limits of reenactment should not necessarily be seen as the limits of historical explanations. Rather, in cases of extreme cultural differences the reenactment strategy has to be supplemented by theoretical considerations. Using as an example the debate between Christopher Browning and Daniel Goldhagen about the motivation of ordinary policemen for participating in the extermination of Jews in Eastern Europe, I will distinguish between the strategy of cognitive extrapolation and psychological theory proper.

II. The centrality of reenactment: lessons from contemporary philosophy of mind and language

In order to appreciate the force of Collingwood's position it is necessary to reconstruct and refine his arguments for reenactment, which are scattered throughout *The Idea of History*. For this purpose, and because Collingwood does not regard reenactment merely as the method of history but as *the* general method to study other minds,[3] it is instructive to situate him in the contemporary debate about the nature of folk psychology as it is discussed between proponents of simulation theory and theory theory. In this context, the term "folk psychology" refers to the conceptual repertoire of mental and psychological categories that ordinary people, without any specific psychological training, have available in order to understand their own and somebody else's behavior. We (including children) explain, for example, somebody's turning red in the face and screaming by saying that he is angry, or by predicting that Professor X will try to publish as much as possible because she wants to get tenure.

The main issue in the debate between simulation theory and theory theory is the question of how best to account for our folk-psychological capacity to interpret, predict, and explain another person's actions and thoughts in a psychologically realistic manner. That is, how should the psychological mechanisms that allow us to apply mental state terminology for the purpose of prediction and explanation be depicted? Roughly described, most theory theorists maintain that our folk-psychological ability is based, at least tacitly, on a theory about human psychology and its belief/desire generalizations (such as that, *ceteris paribus*, somebody will do x if he or she desires y and believes that x is the most apt means to y). Our prediction or explanation that somebody will try to publish as much as possible is thus based on an implicit inference that uses an instance of this general and theoretical scheme. We conclude that Professor X will try to publish as much as possible because she desires to get tenure and she believes that in order to gain tenure one has to publish as much as possible; behind this conclusion is our general claim that everybody who has these beliefs and desires will, *ceteris paribus*, publish as much as possible.

Simulation theorists, on the other hand, argue for a version of Collingwood's reenactment theory, a version couched in the vocabulary of contemporary cognitive science. They conceive of our understanding of another person as arising from the active involvement of our own practical deliberative capacity, not from theoretical knowledge about other human beings. We do not understand another person by appealing to an abstract theory but by putting ourselves in the shoes of the other person, imagining the world "as it would appear from his point of view" and "then deliberate, reason and see what decision emerges."[4] With Stich and Nichols, one can characterize simulation in a more fine-grained manner and distinguish further between an "actual situation simulation" and a "pretense-driven-off-line simulation."[5] In the first kind of simulation, we predict the action of another person by putting ourselves in a situation very similar to the one he or she is in and observe how we react. For example, we predict how another person might solve a problem in arithmetic by solving it ourselves. Here we predict another person's behavior in light of thoughts we actually have. In pretense-driven simulation, on the other hand, we take into account the relevant differences between ourselves and our target by feeding our own decision system with pretend beliefs and desires and run it "off-line," that is, without our decision system actually determining our course of action or changing any beliefs that we hold. For example I might be able to predict how a person will act when he or she believes that the earth is flat even though I do not actually share that belief and would never act on such a belief. Furthermore, in arriving at this prediction I do not appeal to any psychological generalizations. For that very reason both types of simulation are, in Goldman's terms, process-driven, not theory-driven.

Simulation theorists argue for their claims in fundamentally two ways. First, they point to psychological experiments done by child psychologists and claim that simulation can account better for some of their results. Second, they provide *a priori* reasons by arguing that the nature of thought makes simulation essential for understanding other minds. Collingwood belongs to the second group. He claims that, because of the subject matter, historians cannot be satisfied with observing regularities between events from an external physical perspective. Historians have to grasp the "inside" or the thought-side of an event in order to understand it as a purposeful human action. However, Collingwood does not sufficiently argue against a possible theory theory position in the philosophy of history. Granted that one has to understand what motivations caused a particular action in order to understand why certain agents did what they did; but why is such explanatory understanding not at least implicitly guided by a folk-psychological theory? Nothing that Collingwood explicitly said shows that historians do not rely on a tacit theory, which they acquire in their day-to-day encounters with other people.

Collingwood would probably answer that historians have to understand how human agents in a certain situation are rationally motivated but not nomologically compelled to act.[6] Thus, "historical thought, thought about rational activity is free from the domination of natural science, and rational activity is free from the domination of nature."[7] Yet again one has to be careful in drawing a direct conclusion about the necessity of simulation or reenactment from this observation alone. Pointing out that understanding a rational action means to place it in the context of normative considerations about the appropriateness of an action reveals only a difference in the logical structure between action explanations and other explanations of events in the natural sciences. It does not automatically imply an epistemic or methodological difference in such explanations, since it is compatible with a theory theory position that belief/desire explanations invoke generalizations not as laws but as prescriptive rules specifying what it would mean to be rational.

However, in Collingwood one can find suggestions for two further arguments for re-enactment that show this construal of the theory theory position to be lacking. The first I shall call "the argument from the essential contextuality of rational thought." Jane Heal also promotes this strategy in the context of contemporary simulation theory. The second strategy I shall call "the argument from the essential indexicality of thought."

The essential contextuality of rational thought

Heal draws her simulationist conclusions from the observation that the epistemic justification of contentful mental states is holistic and context dependent, that is, "no thought, whatever its subject matter, can be ruled out *a priori* as certainly irrelevant to a given question."[8] The theory theory view could, hence, be right only if we have a general theory that would enable us to predict which thoughts are epistemically relevant in a specific context. Yet it is empirically not very likely that we possess tacitly such a complex theory of relevance. Moreover, even if we possess such a theory, its possession alone does not guarantee that we would apply it correctly in the relevant circumstances. In this context, a regress of theories threatens, which can only be avoided by appealing to a non-theoretical capacity.[9] Elsewhere I have argued that Aristotle and Wittgenstein's rule-following considerations imply these conclusions.[10] Moreover, even if we were to assume for a moment counterfactually that we have general standards or expectations that govern our behavior in every situation, these standards—whether tacit or explicit—can only be formulated on a very general level. These general standards are therefore to a certain extent open-ended. Each application requires a practical capacity to recognize which rule is relevant for a particular situation and the capacity to apply these rules appropriately afterwards. Hence, recognizing how another person might use such a rule would require using the same practical know-how applied during a process of simulation. No purely theoretical knowledge is therefore sufficient for the task of explaining others' behavior.

These considerations gain even more weight if one recognizes that in normal situations agents not only apply one rule to a particular situation but they have to consider and weigh a variety of sometimes conflicting rules. Collingwood recognizes this fact in Chapter Nine of his *Autobiography*. There he argues that only historical knowledge can provide the "insight" that would enable us to avoid another war such as World War I, for which he holds a "civilization based upon natural science" responsible. Even though he maintains, somewhat contrary to the spirit of Wittgenstein, that "if ready-made rules for dealing with situations of specific types are what you want, natural science is the kind of thing which can provide them,"[11] he nevertheless emphasizes that we are rationally compelled to act in situations for which we do not have ready-made rules, and in situations in which we are not content with applying a known rule because we have to negotiate the application of that rule with other relevant normative considerations:

> Thus everybody has certain rules according to which he acts in dealing with his tailor. These rules are, we will grant, soundly based on experience. . . . But so far as he acts according to these rules, he is dealing with his tailor only in his capacity as a tailor, not as John Robinson, aged sixty, with a weak heart and a consumptive daughter, a passion for gardening and an overdraft at the bank.[12]

Collingwood draws the conclusion that only through reenactment and the simulative involvement of our own practical judgments are we able to grasp the rationality of actions in situations in which multiple normative considerations have to be negotiated.

The Essential Indexicality of Rational Thought

A second argument for reenactment or simulation is suggested by Collingwood's claim that our recognition of a thought cannot be conceived as being similar to the perception of an external object. Conceiving of our recognition of a thought on the model of object perception does not allow us to grasp that a thought is a mental state of a particular person, a state that orients this person towards the world. For that very reason it also does not allow us to understand how a thought can rationally motivate an agent to act in a certain manner in this world. Collingwood thus emphasizes that we can recognize a thought as a thought only by grasping it as the thought *of someone*, that is, as a mental act or state that a person recognizes as his or her own.[13]

Collingwood's assertions about the subjectivity of thought are best understood in light of considerations about the essential and irreducible role of first-person concepts in our cognitive system. This role has been recognized by thinkers as diverse as Descartes, Kant, Perry, and most recently by Burge. As Kant maintained against Hume, in order for thoughts to be recognized as constituting a conception about the world, they cannot be understood merely as temporarily succeeding events in an ever-changing stream of consciousness. To express it more radically, such a conception of thought would not even allow us to understand the stream of consciousness as a singular stream of consciousness. It would be better described as a flickering of radically separated conscious events. For Kant, it was the fundamental mistake of empiricist epistemology that it could not account for the possibility of the unity of consciousness that it presupposed in taking sensory experience as the basis of all knowledge. Empiricists overlook what he calls the transcendental unity of apperception, that is, the ability to recognize one's thoughts as one's own or, as Kant says, that "it must be possible for the 'I think' to accompany all of my representation."[14]

One can accept these insights without accepting Kant's postulation of a noumenal world or his attempt to derive *synthetic a priori* principles from such considerations. Kant is right in insisting that thoughts can be understood to be about a world only insofar as they are part of a subjective perspective on this world. More importantly, if thoughts did not provide a subjective perspective on the world, they could not be understood to rationally compel an agent to act in the world, especially if we conceive of actions as the result of active deliberation. Without the unity of consciousness, provided by the ability to recognize thoughts in my mind as my own, I would lack the ability to rationally organize my own thoughts, since I would lack the ability even to recognize that an incoherence between thoughts might require an epistemic solution. Recognizing that two thoughts contradict each other does not compel me to revise any of my own beliefs unless such a contradiction is recognized as a contradiction between *my* thoughts. Burge is thus right when he maintains that only in light of the use of the I-concept can we fully understand ourselves as being critical reasoners, that is, as "reasoners who are moved by reasons." As he puts it: "Recognition that a thought is one's own—taking up the subjectivity and proprietary ownership in the first person concept—is the only basis for conceptually expressing having a rationally immediate and necessary reason to tend a point of view, to make the reasons effective on the attitude they evaluate."[15]

Moreover, as John Perry has shown,[16] this immediacy can only be understood in light of an essential—that is, unanalyzable and irreplaceable—use of the first-person pronoun, or, as philosophers and linguists like to call it, the first-person *indexical*. Our knowledge of what the expression "I" and other indexical expressions like "here," "now," "today," and so on refer to depends on our knowledge of certain features of the context in which these terms were uttered. "I" always refers to the speaker of an utterance. For that very reason, we do not have any difficulty in recognizing that the utterance "I am not a crook" uttered by President Nixon has the same semantic content as the sentence "Mr Nixon is not a crook." Nevertheless, thoughts using the I-concept or first-person indexical play a special psychological role that cannot be captured by semantically equivalent thoughts. To use one of Perry's well-known examples, only if I recognize that it is I who is unintentionally making a mess will I have a reason to stop engaging in the behavior that causes the mess. No uniquely identifying description of me like "The only person in aisle 5 in Shaw's supermarket in Sturbridge, MA on June 15, 2001 at 4:45pm is making a mess" can replace the first-person indexical in its psychological efficacy. In order to have a reason for changing my behavior based on this description, I would first have to recognize that it is I who is described in this manner. Similar remarks apply to attempts to replace the "I" with "the person who is making this utterance" or "the person who is having this thought."

These considerations have direct implications for the asserted centrality of simulation for our understanding of others as rational agents, as Kant seemed to have explicitly recognized:

> It is obvious that, if I wish to represent to myself a thinking being, I must put myself in his place, and thus substitute, as it were, my own subject for the object I am seeking to consider (which does not occur in any other investigation), and that we demand the absolute unity of the subject of a thought, only because we otherwise could not say, "I think" (the manifold in one representation). For although the whole of the thought could be divided and distributed among many subjects, the subjective "I" can never be thus divided and distributed, and it is this "I" that we presuppose in all thinking.[17]

Understanding why others should change their behavior or attitude in light of their thoughts requires treating them as recognizing these thoughts as their own. The only model we have for such a capacity is our own use of the first-person concept.

Two points follow from this. First, in order to recognize the thoughts of others as indeed *their* thoughts, I must be able to see how these thoughts could be *my* thoughts. That is, only by being able to assign these thoughts to myself can I be in a position to take them to be the thoughts of another. (Consider the mutterings of a mental patient: do they in fact express ultimately coherent thought of the patient, or are they simply random vocables? Only if we are able to see how the purported content of these vocables could in fact be meaningful *for us* would we be able to say they are contentful thoughts of the patient.) Second, it further follows that ascertaining what in fact the particular contents of these thoughts are (assuming them to be actual thoughts) requires that we grasp what they would say to us if we had them, that we appreciate how they would motivate us if we had them. (Thus, to invoke Perry's earlier example, we can appreciate the meaning of Perry's saying to himself "I am making a mess" only if for us "making a mess" is a thought that motivates us to avoid certain behavior or to undertake other behavior like cleaning up.) The basic point here is that in determining whether an apparent thought of another is indeed a thought, and in determining the contents of this thought, we must take the other's thoughts as our own.

I would therefore suggest that Collingwood's emphasis on reenactment in *The Idea of History* is fully compatible with his view of history in the recently rediscovered manuscript *The Principles of History*, even though in the latter he does not mention reenactment as the method that distinguishes the historical sciences from the natural sciences. For in *Principles* he is adamant that the historical sciences, in contrast to the natural sciences, are "criteriological." They explain human agency not by appealing to mere regularities but in light of normative distinctions such as true or false, wise or foolish, right or wrong, and rational or irrational. If I am right, one's actions and thoughts can be conceived of as being guided by such normative distinctions only insofar as one recognizes one's thoughts as one's own, since one would not otherwise be in a position to accept their normative force. Only in this manner is it indeed conceivable how agents could find certain of their thoughts to compel an action rationally, because otherwise they would be in no position to recognize how their actions could violate what is rationally demanded by their own thoughts and normative commitments. It is exactly this reflective capacity that allows us to account for our ability to stand corrected in light of a justified critique by others. Understanding rational agency that can be normatively evaluated from the perspective of another person is thus possible only in light of one's own practical deliberation and use of the I-concept. I only understand how thoughts can rationally motivate action if I understand how they would motivate me if they were my thoughts.

In light of these considerations, one can also understand Collingwood's claim that all reenactment is critical. Collingwood would disagree with contemporary simulation theorists who stress that simulation is performed off-line, that is, without having any effect on our own cognitive structure. For contemporary thinkers simulation tends to happen in a detached mode. We model the other person's thought by using our own cognitive mechanisms without fully engaging them. Collingwood might have called such a conception of reenactment a positivist or scientistic conception of reenactment because it still does not completely characterize the difference between using reenactment for understanding other agents and a more detached theoretical study of a particular domain under investigation. If we understand how a thought can be a reason only by reenacting it as our own thought, then this forces us also to take a position on the having of this thought. Reenactment can indeed have repercussions for our own thinking about the world. In emphasizing the critical aspect of reenactment, Collingwood is closer to the continental-hermeneutic tradition represented prominently by Hans Georg Gadamer than to contemporary simulation theorists who fail to grasp the repercussions that reenactment might have on the reenactor's own cognitive system.

III. The scope of reenactment: reenactment or fusion of horizons?

Yet despite their mutual recognition that historical knowledge affects our own worldview, Gadamer rejects Collingwood's notion of reenactment as the appropriate conception of understanding. Gadamer explicitly acknowledges that his own conception of interpretation is deeply indebted to Collingwood's conception of the logic between question and answer in the *Autobiography*. Nevertheless, he argues that Collingwood's conception of reenactment is still too closely related to "the cognitive ideal familiar to us from the knowledge of nature, where we understand a process only when we are able to reproduce it artificially."[18] Collingwood has not fully made the transition from "the narrowness of psychology to historical hermeneutics." Even though he has grasped that the historian cannot abstract completely from his present perspective, he does not sufficiently grasp the implications of this insight, that is, "the dimension of hermeneutic mediation which is passed through in every act of understanding still escapes him."[19]

Since Gadamer's hermeneutic position, developed in *Truth and Method*, and his rejection of a psychologistic conception of understanding, have been so central and influential for the contemporary theory of interpretation, it is important for the purposes of this paper to evaluate the scope of his arguments against reenactment. Even though Gadamer is mainly concerned with the interpretation of texts, in objecting to conceiving of the author's original intention as the fixed standard of interpretation, he suggests two principal arguments against the idea that in interpreting we rethink another person's thoughts: one epistemological and the other ontological.

First, Gadamer argues that a conception of understanding as rethinking the thoughts of others assumes that we could reconstruct an author's original intention or thoughts independently of an interpretation of the text or historical artifacts, and in a manner that abstracts from our own perspective of the world. For Gadamer such a conception of interpretation denies the condition of the possibility of understanding, namely, that something can count as meaningful only insofar as it is meaningful *for us*. Second, and equally important, to judge a text or even a past action in light of an author's or agent's intention misidentifies the ontological location of meaning. Historical "texts" and works of art do not constitute independent units of meaning and significance; instead, their meaning resides with their own history of reading and performances—what Gadamer calls their *Wirkungsgeschichte* or the history of effect. It is exactly the meaning of the text that has to be regarded as the object of hermeneutic understanding:

> Our understanding of written tradition per se is not such that we can simply presuppose that the meaning we discover in it agrees with what the author intended. Just as the events in history do not in general manifest any agreement with the subjective ideas of the person who stands and acts within history, so the sense of a text in general reaches far beyond what its author originally intended.[20]

Gadamer therefore conceives of hermeneutic understanding not as revealing a psychological entity, such as an author's intention, but as trying to recognize the objective content of the text, "die Sache selbst," as he likes to say. Gadamer agrees with Collingwood that one can grasp this content only if one understands it as an answer to a particular question. This requires the involvement of one's own cognitive system, since hermeneutic understanding happens only if one gives these questions serious consideration. Gadamer likens this hermeneutic process to "dialogue with the text,"[21] and not with the author. It is the attempt to work out a perspective from which the whole text makes sense through the dialectical movement of whole and part that constitutes the hermeneutic circle. The interpretive process can never completely abstract from the prejudices of the interpreter, yet it requires a certain openness and willingness to recognize that some of one's own presuppositions might have to be abandoned in order to grasp the perspective of the text. Nevertheless, for the above reasons the hermeneutic process cannot be characterized as a psychological reenactment of thoughts of particular agents but has to be better understood as a fusion of horizons.[22]

Insofar as the interpretations of works of art, literary works, legal texts, and religious texts such as the Bible are concerned, Gadamer's critique of Collingwood is in my opinion quite plausible, especially his ontological argument. Gadamer seems to be right in insisting that we are not primarily interested in recovering the author's intentions in reading such texts. Collingwood himself seems to admit as much, for example when he says that there is no history of artistic problems—problems the artist intended to solve—but only a history of artistic achievement;[23] if this is the case, the use of the reenactment terminology is misleading as an analysis of the interpretation of such texts. Nevertheless, Gadamer's critique does not apply wholeheartedly to historical explanations. He tends to view historical understanding incorrectly merely as "a kind of literary/philological criticism writ large."[24]

Whereas one has to agree with Gadamer that the historical significance of an event cannot be reduced to what agents intended at the time of their actions—the historical significance, for example, of Chamberlain's appeasement politics appears certainly to be different when commented on after 1945 than at the time of its implementation – historians provide an account of individual behavior in terms of its reasons. They are in the business of answering questions like "What were the reasons for Chamberlain's politics of appeasement?" In providing such an account of individual agency we commit ourselves to a realistic understanding of our ordinary scheme of folk-psychological and *rationalizing action explanation*, as I will call our practice of explaining actions in terms of the agent's reasons, beliefs, and desires, setting aside any Freudian interpretations of that phrase. Rationalizing explanations of actions are adequate only if they mention reasons that caused individuals to act at a particular time and place. Thus Gadamer's objection that taking the author's intention as the standard of interpretation misidentifies the ontological location of meaning rests on an insufficient appreciation of fundamental differences among various objects of interpretation. Interpreting behavior as rational action conceptually requires taking into account the intentions of individual agents as the causes of their actions. On the other hand, authorial intentions are not the primary focus of interpretations of literary texts and works of art because these writings cannot be easily modeled on the basis of well-understood speech acts like assertions (where speaker intention is the primary focus, since we understand assertions only insofar as we grasp the belief the speaker intended to express).

Even if Gadamer would have to admit the above point for conceptual reasons, he could still maintain that rationalizing action explanations on Collingwood's reenactment model are in principle impossible because in trying to reconstruct the intentions and thoughts of agents from the past, we can never abstract from our own perspective. For that very reason, it is an illusion to think that we can rethink Plato's thoughts. All we can do is to think thoughts that Plato's texts demand us to think by initiating a process Gadamer describes as the fusion of horizons with the text. Nevertheless, it is not clear why such a "fusion of horizons," in which I recognize that Plato's text does not share all of my presuppositions, should not allow me to reenact Plato's thoughts. This conclusion would only follow if one subscribes to a very radical form of meaning holism or holism of the mental according to which the identity of one's thought is completely determined by its relation to all of one's other thoughts. According to this conception of holism one could share one belief only if one shares all the beliefs of the other person. I am not sure whether Gadamer himself would subscribe to this radical form of holism. If one subscribes to it, it follows that we could never think the thoughts of another person whether living or dead, since no two persons as a matter of fact share all of their beliefs, desires, values, and so on. Yet only such a radical version of holism provides a good reason for maintaining that I cannot think the same thoughts as another person in the past or present.

Collingwood correctly rejects this radical form of holism.[25] A sensible conception of meaning holism only implies that the primary unit of meaning is a particular structured set of sentences, since the attribution of meaning to one sentence can only be justified in the context of the interpretation of other sentences. The thesis of meaning holism does not assert that one cannot have the concept of a belief about the earth if one does not know anything about modern astronomy or physics. All it entails is that in order to have a belief one must have a language or belief system that has a certain amount of structure and complexity. It implies that we can never attribute just one belief to another person. In attributing a particular belief to another person, the interpreter thus has to be sensitive to how this particular belief is integrated into the belief system of the interpretee in comparison to the integration of that belief into the interpreter's own belief system.

Thus if Gadamer's objections do not show that it is in principle impossible to rethink another person's thought, and if the considerations in the first section are correct, reenactment has to play a central role in historical explanations. It is only in this manner that we can understand the rationally compelling nature of reason explanations and their accounts of human actions.

IV. The limits of reenactment and the relativity of historical explanations

Even if one agrees with the above considerations about the methodological centrality of reenactment for the explanation of actions—and thus at least for certain kinds of historical explanations—one also has to recognize that Collingwood's emphasis on reenactment as *the* historical method in *The Idea of History* is certainly one-sided. First, as has been shown, one should explicitly limit the scope of reenactment to the explanation of individual actions. Furthermore, the task of historians is not exhausted by explaining individual actions at a particular time and place; they also have to construct a narrative of a particular period, a task that Collingwood describes without going into great detail as the task of the historical imagination. In this article I cannot address the complex issues involved in the question of how these narratives explain or whether historical narratives can be understood in a realistic manner. Gadamer is certainly correct in maintaining that historical narratives do not characterize the historical process merely from the perspective of the individual agent. But regardless of the limits of reenactment in historical narratives, I would like to conclude by discussing the limits of reenactment even in accounting for individual agency. In particular, I want to adumbrate the relation between reenactment and the use of theory, as well as what I call the relativity of historical explanation due to the reenactment method. These issues are not sufficiently discussed by either Collingwood or contemporary simulation theorists.

Collingwood, more than contemporary simulation theorists, is quite aware of the fact that, if historians depend only on the reenactment method, then they cannot find all periods of history intelligible.[26] The holistic constitution of thought implies a certain limitation of the simulation or reenactment strategy in case a large number of background assumptions are not shared between the interpreter and interpretee. Here one might think of the differences between a person with a modern scientific outlook and a devout religious believer, between a political conservative or liberal, or even persons within one discipline committed to very different paradigms. Differences in these relevant background beliefs can mean very different judgments about what aspect of a situation should count as relevant and which reaction would count as appropriate. Reenactment could help here only if it were indeed possible to retool our holistic belief system very easily. We certainly can be trained in very different traditions, research methods, or social roles, but it is implausible and unrealistic to assume that our cognitive system is flexible without constraint. It is also unrealistic to assume that great cognitive and cultural differences can be overcome by adding a few pretend beliefs and desires. The method of reenactment has to be supplemented by different degrees of theoretical considerations in order to explicate the rationally compelling nature of the actions in question, or in order to provide a third-person causal account of them. I will illustrate these claims by analyzing Christopher Browning and Daniel Goldhagen's attempts to explain the behavior of the "ordinary" men of Police Battalion 101 in World War II.[27] Here I am not interested in the correctness of either Goldhagen or Browning's explanations; rather I am interested how both authors try to overcome the limitations of reenactment.

The explanatory problem for Goldhagen and Browning consists in explaining why most of these men participated rather willingly in the extermination campaign against Jews in Eastern Europe, even though they could not be regarded as particularly ideologically committed Nazis and even though they did not face severe punishment such as the death penalty if they wanted to excuse themselves. Their behavior does not seem to be reenactable by us. Nevertheless, Goldhagen still tries to account for the actions of the police battalion within the ordinary belief/desire framework by providing reasons (even though morally repugnant reasons) for their behavior. He suggests that Germans of that time have to be characterized by a very different set of beliefs and habits, which he characterizes as eliminative anti-Semitism. His interpretive strategy follows the model of interpretation that I have characterized elsewhere as the interplay between projecting oneself in a specific situation and cognitive extrapolation.[28] I understand cognitive extrapolation as the capacity to extrapolate the reaction of another person from my own reactions in a certain situation in light of my second-order ability to recognize relevant differences in our background assumptions and belief systems. It is exactly this second-order capacity that is overlooked by Collingwood and contemporary simulation theorists. In using the strategy of cognitive extrapolation, one still tries to account for the behavior of another person as a "rationally compelling" action. However, one does not find the action intelligible because one is able to reenact the agent's thoughts on a first-order level, but because one can predict it based on one's knowledge of how one would react in such a situation and one's reflective understanding of the difference between the relevant cognitive and cultural background assumptions. Furthermore, such cognitive extrapolation presupposes an implicit theoretical grasp of the causal efficacy and interaction of various mental states. Otherwise we could not account for the explanatory power of such an interpretive strategy. Only in light of an implicit folk-psychological framework theory about how minds in general work are we able to overcome the limitation of a purely reenactive or simulative strategy and rationalize certain actions.

Browning, on the other hand, leaves the realm of rationalizing explanations and appeals to what Collingwood would call a psychology of "blind impulses." He opts for a purely third-person explanatory perspective in suggesting that we have to go beyond a conception of ordinary belief/desire psychology in order to explicate the behavior of the men in the police battalion. In this context Browning appeals to Milgram's obedience and Zimbardo's prison experiments, that is, to psychological theories about how situational factors might influence a person's behavior.

Both strategies belong properly to the realm of historical explanations. That this is so shows that Collingwood overemphasizes the difference between historical explanation and theoretical explanation in the natural sciences. Nevertheless, even for Goldhagen and Browning the explanatory problem is set by the failed attempt to reenact the behavior of Police Battalion 101. Further theoretical strategies are appealed to only in case reenactment is not possible. Which of these theoretical strategies is ultimately judged to be successful depends on how it "fits" with the historical evidence and our other knowledge of human behavior. More important for my purposes, a historian's account of individual agency is always relative to the attempt to reenact the thought process of others and the difficulties he or she faces in such an attempt, which depends on the degree of difference between their respective belief systems and cultural background assumptions. In this sense, Collingwood is right to maintain that the past is always the present's past. Yet this does not mean that the historian does not describe real causal processes. It only implies that the description of these processes—and what one considers to be particularly salient in one's historical account of individual agency—is relative to our habits of thought and the difficulties we face in reenacting another person's thought.

To end, I would like to add a brief word of caution. The above account of interpretation as a dialectical interplay between reenactment, cognitive extrapolation, and other theoretical considerations should not be taken as a description of an algorithmic decision procedure that determines when to use reenactment and when to supplement reenactment with various theoretical considerations. Such decisions—similar to scientific revolutions à la Kuhn—are in the end irreducible practical decisions that depend on the degree of dissatisfaction felt with making sense of agents, given the cultural perspective of the researcher, the historical evidence, and the availability of various theoretical resources. In light of their different background assumptions, researchers might not even agree on what aspect of another person's behavior deserves special explanatory attention. A devout Christian, for example, might have a very different attitude towards the magical practices of the Azande than a person writing from a predominantly scientific perspective such as Evans-Pritchard. For that very reason he or she might have described their practices in a very different manner and from a different "baseline," so to speak. Gadamer is right to insist that interpretation is an openended and pluralistic enterprise. Interpretive disputes that are dependent on different interpretive baselines are certainly not easily resolvable. Yet this does not imply that one should adopt a position of interpretive relativism. Even though the structure of an interpretation is dependent on the interpreter's outlook, various interpretations can still be compared with one another and judged to be better or worse, compatible or incompatible given the historical evidence and the consistency of the interpretation itself. Furthermore, this critical evaluation will be driven by our ability or inability to reenact the thoughts of other persons, this time not only the thoughts of the agent whose action we try to explain, but also the thoughts of other interpreters.

I have attempted to show that Collingwood is right in claiming that reenactment is of central importance for the historical understanding and explanation of individual agency. Gadamer's critique of Collingwood rests in the end on an insufficient appreciation of the various objects of historical understanding. Yet Collingwood underestimates the role of various theoretical considerations required to overcome the inherent limitations of the reenactment method. While recognizing that reenactment has to be seen as the basic default method, our understanding and explanation of individual agency is better conceived as the creative interplay of reenactment and various theoretical considerations. Furthermore, this insight contains the seed for a realistically grounded conception of historical narratives, if one agrees with Collingwood that the explanation of individual agency is of central importance for such narratives.

Notes

1 See Carl Hempel, *Aspects of Scientific Explanations* (New York: Free Press, 1965), and David-Hillel Ruben, *Explaining Explanation* (London: Routledge, 1990).

2 For an excellent analysis of Collingwood's claim regarding the scope of reenactment, see W. H. Dray, *History as Re-enactment* (Oxford: Oxford University Press, 1995).

3 R. G. Collingwood, *The Idea of History* [1945] (Oxford: Oxford University Press, 1994), 219.

4 Jane Heal, "Replication and Functionalism," in *Folk Psychology*, ed. Martin Davies and Tony Stone (Oxford: Blackwell Publishers, 1995), 47 and Alvin Goldman, "Interpretation Psychologized," in *ibid.*, 85. For a distinct and radical version of simulation theory, see also Robert Gordon, "Folk Psychology as Simulation," in *ibid.*, 60–73; and " 'Radical' Simulationism," in *Theories of Theories of Mind*, ed. Peter Carruthers and Peter Smith (Cambridge, Eng.: Cambridge University Press, 1996), 11–21.

5 Stephen Stich and Shaun Nichols, "Cognitive Penetrability, Rationality and Restricted Simulation," *Mind and Language* 12 (1997), 297–326.

6 Collingwood, *The Idea of History*, 316.

7 *Ibid.*, 318.

8 Heal, "Simulation, Theory and Content," in Carruthers and Smith, eds., *Theories of Theories of Mind*, 79.

9 Heal, "Simulation, Theory and Content," 83f.

10 Karsten Stueber, "Understanding Other Minds and the Problem of Rationality," in *Empathy and Agency: The Problem of Understanding in the Human Sciences*, ed. Hans Herbert Kögler and Karsten Stueber (Boulder: Westview Press, 2000), 144–162.

11 R. G. Collingwood, *Autobiography* (Oxford: Oxford University Press, 1939), 101.

12 *Ibid.*, 104.

13 For these suggestions in Collingwood, see *The Idea of History*, 291 and 292.

14 Immanuel Kant, *Critique of Pure Reason*, transl. Norman Kemp Smith (London: Macmillan, 1953), B131.

15 Tyler Burge, "Reason and the First Person," in *Knowing Our Own Minds*, ed. C. Wright, B. Smith, and C. Macdonald (Oxford: Clarendon Press, 1998), 256.

16   John Perry, "The Problem of the Essential Indexical," in *The Problem of the Essential Indexical and Other Essays* (Oxford: Oxford University Press, 1993), 33–52.

17   Kant, *Critique of Pure Reason*, A353–354.

18   Hans-Georg Gadamer, *Truth and Method*, 2nd rev. edition (New York: Crossroad Publishing, 1989), 373.

19   *Ibid.*, 513 and 516. See also Collingwood's claim that "the historian himself . . . is part of the process he is studying, has his own place in that process, and can see it only from the point of view which at the present moment he occupies." *The Idea of History*, 248.

20   Gadamer, *Truth and Method*, 372.

21   *Ibid.*, 368.

22   *Ibid.*, 306.

23   Collingwood, *The Idea of History*, 314.

24   Gadamer, *Truth and Method*, 339.

25   See Collingwood, *The Idea of History*, 284–301.

26   Collingwood, *The Idea of History*, 218–219.

27   Christopher Browning, *Ordinary Men: Reserve Battalion 101 and the Final Solution in Poland* (New York: HarperCollins, 1992), and Daniel Goldhagen, *Hitler's Willing Executioners: Ordinary Germans and the Holocaust* (New York: Alfred A. Knopf, 1996).

28   See my "Understanding Other Minds and the Problem of Rationality," especially 154–160.

PART IV

Rationality and choice

T HE THEORY OF RATIONAL CHOICE IS the most refined and influential theoretical paradigm in the social sciences. Although its origins date back to the Neoclassical revolution in economics of the 1870s, rational choice theory has established its prominence primarily during the last half century or so. Since the 1950s not only it has become the mainstream theoretical approach in economic science, but has extended its influence in several other disciplines. Political science has been particularly receptive, but there is virtually no human science where rational choice theory has not had some impact, from sociology to anthropology, law, history, international relations, and even biology. Much of this success is due to the development of game theory, the branch of the theory of choice that deals with the strategic interaction of a finite (usually small) number of agents. While Neoclassical theory was chiefly concerned with the analysis of market behaviour, game theory has allowed the extension of the domain of rational choice theory to many situations that were once considered impermeable to economic analysis.

Because of its many successes (from a sociological point of view, at least) the theory of rational choice has always been the subject of intense philosophical scrutiny. On the one hand, the "imperialistic" ambitions of rational choice theorists have faced a strong resistance from neighbour "colonized" disciplines. Such resistance has often made use of philosophical arguments to question the alleged scientific superiority of the rational choice approach, which in turn has been forced to clarify and defend its methodological and ontological premises to rebut the attacks (e.g. Green and Shapiro 1994, Friedman ed. 1996). On the other hand, game theory has become fertile ground for the encounter of philosophers and social scientists interested in normative issues, particularly the definition of rational norms of conduct (practical rationality) and of principles of distributive justice (see Hausman and McPherson 2006 for an excellent introduction).

While all these topics are worthy of philosophical attention and have generated lively on-going debates in the philosophy of economics, in this anthology we focus on the philosophical debates fostered by the rise of game theory *as a positive scientific theory* over the last three decades. Game theory is a product of the massive investments in scientific research that took place especially in the United States during World War II. Its official date of birth is the publication of a monograph on *The Theory of Games and Economic Behavior* (1944) by the mathematician John von Neumann and the economist Oskar Morgenstern. In *The Theory of Games* von Neumann and Morgenstern not only provided a taxonomy and seminal analysis of several strategic games, but also formalized the theory of individual decision-making and extended its application to the domain of risky choice.

For over a decade after the end of the war the theory of games attracted some of the best scholars in the field of mathematics, economics, psychology, and philosophy. Its dissemination outside a small group of specialists, however, was hampered by various factors: the research priority of economic theorists, to begin with, whose research efforts mainly concentrated on general equilibrium analysis; and the secrecy imposed by the Pentagon, which funded game theory research during the Cold War. Moreover, rational choice theory outside economics was often conflated with the "positivistic" trends that more or less at the same time were becoming fashionable (but controversial) in the social sciences. Resistance to game theory thus partly overlapped with the anti-positivistic reactions of the 1960s and 1970s.

The identification of rational choice analysis with positivistic social science, however, is highly debatable. On the surface game theory (and economic theory more generally) seems to satisfy the criteria that the positivists considered the hallmarks of "good" science, such as the use of formal mathematical models and the formulation of precise predictions that can in principle be tested empirically. There are also striking *dis*analogies, though: while the positivists portrayed science as aimed at the discovery of universal laws of association among events, for example, such laws do not figure prominently in the theory of rational choice. Like biologists, game theorists are primarily devoted to the construction of idealized models and, arguably, the identification of mechanisms that explain (at least part of) the observed behaviour of real human agents (on mechanisms see also the chapters in Part II). From a historical point of view, moreover, the rational choice approach grew in close association with anti-empiricist approaches in the philosophy of social science. During the *Methodenstreit* of the late nineteenth and early twentieth century, for example, rational choice analysis was promoted by theorists such as Carl Menger and Ludwig von Mises who advocated the primacy of pure theory over the search for empirical regularities, against the German Historical and the American Institutionalist schools of economics.

Von Mises (1949), in particular, argued that choice is necessarily explained by individual beliefs and desires, and attributed to this methodological rule the status of a transcendental principle that is a priori valid for the interpretation of all human action. Very similar arguments can be found in the writings of the "hermeneutic" school (Collingwood 1946, Dray 1957 – see also Part III) and in the work of philosophers who have questioned positivism in the social sciences. The most famous example is probably Donald Davidson's claim that the study of human behaviour ought to make use of normative principles – such as the principle of rationality – that do not describe an objective state of affairs but rather belong to the interpretative tools of folk psychology (cf. Davidson 1984, 2004). According to this view, rational choice theory (even its more mathematical manifestations) falls in the hermeneutic rather than the positivistic camp of social science methodology.

In light of all this, philosophers of social science have given up trying to fit the rational choice approach within the straight-jacket of some preconceived philosophical theory of science. Making sense of rational choice theory requires the development of philosophical categories that are appropriate for *this* particular scientific enterprise. The first chapter in Part IV of the anthology offers an overview of the main theoretical results in the area of game and decision theory during the 1950s, 1960s and 1970s. John Harsanyi, co-recipient of the 1994

Nobel Prize in economics, was one of the giants of the first generation of game theorists. He made important contributions to the analysis of games of incomplete information, but he is known to philosophers mainly for his attempt to defend a sophisticated form of utilitarian moral theory using the tools of the modern theory of decision under risk (Harsanyi 1977). He also formulated a utilitarian version of the "veil of ignorance" argument that would later be rediscovered, suitably modified, by John Rawls (1971). Harsanyi's chapter introduces the main concepts used by game theorists to analyse the strategic interaction of rational players – including utility maximization and consistency of preferences, Nash equilibrium, and perfect equilibrium in sequential games. The discussion is non-technical and gives a taste of both the successes and the challenges faced by game theory during its early phase of development.

The second chapter, by Daniel Kahneman, is representative of a major shift in contemporary rational choice research. While up until the 1970s game and decision theory research focused mainly on the solution of theoretical and conceptual puzzles, since the 1980s the emergence of experimental and behavioural economics has established a prolific partnership between theoretical analysis and empirical research (Camerer 2003, Guala 2005). Kahneman – a psychologist by training – led with his collaborator Amos Tversky a sustained programme aimed at testing empirically the models of decision and game theory using a variety of controlled and field experiments (Kahneman et al. eds. 1982 , Kahneman and Tversky eds. 2000). The experiments have highlighted significant and systematic deviations of the choices of real human beings from the predictions of the theory, and have been explained using descriptive models of decision-making that depart in some respects from the assumption of full rationality. The chapter reprinted in this anthology is an excerpt from Kahneman's 2002 Nobel lecture, where these results are interpreted in light of a fundamental distinction between two cognitive systems or mechanisms that govern individual choice – an automatic and relatively rigid system that uses cognitive and emotional "shortcuts" for fast and cheap decision-making, vs. a reflective, slower and more flexible system that is in charge of complex and computationally demanding decisions. The behaviour of human decision-makers results from the interaction between these two systems and can diverge more or less from the predictions of the theory of rational choice depending on the relative contribution of each system in each decision context.

The work of Kahneman and his collaborators has had an enormous impact in the social sciences. During the 1980s and 1990s it has made social scientists increasingly aware of both the fertility and the limitations of the rational choice approach. On the one hand, Tversky and Kahneman have defended the validity of orthodox game and decision theory from a norma-tive perspective, and have highlighted its heuristic value. Many of the empirical phenomena discovered by behavioural economists and psychologists would have never been discovered without a theory of perfect rationality providing a benchmark of normatively correct behaviour (Schotter 2006). On the other hand, experimenters have demonstrated that "pure" rational choice theory is unable to account for the behaviour of real human beings in several contexts, and that major payoffs are forthcoming by contaminating game theory with cognitive psychology, biology, and neuroscience (Ross 2005, Gintis 2009).

Critics of the Kahneman-Tversky school highlight the fact that many of the apparent irrationalities documented by psychologists can be explained as misapplications, in artificial laboratory contexts, of rules of thumb that are in fact well-adapted to the solution of problems in the "real world" (Gigerenzer 1991, Gigerenzer et al. 1999, Binmore 1999). A theory of individual choice should then be able to account for the behaviour of human beings in the "ecologically valid" contexts in which the rules of thumb have evolved. PhilipPettit in the third chapter of this section takes a similar stance: having reviewed substantial and important differences between the mechanisms of human decision-making and those depicted in rational choice models, he argues that the theory still retains a genuine explanatory role in economics and social science. Like functional explanations in biology, rational choice models capture the workings of "virtual mechanisms" that bring behaviour in line with the actor's interests, whenever external factors not represented in these models encourage deviations from the rational path. This interpretation, according to Pettit, is able to explain why rational choice models often fail to describe the *processes* but succeed in describing the *outcomes* (the behavioural patterns) of human choice.

While Pettit emphasises the internal forces that contribute to generate behaviour consistent with rational choice theory (self-interest and rationality, roughly corresponding to Kahneman's "System 2"), other philosophers and social scientists highlight the role played by *external* factors aiding decision-making. Using a fashionable term from cognitive science, they have argued that rational choice models are most successful in those contexts where individual actors rely on "cognitive scaffoldings" that simultaneously constrain and support their decisions (Clark 1997, Ferejohn and Satz 1994). These scaffoldings can take the form of a mathematical formula or a computer programme such as those used by stock-market traders to calculate the price of an option (McKenzie 2006), or of a social institution – a set of rules enforced by formal or informal sanctions – prescribing what ought to be done in a situation of a given kind (Smith 2008).

Francesco Guala describes how game theory and experiments were used to design and construct a market institution of this kind – an auction used to sell telecommunication licences in the mid-1990s. While theory alone could not provide specific advice on a number of design issues, together with empirical data it gave valuable insights into the various ways in which the behaviour of bidders could deviate from economic optimality, and contributed to the creation of a system of rules that work smoothly and (arguably) efficiently to allocate the spectrum rights. The case of the FCC auctions has since been discussed critically by philosophers and historians of science who have questioned the auctions' "technological" success (Mirowski and Nik-Khah 2007), but has also stimulated the development of an original interpretation of game theory – the "open-formulae" account – that can make sense of the peculiar use of economic models for institutional design (Alexandrova 2008).

Further reading

Useful discussions of economic imperialism can be found in Lazear (2000) and Mäki (2001). On the history of game theory, see Leonard (1995) and Mirowski (2002). There are several good introductions to individual decision theory, such as Anand (1993). Game theory textbooks for beginners include Gibbons (1992) and Binmore (1992), but philosophers may find the style of presentation of Hargreaves Heap and Varoufakis (2004) particularly attractive for their use of a variety of examples taken from moral theory and political philosophy. The interpretation of game theory models is discussed critically by Sugden (2000) and Grüne and Schweinzer (2008). Influential early critical discussions of rational choice theory include Sen (1976), Elster (1984, 1985). On the use of experiments in game theory and behavioural economics, see also Sugden (2005), Hausman (2005), and Guala (2006). For a response to the critics of the "heuristics and biases" programme see Kahneman and Tversky (1996). Roth (2002) illustrates the "engineering" aspects of rational choice theory.

References

Alexandrova, A. (2008) "Making Models Count," *Philosophy of Science* 75: 383–404.

Anand, P. (1993) *Foundations of Rational Choice Under Risk,* Oxford, Oxford University Press.

Binmore, K. (1992) *Fun and Games: A Text on Game Theory.* Lexington, MA: Heath.

Binmore, K. (1999) "Why Experiment in Economics?", *Economic Journal* 109: F16–24.

Camerer, C. (2003) *Behavioral Game Theory.* Princeton: Princeton University Press.

Clark, A. (1997) *Being There: Putting Brain, Body, and World Together.* Cambridge, Mass.: MIT Press.

Collingwood, R.G. (1946) *The Idea of History,* Oxford: Oxford University Press.

Davidson, D. (1984) *Inquiries into Truth and Interpretation.* Oxford: Oxford University Press.

Davidson, D. (2004) *Problems of Rationality.* Oxford: Oxford University Press.

Dray, W. (1957) *Laws and Explanation in History.* Oxford: Oxford University Press.

Elster, J. (1984) *Sour Grapes: Studies in the Subversion of Rationality.* Cambridge: Cambridge University Press.

Elster, J. (1985) *Ulysses and the Syrens: Studies in Rationality and Irrationality.* Cambridge: Cambridge University Press.

Ferejohn, J. and Satz, D. (1994) "Rational Choice and Social Theory," *Journal of Philosophy* 91: 71–87.

Friedman, Jeffrey (ed.) (1996), *The Rational Choice Controversy,* New Haven: Yale University Press.

Gibbons, R. (1992) *Game Theory for Applied Economists.* Princeton: Princeton University Press.

Gigerenzer, G. (1991) "How to Make Cognitive Illusions Disappear: Beyond 'Heuristics and Biases,'" *European Review of Social Psychology* 2: 83–115.

Gigerenzer, G., Todd, P.M., and the ABC Research Group (1999) *Simple Heuristics that Make Us Smart.* Oxford: Oxford University Press.

Gintis, H. (2009) *The Bounds of Reason: Game Theory and the Unification of the Behavioral Sciences.* Princeton: Princeton University Press.

Green, Donald and Ian Shapiro (1994) *Pathologies of Rational Choice Theory,* New Haven, Yale University Press.

Grüne, T. and Schweinzer, P. (2008) "The Role of Stories in Applying Game Theory," *Journal of Economic Methodology* 15: 131–46

Guala, F. (2005) *The Methodology of Experimental Economics.* Cambridge: Cambridge University Press.

Guala, F. (2006) "Has Game Theory Been Refuted?" *Journal of Philosophy* 103: 239–63.

Hargreaves Heap, S. and Varoufakis, I. (2004) *Game Theory: A Critical Text.* London: Routledge.

Harsanyi, J. (1977) "Morality and the Theory of Rational Behavior," in Sen, A. and Williams, B. (eds. 1982) *Utilitarianism and Beyond.* Cambridge: Cambridge University Press.

Hausman, D.M. (2005) "'Testing' Game Theory." *Journal of Economic Methodology* 12: 211–23.

Hausman, D.M. and McPherson, M.S. (2006) *Economic Analysis, Moral Philosophy and Public Policy.* New York: Cambridge University Press.

Kahneman, D., Slovic, P. and Tversky, A. (eds. 1982) *Judgment under Uncertainty: Heuristics and Biases.* Cambridge: Cambridge University Press.

Kahneman, D. and Tversky, A. (1996) "On the Reality of Cognitive Illusions," *Psychological Review* 103: 582–91.

Kahneman, D. and Tversky, A. (eds.) (2000) *Choices, Values, and Frames.* Cambridge: Cambridge University Press.

Lazear, E.P. (2000) "Economic Imperialism," *Quarterly Journal of Economics* 115: 99–146.

Leonard, R.J. (1995) "From Parlor Games to Social Science: Von Neumann, Morgenstern, and the Creation of Game Theory 1928–1944," *Journal of Economic Literature* 33: 730–61.

Mäki, U. (2001) "Explanatory Unification: Double and Doubtful," *Philosophy of the Social Sciences* 31: 488–506.

McKenzie, D. (2006) *An Engine, Not a Camera: How Financial Models Shape Markets.* Cambridge, MA: MIT Press.

Mirowski, P. (2002) *Machine Dreams: Economics Becomes a Cyborg Science.* Cambridge: Cambridge University Press.

Mirowski, P. and Nik-Khah, E. (2007) "Markets Made Flesh: Callon, Performativity, and a Crisis in Science Studies, Augmented with Consideration of the FCC Auctions," in D. MacKenzie, F. Muniesa and L. Siu (eds.) *Do Economists Make Markets?* Princeton: Princeton University Press.

Rawls, J. (1971) *A Theory of Justice.* New York: Oxford University Press.

Ross, D. (2005) *Economic Theory and Cognitive Science: Microexplanation.* Cambridge, MA: MIT Press.

Roth, A.E. (2002) "The Economist as Engineer: Game Theory, Experimentation, and Computation as Tools for Design Economics," *Econometrica* 70: 1341–78.

Schotter, A. (2006) "Strong and Wrong: The Use of Rational Choice Theory in Experimental Economics," *Journal of Theoretical Politics* 18: 498–511.

Sen, A. (1976) "Rational Fools: A Critique of the Behavioral Foundations of Economic Theory," *Philosophy and Public Affairs* 6: 317–44.

Smith, V. (2008) *Rationality in Economics*. Cambridge: Cambridge University Press.

Sugden, Robert (2000) "Credible Worlds: The Status of Theoretical Models in Economics," *Journal of Economic Methodology* 7: 1–31.

Sugden, R. (2005) "Experiments as Exhibits and Experiments as Tests," *Journal of Economic Methodology* 12: 291–302.

von Mises, L. (1949) *Human Action*. New Haven: Yale University Press.

von Neumann, J. and Morgenstern, O. (1944) *The Theory of Games and Economic Behavior*. Princeton: Princeton University Press.

Chapter 14

JOHN C. HARSANYI

ADVANCES IN UNDERSTANDING RATIONAL BEHAVIOR

1. Introduction

THE CONCEPT OF RATIONAL BEHAVIOR (or of practical rationality) is of considerable philosophical interest. It plays an important role in moral and political philosophy, while the related concept of theoretical rationality is connected with many deep problems in logic, epistemology, and the philosophy of science. Both practical and theoretical rationality are important concepts in psychology and in the study of artificial intelligence. Furthermore, rational-behavior models are widely used in economics and, to an increasing extent, also in other social sciences. This fact is all the more remarkable since rationality is a normative concept and, therefore, it has been claimed (incorrectly, as I shall argue) that it is out of place in non-normative, empirically oriented studies of social behavior.

Given the important role that the concept of rationality plays in philosophy and in a number of other disciplines, I have thought it may be of some interest to this interdisciplinary audience if I report on some work in decision theory and in game theory that holds out the prospect of replacing our common-sense notion of rational behavior by a much more general, much more precise, and conceptually very much richer notion of rationality. I feel that successful development of an analytically clear, informative, and intuitively satisfactory concept of rationality would have significant philosophical implications.

I shall first discuss the common-sense notion of rational behavior. Then, I shall briefly describe the rationality concepts of classical economic theory and of Bayesian decision theory. Finally, I shall report on some, mostly very recent, results in game theory, which, I believe, are practically unknown to non-specialists. Of course, within the space available, I cannot do more than draw a sketchy and very incomplete picture of the relevant work – a picture no doubt strongly colored by my own theoretical views.

2. The means–ends concept of rational behavior

In everyday life, when we speak of 'rational behavior', in most cases we are thinking of behavior involving a choice of the best *means* available for achieving a given *end*. This implies that, already at a common-sense level, rationality is a *normative* concept: it points to what we *should* do in order to attain a given end or objective. But, even at a common-sense level, this concept of rationality does have important *positive* (non-normative) applications: it is used for *explanation*, for *prediction*, and even for mere *description*, of human behavior.

Indeed, the assumption that a given person has acted or will act rationally, often has very considerable explanatory and predictive power, because it may imply that we can explain or predict a large number of possibly very complicated facts about his behavior in terms of a small number of rather simple hypotheses about his goals or objectives.

For example, suppose a given historian comes to the conclusion that Napoleon acted fairly rationally in a certain period. This will have the implication that Napoleon's actions admit of explanation in terms of his political and military objectives – possibly in terms of a rather limited number of such objectives – and that other, often less easily accessible, psychological variables need not be used to any major extent to account for his behavior. On the other hand, if our historian finds that Napoleon's behavior was not very rational, then this will imply that no set of reasonably well-defined policy objectives could be found that would explain Napoleon's behavior, and that any explanation of it must make use of some 'deeper' motivational factors and, ultimately, of some much more specific assumptions about the psychological mechanisms underlying human behavior.

Yet, we do make use of the notion of rationality also in cases where we are not interested in an explanation or prediction of human behavior, but are merely interested in providing an adequate *description* of it. For instance, any historical narrative of Napoleon's political and military decisions will be seriously incomplete, even at a descriptive level, if it contains no discussion of the rationality or irrationality of these decisions. Thus, it will not be enough to report that, in a particular battle, Napoleon attacked the enemy's right wing. Rather, we also want to know whether, under the existing conditions, this attack was a sensible (or perhaps even a brilliant) tactical move or not.

Philosophers, and social scientists outside the economics profession, have often expressed puzzlement about the successful use of the normative concept of rational behavior in positive economics – and, more recently, also in other social sciences[1] – for explanation and prediction, and even for mere description, of human behavior. But there is really nothing surprising about this. All it means is that human behavior is mostly *goal-directed*, often in a fairly consistent manner, in many important classes of social situations. For example, suppose that people are *mainly* after money in business life (even if they do also have a number of other objectives), or are mainly after election or re-election to public office in democratic politics, or are mainly after social status in many social activities, or are mainly after national self-interest in international affairs – at least that these statements are true as a matter of reasonable first approximation. Then, of course, it is in no way surprising if we can explain and sometimes even predict, and can also meaningfully describe, their behavior in terms of the assumption that they are after money, or after public office, or after social status, or after national self-interest.

Even if the subject matter of our investigation were not human behavior, but rather the behavior of goal-pursuing robots, a model of 'rational' (i.e. goal-pursuing) robot behavior would be a very valuable analytical tool. Of course, just as in the case of human beings, such a rationalistic model would only work with highly 'rational' (i.e. with very well-functioning) robots. To explain the behavior of a robot with a faulty steering mechanism, we would need a more complicated model, based on fairly detailed assumptions about the robot's internal structure and operation.

To be sure, while we could at least conceive of a perfectly well-constructed goal-pursuing robot, completely consistent and completely single-minded in working for his pre-established goal, human beings are seldom that consistent. In some situations, they will be deflected from their objectives by Freudian-type emotional factors, while in others they will fail to pursue any well-defined objectives altogether. Moreover, even if they do aim at well-defined objectives, their limitatious in computing (information-processing) ability may prevent them from discovering the most effective strategies (or any reasonably effective strategies) for achieving these objectives. (Of course, any robot of less than infinite structural complexity will be subject to similar computational limitations. But he may not be subject to anything resembling emotional problems.)

Obviously, this means that in *some* situations models of rational behavior will not be very useful in analyzing human behavior – except perhaps after substantial modification (e.g. along the lines suggested by Simon's (1960) theory of limited rationality). Clearly, it is an empirical question what types of social situations lend themselves, and to what extent, to analysis in terms of rational-behavior models. But recent work in political science, in international relations, and in sociology, has shown that a much wider range of social situations seems to admit of rationalistic analysis than most observers would have thought even ten years ago.[2]

3. The rational-behavior model of economic theory

Even at a common-sense level, the means-ends model is not the only model of rational behavior we use. Another, though perhaps less important, model envisages rational behavior as choosing an object (or a person) satisfying certain stipulated formal (possibly non-causal) *criteria*. For instance, if my aim is to climb the highest mountain in California, then it will be rational for me to climb Mount Whitney, and it will be irrational for me to climb any other mountain. But we would not normally say that climbing Mount Whitney is a *means* to climbing the highest mountain in California, because my climbing of Mount Whitney does not causally *lead* to a climbing of the highest mountain. Rather, it already *is* a climbing of the highest mountain. It is a rational action in the sense of being an action (and, indeed, the only action) satisfying the stipulated criterion.[3]

Thus, it would be rather artificial to subsume criterion-satisfying behavior under the means-ends model of rationality. It is more natural to do the converse, and argue that looking for a means to a given end is a special case of looking for an object satisfying a particular criterion, viz. the criterion of being causally effective in attaining a given end.

This implies that the means-ends concept of rational behavior is too narrow because it fails to cover criterion-satisfying behavior. An even more important limitation of this concept lies in the fact that it restricts rational behavior to a choice among alternative *means* to a given end, and fails to include a rational choice among alternative *ends*. Therefore, it cannot explain why a given person may shift from one end to another.

To overcome this limitation, already 19th and early 20th century economists introduced a broader concept of rationality which defines rational behavior as a choice among alternative ends, on the basis of a given set of *preferences* and a given set of *opportunities* (i.e. a given set of available alternatives). If I am choosing a given end (or a given set of mutually compatible ends, which can be described as a unique composite end), then typically I have to give up many alternative ends. Giving up these alternative ends is the *opportunity cost* of pursuing this particular end. Thus, under this model, rational behavior consists in choosing one specific end, after careful consideration and in full awareness of the opportunity costs of this choice.

This model will often enable us to explain why a given individual has changed over from pursuing one objective to pursuing another, even if his basic preferences have remained the same. The explanation will lie in the fact that the opportunity costs of various possible objectives (i.e. the advantages and the disadvantages associated with them) have changed, or at least the information he has about these opportunity costs has done so.

For example, a given person may seek admission to a particular university, but then may change his mind and fail to attend. He may do so because the tuition fees or other monetary costs have increased; or because the studies he would have to undertake have turned out to be harder or less interesting than he thought they would be; or because he has received unfavorable information about the hoped-for economic advantages of a university degree, etc. All these explanations are compatible with the assumption that, during the whole period, his basic preferences remained the same, and that only the situation (i.e. his opportunity costs), or his information about the situation, have changed.[4]

It is easy to verify that the preferences-opportunities model includes both the means-ends model and the criterion-satisfaction model as special cases.

An important result of economic theory has been to show that, if a given person's preferences satisfy certain consistency and continuity axioms, then these preferences will admit of representation by a well-defined (and, indeed, continuous) utility function. (For proof, see Debreu, 1959, pp. 55–59.) Accordingly, for such a person, rational behavior – as defined by the preferences-opportunities model – will be equivalent to *utility-maximization* (utility-maximization theorem).

4. Bayesian decision theory

Classical economic theory was largely restricted to analyzing human behavior under *certainty*, i.e. under conditions where the decision maker can uniquely predict the outcome of any action he may take (or where one can assume this to be the case at least as a matter of first approximation). It has been left to modern decision theory to extend this analysis to human behavior under risk and under uncertainty.

Both risk and uncertainty refer to situations where the decision maker cannot always uniquely predict the outcomes of his action. But, in the case of *risk*, he will know at least the objective probabilities associated with all possible outcomes. In contrast, in the case of *uncertainty*, even some or all of these objective probabilities will be unknown to him (or may even be undefined altogether).

The utility maximization model provides a satisfactory characterization of rational behavior under certainty, but fails to do so under risk and under uncertainty. This is so because it is not sufficient to assume that any given lottery (whether it is a 'risky' lottery involving known probabilities, or is an 'uncertain' lottery involving unknown probabilities) will have a well-defined numerical utility to the decision maker. Rather, we need a theory specifying *what value* this utility will have, and how it will depend on the utilities associated with the various prizes. This is exactly what decision theory is trying to specify.

The main conclusion of decision theory is this. If the decision maker's behavior satisfies certain consistency and continuity axioms (a larger number of axioms than we needed to establish the utility-maximization theorem in the case of certainty), then his behavior will be equivalent to *maximizing his expected utility*, i.e. to maximizing the mathematical expectation of his cardinal utility function. In the case of *risk*, this expected utility can be defined in terms of the relevant objective probabilities (which, by assumption, will be known to the decision maker). On the other hand, in the case of *uncertainty*, this expected utility must be defined in terms of the decision maker's own subjective probabilities whenever the relevant objective probabilities are unknown to him (expected-utility maximization theorem).[5]

This result leads to the *Bayesian* approach to decision theory, which proposes to define rational behavior under risk and under uncertainty as expected-utility maximization.[6]

Besides the axioms used already in the case of certainty, we need one additional consistency axiom to establish the expected-utility maximization theorem in the cases of risk and of uncertainty. This axiom is the *sure-thing principle*, which can be stated as follows. "Let X be a bet[7] that would yield a given prize x to the decision maker if a specified event E took place (e.g. if a particular horse won the next race). Let Y be a bet that would yield him another prize y, which he *prefers* over x, if this event E took place. There are no other differences between the two bets. Then, the decision maker will consider bet Y to be *at least as desirable* as bet X." (Actually, unless he assigns zero probability to event E, he will no doubt positively *prefer* bet Y, which would yield the more attractive prize y, if event E took place. But we do not need this slightly stronger assumption.)

In my opinion, it is hard to envisage any rational decision maker who would knowingly violate the sure-thing principle (or who would violate the – somewhat more technical – continuity axiom we need to prove the expected-utility maximization theorem). This fact is, of course, a strong argument in favor of the Bayesian definition of rational behavior. Another important argument lies in the fact that all alternative definitions of rational behavior (and, in particular, all definitions based on the once fashionable maximin principle and on various other related principles) can be shown to lead to highly irrational decisions in many practically important situations. (See Radner and Marschak, 1954; also Harsanyi, 1975a.)

In the case of risk, acceptance of Bayesian theory is now virtually unanimous. In the case of uncertainty, the Bayesian approach is still somewhat controversial, though the last two decades have produced a clear trend toward its growing acceptance by expert opinion. Admittedly, support for Bayesian theory is weaker among scholars working in other fields than it is among decision theorists and game theorists. (I must add that some of the criticism directed against the Bayesian approach has been rather uninformed, and has shown a clear lack of familiarity with the relevant literature.)

5. A general theory of rational behavior

Whatever the merits of the rationality concept of Bayesian decision theory may be, it is still in need of further generalization, because it does not adequately cover rational behavior in *game situations*, i.e. in situations where the outcome depends on the behavior of two or more rational individuals who may have partly or wholly divergent interests. Game situations may be considered to represent a special case of uncertainty, since in general none of the players will be able to predict the outcome, or even the probabilities associated with different possible outcomes. This is so because he will not be able to predict the strategies of the other players, or even the probabilities associated with their various possible strategies. (To be sure, as we shall argue, at least in principle, game-theoretical analysis does enable each player to discover the solution of the game and, therefore, to predict the strategies of the other players, provided that the latter will act in a rational manner. But the point is that, prior to such a game-theoretical analysis, he will be unable to make such predictions.)

Game theory defines rational behavior in game situations by defining solution concepts for various classes of games.

Since the term 'decision theory' is usually restricted to the theory of rational behavior under risk and under uncertainty, I shall use the term *utility theory* to describe the broader theory which includes both decision theory and the theory of rational behavior under certainty (as established by classical economic theory).

Besides utility theory and game theory, I propose to consider *ethics*, also, as a branch of the general theory of rational behavior, since ethical theory can be based on axioms which represent specializations of some of the axioms used in decision theory (Harsanyi, 1955).

Thus, under the approach here proposed, the *general theory of rational behavior* consists of three branches:

(1) *Utility theory*, which is the theory of *individual* rational behavior under certainty, under risk, and under uncertainty. Its main result is that, in these three cases, rational behavior consists in *utility maximization* or *expected-utility maximization*.

(2) *Game theory*, which is the theory of rational behavior by *two or more* interacting rational individuals, each of them determined to maximize his own interests, whether selfish or unselfish, as specified by his own utility function (payoff function). (Though some or all players may very well assign high utilities to clearly altruistic objectives, this need not prevent a conflict of interest between them since they may possibly assign high utilities to quite *different*, and perhaps strongly conflicting, altruistic objectives.)

(3) *Ethics*, which is the theory of rational moral value judgments, i.e. of rational judgments of preference based on impartial and impersonal criteria. I have tried to show that rational moral value judgments will involve *maximizing* the *average utility level* of all individuals in society. (See Harsanyi, 1953, 1955, 1958, 1975a, and 1975b.)

Whereas game theory is a theory of possibly conflicting (but not necessarily selfish) *individual* interests, ethics can be regarded as a theory of the *common* interests (or of the general welfare) of society as a whole.

6. Games with incomplete information

We speak of a game with *complete information* if the players have full information about all *parameters* defining the game, i.e. about all variables fully determined *before* the beginning of the game. These variables include the players' payoff functions (utility functions), the strategical possibilities available to each player, and the amount of information each player has about all of these variables. We speak of a game with *incomplete information* if some or all of the players have less than full information about these parameters defining the game.

This distinction must not be confused with another, somewhat similar distinction. We speak of a game with *perfect information* if the players always have full information about the *moves* already made in the game, including the *personal moves* made by the individual players and the *chance moves* decided by chance. Thus, perfect information means full information about all game events that took part *after* the beginning of the game. We speak of a game with *imperfect information* if some or all players have less than full information about the moves already made in the game.

It was a major limitation of classical game theory that it could not handle games with *incomplete* information (though it did deal both with games involving perfect and imperfect information). For, many of the most important real-life game situations are games with incomplete information: the players may have only limited knowledge of each other's payoff functions (i.e. of each other's real objectives within the game), and may also know very little about the strategies as well as the information available to the other players.

In the last few years we have discovered how to overcome this limitation. How this is done can be best shown in an example. Suppose we want to analyze arms control negotiations between the United States and the Soviet Union. The difficulty is that neither side really knows the other side's true intentions and technological capabilities. (They may have reasonably good intelligence estimates about each other's weapon systems in actual use, but may know very little about any new military inventions not yet used in actual weapon production.) Now we can employ the following model. The American player, called A, and the Russian player, called R, both can occur in the form of a number of different possible 'types'. For instance, the Russian player could be really R_1, a fellow with very peaceful intentions but with access to very formidable new weapon technologies; and with the expectation that the American player will also have peaceful intentions, yet a ready access to important new technologies. Or, the Russian player could be R_2, who is exactly like R_1, except that he expects the American player to have rather aggressive intentions. Or, the Russian player could be R_3, who shows still another possible combination of all these variables, etc.

Likewise, the American player could be of type A_1 or A_2 or A_3, etc., each of them having a different combination of policy objectives, of access to new technologies, and of expectations about Russian policy objectives and about Russian access to new technologies. (We could, of course, easily add still further variables to this list.)

The game is played as follows. At the beginning of the game, nature conducts a lottery to decide which particular types of the American player and of the Russian player (one type of each) will actually participate in the game. Each possible combination (A_i, R_j) of an American player type and of a Russian player type have a pre-assigned probability p_{ij} of being selected. When a particular pair (A_i, R_j) has been chosen, they will actually play the game. Each player will know his own type but will be ignorant of his opponent's actual type. But, for any given type of his opponent, he will be able to assign a numerical probability to the possibility that his opponent is of this particular type, because each player will know the probability matrix $P = (p_{ij})$.

What this model does is to reduce the original game with *incomplete* information, G, to an artificially constructed game with *complete* information, G^*. The *incomplete* information the players had in G about the basic parameters of the game is represented in the new game G^* as *imperfect* information about a certain chance move at the beginning of the game (viz. the one which determines the types of the players). As the resulting new game G^* is a game with complete (even if with imperfect) information, it is fully accessible to the usual methods of game-theoretical analysis.

The model just described is not the most general model we use in the analysis of games with incomplete information. It makes the assumption that all players' expectations about each other's basic characteristics (or, technically speaking, all players' subjective probability distributions over all possible types of all other players) are sufficiently consistent to be expressible in terms of one basic probability matrix $P = (p_{ij})$. We call this the assumption of *mutually consistent expectations*. In many applications, this is a natural assumption to make and, whenever this is the case, it greatly simplifies the analysis of the game. (See Harsanyi, 1967–68.)

There are, however, cases where this assumption seems to be inappropriate. As Reinhard Selten has pointed out (in private communication – cf. Harsanyi, 1967–68, pp. 496–497), even in such cases, the game will admit of analysis in terms of an appropriate probabilistic model, though a more complicated one than would be needed on the assumption of consistent expectations.

7. Non-cooperative games and equilibrium points: the prisoner's dilemma problem

We have to distinguish between *cooperative* games, where the players can make fully binding and enforceable commitments (fully binding promises, agreements, and threats, which absolutely *have* to be implemented if the stipulated conditions arise), and *non-cooperative* games, where this is not the case. In real life, what makes commitments fully binding is usually a law-enforcing authority. But in some cases prestige considerations (a fear of losing face) may have similar effects.

Nash (1950 and 1951), who first proposed this distinction, defined cooperative games as games with enforceable commitments *and* with free communication between the players. He defined non-cooperative games as games without enforceable commitments *and* without communication. These were somewhat misleading definitions. Presence or absence of free communication is only of secondary importance. The crucial issue is the possibility or impossibility of binding and enforceable agreements. (For example, in the prisoner's dilemma case, as I shall argue below, the cooperative solution will be unavailable to the players if no enforceable agreements can be made. This will be true regardless of whether the players can talk to each other or not.)

In a cooperative game, the players can agree on any possible combination of strategies since they can be sure that any such agreement would be kept. In contrast, in a non-cooperative game, only self-enforcing agreements are worth making because only self-enforcing agreements have any real chance of implementation.

A self-enforcing agreement is called an equilibrium point. A more exact definition can be stated as follows. A given strategy of a certain player is called a *best reply* to the other players' strategies if it maximizes this player's payoff so long as the other players' strategies are kept constant. A given combination of strategies (containing exactly one strategy for each player) is called an *equilibrium point* if every player's strategy is a best reply to all other players' strategies. The concept of an equilibrium point, also, is due to Nash (1950, 1951).

For example, suppose that the following two-person game is played as a non-cooperative game, so that no enforceable agreements can be made:

	B_1	B_2
A_1	2, 2	0, 3
A_2	3, 0	1, 1

This type of game is called a prisoner's dilemma. (For an explanation of this name, see Luce and Raiffa, 1957, pp. 94–95.)

In this game, the strategy pair (A_2, B_2) is an equilibrium point, because player 1's best reply to B_2 is A_2, whereas player 2's best reply to A_2 is B_2. Indeed, the game has no other equilibrium point. If the two players use their equilibrium strategies A_2 and B_2, then they will obtain the payoffs (1, 1).

Obviously, both players would be better off if they could use the strategies A_1 and B_1, which would yield them the payoffs (2, 2). But these two strategies do not form an equilibrium point. Even if the two players explicitly *agreed* to use A_1 and B_1, they would not do so, and would *know* they would not do so. Even if we assumed for a moment that the two players did expect the strategy pair (A_1, B_1) to be the outcome of the game, *this very expectation would make them use another strategy pair* (A_2, B_2) instead. For instance, if player 1 expected player 2 to use strategy B_1, he himself would not use A_1 but would rather use A_2, since A_2 would be his best reply to player 2's expected strategy B_1. Likewise, if player 2 expected player 1 to use A_1, he himself would not use B_1 but would rather use B_2, since B_2 would be his best reply to player 1's expected strategy A_1.

Of course, if the game were played as a cooperative game, then agreements would be fully enforceable, and the two players would have no difficulty in agreeing to use strategies A_1 and B_1 so as to obtain the higher payoffs (2, 2). Once they agreed on this, they could be absolutely sure that this agreement would be fully observed.

Thus, we must conclude that, if the game is played as a non-cooperative game, then the outcome will be the equilibrium point (A_2, B_2), which is often called the *non-cooperative solution*. On the other hand, if the game is played as a cooperative game, then the outcome will be the non-equilibrium point strategy pair (A_1, B_1), which is called the *cooperative solution*.

More generally, the solution of a non-cooperative game must always be an equilibrium point. In other words, each player's solution strategy must be a best reply to the other players' solution strategies. This is so because the solution, by definition, must be a strategy combination that the players can rationally *use*, and that they can also rationally *expect* one another to use. But, if any given player's solution strategy were *not* his best reply to the other players' solution strategies, then the very expectation that the other players would use their solution strategies would make it rational for this player *not* to use his solution strategy (but rather to use a strategy that was a best reply to the solution strategies he expected the other players to use). Hence, the alleged 'solution' would not satisfy our definition of a solution.

This argument does not apply to a cooperative game, where each player can irrevocably commit himself to using a given strategy even if the latter is *not* a best reply to the other players' strategies. But it does apply to any non cooperative game, where such a commitment would have no force.

This conclusion is accepted by almost all game theorists. It is, however, rejected by some distinguished scholars from other disciplines, because it seems to justify certain forms of socially undesirable non-cooperative behavior in real-life conflict situations. Their sentiments underlying this theoretical position are easy to understand and deserve our respect, but I cannot say the same thing about their logic. I find it rather hard to comprehend how anybody can deny that there is a fundamental difference between social situations where agreements are strictly enforceable and social situations where this is not the case; or how anybody can deny that, in situations where agreements are wholly unenforceable, the participants may often have every reason to distrust each other's willingness (and sometimes even to distrust each other's very ability) to keep agreements, in particular if there are strong incentives to violate these agreements.

To be sure, it is quite possible that, in a situation that *looks like* a prisoner's dilemma game, the players will be able to achieve the cooperative solution. Usually this will happen because the players are decent persons and therefore attach considerable disutility to using a non-cooperative strategy like A_2 or B_2 when the other player uses a cooperative strategy like A_1 or B_1. Of course, if the players take this attitude, then this will change the payoff matrix of the game. For instance, suppose that both players assign a disutility of 2 units to such an outcome. This will reduce the utility payoff that player 1 associates with the outcome (A_2, B_1) to $3 - 2 = 1$. Likewise, it will also reduce the utility payoff that player 2 associates with the outcome (A_1, B_2) to $3 - 2 = 1$. (If the players assigned a special disutility to violating an agreement, and then actually agreed to use the strategy pair (A_1, B_1), this would have similar effects on the payoff matrix of the game.) Consequently, the game will now have the following payoff matrix:

	B_1	B_2
A_1	2, 2	0, 1
A_2	1, 0	1, 1

This new game, of course, is no longer a prisoner's dilemma since now both (A_1, B_1) and (A_2, B_2) are equilibrium points. Hence, even if the game remains formally a non-cooperative game without enforceable agreements, the players will now have no difficulty in reaching the outcome (A_1, B_1), which we used to call the cooperative solution, so as to obtain the payoffs (2, 2). This conclusion, of course, is fully consistent with our theory because now (A_1, B_1) *is* an equilibrium point.

This example shows that we must clearly distinguish between two different problems. One is the problem of whether a game that *looks like* a prisoner's dilemma *is* in fact a prisoner's dilemma: does the proposed payoff matrix of the game (which would make the game a prisoner's dilemma) correctly express the players' true payoff functions, in accordance with their real preferences and their real strategy objectives within the game? This is *not* a game-theoretical question, because game theory regards the players' payoff functions as *given*. It is, rather, an empirical question about the players' psychological makeup. The other question *is* a game-theoretical question: it is the question of how to define the solution of the game, once the payoff matrix has been correctly specified. A good deal of confusion can be avoided if these two questions are kept strictly apart.

As a practical matter, social situations not permitting enforceable agreements often have a socially very undesirable incentive structure, and may give rise to many very painful human problems. But these problems cannot be solved by arguing that people should act as if agreements were enforceable, even though they are not; or that people should trust each other, even though they have very good reasons to withhold this trust. The solution, if there is one, can only lie in actually providing effective incentives to keep agreements (or in persuading people to assign high utility to keeping agreements, even in the absence of external incentives). What we have to do, if it can be done, is to *change* non-cooperative games into cooperative games by making agreements enforceable, rather than pretend that we live in a make-believe world, where we can take non-cooperative games as they are, and then analyze them simply as if they were cooperative games, if we so desire.

I have discussed at some length the principle that the solution of a non-cooperative game must be an equilibrium point, because this principle will play an important role in the game-theoretical investigations I am going to report on.

8. Perfect equilibrium points

After Nash's discovery of the concept of equilibrium points in 1950, for many years game theorists were convinced that the only rationality requirement in a non-cooperative game was that the players' strategies should form an equilibrium point. But in 1965 Reinhard Selten proposed counterexamples to show that even equilibrium points might involve irrational behavior (Selten, 1965). He has suggested that only a special class of equilibrium points, which he called *perfect* equilibrium points, represent truly rational behavior in a non-cooperative game.

Since the difference between perfect and imperfect equilibrium points is obscured in the normal-form representation,[8] let us consider the following two-person non-cooperative game, given in extensive form (game-tree form):

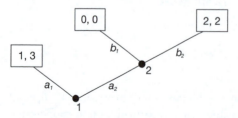

In this game, the first move belongs to player 1. He can choose between moves a_1 and a_2. If he chooses a_1, then the game will end with the payoffs (1, 3) to the two players, without player 2 having any move at all. On the other hand, if player 1 chooses move a_2, then player 2 has a choice between moves b_1 and b_2. If he chooses the former, then the game will end with the payoffs (0, 0); while if he chooses the latter, then the game will end with the payoffs (2, 2). The normal form of this game is as follows:

	B_1	B_2
A_1	1, 3	1, 3
A_2	0, 0	2, 2

The players' strategies have the following interpretation. Strategy A_1 (or A_2) means that player 1 will choose move a_1 (or a_2) at the beginning of the game. On the other hand, strategy B_1 (or B_2) means that player 2 will choose move b_1 (or b_2) *if player 1 chooses move a_2* (while if player 1 chooses move a_1, then player 2 will do nothing). Player 2's strategies can be described only in terms of these *conditional* statements since he will have a move only if player 1 chooses move a_2.

A look at the normal form will reveal that the game has two pure-strategy equilibrium points, *viz.* $E_1 = (A_1, B_1)$ and $E_2 = (A_2, B_2)$. E_2, is a perfectly reasonable equilibrium point. But, as I propose to show, E_1 is not: it involves irrational behavior, and irrational expectations by the players about each other's behavior.

In fact, player 1 will use strategy A_1 (as E_1 requires him to do) only if he expects player 2 to use strategy B_1. (For if player 2 used B_2, then player 1 would be better off by using A_2.) But it is *irrational* for player 1 to expect player 2 to use strategy B_1, i.e. to expect player 2 to make move b_1 should player 1 himself make move a_2. This is so because move b_1 will yield player 2 only the payoff 0, whereas move b_2 would yield him the payoff 2.

To put it differently, player 2 will obviously prefer the outcome (A_1, B_1), yielding him 3 units of utility, over the outcome (A_2, B_2), yielding him only 2 units. Therefore, player 2 may very well try to induce player 1 to use strategy A_1, i.e. to make move a_1: for instance, he may threaten to use strategy B_1, i.e. to punish player 1 by making move b_1, should player 1 counter his wishes by making move a_2. But the point is that this would *not* be a credible threat because, by making move b_1, player 2 would not only punish player 1 but rather would just as much punish himself. This is so because move b_1 would reduce *both* of their payoffs to 0 (while the alternative move b_2 would give both of them payoffs of 2 units).

To be sure, if player 2 could irrevocably *commit* himself to punish player 1 in this way, and could do this *before* player 1 had made his move, then it would be rational for player 2 to make such a commitment in order to deter player 1 from making move a_2. But, in actual fact, player 2 cannot make such a commitment because this is a non-cooperative game. On the other hand, if player 2 is *not* compelled by such a prior commitment to punish player 1, then he will have no incentive to do so since, once player 1 has made his move, player 2 cannot gain anything by punishing him at the cost of reducing his own payoff at the same time.

To conclude, $E_1 = (A_1, B_1)$ is an irrational equilibrium point because it is based on the unreasonable assumption that player 2 would punish player 1 if the latter made move a_2 – even though this punishing move would reduce not only player 1's payoff but also player 2's own payoff. Following Selten's proposal, we shall call such unreasonable equilibrium points *imperfect* equilibrium points. In contrast, equilibrium points like $E_2 = (A_2, B_2)$, which are not open to such objections, will be called *perfect* equilibrium points.

The question naturally arises how it is possible that an equilibrium point should use a highly irrational strategy like B_1 as an equilibrium strategy at all. The answer lies in the fact that, as long as the two players follow their equilibrium strategies A_1 and B_1, player 2 will never come in a position *where he would have to make the irrational move b_1* prescribed by strategy B_1. For, strategy B_1 would require him to make move b_1 only if player 1 made move a_2. But this contingency will never arise because player 1 follows strategy A_1 (which requires him to make move a_1 rather than a_2).[9]

In other words, strategy B_1 would require player 2 to make move b_1 only if the game reached the point marked by 2 on our game tree[10] (since this is the point where he had to choose between moves b_1 and b_2). But, so long as the players follow the strategies A_1 and B_1, this point will never be reached by the game.

This fact suggests a mathematical procedure for eliminating imperfect equilibrium points from the game. All we have to do is to assume that, whenever any player tries to make a specific move, he will have a very small but positive probability e of making a 'mistake', which will divert him into making another move than he wanted to make, so that *every* possible move will occur with some positive probability. The resulting game will be called a *perturbed game*. As a result of the players' assumed 'mistakes', in a perturbed game every point of the game tree will always be reached with a positive probability whenever the game is played. It can be shown that, if the game is perturbed in this way, only the perfect equilibrium points of the original game will remain equilibrium points in the perturbed game, whereas the imperfect equilibrium points will lose the status of equilibrium points. (More exactly, we can find the perfect equilibrium points of the original game if we take the equilibrium points of the perturbed game, and then let the mistake probabilities e go to zero.)

Thus, in our example, suppose that, if player 1 tries to use strategy A_1, then he will be able to implement the intended move a_1 only with probability $(1 - e)$, and will be forced to make the unintended move a_2 with the remaining small probability e. Consequently, it will not be costless any more for player 2 to use strategy B_1 when player 1 uses A_1. This is so because now player 1 will make move a_2 with a positive probability and, therefore, player 2 will have to counter this by making the costly move b_1, likewise with a positive probability. As a result, strategy B_1, will no longer be a best reply to A_1, and (A_1, B_1) will no longer be an equilibrium point.

The difference between perfect and imperfect equilibrium points can be easily recognized in the extensive form of a game but is often hidden in the normal form. This implies that, contrary to a view that used to be the commonly accepted view by game theorists, the normal form of the game in general fails to provide all the information we need for an adequate game-theoretical analysis of the game, and we may have to go back to the extensive form to recover some of the missing information.

On the other hand, if the normal form often contains too little information, the extensive form usually contains far too much, including many unnecessary details about the chance moves and about the time sequence in which individual moves have to be made. For this reason, Reinhard Selten and I have defined an intermediate game form, called the *agent normal form*, which omits the unnecessary details but retains the essential information about the game. (We obtain the agent normal form if we replace each player by as many 'agents' as the number of his information sets in the game, and then construct a normal form with these agents as the players.) For a more extensive and more rigorous discussion of perfect equilibrium points and of the agent normal form, see Selten (1975).

Notes

1   For references, see Harsanyi (1969, p. 517, footnote 8).
2   See footnote 1.
3   The concept of criterion-satisfying behavior is probably not very important in everyday life. But it is very important in ethics (see Harsanyi, 1958).
4   Of course, in many cases, when a person has changed his goals, the most natural explanation will be that his preferences themselves have changed. In such cases, the model of rational behavior will

be inapplicable, or at least will have to be supplemented by other explanatory theories, e.g. by learning theory, etc.

5   A very simple proof of this theorem for *risk* is given by Luce and Raiffa (1957, pp. 23–31). [. . .] A simple proof of the theorem for *uncertainty* is found in Anscombe and Aumann (1963).

6   The term 'Bayesian approach' is often restricted to the proposal of using expected-utility maximization as a definition of rational behavior in the case of *uncertainty*, where expected utility must be computed in terms of *subjective* probabilities.

7   The terms 'bet' and 'lottery' will be used interchangeably.

8   For a non-technical explanation of the terms 'normal form' and 'extensive form', see Luce and Raiffa (1957, Chapter 3).

9   From a logical point of view, strategy B_1 does satisfy the formal criteria for an equilibrium strategy because, in applying these criteria, the conditional statement defining strategy B_1 ('player 2 would make move b_1 if player 1 made move a_2') is interpreted as *material implication*. In contrast, B_1 fails to satisfy our informal criteria for a 'rational' strategy because, in applying these latter criteria, the same conditional statement is automatically interpreted as a *subjunctive conditional*.

10 We say that a given point of the game tree is *reached* by the game if it either represents the starting position in the game or is reached by a branch representing an actual move by a player or by chance. Thus, in our example, the point marked by 1 is always reached whereas the point marked by 2 is reached only if player 1 chooses to make move a_2 (rather than move a_1).

Bibliography

Anscombe, F. J. and Aumann, R. J.: 1963, 'A Definition of Subjective Probability', *Annals of Mathematical Statistics* **34**, 199–205.

Debreu, G.: 1959, *Theory of Value*, John Wiley & Sons, New York.

Harsanyi, J. C.: 1953, 'Cardinal Utility in Welfare Economics and in the Theory of Risk-taking', *Journal of Political Economy* **61**, 434–435.

Harsanyi, J. C.: 1955, 'Cardinal Welfare, Individualistic Ethics, and Interpersonal Comparisons of Utility', *Journal of Political Economy* **63**, 309–321.

Harsanyi, J. C.: 1958, 'Ethics in Terms of Hypothetical Imperatives', *Mind* **47**, 305–316.

Harsanyi, J. C.: 1967–68, 'Games with Incomplete Information Played by 'Bayesian' Players', *Management Science* **14**, 159–182, 320–334, and 486–502.

Harsanyi, J. C.: 1969, 'Rational-Choice Models of Political Behavior vs. Functionalist and Conformist Theories', *World Politics* **21**, 513–538.

Harsanyi, J. C.: 1975a, 'Can the Maximin Principle Serve as a Basis for Morality? A Critique of John Rawls's Theory', *American Political Science Review* **59**, 594–606.

Harsanyi, J. C.: 1975b, 'Nonlinear Social Welfare Functions', *Theory and Decision* **7**, 61–82.

Luce, R. D. and Raifla, H.: 1957, *Games and Decisions*, John Wiley & Sons, New York.

Nash, J. F.: 1950, 'Equilibrium Points in *n* Person Games', *Proceedings of the National Academy of Sciences, U.S.A.* **36**, 48–49.

Nash, J. F.: 1951, 'Non Cooperative Games', *Annals of Mathematics* **54**, 286–295.

Radner, R. and Marsehak, J.: 1954, 'Note on Some Proposed Decision Criteria', in R. M. Thrall *et al.*, *Decision Processes*, John Wiley & Sons, New York, 1954, pp. 61–68.

Selten, R.: 1965, 'Spieltheoretische Behandlung eines Oligopolmodells mit Nachfrageträgheit', *Zeitschrift für die gesamte Staatswissenschaft* **121**, 301–324 and 667–689.

Selten, R.: 1975, 'Reexamination of the Perfeetness Concept for Equilibrium Points in Extensive Games', *International Journal of Game Theory* **4**, 25–55.

Simon, H. A.: 1960, *The New Science of Management Decision*, Harper & Brothers, New York.

Chapter 15

DANIEL KAHNEMAN

MAPS OF BOUNDED RATIONALITY
Psychology for behavioral economics

THE WORK CITED BY THE NOBEL committee was done jointly with Amos Tversky (1937–1996) during a long and unusually close collaboration. Together, we explored the psychology of intuitive beliefs and choices and examined their bounded rationality. Herbert A. Simon (1955, 1979) had proposed much earlier that decision makers should be viewed as boundedly rational, and had offered a model in which utility maximization was replaced by satisficing. Our research attempted to obtain a map of bounded rationality, by exploring the systematic biases that separate the beliefs that people have and the choices they make from the optimal beliefs and choices assumed in rational-agent models. The rational-agent model was our starting point and the main source of our null hypotheses, but Tversky and I viewed our research primarily as a contribution to psychology, with a possible contribution to economics as a secondary benefit. We were drawn into the interdisciplinary conversation by economists who hoped that psychology could be a useful source of assumptions for economic theorizing, and indirectly a source of hypotheses for economic research (Richard H. Thaler, 1980, 1991, 1992). These hopes have been realized to some extent, giving rise to an active program of research by behavioral economists (Thaler, 2000; Colin Camerer et al., forthcoming; for other examples, see Kahneman and Tversky, 2000).

My work with Tversky comprised three separate programs of research, some aspects of which were carried out with other collaborators. The first explored the heuristics that people use and the biases to which they are prone in various tasks of judgment under uncertainty, including predictions and evaluations of evidence (Kahneman and Tversky, 1973; Tversky and Kahneman, 1974; Kahneman et al., 1982). The second was concerned with prospect theory, a model of choice under risk (Kahneman and Tversky, 1979; Tversky and Kahneman, 1992) and with loss aversion in riskless choice (Kahneman et al., 1990, 1991; Tversky and Kahneman, 1991). The third line of research dealt with framing effects and with their implications for rational-agent models (Tversky and Kahneman, 1981, 1986). The present essay revisits these three lines of research in light of recent advances in the psychology of intuitive judgment and choice. Many of the ideas presented here were anticipated informally decades ago, but the attempt to integrate them into a coherent approach to judgment and choice is recent.

Economists often criticize psychological research for its propensity to generate lists of errors and biases, and for its failure to offer a coherent alternative to the rational-agent model. This complaint is only partly justified: psychological theories of intuitive thinking cannot match the elegance and precision of formal normative models of belief and choice, but this is just another way of saying that rational models are psychologically unrealistic. Furthermore, the alternative to simple and precise models is not chaos. Psychology offers integrative concepts and mid-level generalizations, which gain credibility from their ability to explain ostensibly different phenomena in diverse domains. In this spirit, the present essay offers a unified treatment of intuitive judgment and choice, which builds on an earlier study of the relationship between preferences and attitudes (Kahneman et al., 1999) and extends a model of judgment heuristics recently proposed by Kahneman and Shane Frederick (2002). The guiding ideas are (i) that most judgments and most choices are made intuitively; (ii) that the rules that govern intuition are generally similar to the rules of perception. Accordingly, the discussion of the rules of intuitive judgments and choices will rely extensively on visual analogies.

[. . .]

I. The architecture of cognition: two systems

The present treatment distinguishes two modes of thinking and deciding, which correspond roughly to the everyday concepts of reasoning and intuition. Reasoning is what we do when we compute the product of 17 by 258, fill an income tax form, or consult a map. Intuition is at work when we read the sentence "Bill Clinton is a shy man" as mildly amusing, or when we find ourselves reluctant to eat a piece of what we know to be chocolate that has been formed in the shape of a cockroach (Paul Rozin and Carol Nemeroff, 2002). Reasoning is done deliberately and effortfully, but intuitive thoughts seem to come spontaneously to mind, without conscious search for computation, and without effort. Casual observation and systematic research indicate that most thoughts and actions are normally intuitive in this sense (Daniel T. Gilbert, 1989, 2002; Timothy D. Wilson, 2002; Seymour Epstein, 2003).

Although effortless thought is the norm, some monitoring of the quality of mental operations and overt behavior also goes on. We do not express every passing thought or act on every impulse. But the monitoring is normally lax, and allows many intuitive judgments to be expressed, including some that are erroneous (Kahneman and Frederick, 2002). Ellen J. Langer et al. (1978) provided a well-known example of what she called "mindless behavior." In her experiment, a confederate tried to cut in line at a copying machine, using various preset "excuses." The conclusion was that statements that had the form of an unqualified request were rejected (e.g., "Excuse me, may I use the Xerox machine?"), but almost any statement that had the general form of an explanation was accepted, including "Excuse me, may I use the Xerox machine because I want to make copies?" The superficiality is striking.

Frederick (2003, personal communication) has used simple puzzles to study cognitive self-monitoring, as in the following example: "A bat and a ball cost $1.10 in total. The bat costs $1 more than the ball. How much does the ball cost?" Almost everyone reports an initial tendency to answer "10 cents" because the sum $1.10 separates naturally into $1 and 10 cents, and 10 cents is about the right magnitude. Frederick found that many intelligent people yield to this immediate impulse: 50 percent (47/93) of a group of Princeton students and 56 percent (164/293) of students at the University of Michigan gave the wrong answer. Clearly, these respondents offered their response without first checking it. The surprisingly high rate of errors in this easy problem illustrates how lightly the output of effortless associative thinking is monitored: people are not accustomed to thinking hard, and are often content to trust a plausible judgment that quickly comes to mind. Remarkably, Frederick has found that errors in this puzzle and in others of the same type were significant predictors of high discount rates.

In the examples discussed so far, intuition was associated with poor performance, but intuitive thinking can also be powerful and accurate. High skill is acquired by prolonged practice, and the performance of skills is rapid and effortless. The proverbial master chess player who walks past a game and declares "white mates in three" without slowing is performing intuitively (Simon and William G. Chase, 1973), as is the experienced nurse who detects subtle signs of impending heart failure (Gary Klein, 1998; Atul Gawande, 2002).

The distinction between intuition and reasoning has recently been a topic of considerable interest to psychologists (see, e.g., Shelly Chaiken and Yaacov Trope, 1999; Gilbert, 2002; Steven A. Sloman, 2002; Keith E. Stanovich and Richard F. West, 2002). There is substantial agreement on the characteristics that distinguish the two types of cognitive processes, for which Stanovich and West (2000) proposed the neutral labels of System 1 and System 2. The scheme shown in Figure 15.1 summarizes these characteristics. The operations of System 1 are fast, automatic, effortless, associative, and often emotionally charged; they are also governed by habit, and are therefore difficult to control or modify. The operations of System 2 are slower, serial, effortful, and deliberately controlled; they are also relatively flexible and potentially rule-governed.

The difference in effort provides the most useful indications of whether a given mental process should be assigned to System 1 or System 2. Because the overall capacity for mental effort is limited, effortful processes tend to disrupt each other, whereas effortless processes neither cause nor suffer much interference when combined with other tasks. For example, a driver's ability to conduct a conversation is a sensitive indicator of the amount of attention currently demanded by the driving task. Dual tasks have been used in hundreds of psychological experiments to measure the attentional demands of different mental activities (for a review, see Harold E. Pashler, 1998). Studies using the dual-task method suggest that the self-monitoring function belongs with the effortful operations of System 2. People who are occupied by a

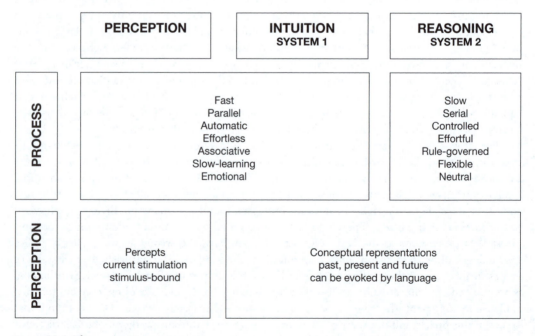

Figure 15.1 Three cognitive systems

demanding mental activity (e.g., attempting to hold in mind several digits) are much more likely to respond to another task by blurting out whatever comes to mind (Gilbert, 1989). The phrase that "System 2 monitors the activities of System 1" will be used here as shorthand for a hypothesis about what would happen if the operations of System 2 were disrupted. For example, it is safe to predict that the percentage of errors in the bat-and-ball question will increase, if the respondents are asked this question while attempting to keep a list of words in their active memory.

In the language that will be used here, the perceptual system and the intuitive operations of System 1 generate *impressions* of the attributes of objects of perception and thought. These impressions are not voluntary and need not be verbally explicit. In contrast, *judgments* are always explicit and intentional, whether or not they are overtly expressed. Thus, System 2 is involved in all judgments, whether they originate in impressions or in deliberate reasoning. The label "intuitive" is applied to judgments that directly reflect impressions.

Figure 15.1 illustrates an idea that guided the research that Tversky and I conducted from its early days: that intuitive judgments occupy a position—perhaps corresponding to evolutionary history—between the automatic operations of perception and the deliberate operations of reasoning. All the characteristics that students of intuition have attributed to System 1 are also properties of perceptual operations. Unlike perception, however, the operations of System 1 are not restricted to the processing of current stimulation. Like System 2, the operations of System 1 deal with stored concepts as well as with percepts, and can be evoked by language. This view of intuition suggests that the vast store of scientific knowledge available about perceptual phenomena can be a source of useful hypotheses about the workings of intuition. The strategy of drawing on analogies from perception is applied in the following section.

II. The accessibility dimension

A defining property of intuitive thoughts is that they come to mind spontaneously, like percepts. The technical term for the ease with which mental contents come to mind is *accessibility* (E. Tory Higgins, 1996). To understand intuition, we must understand why some thoughts are accessible and others are not. The remainder of this section introduces the concept of accessibility by examples drawn from visual perception.

Consider Figures 15.2a and 15.2b. As we look at the object in Figure 15.2a, we have immediate impressions of the height of the tower, the area of the top block, and perhaps the volume of the tower. Translating these impressions into units of height or volume requires a deliberate operation, but the impressions themselves are highly accessible. For other attributes, no perceptual impression exists. For example, the total area that the blocks would cover if the tower were dismantled is not perceptually accessible, though it can be estimated by a deliberate procedure, such as multiplying the area of a block by the number of blocks. Of course, the situation is reversed with Figure 15.2b. Now the blocks are laid out and an impression of total area is immediately accessible, but the height of the tower that could be constructed with these blocks is not.

Some relational properties are accessible. Thus, it is obvious at a glance that Figures 15.2a and 15.2c are different, but also that they are more similar to each other than either is to Figure 15.2b. And some statistical properties of ensembles are accessible, while others are not. For an example, consider the question "What is the average length of the lines in Figure 15.3?" This question is easy. When a set of objects of the same general kind is presented to an observer—whether simultaneously or successively—a representation of the set is computed automatically, which includes quite precise information about the average (Dan Ariely, 2001;

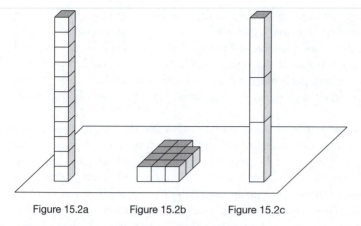

Figure 15.2a   Figure 15.2b   Figure 15.2c

Figure 15.2 Examples of differential accessibility

Sang-Chul Chong and Anne Treisman, 2003). The representation of the prototype is highly accessible, and it has the character of a percept: we form an impression of the typical line without choosing to do so. The only role for System 2 in this task is to map the impression of typical length onto the appropriate scale. In contrast, the answer to the question "What is the total length of the lines in the display?" does not come to mind without considerable effort.

As the example of averages and sums illustrates, some attributes are more accessible than others, both in perception and in judgment. Attributes that are routinely and automatically produced by the perceptual system or by System 1, without intention or effort, have been called *natural assessments* (Tversky and Kahneman, 1983). Kahneman and Frederick (2002) compiled a partial list of these natural assessments. In addition to physical properties such as size, distance, and loudness, the list includes more abstract properties such as similarity, causal propensity, surprisingness, affective valence, and mood.

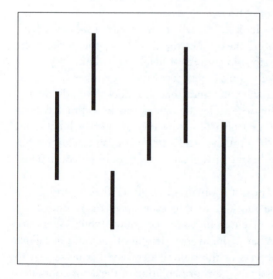

Figure 15.3 Differential accessibility of statistical properties

The evaluation of stimuli as good or bad is a particularly important natural assessment. The evidence, both behavioral (John A. Bargh, 1997; Robert B. Zajonc, 1998) and neuro-physiological (e.g., Joseph E. LeDoux, 2000), is consistent with the idea that the assessment of whether objects are good (and should be approached) or bad (should be avoided) is carried out quickly and efficiently by specialized neural circuitry. A remarkable experiment reported by Bargh (1997) illustrates the speed of the evaluation process, and its direct link to approach and avoidance. Participants were shown a series of stimuli on a screen, and instructed to respond to each stimulus as soon as it appeared, by moving a lever that blanked the screen. The stimuli were affectively charged words, some positive (e.g., LOVE) and some aversive (e.g., VOMIT), but this feature was irrelevant to the participant's task. Half the participants responded by pulling the lever toward themselves, half responded by pushing the lever away. Although the response was initiated within a fraction of a second, well before the meaning of the stimulus was consciously registered, the emotional valence of the word had a substantial effect. Participants were relatively faster in pulling a lever toward themselves (approach) for positive words, and relatively faster pushing the lever away when the word was aversive. The tendencies to approach or avoid were evoked by an automatic process that was not under conscious voluntary control. Several psychologists have commented on the influence of this primordial evaluative system (here included in System 1) on the attitudes and preferences that people adopt consciously and deliberately (Zajonc, 1998; Kahneman et al., 1999; Paul Slovic et al., 2002; Epstein, 2003).

The preceding discussion establishes a dimension of accessibility. At one end of this dimension we find operations that have the characteristics of perception and of the intuitive System 1: they are rapid, automatic, and effortless. At the other end are slow, serial, and effortful operations that people need a special reason to undertake. Accessibility is a continuum, not a dichotomy, and some effortful operations demand more effort than others. Some of the determinants of accessibility are probably genetic; others develop through experience. The acquisition of skill gradually increases the accessibility of useful responses and of productive ways to organize information, until skilled performance becomes almost effortless. This effect of practice is not limited to motor skills. A master chess player does not see the same board as the novice, and visualizing the tower in an array of blocks would also become virtually effortless with prolonged practice.

The impressions that become accessible in any particular situation are mainly determined, of course, by the actual properties of the object of judgment: it is easier to see a tower in Figure 15.2a than in Figure 15.2b, because the tower in the latter is only virtual. Physical salience also determines accessibility: if a large green letter and a small blue letter are shown at the same time, "green" will come to mind first. However, salience can be overcome by deliberate attention: an instruction to look for the small object will enhance the accessibility of all its features.

Analogous effects of salience and of spontaneous and voluntary attention occur with more abstract stimuli. For example, the statements "Team A beat team B" and "Team B lost to team A" convey the same information, but because each sentence draws attention to its grammatical subject, they make different thoughts accessible. Accessibility also reflects temporary states of associative activation. For example, the mention of a familiar social category temporarily increases the accessibility of the traits associated with the category stereotype, as indicated by a lowered threshold for recognizing behaviors as indications of these traits (Susan T. Fiske, 1998).

As designers of billboards know well, motivationally relevant and emotionally arousing stimuli spontaneously attract attention. Billboards are useful to advertisers because paying attention to an object makes all its features accessible—including those that are not linked to its primary motivational or emotional significance. The "hot" states of high emotional and motivational arousal greatly increase the accessibility of thoughts that relate to the immediate emotion and to the current needs, and reduce the accessibility of other thoughts (George Loewenstein, 1996, 2000; Jon Elster, 1998). An effect of emotional significance on accessibility was demonstrated in an important study by Yuval Rottenstreich and Christopher K. Hsee (2001), which showed that people are less sensitive to variations of probability when valuing chances to receive emotionally loaded outcomes (kisses and electric shocks) than when the outcomes are monetary.

Figure 15.4 (adapted from Jerome S. Bruner and A. Leigh Minturn, 1955) includes a standard demonstration of the effect of context on accessibility. An ambiguous stimulus that is perceived as a letter within a context of letters is instead seen as a number when placed within a context of numbers. More generally, expectations (conscious or not) are a powerful determinant of accessibility.

Another important point that Figure 15.4 illustrates is the complete suppression of ambiguity in conscious perception. This aspect of the demonstration is spoiled for the reader who sees the two versions in close proximity, but when the two lines are shown separately, observers will not spontaneously become aware of the alternative interpretation. They "see" the interpretation of the object that is the most likely in its context, but have no subjective indication that it could be seen differently. Ambiguity and uncertainty are suppressed in intuitive judgment as well as in perception. Doubt is a phenomenon of System 2, an awareness of one's ability to think incompatible thoughts about the same thing. The central finding in studies of intuitive decisions, as described by Klein (1998), is that experienced decision makers working under pressure (e.g., firefighting company captains) rarely need to choose between options because, in most cases, only a single option comes to mind.

The compound cognitive system that has been sketched here is an impressive computational device. It is well-adapted to its environment and has two ways of adjusting to changes: a short-term process that is flexible and effortful, and a long-term process of skill acquisition that eventually produces highly effective responses at low cost. The system tends to see what it expects to see—a form of Bayesian adaptation—and it is also capable of responding effectively to surprises. However, this marvelous creation differs in important respects from another paragon, the rational agent assumed in economic theory. Some of these differences are explored in the following sections, which review several familiar results as effects of accessibility. Possible implications for theorizing in behavioral economics are explored along the way.

Figure 15.4 An effect of context on accessibility

III. Changes or states: prospect theory

A general property of perceptual systems is that they are designed to enhance the accessibility of changes and differences. Perception is *reference-dependent:* the perceived attributes of a focal stimulus reflect the contrast between that stimulus and a context of prior and concurrent stimuli. This section will show that intuitive evaluations of outcomes are also reference-dependent.

The role of prior stimulation is familiar in the domain of temperature. Immersing the hand in water at 20°C will feel pleasantly warm after prolonged immersion in much colder water, and pleasantly cool after immersion in much warmer water. Figure 15.5 illustrates reference-dependence in vision. The two enclosed squares have the same luminance, but they do not appear equally bright. The point of the demonstration is that the brightness of an area is not a single-parameter function of the light energy that reaches the eye from that area, just as the experience of temperature is not a single-parameter function of the temperature to which one is currently exposed. An account of perceived brightness or temperature also requires a parameter for a reference value (often called adaptation level), which is influenced by the context of current and prior stimulation.

From the vantage point of a student of perception, it is quite surprising that in standard economic analyses the utility of decision outcomes is assumed to be determined entirely by the final state of endowment, and is therefore reference-independent. In the context of risky choice, this assumption can be traced to the brilliant essay that first defined a theory of expected utility (Daniel Bernoulli, 1738). Bernoulli assumed that states of wealth have a specified utility, and proposed that the decision rule for choice under risk is to maximize the expected utility of wealth (the moral expectation). The language of Bernoulli's essay is prescriptive—it speaks of what is sensible or reasonable to do—but the theory was also intended as a description of the choices of reasonable men (Gerd Gigerenzer et al., 1989). As in most modern treatments of decision-making, Bernoulli's essay does not acknowledge any tension between prescription and description. The proposition that decision makers evaluate outcomes by the utility of final asset positions has been retained in economic analyses for almost 300 years. This is rather remarkable, because the idea is easily shown to be wrong; I call it Bernoulli's error.

Tversky and I constructed numerous thought experiments when we began the study of risky choice that led to the formulation of prospect theory (Kahneman and Tversky, 1979).

Figure 15.5 Reference-dependence in the perception of brightness

Examples such as Problems 1 and 2 below convinced us of the inadequacy of the utility function for wealth as an explanation of choice:

Problem 1

Would you accept this gamble?
50% chance to win $150
50% chance to lose $100
Would your choice change if your overall wealth were lower by $100?

There will be few takers of the gamble in Problem 1. The experimental evidence shows that most people will reject a gamble with even chances to win and lose, unless the possible win is at least twice the size of the possible loss (e.g., Tversky and Kahneman, 1992). The answer to the second question is, of course, negative. Next consider Problem 2:

Problem 2

Which would you choose?
lose $100 with certainty
or
50% chance to win $50
50% chance to lose $200
Would your choice change if your overall wealth were higher by $100?

In Problem 2, the gamble appears much more attractive than the sure loss. Experimental results indicate that risk-seeking preferences are held by a large majority of respondents in problems of this kind (Kahneman and Tversky, 1979). Here again, the idea that a change of $100 in total wealth would affect preferences cannot be taken seriously.

We examined many choice pairs of this type in our early explorations, and concluded that the very abrupt switch from risk aversion to risk seeking could not plausibly be explained by a utility function for wealth. Preferences appeared to be determined by attitudes to gains and losses, defined relative to a reference point, but Bernoulli's theory and its successors did not incorporate a reference point. We therefore proposed an alternative theory of risk, in which the carriers of utility are gains and losses—changes of wealth rather than states of wealth. One novelty of prospect theory was that it was explicitly presented as a formal descriptive theory of the choices that people actually make, not as a normative model. This was a departure from a long history of choice models that served double duty as normative logics and as idealized descriptive models.

The distinctive predictions of prospect theory follow from the shape of the value function, which is shown in Figure 15.6. The value function is defined on gains and losses and is characterized by three features: (1) it is concave in the domain of gains, favoring risk aversion; (2) it is convex in the domain of losses, favoring risk seeking; (3) most important, the function is sharply kinked at the reference point, and *loss-averse*—steeper for losses than for gains by a factor of about 2–2.5 (Kahneman et al., 1991; Tversky and Kahneman, 1992).

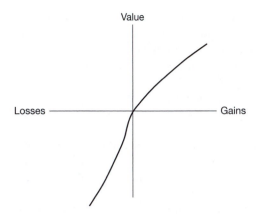

Figure 15.6 A schematic value function for changes

If Bernoulli's formulation is transparently incorrect as a descriptive model of risky choices, as has been argued here, why has this model been retained for so long? The answer appears to be that the assignment of utility to wealth is an aspect of rationality, and therefore compatible with the general assumption of rationality in economic theorizing (Kahneman, 2003a). Consider Problem 3:

Problem 3

Two persons get their monthly report from a broker:
A is told that her wealth went from 4M to 3M
B is told that her wealth went from 1M to 1.1M
Who of the two individuals has more reason to be satisfied with her financial situation? Who is happier today?

Problem 3 highlights the contrasting interpretations of utility in theories that define outcomes as states or as changes. In Bernoulli's analysis only the first of the two questions of Problem 3 is relevant, and only long-term consequences matter. Prospect theory, in contrast, is concerned with short-term outcomes, and the value function presumably reflects an anticipation of the valence and intensity of the emotions that will be experienced at moments of transition from one state to another (Kahneman, 2000a, b; Barbara Mellers, 2000). Which of these concepts of utility is more useful? The cultural norm of reasonable decision-making favors the long-term view over a concern with transient emotions. Indeed, the adoption of a broad perspective and a long-term view is an aspect of the meaning of rationality in everyday language. The final-states interpretation of the utility of outcomes is therefore a good fit for a rational-agent model.

These considerations support the normative and prescriptive status of the Bernoullian definition of outcomes. On the other hand, an exclusive concern with the long term may be prescriptively sterile, because the long term is not where life is lived. Utility cannot be divorced from emotion, and emotions are triggered by changes. A theory of choice that completely ignores feelings such as the pain of losses and the regret of mistakes is not only descriptively unrealistic, it also leads to prescriptions that do not maximize the utility of outcomes as they are actually experienced— that is, utility as Bentham conceived it (Kahneman, 1994, 2000a; Kahneman et al., 1997).

Bernoulli's error—the idea that the carriers of utility are final states—is not restricted to decision-making under risk. Indeed, the incorrect assumption that initial endowments do not matter is the basis of Coase's theorem and of its multiple applications (Kahneman et al., 1990). The error of reference-independence is built into the standard representation of indifference maps. It is puzzling to a psychologist that these maps do not include a representation of the decision maker's current holdings of various goods—the counterpart of the reference point in prospect theory. The parameter is not included, of course, because consumer theory assumes that it does not matter.

The core idea of prospect theory—that the value function is kinked at the reference point and loss averse—became useful to economics when Thaler (1980) used it to explain riskless choices. In particular, loss aversion explained a violation of consumer theory that Thaler identified and labeled the "endowment effect": the selling price for consumption goods is much higher than the buying price, often by a factor of 2 or more. The value of a good to an individual appears to be higher when the good is viewed as something that could be lost or given up than when the same good is evaluated as a potential gain (Kahneman et al., 1990, 1991; Tversky and Kahneman, 1991).

When half the participants in an experimental market were randomly chosen to be endowed with a good (a mug) and trade was allowed, the volume of trade was about half the amount that would be predicted by assuming that value was independent of initial endowment (Kahneman et al., 1990). Transaction costs did not explain this counterexample to the Coase theorem, because the same institution produced no indication of reluctance to trade when the objects of trade were money tokens. The results suggest that the participants in these experiments did not value the mug as an object they could have and consume, but as something they could get, or give up. Interestingly, John A. List (2003a, b) found that the magnitude of the endowment effect was substantially reduced for participants with intense experience in the trading of sports cards. Experienced traders (who are also consumers) showed less reluctance to trade one good for another—not only sports cards, but also mugs and other goods—as if they had learned to base their choice on long-term value, rather than on the immediate emotions associated with getting or giving up objects.

Reference-dependence and loss aversion help account for several phenomena of choice. The familiar observation that out-of-pocket losses are valued much more than opportunity costs is readily explained, if these outcomes are evaluated on different limbs of the value function. The distinction between "actual" losses and losses of opportunities is recognized in many ways in the law (David Cohen and Jack L. Knetsch, 1992) and in lay intuitions about rules of fairness in the market (Kahneman et al., 1986). Loss aversion also contributes to the well-documented status-quo bias (William Samuelson and Richard Zeckhauser, 1988). Because the reference point is usually the status quo, the properties of alternative options are evaluated as advantages or disadvantages relative to the current situation, and the disadvantages of the alternatives loom larger than their advantages. Other applications of the concept of loss aversion are documented in several chapters in Kahneman and Tversky (2000).

IV. Framing effects

In the display of blocks in Figure 15.2, the same property (the total height of a set of blocks) was highly accessible in one display and not in another, although both displays contained the same information. This observation is entirely unremarkable—it does not seem shocking that some attributes of a stimulus are automatically perceived while others must be computed, or that the same attribute is perceived in one display of an object but must be computed in another. In the context of decision-making, however, similar observations raise a significant challenge to the rational-agent model.

The assumption that preferences are not affected by inconsequential variations in the description of outcomes has been called extensionality (Kenneth J. Arrow, 1982) and invariance (Tversky and Kahneman, 1986), and is considered an essential aspect of rationality. Invariance is violated in *framing effects*, where extensionally equivalent descriptions lead to different choices by altering the relative salience of different aspects of the problem. Tversky and Kahneman (1981) introduced their discussion of framing effects with the following problem:

The Asian disease

Imagine that the United States is preparing for the outbreak of an unusual Asian disease, which is expected to kill 600 people. Two alternative programs to combat the disease have been proposed. Assume that the exact scientific estimates of the consequences of the programs are as follows:

If Program A is adopted, 200 people will be saved

If Program B is adopted, there is a one-third probability that 600 people will be saved and a two-thirds probability that no people will be saved

---

In this version of the problem, a substantial majority of respondents favor Program A, indicating risk aversion. Other respondents, selected at random, receive a question in which the same cover story is followed by a different description of the options:

If Program A' is adopted, 400 people will die

If Program B' is adopted, there is a one-third probability that nobody will die and a two-thirds probability that 600 people will die

---

A substantial majority of respondents now favor Program B', the risk-seeking option. Although there is no substantive difference between the versions, they evoke different associations and evaluations. This is easiest to see in the certain option, because outcomes that are certain are overweighted relative to outcomes of high or intermediate probability (Kahneman and Tversky, 1979). Thus, the certainty of saving people is disproportionately attractive, while accepting the certain death of people is disproportionately aversive. These immediate affective responses respectively favor A over B and B' over A'. As in Figures 15.2a and 15.2b, the different representations of the outcomes highlight some features of the situation and mask others.

In an essay about the ethics of policy, Thomas C. Schelling (1984) presented a compellingly realistic example of the dilemmas raised by framing. Schelling reports asking his students to evaluate a tax policy that would allow a larger child exemption to the rich than to the poor. Not surprisingly, his students found this proposal outrageous. Schelling then pointed out that the default case in the standard tax table is a childless family, with special adjustments for families with children, and led his class to agree that the existing tax schedule could be rewritten with a family with two children as the default case. In this formulation, childless families would pay a surcharge. Should this surcharge be as large for the poor as for the rich? Of course not. The two versions of the question about how to treat the rich and the poor both trigger an intuitive preference for protecting the poor, but these preferences are incoherent. Schelling's problem highlights an important point. Framing effects are not a laboratory curiosity, but a ubiquitous reality. The tax table must be framed one way or another, and each frame will increase the accessibility of some responses and make other responses less likely.

There has been considerable interest among behavioral economists in a particular type of framing effect, where a choice between two options A and B is affected by designating either A or B as a default option. The option designated as the default has a large advantage in such choices, even for decisions that have considerable significance. Eric J. Johnson et al. (1993) described a compelling example. The states of Pennsylvania and New Jersey both offer drivers a choice between an insurance policy that allows an unconstrained right to sue, and a less expensive policy that restricts the right to sue. The unconstrained right to sue is the default in Pennsylvania, the opposite is the default in New Jersey, and the takeup of full coverage is 79 percent and 30 percent in the two states, respectively. Johnson and Daniel G. Goldstein (2003) estimate that Pennsylvania drivers spend 450 million dollars annually on full coverage that they would not purchase if their choice were framed as it is for New Jersey drivers.

Johnson and Goldstein (2003) also compared the proportions of the population enrolled in organ donation programs in seven European countries in which enrollment was the default and four in which non-enrollment was the default. Averaging over countries, enrollment in donor programs was 97.4 percent when this was the default option, 18 percent otherwise. The passive acceptance of the formulation given has significant consequences in this case, as it does in other recent studies where the selection of the default on the form that workers completed to set their 401(k) contributions dominated their ultimate choice (Brigitte Madrian and Dennis Shea, 2001; James J. Choi et al., 2002).

The basic principle of framing is the passive acceptance of the formulation given. Because of this passivity, people fail to construct a canonical representation for all extensionally equivalent descriptions of a state of affairs. They do not spontaneously compute the height of a tower that could be built from an array of blocks, and they do not spontaneously transform the representation of puzzles or decision problems. Obviously, no one is able to recognize "137 × 24" and "3,288" as "the same" number without going through some elaborate computations. Invariance cannot be achieved by a finite mind.

The impossibility of invariance raises significant doubts about the descriptive realism of rational-choice models (Tversky and Kahneman, 1986). Absent a system that reliably generates appropriate canonical representations, intuitive decisions will be shaped by the factors that determine the accessibility of different features of the situation. Highly accessible features will influence decisions, while features of low accessibility will be largely ignored—and the correlation between accessibility and reflective judgments of relevance in a state of complete information is not necessarily high.

A particularly unrealistic assumption of the rational-agent model is that agents make their choices in a comprehensively inclusive context, which incorporates all the relevant details of the present situation, as well as expectations about all future opportunities and risks. Much evidence supports the contrasting claim that people's views of decisions and outcomes are normally characterized by "narrow framing" (Kahneman and Daniel Lovallo, 1993), and by the related notions of "mental accounting" (Thaler, 1985, 1999) and "decision bracketing" (Daniel Read et al., 1999).

The following are some examples of the prevalence of narrow framing. The decision of whether or not to accept a gamble is normally considered as a response to a single opportunity, not as an occasion to apply a general policy (Gideon Keren and Willem A. Wagenaar, 1987; Tversky and Donald A. Redelmeier, 1992; Kahneman and Lovallo, 1993; Shlomo Benartzi and Thaler, 1999). Investors' decisions about particular investments appear to be considered in isolation from the remainder of the investor's portfolio (Nicholas Barberis et al., 2003). The time horizon that investors adopt for evaluating their investments appears to be unreasonably short—an observation that helps explain the equity-premium puzzle (Benartzi and Thaler, 1995). Finally, the prevalence of the gain/loss framing of outcomes over the wealth frame, which was discussed in the previous section, can now be seen as an instance of narrow framing. A shared feature of all these examples is that decisions made in narrow frames depart far more from risk neutrality than decisions that are made in a more inclusive context.

The prevalence of narrow frames is an effect of accessibility, which can be understood by referring to the displays of blocks in Figure 15.2. The same set of blocks is framed as a tower in Figure 15.2a, and as a flat array in Figure 15.2b. Although it is possible to "see" a tower in Figure 15.2b, it is much easier to do so in Figure 15.2a. Narrow frames generally reflect the structure of the environment in which decisions are made. The choices that people face arise one at a time, and the principle of passive acceptance suggests that they will be considered as they arise. The problem at hand and the immediate consequences of the choice will be far more accessible than all other considerations, and as a result decision problems will be framed far more narrowly than the rational model assumes.

[. . .]

VIII. Concluding remarks

The rational agent of economic theory would be described, in the language of the present treatment, as endowed with a single cognitive system that has the logical ability of a flawless System 2 and the low computing costs of System 1. Theories in behavioral economics have generally retained the basic architecture of the rational model, adding assumptions about cognitive limitations designed to account for specific anomalies. For example, the agent may be rational except for discounting hyperbolically, evaluating outcomes as changes, or a tendency to jump to conclusions.

The model of the agent that has been presented here has a different architecture, which may be more difficult to translate into the theoretical language of economics. The core ideas of the present treatment are the two-system structure, the large role of System 1 and the extreme context-dependence that is implied by the concept of accessibility. The central characteristic of agents is not that they reason poorly but that they often act intuitively. And the behavior of these agents is not guided by what they are able to compute, but by what they happen to see at a given moment.

These propositions suggest heuristic questions that may guide attempts to predict or explain behavior in a given setting: "What would an impulsive agent be tempted to do?" "What course of action seems most natural in this situation?" The answers to these questions will often identify the judgment or course of action to which most people will be attracted. For example, it is more natural to join a group of strangers running in a particular direction than to adopt a contrarian destination. However, the two-system view also suggests that other questions should be raised: "Is the intuitively attractive judgment or course of action in conflict with a rule that the agent would endorse?" If the answer to that question is positive, then "How likely is it in the situation at hand that the relevant rule will come to mind in time to override intuition?" Of course, this mode of analysis also allows for differences between individuals, and between groups. What is natural and intuitive in a given situation is not the same for everyone: different cultural experiences favor different intuitions about the meaning of situations, and new behaviors become intuitive as skills are acquired. Even when these complexities are taken into account, the approach to the understanding and prediction of behavior that has been sketched here is simple and easy to apply, and likely to yield hypotheses that are generally plausible and often surprising. The origins of this approach are in an important intellectual tradition in psychology, which has emphasized "the power of the situation" (Lee Ross and Nisbett, 1991).

The present treatment has developed several themes: that intuition and reasoning are alternative ways to solve problems, that intuition resembles perception, that people sometimes answer a difficult question by answering an easier one instead, that the processing of information is often superficial, that categories are represented by prototypes. All these features of the cognitive system were in our minds in some form when Amos Tversky and I began our joint work in 1969, and most of them were in Herbert Simon's mind much earlier. However, the role of emotion in judgment and decision making received less attention in that work than it had received before the beginning of the cognitive revolution in psychology in the 1950s. More recent developments have restored a central role to emotion, which is incorporated in the view of intuition that was presented here. Findings about the role of optimism in risk taking, the effects of emotion on decision weights, the role of fear in predictions of harm, and the role of liking and disliking in factual predictions—all indicate that the traditional separation between belief and preference in analyses of decision making is psychologically unrealistic.

Incorporating a common sense psychology of the intuitive agent into economic models will present difficult challenges, especially for formal theorists. It is encouraging to note, however, that the challenge of incorporating the first wave of psychological findings into economics appeared even more daunting 20 years ago, and that challenge has been met with considerable success.

References

Ariely, Dan. "Seeing Sets: Representation by Statistical Properties." *Psychological Science*, March 2001, *12*(2), pp. 157–62.

Arrow, Kenneth J. "Risk Perception in Psychology and Economics." *Economic Inquiry*, January 1982, *20*(1), pp. 1–9.

Barberis, Nicholas; Huang, Ming and Thaler, Richard H. "Individual Preferences, Monetary Gambles and the Equity Premium." National Bureau of Economic Research (Cambridge, MA) Working Paper No. W9997, May 2003.

Bargh, John A. "The Automaticity of Everyday Life," in Robert S. Wyer, Jr., ed., *The automaticity of everyday life: Advances in social cognition*, Vol. 10. Mahwah, NJ: Erlbaum, 1997, pp. 1–61.

Benartzi, Shlomo and Thaler, Richard H. "Myopic Loss Aversion and the Equity Premium Puzzle." *Quarterly Journal of Economics*, February 1995, *110*(1), pp. 73–92.

Benartzi, Shlomo and Thaler, Richard H. "Risk Aversion or Myopia? Choices in Repeated Gambles and Retirement Investments." *Management Science*, March 1999, *47*(3), pp. 364–81.

Bernoulli, Daniel. "Exposition of a New Theory on the Measurement of Risk." *Econometrica*, January 1954, *22*(1), pp. 23–36. (Original work published 1738.)

Bruner, Jerome S. and Minturn, A. Leigh. "Perceptual Identification and Perceptual Organization." *Journal of General Psychology*, July 1955, *53*, pp. 21–28.

Camerer, Colin F.; Loewenstein, George and Rabin, Matthew, eds. *Advances in behavioral economics*. Princeton, NJ: Princeton University Press (forthcoming).

Chaiken, Shelly and Trope, Yaacov, eds. *Dual-process theories in social psychology*. New York: Guilford Press, 1999.

Choi, James J.; Laibson, David; Madrian, Brigitte and Metrick, Andrew. "Defined Contribution Pensions: Plan Rules, Participant Decisions and the Path of Least Resistance," in James M. Poterba, ed., *Tax policy and the economy*, Vol. 16. Cambridge, MA: MIT Press, 2002, pp. 67–113.

Chong, Sang-Chul and Treisman, Anne. "Representation of Statistical Properties." *Vision Research*, February 2003, *43*(4), pp. 393–404.

Cohen, David and Knetsch, Jack L. "Judicial Choice and Disparities Between Measures of Economic Value." *Osgoode Hall Law Review*, 1992, *30*(3), pp. 737–70.

Elster, Jon. "Emotions and Economic Theory." *Journal of Economic Literature*, March 1998, *26*(1), pp. 47–74.

Epstein, Seymour. "Cognitive-Experiential Self-Theory of Personality," in Theodore Millon and Melvin J. Lerner, eds., *Comprehensive handbook of psychology, volume 5: Personality and social psychology*. Hoboken, NJ: Wiley & Sons, 2003, pp. 159–84.

Fiske, Susan T. "Stereotyping, Prejudice, and Discrimination," in Daniel T. Gilbert, Susan T. Fiske, and Gardner Lindzey, eds., *The handbook of social psychology*, 4th Ed., Vol. 1. New York: McGraw-Hill, 1998, pp. 357–411.

Gawande, Atul. *Complications: A surgeon's notes on an imperfect science*. New York: Metropolitan Books, 2002.

Gigerenzer, Gerd; Swijtink, Zeno; Porter, Theodore; Daston, Lorraine; Beatty, John and Kruger, Lorenz. *The empire of chance: How probability changed science and everyday life*. Cambridge: Cambridge University Press, 1989.

Gilbert, Daniel T. "Thinking Lightly About Others: Automatic Components of the Social Inference Process," in James S. Uleman and John A. Bargh, eds., *Unintended thought*. Englewood Cliffs, NJ: Prentice-Hall, 1989, pp. 189–211.

Gilbert, Daniel T. "Inferential Correction," in Thomas Gilovich, Dale Griffin, and Daniel Kahneman, eds., *Heuristics and biases: The psychology of intuitive thought*. New York: Cambridge University Press, 2002, pp. 167–84.

Higgins, E. Tory. "Knowledge Activation: Accessibility, Applicability, and Salience," in E. Tory Higgins and Arie W. Kruglanski, eds., *Social psychology: Handbook of basic principles*. New York: Guilford Press, 1996, pp. 133–68.

Johnson, Eric J. and Goldstein, Daniel G. "Do Defaults Save Lives?" Working paper, Center for Decision Sciences, Columbia University, 2003.

Johnson, Eric J.; Hershey, John; Meszaros, Jacqueline and Kunreuther, Howard. "Framing, Probability Distortions, and Insurance Decisions." *Journal of Risk and Uncertainty*, August 1993, 7(1), pp. 35–51.

Kahneman, Daniel. "New Challenges to the Rationality Assumption." *Journal of Institutional and Theoretical Economics*, March 1994, 150(1), pp. 18–36.

Kahneman, Daniel. "Evaluation by Moments: Past and Future," in Daniel Kahneman and Amos Tversky, eds., *Choices, values, and frames*. New York: Cambridge University Press, 2000a, pp. 693–708.

Kahneman, D. Experienced utility and objective happiness: A moment-based approach. In D. Kahneman & A. Tversky (Eds.), *Choices, values, and frames* New York: Cambridge University Press, 2000b, pp. 673–692.

Kahneman, Daniel. "A Psychological Perspective on Economics." *American Economic Review*, May 2003a (*Papers and Proceedings*), 93(2), pp. 162–68.

Kahneman, Daniel and Frederick, Shane. "Representativeness Revisited: Attribute Substitution in Intuitive Judgment," in Thomas Gilovich, Dale Griffin, and Daniel Kahneman, eds., *Heuristics and biases: The psychology of intuitive thought*. New York: Cambridge University Press, 2002, pp. 49–81.

Kahneman, Daniel; Fredrickson, Barbara L.; Schreiber, Charles A. and Redelmeier, Donald A. "When More Pain is Preferred to Less: Adding a Better End." *Psychological Science*, November 1993, 4(6), pp. 401–05.

Kahneman, Daniel; Knetsch, Jack and Thaler, Richard. "Fairness as a Constraint on Profit-seeking: Entitlements in the Market." *American Economic Review*, September 1986, 76(4), pp. 728–41.

——. "Experimental Tests of the Endowment Effect and the Coase Theorem." *Journal of Political Economy*, December 1990, 98(6), pp. 1325–48.

——. "The Endowment Effect, Loss Aversion, and Status Quo Bias: Anomalies." *Journal of Economic Perspectives*, Winter 1991, 5(1), pp. 193–206.

Kahneman, Daniel and Lovallo, Daniel. "Timid Choices and Bold Forecasts: A Cognitive Perspective on Risk Taking." *Management Science*, January 1993, 39(1), pp. 17–31.

Kahneman, Daniel; Ritov, Ilana and Schkade, David. "Economic Preferences or Attitude Expressions? An Analysis of Dollar Responses to Public Issues." *Journal of Risk and Uncertainty*, December 1999, 19(1–3), pp. 203–35.

Kahneman, Daniel; Slovic, Paul and Tversky, Amos, eds. *Judgment under uncertainty: Heuristics and biases*. New York: Cambridge University Press, 1982.

Kahneman, Daniel and Tversky, Amos. "On the Psychology of Prediction." *Psychological Review*, July 1973, 80(4), pp. 237–51.

——. "Prospect Theory: An Analysis of Decisions Under Risk." *Econometrica*, March 1979, 47(2), pp. 263–91.

——, eds. *Choices, values, and frames*. New York: Cambridge University Press, 2000.

Kahneman, Daniel; Wakker, Peter P. and Sarin, Rakesh. "Back to Bentham? Explorations of Experienced Utility." *Quarterly Journal of Economics*, May 1997, 112(2), pp. 375–405.

Keren, Gideon and Wagenaar, Willem A. "Violations of Utility Theory in Unique and Repeated Gambles." *Journal of Experimental Psychology: Learning, Memory, and Cognition*, July 1987, 13(3), pp. 387–91.

Klein, Gary. *Sources of power: How people make decisions*. Cambridge, MA: MIT Press, 1998.

Langer, Ellen J.; Blank, Arthur and Chanowitz, Benzion. "The Mindlessness of Ostensibly Thoughtful Action: The Role of 'Placebic' Information in Interpersonal Interaction." *Journal of Personality and Social Psychology*, June 1978, *36*(6), pp. 635–42.

LeDoux, Joseph E. "Emotion Circuits in the Brain." *Annual Review of Neuroscience*, March 2000, *23*, pp. 155–84.

List, John A. "Does Market Experience Eliminate Market Anomalies?" *Quarterly Journal of Economics*, February 2003a, *118*(1), pp. 47–71.

List, John A. "Neoclassical Theory Versus Prospect Theory: Evidence From the Marketplace." National Bureau of Economic Research (Cambridge, MA) Working Paper No. W9736, 2003b; *Econometrica*, 2004 (forthcoming).

Loewenstein, George. "Out of Control: Visceral Influences on Behavior." *Organizational Behavior and Human Decision Processes*, March 1996, *65*(3), pp. 272–92.

———. "Emotions in Economic Theory and Economic Behavior." *American Economic Review*, May 2000 (*Papers and Proceedings*), *90*(2), pp. 426–32.

Madrian, Brigitte and Shea, Dennis. "The Power of Suggestion: Inertia in 401(k) Participation and Savings Behavior." *Quarterly Journal of Economics*, November 2001, *116*(4), pp. 1149–87.

Mellers, Barbara. "Choice and the Relative Pleasure of Consequences." *Psychological Bulletin*, November 2000, *126*(6), pp. 910–24.

Pashler, Harold E. *The psychology of attention*. Cambridge, MA: MIT Press, 1998.

Read, Daniel; Loewenstein, George and Rabin, Matthew. "Choice Bracketing." *Journal of Risk and Uncertainty*, December 1999, *19*(1–3), pp. 171–97.

Ross, Lee and Nisbett, Richard E. *The person and the situation*. New York: McGraw-Hill, 1991.

Rottenstreich, Yuval and Hsee, Christopher K. "Money, Kisses and Electric Shocks: On the Affective Psychology of Risk." *Psychological Science*, May 2001, *12*(3), pp. 185–90.

Rozin, Paul and Nemeroff, Carol. "Sympathetic Magical Thinking: The Contagion and Similarity Heuristics," in Thomas Gilovich, Dale Griffin, and Daniel Kahneman, eds., *Heuristics and biases: The psychology of intuitive thought*. New York: Cambridge University Press, 2002, pp. 201–16.

Samuelson, William and Zeckhauser, Richard. "Status Quo Bias in Decision Making." *Journal of Risk and Uncertainty*, March 1988, *1*(1), pp. 7–59.

Schelling, Thomas C. *Choice and consequence: Perspectives of an errant economist*. Cambridge, MA: Harvard University Press, 1984.

Simon, Herbert A. "A Behavioral Model of Rational Choice." *Quarterly Journal of Economics*, February 1955, *69*(1), pp. 99–118.

Simon, Herbert A. "Information Processing Models of Cognition." *Annual Review of Psychology*, February 1979, *30*, pp. 363–96.

Simon, Herbert A. and Chase, William G. "Skill in Chess." *American Scientist*, July 1973, *61*(4), pp. 394–403.

Sloman, Steven A. "Two Systems of Reasoning," in Thomas Gilovich, Dale Griffin, and Daniel Kahneman, eds., *Heuristics and biases: The psychology of intuitive thought*. New York: Cambridge University Press, 2002, pp. 379–96.

Slovic, Paul; Finucane, Melissa; Peters, Ellen and MacGregor, Donald G. "The Affect Heuristic," in Thomas Gilovich, Dale Griffin, and Daniel Kahneman, eds., *Heuristics and biases: The psychology of intuitive thought*. New York: Cambridge University Press, 2002, pp. 397–420.

Stanovich, Keith E. and West, Richard F. "Individual Differences in Reasoning: Implications for the Rationality Debate?" *Behavioral and Brain Sciences*, October 2000, *23*(5), pp. 645–65.

Stanovich, Keith E. and West, Richard F. "Individual Differences in Reasoning: Implications for the Rationality Debate?" in Thomas Gilovich, Dale Griffin, and Daniel Kahneman, eds., *Heuristics and biases: The psychology of intuitive thought*. New York: Cambridge University Press, 2002, pp. 421–40.

Thaler, Richard H. "Toward a Positive Theory of Consumer Choice." *Journal of Economic Behavior and Organization*, March 1980, *1*(1), pp. 36–90.

Thaler, Richard H. "Mental Accounting and Consumer Choice." *Marketing Science*, Summer 1985, *4*(3), pp. 199–214.

Thaler, Richard H. *Quasi rational economics*. New York: Russell Sage Foundation, 1991.

Thaler, Richard H. *The winner's curse: Paradoxes and anomalies of economic life*. New York: Free Press, 1992.

Thaler, Richard H. "Mental Accounting Matters." *Journal of Behavioral Decision Making*, July 1999, *12*(3), pp. 183–206.

Thaler, Richard H. "Toward a Positive Theory of Consumer Choice," in Daniel Kahneman and Amos Tversky, eds., *Choices, values, and frames*. New York: Cambridge University Press, 2000, pp. 268–87.

Tversky, Amos and Kahneman, Daniel. "Judgment under Uncertainty: Heuristics and Biases." *Science*, September 1974, *185*(4157), pp. 1124–31.

Tversky, Amos and Kahneman, Daniel. "The Framing of Decisions and the Psychology of Choice." *Science*, January 1981, *211*(4481), pp. 453–58.

Tversky, Amos and Kahneman, Daniel. "Extensional Versus Intuitive Reasoning: The Conjunction Fallacy in Probability Judgment." *Psychological Review*, October 1983, *90*(4), pp. 293–315.

Tversky, Amos and Kahneman, Daniel. "Rational Choice and the Framing of Decisions." *Journal of Business*, October 1986, *59*(4), pp. S251–78.

Tversky, Amos and Kahneman, Daniel. "Loss Aversion in Riskless Choice: A Reference-Dependent Model." *Quarterly Journal of Economics*, November 1991, *106*(4), pp. 1039–61.

Tversky, Amos and Kahneman, Daniel. "Advances in Prospect Theory: Cumulative Representation of Uncertainty." *Journal of Risk and Uncertainty*, October 1992, *5*(4), pp. 297–323.

Tversky, Amos and Redelmeier, Donald A. "On the Framing of Multiple Prospects." *Psychological Science*, May 1992, *3*(3), pp. 191–93.

Wilson, Timothy D. *Strangers to ourselves: Discovering the adaptive unconscious.* Cambridge, MA: Harvard University Press, 2002.

Zajonc, Robert B. "Emotions," in Daniel T. Gilbert, Susan T. Fiske, and Gardner Lindzey, eds., *Handbook of social psychology*, 4th Ed., Vol. 1. New York: Oxford University Press, 1998, pp. 591–632.

Chapter 16

PHILIP PETTIT

THE VIRTUAL REALITY OF
HOMO ECONOMICUS

THE ECONOMIC EXPLANATION OF individual behaviour, even behaviour outside the traditional province of the market, projects a distinctively economic image on the minds of the agents involved. It suggests that, in regard to motivation and rationality, they conform to the profile of homo economicus. But this suggestion, by many lights, flies in the face of common sense; it conflicts with our ordinary assumptions about how we each feel and think in most situations, certainly most non-market situations, and about how that feeling and thought manifests itself in action. What, then, to conclude? That common sense is deeply in error on these matters? That, on the contrary, economics is in error—at least about non-market behaviour—and common sense sound? Or that some form of reconciliation is available between the two perspectives? This paper is an attempt to defend a conciliationist position.

The paper is in four sections. In the first section I describe the economic mind that is projected in economic explanation, whether explanation of market or non-market behaviour. In the second section I argue that this is not the mind that people manifest in most social settings and, in particular, that it is not the mind that common sense articulates. In the third section I show that nevertheless the economic mind may have a guaranteed place in or around the springs of human action; it may have a virtual presence in the generation of action, even action on which it does not actually impact. And then in the last section I show that where the economic mind has such a virtual presence, that is enough to license an important variety of economic explanation: the explanation of the resilience or robustness of certain patterns rather than the explanation of their emergence or continuance. I believe that this is the variety of explanation which is pursued generally in the economics—if you like, in the rational-choice explanation—of social or non-market behaviour.

1. The thesis of the economic mind

There are two sorts of assumptions that economists make about the minds of the agents with whom they are concerned. First, content-centred assumptions about the sorts of things that the agents desire: about which things they prefer and with what intensities. And, second, process-centred assumptions about the way in which those desires, those degrees of preference, issue in action.

The process-centred assumptions boil down to the assumption that people's actions serve their desires well, given their beliefs about such matters as the options available, the likely consequences of different options, and so on. There are different theories as to what it is for an action or choice to serve an agent's desires well, given the agent's beliefs: about what it is for an agent to be rational. Many economists work with relatively simple models but the family of theories available is usefully exemplified by Bayesian theories of rationality (Eells 1982). According to Bayesian theory, an action is rational just in case it maximises the agent's expected utility.

The Bayesian idea is that every agent has a utility function that identifies a certain degree of utility, a certain intensity of preference, for every way the world may be—every prospect— and a probability function that determines, for each option and for each prospect, the probability that the choice of that option would lead to the realisation of that prospect. An action will maximise the agent's expected utility just in case it has a higher expected utility than alternative options, where we determine the expected utility of an option as follows: we take the prospects with nonzero probability associated with the option; we multiply the utility of each prospect by the fraction representing the probability of its being realised in the event of the option's being chosen; and we add those products together.

So much for the assumptions that economists make about the way desires or preferences lead to action. What now of the assumptions that they make about the content of what human beings prefer or desire? The main question here is how far economists cast human beings as egocentric in their desires. In order to discuss it, we need some distinctions between different theses that each ascribe a certain egocentricity.

1. Self-centredness. This relatively weak claim says that people do what they do as a result of their own desires or utility functions. They do not act on the basis of moral belief alone; such belief issues in action, only if accompanied by a suitable desire. And they do not act just on the basis of perceiving what other people desire; the perception that someone desires something can lead to action only in the presence of a desire to satisfy that other person.
2. Weak non-tuism. This is a stronger claim, in the sense that it presupposes the first but represents people as intuitively more egocentric still. People's desires bear on how others behave and on what happens to others, so the thesis goes, but such desires are not affected by perceptions of what those agents desire, even for themselves; people's utility functions, as it is often put, are independent of one another (Gauthier 1986, 87).
3. Strong non-tuism. A stronger claim again: people's desires do not extend, except instrumentally, to others. Not only do people take no account of what others desire in forming their own desires in regard to others; any desires they have for what others should do, or for what should happen to others, are motivated ultimately by a desire for their own satisfaction (Gauthier 1986, 311).
4. Self-regardingness. A thesis that presupposes 1 but represents an alternative way of strengthening it to that represented by 2 and 3. People's non-instrumental desires may extend to others, and they may be responsive to the perceived desires of others—2 and 3 may be false—but the more that the desires bear on their own advantage, the stronger they are; in other words, people are relatively self-regarding in their desires.

Economists almost universally accept the first, self-centredness thesis. Agents who are rational in any economically recognisable sense cannot be led to action just by moral belief or the perception of what another desires or anything of the sort; such belief or perception may affect what they do but only through first affecting what they desire. Some thinkers toy with the possibility that agents may be capable of putting themselves under the control of something other than their own desires: for example, Mark Platts (1980) when he imagines that moral belief may motivate without the presence of desire; Amartya Sen (1982, Essay 4) when he speaks of the possibility of commitment; and Frederic Schick (1984) when he canvases the notion of sociality. But economists are probably on the side of common sense in urging that all action is mediated via the desires of the agent (Pettit 1993, ch. 1). In any case, that is what I shall assume in what follows. There is a conflict between economics and common sense, as I shall be arguing, but it does not arise in respect of this first thesis.

Do economists go beyond the rather uncontroversial form of self-centredness articulated in thesis 1? They certainly do so to the extent that certain versions of the axioms of consumer-choice theory go beyond minimal requirements of rationality, self-centredness included, and imply features like the downward-sloping demand curve. But that is not the issue. The question is whether economists go beyond the postulate of self-centredness in postulating any of the more egoistic theses, 2 to 4.

Many economic theories endorse weak and strong non-tuism. They do so to the extent that various economic models assume that any good I do you is, from my point of view, an externality for which ideally I would want to extract payment: an external benefit that I would ideally want to appropriate for myself (or "internalise") (Gauthier 1986, 87). But this seems to be a feature of particular models and not an assumption that is essentially built into the economic way of thinking. And it is a feature that affects only some of the standard results of the theories in question, not all of them (Sen 1982, p. 93). I am not inclined to regard it as a deep feature of economic thinking. It may have little or no presence, for example, in the application of economic thought to social life outside the market.

Some may say that there is a deeper reason than the frequent use of non-tuistic assumptions for thinking that economic thinking is strongly non-tuistic in nature. The deeper reason, according to these theorists, is that in holding that agents act so as to satisfy their desires, economists assume that agents act for the sake of achieving their own desire-satisfaction: that is, for the sake of attaining a certain benefit for themselves. Anthony Downs gives countenance to this line of thought when, ironically enough, he tries to explain how economists can make sense of altruism. "There can be no simple identification of acting for one's greatest benefit with selfishness in the narrow sense because self-denying charity is often a great source of benefits to oneself. Thus our model leaves room for altruism in spite of its basic reliance upon the self-interest axiom" (Downs 1957, p. 37).

The line of thought in Downs's remark is confused. Accepting the economic theory of rationality may mean believing that people maximise expected utility but it does not mean believing that they act for their own greatest benefit. That persons maximise expected utility means that they act in the way that best serves their desires, according to their beliefs, but not that they do so for the sake of maximum desire-satisfaction and, in that sense, for the sake of their greatest benefit. When I act on a desire to help an elderly person across the road, I act so as to satisfy that desire but I do not act for the sake of such satisfaction; I act for the sake of helping the elderly person. To think otherwise would be to confuse the sense in which I seek desire-satisfaction in an ordinary case like this and the sense in which I seek it when I relieve the longing for a cigarette by smoking or the yearning for a drink by going to the pub.

I am prepared to concede, then, that while economics postulates self-centredness in the sense of thesis 1, it does not necessarily suppose that people are non-tuistic in the senses defined in theses 2 and 3. But, to come now to thesis 4, I do think that the discipline is committed to the assumption that people's self-regarding desires are generally stronger than their other-regarding ones: that in this sense people are relatively self-regarding in their desires. Whenever there is a conflict between what will satisfy me or mine and what will satisfy others, the assumption is that in general I will look for the more egocentric satisfaction. I may do so through neglecting your interests in my own efforts at self-promotion, or through helping my children at the expense of yours, or through jeopardising a common good for the sake of personal advantage, or through taking the side of my country against that of others. The possibilities are endless. What unites them is that in each case I display a strong preference for what concerns me or mine, in particular a preference that is stronger than a countervailing preference for what concerns others.

The assumption that people are relatively self-regarding in their desires shows up in the fact that economists tend only to invoke relatively self-regarding desires in their explanations and predictions. They predict that as it costs more to help others, there will be less help given to others, that as it becomes personally more difficult to contribute to a common cause—more difficult, say, to take litter to the bin—there will be a lesser level of contribution to that cause, and so on. They offer invisible-hand explanations under which we are told how some collective good is attained just on the basis of each pursuing their own advantage. And they specialise in prisoner's-dilemma accounts that reveal how people come to be collectively worse off, through seeking each to get the best possible outcome for themselves.

It may be said against this that I am focussing on purely contingent aspects of economic explanations: that there is no reason why economists should not develop their explanations on the basis of other-regarding desires as well. Perhaps fewer people will put their litter in a bin that becomes more difficult to access. But, equally, fewer people will put their litter in a bin, if it comes to be generally believed that littering is not so bad after all: say if it comes to be believed, however improbably, that littering has some good environmental side-effects. Or so any economist should be prepared to admit.

This observation shows that economists can and should recognise the relevance of relatively other-regarding desires. But it does not demonstrate that they must take those desires to be potentially just as powerful as self-regarding preferences. And the explanatory practice of economists manifests the contrary belief. The working assumption behind economic explanation is that, however much people may care for others, care for a collective good, or care for some moral principle, their self-concern is likely to outweigh the effects of such care, if it comes into conflict with it. That is why it must be a miracle in the economics textbook if some aggregate or collective pattern emerges or continues when the available self-regarding reasons argue against people's doing the things that the pattern requires.

The belief that people are relatively self-regarding shows up in other aspects of economic thought too. It may be behind the assumption of economic policy-makers and institutional designers that no proposal is plausible unless it can be shown to be "incentive-compatible": that is, unless it can be shown that people will have self-regarding reasons for going along with what the proposal requires.[1] And it may be at the root of the Paretian or quasi-Paretian assumption of normative or welfare economics that it is uncontroversially a social benefit if things can be changed so that all preferences currently satisfied continue to be satisfied and if further preferences are satisfied as well. This assumption is plausible if the preferences envisaged are self-regarding, for only envy would seem to provide a reason for denying that it is a good if some people can get more of what they want for themselves without others getting less. But the assumption is not at all plausible if the preferences also include other-regarding preferences, as we shall see in a moment. And so the Paretian assumption manifests a further, deeper belief: that the preferences with which economics is concerned are self-regarding ones.

The Paretian assumption is not plausible—certainly not as uncontroversial as economists generally think—when other-regarding preferences are involved, for reasons to which Amartya Sen (1982, Essay 2) has directed our attention. Consider two boys, Nasty and Nice, and their preferences in regard to the distribution of two apples, Big and Small. Nasty prefers to get Big no matter who is in control of the distribution. Nice prefers to get Small if he is in control—this, because he is other-regarding and feels he should give Big away if he is in charge—but prefers to get Big, if Nasty is in control: he is only human, after all. The Paretian assumption suggests—under the natural individuation of options (Pettit 1991)—that it is better to have Nice control the distribution rather than Nasty. If we put Nice in control, then that satisfies Nasty—he gets Big—and it satisfies Nice as well: Nice's preference for having Big if Nasty is in control does not get engaged and Nice's preference for having Small—for giving Big away—if he is in control himself, is satisfied. But this is clearly crazy: it means that we are punishing Nice for being nice, in particular for having other-regarding preferences; and this, while apparently attempting just to increase preference-satisfaction in an impartial manner. The lesson is that the Paretian assumption is not plausible once other-regarding preferences figure on the scene and so, if economists think that it is plausible—think indeed that it is uncontroversial—that suggests that they only have self-regarding preferences in view.

The upshot of all this, then, is that economists present human agents as relatively self-regarding creatures who act with a view to doing as well as possible by their predominantly self-regarding desires. These desires are usually assumed to be desires for what is loosely described as economic advantage or gain: that is, roughly, for advantage or gain in the sorts of things that can be traded. But self-interested desires, of course, may extend to other goods too, and there is nothing inimical to economics in explaining patterns of behaviour by reference, say, to those non-tradable goods that consist in being well loved or well regarded (Pettit 1990, Brennan and Pettit 1993). The economic approach is tied to an assumption of relative self-interest but not to any particular view of the dimensions in which self-interest may operate.

2. The conflict with common sense

Does the picture fit? Are human beings rational centres of predominantly self-interested concern? It would seem not. Were human agents centres of this kind, then we would expect them to find their reasons for doing things predominantly in considerations that bear on their own advantage.[2] But this isn't our common experience, or so at least I shall argue.

Consider the sorts of considerations that weigh with us, or seem to weigh with us, in a range of common-or-garden situations. We are apparently moved in our dealings with others by considerations that bear on their merits and their attractions, that highlight what is expected of us and what fair play or friendship requires, that direct attention to the good we can achieve together or the past that we share in common, and so on through a complex variety of deliberative themes. And not only are we apparently moved in this non-egocentric way. We clearly believe of one another—and take it, indeed, to be a matter of common belief—that we are generally and reliably responsive to claims that transcend and occasionally confound the calls of self-interest. That is why we feel free to ask each other for favours, to ground our projects in the expectation that others will be faithful to their past commitments, and to seek counsel from others in confidence that they will present us with a more or less impartial rendering of how things stand.

Suppose that people believed that they were each as self-interested as economists appear to assume; suppose that this was a matter of common belief amongst them. In that case we would expect much of the discourse that they carry on with one another to assume the shape of a bargaining exchange. We would expect each of them to try to persuade others to act in a certain way by convincing them that it is in their personal interest to act in that way: this, in good part, by convincing them that they, the persuaders, will match such action appropriately, having corresponding reasons of personal advantage to do so. Under the economic supposition, there would be little room for anyone to call on anyone else in the name of any motive other than self-interest.

The economic supposition may be relevant in some areas of human exchange, most saliently in areas of market behaviour. But it clearly does not apply across the broad range of human interaction. The normal mode under which people exchange with one another is closer to the model of a debate than the model of a bargain. It involves them in each presenting to the other considerations that, putatively, they both recognise as relevant and potentially persuasive. I do not call on you in the name of what is merely to your personal advantage; did I do so, that could be a serious insult. I call on you in the name of your commitment to certain ideals, your membership in certain groups, your attachment to certain people. I call on you, more generally, under the assumption that, like me, you understand and endorse the language of loyalty and fair play, kindness and politeness, honesty and straight talking. This language often has a moral ring but the terminology and concepts involved are not confined to the traditional limits of the moral; they extend to all the terms in which our culture allows us to make sense of ourselves, to make ourselves acceptably intelligible, to each other.

One way of underlining this observation is to consider how best an ethnographer might seek to make sense of the ways in which people conduct their lives and affairs. An ethnographer who came to the shores of a society like ours—a society like one of the developed democracies—would earn the ridicule of professional colleagues if they failed to take notice of the rich moral and quasi-moral language in which we ordinary folk explain ourselves to ourselves and ourselves to one another: the language, indeed, in which we take our bearings as we launch ourselves in action. But if it is essential for the understanding of how we ordinary folk behave that account is taken of that language, then this strongly suggests that economists must be mistaken—at least they must be overlooking some aspect of human life—when they assume that we are a relatively self-regarding lot.

The claim that ordinary folk are oriented towards a non-egocentric language of self-explanation and self-justification does not establish definitively, of course, that they are actually not self-regarding. We all recognise the possibilities of rationalisation and deception that such a language leaves open. Still, it would surely be miraculous that that language succeeds as well as it does in defining a stable and smooth framework of expectation, if as a matter of fact people's sensibilities do not conform to its contours: if, as a matter of fact, people fall systematically short—systematically and not just occasionally short—of what it suggests may be taken for granted about them.

We are left, then, with a problem. The economic mind is that of a relatively self-regarding creature. But the mind that people display towards one another in most social settings, the mind that is articulated in common conceptions of how ordinary folk are moved, is saturated with concerns that dramatically transcend the boundaries of the self. So how, if at all, can the economic mind be reconciled with the common-or-garden mind?[3]

3. The economic mind as a virtual presence

The obvious answer for would-be conciliationists is to say that whereas ordinary folk conform in most contexts to the picture of the common mind, the economic mind is still implicitly present in such contexts. But how to interpret this? What does it mean to say that the economic mind is implicitly present: that people are implicitly but not explicitly oriented towards the self-regarding concerns that economists privilege?

The main model of the implicit-explicit distinction is drawn from a visual analogy. It suggests that an explicit concern is something focal, something directed to the centre of a subject's field of vision, whereas an implicit concern is a concern for what lies at the edge of that field: a concern for what is peripherally rather than focally tracked. If I explicitly desire something, my desire is explicit in the sense in which I am explicitly aware of the computer screen in front of me; if I implicitly desire something, my desire is implicit in the sense in which I am—or was a moment ago—only implicitly aware of the telephone at the edge of my desk. Does this model help in explicating the idea that even if people are not always explicitly of an economic turn of mind, they are at least implicitly so?

The model certainly gives us a picture of what it might mean to say that implicitly people are economically minded. It would mean that even as people pay attention to the sorts of concerns engaged in ordinary exchanges with others, even as they keep their eyes on the needs of a friend, the job that has to be done, the requirements of fairness, they invariably conduct some peripheral scanning of what their own advantage dictates that they should do. The model does not deny the appearance of more or less other-regarding deliberation but it does debunk that appearance. It suggests that whether they are aware of it or not, those who practise other-directed deliberation indulge a more self-directed style of reflection in the shadows of the mind, on the boundaries of their attention. Gary Becker (1976, p. 7) comes close to endorsing this model when he writes: "the economic approach does not assume that decision units are necessarily conscious of their own efforts to maximize or can verbalize or otherwise describe in an informative way reasons for the systematic patterns in their behavior. Thus it is consistent with the emphasis on the subconscious in modern psychology."

But the focal-peripheral interpretation of the claim that people are implicitly self-regarding does not make the claim seem particularly compelling. We all admit that people profess standards from which they often slip and that their slipping does usually relate to an awareness, perhaps a deeply suppressed awareness, of the costs of complying with the standards. We all admit, in other words, that weakness of will and self-deception are pretty commonplace phenomena. But what the focal-peripheral model would suggest is that the whole of human life is shot through with this sort of failure: that what we take to be a more or less occasional, more or less localised, sort of pathology actually represents the normal, healthy state of the human organism. That is a fairly outrageous claim. Most economists would probably be shocked to hear that the view of the human subject which they systematically deploy is about as novel, and about as implausible, as the picture projected in classical Freudianism.

But if we reject the focal-peripheral way of reconciling the economic and the common mind, are we forced to choose between the two pictures of the human subject? Are we forced to choose between economic science and common sense? Happily, I think not. There is a second, less familiar model of the implicit-explicit distinction that is available in the literature and it promises a different, more attractive mode of reconciliation.

I call this the virtual-actual model. One area where it is sometimes deployed—though not in so many words—is in explaining the sense in which I may implicitly believe that 2 times 101 is 202, even when I have never given a thought to that particular multiplication; or, to take another example, the sense in which I may implicitly believe that Europe has more than ten million inhabitants, when I have only ever thought about the population of individual countries. I implicitly believe these things in the sense that I am so disposed—specifically, I am so familiar with elementary arithmetic or with the population figures for European countries—that even the most casual reflection is sufficient to trigger the recognition that indeed 2 times 101 is 202, indeed the population of Europe is more than ten million. I virtually believe the propositions in question—virtually, not actually—but the virtuality or potentiality in question is so close to realisation that ordinary usage scarcely marks the shortfall.

I propose that if we are to follow the familiar conciliationist route of describing people as economically minded, but not always in an explicit fashion, we should try to spell out this claim by reference to the virtual-actual model, not the peripheral-focal one. I think that it is not implausible that people are virtually self-regarding in most contexts of choice, even if they are not actually so. It is generally agreed that actual self-regard plays a great part in market and related behaviour but that it does not have the same sort of presence—if it has a presence at all—in other contexts: for example, in contexts of ordinary family or friendly interaction, in contexts of political decision, or in contexts of group behaviour. What I suggest is that in such non-market contexts self-regard may still have an important presence: it may be virtually if not actually there; it may be waiting in the wings, even if it is not actually on stage.

Here is how self-regard might have a virtual presence in such contexts. Suppose, first of all, that people are generally content in non-market contexts—we can restrict our attention to these—to let their actions be dictated by what we might call the cultural framing of the situation in which they find themselves. A friend asks for a routine level of help and, in the absence of urgent business, the agent naturally complies with the request; it would be unthinkable for someone who understands what friendship means to do anything else. There is an election in progress and, the humdrum of everyday life being what it is, the agent spontaneously makes time for going to the polls; that is manifestly the thing to do, under ordinary canons of understanding, and the thing to do without thinking about it. Someone has left a telephone message asking for a return call about some matter and the agent doesn't hesitate to ring back; even if aware that there is nothing useful they can tell the original caller, they shrink from the impoliteness, in their culture, of ignoring the call. In the pedestrian patterns of day-to-day life, the cultural framing of any situation will be absolutely salient to the ordinary agent and the ordinary agent will more or less routinely respond. Or so at least I am prepared to assume.

But that is only the first part of my supposition. Suppose, in the second place, that despite the hegemony of cultural framing in people's everyday deliberations and decisions, there are certain alarm bells that make them take thought to their own interests. People may proceed under more or less automatic, cultural pilot in most cases but at any point where a decision is liable to cost them dearly in self-regarding terms, the alarm bells ring and prompt them to consider personal advantage; and heeding considerations of personal advantage leads people, generally if not invariably, to act so as to secure that advantage: they are disposed to do the relatively more self-regarding thing.

Under these suppositions, self-regard will normally have no actual presence in dictating what people do; it will not be present in deliberation and will make no impact on decision. But it will always be virtually present in deliberation, for there are alarms which are ready to ring at any point where the agent's interests get to be possibly compromised and those alarms will call up self-regard and give it a more or less controlling deliberative presence. The agent will run under cultural pilot, provided that pilot does not carry them into terrain that is too dangerous from a self-interested point of view. Let such terrain come into view, and the agent will quickly return to manual; they will quickly begin to count the more personal losses and benefits that are at stake in the decision at hand. This reflection may not invariably lead to self-regarding action—there is such a thing as self-sacrifice, after all—but the assumption is that it will do so fairly reliably.

If the suppositions I have described were realised, then it would be fair to say that people are implicitly self-regarding: that they implicitly conform to the image of the economic mind. The reason is that under the model of virtual self-regard, no action is performed without self-regarding consideration unless it fails to ring certain alarms: that is, unless it promises to do suitably well in self-regard terms. What it is to do suitably well may vary from individual to individual, of course, depending on their expectations as to what is feasible and depending on their self-regarding aspirations: depending on how much they want for themselves, and with what intensity. But the point is that regardless of such variations, the model of virtual self-regarding control does privilege self-regard in a manner that conforms to the image of the economic mind. Another way of putting this point is to say that under the model described, an agent will generally be moved by certain considerations only if they satisfy a certain negative, self-regarding condition: only if they do not tend to lead the agent towards a certain level of self-sacrifice. Let the considerations push the agent below the relevant self-regarding level of aspiration and the alarm bells will ring, causing the agent to rethink and probably reshape the project at hand.

The position which self-regard is given under the model of virtual self-regarding control is rather like that which it enjoys under Herbert Simon's (1978) model of satisficing as distinct from maximising behaviour. People do pretty well in self-regarding terms, even if they do not do as well as possible. And it may even be that virtual self-regarding control enables them to do as well as possible in egocentric terms, for the absence of self-regarding calculation in most decisions represents a saving in time and trouble—these are virtues emphasised by Simon— and it may also secure other benefits: it may earn a greater degree of acceptance and affection, for example, than would a pattern of relentless calculation.

But is the model of virtual self-regarding control, in particular the scenario of the alarm bells, a plausible one? The question divides in two. First, is there any arrangement under which we can imagine that such alarms are put in place? And second, if there is, can we plausibly maintain that those alarms will reliably serve to usher self-regarding deliberation into a controlling position in the generation of behaviour?

The alarms required will have to be informational; they will have to be signals that this is the sort of situation where the agent's advantage may be compromised, if cultural framing is given its head. So are there signals available in ordinary contexts that might serve to communicate this message? Clearly, there are. Consider the fact that a decision situation is non-routine; or that it is of a kind in which the agent's fingers were already burned; or that it is a situation in which the agent's peers—others who might be expected to fare about as well—do generally better than the agent; or that some conventional or other assurances as to the responses of others are lacking. Any such facts can serve as signals that the agent's personal advantage may be in especial danger. Indeed it is hard to imagine a situation in which the agent's interests were likely to be compromised in significant measure by culturally framed demands—compromised in a measure that the agent would not generally tolerate—without such signals being present. Certainly it is reasonable to assume that generally there will be signals available in such situations that the agent should take care: signals to the effect that this is a situation where that framing is liable to serve the agent less well than it ordinarily does.

The other question is whether it is plausible, given the availability of signals of this kind, to postulate that the signals will generally tip agents into a self-regarding sort of deliberation: a sort of deliberation that is normally sidelined in favour of fidelity to the cultural frame. This issue is wholly an empirical matter but it is an issue on which the weight of received opinion speaks unambiguously. It has been common wisdom for at least two thousand years of thinking about politics that few are proof against temptation and few, therefore, are likely to ignore signals that their self-interest may be endangered. Human beings may be capable of reaching for the stars but, except for some romantic strands of thought, all the streams in the Western tradition of thinking suggest that if there is opportunity for individuals to further their own interests, then they can generally be relied upon, sooner or later, to exploit that opportunity:

all power corrupts. The main theme of the tradition is summed up in the lesson that no one can be entrusted with the ring of Gyges that Plato discusses: the ring that renders a person invisible and that makes it possible for him to serve his own interests with impunity, at whatever cost to the interests of others.

These lines of thought give support, therefore, to the picture described above. They suggest that it is very plausible to think that even when people pay no actual attention to relatively self-regarding considerations, still those considerations have a certain presence and relevance to how people behave. They are virtually present, in the sense that if the behaviour rings the alarm bells of self-interest—and there will be plenty such bells to ring—the agent will give heed and will tend to let self-regarding considerations play a role in shaping what is done.[4]

Under the emerging picture, then, there is a sense in which people are always at least implicitly of the self-regarding cast of mind projected by economists; if they are not actually self-regarding in their mode of deliberation, they are virtually so: if self-regard does not actually occupy the pilot's seat, it is always there in the co-pilot's, ready to assume control. The picture is a rather non-idealistic representation of human beings but it is not unnecessarily bleak. It emphasises that in the normal run, people are not calculating or self-concerned: they articulate their lives and relationships in the currency of received values and they generally conform to the requirements of those values. Where it goes non-idealistic, it does so only in the spirit of what we might call the Gyges axiom: the principle that virtue—fidelity to the demands of the cultural frame—is fragile and generally survives only under conditions in which it is not manifestly against the interests of the agent, only under conditions in which the alarm bells do not ring.

There are two further points to put to those who worry about the alleged non-idealism of our picture. First, the picture leaves open the possibility that in many cases some individuals will not heed the alarms and will stick to what the culturally framed situation requires, by criteria of common values, through the thick and the thin of self-sacrifice. And, second, the picture leaves room for the Aristotelian principle that people become virtuous, become lovers of virtuous ways, through habituation in those ways. It leaves room, not just for the possibility that some people will be relatively heedless of the alarms described, but for the possibility that such heedlessness may be facilitated in increasing measure by a regime in which the alarms only rarely ring: a regime in which things are well designed and people are free, in the silence of self-regard, to develop an attachment to doing that which by the common values of the culture is what the situation requires.

4. The economic mind as an explanatory principle

We saw in the first section that the economic mind is distinctively self-regarding and in the second that it contrasts in this respect with the common mind: the mind as articulated in common ways of thinking. The last section gave us a picture under which it seems possible to reconcile these two points of view: the points of view associated respectively with economics and common sense. The common-sense viewpoint is valid to the extent that ordinary folk manage their affairs most of the time without adverting to their own interests; they are guided in their decisions by what is required of them under the cultural framing of the situations in which they find themselves. The economic viewpoint is valid to the extent that even when this is so, even when people are not explicitly self-regarding in their deliberations, still self-regard has a virtual presence; it is there, ready to affect what people do, in the event that any of the alarm bells of self-interest ring.

The question which now arises, however, is how far the merely virtual presence of self-regard is supposed to legitimate the economic explanatory enterprise: the enterprise of explaining various patterns in human affairs by reference to rational self-regard. That self-regarding considerations have a virtual as distinct from an actual presence in human deliberation means that they are not actual causes of anything that the agents do. They may be standby causes of certain patterns of behaviour: they may be potential causes that would serve to sustain those patterns, did the actual causes fail. But it is not clear how anything is to be explained by reference to causes of such a would-be variety. After all, explanation is normally taken to uncover the factors operative in the production of the events and patterns to be explained; it is normally taken to require a reference to actual causal history (Lewis 1986, Essay 22).

This difficulty can be underlined by considering the explananda that economic investigation is ordinarily taken to be concerned with in the non-market area. These are, first, the emergence of certain phenomena or patterns in the past and, second, their continuation into the present and future. The explanation of the emergence of any phenomenon—say, the emergence of a norm or institution—clearly requires a reference to the factors that were operative in bringing it into existence. And the explanation of the continuation of any phenomenon, equally clearly, requires a reference to the factors that keep it there. So how could a reference to virtual self-regard serve to explain anything? In other words, how can our model of the common-cum-economic mind serve to make sense of the explanatory claims of economics, in particular of the economics of non-market behaviour: of behaviour that is motored by the perception of what situations demand, under relevant cultural frames, not by considerations of self-regard?

The answer, I suggest, is that while virtual self-regard may be of no use in explaining the emergence or continuation of any pattern of behaviour, it can be of great utility in explaining a third explanandum: the resilience of that pattern of behaviour under various shocks and disturbances.

Imagine a little set-up in which a ball rolls along a straight line—this, say, under Newton's laws of motion—but where there are little posts on either side that are designed to protect it from the influence of various possible but non-actualised forces that might cause it to change course; they are able to damp incoming forces and if such forces still have an effect they are capable of restoring the ball to its original path. The posts on either side are virtual or standby causes of the ball's rolling on the straight line, not factors that have an actual effect. So can they serve an explanatory purpose? Well, they cannot explain the emergence or the continuation of the straight course of the rolling ball. But they can explain the fact—and, of course, it is a fact—that not only does the ball roll on a straight line in the actual set-up, it sticks to more or less that straight line under the various possible contingencies where perturbing forces appear and even have a temporary effect. They explain the fact, in other words, that the straight rolling is not something fragile, not something vulnerable to every turn of the wind, but rather a resilient pattern: a pattern that is robust under various contingencies and that can be relied upon to persist.

The resilience explained in this toy example may be a matter of independent experience, as when I discover by induction—and without understanding why—that the ball does keep returning to the straight line. But equally the resilience may only become salient on recognising the explanatory power of the posts: this, in the way in which the laws that a theory explains may only become salient in the light of the explanatory theory itself. It does not matter which scenario obtains. In either case the simple fact is that despite their merely standby status, the posts serve to resolve an important matter of explanation. They explain, not why the pattern emerged at a certain time, nor why it continues across a certain range of times, but why it continues across a certain range of contingencies: why it is modally, as distinct from temporally, persistent.

The lesson of our little analogy should be clear. As a reference to the virtually efficacious posts explains the resilience with which the ball rolls on a straight line, so a reference to a merely virtual form of self-regard may explain the resilience with which people maintain certain patterns of behaviour. Imagine a given pattern of human behaviour whose continuation is actually explained by the cultural framing under which people view the relevant situations or, more prosaically, by people's sheer inertia. Suppose that that pattern of behaviour has the modal property of being extremely robust under various contingencies: say, under the contingency that some individuals peel away and offer an example of an alternative pattern. The factors that explain its actually continuing may not explain this robustness or resilience; there may be no reason why the example of mutant individuals should not display a new way of viewing the situation, for example, or should not undermine the effects of inertia. So how to explain the resilience of the pattern? Well, one possible explanation would be that as the contingencies envisaged produce a different pattern of behaviour, the alarm bells of self-interest ring—this, because of the contrast between what different individuals are doing—and the self-regarding deliberation that they prompt leads most of the mutants and would-be mutants back towards the original pattern.

The analogy with the rolling ball serves to show how in principle the model of virtual self-regard may leave room for the economic explanation of behaviour that is not actively generated by considerations of self-regard. But it may be useful, in conclusion, to illustrate the lesson more concretely.

David Lewis's (1969) work on convention is often taken as a first-rate example of how economic explanation can do well in making sense of a phenomenon outside the traditional economic domain of the market. He invokes the fact that conventions often serve to resolve certain problems of coordination—problems of a kind that can be nicely modelled with game-theory techniques—in explanation of such conventions. But what is supposed to be explained by Lewis's narrative? Lewis is clearly not offering a historical story about the emergence of conventions. And, equally clearly, he is not telling a story about the factors that actually keep the conventions in place; he freely admits that people may not be aware of the coordination problem solved by conventional behaviour and may stick to that behaviour for any of a variety of reasons: reasons of inertia, perhaps, or reasons of principle or ideology that may have grown up around the convention in question.

The best clue to Lewis's explanatory intentions comes in a remark from a later article when he considers the significance of the fact that actually conventional behaviour is mostly produced by blind habit. "An action may be rational, and may be explained by the agent's beliefs and desires, even though that action was done by habit, and the agent gave no thought to the beliefs or desires which were his reasons for action. If that habit ever ceased to serve the agent's desires according to his beliefs, it would at once be overridden and corrected by conscious reasoning" (Lewis 1983, p. 181). This remark gives support to the view that what Lewis is explaining about convention, by his own lights, is not emergence or continuance but resilience. He implies that the servicing of the agent's—as it happens, self-regarding—desires is not the actual cause of the conventional behaviour but a standby cause: a cause that would take the place of a failing habit, so long as the behaviour remains suitable; this, in the way that Lewis says it would displace the remaining habit at the point where the behaviour becomes unsuitable. And if the servicing of self-regard is a standby cause of this kind, then what it is best designed to explain is the resilience, where there is resilience, of the conventional behaviour.

But it is not only the Lewis explanation of conventional behaviour that lends itself to this gloss. Can we explain American slave-holding by reference to economic interests (Fogel and Engerman 1974, p. 4), when slave-holders articulated their duties, and conducted their business, in terms of a more or less religious ideology? Yes, to the extent that we can explain why slave-holding was a very resilient institution up to the time of the civil war; we can explain why the various mutants and emancipationists never did more than cause a temporary crisis. Can we explain the failure of people to oppose most oppressive states as a product of free-rider reasoning (North 1981. pp. 31–32), when it is granted that they generally used other considerations to justify their acquiescence? Yes, so far as the free-riding variety of self-regarding reasoning would have been there to support non-action, to make non-action resilient, in any situation where the other, actual reasons failed to do so and alarm bells rang. Can we invoke considerations of social acceptance to explain people's abiding by certain norms, as I have tried to do elsewhere (Pettit 1990), when I freely grant that it is considerations of a much less prudential kind that keep most people faithful to such norms? Yes, we certainly can. Self-regarding considerations of social acceptance can ensure that normative fidelity is robust or resilient if they come into play whenever someone begins to deviate, or contemplate deviation, and if they serve in such cases to restore or reinforce compliance.

The upshot will be clear. We can make good sense of economic explanation, even explanation of non-market behaviour, in terms of the model of virtual self-regard whereby the economic mind is reconciled with the common mind. That model recommends itself, then, on at least two grounds. It shows that the assumptions which economists make about the human mind, in particular about human motivation, can be rendered consistent with the assumptions of commonplace, everyday thinking. And it shows that so interpreted, the assumptions motivate a promising and indeed developing program for economic explanation: and explanation, not just in the traditional areas of market behaviour, but across the social world more generally.

Notes

1. In fairness, however, I should note that this search for incentive-compatibility could be motivated—reasonably or not—by the belief that however other-regarding most people are, policies should always be designed to be proof against more self-regarding "knaves." See Brennan and Buchanan (1981).

2. Some might say that under the assumption that human beings are rational centres of predominantly self-regarding concern—this, in a Bayesian sense—we ought to expect that they would be, not only self-concerned, but also calculating: we ought to expect that they would think in terms of the ledger of probabilities and utilities that figure in Bayesian decision theory. I do not go along with this. Bayesian decision theory says nothing on how agents manage to maximise expected utility; it makes no commitments on the style of deliberation that agents follow. See Pettit 1991.

3. This problem may be dismissed by some thinkers on the ground that the literature on conditional cooperation shows how economically rational individuals may cooperate out of purely self-regarding motives (Axelrod 1984, Pettit and Sugden 1989). But that would be a mistake. This literature shows that economically rational individuals may come to behave cooperatively, not that they will come to think and talk in a cooperative way.

4. The picture of virtual self-regard may be modified by being made subject to certain boundary conditions. It might be held, for example, that the picture does not apply universally, only under certain structural arrangements: say, that it does not apply in family life, only in relations of a more public character. For related ideas see Satz and Ferejohn (1994).

References

Axelrod, Robert 1984. *The Evolution of Cooperation*, New York: Basic Books.

Becker, Gary 1976. *The Economic Approach to Human Behaviour*, Chicago: University of Chicago Press.

Brennan, H. G. and J. M. Buchanan 1981. "The Normative Purpose of Economic 'Science': Rediscovery of an Eighteenth Century method." *International Review of Law and Economics*, vol 1, 155–66.

Brennan, H. G. and J. M. Buchanan and Philip Pettit 1993. "Hands Invisible and Intangible," *Synthese*, vol. 94, 1993, pp. 191–225.

Downs, Anthony 1957. *An Economic Theory of Democracy*. New York: Harper.

Eells, Ellery 1982. *Rational Decision and Causality*, Cambridge: Cambridge University Press.

Fogel, R. W. and S. L. Engermann 1974. *Time on the Cross: The Economics of American Negro Slavery*. Soston: Little, Brown.

Gauthier, David 1986. *Morals by Agreement*. Oxford: Oxford University Press.

Lewis, David 1969 *Convention*. Cambridge, MA: M.I.T. Press.

Lewis, David 1983/86. *Philosophical Papers*, vols. 1 & 2. New York: Oxford University Press.

North, Douglas 1981. *Structure and Change in Economic History*. New York: Norton.

Pettit, Philip 1990. "*Virtus Normativa*: Rational Choice Perspectives," *Ethics*, vol. 100, pp. 725-55.

Pettit, Philip 1991. "Decision Theory and Folk Psychology," in Michael Bacharach and Susan Hurley, eds., *Essays in the Foundations of Decision Theory*, Oxford: Basil Blackwell, pp. 147-75.

Pettit, Philip 1993. *The Common Mind: An Essay on Psychology, Society and Politics*. New York: Oxford University Press.

Pettit, Philip and Robert Sugden 1989. "The Backward Induction Paradox," *Journal of Philosophy*, vol. 86, 1989, pp. 169–82.

Platts, Mark 1980. *Ways of Meaning*. London: Routledge.

Satz, Debra and John Ferejohn 1994. "Rational Choice and Social Theory," *Journal of Philosophy*, vol. 91, pp. 71–87.

Schick, Frederic 1984. *Having Reasons: An Essay on Rationality and Sociality*, Princeton, NJ: Princeton University Press.

Sen, Amartya 1982. *Choice, Welfare and Measurement*. Oxford: Blackwell

Simon, Herbert 1978. "Rationality as Process and as Product of Thought," *American Economic Review* vol. 68, pp. 1–16.

Chapter 17

FRANCESCO GUALA

BUILDING ECONOMIC MACHINES
The FCC auctions

DEBATES IN THE PHILOSOPHY OF the social sciences rely too often on *a priori* argumentation, or take off from considerations of purely theoretical scientific practice. In contrast, the philosophy of the natural sciences has been massively influenced by the detailed studies of concrete scientific practice made by historians and sociologists during the past three decades.[1] Descriptive work of the latter kind can affect philosophical views of science (for example, a realist or an instrumentalist viewpoint) without necessarily engaging directly in abstract philosophical arguments. This paper is intended as a contribution to this sort of literature, setting the empirical ground for philosophical theorising about the social sciences.

The case study comes from a sub-field of rational choice theory known as the theory of 'mechanism design'. The second ambition of this paper, then, is to try to intervene in the debate on rational choice modelling and the metaphysics of social mechanisms.[2] The argument stems from the assumption that we know best what we have built ourselves, and therefore that, whenever possible, interpretations of a scientific theory (in the natural *and* in the social sciences) should take applied science as their point of departure. Given that successful technological applications have the power to drive entire research programmes at once, it is particularly important to ask what kind of interpretation of rational choice theory is warranted by its applied branches.

I shall examine one of the most publicised applications of rational choice theory to date: the construction in 1993–94 of a new market institution, by means of which the Federal Communication Commission (an agency of the US government, FCC from now on) would allocate a unique kind of goods. I shall therefore focus on auction theory, a branch of game theory that 'is closer to applications than is most frontier mathematical economics' (McAfee and McMillan, 1987, p. 700). As it will turn out, 'being close to applications' is not quite the same as 'being straightforwardly applicable'.

1. Background of the FCC auction

A 'decentralising wave' hit the American economy in the late 1980s. A new political imperative prescribed the replacement, whenever feasible, of centralised, bureaucratic systems of allocation by market processes. Before this wave reached the telecommunications industry, licences for wireless Personal Communication Systems (PCS)—providing the right to use a portion of the airwave spectrum for radio communication, or telephones, portable faxing machines, and so on—were assigned *via* an administrative hearing process. Each potential user had to apply to the FCC and convince them of their case; a commission would then decide to whom the licence should have gone. Such a method had a number of drawbacks: above all, it was slow, cumbersome, non-transparent, and gave licences away for free instead of selling them for their market value. In 1982 the Congress decided to reform the system and make it faster by using lotteries: each licence was randomly assigned to one of the companies which had applied for it.

The lottery system was quicker, but had other defects: in particular, some companies would participate even though they were not interested in a licence, just to resell it and make large profits out of it. A secondary market was thus created in which licences were resold by lucky winners to those who would really use them. The lottery system generated an unjust and unjustified distribution of income from the controller of the airwaves (the USA) to individuals who had done nothing to deserve it.[3] In July 1993 the Congress decided that the lottery system had to be replaced by a market institution, and the FCC was faced with the problem of identifying and implementing within ten months the best auction system for selling their licences.

The problem of devising a suitable kind of auction was far from trivial, and previous experiences in New Zealand and Australia had shown that it is also a delicate one: a badly conceived reform could lead to disastrous results.[4] As a journalist put it, 'when government auctioneers need worldly advice, where can they turn? To mathematical economists of course', and 'as for the firms that want to get their hands on a sliver of the airwaves, their best bet is to go out first and hire themselves a good game theorist'.[5] In September 1993 the FCC issued a 'Notice of Proposed Rule Making' setting out the goals to be achieved by the auctions, tentatively proposing a design, and asking for comments and suggestions from potential bidders.

Soon a number of economists (Robert Wilson, Paul Milgrom, Charles Plott, Preston McAfee, Jeremy Bulow, Mark Isaac, Robert Weber, John Ledyard and many others) got involved in the problem as companies' advisors. The aims to be pursued in auctioning PCS acted as constraints on the work of the consultants. The auction was intended to achieve an efficient allocation (making sure that the spectrum rights went to those companies that most valued them and could make best use of them), to prevent monopolies, and to promote small businesses, rural telephone companies, minority-owned and women-owned firms (as prescribed by the Government and the FCC policy). Moreover, it was understood that the volume of revenue raised by the auctioneer (the FCC) was an important factor to be taken into account. The target was thus set right at the beginning of the enterprise. It took the form of an economic 'phenomenon' to be created from scratch, with certain specific characteristics that made it valuable in the FCC's eyes. The following story is a *tour de force* from this preliminary identification of the target to the final product (the FCC auction as it was eventually implemented in July 1994), through a series of theoretical models, experimental systems, simulations, public and private demonstrations of the properties of different economic machines.

2. Mechanism design

The FCC enterprise is a typical case of a '*mechanism design*' problem. The term 'mechanism' is widely used in the social sciences, in various and often inconsistent ways.[6] In this paper I shall stick to the conventional usage in philosophy of science: mechanisms are abstract or concrete structures endowed with their own specific causal properties. Putting mechanisms to work generates '*processes*'.[7] According to a widely shared view of scientific knowledge, the main task of the theorist is to explain spontaneously occurring and experimental processes, by designing an appropriate model for each kind of mechanism and the phenomena it generates. The FCC case belongs to an altogether different kind of scientific activity, proceeding in the opposite direction, *from models to mechanisms and processes.*

> Designs are motivated by . . . a mathematical model, a body of theory . . . that is perhaps completely devoid of operational detail. The task is to find a system of institutions—the rules for individual expression, information transmittal, and social choice— . . . that mirrors the behavioural features of the mechanism. The theory suggests the existence of [mechanisms and] processes that perform in certain (desirable) ways, and the task is to find them. This is a pure form of institutional engineering.
> (Plott, 1981, p. 134)

Theory can be used to produce new technology, by shaping the social world so as to mirror a model in all its essential aspects. The 'idealised' character of a theory may thus be a virtue rather than a defect, as the explicit role of theory is to point to a possibility. Theory *projects*, rather than describing what is already there.

The mechanisms we shall be concerned with are market institutions. Mechanism design is often motivated by the will to replace centralised, expensive or inefficient systems of regulation with 'better' (i.e. decentralised, cheaper or more efficient) ones. The problem is analogous to deciding whether to direct traffic using policemen rather than traffic lights or roundabouts. Each system has advantages and drawbacks in terms of cost, ambiguity of the rules, propensity to generate confusion and mistakes, costs of enforcement, and so on.

The theory of mechanism design involves both the study of the functioning of different institutions, and their evaluation. It is an enterprise between theoretical and applied economics, which requires first stating clearly the goals to be achieved by the mechanism, and then finding the best means to achieve them in the case at hand. Rational choice theory is an extremely valuable analytical tool in this enterprise. Once the environment (agents' preferences) is defined, it is possible to think of institutional rules as defining a game, which the agents are facing and trying to solve rationally. Ideally, it should be possible to predict exactly what outcome will be achieved by a given mechanism in a given environment by means of equilibrium analysis.

3. The role of theory

When the FCC started auctioning in 1994, the results were immediately hailed as a major success, if only for the huge sums of money gained by the Federal Government ($23 billion between 1994 and 1997). Most of the glory went to the theorists who had helped design the auction mechanism. The FCC auction was claimed to be 'the most dramatic example of game theory's new power', 'a triumph not only for the FCC and the taxpayers, but also for game theory (and game theorists)', and so on.[8] It would be mistaken, however, to think of the FCC auction's design as entirely theory-driven, dictated by auction theory. Auctions like those for PCS are in fact a typical example of what game theory is *not* very good at modelling.

Game-theoretic accounts of auction mechanisms date back to the sixties, thanks mainly to the pioneering work of William Vickrey (1961). Vickrey solved an auction game known as the 'independent private values model', where each bidder is supposed to be aware exactly of the value of the auctioned item, but does not know its value to other bidders. Such an assumption seems to be satisfied in auctions of, say, antiques, that will be privately enjoyed by buyers who do not intend to resell them. Wilson (1977) and then Milgrom and Weber (1982) extended Vickrey's private value model to other important cases. Auctions are modelled as non-cooperative games played by expected-utility-maximising bidders. The players are assumed to adopt equilibrium strategies—in the standard sense of a Bayes-Nash equilibrium in which, given everyone else's moves, no player can do better than she is presently doing by changing her strategy.[9]

After more than two decades of theoretical development, the theory of auctions still relies on a number of restrictive assumptions, and can by no means be applied to all cases. The most important and disturbing feature of the commodities (the PCS licences) to be auctioned by the FCC is their being (in economists' jargon) sometimes 'complementary' (such as licences to provide the same service to different contiguous regions) and sometimes 'perfect substitutes' (licences for different spectrum bands which can provide the same service) for one another. Thus the value of an individual licence may be strictly dependent on the buyer's owning one or more of the other items: the value of a 'package' could differ from the sum of the values of the individual items that are in it. This is due to a number of characteristics of the airwaves industry, from fixed-cost technology to customer-base development, from problems of inter-ferences to the use of different standards by different companies (McMillan, 1994, p. 150). For all these reasons a licence for transmitting in a certain region is in general more or less valuable depending on whether one owns the licence for a neighbouring area or not.

Complementarities are one of economists' nightmares, because models of competitive markets with goods of this kind in general do not have a unique equilibrium and are unstable. No theorem in auction theory tells you what kind of institution will achieve an efficient outcome. The theory is from this point of view incomplete: there does not exist a prediction for auctions with interdependent goods. The first issue to be tackled by the consultants when they started work in 1993 was whether to use a traditional bidding mechanism or to create something new, an institution designed 'ad hoc' for the specific problem at hand. Although conservative considerations of reliability pulled in the first direction, the peculiar features of the airwaves industry seemed to require the second approach. In the Notice of Proposed Rule Making of September 1993, the FCC suggested the implementation of an auction system in two stages (a 'combinatorial auction'), in which goods are initially auctioned in packages (with a sealed-bid mechanism) and then, later on, on an individual basis. This procedure seemed to solve the problem of aggregation in a straightforward way: the items are assigned to the winners of either the first or the second auction depending on which one guarantees more revenue to the seller. If bidders really value a package more than the individual items in isolation (as the complementarity hypothesis suggests), then the procedure should provide an incentive for aggregation.

Paul Milgrom and Robert Wilson on the one hand, and Preston McAfee on the other (consulting for Pacific Bell and AirTouch Communications respectively), objected to such a solution, and proposed an alternative mechanism called 'simultaneous ascending-bid auction'. In a *simultaneous* auction several markets are open at the same time, and bidders can operate in all of them at once. In an *ascending* auction bidders continue to make their offers until the market is closed—which usually means until no new offers are put forward. Simultaneity and the ascending form allow each bidder to collect valuable information about the behaviour of other firms as well as about her own chance of constructing the aggregation of items she most prefers. Bidders can thus switch during the auction to less preferred combinations as soon as they realise they will not be able to achieve their primary objective. Moreover, an ascending-bid (as opposed to a sealed-bid) system is supposed to reduce the 'winner's curse' phenomenon, because by keeping an eye on each other's bids buyers can make a better conjecture about what the evaluations of the other bidders (and thus the real value of the licences) are. The proposed mechanism however had some worrying features: notably, it looked at first sight rather complicated, and it had never been tried before.

On behalf of Pacific Bell, Milgrom and Wilson sent a document to the FCC arguing that a combinatorial process in two stages like the one proposed in the September 1993 Notice was to be discarded. Their arguments are representative of the kind of reasoning used by theorists in order to select the 'right' design for the FCC case. It is worth spending some time reviewing at least one of them, because it sheds interesting light on the role played by game theory in the design process.

Milgrom and Wilson argued, among other things, that a combinatorial institution may give rise to free-riding situations.[10] Suppose there are three bidders: One, Two and Three. One's willingness to pay for item A is 4, whereas he is not eligible to buy item B nor the package consisting of A and B together. Bidder Two's willingness to pay is symmetrical: 4 for B, and not eligible for A or AB. Bidder Three, in contrast, is willing to pay $1+e$ for A, $1+e$ for B, and $2+e$ for AB (with e small and positive). The payoffs are represented in the following matrix:

	A	B	AB
One	4	—	—
Two	—	4	—
Three	1+e	1+e	2+e

The only efficient allocation is in this case the one assigning A to One, and B to Two. In an ascending simultaneous auction, bidder Three bids 1 for each item, bidders One and Two bid just enough for Three to give up, and then acquire A and B respectively: the efficient outcome is a sub-game perfect equilibrium of the simultaneous ascending mechanism.

Milgrom and Wilson turned then to the two-stages combinatorial design. Under this institutional arrangement, bidder Three does not have an incentive to bid on A and B individually; he just participates in the auction for package AB, where he bids $2+e$. Player One can win the individual auction for A by bidding 1, and so can Two win the auction for B. But then the package would go to player Three. One and Two have therefore an interest to raise the total value of A and B by bidding more on at least one of them, but would like the other to do so in order to minimise their own costs. Milgrom and Wilson showed that such a free-rider situation has a mixed-strategy equilibrium that is inefficient. Bidders One and Two each face a sub-game which can be represented by the following payoff matrix:

	Raise bid	Don't raise
Raise bid	2,2	2,3
Don't raise	3,2	0,0

By backward induction, it can be proven that this sub-game has an equilibrium in which each bidder plays 'Raise the bid' with probability $2/3$ and 'Don't raise' with probability $1/3$. But then there is a $1/9$ probability of Three getting both A and B by paying just $1/4$ of what bidders One and Two would jointly pay for them (Milgrom, 1998, p. 15).

Such an argument clearly makes use of game theory, but does not follow from a *general* game-theoretic model of combinatorial auctions. Lacking a comprehensive theory of these processes, the economists engaged in the FCC enterprise relied on a number of independent theoretical insights and local analyses of how players are supposed to behave when solving certain tasks in isolation. 'The spectrum sale is more complicated than anything in auction theory', as two of the protagonists admit (McAfee and McMillan, 1996, p. 171). The relation between theoretical reasoning and the final implementation of the auction is well summarised by the following remarks:

The FCC auctions provide a case study in the use of economic theory in public policy. They have been billed as the biggest-ever practical application of game theory. Is this valid? A purist view says it is not. There is no theorem that proves the simultaneous ascending auction to be optimal. The setting for the FCC auctions is far more complicated than any model yet, or ever likely to be, written down. Theory does not validate the auction form the FCC chose to implement. The purist view, however, imposes too high a standard. The auction form was designed by theorists. The distinction between common-value and independent-value auction settings helped clarify thinking. The intuition developed by modelling best responses in innumerable simple games was crucial in helping the auction designers anticipate how bidders might try to outfox the mechanism.

(McMillan et al., 1997, p. 429)

Theory played a crucial role in the design, but only if we interpret the term 'theory' in a loose sense. 'The auction designers based their thinking on a range of models, each of which captures a part of the issue' (McAfee and McMillan, 1996, p. 171). It is true that 'Game theory played a central role in the analysis of rules' and 'ideas of Nash equilibrium, rationalisability, backward induction, and incomplete information . . . were the real basis of daily decisions about the details of the auction design' (Milgrom, 1995, pp. 19–20), but

> . . . the real value of the theory is in developing intuition. The role of theory, in any policy application, is to show how people behave in various circumstances, and to identify the tradeoffs involved in altering those circumstances. What the theorists found to be the most useful in designing the auction and advising the bidders was not complicated models that try to capture a lot of reality . . . Instead, a focused model that isolates a particular effect and assumes few or no special functional forms is more helpful in building understanding.
>
> (McAfee and McMillan, 1996, p. 172)

The other side of the coin is that it is impossible to define the exact form of the rules to be used, and theory never gives you the whole picture of the complicated process at any time. For this reason, it is true that 'the auctions would not have taken the shape they did were it not for the economic knowledge brought to the design process' (McMillan et al., 1997, p. 429)—but only if we extend the meaning of 'economic knowledge' well beyond the theoretical realm. Indeed, today 'much of what we know about multi-unit auctions with interdependencies [i.e. complementarities] comes from experiments' (McMillan, 1994).

4. Constructing and controlling 'microeconomic systems'

Although its roots go back to the eighteenth century, experimental economics as practised nowadays is entirely a post-Second World War phenomenon. It is worth introducing some of its basic methodological tenets, and not only because they have an independent interest and will provide some taste of what an economic laboratory experiment is; the methodology of experimental economics is illuminating also in order to understand when, where and how game theoretic models can be made to work in the lab and—by extension—in the 'real world' once the latter has been properly engineered. The key concept here is that of a 'microeconomic system'.

The idea that heterogeneous knowledge is required in order to run and correctly interpret an experiment is hardly new. Like many other philosophical insights, it goes back at least to

Pierre Duhem, who first noticed that a 'cluster' of independent hypotheses about the functioning of instruments, measurement procedures and so on is involved in experimental science. More recently, it has become common to stress the non-theoretical, practical, tacit character of much experimental knowledge.[11] In economics, a 'correctly performed' experiment is one that the experimenter is able to control and interpret properly. A set of precepts and rules have been devised which define the concept of a 'good' experimental system. These rules are partly independent from the theories under test, and rely heavily on the experimenter's judgement for their application.

In 1993 Pacific Bell hired a group of economists from Caltech, led by Charles Plott, to run a series of experiments that would test some theoretical insights, thus helping to choose the best design and to implement it operationally. Initially, the role of experiments was to help choose among the two institutions (the 'combinatorial' and the 'continuous ascending' auctions), for which neither a comprehensive theoretical analysis nor empirical data existed. The main concern, from the FCC and the advisors' point of view, was with efficiency. By theoretical means, it is impossible to prove that the allocation generated by the continuous ascending auction is efficient. By observing a 'real world' process, very few hints about whether the outcome is efficient or not can be gained, because of the unobservable nature of bidders' valuations. Experiments, in contrast, allow the 'induction' of known values on subjects, and thus enable one to check whether an institution really allocates the goods to those who value them most. The Caltech team made use of what they call 'testbed' experiments:

> An experimental 'testbed' is a simple working prototype of a process that is going to be employed in a complex environment. The creation of the prototype and the study of its operation provides a joining of theory, observation and the practical aspects of implementation, in order to create something that works.
>
> (Plott, 1996, p. 1)

Experimental testbeds must, of course, be designed in an appropriate way. They must, first of all, fulfil the requirements of 'Induced Value Theory', an approach to experimentation originally due to the economist Vernon Smith (1976, 1982, 1987). Induced Value Theory consists of five 'precepts', 'a proposed set of sufficient conditions for a valid controlled micro-economic experiment' (Smith, 1982, p. 261). Two of them, *saliency* and *non-satiation*, are supposed to 'allow us to assert that we have created a microeconomic system . . . in the laboratory' (Smith, 1987, p. 108). A 'microeconomic system' is defined by the characteristics of the agents (their tastes, knowledge and commodity endowments), and by some institution regulating their decisions. The saliency requirement prescribes that the outcomes of an experiment be a function of agents' decisions only, and that the rewards be a (monotonically increasing) function of the outcomes. Non-satiation prescribes to set the rewards so that the agents strictly prefer more rewards to less in all cases.

The concept of microeconomic system is quite interesting from a philosophical point of view. The construction of a laboratory microeconomy enables one to test a theory in an 'ideal' situation, in which the agents' utility functions have only experimental rewards as arguments and are monotonically increasing with them. A microeconomic system is supposed to be a system that economists know how to interpret, which is 'transparent' to economic analysis. Furthermore, this notion plays a rhetorical role in suggesting that the laboratory systems are 'real' economic systems, in the sense that they do not differ from 'real-world' economies in any respect that is deemed relevant by standard economic theory.

Two other precepts of Induced Value Theory aim at making sure that subjects' preferences for the reward medium are not 'disturbed' by any other interfering motive. As Smith puts it, they 'assure that we have created a controlled microeconomy' (Smith, 1987, p. 108). The simplest incentive method, one used for instance in auction experiments, consists in telling each subject her own reservation price, and then paying (or getting from) her the amount she has been able to gain (or lose) during the market experiment. Control on preferences is achieved by carefully designing the experiment so as to shield it from possible disturbances. For example, experimenters make sure that the subjects do not care about what others gain or lose (precept of *privacy*) by isolating one subject from another; they try to compensate for the cost of decision-making by paying them extra money on top of what subjects gain or lose; they prevent subjects from attaching game-value to transactions (*dominance*) by making possible losses relevant, and so on. Notice that whereas the goals to be achieved (as specified by the precepts) are rather precise, *how* to achieve them is not. A lot is left to intuition, personal judgement, experience and practical knowledge. Not surprisingly, then, whether the precepts have been fulfilled in particular cases is often a matter of controversy.

Privacy and dominance impose constraints on agents, which are rather severely disciplined. The precepts of induced value theory define an 'artificial' situation: it is simply not true that saliency, non-satiation, privacy and dominance are in general instantiated in non-laboratory economic situations. These requirements, however, are crucial in the process of applying highly abstract models to concrete cases: they help to build, on the one hand, the experimental counterpart of the theoretical restrictions that make demonstrations from economic models possible; and, on the other, the (extra-theoretical) 'background conditions' which enable economic relationships to hold (when they hold at all, of course) in the real world. Let me try to be more precise.

The rigour of economics' *theoretical* demonstrations is usually achieved by imposing a high number of assumptions, postulates, premises, and so on, which collectively contribute to the derivation of some precise economic proposition. Thus, for example, the existence of efficient equilibria may be proved by assuming that the market is perfectly competitive, that it is populated by rational and self-interested economic agents, that such agents have consistent preferences, that a Walrasian auctioneer is there to match supply and demand, that the costs of transacting are negligible, and so on. Even a simple model of supply and demand requires a rather fine-grained description of the circumstances, in order to come out with the claim that an efficient equilibrium price will clear the (fictional) market.

But theoretical models do not provide the rules to *materially* construct the markets they (partially) describe. First of all, the basic components of partial equilibrium explanations, such as for instance the law of demand (agents demand more quantity as the price diminishes) are *ceteris paribus* in character.[12] The quantity demanded is, for example, typically assumed to depend only on the price of the goods, and an accurate design of the experiment (namely one that follows the precepts of Induced Value Theory) is supposed to fulfil such conditions. Secondly, some concepts that are used as restrictions in the model need *other* background conditions for their material instantiation. The *homo oeconomicus* of most Neoclassical models, for example, can operate only in an appropriate environment. Real human beings are more likely to behave in a self-interested manner if they do not know what the consequences of their actions will be for the other players (see the requirement of privacy above). They tend to act more rationally if the problem-situation is well specified and they have had enough time to practise with it, and so on. The important point, to repeat, is that not *all* such conditions are listed by the generic, basic theory. In some cases, economic wisdom guides experimental practice in identifying the features which allow abstract economic concepts to become instantiated in real, flesh-and-bones economic entities. Saliency, non-satiation, privacy and dominance, as well as the prescription to use experienced subjects, belong to this body of knowledge. These guidelines are not *part of* economic theory, but rather tell us (roughly) how to construct real economic systems faithful to our abstract models.

To sum up, at the most abstract level, we have highly theoretical concepts such as competitive equilibrium. These are embedded in a structure of deductive reasoning from a set of strict assumptions identifying the conditions under which those concepts may be deductively demonstrated. It must be stressed that the description of the sufficient structure for effects like efficient equilibria to obtain is still abstract. The 'real world' counterparts of theoretical entities such as the rational economic men of our models are instantiated only under further restrictive arrangements. These arrangements define the bottom level of concreteness for the applicability of economic models. Economists are guided by experimental, practical, as well as theoretical knowledge in designing their experiments so that these background conditions are satisfied. The circumstances in which an economic system maintains its own structural properties may, however, be quite narrow and fragile. This is, of course, of great concern to the economic engineer, whose machines are supposed to work for several years, in different contexts and without the constant supervision of their manufacturer.

5. Testing the robustness of alternative designs

In early 1994 the Caltech group ran a series of comparative efficiency tests of the simultaneous ascending auction versus a combinatorial sealed-bid plus sequential continuous design. The results were interpreted as favourable to the former (Plott, 1997).[13] In this first stage, experimenters were particularly interested in observing the functioning of the two bidding institutions in their 'bare-bone' versions, in order to become familiar with their fundamental properties and flaws. Comparative testing of institutions in their simplest versions, however, was also instrumental in allowing the first operational details and problems to emerge. The mechanisms were for the first time transported from the abstract world of ideas to the laboratory. Some 'flesh' was added to transform the fundamental insights into working processes, flesh which might have modified, impeded or hidden some of the systems' structural dispositions. These experiments could therefore be seen as tests of the combinatorial and the ascending continuous auctions—but 'tests' of a peculiar kind, because the mechanisms themselves, rather than any theoretical model, were subject to examination. The issue was not whether some theory about an institution was to be discarded, but whether one rather than another institution should have been chosen for its properties, despite the fact that no thorough theoretical understanding of its functioning was available.

At the first step of 'concretisation', not surprisingly, experimentalists spotted problems that the theorists had not (and probably could not have) anticipated. Plott and his collaborators implemented the combinatorial design by running so-called 'Japanese auctions' combined with a sealed-bid pre-auction. In the first round a sealed-bid offer is made for a package of items, which are then auctioned individually in the second round: in a Japanese auction the auctioneer announces higher and higher prices and the bidders 'drop out' one after another; the last one to remain in the auction wins the item and pays the second highest bid value. If the aggregate value of the individually sold items exceeds that of the package, the results of the sealed-bid auction are disregarded; otherwise, the items are sold as a package.

One problem with this procedure is that some bidders have an interest in staying in the Japanese auction well above their reservation price, in order to raise the prices and overcome a sealed-bid pre-offer. This may push the price 'too high' and cause a bubble effect. The risk of staying in the auction above your reservation price, however, increases as the number of bidders that are participating diminishes. For this reason, information is crucial: players must not know how many others are still competing. Not to communicate explicitly how many bidders are still in the game, however, does not constitute a sufficient form of shielding: one has to be careful that *any* possible information flow be stopped. The click of a key, a 'blink' on the computer screen in coincidence with bidders' drop-out or even a door slamming when they leave the room is enough to give valuable hints to the other participants. These practical problems were actually discovered by Plott and his team only thanks to laboratory work, and the Japanese auction design was accordingly abandoned in favour of the continuous auction design.

The problem above is one of 'robustness'. The combinatorial auction, in other words, is not only out-performed by the continuous ascending auction in terms of efficiency, but is also difficult to implement correctly. It is a 'delicate' process, and small imperfections (in shielding the flow of information, for example) may cause it to break down altogether. One can distinguish cases of 'environmental' robustness, like the one above, from cases of 'personality' robustness:[14] economists' assumptions in modelling economic agents may be *for the most part* accurate, but in more or less marginal instances real behaviour may diverge from the model's predictions. Environmental robustness, in other words, is a function of an institution's capacity to work properly in a number of different environments. Personality robustness, in contrast, depends on its capacity to work with a range of real players, who may behave slightly differently from the ideal rational maximising agents postulated by game theoretic models.

Confusion and misunderstanding of the rules are also sources of concern in the implementation of mechanisms, not least because they may generate legal quarrels. Testbed experiments allowed the spotting of those critical moments when subjects may need help from the auctioneer in order to understand some detail of the auction. The problem is not just whether a certain abstract model fits reality (or whether reality can be made to fit the model), but also *how* it fits. The question is how fragile such a fit is, how sensitive to little imperfections, mistakes, and so on.

Another important role of laboratory experiments consisted in helping to develop the appropriate software. Game theory, of course, does not specify whether an auction should be run with mere pencil and paper support, or with computers. Electronic auctions are in general privileged because they facilitate analysis of data and enforcement of the rules: one can, for instance, design a software which does not accept bidding below the highest standing bid of the previous round, thus controlling automatically for errors and saving precious time. But no specific software for the continuous ascending auction was available at the time, and a new one had to be created *ad hoc*. The data of testbed experiments, elaborated by means of an independently designed programme, were used as inputs into the final software to be used in the real FCC auctions. By means of such 'parallel checking' (Plott, 1997, pp. 627–31) the consultants made sure that the FCC software worked properly and delivered correct data in a reliable fashion. Trained students were employed to investigate the properties of the software. They used diaries and notebooks to keep track of all the problems that could arise, and were then asked to answer a questionnaire surveying the most likely sources of 'bugs'. The process must be 'idiot-proof': 'robust' to the people who use it, who may create a number of bizarre problems (to the extent of crashing the whole network) or make unpredictable moves in playing their game.

The enterprise of building a 'properly working' institution in the laboratory thus shows that small variations can make a big difference indeed. 'The exact behaviour of the auctions can be sensitive to very subtle details of how the auction process operates' (Plott, 1997, p. 620). To understand why a mechanism may be chosen for reasons that differ from its theoretical properties, one has to recall that those properties are defined at a certain (usually high) level of abstraction. An institution producing desirable allocations when correctly built may nevertheless be very difficult to build correctly.

Compared with other applied disciplines, economic engineering is peculiar in at least two respects: first, once the basic causal structure has been chosen (for example, the combinatorial auction design), the economic engineer has very little room for manoeuvre, in terms of the corrections, modifications and interventions which are allowed. The materials are for the most part given because agents should not, for instance, be forced to change their preferences— although some kinds of preferences (such as collusive or altruistic ones) can be *ruled out* by design (see above). The principal way in which the economist can intervene in the problem-situation is by defining the rules of the institution. Secondly, as we have seen, in the FCC case the designers were lacking theory to guide the implementation. It was not just a matter of 'adding matter' to an abstract causal structure, but rather of adding matter while understanding and shaping the causal structure itself.

6. Testing the rules

The Caltech experiments were used differently in different phases of the project. First, as we have seen, they were instrumental in choosing between the Milgrom–Wilson–McAfee design and the initial FCC proposal. Secondly, testbeds were used to transform the abstract design into a real process that could perform the required task reliably in the environment where the auction was to be implemented. Finally, experimental data were most valuable in interpreting and checking the results of the first *real* auctions run by the FCC. Before coming to that, however, it is worth looking at some of the experiments run by Plott and his team in order to check the joint effect of the rules that would have regulated the FCC auctions.

Mechanism designers see the rules as a device for defining the strategic situation which bidders face and to which they are supposed to react rationally. Unfortunately, in the case of spectrum licences, theorists were unable to solve the whole game, and thus had to rely on the analysis of single sub-games in a piecemeal manner. How the pieces would have interacted once put together remained an open issue, about which theorists had relatively little to say. Experiments can be used to move gradually from the world of paper and ideas to the real world, without losing the desired structural properties of a mechanism on the way. The enterprise is similar to that of designing a space probe: it would be too costly to proceed on a trial-and-error basis, and perform a series of full-scale tests.

The structure of the continuous ascending auction has so far been sketched at a most abstract level. The details of the design were in fact much more complicated. Preston McAfee, Robert Wilson and Paul Milgrom were mainly responsible for writing the detailed rules that were to regulate bidding in all its various aspects, and which eventually were put together in a lengthy document. The most important—and debated—rules concerned increments, withdrawals, eligibility, waivers and activity.

The simultaneous ascending auction proceeds in rounds. At every round, the players offer their bids, which are scrutinised by the auctioneer, and then are presented with the results. The feedback includes a list of the bids presented at that round and by whom, the value of the 'standing high bid', and the minimum bid allowed for the next round. The minimum allowed bid is calculated by adding to the standing high bid a fixed proportion (5% or 10%, usually) called the *bid increment*. A bid is said to be eligible if it is higher than the minimum bid allowed in that round and it is presented by an *eligible bidder*. Each bidder, in fact, must at the beginning of the auction make a deposit proportional to the number of licences she wants to bid for (each item is auctioned on a different market). Such a deposit establishes her 'initial eligibility', i.e. the number of markets she can enter.

The idea of eligibility was introduced not only to prevent problems such as those that occurred in the New Zealand auctions (where bidders who were not really interested in the licences participated and then resold the licences to others), but also to regulate the time-length of the auction. Eligibility constrains a bidder's activity in an ingenious manner. A bidder is said to be *active* if she either has the highest standing bid from the previous round, or is submitting an eligible bid. The activity cannot exceed a bidder's initial eligibility, but bidders also have an incentive not to remain below a certain level of activity. In the first round, in fact, a buyer must bid at least a certain fraction of her initial eligibility; if she does not, her eligibility is reduced in the next round. Such a procedure is supposed to increase the transparency of the auction (by forcing companies to commit early on), and to speed it up by preventing 'wait and see' strategies on the part of bidders. The possibility of mistakes is taken into account by providing bidders with five '*waivers*' of the activity rules. Bidders could also *withdraw* a bid, but with the risk of paying the difference between the final selling price (as elicited in a further round) and the withdrawn bid if the latter should exceed the former.

The rules regulating activity were motivated by the worry that bidders could have a strategic interest in slowing down the pace of the auction.[15] The time-length of an auction depends on two factors: the number of rounds played and the interval between rounds. According to the Milgrom–Wilson design, each auction is supposed to stop after a certain period and start again the next day, until no new eligible bids are received. The idea of having subsequent 'rounds' was motivated by the thought that companies may need time to revise their strategies, reflect on their budgets, and thus avoid 'winner's curse' phenomena. As Paul Milgrom put it, 'there are billions of dollars at stake here, and there is no reason to rush it when we are talking about permanently affecting the structure of a new industry'.[16]

The FCC, however, was quite concerned about the time problem, not least for practical reasons (booking a big hotel to run an auction, for instance, costs money). Whereas theory gave no indication of how long a continuous ascending auction might go on for, experiments allowed the testing of different rules, with rounds taking place at different intervals. One possible solution was to impose big increments above the highest standing bid, so as to identify the winners quickly. In experiments, however, it was observed that big increments sometimes eliminated bidders too quickly, causing their eligibility to drop and therefore creating a 'demand killing' effect (Plott, 1997, p. 633). Such an interaction between the increment rule and the eligibility rule could hardly have been predicted without experiments. Without a general theory of simultaneous ascending auctions, theorists could rely only on a number of independent insights about the effects of different rules, but could not exactly figure out what would happen were all the rules implemented at the same time.

> The concepts of withdrawals, eligibility, increments, and announcement of stage changes, all involve reasonable sounding concepts when considered alone, but there remain questions about how they might interact together, with other policies, or with the realities of software performance. Can one waiver and bid at the same time? What happens if you withdraw at the end of the auction—can the auction remain open so the withdrawal can be cleared? How shall a withdrawal be priced?
>
> (Plott, 1997, p. 629)

The answers to these questions were partly sought in the laboratory. 'The complex ways the rules interact, and the presence of ambiguities, do not become evident until one tries to actually implement the rules in an operational environment' (Plott, 1997, p. 628). More time between rounds might allow bidders to put forward sensible bids, but more frequent rounds might also shorten the process considerably. And would either of these solutions affect efficiency? Plott and his collaborators eventually found that total time was principally a function of the number of rounds, and auctions going on for more than one hundred rounds were observed in the laboratory. The Caltech team thus tried to vary the interval between rounds, and concluded that to have more frequent rounds did not affect efficiency in their laboratory experiments (Plott, 1997, pp. 632–633).

The Milgrom–Wilson–McAfee rules also involved the possibility of withdrawals, in case a winner decided *a posteriori* that the price was not worth the item bought, or that she could not achieve the preferred aggregation: the item would be 'sold back to the market' and the withdrawing bidder would pay the difference between her bid and the final price to the FCC. Withdrawals and losses can, however, cause 'cycles': an item may be bought and resold, and bought and resold and so on until someone is satisfied with the price. Experiments were used to create cycles in the laboratory (see Figure 17.1) in order to see whether they could arise in practice, to study the conditions (the parameters) under which they can be generated, and how they behave (for how long they go on before disappearing, for instance).

Theoretical and empirical insights, to sum up, provided initially just a few rough 'causal stories' about the functioning of certain bits of the institution. Thanks to previous experiments, it was known that more transparent mechanisms (like the English system) tend to prevent 'winner's curse' effects better than 'less transparent' ones do (such as sealed-bid auctions). It was also known that imposing no entry fee would have encouraged opportunistic bidders to

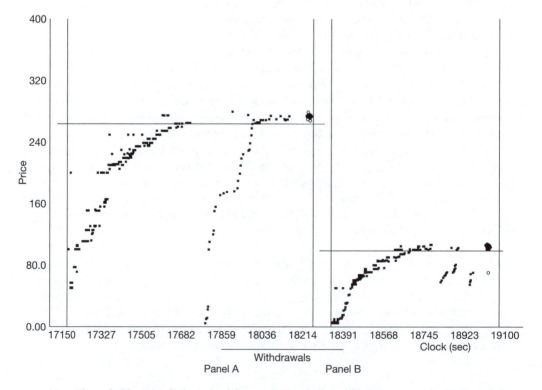

Figure 17.1 Three bidding 'cycles' in the laboratory. Reproduced by permission from Plott (1997), p. 625. © 1997 The Massachusetts Institute of Technology.

participate. It was conjectured that under some circumstances some bidders might have an interest (opposite to the FCC's) in delaying the auction—and so on. These insights do not jointly pin down the structure of the best possible institution in all its aspects. They just convey information about what certain components do in certain cases, when acting in isolation. Instead of laying down the structure of the auction on paper, it was displayed at work in the laboratory. The job of checking that the different components had been put together in the 'right' way (that they *could* be put together in the right way, to begin with), and that they worked smoothly in practice was done by running demonstrations in the lab.

7. Checking external validity

The consultants eventually monitored a *real* FCC auction (which took place in Washington, DC, in October 1994)[17] to check whether the transposition of the Milgrom–Wilson simultaneous ascending auction mechanism from the world of theory to the real world *via* the laboratory had been successful—or, to put it differently, whether 'external validity' had been achieved.[18] The expertise achieved in the lab was invaluable for this. Experiments had taught that, especially in the first rounds, 'regardless of the amount of preparation and testing, things happen', and 'decisions must be made on the spot from experience and judgement' (Plott, 1997, p. 631). A committee of consultants was thus formed, to supervise the FCC auction and intervene at any time to assist the participants. Any inconvenience that arose in testbeds was likely to be spotted by the trained eye of the experimenters.

Laboratory tests with similar parameters to those supposed to be the case in the real auction were run beforehand so that the results could be compared after the event. The experimental auctions had been constructed so as to have the same number of players, the same number of items auctioned, complementarities such as those presumably existing in the 'real' market, a similar number of rounds,[19] similar (although fictional) values, and so on. Then, a large amount of data collected both in the lab and in the real auction was systematically analysed and compared. This data included bidding patterns, pricing trajectories, the rise of 'bubbles', the formation of sensible licence aggregations, the fact that similar items sold for similar prices, the absence of post-auction resale, and several other phenomena of interest.[20]

[. . .]

8. Rational choice technology

The FCC auctions were a success. They were successful not just politically but also from a scientific viewpoint. They provided a solution to a complicated problem, and have inspired other projects as a benchmark example of economic engineering. This does not mean that the implemented institution was absolutely flawless: it could be improved and some work is still being done on rules, for example to prevent collusive bidding.[21] But the solutions devised by the FCC consultants stood on firm ground, probably as firm as our best science and technology can be.

As stated in the introduction, this article is not intended to discuss the various philosophical interpretations of rational choice theory in any depth. That is a project worth a separate paper. However, some tentative remarks can be provided that go in that direction. First, several aspects of this case study seem to rule out an instrumentalist interpretation of the local models that guided economists' work as FCC consultants. To build a successful auction one needs to pay attention to the computational abilities and preferences of its users. One has to make sure that the tasks the bidders face are not too complicated or the rules unclear. Bidders' reactions to possible strategic situations must be analysed in the light of realistic cognitive capacities at the individual level. One cannot just presume that buyers behave 'as if' they were rational. Bidders must react adequately to new situations and sometimes be creative in devising new strategies, as opposed to just relying on established routines. The economic engineer must design a mechanism keeping individuals' *real* capacities in mind. On the other hand, it is by designing and implementing an adequate mechanism that the engineer ensures that rational choice models can work. Since it is partly in virtue of the structure of the situation that economic agents behave rationally, a great part of economic engineering is devoted to ensuring that the structure is 'right' (and experiments, as we have seen, are invaluable for that).[22]

One should also keep in mind that bidding teams in the real FCC auctions included professional game theorists hired by firms in order to maximise their chances of putting together a profitable aggregation.[23] This way, the classical game-theoretic assumptions of rationality and common knowledge of rationality (everybody knows that everybody is rational, and that everybody knows that everybody knows . . .) were most likely to be satisfied. This suggests a more general point: due to the partly self-referential character of social concepts, for the construction of a stable and reliable socio-economic mechanism to be possible at all, adequate self-perpetuating mechanisms must be set in place.[24] The institution assumes behaviour with certain formal characteristics on the agents' part, but each agent must also know these assumptions, and must be confident that the other agents are willing and capable of fulfilling the mechanism's requirements.

Finally, it is a common strategy to attack rational choice theory by pointing out that it is either false or void of empirical content as a (general) theory of human behaviour. 'General' is between brackets because it is usually taken for granted that absolute generality must be the goal of every respectable scientific theory. But neither charge does justice to the rational choice approach. There *can* be reliable economic mechanisms, as stable, fine-tuned and robust as we need them to be. But they seem to be hardly spontaneous nor common—they are mostly constructed with ingenuity in the abstract realm of theory, sometimes even repeatedly tried in a university lab. Perhaps there exists some more general account of human behaviour and decision-making, which can include rational choice theory as a sub-case. Consider that rational choice models seem to possess just enough detail to be translatable into operational mechanisms. But nevertheless a lot of 'filling out' is needed before the mechanism is ready to operate. And that seems to be the case with any account of human behaviour. The question is not merely one of choosing between accounts with a general as against a limited domain of application, but rather one of trading off between abstract and concrete models, which need more or less filling out in order to be transformed into useful and robust social technology.

Notes

1 See Hacking (1983) and Cartwright (1999) for some representative examples of the new, practice-based, philosophy of science of the 1980s and 1990s.
2 A good overview of the rational choice theory debate can be found in Friedman (1996). On social mechanisms, see 7 below. I'll leave it to the reader to appreciate to what extent these two debates suffer from the defects highlighted in the main text above.
3 According to the US Department of Commerce, more than $45 billion were gained by opportunistic lottery winners in the 1980s (see McMillan, 1994, p. 147, n. 3). For a comparison of the auction method of allocation with other methods such as lotteries or administrative hearings, as well as for a discussion of the pros and cons of auctioning licenses, see McMillan (1995).
4 McMillan (1994, p. 147) and Milgrom (1995, pp. 4–11) tell the stories of these earlier design failures.
5 *The Economist*, July 23, 1994, p. 70; quoted in McAfee and McMillan (1996), p. 159.
6 One of the sources of confusion is the question of whether 'mechanisms' are social entities or representations. The ambiguity is generalised, even in advanced textbooks. Mas-Colell *et al.*, for instance,

in the very same page define a mechanism as 'the formal *representation* of . . . an institution' (more precisely: a collection of strategy sets and an outcome function from the Cartesian product of the strategy sets to the set of alternatives) and shortly after claim that 'a mechanism can be seen as an *institution* with rules governing the procedure for making collective choice' (Mas-Colell, Whinston and Green, 1995, p. 866; my italics).

7   The views on economic mechanisms and machines that inform this essay are closest to those of Cartwright (1999) and Dupré (2001). The distinction between mechanisms and processes is due to Salmon (1984), but see also Machamer, Darden and Craver (2000). On socio-economic mechanisms in particular, see Lawson (1997) and the essays collected in Hedström and Swedberg (1998), although Pierre Salmon (1998) and his commentators are perhaps more illuminating.

8   The above quotes are from *Fortune*, 6 February, 1995, p. 36, cited by McAfee and McMillan (1996), p. 159, who report on other similar reactions. Other references can be found in Milgrom (1995).

9   For an introduction to auction theory, see Milgrom (1989); for a more comprehensive survey, see McAfee and McMillan (1987).

10   The example is presented in Milgrom (1998, 2000).

11   See, for example, Hacking (1983) and Collins (1985), and the essays in Pickering (1992).

12   Hausman (1989) gives a convincing account of why demand and supply explanations are to be interpreted as causal in character, and how the explaining principles are to be read as including a *ceteris paribus* clause.

13   But see Ledyard, Porter and Rangel (1997) for a somewhat different conclusion. John Ledyard is part of a minority of economists who favour the combinatorial over the simultaneous ascending mechanism.

14   See Schotter (1995) for this distinction and some useful discussion.

15   Milgrom (1998) provides an example and a game-theoretic argument in support of such a hypothesis.

16   'Access to Airwaves: Going, Going, Gone', *Stanford Business School Magazine*, June 1994.

17   For a detailed analysis and discussion of the early FCC auctions, see Cramton (1995, 1997, 1998), Ayres and Cramton (1996) and Milgrom (1995). The data of all the auctions run by the FCC is available on-line at *www.fcc.gov/wtb/auctions*.

18   In experimental economics, the problem of external validity is often referred to as the problem of 'parallelism'.

19   The FCC, though, interrupted the final testbed experiments before their completion. One last round of bidding was unexpectedly called, and this probably accounts for the sudden rise in prices (see Plott, 1997, p. 636, n. 6).

20   See also Cramton (1995, 1997, 1998).

21   Some companies, for example, devised sophisticated signalling systems using the last few digits of their bids, in order to communicate to other competitors their willingness to cooperate (Cramton and Schwartz, 2000).

22   A similar point on the importance of structure for rational choice models has been made by Satz and Ferejohn (1994), but it is my contention that the FCC case warrants a stronger interpretation than their mild instrumentalism (or 'moderate externalism').

23   Peter Cramton (1995, 1997) has provided some interesting accounts of the early auctions, written from an insider's perspective—Cramton was part of the PageNet bidding team.

24   For a more detailed illustration of this point, see Barnes (1983).

References

Ayres, I. and Cramton, P. (1996) 'Deficit Reduction through Diversity: A Case Study of How Affirmative Action at the FCC Increased Auction Competition', *Stanford Law Review* **48**, 761–815.

Barnes, B. (1983) 'Social Life as Bootstrapped Induction', *Sociology* **17**, 524–545.

Cartwright, N. (1999) *The Dappled World* (Cambridge: Cambridge University Press).

Collins, H. M. (1985) *Changing Order* (London: Sage).

Cramton, P. C. (1995) 'Money Out of Thin Air: The Nationwide Narrowband PCS Auction', *Journal of Economics and Management Strategy* **4**, 267–343.

Cramton, P. C. (1997) 'The FCC Spectrum Auctions: An Early Assessment', *Journal of Economics and Management Strategy* **6**, 431–495.

Cramton, P. C. (1998) 'The Efficiency of the FCC Spectrum Auctions', *Journal of Law and Economics* **41**, 727–736.

Cramton, P. and Schwartz, J. (2000) 'Collusive Bidding: Lessons from the FCC Spectrum Auction', *Journal of Regulatory Economics* **17**, 229–252.

Dupré, J. (2001) 'Economics without Mechanism', in U. Mäki (ed.), *The Economic World View* (Cambridge: Cambridge University Press).

Friedman, J. (ed.) (1996) *The Rational Choice Controversy* (New Haven: Yale University Press).

Hacking, I. (1983) *Representing and Intervening* (Cambridge: Cambridge University Press).

Harrison, G. (1989) 'Theory and Misbehavior of First-Price Auctions', *American Economic Review* **79**, 749–762.

Hausman, D. M. (1989) 'Supply and Demand Explanations and Their *Ceteris Paribus* Clauses', *Review of Political Economy* **2**, 168–187.

Hedström, P. and Swedberg, R. (eds) (1998) *Social Mechanisms* (Cambridge: Cambridge University Press).

Lawson, T. (1997) *Economics and Reality* (London: Routledge).

Ledyard, J. O., Porter, D. and Rangel, A. (1997) 'Experiments Testing Multiobject Allocation Mechanisms', *Journal of Economics and Management Strategy* **6**, 639–675.

Machamer, P., Darden, L. and Craver, C. F. (2000) 'Thinking about Mechanisms', *Philosophy of Science* **67**, 1–25.

Mas-Colell, A., Whinston, M. D. and Green, J. R. (1995) *Microeconomic Theory* (Oxford: Oxford University Press).

McAfee, R. P. and McMillan, J. (1987) 'Auctions and Bidding', *Journal of Economic Literature* **25**, 699–738.

McAfee, R. P. and McMillan, J. (1996) 'Analyzing the Airwaves Auction', *Journal of Economic Perspectives* **10**, 159–175.

McMillan, J. (1994) 'Selling Spectrum Rights', *Journal of Economic Perspectives* **8**, 145–162.

McMillan, J. (1995) 'Why Auction the Spectrum?', *Telecommunications Policy* **19**, 191–199.

McMillan, J., Rotschild, M. and Wilson, R. (1997) 'Introduction', *Journal of Economics and Management Strategy* **6**, 425–430.

Milgrom, P. (1989) 'Auctions and Bidding: A Primer', *Journal of Economic Perspectives* **3**, 3–22.

Milgrom, P. (1995) 'Auctioning the Radio Spectrum', in *Auction Theory for Privatization* (Cambridge: Cambridge University Press), forthcoming (available on-line at *www. market-design.com / library.html*).

Milgrom, P. (1998) 'Game Theory and the Spectrum Auctions', *European Economic Review* **42**, 771–778.

Milgrom, P. (2000) 'Putting Auction Theory to Work: The Simultaneous Ascending Auction', *Journal of Political Economy* **108**, 245–272.

Milgrom, P. and Weber, R. (1982) 'A Theory of Auctions and Competitive Building', *Econometrics* **50**, 1089–1122.

Pickering, A. (ed.) (1992) *Science as Practice and Culture* (Chicago: University of Chicago Press).

Plott, C. R. (1981) 'Experimental Methods in Political Economy: A Tool for Regulatory Research', in A. R. Ferguson (ed.), *Attacking Regulatory Problems* (Cambridge, MA: Ballinger), pp. 117–143.

Plott, C. R. (1996) 'Laboratory Experimental Testbeds: Application to the PCS Auction', *Social Science Working Paper 957* (Pasadena: California Institute of Technology).

Plott, C. R. (1997) 'Laboratory Experimental Testbeds: Application to the PCS Auction', *Journal of Economics and Management Strategy* **6**, 605–638.

Roth, A. E. (1991) 'Game Theory as a Part of Empirical Economics', *Economic Journal* **101**, 107–114.

Salmon, P. (1998) 'Free Riding as a Mechanism', in R. E. Backhouse, D. M. Hausman, U. Mäki and A. Salanti (eds), *Economics and Methodology: Crossing Boundaries* (London: Macmillan), pp. 62–87.

Salmon, W. C. (1984) *Scientific Explanation and the Causal Structure of the World* (Princeton: Princeton University Press).

Satz, D. and Ferejohn, J. (1994) 'Rational Choice and Social Theory', *Journal of Philosophy* **91**, 71–87.

Schotter, A. (1995) 'A Practical Person's Guide to Mechanism Selection: Some Lessons from Experimental Economics', working paper, C. V. Starr Center for Applied Economics, New York University.

Smith, V. L. (1976) 'Experimental Economics: Induced Value Theory', *American Economic Review* **66**, 274–277.

Smith, V. L. (1982) 'Microeconomic Systems as an Experimental Science', *American Economic Review* **72**, 923–955.

Smith, V. L. (1987) 'Experimental Methods in Economics', in J. Eatwell, M. Milgate and P. Newman (eds), *The New Palgrave: Allocation, Information and Markets* (London: Macmillan), pp. 94–111.

Vickrey, W. (1961) 'Counterspeculation, Auctions, and Competitive Sealed Tenders', *Journal of Finance* **16**, 8–37.

Wilson, R. (1977) 'A Bidding Model of Perfect Competition', *Review of Economic Studies* **4**, 511–518.

PART V

Methodological individualism

T HE DISCUSSIONS OF RATIONALITY in the previous section focused on how individual people make decisions in various sorts of situations, including situations in which the best choice depends on what other people do. This topic is of interest from a social science perspective because the behaviors of social groups are often presumed to be the product of many interacting individual decisions. If that is right, then it would seem that social scientists could explain larger scale social phenomena, such as economic cycles, corruption, and crime rates, in terms of models that focus on individuals. That is precisely what methodological individualism advocates: explaining social processes in terms of complex interactions among individual agents. Methodological individualism may seem like an abstruse issue of social science method, yet it has political dimensions that can excite impassioned reactions in its proponents and detractors. Some advocates of political liberalism, particularly Karl Popper, saw methodological individualism as essential to a defense of human liberty and the opposition to fascism. To deny methodological individualism, Popper thought, would be to represent individuals as mindless drones who are powerless to initiate social change. In contrast, philosophers and social scientists sympathetic to the Marxist tradition tend to view methodological individualism as kind of smoke screen that functions to maintain a repressive status quo by diverting attention from pervasive and deeply entrenched social structures that constrain and shape individual decisions. Although the chapters included in this section rarely address these political overtones of methodological individualism explicitly, making note of them is helpful for appreciating how a seemingly abstract question could inspire such fervent debate.

A few conceptual distinctions will be helpful in articulating the debate about methodological individualism more clearly. Discussions of this topic in the philosophy of social science commonly distinguish between two types of individualisms in addition to methodological: ontological and semantic. Ontological individualism is the claim that all social processes are composed of complex interactions among individual people. For example, a market consists of a number of people making series of interconnected economic exchanges; the market is not some entity over and above these individual actions, it just *is* them. The point of ontological individualism, therefore, is to deny that there is some level of social reality that transcends the people who compose the society. A number of philosophers grant ontological individualism but deny that it leads to methodological individualism. Notice that methodological individualism is a claim about what sort of explanations social scientists should strive for. But it is far from clear that it is always best to explain things in terms of their basic components. For example, if the component parts are very numerous and not easily observed, then explanations in terms of the basic components might not be a practical possibility. In addition, the phenomena might not depend on the exact arrangement of the individual components, in which case an extensive description of individual level details could be misleading from an explanatory perspective. Consider Emile Durkheim's (1897) hypothesis that suicide rates are inversely related to social solidarity. There are a number of different ways that strong networks of social support can exert a preventive effect on suicide, and it would presumably be possible to devise individual level models to represent various ways that could work. However, a critic of methodological individualism might insist that focusing on such details would cause one to miss the forest for the trees, that is, to fail to see the broader pattern as a result of an excessive emphasis on minutiae. This second objection is often labeled the "multiple realizability argument." There are several ways that one might respond to the multiple realizability argument, but the important point for the present purposes is that one cannot move immediately from ontological claims about the basic constituents of social reality to methodological claims about social science explanation. Some additional philosophical work is required to bridge that gap.

Semantic individualism is the claim that every important social science concept can be defined solely by reference to individuals and their interactions. Consider the concept of social solidarity. If semantic individualism is true, it would be possible to define social solidarity in terms of, say, the density and quality of connections among a collection of individuals. Critics often claim that methodological individualism is committed to semantic individualism and that semantic individualism is false (Kincaid 1996). A common objection to semantic individualism charges that any attempt to define a group level social term via individual concepts will inevitably presuppose some social level concepts. For example, an individualist definition of social solidarity would have to distinguish between significant connections (e.g. a visit from a friend) and insignificant ones (e.g. being told "have a nice day" by a cashier at a supermarket). But distinctions of this kind would presuppose a number of social norms concerning such things as friendship and the impersonal nature of economic exchanges. (Social norms and institutions are, of course, social rather than individual-level concepts.)

In reply to this objection a defender of methodological individualism might deny that presupposing social concepts is necessarily a problem. After all, no single explanation can explain everything, so background assumptions are necessary for any approach. Thus, one might claim that presupposing social concepts would be a problem for methodological individualism only if there were some reason to think that the presupposed concepts would stubbornly resist individualist analysis. Another possible response would be to deny that methodological individualism is committed to semantic individualism. Critics defend this link on the grounds that methodological individualism aims to reduce all group level social theories to theoretical models framed in terms of individuals. This reduction is assumed to require defining all social concepts via individualist ones and then deriving the group level generalizations (e.g. that suicide rates are inversely correlated with social solidarity) from claims about individuals. But it is by no means clear that methodological individualism must aim for reductionism in this sense. For example, the methodological individualist might regard some important social concepts as vague and open-ended and hence not susceptible to any precise definition at all. Rather than aiming to analyze every group level social concept by individualist means, an advocate of methodological individualism might propose replacing some social level concepts with distinct and more clearly defined individual level concepts that allow for more accurate explanations.

The issues and arguments sketched above surface at various points in the chapters included in this section. The first chapter, by Steven Lukes, is a classic critique of methodological individualism. Lukes begins by distinguishing methodological individualism from the ontological thesis that individual persons are the basic constituents of the social world and from the semantic thesis that any meaningful statement about social phenomena can be translated into claims about individual persons and their interactions. Lukes also points out that methodological individualism should not be confused with the political doctrine that the chief goal of social policies should be the satisfaction of individual preferences. However, the central argument of Lukes' chapter is that individual level explanations of social phenomena are possible only if they already presume a background of social context, norms, and institutions. Descriptions of individuals that do not implicitly or explicitly include such background (e.g. descriptions of overt bodily movements) will be incapable of explaining any interesting social processes. Notice that Lukes' argument is very similar to the objection to semantic individualism sketched above.

The next chapter, by Martin van Hees, defends methodological individualism from criticisms arising from a school of thought known as "the new institutionalism." The new institutionalism stresses the role of institutions—such as a government agency, a stock exchange, a military chain of command, and so on—in shaping, constraining, and imparting significance to individual behavior. Moreover, the new institutionalism denies that institutions can be explained by models that focus solely on individuals and their interactions, because the actions and decisions of individuals only make sense within the context of a presupposed institution. The new institutionalist objection to methodological individualism, therefore, is quite similar to Lukes' argument. Both insist that individual level explanations must inevitably presuppose a broader social context. Van Hees agrees with this claim but proposes that the institutional context in any individualist explanation can be accounted for by another individualist explanation that assumes a distinct institutional context. Thus, although some institutional context is invariably assumed, there is, according to van Hees, no particular institutional context that cannot be given an individualist explanation. Van Hees proposes that game theory provides a number of useful models for representing institutional contexts and their role in shaping actions.

The third chapter, by Keith Sawyer, looks to philosophy of mind for inspiration about methodological individualism. Non-reductive materialism is a familiar position in the philosophy of mind that agrees with materialism that there is no immaterial soul—the mind is just the product of processes occurring in our brain—but nevertheless rejects reductionism. Non-reductive materialism appeals to the multiple realizability argument to explain how reductionism could be false even if materialism is true. Likewise, Sawyer proposes that multiple realizability undermines methodological individualism even if the social world is composed solely of individual persons and their interactions, a position he dubs non-reductive individualism. Sawyer's argument assumes that methodological individualism entails semantic individualism, and then uses the multiple realizability argument to attempt to show that semantic individualism is false. To see the idea, consider the concept of social solidarity. Sawyer would agree that as a result of multiple realizability and "wild disjunction," there are jumbles of distinct kinds of individual level processes that can be instances of, or realize, social solidarity. In one case, social solidarity might mean having close friends to confide in, while in another it might mean sharing a sense of national unity with millions of people the vast majority of whom one has never met. Thus, Sawyer's argument is that natural kinds at the social level often do not correspond to any natural grouping definable in terms of individuals and their interactions.

Further reading

See Udehn (2001) for a very thorough historical overview of the literature on methodological individualism. For discussions of methodological individualism in relation to economics, see Hodgson (2007), Hoover (1995). Several authors in addition to Sawyer use some version of the multiple realizability argument to criticize methodological individualism, including Jones (1996), Kincaid (1996), Little (1991), Pettit (1993, 1998). For discussions of how methodological individualism might proceed despite multiple realizability, see Steel (2006), Zahle (2003), van Bouwel (2004). For some reasonably recent defenses of methodological individualism, see Bouvier (2002), Elster (1989), Walsh (1997). For discussions of "analytical Marxism," which attempts to interpret Marxist ideas from the perspective if methodological individualism, see Elster (1985), Farrely (2005), Kumar (2008), Veneziani (2008). For discussions of whether ontological individualism is false and social properties are "emergent," see Elder-Vass (2007), Epstein (2008, 2009), Førland (2008), Porpora (2007).

References

Bouvier, A. (2002) "An Epistemological Plea for Methodological Individualism and Rational Choice Theory in Cognitive Rhetoric," *Philosophy of the Social Sciences* 32: 51–70.

Durkheim, E. (1897) *Suicide: A Study in Sociology*. New York: Free Press.

Elder-Vass, D. (2007) "For Emergence: Refining Archer Account of Social Structure," *Journal for the Theory of Social Behavior* 37: 25–44.

Elster, J. (1985) *Making Sense of Marx*. Cambridge: Cambridge University Press.

—— (1989) *Nuts and Bolts for the Social Sciences*. Cambridge: Cambridge University Press.

Epstein, B. (2008) "When Local Models Fail," *Philosophy of the Social Sciences* 38: 3–24.

—— (2009) "Ontological Individualism Reconsidered," *Synthese* 166: 187–213.

Farrely, C. (2005) "Historical Materialism and Supervenience," *Philosophy of the Social Sciences* 35: 420–46.

Førland, T. (2008) "Mentality as Social Emergent: Can Zeitgeist have Explanatory Power?" *History and Theory* 47: 44–56.

Hodgson, G. (2007) "Meanings of Methodological Individualism," *Journal of Economic Methodology* 14: 211–26.

Hoover, K. (1995) "Is Macroeconomics for Real?" *The Monist* 78: 235–57.

Jones, T. (1996) "Methodological Individualism in Proper Perspective," *Behavior and Philosophy* 24: 119–28.

Kincaid, H. (1996) *Philosophical Foundations of the Social Sciences*. New York: Cambridge University Press.

Kumar, C. (2008) "A Pragmatist Spin on Analytical Marxism and Methodological Individualism", *Philosophical Papers* 37: 185–211.

Little, D. (1991) *Varieties of Social Explanation*. Westview Press.

Pettit, P. (1993) *The Common Mind*. New York: Oxford University Press.

Pettit, P. (1998) Defining and Defending Social Holism," *Philosophical Explorations* 1: 169–84.

Porpora, D. (2007) "On Elder-Vass: Refining a Refinement," *Journal for the Theory of Social Behavior* 37: 195–99.

Kumar, C. (2008) "A Pragmatist Spin on Analytical Marxism and Methodological Individualism," *Philosophical Papers* 37: 185–211.

Steel, D. (2006) "Methodological Individualism, Explanation, and Invariance," *Philosophy of the Social Sciences* 36: 440–63.

Udehn, L. (2001) *Methodological Individualism: Background, History, and Meaning*. New York, NY: Routledge.

Van Bouwel, J. (2004) "Individualism and Holism, Reduction and Pluralism: A Comment on Keith Sawyer and Julie Zahle," *Philosophy of the Social Sciences* 34: 525–35.

Veneziani, R. (2008) "A Future for (Analytical) Marxism?" *Philosophy of the Social Sciences* 38: 388–99.

Walsh, A. (1997) "Methodological Individualism and Vertical Integration in the Social Sciences," *Behavior and Philosophy* 25: 121–36.

Zahle, J. (2003) "The Individualism-Holism Debate on Intertheoretic Reduction and the Argument from Multiple Realization," *Philosophy of the Social Sciences* 33: 77–99.

Chapter 18

STEVEN LUKES

METHODOLOGICAL INDIVIDUALISM RECONSIDERED

I

IN WHAT FOLLOWS I DISCUSS and (hopefully) render harmless a doctrine which has a very long ancestry, has constantly reappeared in the history of sociology and still appears to haunt the scene. It was first clearly articulated by Hobbes, who held that 'it is necessary that we know the things that are to be compounded, before we can know the whole compound' for 'everything is best understood by its constitutive causes', the causes of the social compound residing in 'men as if but even now sprung out of the earth, and suddenly, like mushrooms, come to full maturity, without all kind of engagement to each other'.[1] It was taken up by the thinkers of the Enlightenment, among whom, with a few important exceptions (such as Vico and Montesquieu) an individualist mode of explanation became pre-eminent, though with wide divergencies as to what was included, and how much was included, in the characterization of the explanatory elements. It was confronted by a wide range of thinkers in the early nineteenth century, who brought to the understanding of social life a new perspective, in which collective phenomena were accorded priority in explanation. As de Bonald wrote, it is 'society that constitutes man, that is, it forms him by social education . . .'[2] or, in Comte's words, a society was 'no more decomposable into *individuals* than a geometric surface is into lines, or a line into points'.[3] For others, however, such as Mill and the Utilitarians, 'the laws of the phenomena of society are, and can be, nothing but the actions and passions of human beings', namely 'the laws of individual human nature'.[4] This debate has recurred in many different guises—in the dispute between the 'historical' school in economics and the 'abstract' theory of classical economics, in endless debates among philosophers of history and between sociologists and psychologists,[5] and, above all, in the celebrated controversy between Durkheim and Gabriel Tarde.[6] Among others, Simmel[7] and Cooley[8] tried to resolve the issue, as did Gurvitch[9] and Ginsberg,[10] but it constantly reappears, for example in reactions to the extravagantly macroscopic theorizing of Parsons and his followers[11] and in the extraordinarily muddled debate provoked by the wide-ranging methodological polemics of Hayek and Popper.[12]

What I shall try to do here is, first, to distinguish what I take to be the central tenet of methodological individualism from a number of different theses from which it has not normally been distinguished; and second, to show why, even in the most vacuous sense, methodological individualism is implausible.

Let us begin with a set of truisms. Society consists of people. Groups consist of people. Institutions consist of people plus rules and roles. Rules are followed (or alternatively not followed) by people and roles are filled by people. Also there are traditions, customs, ideologies, kinship systems, languages: these are ways people act, think and talk. At the risk of pomposity, these truisms may be said to constitute a theory (let us call it 'Truistic Social Atomism') made up of banal propositions about the world that are analytically true, i.e. in virtue of the meaning of words.

Some thinkers have held it to be equally truistic (indeed, sometimes, to amount to the same thing) to say that facts about society and social phenomena are to be explained solely in terms of facts about individuals. This is the doctrine of methodological individualism. For example, Hayek writes:

> there is no other way toward an understanding of social phenomena but through our understanding of individual actions directed toward other people and guided by their expected behaviour.[13]

Similarly, according to Popper,

> . . . all social phenomena, and especially the functioning of all social institutions, should always be understood as resulting from the decisions, actions, attitudes, etc., of human individuals, and . . . we should never be satisfied by an explanation in terms of so-called 'collectives' . . .[14]

Finally we may quote Watkins's account of 'the principle of methodological individualism':

> According to this principle, the ultimate constituents of the social world are individual people who act more or less appropriately in the light of their dispositions and understanding of their situation. Every complex social situation, institution or event is the result of a particular configuration of individuals, their dispositions, situations, beliefs, and physical resources and environment.

It is worth noticing, incidentally, that the first sentence here is simply a (refined) statement of Truistic Social Atomism. Watkins continues:

> There may be unfinished or half-way explanations of large-scale social phenomena (say, inflation) in terms of other large-scale phenomena (say, full employment); but we shall not have arrived at rock-bottom explanations of such large-scale phenomena until we have deduced an account of them from statements about the dispositions, beliefs, resources and inter-relations of individuals. (The individuals may remain anonymous and only typical dispositions etc., may be attributed to them.) And just as mechanism is contrasted with the organicist idea of physical fields, so methodological individualism is contrasted with sociological holism or organicism. On this latter view, social systems constitute 'wholes' at least in the sense that some of their large-scale behaviour is governed by macro-laws which are essentially *sociological* in the sense that they are *sui generis* and not to be explained as mere regularities or tendencies resulting from the behaviour of interacting individuals. On the contrary, the behaviour of individuals should (according to sociological holism) be explained at least partly in terms of such laws (perhaps in conjunction with an account, first of individuals' roles within institutions, and secondly of the functions of institutions with the whole social system). If methodological individualism means that human beings are supposed to be

the only moving agents in history, and if sociological holism means that some superhuman agents or factors are supposed to be at work in history, then these two alternatives are exhaustive.[15]

Methodological individualism, therefore, is a prescription for explanation, asserting that no purported explanations of social (or individual) phenomena are to count as explanations, or (in Watkins's version) as rock-bottom explanations, unless they are couched wholly in terms of facts about individuals.

It is now necessary to distinguish this theory from a number of others, from which it is usually not distinguished. It has been taken to be the same as any or all of the following:

(1) Truistic Social Atomism. We have seen that Watkins, for example, seems to equate this with methodological individualism proper.
(2) A theory of meaning to the effect that every statement about social phenomena is either a statement about individual human beings or else it is unintelligible and therefore not a statement at all. This theory entails that all predicates which range over social phenomena are definable in terms of predicates which range only over individual phenomena and that all statements about social phenomena are translatable without loss of meaning into statements that are wholly about individuals. As Jarvie has put it, ' "Army" is merely a plural of soldier and *all* statements about the Army can be reduced to statements about the particular soldiers comprising the Army'.[16]

    It is worth noticing that this theory is only plausible on a crude verificationist theory of meaning (to the effect that the meaning of p is what confirms the truth of p). Otherwise, although statements about armies are true only in virtue of the fact that other statements about soldiers are true, the former are not equivalent in meaning to the latter, nor *a fortiori* are they 'about' the subject of the latter.
(3) A theory of ontology to the effect that in the social world only individuals are real. This usually carries the correlative doctrine that social phenomena are constructions of the mind and 'do not exist in reality'. Thus Hayek writes, 'The social sciences . . . do not deal with "given" wholes but their task is to constitute these wholes by constructing models from the familiar elements—models which reproduce the structure of relationships between some of the many phenomena which we always simultaneously observe in real life. This is no less true of the popular concepts of social wholes which are represented by the terms current in ordinary language; they too refer to mental models . . .'[17] Similarly, Popper holds that 'social entities such as institutions or associations' are 'abstract models constructed to interpret certain selected abstract relations between individuals'.[18]

    If this theory means that in the social world only individuals are observable, it is evidently false. Some social phenomena simply can be observed (as both trees and forests can): and indeed, many features of social phenomena are observable (e.g. the procedure of a court) while many features of individuals are not (e.g. intentions). Both individual and social phenomena have observable and non-observable features. If it means that individual phenomena are easy to understand, while social phenomena are not (which is Hayek's view), this is highly implausible: compare the procedure of the court with the motives of the criminal. If the theory means that individuals exist independently of, e.g., groups and institutions, this is also false, since, just as facts about social phenomena are contingent upon facts about individuals, the reverse is also true. Thus, we can only speak of soldiers because we can speak of armies: only if certain statements are true of armies are others true of soldiers. If the theory means that all social phenomena are fictional and all individual phenomena are factual, that would entail that all assertions about social phenomena are false, or else neither true nor false, which is absurd. Finally, the theory may mean that only facts about individuals are explanatory, which alone would make this theory equivalent to methodological individualism.

(4) A negative theory to the effect that sociological laws are impossible, or that law-like statements about social phenomena are always false. Hayek and Popper sometimes seem to believe this, but Watkins clearly repudiates it, asserting merely that such statements form part of 'half-way' as opposed to 'rock-bottom' explanations.

This theory, like all dogmas of the form 'x is impossible' is open to refutation by a single counter-instance. Since such counter-instances are readily available[19] there is nothing left to say on this score.

(5) A doctrine that may be called 'social individualism' which (ambiguously) asserts that society has as its end the good of individuals. When unpacked, this may be taken to mean any or all of the following: (a) social institutions are to be explained as founded and maintained by individuals to fulfil their ends, consciously framed independently of the institutions (as in, e.g., Social Contract theory); (b) social institutions in fact satisfy individual ends; (c) social institutions ought to satisfy individual ends. (a) is not widely held today, though it is not extinct; (b) is certainly held by Hayek with respect to the market, as though it followed from methodological individualism; and (c) which, interpreting 'social institutions' and 'individual ends' as a non-interventionist state and express preferences, becomes political liberalism, is clearly held by Popper to be uniquely consonant with methodological individualism.

However, neither (b) nor (c) is logically or conceptually related to methodological individualism, while (a) is a version of it.

II

What I hope so far to have shown is what the central tenet of methodological individualism is and what it is not. It remains to assess its plausibility.

It asserts (to repeat) that all attempts to explain social and individual phenomena are to be rejected (or, for Watkins, rejected as rock-bottom explanations) unless they refer exclusively to facts about individuals. There are thus two matters to investigate: (1) what is meant by 'facts about individuals'; and (2) what is meant by 'explanation'?

(1) What is a fact about an individual? Or, more clearly, what predicates may be applied to individuals? Consider the following examples:

(i)   genetic make-up; brain-states
(ii) aggression; gratification; stimulus-response
(iii) co-operation; power; esteem
(iv) cashing cheques; saluting; voting.

What this exceedingly rudimentary list shows is at least this: that there is a continuum of what I shall henceforth call individual predicates from what one might call the most non-social to the most social. Propositions incorporating only predicates of type (i) are about human beings *qua* material objects and make no reference to and presuppose nothing about consciousness or any feature of any social group or institution. Propositions incorporating only individual predicates of type (ii) presuppose consciousness but still make no reference to and presuppose nothing about any feature of any social group or institution. Propositions incorporating only individual type (iii) do have a minimal social reference: they presuppose a social context in which certain actions, social relations and/or mental states are picked out and given a particular significance (which makes social relations of certain sorts count as 'co-operative', which makes certain social positions count as positions of 'power' and a certain set of attitudes count as 'esteem'). They still do not presuppose or entail any particular propositions about any particular form of group or institution. Finally, propositions incorporating only individual predicates of type (iv) are maximally social, in that they presuppose and sometimes directly entail propositions about particular types of group and institution. ('Voting Labour' is at an even further point on the continuum.)

Methodological individualism has frequently been taken to confine its favoured explanations to any or all of these sorts of individual predicates. We may distinguish the following four possibilities.

(i) Attempts to explain in terms of type (i) predicates. A good example is H. J. Eysenck's *Psychology of Politics*.[20] According to Eysenck, 'Political actions are actions of human beings; the study of the direct cause of these actions is the field of the study of psychology. All other social sciences deal with variables which affect political action indirectly'.[21] (Compare this with Durkheim's famous statement that 'every time that a social phenomenon is directly explained by a psychological phenomenon, we may be sure that the explanation is false'.)[22] Eysenck sets out to classify attitudes along two dimensions—the Radical-Conservative and the Tough-minded-Tender-minded—on the basis of evidence elicited by carefully-constructed questionnaires. Then, having classified the attitudes, his aim is to *explain* them by reference to antecedent conditions and his interest here is centred upon the modifications of the central nervous system.

(ii) Attempts to explain in terms of type (ii) predicates. Examples are Hobbes's appeal to appetites and aversions, Pareto's residues and those Freudian theories in which sexual activity is seen as a type of undifferentiated activity that is (subsequently) channelled in particular social directions.

(iii) Attempts to explain in terms of type (iii) predicates. Examples are those sociologists and social psychologists (from Trade to Homans[23]) who favour explanations in terms of general and 'elementary' forms of social behaviour, which do invoke some minimal social reference but are unspecific as to any particular form of group or institution.

(iv) Attempts to explain in terms of type (iv) predicates. Examples of these are extremely widespread, comprising all those who appeal to facts about concrete and specifically located individuals in order to explain. Here the relevant features of the social context are, so to speak, built into the individual. If one opens almost any empirical (though not theoretical) work of sociology, or history, explanations of this sort leap to the eye.

Merely to state these four alternative possibilities is to suggest that their differences are more important than their similarities. What do they show about the plausibility of methodological individualism? To answer this it is necessary to turn to the meaning of 'explanation'.

(2) To explain something is (at least) to overcome an obstacle—to make what was unintelligible intelligible. There is more than one way of doing this.

It is important to see, and it is often forgotten, that to *identify* a piece of behaviour, a set of beliefs, etc., is sometimes to explain it. This may involve seeing it in a new way, picking out hidden structural features. Consider an anthropologist's interpretation of sacrifice or a sociological study of bureaucracy. Often explanation resides precisely in a successful and sufficiently wide-ranging identification of behaviour or types of behaviour (often in terms of a set of beliefs). Again, to take an example from Mandelbaum,[24] a Martian visiting earth sees one man mark a piece of paper that another has handed him through some iron bars: on his being told that the bank-teller is certifying the withdrawal slip he has had the action explained, through its being identified. If the methodological individualist is saying that no explanations are possible (or rock-bottom) except those framed exclusively in terms of individual predicates of types, (i), (ii) and (iii), i.e., those not presupposing or entailing propositions about particular institutions and organizations, then he is arbitrarily ruling out (or denying finality to) most ordinarily acceptable explanations, as used in everyday life, but also by most sociologists and anthropologists for most of the time. If he is prepared to include individual predicates of type (iv), he seems to be proposing nothing more than a futile linguistic purism. Why should we be compelled to talk about the tribesman but not the tribe, the bank-teller but not the bank? Moreover, it would be a mistake to underestimate the difficulty or the importance of explanation by identification. Indeed, a whole methodological tradition (from Dilthey through Weber to Winch) holds this to be the characteristic mode of explanation in social science.

Another way of explaining is to deduce the specific and particular from the general and universal. If I have a body of coherent, economical, well-confirmed and unfalsified general laws from which, given the specifications of boundary and initial conditions, I predict (or retrodict) x and x occurs, then, in one very respectable sense, I have certainly explained x. This is the form of explanation which methodological individualists characteristically seem to advocate, though they vary as to whether the individual predicates which are uniquely to constitute the general laws and specifications of particular circumstances are to be of types (i), (ii), (iii) or (iv).

If they are to be of type (i), either of two equally unacceptable consequences follows. Eysenck writes, 'It is fully realized that most of the problems discussed must ultimately be seen in their historical, economic, sociological, and perhaps even anthropological context, but little is to be gained at the present time by complicating the picture too much.'[25] But the picture is already so complicated at the very beginning (and the attitudes Eysenck is studying are only identifiable in social terms); the problem is how to simplify it. This could logically be achieved either by developing a theory which will explain the 'historical, economic, sociological . . . anthropological context' exclusively in terms of (e.g.) the central nervous system or by demonstrating that this 'context' is simply a backdrop against which quasi-mechanical psychological forces are the sole causal influences at work. Since, apart from quaint efforts that are of interest only to the intellectual historian, no-one has given the slightest clue as to how either alternative might plausibly be achieved, there seems to be little point in taking it seriously, except as a problem in philosophy. Neuro-physiology may be the queen of the social sciences, but her claim remains entirely speculative.

If the individual predicates are to be of type (ii), there is again no reason to find the methodological individualist's claim plausible. Parallel arguments to those for type (i) predicates apply: no-one has yet provided any plausible reason for supposing that, e.g., (logically) pre-social drives uniquely determine the social context or that this context is causally irrelevant to their operation. As Freud himself saw, and many neo-Freudians have insisted, the process of social channelling is a crucial part of the explanation of behaviour, involving reference to features of both small groups and the wider social structure.

If the individual predicates are to be of type (iii), there is still no reason to find the methodological individualist's claim plausible. There may indeed be valid and useful explanations of this type, but the claim we are considering asserts that all proper, or rock-bottom, explanations must be. Why rule out as possible candidates for inclusion in an *explicans* (statement of general laws + statement of boundary and initial conditions) statements that are about, or that presuppose or entail other statements that are about, social phenomena? One reason for doing so might be a belief that, in Hume's words, 'mankind are . . . much the same in all times and places'.[26] As Homans puts it, the characteristics of 'elementary social behaviour, far more than those of institutionalized behaviour, are shared by all mankind':

Institutions, whether they are things like the physician's role or things like the bureaucracy, have a long history behind them of development within a particular society; and in institutions societies differ greatly. But within institutions, in the face-to-face relations between individuals . . . characteristics of behaviour appear in which mankind gives away its lost unity.[27]

This may be so, but then there are still the differences between institutions and societies to explain.

Finally, if the claim is that the individual predicates must be of type (iv), then it appears harmless, but also pointless. Explanations, both in the sense we are considering now and in the sense of identifications, may be wholly couched in such predicates but what uniquely special status do they possess? For, as we have already seen, propositions incorporating them presuppose and/ or entail other propositions about social phenomena. Thus the latter have not really been eliminated; they have merely been swept under the carpet.

It is worth adding that since Popper and Watkins allow 'situations' and 'inter-relations between individuals' to enter into explanations, it is difficult to see why they insist on calling their doctrine 'methodological individualism'. In fact the burden of their concerns and their arguments is to oppose certain sorts of explanations in terms of social phenomena, which they regard as wicked. They are against 'holism' and 'historicism', but opposition to these doctrines does not entail acceptance of methodological individualism. For, in the first place, 'situations' and 'inter-relations between individuals' can be described in terms which do not refer to individuals, without holist or historicist implications. And secondly, it may be impossible to describe them in terms which do refer to individuals, and yet reference to them may be indispensable to an explanation, either as part of an identifying explanation, or in the statement of a general law or of initial and boundary conditions.

Notes

1   *The English Works of Thomas Hobbes*, ed. Sir William Molesworth, London, John Bohn, 1839–44, vol. I, p. 67; vol. II, pp. xiv, 109.
2   L. de Bonald, *Théorie du Pouvoir*, Paris, Librairie d'Adrien le Clere, 1854, vol. I, p. 103.
3   A. Comte, *Système de Politique Positive*, Paris, L. Mathias, 1951, vol. II, p. 181.
4   J. S. Mill, *A System of Logic*, 9th edn., London, Longmans, Green and Co., 1875, vol. II, p. 469.
5   See D. Essertier, *Psychologie et Sociologie*, Paris, Centre de Documentation Sociale de l'Ecole Normale Supérieure, 1927.
6   Cf. E. Durkheim, *Les Règles de la Méthode Sociologique*, Paris, Alcan and P.U.F., 1895; 15th edn., 1963, and G. Tarde, *Les Lois Sociales*, Paris, Alcan, 1898.
7   See *The Sociology of George Simmel* tr. and ed. with introd. by K. H. Wolff, Glencoe, Ill., Free Press, 1950, esp. chs. I, II and IV (e.g. 'Let us grant for the moment that only individuals "really" exist. Even then, only a false conception of science could infer from this "fact" that any knowledge which somehow aims at synthesizing these individuals deals with merely speculative abstractions and unrealities', pp. 4–5).
8   See C. H. Cooley, *Human Nature and the Social Order*, New York, Scribner's, 1912. For Cooley, society and the individual are merely 'the collective and distributive aspects of the same thing' (pp. 1–2).
9   See G. Gurvitch, 'Les Faux Problèmes de la Sociologie au XIXᵉ Siècle' in *La Vocation Actuelle de la Sociologie*, Paris, Presses Universitaires de France, 1950, esp. pp. 25–37.
10   See M. Ginsberg, 'The Individual and Society' in *On the Diversity of Morals*, London, Heinemann, 1956.
11   See G. C. Homans, 'Bringing Men Back In', *Amer. Soc. Rev.*, vol. 29 (1964), and D. H. Wrong, 'The Over-socialized Conception of Man in Modern Sociology', *ibid.*, vol. 26 (1961).
12   See the following discussions: F. A. Hayek, *The Counter-Revolution of Science*, Glencoe, Ill., Free Press, 1952, chs. 4, 6 and 8; K. R. Popper, *The Open Society and its Enemies*, London, Routledge, 1945, ch. 14, and *The Poverty of Historicism*, London, Routledge, 1957, chs. 7, 23, 24 and 31; J. W. N. Watkins,

'Ideal Types and Historical Explanation', *Brit. J. Phil. Sci.*, vol. 3 (1952), reprinted in H. Feigl and M. Brodbeck, *Readings in the Philosophy of Science*, New York, Appleton Century-Crofts, 1953; 'The Principle of Methodological Individualism (note), ibid., vol. 3 (1952); 'Historical Explanation in the Social Sciences', ibid., vol. 8 (1957); M. Mandelbaum, 'Societal Laws', ibid., vol. 8 (1957); L. J. Goldstein, 'The Two Theses of Methodological Individualism' (note), ibid., vol. 9 (1958); Watkins, 'The Two Theses of Methodological Individualism' (note), ibid., vol. 9 (1959); Goldstein, 'Mr. Watkins on the Two Theses' (note), ibid., vol. 10 (1959); Watkins, 'Third Reply to Mr. Goldstein' (note), ibid., vol. 10 (1959); K. J. Scott, 'Methodological and Epistemological Individualism' (note), ibid., vol. 11 (1961); Mandelbaum, 'Societal Facts', *Brit. J. Soc.*, vol. 6 (1955); E. Gellner, 'Explanations in History', *Proc. Aristotelian Soc.*, supplementary vol. 30 (1956). (These last two articles together with Watkins's 1957 article above are reprinted in P. Gardiner (ed.), *Theories of History*, Glencoe, Ill., Free Press, 1959, together with a reply to Watkins by Gellner. Gellner's paper is here retitled 'Holism and Individualism in History and Sociology'.) M. Brodbeck, 'Philosophy of the Social Sciences', *Phil. Sci.*, vol. 21 (1954); Watkins, 'Methodological Individualism: A Reply' (note), ibid., vol. 22 (1955); Brodbeck, 'Methodological Individualisms: Definition and Reduction', ibid., vol. 25 (1958); Goldstein, 'The Inadequacy of the Principle of Methodological Individualism', *J. Phil.*, vol. 53 (1956); Watkins, 'The Alleged Inadequacy of Methodological Individualism' (note), ibid., vol. 55 (1958); C. Taylor, 'The Poverty of the Poverty of Historicism', *Universities and Left Review*, 1958 (Summer) followed by replies from I. Jarvie and Watkins, ibid., 1959 (Spring); J. Agassi, 'Methodological Individualism', *Brit. J. Soc.*, vol. 11 (1960); E. Nagel, *The Structure of Science*, London, Routledge, 1961, pp. 535–46; A. C. Danto, *Analytical Philosophy of History*, Cambridge, Cambridge University Press, 1965, ch. XII; and W. H. Dray, 'Holism and Individualism in History and Social Science' in P. Edwards (ed.) *The Encyclopedia of Philosophy*, New York, Macmillan and Free Press, 1967.

13   *Individualism and Economic Order*, London, Routledge, 1949, p. 6.
14   *The Open Society*, 4th edn., vol. II, p. 98.
15   'Historical Explanation in the Social Sciences' in Gardiner (ed.), op. cit., p. 505. Cf. 'large-scale *social* phenomena must be accounted for by the situations, dispositions and beliefs of individuals. This I call methodological individualism'. Watkins, 'Methodological Individualism: A Reply', *Phil. Sci.*, vol. 22 (1955) (see note 12), p. 58.
16   Art. cit., p. 57.
17   *The Counter-Revolution of Science*, p. 56.
18   *The Poverty of Historicism* (paperback edition), 1961, p. 140.
19   Popper himself provides some: see *The Poverty of Historicism*, pp. 62–3.
20   London, Routledge, 1954.
21   Op. cit., p. 10.
22   Op. cit., p. 103.
23   See *Social Behaviour: its Elementary Forms*, London, Routledge, 1961.
24   Art. cit.
25   Op. cit., p. 8.
26   D. Hume, *Essays Moral and Political*, ed. T. H. Green and T. H. Grose, London, Longmans, Green and Co., 1875, vol. II, p. 68.
27   Op. cit., p. 6.

Chapter 19

MARTIN VAN HEES

EXPLAINING INSTITUTIONS
A defence of reductionism

1. Introduction

IN THE EARLIER DAYS OF ITS development, two important spokesmen for new institutionalism said that this approach to the study of social and political phenomena 'is far from coherent or consistent; it is not completely legitimate; but neither can it be entirely ignored' (March & Olsen 1984: 734). These words still seem to be highly relevant. New institutionalism cannot be ignored. It purports to reshape our thinking about topics as divergent as local governments, legislative processes, public law, the origins of the state, international cooperation, bureaucratic policy making, and so on. The approach has not only influenced the study of politics and public administration, but it also has had an influence on such related disciplines as law, organization theory, economics and sociology. Furthermore, the stream of new institutional publications reveal that the number of scientists adopting this approach is still increasing. However, although new institutionalism cannot be ignored, speaking of the *new* institutional approach would suggest a greater consensus among its followers than can in fact be found. There is not only a wide diversity of opinions about the essentials of one of the central notions (if not the central notion) of the paradigm, namely that of an institution, but also with respect to the appropriate way of carrying out institutional analyses (DiMaggio & Powell 1991).

The picture must not be drawn too pessimistically, though. The existence of common themes is evident. It is almost trivial to say that new institutionalists are first and foremost interested in the role that institutions play in our understanding of social and political events. Broadly speaking, this interest in institutions can be seen to result in two lines of research. The first research line is one in which institutions are described and analysed in increasing detail. Since institutions determine the way individuals act, the detailed specification of the characteristics of the institutional context in which individuals act leads to a better understanding of that human behaviour. An important example of the sophisticated analysis of the institutional setting which this line of research yields is given in the context of the analysis of legislative processes. One of the central results of the formal theory of voting is the ubiquity of instability under the majority rule (McKelvey 1976). Shepsle has argued convincingly that the abstract model of the decision-making process on which this negative result rests contradicts the actual practice of legislative decision making in which the outcome is to a large extent determined by rules of jurisdiction and amendment control (Shepsle 1979, 1986). Taking account of those rules yields a more detailed description of the legislative process. Such a less abstract description of the institutional context may provide an explanation for the existence of political stability, that is, it may show that, under these particular institutional arrangements, individuals will adopt strategies that do form an equilibrium. In this first type of institutional analysis, new institutionalism can be seen as supplementary to conventional theories explaining human behaviour; it provides a more detailed description of the context in which the behaviour takes place. However, the institutional arrangements are still defined *exogenously*, that is, they form the given setting in which individuals perform actions.

A second line of research within new institutionalism emphasizes the importance of *endogenous* treatments of institutions. In this view, institutional arrangements should not only play a role insofar as they form the context in which agents act; the institutional context should itself be subject to explanation. Explanations of the existence of institutions cannot be reduced to the behaviour of individuals because the actions, goals, preferences, beliefs of individuals are them-selves characteristics of the institutional setting. According to these theorists, new institutionalism should depart from those conceptions of political life which are 'inclined to see political phenomena as the aggregate consequences of individual behavior, less inclined to ascribe the outcomes of politics to organizational structures' (March & Olsen 1989: 3). New institutionalism must go 'beyond' reductionist explanations such as those exemplified by, for instance, rational choice theory (Scharpf 1983: 11; March & Olsen 1984: 735–6; Smith 1988: 95; March & Olsen 1989: 8–16; Thelen & Steinmo 1992: 7–10).

In this paper we examine the claim that the concern with endogenous institutional variables entails the transcendence of reductionist accounts of social and political phenomena. We shall argue that the claim cannot be sustained. In fact, we argue that there are very strong reasons in favour of a reductionist analysis of institutions. First, we show that the dimensions new institutionalists sometimes merely implicitly ascribe to institutions can be systematically distinguished and analysed in terms of the characteristics of the reductionist models offered by rational choice theory, and in particular by game theory. The new institutional concern with contextual factors thus can be (and often already has been) dealt with by a reductionist framework. Second, we argue that rational choice theory not only provides very useful tools for the study of individual behaviour *within* an institutional context, but that it is also perfectly capable of analysing decision making *about* institutional arrangements. As long as at least some exogenous variables are allowed, the required endogenous treatment of institutional variables can be realized in a reductionist framework.

The plan of this paper is as follows. In Section 2 we discuss the meaning of the terms 'methodological individualism' and 'reductionism'. After having made clear what we understand by these terms, we describe in Section 3 some of the essentials of game theory, the textbook example of a theory based on the principle of methodological individualism. In Section 4 we turn to new institutionalism and examine what new institutionalists capture under the term 'institutions'. In Section 5 it is argued that new institutionalism, insofar as it is characterized by a concern with the endogenous treatment of institutions, does not go 'beyond' reductionism at all. The new institutional emphasis on the importance of the institutional setting should, in our perspective, not be seen as an argument for removing the restrictions allegedly set by the reductionist scheme of explanations used in rational choice theory. It should be interpreted in the same way as the new institutional concern with institutions has been treated in the first new institutional line of research distinguished above, to wit, as an impetus leading to the refinement of reductionist explanations, not as the driving force of a new non-reductionist paradigm.

2. Methodological individualism and reductionism

One of the perennial controversies in the history of the social sciences is between proponents and opponents of methodological individualism. Almost every social scientist has in one way or another, sometimes *ad nauseam*, been confronted with the issue. Furthermore, almost every researcher takes (knowingly or unknowingly) a stand in the debate. The position one adopts is not without importance since it has profound consequences for the way one studies social phenomena and, consequently, for one's understanding of the nature of social events. Like many other important concepts, the notion of methodological individualism (MI) is used in different and contrasting ways (Lukes 1973; Bhargava 1992). These differences, however, have not always been made clear and, as a result, the debate is sometimes confused. Proponents and opponents of MI dispute about different issues, and defenders of MI disagree no less about what to defend than opponents do about what to attack. Yet, for the purpose of a proper appraisal of the idea, it should be clear what kind of interpretations are possible and which type of MI is under consideration. To introduce some order, let us first consider the distinction between the so-called *ontological* and *explanatory* variants of MI (Bhargava 1992).

Ontological interpretations of MI rest on the claim that no social entities exist *other than those* that can be defined in terms of individuals and their properties. In the ontological view, it is nonsensical to speak about social entities as having a nature of their own. In this interpretation, MI is the 'denial that there are such undefinable group properties or such superentities' (Brodbeck 1968: 283) or the view that 'the ultimate constituents of the social world are individual people' (Watkins 1968: 270). However, since assumptions about the nature of reality or the status of social phenomena need not have any direct relation to the way we do research (Friedman 1968) and since the new institutional critique of reductionism and MI is first and foremost about methodological issues we shall restrict ourselves to those forms of MI that focus directly on methodological issues, leaving aside the ontological interpretations.

Explanatory variants of MI have as their core elements ideas about the proper way of explaining social events. These ideas boil down to the statement that social events should ultimately be explained in terms of individuals and their properties. However, since there are different types of explanation within the social sciences, there are also different opinions about what counts as valid instances of these strands of MI (Bhargava 1992). We shall restrict our attention to what can be called 'mainstream' MI: the view according to which social phenomena should be explained in terms of theories of individual action. In this view 'the methodological individualist claims that all true theories of social science are *reducible* to theories of individual human action, plus boundary conditions specifying the conditions under which persons act' (Nozick 1977: 353).

Classic instances of this form of MI are contractarian political theories. For instance, Thomas Hobbes is often mentioned as one of the founding fathers of MI on the basis of the political theory presented in *Leviathan*. In Hobbes' theory, the sovereign state results from the actions and deliberations of individuals. When confronted with the hardships of the state of nature, individuals decide to make a contract to institute the Leviathan and thereby leave the state of nature. The emergence of the state as a social phenomenon is explained in terms of a theory about the way individuals act in a state of nature. The state is an *intended* result of that behaviour. Other examples of mainstream MI are theories that explain social phenomena in terms of *unintended* consequences of the behaviour of individuals. In these explanations, a social phenomenon is a by-product of individual actions. For instance, beach congestion on a sunny afternoon is the unintended consequence of individuals deciding, independently of one another, to take a swim. Or, to formulate a less trivial example of the same phenomenon, the environmental crisis with which modern society is confronted can be considered to be the unintended result of such isolated human actions as driving a car, reading a book, eating meat, keeping pets, and so on (Hardin 1968; Schelling 1978).

An explanation of a social phenomenon in line with MI is always in terms of some general theory about individuals. The theory can be applied only if the boundary conditions under which it operates are known. Some of these conditions have to do with the constraints within which choices are made. For instance, if we explain the behaviour of bureaucrats on the basis of some budget-maximizing principle, we need to know what the range of actions of the bureaucrats is, what the consequences of the various actions in terms of the bureaucrats' budgets are, whether there are any competitive pressures, etc. It may well be the case that policy x would maximize the bureaucrats' budgets although it is not adopted by them: the policy may, for some other reason, not be feasible. Thus, constraints effectuate and shape the choices made by individuals. Let us for the moment refer to all more or less permanent determinants of the behaviour of individuals as the *institutional setting* or simply as the *institution* (we give a more detailed specification of the features of an institutional setting in Section 4). This setting determines the boundary conditions under which the general theory of human behaviour is to be applied. If the social event to be explained is itself an institution, then we can say that institutions are explained in terms of a general theory of individual behaviour *within* an institutional setting. Depending on the scope and depth one intends the analysis to have, one can also try to explain the institutions constraining individual actions. However, in order to do so along the lines of MI, one again has to define the institutional setting within which the emergence of those institutions are explained. To explain a particular phenomenon one invokes a general theory in combination with information about the institutional setting. That institution can also be explained in terms of a general theory and some other institutional setting. In order to obtain an even more detailed explanation one may explain this other institution in terms of yet another institution, etc.

Thus, we see that MI in fact embraces the view that social events can never be explained solely in individual terms. An explanation along the lines of MI always requires a combination of a general theory of human action *plus* a specification of the boundary conditions under which the theory is effective. These boundary conditions need not be about individuals, relations between individuals or properties of individuals, but may well be social phenomena. One of the essentials of MI, however, is that any explanation of these boundary conditions, or, more generally, the institutional setting, should itself be in terms of a general theory of individual human behaviour.

MI is a specific form of reductionism. Reductionism demands that an event at level x should always be explained on the basis of a general theory about phenomena occurring at a lower level of analysis. Reductionist explanations abound in contemporary research. To give but one example, in the theory of international relations it is quite common to conceive of national states as agents to which motives can be ascribed without further reducing those motives to something on the level of the individual (say the preferences of the members of the cabinet). For instance, phenomena such as the emergence of institutional arrangements are then explained on the basis of the motives of the states participating in those arrangements (Axelrod & Keohane 1985). As with MI, the demand for an explanation in terms of a general theory on a lower level of analysis does *not* imply that higher level phenomena may not appear in the explanation. On the contrary, boundary conditions should be stipulated that specify the constraints within which (individual or collective) agents act. Thus, the structure of other reductionist explanations is similar to that of MI, but the levels of analysis may differ.

3. Methodological individualism illustrated: game theory

A representative type of MI is formed by those theories in which individual rationality plays an important role. Later we shall relate the new institutional concerns to the reductionist analysis of institutions offered by rational choice theory, in particular game theory. In order to do so, we outline in this section some of the essential features of game theory.

Game theory is that part of rational choice theory that focuses particularly on the strategic aspects of decision making; it is concerned with the interdependence of human behaviour. A game-theoretic analysis of a decision situation proceeds in two steps. First, the characteristics of the decision situation are described. One way of doing so is in terms of a *game in normal form*. It consists of the following ingredients:

(1) a set of *individuals*;
(2) for each individual a set of *strategies* available to him or her;
(3) a *procedure* that assigns an outcome to each possible combination of individual strategies (each 'play of the game');
(4) the individual *preferences* regarding the set of possible outcomes.

The specification of a game belongs to the *descriptive part* of a game-theoretic model, in which the assumption of individual rationality already plays a role. It is assumed that the individual preference relations are orderings, i.e., are complete and transitive. In other words, an individual can compare any two alternatives with each other (completeness), and if a person happens to prefer x to y and y to z, then the person also prefers x to z (transitivity).

A game-theoretic model not only contains a descriptive part, but also a *solution part*. In this part the postulate of individual rationality plays a more prominent role. Conjectures are made about what outcomes will be likely if the game is played by rational individuals. To do so a solution concept is employed. Well-known solution concepts are Nash equilibrium, dominance solvability, natural outcome, and so on. A solution concept is, essentially, a set of conditions that a theorist imposes on strategy combinations. The conditions are presumed to reduce the set of all possible plays of the game to those that can actually be expected to occur if individuals act rationally. In other words, each of the various solution concepts can be interpreted as a possible 'translation' of the principle of individual rationality. For instance, a Nash equilibrium of a game is defined as a play in which none of the individuals can secure a more preferred outcome if the others stick to their strategies. It expresses the view that rationality means that each individual will use his or her best response to the other person's actions.

It should be emphasized that different game theorists adopt different solution concepts; there is not one particular solution concept that is considered to be superior to all others. The reasons are well known. First, for almost any solution concept one can define games in which the concept does not work: in that particular game there is no strategy combination satisfying the conditions defined by that particular solution concept. If one nevertheless wants to predict the outcomes of such games one must invoke some other solution concept. Second, there are often situations conceivable in which the particular solution concept yields too many possible solutions. The set of possible plays is then barely reduced and, as a result, the predictive power of the model is limited. Third, like all translations, translations of the postulate of individual rationality in terms of a particular solution concept can sometimes be disputed. One can often construct examples in which the particular concept leads to outcomes that are counterintuitive.

Despite these difficulties, the basic form of a game-theoretic explanation of a social event should be clear. It is completely in line with MI. Individuals make choices within a set of boundary conditions. The general theory of human action stipulates that individuals act rationally, that is, the preferences of individuals have certain formal characteristics and the individual actions will correspond to some specified solution concept. If the explanation demands, the boundary conditions within which individuals act can also be explained in game-theoretic terms. For instance, suppose we are trying to give a game-theoretic account of why the defence expenditures are of amount x at time t_2. Suppose, furthermore, that the range of actions of the politicians who make decisions about the budget is restricted. Parts of the budget are fixed due to prior commitments. If we are primarily interested in the changes in the budget compared with some earlier time period, say t_1, then a possible explanation might be in terms of the strategic choices made by politicians between t_1 and t_2. On the other hand, if we want to explain the whole array of defence expenditures, then we also have to explain those parts of the budget that have been decided upon a long time ago, say at t_0. Although such an explanation would be more elaborate than the one focusing on the decisions made at time t_1 alone, there is no reason to believe that such a more elaborate explanation could not be carried out with the help of game-theoretic models. In fact, such models have existed as long as game theory; these are models in which a *game in extensive form* describes the situation at hand. A game in extensive form consists of a decision tree in which the nodes represent points in time at which choices are made. The game models the decision process as a sequence of individual choices. Since, at each node, new boundary conditions may arise (determining which individuals can choose, what choices individuals can make, to what nodes in the tree those choices may lead, etc.), individuals can be said to make decisions about, among other things, boundary conditions. A game in extensive form consists of a decision tree in which at each node at most one individual makes a choice. To model decision making about boundary conditions one can also make use of so-called *simultaneous games*, that is, games consisting of decision nodes ('subgames') at which several individuals make their choices simultaneously (Shubik 1982: 47; van Hees 1995).

It is often the case that such more elaborate games can be reduced to a game in normal form by defining a strategy as a sequence of choices made by an individual at different points in time. One can, for instance, model decision making about the defence expenditures at time t_2 as a decision process in which individuals make decisions both at time t_0 and at t_1. The strategy adopted at time t_0 is then simply a description of actions taken at time t_0 and t_1 ('Always vote against defence expenditures' or 'Vote yes for making of commitments at time t_0. Decide against additional changes in the budget at t_1 if commitments are actually made at t_0. Approve additional changes if commitments are not made'. And so on.)

Before we consider the question of how such a purely reductionist framework as game theory can contribute to our understanding of institutions, we return to new institutionalism and examine what new institutionalists have understood by the term 'institutions'.

4. New institutionalism and institutions

To assess the claim that the new institutional concerns imply the transcendence of reductionism, we have to make clear what it is that new institutionalists conceive to be the central object of their study – what they have in mind when they speak about institutions. Regrettably, new institutionalists use the term in different and sometimes inconsistent ways (Ostrom 1986a: 4). We shall not try to give a systematic account of the various types of definition employed by new institutionalists, nor shall we try to distil some kind of basic definition. The state of the art does not seem to justify such analytic rigour yet. Instead, we shall draw a rather impressionistic picture of what new institutionalists refer to when they speak about institutions.

We distinguish three dimensions – structural, procedural, and behavioural – which can be seen to play a role in new institutional interpretations of the notion of an institution.

The *structural* dimension of institutions refers to all those phenomena that persist over a period of time and that form the constraints within which individuals act and interact. For instance, political parties can be construed as institutions in this structural sense. They determine a politician's range of actions. Some of the actions the politician might want to take may not be feasible, given his party's platform, for instance. Another example of such structural aspects is the legal system of a society. It determines the admissibility of courses of action and thereby restricts the range of actions of individuals. Structural aspects are not always defined explicitly. Important forms of informal constraints, for instance, are those that influence a person's preferences: the subtle ways in which the opinions of friends, family, teachers, etc., influence our thinking about and evaluation of the actions we can take. Other types of important informal constraints are, for instance, the roles individuals are assumed to be playing, or the channels through which communication between individuals take place.

The *procedural* dimension refers to mechanisms which systematically transform the actions taken by individuals into particular results. In a legislative context, for instance, the procedure may be the method used to amalgamate votes into a collective outcome. Thus we can consider the method of majority voting as an institution in the procedural sense. Procedural aspects refer not only to the mechanism through which decision making *within* committees takes place, but also to the way committees are mutually related and to the effect that these mutual relations have on the way decisions are made. The long legislative road through subcommittees, commit-tees, legislative chambers etc. forms an example of such procedural aspects. We need not think of voting rules alone, however. The mechanism can also be a legal rule attaching sanctions to violations of obligations.

Finally, some of the definitions offered by new institutionalists are framed in terms of behavioural regularities or patterns of human behaviour. For instance, Rowe states that 'social institutions are in fact nothing more than agents rationally following rules of action, and being believed by others to do so' (Rowe 1989: 5; see also Schotter 1981). We shall call these patterns or regularities the *behavioural* dimension of institutions. Examples of behavioural institutional aspects are conventions, which are regularities in conduct that emerge spontaneously when individuals in a group are engaged in an ongoing relationship with each other. Such conventions facilitate processes of mutual adjustment and learning, thus reducing the complexity of the social situation.

It should be clear that these three dimensions are closely related. Consider systems of norms, for instance: norms obviously belong to the institutional setting in which action takes place. In fact, each of the three types of institutional aspects is relevant to the study of norms. A norm like 'you shall refrain from doing *x*' has structural aspects ('I may not do *x* and therefore my range of actions is restricted'), procedural aspects ('if you do *x* you will be sanctioned') and behavioural aspects ('people tend not to do *x*'). Note, furthermore, that the rule-oriented character of institutions plays a crucial role in each of the three dimensions. The structural aspects of an institution do not refer to temporary constraints – they delimit the range of possible actions over a *longer period of time*. Procedural aspects translate individual actions *systematically* into a social outcome. Finally, the behavioural dimension refers to *patterns* of behaviour, not to incidental actions.

Not every definition of institutions offered by new institutionalists is framed in terms of all of these dimensions (nor need it be so from a nominalistic point of view). New institutionalism is less characterized by a consensus about the proper way of identifying and defining institutions than by an overall concern to go beyond 'institution-free' explanations. The thrust of the new institutional argument is that the mainstream approaches within the social sciences do not pay sufficient attention to the institutional setting in which social events are embedded. As we have seen, this means for some authors that an explanation of a social event should not take the institutional framework as a set of exogenously given independent variables, but should take that framework as one of the things which itself is in need of explanation. We shall now turn to the question of whether this does indeed imply that reductionism should be abandoned.

5. New institutionalism and reductionism

In the previous sections we have given the central outlines of the methodological positions usually referred to as methodological individualism or, more generally, reductionism. Furthermore, we have described some fundamental concepts of a reductionist approach *par excellence*: game theory. Finally, a sketch was given of the various dimensions new institutionalists have ascribed to institutions. We are now able to address the question of whether new institutionalism should transcend reductionist modes of explanations, as has been claimed by some new institutionalists.

To do so, we first examine the definition and analysis of institutions in the reductionist explanations offered by game theorists. Each of the dimensions ascribed to institutions by new institutionalists can be described in game-theoretic terms. First of all, consider the *structural dimension*. As we have seen, it refers to all those constraints within which individuals act. What are those constraints? We distinguish three types: those relating to the *individuals* partaking in the decision process; those relating to the *strategies* available to the individuals making choices; and those relating to the *preferences* of the individuals. Constraints determining which individuals participate can have a wide variety of forms. They can be physical ('Mr X is ill and therefore does not participate'), legal ('Mr X does not have the right to make this type of contract'), moral ('Mr X should not interfere'), etc. Furthermore, there are constraints demarcating the sets of individual strategies, that is, determining what an individual can and cannot, or may and may not do (van Hees 1995). Again a multitude of forms exists: examples are legal arrangements like power-conferring rules, mechanisms influencing the amount of information an individual has or the individual's capacity to deal with information, the communication channels in society, etc. Finally, there are constraints related to the preferences of an individual. One can think, for instance, of mechanisms of socialization as processes of preference formation.

The relation of the *procedural dimension* to a game is obvious. It is defined by the *procedure* through which the individual strategies are linked with outcomes. The notions to which the first two institutional dimensions are related are precisely the factors of which the descriptive part of a game-theoretic model is composed: procedures, individuals, strategies, preferences. Since a game consists of these four components, we can also say that structural and procedural aspects of institutions are described by the game (whether in normal or extensive form).

The third dimension of institutions, the *behavioural dimension*, is related to the way individuals act. As we have seen, assumptions about the way individuals act belong to the solution part of a game-theoretic model. Game theorists have always been keenly aware of the close relationship between the solution part of a game-theoretic model and the institutional setting of a society. The founding fathers of game theory themselves stated that the solution part expresses the 'accepted standard of behaviour' or the 'established order of society' (Von Neumann & Morgenstern 1944: 41).

Thus each of the various institutional dimensions can be interpreted in game-theoretic terms. The structural and procedural dimensions are defined in terms of the descriptive part of a game-theoretic model – the specification of the game – whereas the behavioural dimension is captured by the solution part of the model. There seems to be no ground for the claim that the confines of game-theoretic models are too narrow to permit the analysis of institutions. On the contrary, the components of a game-theoretic model correspond nicely with the various aspects that new institutionalists have attributed to institutions. Game theory can be used to model the various dimensions of institutions in a coherent and systematic way.

Game theory can also be used to explain the existence of institutions and thus to provide an *endogenous* treatment of institutions. As we saw in Section 2, explanations along the lines of (explanatory) methodological individualism are in terms of the interplay between a set of boundary conditions and a theory of human behaviour. If the explanation demands, those boundary conditions which can be said to be of *first order* can themselves be subject to explanation. The only limitation thereby is that boundary conditions of the first order should also be explained through the combination of a general theory of human action and a set of boundary conditions. The latter conditions – the *second-order* conditions – can also be formulated endogenously. Now it becomes obvious that the claim that new institutionalism goes beyond methodological individualism and reductionism, because it treats institutional variables endogenously, is based on a naive and distorted picture of those methodological positions. The claim would only be justified if reductionism precludes explanations in which no conditions of second or higher order occur. However, we have seen in our exposition of reductionism that this is not the case. Reductionism does not preclude the explanation of the institutional settings within which individuals (or, for that matter, groups of individuals) act. Hence, new institutionalism is, insofar as it is characterized by a concern with higher-order explanations, perfectly compatible with reductionism.

First, consider the structural aspects of an institution. As we have seen, a game is an abstract way of describing a decision situation. It may well be the case that the decision situation at hand is one in which the objects of choice themselves are games; the decision situation should then be modelled as a a game consisting of a sequence of subgames, that is, a simultaneous game. The play of the first subgame determines the subgame that will be played next, and so on. Each subgame contains a specification of individuals and strategies. A model thus results which can be used to explain the emergence of structural aspects of institutions: players and strategies. Take, for instance, intraparty decision making about the division of labour among members of parliament. The division of labour not only determines which strategies each representative has (person x is or is not allowed to speak on behalf of his party) but also which representatives do and do not participate in the various stages of the process of parliamentary decision making (person x is or is not a member of this particular subcommitee).

It may seem less obvious that preferences can also be treated endogenously. Although the importance of preference formation processes has often been emphasized, preferences usually belong to the exogenous variables of rational choice models. This does not mean, however, that it is not possible to study these processes within a rational choice framework, nor that such research has not yet been carried out. In fact, at least three routes can be explored. First, approaches exist in which an individual has several sets of preferences that mutually influence each other (Thaler & Shefrin 1981; Kuran 1991). For instance, in their analysis of the notion of self control, Thaler and Shefrin make use of a model of intertemporal choice in which an individual is seen both as a farsighted 'planner' who wants to realize his long-term preferences and as a myopic 'doer' who is only concerned with short-term gains. Since the planner's long-term preferences are a function of the doer's short-term preferences, the planner can satisfy his preferences by, among other things, modifying those short-term preferences. A second route of analysing endogenous preferences is in terms of models of incomplete information (Cohen & Axelrod 1984; Gerber & Jackson 1993). In these models individuals change their preferences if it becomes clear that their earlier preferences were based on incorrect beliefs concerning the characteristics of the decision situation. Finally, one can explain preferences on the basis of the other structural institutional aspects. Assuming that different types of players have different types of preferences, one can use models that explain the selection of players to account for the existing preferences. If, for instance, risk-averse politicians are more successful than their more risk-taking colleagues, then – given the appropriate setting – politicians of the latter kind will disappear from the political arena.

Hence, each of the structural aspects of institutions – constraints determining the set of individuals, the strategies and the preferences – can in principle be treated endogenously in game theory. Now consider the procedural dimension. By focusing on the procedures used to link the various subgames of a game, one sees that the model also enables one to study the selection of a procedure for making decisions – it permits the analysis of *constitutional decision making*. Indeed, constitutional decision making has always been an important subject for rational choice theorists (Buchanan & Tullock 1962; Eichberger & Pethig 1994). Finally, not only the descriptive part of a game-theoretic model can be subject to choice; the same can in principle be said of the solution part. For instance, among game theorists it is well known that specific relationships between principles of rationality and patterns of choice can be considered as resulting from processes of adaptive behaviour in a dynamic context. During the play of a game, conventions may arise concerning the way the play should be played (Taylor 1976; Schotter 1981).

Thus we conclude that each of the institutional dimensions can be defined endogenously in a game-theoretic model. Adopting game-theoretic models does not entail anything about the permitted level of analysis of the independent variables. A game-theoretic explanation – whether in terms of a game in extensive or normal form – is not automatically restricted to the first, most basic order. There is only one limit to what game theory can do in this respect: *in the end* game theory should have at least *some* exogenously given institutional factors on the basis of which the other institutional variables are explained. There should be at least one initial point at which the game starts and hence there should also be at least one exogenously given specification of individuals, strategies, procedure, and preferences. Although game-theoretic explanations are not necessarily of the first order, they must be of *some* order. The fact that game-theoretic explanations should in the end take at least some institutional factors as exogenously given, can only be considered to be a drawback if it is claimed that chains of explanations can always be extended up to a point at which no further institutional variables are needed, that is, to some rock-bottom point at which only individually related phenomena play a role. However, this claim is not only rather dubious, it also takes reductionism to its extremes: social phenomena should in the end be explained *only* in terms of individuals, their relations and their properties. At this basic level references should no longer be made to the institutional context. In other words the new institutional rejection of methodological individualism as adopted by rational choice theorists can only be justified if an even more rigorous form of methodological individualism is adopted. Insofar as new institutionalism is able to go beyond the reductionism of rational choice theorists, it is led to embrace a more radical form of reductionism. It is highly improbable that new institutionalists are willing to justify, let alone adopt, such an extreme position.

6. Conclusion

It cannot be emphasized enough that we do not want to dismiss the new institutional concern with institutions *per se*. Underlying new institutionalism is the basic assumption that the study of institutional arrangements contributes considerably to our understanding of social life. For this reason, the analysis of human behaviour within an institutional context and the explanation of the existence of that setting itself are important. In our opinion, it is indeed a truism that both the analysis and explanation of institutions should play an essential role in political science and in the related disciplines. The quest for ever more detailed explanations of the way individuals make decisions within institutional contexts is therefore an important and valuable enterprise. Hence, phenomena such as the inclusion and exclusion of individuals, the formation of preferences, the distribution of power, the choice of rules and procedures, the emergence of patterns of behaviour, and so on, are important topics, the study of which should play an essential role in any of the social sciences.

We started our exposition of new institutionalism by distinguishing two lines of new institutional research. In the first line, new institutionalism is seen as a demand to focus in greater detail on the institutional framework in which human behaviour occurs. It thus forms a welcome contribution to existing modes of explanation within the social sciences, including rational choice theory (Ostrom 1991). In the second line of research it is claimed that any mode of explanation that will try to do justice to the importance of institutional arrangements should abandon reductionist modes of explanations. We have concentrated on this second line of research. In our assessment of its claim we started with an exposition of a specific form of reductionism: methodological individualism. It was shown that this form of reductionism does not entail that social events should be explained in individual terms alone. Methodological individualism requires not only a general theory of human action but also a specification of the boundary conditions under which that theory applies. These boundary conditions need not be defined exclusively in individualistic terms; they may well describe institutional arrangements. The institutional arrangements that form the boundary conditions can themselves be the objects of explanation within a reductionist framework. In that event they are seen as arising from the combination of a theory of human behaviour to a set of second-order boundary conditions. These second-order conditions can be explained on the basis of conditions of an even higher order, and these higher-order conditions can themselves also be explained in terms of conditions of a yet higher order. It follows that reductionism permits the endogenous treatment of institutions. This conclusion is illustrated by the reductionist approach adopted by rational choice theorists. First of all, the notion of a game-theoretic model provides a coherent and systematic account of the various institutional dimensions distinguished in the literature. Furthermore, game theory provides an excellent tool for the endogenous treatment of institutions. Indeed, game-theoretic models in which decisions about institutional arrangements are made form an important part of game theory. This is, of course, not to say that new institutionalism is nothing but a particular form of rational choice theory, or that any social theorist interested in the analysis of institutions should embrace the rational choice framework. Rational choice theory does have its problems. For instance, we have already touched on the existence of situations in which the standard solution concepts lack predictive power because they yield too many equilibria or no equilibrium at all. However, the fact that the theory is confronted with these problems does not imply that they cannot be solved *within* the rational choice framework.

What we do hope to have established is that, for the question of what institutions are, for how institutions emerge, and for how they effect individual behaviour there are good reasons for adopting the reductionist framework offered by rational choice theory. The study of institutions does not imply the necessity of new modes of scientific explanations or new paradigms.

References

Axelrod, R. & Keohane, R.O. (1985). Achieving cooperation under anarchy: Strategies and institutions, *World Politics* 38: 226–254.

Bhargava, R. (1992). *Individualism in social science: Forms and limits of a methodology*. Oxford: Clarendon.

Brodbeck, M. (1968). Methodological individualisms: Definitions and reduction, pp. 280–304, in M. Brodbeck (ed.), *Readings in the philosophy of the social sciences*. New York: Macmillan.

Buchanan, J.M. & Tullock, G. (1962). *The calculus of consent: Logical foundations of constitutional democracy*. Ann Arbor: University of Michigan Press.

Cohen, M.D. & Axelrod, R. (1984). Coping with complexity: The adaptive value of changing utility, *American Economic Review* 74: 30–42.

DiMaggio, P.J. & Powell, W.W. (1991). Introduction, pp. 1–38, in: P.J. DiMaggio & W.W. Powell (eds.), *The new institutionalism in organizational analysis*. Chicago: University of Chicago Press.

Eichberger, J. & Pethig, R. (1994). Constitutional choice of rules, *European Journal of Political Economy* 10: 311–337.

Friedman, M. (1968). The methodology of positive economics, pp. 508–528, in: M. Brodbeck (ed.), *Readings in the philosophy of the social sciences*. New York: Macmillan.

Gerber, E.R. & Jackson, J.E. (1993). Endogenous preferences and the study of institutions, *American Political Science Review* 87: 639–656.

Hardin, G. (1968). The tragedy of the commons, *Science* 162: 1243–1248.

Kuran, T. (1991). Cognitive limitations and preference evolution. *Journal of Institutional and Theoretical Economics*, 147: 241–273.

Lukes, S. (1973). Methodological individualism reconsidered, pp. 119–129, in: A. Ryan (ed.), *The philosophy of the social explanation*, London: Oxford University Press.

March, J.G. & Olsen, J.P. (1984). The new institutionalism: Organizational factors in political life, *American Political Science Review* 78: 734–749.

March, J.G. & Olsen, J.P. (1989). *Rediscovering institutions. The organizational basis of politics*. London: Macmillan.

McKelvey, R.D. (1976). Intransitivities in multidimensional voting models and some implications for agenda control, *Journal of Economic Theory* 12: 472–482.

Nozick, R. (1977). On Austrian methodology, *Synthese* 36: 353–392.

Ostrom, E. (1986a). An agenda for the study of institutions, *Public Choice* 48: 3–25.

Ostrom, E. (1991). Rational choice theory and institutional analysis: Toward complementarity, *American Political Science Review* 85: 237–243.

Rowe, N. (1989). *Rules and institutions*, Ann Arbor: Michigan University Press.

Scharpf, F.W. (1983). Zur Bedeutung institutioneller Forschungsansätze, pp. 9–20, in: F.W. Scharpf & M. Brockmann (eds.), *Institutionelle Bedingungen der Arbeitsmarkt- und Beschäftigungspolitik*. Frankfurt: Campus.

Schelling, Th. (1978). *Micromotives and macrobehavior*. New York: Norton.

Schotter, A. (1981). *The economic theory of social institutions*. Cambridge: Cambridge University Press.

Shepsle, K.A. (1979). Institutional arrangements and equilibrium in multidimensional voting models, *American Journal of Political Science* 23: 27–59.

Shepsle, K.A. (1986). The positive theory of legislative institutions: An enrichment of social choice and spatial models, *Public Choice* 50: 135–178.

Shubik, M. (1982). *Game theory in the social sciences. Concepts and solutions*. Cambridge: MIT.

Smith, R.M. (1988). Political jurisprudence, the 'New Institutionalism', and the future of public law, *American Political Science Review* 82: 89–108.

Taylor, M. (1976). *Anarchy and cooperation*. London: John Wiley.

Thaler, R.H. & Shefrin, H.M. (1981). An economic theory of self-control, *Journal of Political Economy* 89: 392–406.

Thelen, K. & Steinmo, S. (1992). Historical institutionalism in comparative politics, pp. 1–32, in S. Steinmo, K. Thelen & F. Longstreth (eds.), *Structuring politics: Historical institutionalism in comparative analysis*. Cambridge: Cambridge University Press.

van Hees, M. (1995). *Rights and decisions. Formal models of law and liberalism*. Dordrecht: Kluwer.

Von Neumann, J. & Morgenstern, O. (1944). *Theory of games and economic behaviour*. Princeton: Princeton University Press.

Watkins, J.W.N. (1968). Methodological individualism and social tendencies, pp. 254–269, in: May Brodbeck (ed.), *Readings in the philosophy of the social sciences*. New York: Macmillan.

Chapter 20

KEITH SAWYER

NONREDUCTIVE INDIVIDUALISM
Part I – Supervenience and wild disjunction

THE TENSION BETWEEN individualism and collectivism is central to contemporary sociological theory and practice. The debate occurs at two levels: an ontological level, concerning arguments about what entities and properties exist in the world, and a methodological or epistemological level, concerning the proper way to proceed in scientific practice. In this article, I draw on several decades of established argument in the philosophy of mind to explore and clarify these long-standing ontological and methodological issues in sociology.

Individualists, such as rational choice theorists and exchange theorists, make both ontological and methodological claims for their approach. *Ontological individualism* is the stance that only individuals exist; sociological objects and properties are nothing but combinations of the individual participants and their properties. *Methodological individualism* is an epistemological stance that argues that every event that sociology explains can be explained in terms of individuals, and every law in sociology can be explained by laws concerning individuals (Coleman 1990, 20; Hempel 1965, 258–64; Homans 1964). Early statements of methodological individualism by Popper, Hayek, and Watkins were soon criticized (e.g., Gellner [1956] 1968; Goldstein [1958] 1973; Mandelbaum 1955); contemporary methodological individualists have responded vigorously to these criticisms (e.g., Macdonald and Pettit 1981; Quinton 1975–76; Mellor 1982). Despite this long history, the debate remains confused and unresolved (cf. Bhargava 1992; Ruben 1985, 132). For example, upon examination, many of the arguments for methodological individualism seem in fact to be arguments for ontological individualism, yet one can accept ontological individualism and still reject methodological individualism. The logical error of making ontological arguments in support of methodological claims is quite common in the philosophy of social science and is found in Popper's (1962) confusion of materialist metaphysics with epistemology (e.g., p. 341), in Elster's (1985) methodologically individualist reading of Marx, and in Giddens's (1984) attacks on structural sociology (e.g., chap. 4).

In opposition to individualism, contemporary collectivist paradigms in sociology include network theory, structural sociology, sociological realism, and neofunctionalism. Structuralists, for example, argue that social phenomena can be studied objectively and scientifically without a concern for individual-level properties (e.g., Blau 1970, 1977; Mayhew 1980). Like individualists, collectivists have not been clear about the degree to which their stance is ontological or methodological. As a result, several theorists have accused structuralists of hypostatizing or reifying sociological concepts (Collins 1981; Giddens 1984; King 1999). These critics claim that the structuralist method assumes that society is ontologically autonomous of individuals, when in fact it is nothing more than a descriptive convenience for sociologists (e.g., King 1999, 272). Are structural sociologists claiming that sociological terms and concepts are real, or are they making the weaker argument that sociologists need them for explanation? If the latter, then sociological terms and concepts would seem to be nothing more than descriptive conveniences, and they would seem to be epiphenomenal. If one makes only methodological claims for the usefulness of sociological terms and concepts, then those terms and concepts cannot have causal power. Yet many structuralists speak as if sociological phenomena can exert causal power over individuals. If collective phenomena can exert causal power, then they must be real, and the theorist must provide philosophical arguments to justify this sociological realism.

In fact, several contemporary sociological theorists who reject individualism have made realist arguments (e.g., Archer 1995; Bhaskar [1975] 1979; Keat and Urry 1975). The unresolved difficulty facing sociological realists is the problem of a *dualist ontology*: if both social entities and individuals are real, then it seems that one has two distinct ontological orders. Without a more robust foundational account, an ontologically individualist sociology has no grounds for proposing social causal laws. Due to such difficulties, sociological realism is not widely held by contemporary philosophers of social science, and many prominent schools of sociological theory—including methodological individualism, subjectivism, and interpretivism—are antirealist concerning the social.

In this article, I draw on contemporary philosophy of mind to provide a novel integration of the individualist and collectivist positions. I draw on philosophical discussions of supervenience, multiple realizability, and wild disjunction to provide a philosophical argument to ground collectivist macrosociology, one that grants to individualists their primary ontological concerns yet holds that sociology may of necessity be irreducible to laws and terms concerning individuals. I refer to this position as *nonreductive individualism* (NRI) by analogy with the consensus position in philosophy of mind, *nonreductive materialism*. Nonreductive materialism developed over the past thirty years as a theory concerning the mind-brain relation. As a result of debates beginning in the 1960s and continuing through the 1990s, arguments for nonreductive materialism largely convinced philosophers of mind to reject *eliminative materialism*, the physicalist stance that higher-level discourse is incorrect and unnecessary and should be replaced with the lower-level discourse. Nonreductive materialism holds to *ontological materialism*, the belief that all that exists is matter, thus rejecting various forms of Cartesian dualism and vitalism. However, nonreductive materialism argues that mental properties and states are irreducible to physical properties and states and that the science of the mind is autonomous from the science of neurons.

Although these arguments have focused on the mind-brain relation, many philosophers believe that they can be generalized to apply to any hierarchically ordered sets of properties (Fodor 1989; Humphreys 1997, 3; Jackson and Pettit 1992, 107; Kincaid 1997, 76; Yablo 1992, 247, n. 5). Yet the implications of these well-established arguments have not yet been fully developed by sociological theorists. The concepts of supervenience and multiple realizability have been discussed by some philosophers of social science (Currie 1984; Kincaid 1997; Mellor 1982; MacDonald and Pettit 1981; Pettit 1993), although their influence in sociological theory has been limited. The wild disjunction argument has not been fully explored by these philosophers, and its sociological implications have not been elaborated. Consequently, I elaborate this argument in some detail.

I extend NRI to provide an account of why social causation may necessarily be a part of sociological explanation. A commonly noted problem with ontological individualism is that it seems to result in sociological phenomena that are *epiphenomenal*, or causally inert. Many philosophers of social science who reject methodological individualism nonetheless agree that the social has no causal power. Prior realist and collectivist accounts have left this issue unresolved. I draw on arguments for mental causation from the philosophy of mind to make an argument for social causation that is consistent with ontological individualism, and I conclude that sociologists are justified in forming laws that describe how individuals are affected by social causes and that such laws may be irreducible to the intentions, perceptions, goals, or actions of individuals.

Levels of analysis

Nonreductive materialism draws on a long philosophical tradition of conceiving of the world in terms of *levels of analysis*, as a stratified structure of "levels" or "orders" of entities and their characteristic properties. Higher-level entities are composed of entities belonging to the lower levels; the entities at each level are characterized by a set of properties distinctive to that level (Kim 1993, 337; Wimsatt 1976). Most nonreductive materialists consider these to be not merely layers of discourse about objects and their properties but layers that in some sense actually exist in the world.

A similar conception of levels of analysis has been central to sociological theory at least since Comte proposed his hierarchy of the sciences; the level notion began to receive focused attention in the late 1980s in connection with theories of the micro-macro link, conceived of as the relation between individual and collective entities and properties (Alexander et al. 1987; Archer 1995; Ritzer 1991). Many of these contemporary theorists hold that social phenomena emerge out of interaction between individuals (Edel 1959; Ritzer 1991; Wagner 1964; Wiley 1988), and in some contemporary sociological theories, these emergent social entities and properties are claimed to exert causal force over those constituting individuals (e.g., Archer 1995; see Sawyer 2001).

Physicalist reductionists accept that there may be some practical use to levels of analysis as realms of scientific discourse but hold that these levels do not actually exist in the world. If all objects are physical, then how can so-called higher-level properties of entities and events be anything more than physical properties? And more critically, how can these higher-level properties or entities have causal powers, above and beyond the causal powers of physical matter? This is the crux of the contemporary debate between identity theorists and nonreductive materialists in the philosophy of mind. In the following, I draw on well-established arguments in the philosophy of mind to argue for a form of *property dualism*, which holds that social properties may be irreducible to individual properties, even though social entities consist of nothing more than individuals.

Type and token identity

The mind-brain identity thesis holds that the mental is identical with the physical (one canonical statement is Smart 1959). In response, nonreductive philosophers of mind partially accepted this claim but counterproposed a distinction between *type identity* and *token identity*. The nonreductionists pointed out that the initial statement of the identity thesis was actually a claim for "type identity": all mental types, or properties are identical to physical properties, or more generally all properties are identical to physical properties. Nonreductionists reject type identity but accept token identity, and likewise, NRI accepts token identity:

Token identity: There is only one kind of event in the universe, regardless of the terms, concepts, or laws used to describe those events. Events are unrepeatable, dated, countable particulars, or tokens. However, a single event may be referred to under multiple descriptions (following Davidson, 1970).

This thesis presupposes an ontology in which it is objects that have properties, and it is properties that carry causal powers; however, it is events that are the relata of causal transactions. I take an event to be the instantiation of properties by an object at a time. Critically, token identity does not entail type identity of events. A type of event is a class or kind of event that has instances, and we understand an event as a type relative to a taxonomy. Individual token events can be instances of multiple types; the event type "a group eating in a restaurant" may be instantiated in a token event that also instantiates the event type "a meeting of a reading club." Even though these types may be instantiated in the same token, the types are not identical; a group eating in a restaurant is not always a meeting of a reading club. In addition to token events that instantiate multiple social event types, a single event token can instantiate both social event types and individual event types; the event token that instantiates the social type "a meeting of a reading club" may also instantiate individual event types such as "each of the individuals present satisfies hunger by eating" and "some of the individuals present are hoping to make new friends."

Thus, a single event or entity can have both social and individual properties. The collective entity that has the social property "being a church" may also have a collection of individual properties associated with each of its component members, for example, each individual I_n may hold properties "believing in X_n" or "intending Y_n," where the sum total of such beliefs and intentions are (in some sense) constitutive of the social property "being a church."

In the following, I draw on arguments from the philosophy of mind to argue that the relation between social events and individual events is one of token identity but not of type identity. Type identity of events would lead to the reductionism of methodological individualism, in the same way that mind-brain type identity leads to physicalist reductionism. However, token identity without type identity is problematic for methodological individualism. Essentially, I argue that if social types or properties are multiply realized in wildly disjunctive sets of individual properties, methodological individualism cannot be maintained.

Supervenience

Nonreductive materialists argue against type identity using arguments of *supervenience* and *multiple realization*. Although these have largely proceeded as two distinct traditions of discourse, most philosophers agree that these two arguments are compatible (e.g., Heil 1999; Horgan 1981, 405–9; Kim 1984, 262; Lowe 1993, 630; Sarkar 1992). The claim that mental states are physically realized entails the claim that they are physically supervenient. Many nonreductive materialists use elements of both supervenience and multiple realization arguments (Kim 1993, 194–95).

Davidson (1970) noted that token identity entailed supervenience:

Supervenience: If two events are identical with respect to their descriptions at the lower level, then they cannot differ at the higher level. If a collection L of lower-level components with a given set of relations causes higher-level property H to emerge at time t, then on every other occasion when L obtains, H will again obtain.

The social version of supervenience states that if a collection of individual properties with a given set of relations causes a certain social property to obtain on one occasion, then that same collection of individual properties in that same set of relations on another occasion will cause the same social property to obtain. Supervenience is commonly defined in terms of *indiscernability*: higher-level properties supervene on lower-level properties when any two things indiscernible in lower-level properties are indiscernible in higher-level properties (Kim 1997, 188). Note that this implies that an event's properties cannot change at a higher level without also changing at the lower levels. Also note that supervenience is an asymmetric relation between levels; a given social property can conceivably supervene on multiple, different collections of individual properties on different occasions, but the inverse is not the case: A given collection of individual properties will realize the same social property on all occasions.

Davidson's (1970) paper has been extremely influential, and today most philosophers of mind accept that the mind is supervenient on the brain, reject type identity, and accept property dualism. Property dualists argue that "hard" or "liquid" exist as properties of objects like rocks or water, even though they are not properties of the individual atoms composing the object; likewise, property dualists regarding the mental argue that mental properties exist as properties of the brain. A single token brain event can have both mental and physical properties, in the same way that an ocean current can have both fluid-flow properties and molecular properties.

In the same way that an ontological materialist must accept token identity and supervenience regarding the mental-physical relation (cf. Kim 1997; Papineau 1993), an ontological individualist must accept the analogous theses regarding the social-individual relation. To reject either necessarily results in problematic ontological dualisms. For example, to reject token identity, one must maintain that there are two distinct classes of event, social and individual, which could then participate in causal relations with each other. To reject supervenience is to accept ontological dualism and opens one to the criticism of hypostatizing the social group as an entity. This is why the most prominent contemporary sociological realists, Bhaskar (1979) and Archer (1995), implicitly accept both token identity and supervenience (Sawyer 2001).

A few philosophers of social science have suggested that the individual-collective relation is one of supervenience, but these have been cursory treatments and have not addressed the most recent philosophical discussions concerning supervenience. Currie (1984, 357) argued that supervenience provides an argument for the ontological independence of the social, and thus his argument is effectively countered by more recent philosophical commentaries on supervenience, which note that supervenience does not solve any ontological problems and that it is compatible with both reductionist and nonreductionist positions (Heil 1998, 1999; Kim 1997; Lennon and Charles 1992). Kincaid (1997) did not make explicit that the supervenience argument refers to properties rather than to entities such as objects or events; thus, the relation of his argument to NRI is not clear. Mellor (1982, 16) accepted supervenience but argued that it entails reducibility. MacDonald and Pettit (1981, 119–20, 144–45) noted the supervenience argument in passing but claimed that it does not entail nonreductionism and is compatible with methodological individualism. Pettit (1993, 148–54) argued that both the social and the intentional are supervenient on the physical, that social regularities supervene on individual intentional regularities, and that this constituted an argument against collectivism. These claims are similar to more recent reductionist criticisms of supervenience that I review below; these philosophers of mind have argued that token identity and supervenience entail physicialism. By drawing on the responses to these criticisms, I show by analogy that token identity and supervenience do not entail methodological individualism.

Multiple realizability and wild disjunction

Supervenience is consistent with ontological individualism and is noncommittal with respect to the reductionist stance of methodological individualism (Heil 1998, 1999). If supervenience is to be used to ground a nonreductive stance, one must develop a version of the supervenience thesis that argues that the reductionist approach of methodological individualism is not possible for some social properties, despite ontological individualism. I will argue that to reject methodological individualism, one must show how type identity versions of supervenience might not obtain. The argument that convinced most philosophers of mind that the mental could not be reduced to the physical was Putnam and Fodor's *multiple realizability* argument (Fodor 1974; Putnam 1967); nonreduction due to multiple realizability is now the consensus position in the philosophy of mind (Block 1997; Heil 1999). The argument that mental properties are multiply realizable led to the demise of type identity and of eliminative materialism. An acceptance of a parallel argument in sociology would show how one could reject methodological individualism.

Putnam's general idea was inspired by the rapid development of computers and the new field of artificial intelligence. Putnam reasoned that if mental states could be grounded, or "realized," in both carbon-based human brains and in silicon-based digital computers, then those mental states could not be identified with either realization of them. To use the canonical example, being in pain is a mental property that is multiply realizable. Your being in pain depends on and is determined by a particular neurological property, a fish's being in pain depends on and is determined by a very different neurological property, and if a computer were ever developed that could feel pain, that pain would be determined by a silicon-based property.

Social properties are multiply realizable at the individual level (cf. Kincaid 1997, 17–20). For example, the property of "being a church" can be realized by a wide range of organizational structures, cultural practices, and individual beliefs and dispositions. The same is true of properties such as "being a family," "being an organization," and "being an institution." Microsocial properties are no less multiply realizable: examples include "being an argument," "being a conversation," and "being an act of discrimination."

Putnam argued that mental states, types, or kinds are functional types rather than physical types. A mental state like "pain" is defined by its functional properties and thus is a functional type; this functional type can be "realized" (or "implemented" or "executed") by a widely varying range of physical material: a human mind, an octopus mind, or an intelligent robot. Thus, Putnam grounded multiple realizability in *functionalism* by giving mental properties functional definitions rather than reductive definitions in terms of their realizing physical properties. A functionalist holds that what defines a system component are functional properties that are specified in terms of their causal role in relating inputs to outputs, rather than their physical realizations.

Although often mentioned in the same breath, multiple realizability is not identical to functionalism, and multiple realizability does not depend on functionalism. Multiple realization is a descriptive claim about the nature of the organization of the objective world; functionalism is an explanatory account of how that state of affairs came to be. My account in the following is independent of functionalist claims. For example, Horgan extended the multiple realizability concept beyond the usual argument that functional mental states like "pain" are multiply realized, in virtue of having different physical realizations in different species (Horgan 1997). This original claim of Putnam's is fairly easy for a reductionist to handle because he can respond by proposing a species-specific reduction; this was Kim's response in 1989. Horgan's stronger claim is that a mental state could be multiply realized within creatures of the same species (my brain's realization of my pain may not be the same as your brain's realization of your pain). An even stronger claim is that a mental state could be multiply realized within a single organism (my brain's realization of pain at time t_1 may not be the same as my brain's realization of pain at time t_2).

The following account of *wild disjunction* is an account of how this may be. The basic idea is that for any social property, there is in principle an endless sequence of nomologically possible individual-level states such that although each of them "realize" or "implement" the social property, none of them is coextensive with it. In connection with his supervenience argument, Davidson (1970) first noted the implications of wild disjunction for nonreductive materialism. Davidson explained that philosophers of mind in the 1960s rejected definitional behaviorism not simply because its theories failed but rather because there was a pattern to the failures. Reducing a mental event to a purely behavioral description did not work because a simple description of a mental event required a complex, long, provisoladen, disjunctive description in behavioral language. Thus, psychologists rejected behaviorism because they realized that there were probably no nomological connections between the mental and observed behaviors. Consequently, Davidson accepted token identity and supervenience but denied that they entail reducibility through law or definition. This claim is based on his notion of a law: laws refer to event types, defined in terms of physical or mental properties; although a mental event could be picked out using the physical vocabulary alone, there is no purely physical property, no matter how complex, that has the same extension as a mental property. The physical equivalent of a mental property might be a long and uninstructive disjunction; thus, the mental is nomologically irreducible—there may be relations between the mental and the physical, but they are not lawlike (Davidson 1970, 88–92).

In the following, I draw on Fodor's (1974, 1997) elaboration of the wild disjunction argument to show why methodological individualist arguments for type identity are unsuccessful, thus showing that social properties may not be reducible to individual properties. Fodor provided an account of how it is that all of the special sciences have identified macro-level regularities that are realized by mechanisms whose physical substance is typically quite heterogeneous and unimaginably complicated. All of the special sciences—not only sociology and psychology, but also physical sciences such as chemistry and biology—seem to indicate that complex combinations of heterogeneous micro-level components somehow converge on stable macro-level properties.

Let

$$S_1x \rightarrow S_2x \tag{1}$$

be a law of sociology. (1) is intended to be read "all S_1 situations bring about S_2 situations." A classic example is Blau's (1970) statement of Durkheim's ([1893] 1984) law about social differentiation: as the size of a collective increases, the degree of differentiation within the collective will increase. Even some methodological individualists such as Popper accept the existence of social laws; Popper (1957) provided several examples of sociological laws, such as "you cannot have full employment without inflation" and "you cannot introduce a political reform without strengthening the opposing forces, to a degree roughly in ratio to the scope of the reform" (p. 62). A necessary and sufficient condition of the reduction of Equation 1 to a law about individuals is that the formulae (2) and (3) be laws, and a necessary and sufficient condition for methodological individualism to obtain is that all of sociology's laws be so reducible:

$$S_1x \leftrightarrow I_1x \tag{2a}$$
$$S_2x \leftrightarrow I_2x \tag{2b}$$
$$I_1x \rightarrow I_2x. \tag{3}$$

I_1 and I_2 are descriptions of groups in terms of the properties of the component individuals and their relations, and (3) is a law relating these collections of properties and relations. Formulae like (2) are called *bridge laws*. Bridge laws contain properties of both the reduced and the reducing science. Note that the double arrow in the bridge laws (2) are not causal arrows because causation is asymmetric whereas bridge laws must be symmetric. The arrows in bridge laws are identity relations. If type identity of the social and the individual holds, then the relations in (2) are lawful relations of property identity.

Every science has a taxonomy of events in its universe of discourse and a descriptive vocabulary of theoretical and observation properties such that events fall under the laws of the science by virtue of satisfying those properties. Obviously, not every true description of an event is a description in a science's vocabulary of properties. For example, there may be many sociological events that have the property "a church founded in the month of August hires a janitor." However, there is no science that contains "a church founded in the month of August hires a janitor" as part of its descriptive vocabulary. Likewise, there is no sociological law that applies to events in virtue of their being instantiations of the property "a church founded in the month of August hires a janitor." In Fodor's terms, this property is not a *natural kind*, and predicates that express that property are not natural kind predicates. A natural kind is something that exists in the world, and membership in a natural kind is determined by the causal structure of the world (Boyd 1991; Hacking 1991). In the following, I will use the term "natural kind" to refer to both natural kinds and social kinds, to make clear the analogies with the original argument in the philosophy of mind.

If methodological individualism is true, then every sociological natural kind is, or is coextensive with, an individual natural kind (as claimed by Macdonald and Pettit 1981). Every sociological natural kind is an individual natural kind if bridge laws express property identities, and every sociological natural kind is coextensive with an individual natural kind if bridge laws express event identities. This follows from our above characterization of methodological individualism: that every property that appears in a law of sociology must appear as one of the reduced properties in some bridge law. If a law about individuals is related to a sociological law in the way that (3) is related to (1), then every natural kind predicate of sociology is related to a natural kind predicate of individuals in the way that (2) relates S_1 and S_2 to I_1 and I_2.

I will argue that this consequence of methodological individualism cannot be maintained, drawing on Fodor's wild disjunction argument. If the right-hand sides of the bridge laws (2) are wildly disjunctive, then one can accept token identity and supervenience and yet reject methodological individualism.

Sociological natural kind terms such as "church" or "competitive team sport" may involve the disjunction of a large number of otherwise unrelated collections of individual-level properties. "Competitive team sport" is a group-level natural kind term. The regularities observed on the field can be described at a structural level in terms of the positions, patterns, and rules of the game. Token event identity holds; using only individual natural kind terms, the individual-level description of a single token event within, for example, a single token football game might be possible. These properties would include the differing motives for playing; the attitudes about fellow players; the beliefs about the potential outcomes of the game; the unique, potentially idiosyncratic individual calculations of present utility and of future trust and obligations; and each individual's internal representations of the football game and his role within it.

But successful translations of token events into individual terms is not sufficient to ground methodological individualism; it claims not only that a given token event's social description can be reduced but that social event types can be reduced. For example, it claims that one can develop an individual-level description of the natural kind term "competitive team sport" such that all possible tokens of this sociological type can be described in individual terms. A reduction of the group-level natural kind term "competitive team sport" to natural kind terms of individuals would involve the disjunction of all past and potential players' individual properties, in every past and potential competitive team sport, in all of the world's cultures. For these reasons, an individual-level description of the social-level natural kind term "competitive team sport" is likely to be wildly disjunctive.

Likewise, "being a church" could be realized in disjunctive ways in different cultures and social groups. Nonetheless, "being a church" could participate in social laws such as "if a group has the property of being a church, then its degree of solidarity will be higher than groups that do not have this property." This social law is designed to be applicable to all social groups holding the property, regardless of that property's realization in any given society or culture.

If individual-level realizations of sociological properties are wildly disjunctive—and there is much empirical evidence that suggests that they are—then for methodological individualism to be maintained, we have to allow wildly disjunctive right-hand sides of bridge laws:

$$Sx \leftrightarrow I_1x \text{ or } I_2x \text{ or } I_3x \text{ or } \ldots \text{ or } I_nx, \tag{4}$$

where S is a natural kind term of sociology and I_n are natural kind terms of individuals, each corresponding to the properties of all component individuals and their relations for one realization of Sx. In (4), the right-hand side is a disjunction of many natural kind predicates of individuals, but the disjunction is not, itself, a natural kind predicate of individuals.

For cases of reduction in which the bridging relation is like (4), then what corresponds to (3) above—the social law as reduced to individual terms—will not be a law, because the properties appearing in the antecedent and the consequent will not be natural kind predicates. Instead, we will have something like (5):

| Law of sociology: | S_1x | $\rightarrow$ | S_2x | (1) |
| Disjunctive properties: | $I_1x \text{ or } I_2x \text{ or } I_3x \ldots I_nx$ | $\rightarrow$ | $I_1{*}x \text{ or } I_2{*}x \text{ or } I_3{*}x \ldots I_n{*}x$ | (5) |

of individual event types.

Thus, if wild disjunction is empirically correct, then statements such as (5) are the individualist reductions of the laws of sociology:

$$I_1x \text{ or } I_2x \text{ or } I_3x \text{ or } \ldots \text{ or } I_nx \rightarrow I_1{*}x \text{ or } I_2{*}x \text{ or } I_3{*}x \text{ or } \ldots \text{ or } I_n{*}x. \tag{5}$$

In Watkins's (1957) classic phrase, (5) is a "rock bottom" explanation of the social law identified in (1). Methodological individualism can be maintained only by accepting that such laws are the proper business of sociology. Even if we accept that relations such as (5) are the ultimate laws of sociology, we are still left with a rather weak version of methodological individualism; the usual account of methodological individualism holds that natural kind terms of sociology can be nomically translated into natural kind terms of individuals.

Of course, an immortal and all-knowing sociologist might find a combination of properties about individual event types that was, in brute fact, coextensive with the sociological description "a church" or "a competitive team sport." Because we accept ontological individualism—a football game, after all, contains only the people that are playing it—and token identity—each event described by the sociological property "competitive team sport" is identical to an event described by the properties of the constituent individuals—then there must be such a disjunction. But due to wild disjunction, nothing but brute enumeration could convince us of the accuracy of any proposed disjunction.

If methodological individualism is true, then for every sociological natural kind predicate there is a coextensive set of individual natural kind predicates, and the generalization that states this coextension is a law. If wild disjunction holds, then the individual-level disjunction is not a natural kind term, and thus the relations in (5) are not what most scientists mean by laws. If we allow relations such as (5) to be the laws of sociology, there are major epistemological consequences. We no longer know what a law of sociology should look like, and we no longer know what a type or predicate of sociology should look like. This would make it very difficult to do any sociology at all, even sociology that is methodologically individualist.

All methodologically individualist social science theories—agent-based computational modeling, rational choice theory, game theory—are institutionalized gambles that such lawful coextensions can be found. However, there are good grounds for hedging these bets. There are no firm data for any but the grossest and most approximate correspondences between sociological types and individual types. There is an open empirical possibility that what corresponds to the natural kind predicates of sociology may be a heterogeneous and unsystematic disjunction of predicates in individualist language. If so, sociology would not be reducible to individualism in the sense of reduction involved in claims of methodological individualists. If the relation is characterized by wild disjunction, then the attempt to pair sociological structures with individual-level phenomena may be forbiddingly difficult.

Why does macrosociology exist at all? The methodological individualist's answer is entirely epistemological: if only societies were not so complex, if only individuals' motives and mental states were not so hard to determine en masse, if only human communication were not so difficult to understand, then we could study individuals instead of macro phenomena (e.g., Elster 1985, 5–6). Wild disjunction provides an explanation that goes beyond this epistemological claim. Sociology does not exist only because the individual-level decomposition is simply too difficult to fully describe and explain; this would be the case only if the wild disjunction at the lower level had lawful correspondences to the higher-level natural kinds. But if the disjunctive lower-level terms are not lawfully related, then the existence of higher-level science depends not on our epistemological weaknesses but on the way the world is put together: not all natural kind terms of the higher-level science correspond to natural kind terms of the lower-level science (cf. Fodor 1974, 131). Consequently, Fodor described himself as a realist concerning mental properties.

These arguments have been influential and continue to be widely debated in philosophy of mind. Critics of multiple realizability include Sober (1999), who argued for the causal completeness of physics but accepted that there is a place for higher-level explanations, and Millikan (1999), who provided a technical criticism of Fodor's concept of the natural kind. Whether nonreductive materialism warrants mental realism is still unresolved (Heil 1998; Kim 1989, 1997; Lennon and Charles 1992, 14–18). Several critics have noted that multiple realizability and wild disjunction do not entail property dualism and thus do not justify mental realism. Kim (1992), Bealer (1994), and Horgan (1981) argued that just because the lower-level description is wildly disjunctive does not, in itself, explain why the lower-level description cannot be a property; the higher-level property could be identical to the disjunctive property formed by the many realizations at the lower level, and this disjunctive property could be part of a law. Kim argued that such a wildly disjunctive property must be a natural kind, or else we have to deny that higher-level terms and concepts pick out properties and kinds in the world and thus we must reject higher-level realism. Fodor (1997) and Block (1997) more recently responded with defenses of multiple realizability.

The wild disjunction argument has not been applied to sociological theory. Philosophers of social science have occasionally invoked multiple realizability to argue against methodological individualism but without elaborating the implications of wild disjunction (e.g., Currie 1984, 353); as Bhargava (1992, 67) noted, supervenience and multiple realization alone are not sufficient to counter methodological individualism. Ruben (1985, 94–127) rejected the wild disjunction argument against physicalism in the philosophy of mind but then proposed a nonanalogous "alternative realization" argument against individualism that draws on a theory of intentional states. Jackson and Pettit (1992, 103) rejected the multiple realizability claim but without engaging in the above arguments. Kincaid (1997) used multiple realization arguments to argue against methodological individualism; but without the wild disjunction argument, his presentation does not make as strong an argument against individualism. Papineau (1985) denied the applicability of functionalist arguments from philosophy of mind to sociological theory, basing his critique on a notion that multiple realizability arises from selection pressures. But his argument assumed that the only version of multiple realization is a functionalism based on selection pressure arguments (cf. Papineau 1993, 47, n. 9); yet that is not central to the above account. Macdonald and Pettit (1981, 145–47) rejected collectivism by arguing that the different realizations at the individual level are actually instantiations of the same property. They rejected the possibility that there could be a lawful regularity at the social level that would not correspond to a lawful regularity at the individual level; they claimed that any institutional predicates used in the formulation of nomic regularities must be predicates that reduce to individual counterparts. This argument is analogous to Kim's (e.g., 1992) critique of Fodor, in arguing for type identity of social and individual properties.

Conclusion

To summarize, I have defined NRI as an acceptance of token identity and supervenience, combined with the wild disjunction argument that this ontological position does not entail the reductivist program in sociology. Even if token sociological events are identical to token individual events and social properties supervene on individual properties, it does not follow that the natural kind predicates of sociology are coextensive with the natural kind predicates of individualism. Thus, ontological individualism does not guarantee that properties of individuals provide a sufficient vocabulary for sociological theory. In the same way that nonreductive materialism is compatible with the ontological assumptions of materialism—matter is the only substance that exists in the universe—NRI is compatible with the ontological assumptions of individualism—social groups are composed of nothing other than individuals. And like nonreductive materialism, NRI nonetheless argues that sociologists have valid philosophical grounds for developing laws and theories concerning collective phenomena that may not be reducible to laws and theories concerning individuals.

NRI supports collectivism by demonstrating how sociological laws, properties, and types may be irreducible to individual laws, properties, and types. The extent to which wild disjunction holds for any given sociological property is an empirical question that must be resolved through empirical study (cf. Fodor 1974; Kincaid 1997, 13–30). But if it does hold, NRI suggests that collectivism may be a necessary scientific stance because of the structure of the world, not only because of our own epistemological limitations. NRI would then lead to a special type of sociological realism with respect to those properties, a realism that is consistent with ontological individualism.

Fodor and others have used these arguments to argue that mental properties are real, but this remains one of the more controversial elements of the argument. One of the reasons that these arguments are still current in the philosophy of mind is that their resolution is directly relevant to the question of mental causation. The exact nature of one's version of supervenience determines one's attitude toward the possibility of irreducible higher-level causal laws. The import of antirealist criticisms of property dualism is that higher-level properties are causally inert. If so, we still have no account of how mental or social properties could participate in causal laws.

References

Alexander, Jeffrey C., Bernhard Giesen, Richard Münch, and Neil J. Smelser, eds. 1987. *The micro-macro link*. Berkeley: University of California Press.

Archer, Margaret S. 1995. *Realist social theory: The morphogenetic approach*. New York: Cambridge University Press.

Bealer, George. 1994. The rejection of the identity thesis. In *The mind-body problem: A guide to the current debate*, edited by R. Wagner and T. Szubka. Cambridge, UK: Blackwell.

Bhargava, Rajeev. 1992. *Individualism in social science*. New York: Oxford University Press.

Bhaskar, Roy. [1975] 1997. *A realist theory of science*. Reprint, New York: Verso Classics.

———. 1979. *The possibility of naturalism*. Brighton, UK: Harvester.

Blau, Peter M. 1970. A formal theory of differentiation in organizations. *American Sociological Review* 35:201–18.

Blau, Peter M. 1977. A macrosociological theory of social structure. *American Journal of Sociology* 83 (1):26–54.

Block, Ned. 1997. Anti-reductionism slaps back. *Philosophical Perspectives* 11:107–32.

Boyd, Richard. 1991. Realism, anti-foundationalism and the enthusiasm for natural kinds. *Philosophical Studies* 61:127–48.

Coleman, James S. 1990. *Foundations of social theory*. Cambridge, MA: Harvard University Press.

Collins, Randall. 1981. On the microfoundations of macrosociology. *American Journal of Sociology* 86 (5):984–1014.

Currie, Gregory. 1984. Individualism and global supervenience. *British Journal for the Philosophy of Science* 35:345–58.

Davidson, Donald. 1970. Mental events. In *Experience and theory*, edited by L. Foster and J. W. Swanson. Amherst: University of Massachusetts Press.

Durkheim, Emile. [1893] 1984. *The division of labor in society*. Reprint, New York: Free Press. (Originally published as *De la division du travail social: étude sur l'organisation des sociétés supérieures*. Paris: Alcan, 1893.)

Edel, Abraham. 1959. The concept of levels in social theory. In *Symposium on social theory*, edited by L. Gross. Evanston, IL: Row, Peterson and Company.

Elster, Jon. 1985. *Making sense of Marx*. New York: Cambridge University Press.

Fodor, Jerry A. 1974. Special sciences (Or: The disunity of science as a working hypothesis). *Synthese* 28:97–115.

———. 1989. Making mind matter more. *Philosophical Topics* 17 (1):59–79.

———. 1997. Special sciences: Still autonomous after all these years. *Philosophical Perspectives* 11:149–63.

Gellner, Ernest. [1956] 1968. Holism versus individualism. In *Readings in the philosophy of the social sciences*, edited by M. Brodbeck. Reprint, New York: Macmillan Company. (Originally published as Explanations in history. *Proceedings of the Aristotelian Society* 30 (Suppl.):157–76).

Giddens, Anthony. 1984. *The constitution of society: Outline of the theory of structuration*. Berkeley: University of California Press.

Goldstein, L.J. [1958] 1973. Two theses of methodological individualism. In *Modes of individualism and collectivism*, edited by J. O'Neill. Hampshire, UK: Gregg Revivals. (Original work published in *British Journal for the Philosophy of Science* 9.)

Hacking, Ian. 1991. A tradition of natural kinds. *Philosophical Studies* 61:109–26.

Heil, John. 1998. Supervenience deconstructed. *European Journal of Philosophy* 6 (2):146–55.

———. 1999. Multiple realizability. *American Philosophical Quarterly* 36 (3):189–208.

Hempel, Carl G. 1965. *Aspects of scientific explanation and other essays in the philosophy of science*. New York: Free Press.

Homans, George C. 1964. Commentary. *Sociological Inquiry* 34:221–31.

Horgan, Terence. 1981. Token physicalism, supervenience, and the generality of physics. *Synthese* 49:395–413.
———. 1997. Kim on mental causation and causal exclusion. *Philosophical Perspectives* 11:165–84.
Humphreys, Paul. 1997. How properties emerge. *Philosophy of Science* 64:1–17.
Jackson, Frank, and Philip Pettit. 1992. Structural explanation in social theory. In *Reduction, explanation, and realism*, edited by K. Lennon and D. Charles. Oxford, UK: Clarendon.
James, Susan. 1984. *The content of social explanation*. New York: Cambridge University Press.
Keat, Russell, and John Urry. 1975. *Social theory as science*. London: Routledge.
Kim, Jaegwon. 1975. Events as property exemplifications. In *Action theory*, edited by M. Brand and D. Walton. Dordrecht, the Netherlands: D. Reidel.
———. 1984. Epiphenomenal and supervenient causation. *Midwest Studies in Philosophy* 9:257–70.
———. 1989. The myth of nonreductive materialism. *Proceedings and addresses of the American Philosophical Association* 63:31–47.
———. 1992. Multiple realizability and the metaphysics of reduction. *Philosophy and Phenomenological Research* 52:1–26.
———. 1993. The non-reductivist's troubles with mental causation. In *Mental causation*, edited by J. Heil and A. Mele. Oxford, UK: Clarendon.
———. 1997. The mind-body problem: Taking stock after forty years. *Philosophical Perspectives* 11:185–207.
Kincaid, Harold. 1997. *Individualism and the unity of science*. New York: Rowman & Littlefield.
King, Anthony. 1999. The impossibility of naturalism: The antinomies of Bhaskar's realism. *Journal for the Theory of Social Behavior* 29 (3):267–88.
Lennon, Kathleen, and David Charles. 1992. Introduction. In *Reduction, explanation, and realism*, edited by D. Charles and K. Lennon. Oxford, UK: Clarendon.
Lowe, E. J. 1993. The causal autonomy of the mental. *Mind* 102 (408):629–44.
Macdonald, Graham, and Philip Pettit. 1981. *Semantics and social science*. London: Routledge.
Mandelbaum, Maurice. 1955. Societal facts. *British Journal of Sociology* 6 (4): 305–17.
Mayhew, Bruce H. 1980. Structuralism versus individualism, part 1: Shadowboxing in the dark. *Social Forces* 59 (2):335–75.
Mellor, D. H. 1982. The reduction of society. *Philosophy* 57:51–75.
Millikan, Ruth Garrett. 1999. Historical kinds and the "special sciences." *Philosophical Studies* 95 (1/2):45–65.
Papineau, David. 1985. Social facts and psychological facts. In *Popper and the human sciences*, edited by G. Currie and A. Musgrave. Dordrecht, the Netherlands: Martinus Nijhoff.
———. 1993. *Philosophical naturalism*. Oxford, UK: Basil Blackwell.
Pettit, Philip. 1993. *The common mind: An essay on psychology, society, and politics*. Oxford, UK: Oxford University Press.
Popper, Karl R. 1957. *The poverty of historicism*. London: Routledge Kegan Paul.
———. 1962. *Conjectures and refutations*. New York: Basic Books.
Putnam, Hilary. 1967. Psychological predicates. In *Art, mind, and religion: Proceedings of the 1965 Oberlin Colloquium in Philosophy*, edited by W.H. Capitan and D.D. Merrill. Pittsburgh, PA: University of Pittsburgh Press.
Quinton, Anthony. 1975–76. Social objects. *Proceedings of the Aristotelian Society* 76:1–27.
Ritzer, George. 1991. *Metatheorizing in sociology*. Lexington, MA: Lexington Books.
Ruben, David-Hillel. 1985. *The metaphysics of the social world*. Boston: Routledge Kegan Paul.
Sarkar, Sahotra. 1992. Models of reduction and categories of reductionism. *Synthese* 91:167–94.
Sawyer, R. Keith. 2001. Emergence in sociology: Contemporary philosophy of mind and some implications for sociological theory. *American Journal of Sociology* 107:551–85.
Smart, J.J.C. 1959. Sensations and brain processes. *Philosophical Review* 68(2):141–56.
Sober, Elliott. 1999. The multiple realizability argument against reductionism. *Philosophy of Science* 66:542–64.
Wagner, Helmut R. 1964. Displacement of scope: A problem of the relationship between small-scale and large-scale sociological theories. *American Journal of Sociology* 64:571–84.
Watkins, J.W.N. 1957. Historical explanation in the social sciences. *British Journal for the Philosophy of Science* 8:104–17.
Wiley, Norbert. 1988. The micro-macro problem in social theory. *Sociological Theory* 6:254–61.
Wimsatt, William C. 1976. Reductionism, levels of organization, and the mind-body problem. In *Consciousness and the brain*, edited by G. G. Globus, G. Maxwell, and I. Slavodnik. New York: Plenum.
Yablo, Stephen. 1992. Mental causation. *The Philosophical Review* 101 (2):245–79.

PART VI

Norms, conventions, and institutions

INSTITUTIONS ARE A heterogeneous class of entities, ranging from Britons' spontaneous cueing in well-ordered lines to the Sicilian norm of secrecy enforced by the mafia;
from quasi-universal generic arrangements like marriage to highly specific, very complex, and
formally regulated organizations like the European Parliament or the New York Stock
Exchange. It is uncontroversial that studying the nature of these entities is the core business
of the social sciences. And yet, surprisingly, the development of a general theory of institutions
has made little progress until recent times. Partly this was a consequence of disciplinary
specialization: while each branch of the social sciences was busy studying one particular type
of institution (markets for economists, elections for political scientists, food sharing for
anthropologists, etc.), the question of what they all have in common was for a long time
evaded. Each discipline, moreover, explained institutional phenomena using its own concepts
and categories, a lack of coordination that has hindered constructive criticism and the development of a general theoretical framework.

Philosophers have made a decisive contribution to overcome this state of affairs. Not only
have they developed general conceptual tools that can be applied across different disciplinary
domains; they have also highlighted some key empirical issues that call for scientists'
contribution, and have succeeded in recruiting scientists in a new exciting interdisciplinary
research enterprise. As a consequence, contemporary debates in social ontology revolve around
three concepts – *reflexivity*, *performativity*, and *collective intentionality* – that are (in different
ways and to different degrees) shared by most theorists working in this area.

Reflexivity is the thesis that social institutions are constituted by *beliefs about beliefs*. This
idea can be traced back to the classic discussions, by Merton (1957) and others, of self-fulfilling
prophecies and self-defeating predictions in social science. Only recently, however, philosophers
and social scientists have noticed how reflexive beliefs generate not only aberrant phenomena
like the failure of a sound bank, but also robust and virtuous institutions like cueing, exchanging
favours, or getting married. This change of perspective – from the vicious to the beneficial
aspects of mutually sustaining beliefs – owes much on the one hand to technical results in rational
choice theory (e.g. Simon 1957, Schelling 1960) and on the other to the work of philosophers
like David Lewis (1969), Barry Barnes (1983), and Raimo Tuomela (1984, 1995) who have
used the notion of reflexivity to devise general accounts of social ontology.

The first chapter in this section is an excerpt from David Lewis' seminal monograph on social conventions. *Convention* (1969) originated from Lewis' PhD dissertation, written in the 1960s under the supervision of Quine. Lewis was mainly interested in the conventional nature of language, and while shopping for ideas at Harvard happened to attend Thomas Schelling's lectures on game theory. Schelling (1960) had proposed an intriguing solution to one of the most difficult problems of game theory: the multiplicity of equilibria in coordination games. He argued that the selection among these equilibria is often facilitated by apparently irrelevant details that make one of the many solutions of the game *salient*. When this is the case, an equilibrium becomes a "focal point" that attracts players' choices and ensures they are more successful at coordinating than the purely rational calculators of standard game theory.

Developing Schelling's insight, Lewis argued that what makes a coordination solution salient is often just *precedence*, or the history of play. In Britain people drive on the left simply because everybody has done that, up until now; we are writing this chapter in .doc format because this is the format most people use, and so forth. As Schelling put it, "there is [. . .] a strong attraction to the *status quo ante*" (1960: 67–8). A key insight in Lewis' theory is that knowledge of the status quo is public and mutual: I believe that the other drivers drive on the left, they believe that I drive on the left, I believe that they believe that I drive on the left, and so on. In short: because it is *common knowledge* that drivers in Britain drive on the left. Common knowledge, especially in Robert Aumann's later version, has since become a standard technical tool of game theory, but its significance goes well beyond that (see Cubitt and Sugden 2003).

With few exceptions (e.g. Ullmann-Margalit 1977) Lewis' theory had little immediate impact. Lewis went on to make important contributions to other areas of philosophy – especially logic and metaphysics – but did not do any further work in social ontology. By acting as a critical target, however, he fostered the development of an alternative approach – the theory of collective intentionality – that occupies a central place in contemporary social ontology. In the second chapter reprinted in this section, Margaret Gilbert makes a systematic comparison between Lewis' theory and the version of collective intentionality theory she has defended in *On Social Facts* (1989) and several other papers (cf. Gilbert 2000). Gilbert's theory is based on the notion of a *joint commitment* to follow a course of action. It differs from Lewis' account by postulating that individuals adopt a collective perspective – they reason in "we-mode," to use an expression later introduced by Tuomela. The notion of collective intentionality or we-mode reasoning is primitive according to Gilbert and irreducible to the I-mode (individualistic) beliefs and desires of classic rational choice theory.

During the last two decades the notion of collective intentionality has quickly risen to prominence in the philosophy of social science. Philosophers have proposed various analyses of this concept, focusing in particular on the issue of its reducibility to individual intentionality (Tuomela and Miller 1988, Searle 1990, Bratman 1993, Velleman 1997). Economists have developed formal theories of "team reasoning" that solve some conceptual and empirical puzzles of game theory (Sugden 2000, 2003, Bacharach 2006). And social psychologists – in many ways the pioneers in the scientific study of collective intentions – have developed independently a conceptual framework (the theory of "group identity") that accounts for many causal effects observed in the laboratory and in the field (Tajfel 1982, Tajfel and Turner 1986).

We include in the anthology an chapter written by the philosopher who more than anyone else has contributed to disseminate the notion of collective intentionality outside the narrow boundaries of the philosophy of social science. John Searle (1995) extended his earlier work in the philosophy of language – especially John Austin's (1962) concept of *performativity* –

to account for the complexities of social reality in a remarkably simple and elegant fashion. All social facts according to Searle involve a state of collective intentionality, where the members of a group perform an activity in the "we-mode." Beliefs about social entities are also performative, because the existence of social facts depends on a human activity of maintenance of such facts. Having dinner and going to the cinema together, for instance, does not constitute a "date" unless the individuals involved believe they are dating. Dating requires constant "support", so to speak, by an appropriate set of collective intentions.

Institutional facts are a special kind of social facts, endowed with specific functions attributed by the relevant community. (Thus, for example, a piece of paper, metal, or a shell can all be attributed the functional properties of a medium of exchange, i.e. of being money.) For some entity X to count as an institutional thing of type Y it usually has to satisfy some conditions – for example, the condition of being issued by the European Central Bank. Searle's (1995) catchy formula "X counts as Y in C" summarizes this process of creation of the social world from pre-institutional reality plus collective acceptance. (Searle has later amended the formula, but we omit these subtleties here and refer readers to the reprinted chapter.) The process of creation can be reiterated to create several layers of institutional reality: a piece of paper counts as a fine if it has been issued by an officer, who has been appointed by the local police authority, which has been created by the central government, which has been elected by voters, and so on and so forth.

The notions of reflexivity, performativity, and collective intentionality have become central in contemporary social ontology. Much of the debate concerns how these notions should be defined, their mutual relations, and their irreducibility to more fundamental building blocks. There is currently a lot of interest, in particular, in the psychological, biological, and neuro-physiological foundations of philosophers' constructs. Prominent cognitive scientists like Michael Tomasello are trying to outline the evolutionary and ontogenetic pathways of the human capacity to form collective intentions (Tomasello 1999, 2008). Others hope that neuroscience will soon identify the neural basis of "social thinking" (e.g. Becchio and Bertone 2004, Pacherie and Dokic 2006). While a lot of progress has been made in social neuroscience (Adolphs 2003; see also the references in Part III), however it is fair to say that we are still far from identifying the distinctive basis of we-mode vs. I-mode intentionality.

Collective intentionality theory has its critics too. Cristina Bicchieri has constructed a theory of social norms in the tradition of David Lewis, relying on mutual beliefs but sticking firmly to the individualistic perspective of classic game theory. Recall that according to Gilbert (1989) conventions are "quasi-agreements," commitments to follow a course of action that cannot be breached unilaterally by one of the parties involved. Conventions therefore carry an intrinsic "ought," and their violation tends to elicit reproaches and even retaliation from the other members of the community. The rational choice approach instead invites the drawing of a sharp distinction between conventions and norms, where the former are sustained primarily by self-interest, and only the latter are accompanied by an intrinsic "ought." To capture this latter element, Bicchieri postulates a disposition to sanction deviation from norms. Instead of explaining this disposition in a contractarian way, she suggests that sanctions are elicited by frustrated expectations.

In the spirit of Lewis, mutual beliefs and individualistic preferences make most of the work in Bicchieri's theory. Norms are modelled as behavioural rules (or strategies, in game-theoretic terms) that people prefer to follow (a) if they are expected to, and (b) if others follow them too. Bicchieri claims that her account is able to explain all the existing data, but also to predict behaviour that is inconsistent with alternative accounts. There is extensive empirical evidence, in particular, that norm-compliance is conditional on expectations, and social psychologists have developed a number of ingenious ways of manipulating beliefs so as to enhance or reduce norm compliance (cf. Cialdini et al. 1991). Many of these manipulations exploit subtle contextual cues that affect behaviour subliminally and can potentially be used for low-cost policy-making. While the debate is still open and further research is being done, this is clearly an area where the collaboration between philosophy, social science, and cognitive psychology may generate not only theoretical insights but also valuable techniques of social intervention.

Further reading

Lewis' work on conventions has generated an important technical literature at the border between philosophy and game theory, devoted to the definition and refinement of mutual expectations equilibria – see e.g. Bicchieri (1993), Vanderschraaf (1995). Sugden (1998) has argued forcefully that the key to understanding conventions lies in the development of an empirical theory of inductive learning. Although the literature on collective intentionality has become too big to be reviewed here, useful surveys and comparisons of different positions can be found in Tollefsen (2004), Hindriks (2003), Bardsley (2007), Gold and Sugden (2007), and Pettit and Schweikard (2006). Thomasson (2003) has argued that collective intentionality theory has important implications for realism and fallibilism in the social sciences, an issue discussed also by Ruben (1989), Mäki (2008) and Guala (2010). The debate on reflexivity and performativity overlaps partly with another important topic in the philosophy of language and philosophy of social science – the problem of rule-following (or meaning finitism) introduced by Wittgenstein (1953) and later reformulated by Kripke (1982). Although we have not included any specific chapter in the anthology, the interested reader is referred to Pettit (1990b), Bloor (1997), and Kusch (2006). A theory of norms similar to Bicchieri's can be found in Pettit (1990a), while recent empirical work on norms as systems of expectations includes Bicchieri and Xiao (2009), and Dana et al. (2007).

References

Adolphs, Ralph. (2003) "Cognitive Neuroscience of Human Social Behaviour," *Nature Reviews Neuroscience* 4: 165–78.

Austin, J.L. (1962) *How to Do Things with Words.* Oxford: Clarendon Press.

Bacharach, M. (2006) *Beyond Individual Choice: Teams and Frames in Game Theory.* Princeton, NJ: Princeton University Press.

Bardsley, N. (2007) "On Collective Intentions: Collective Action in Economics and Philosophy," *Synthese* 157: 141–59.

Barnes, S.B. (1983) "Social Life as Bootstrapped Induction," *Sociology* 17: 524–45.

Bloor, D. (1997) *Wittgenstein, Rules and Institutions.* London: Routledge.

Becchio, C. and Bertone, C. (2004). "Wittgenstein Running: Neural Mechanisms of Collective Intentionality and We-Mode," *Consciousness and Cognition* 13: 123–33.

Bicchieri, C. (1993) *Rationality and Coordination.* Cambridge: Cambridge University Press.

Bicchieri, C. (2006) *The Grammar of Society.* New York: Cambridge University Press.

Bicchieri, C. and Xiao, E. (2009) "Do the Right Thing: But Only if Others Do So," *Journal of Behavioral Decision Making* 22: 191–208.

Bratman, M. (1993) "Shared Intention," *Ethics* 104: 97–113.

Cialdini, R., Kallgren, C., and Reno R. (1991) "A Focus Theory of Normative Conduct," in *Advances in Experimental Social Psychology, Vol. 24.* Academic Press.

Cubitt, R. and Sugden, R. (2003) "Common Knowledge, Salience and Convention: A Reconstruction of David Lewis's Game Theory," *Economics and Philosophy* 19: 175–210.

Dana, J., Weber, R., and Kuang, J. (2007) "Exploiting the Moral Whiggle Room: Experiments Demonstrating an Illusory Preference for Fairness," *Economic Theory* 33: 67–80.

Gilbert, M. (1989) *On Social Facts*. Princeton, NJ: Princeton University Press.

Gilbert, M. (2000) *Sociality and Responsibility*. Lanham, MD: Rowman & Littlefield.

Gold, N. and Sugden, R. (2007) "Collective Intentions and Team Agency," *Journal of Philosophy* 104: 109–37.

Guala, F. (2010) "Infallibilism and Human Kinds," *Philosophy of the Social Sciences*, 40:244–64.

Hindriks, F.A. (2003) "Social Groups, Collective Intentionality, and Anti-Hegelian Skepticism," in P. Ylikoski and K. Miller (eds.) *Realism in Action*. Dordrecht: Kluwer.

Kripke, S. (1982) *Wittgenstein on Rules and Private Language*. Oxford: Blackwell.

Kusch, M. (2006) *A Sceptical Guide to Meaning and Rules*. Acumen.

Lewis, D.K. (1969) *Convention: A Philosophical Study*. Cambridge, MA: Harvard University Press.

Mäki, U. (2008) "Putnam's Realisms: A View from the Social Sciences," in *Approaching Truth: Essays in Honour of Ikka Niiniluoto*, edited by S. Pihlström, P. Raatikainen, and M. Sintonen. London: College Publications.

Merton, R.K. (1957) "The Self-fulfilling Prophecy," in *Social Theory and Social Structure*. New York: Free Press.

Pacherie, E. and Dokic, J. (2006) "From Mirror Neurons to Joint Actions," *Cognitive Systems Research* 7: 101–12.

Pettit, P. (1990a) "*Virtus Normativa*: Rational Choice Perspectives," *Ethics* 100: 725–55.

Pettit, P. (1990b) "The Reality of Rule-Following," *Mind* 99: 1–21.

Pettit, P. and Schweikard, D. (2006) "Joint Actions and Group Agents," *Philosophy of the Social Sciences* 36: 18–39.

Ruben, D. (1989) "Realism in the Social Sciences," in *Dismantling Truth*, edited by H. Lawson and L. Appignanesi. London: Weidenfeld & Nicolson, pp. 58–75.

Schelling, T. (1960) *The Strategy of Conflict*. Cambridge, MA: Harvard University Press.

Searle, J.R. (1990) "Collective Intentions and Actions," in Cohen, P.R., Morgan, J., and Pollack, M.E. (eds.) *Intentions in Communication*. Cambridge, MA: MIT Press.

Searle, J.R. (1995) *The Construction of Social Reality*. London: Penguin.

Simon, H. (1957) "Bandwagon and Underdog Effects of Election Predictions," in *Models of Man*. New York: Wiley.

Sugden, R. (1998) "The Role of Inductive Reasoning in the Evolution of Conventions," *Law and Philosophy* 17: 377–410.

Sugden, R. (2000) "Team Preferences," *Economics and Philosophy* 16: 174–204.

Sugden, R. (2003) "The Logic of Team Reasoning," *Philosophical Explorations* 6: 165–81.

Tajfel, H. (1982) *Social Identity and Intergroup Relations*. Cambridge: Cambridge University Press.

Tajfel, H. and Turner, J.C. (1986) "The Social Identity Theory of Inter-Group Behavior," in S. Worchel and L. W. Austin (eds.), *Psychology of Intergroup Relations*. Nelson-Hall.

Thomasson, A. (2003) "Realism and Human Kinds," *Philosophy and Phenomenological Research* 68: 580–609.

Tollefsen, D. (2004) "Collective Intentionality," *The Internet Encyclopedia of Philosophy*, www.iep.utm.edu/c/coll-int.htm.

Tomasello, M. (1999) *The Cultural Origins of Human Cognition*. Cambridge, MA: Harvard University Press.

Tomasello, M. (2008) *The Origins of Human Communication*. Cambridge, MA: MIT Press.

Tuomela, R. (1984) *A Theory of Social Action*. Dordrecht: Reidel.

Tuomela, R. (1995) *The Importance of Us*. Stanford: Stanford University Press.

Tuomela, R. and Miller, K. (1988) "We-Intentions," *Philosophical Studies* 53: 367–89.

Ullmann-Margalit, E. (1977) *The Emergence of Norms*. Oxford: Clarendon Press.

Vanderschraaf, P. (1995) "Convention as Correlated Equilibrium," *Erkenntnis* 42: 65–87.

Velleman, J.D. (1997) "How to Share and Intention," *Philosophy and Phenomenological Research* 57: 29–50.

Wittgenstein, L. (1953) *Philosophical Investigations*. Oxford: Blackwell.

Chapter 21

DAVID LEWIS

COORDINATION AND CONVENTION
AND COMMON KNOWLEDGE

1. Sample coordination problems

USE OF LANGUAGE BELONGS to a class of situations with a conspicuous common character: situations I shall call *coordination problems*. I postpone a definition until we have seen a few examples. We begin with situations that might arise between two people—call them "you" and "I."

(1) Suppose you and I both want to meet each other. We will meet if and only if we go to the same place. It matters little to either of us where (within limits) he goes if he meets the other there; and it matters little to either of us where he goes if he fails to meet the other there. We must each choose where to go. The best place for me to go is the place where you will go, so I try to figure out where you will go and to go there myself. You do the same. Each chooses according to his expectation of the other's choice. If either succeeds, so does the other; the outcome is one we both desired.

(2) Suppose you and I are talking on the telephone and we are unexpectedly cut off after three minutes. We both want the connection restored immediately, which it will be if and only if one of us calls back while the other waits. It matters little to either of us whether he is the one to call back or the one to wait. We must each choose whether to call back, each according to his expectation of the other's choice, in order to call back if and only if the other waits.

(3) An example from Hume's *Treatise of Human Nature:* Suppose you and I are rowing a boat together. If we row in rhythm, the boat goes smoothly forward; otherwise the boat goes slowly and erratically, we waste effort, and we risk hitting things. We are always choosing whether to row faster or slower; it matters little to either of us at what rate we row, provided we row in rhythm. So each is constantly adjusting his rate to match the rate he expects the other to maintain.

Now we turn to situations among more than two people.

(4) Suppose several of us are driving on the same winding two-lane roads. It matters little to anyone whether he drives in the left or the right lane, provided the others do likewise. But if some drive in the left lane and some in the right, everyone is in danger of collision. So each must choose whether to drive in the left lane or in the right, according to his expectations about the others: to drive in the left lane if most or all of the others do, to drive in the right lane if most or all of the others do (and to drive where he pleases if the others are more or less equally divided).

(5) Suppose we are campers who have gone looking for firewood. It matters little to anyone in which direction he goes, but if any two go in the same direction they are likely to cover the same ground so that the one who gets there later finds no wood. Each must choose a direction to go according to his expectations about the others: one different from anyone else's.

(6) Suppose several of us have been invited to a party. It matters little to anyone how he dresses. But he would be embarrassed if the others dressed alike and he dressed differently, since he knows that some discreditable explanation for that difference can be produced by whoever is so inclined. So each must dress according to his expectations about the way the others will dress: in a tuxedo if the others will wear tuxedos, in a clown suit if the others will wear clown suits (and in what he pleases if the others will dress in diverse ways).

(7) Suppose we are contented oligopolists. As the price of our raw material varies, we must each set new prices. It is to no one's advantage to set his prices higher than the others set theirs, since if he does he tends to lose his share of the market. Nor is it to anyone's advantage to set his prices lower than the others set theirs, since if he does he menaces his competitors and incurs their retaliation. So each must set his prices within the range of prices he expects the others to set.

(8) An example from Rousseau's *Discours sur l'inégalité:* Suppose we are in a wilderness without food. Separately we can catch rabbits and eat badly. Together we can catch stags and eat well. But if even one of us deserts the stag hunt to catch a rabbit, the stag will get away; so the other stag hunters will not eat unless they desert too. Each must choose whether to stay with the stag hunt or desert according to his expectations about the others, staying if and only if no one else will desert.

(9) Suppose we take it to be in our common interest that some scarce good, say grazing land, should be divided up somehow so that each of us can count on having the exclusive use of one portion. (Suppose nobody ever thinks it would be in his interest to help himself to someone else's portion. The struggle, the harm to his neighbor, the bad example, the general loss of confidence, invariably seem to outweigh any gain.) It matters little to anyone who uses which portion, so long as people never try to use the same portion and no portion ever goes to waste. Each must choose which portion to use according to his expectations about the portions others will use and the portion they will leave for him.

(10) Suppose we are tradesmen. It matters little to any of us what commodities he takes in exchange for goods (other than commodities he himself can use). But if he takes what others refuse he is stuck with something useless, and if he refuses what others take he needlessly inconveniences his customers and himself. Each must choose what he will take according to his expectations about what he can spend—that is, about what the others will take: gold and silver if he can spend gold and silver, U.S. notes if he can spend U.S. notes, Canadian pennies if he can spend Canadian pennies, wampum if he can spend wampum, goats if he can spend goats, whatever may come along if he can spend whatever may come along, nothing if he can spend nothing.

(11) Suppose that with practice we could adopt any language in some wide range. It matters comparatively little to anyone (in the long run) what language he adopts, so long as he and those around him adopt the same language and can communicate easily. Each must choose what language to adopt according to his expectations about his neighbors' language: English among English speakers, Welsh among Welsh speakers, Esperanto among Esperanto speakers, and so on.

2. Analysis of coordination problems

With these examples, let us see how to describe the common character of coordination problems.

Two or more agents must each choose one of several alternative actions. Often all the agents have the same set of alternative actions, but that is not necessary. The outcomes the agents want to produce or prevent are determined jointly by the actions of all the agents. So the outcome of any action an agent might choose depends on the actions of the other agents. That is why—as we have seen in every example—each must choose what to do according to his expectations about what the others will do.

Some combinations of the agents' chosen actions are *equilibria*: combinations in which each agent has done as well as he can given the actions of the other agents. In an equilibrium combination, no one agent could have produced an outcome more to his liking by acting differently, unless some of the others' actions also had been different. No one regrets his choice after he learns how the others chose. No one has lost through lack of foreknowledge.

This is not to say that an equilibrium combination must produce an outcome that is best for even one of the agents (though if there is a combination that is best for everyone, that combination must be an equilibrium). In an equilibrium, it is entirely possible that some or all of the agents would have been better off if some or all had acted differently. What is not possible is that any one of the agents would have been better off if he alone had acted differently and all the rest had acted just as they did.

We can illustrate equilibria by drawing *payoff matrices* for coordination problems between two agents. Call the agents *Row-chooser* and *Column-chooser*. We represent Row-chooser's alternative actions by labeled rows of the matrix, and Column-chooser's by labeled columns. The squares then represent combinations of the agents' actions and the expected outcomes thereof. Squares are labeled with two *payoffs*, numbers somehow measuring the desirability of the expected outcome for Row-chooser and Column-chooser.[1] Row chooser's payoff is at the lower left, Column-chooser's at the upper right.

Thus the matrix of Figure 21.1 might represent a simple version of example (1), where *R1*, *R2*, and *R3* are Row-chooser's actions of going to places *P1*, *P2*, and *P3* respectively, and *C1*, *C2*, and *C3* are Column-chooser's actions of going to places *P1*, *P2*, and *P3* respectively. The equilibria are the three combinations in which Row-chooser and Column-chooser go to the same place and meet there: *R1*, *C1*, *R2*, *C2*, and *R3*, *C3*. For instance, *R2*, *C2* is an equilibrium by definition because Row-chooser prefers it to *R1*, *C2* or *R3*, *C2*, and Column-chooser prefers it to *R2*, *C1* or *R2*, *C3*. Both are indifferent between the three equilibria.

But suppose we change the example so that Row-chooser and Column-chooser care where they go, though not nearly so much as they care whether they meet. The new payoff matrix might be as shown in Figure 21.2. The equilibria remain the same: *R1*, *C1*, *R2*, *C2*, and *R3*, *C3*. But Row-chooser and Column-chooser are no longer indifferent between the equilibria. *R1*, *C1* is the best possible outcome for both; *R3*, *C3* is the worst equilibrium outcome for both, though both prefer it to the nonequilibrium outcomes. Or if the payoff matrix were as shown in Figure 21.3, then *R1*, *C1* would be Row-chooser's best outcome and Column-chooser's worst equilibrium outcome; *R3*, *C3* would be Column-chooser's best outcome and Row-chooser's worst equilibrium outcome. No outcome would be best for both.

[. . .]

	C1	C2	C3
R1	1 / meet / 1	0 / 0	0 / 0
R2	0 / 0	1 / meet / 1	0 / 0
R3	0 / 0	0 / 0	1 / meet / 1

Figure 21.1

	C1	C2	C3
R1	1.5 / meet / 1.5	.2 / .5	0 / .5
R2	.5 / .2	1.2 / meet / 1.2	0 / .2
R3	.5 / 0	.2 / 0	1 / meet / 1

Figure 21.2

	C1	C2	C3
R1	1 / meet / 1.5	.2 / .5	.5 / .5
R2	0 / .2	1.2 / meet / 1.2	.5 / .2
R3	0 / 0	.2 / 0	1.5 / meet / 1

Figure 21.3

3. Solving coordination problems

Agents confronted by a coordination problem may or may not succeed in each acting so that they reach one of the possible coordination equilibria. They might succeed just by luck, although some of them choose without regard to the others' expected actions (doing so perhaps because they cannot guess what the others will do, perhaps because the chance of coordination seems so small as to be negligible). But they are more likely to succeed—if they do—through the agency of a system of suitably concordant mutual expectations. Thus in example (1) I may go to a certain place because I expect you to go there, while you go there because you expect me to; in example (2) I may call back because I expect you not to, while you do not because you expect me to; in example (4) each of us may drive on the right because he expects the rest to do so; and so on. In general, each may do his part of one of the possible coordination equilibria because he expects the others to do theirs, thereby reaching that equilibrium.

If an agent were completely confident in his expectation that the others would do their parts of a certain proper coordination equilibrium, he would have a decisive reason to do his own part. But if—as in any real case—his confidence is less than complete, he must balance his preference for doing his part if the others do theirs against his preferences for acting otherwise if they do not. He has a decisive reason to do his own part if he is *sufficiently* confident in his expectation that the others will do theirs. The degree of confidence which is sufficient depends on all his payoffs and sometimes on the comparative probabilities he assigns to the different *ways* the others might not all do their parts, in case not all of them do. For instance, in the coordination problem shown in Figure 21.4, Row-chooser should do his part of the coordination equilibrium *R1*, *C1* by choosing *R1* if he has more than .5 confidence that Column-chooser will do his part by choosing *C1*. But in the coordination problems shown in Figure 21.5, Row-chooser should choose R1 only if he has more than .9 confidence that Column-chooser will choose *C1*. If he has, say, .8 confidence that Column-chooser will choose *C1*, he would do better to choose *R2*, sacrificing his chance to achieve coordination at *R1*, *C1* in order to hedge against the possibility that his expectation was wrong. And in the coordination problem shown in Figure 21.6, Row-chooser might be sure that if Column-chooser fails to do his part of *R1*, *C1*, at least he will choose *C2*, not *C3*; if so, Row-chooser should choose *R1* if he has more than .5 confidence that Column-chooser will choose *C1*. Or Row-chooser might think that if Column-chooser fails to choose *R1*, he is just as likely to choose *C3* as to choose *C2*; if so, Row-chooser should choose *R1* only if he has more than .9 confidence that Column-chooser will choose *C1*. Or Row-chooser might be sure that if Column-chooser does not choose *C1*, he will choose *C3* instead; if so, Row-chooser's minimum sufficient degree of confidence is about .95. The strength of concordant expectation needed to produce coordination at a certain equilibrium is a measure of the difficulty of achieving coordination there, since however the concordant expectations are produced, weaker expectations will be produced more easily than stronger ones. (We can imagine cases in which so much mutual confidence is required to achieve coordination at an equilibrium that success is impossible. Imagine that a millionaire offers to distribute his fortune equally among a thousand men if each sends him $10; if even one does not, the millionaire will keep whatever he is sent. I take it that no matter what the thousand do to increase their mutual confidence, it is a practical certainty that the millionaire will not have to pay up. So if I am one of the thousand, I will keep my $10.)

We may achieve coordination by acting on our concordant expectations about each other's actions. And we may acquire those expectations, or correct or corroborate whatever expectations we already have, by putting ourselves in the other fellow's shoes, to the best of our ability. If I know what you believe about the matters of fact that determine the likely effects of your alternative actions, and if I know your preferences among possible outcomes and I know that you possess a modicum of practical rationality, then I can replicate your practical reasoning to figure out what you will probably do, so that I can act appropriately.

In the case of a coordination problem, or any other problem of interdependent decision, one of the matters of fact that goes into determining the likely effects of your alternative actions is my own action. In order to figure out what you will do by replicating your practical reasoning, I need to figure out what *you* expect *me* to do.

I know that, just as I am trying to figure out what you will do by replicating your reasoning, so you may be trying to figure out what I will do by replicating my reasoning. This, like anything else you might do to figure out what I will do, is itself part of your reasoning. So to replicate your reasoning, I may have to replicate your attempt to replicate my reasoning.

This is not the end. I may reasonably expect *you* to realize that, unless I already know what you expect me to do, I may have to try to replicate your attempt to replicate my reasoning.

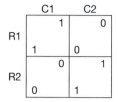

Figure 21.4

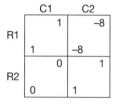 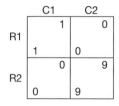 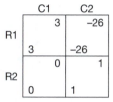

Figure 21.5

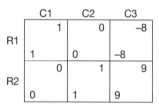

Figure 21.6

So I may expect you to try to replicate my attempt to replicate your attempt to replicate my reasoning. So my own reasoning may have to include an attempt to replicate your attempt to replicate my attempt to replicate your attempt to replicate my reasoning. And so on.

Before things get out of hand, it will prove useful to introduce the concept of *higher-order expectations*, defined by recursion thus:

A first-order expectation about something is an ordinary expectation about it.

An $(n + 1)$th-order expectation about something $(n \geq 1)$ is an ordinary expectation about someone else's nth-order expectation about it.

For instance, if I expect you to expect that it will thunder, then I have a second-order expectation that it will thunder.

Whenever I replicate a piece of your practical reasoning, my second-order expectations about matters of fact, together with my first-order expectations about your preferences and your rationality, justify me in forming a first-order expectation about your action. In the case of problems of interdependent decision—for instance, coordination problems—some of the requisite second-order expectations must be about my own action.

Consider our first sample coordination problem: a situation in which you and I want to meet by going to the same place. Suppose that after deliberation I decide to come to a certain place. The fundamental practical reasoning which leads me to that choice is shown in Figure 21.7. (In all diagrams of this kind, heavy arrows represent implications; light arrows represent causal connections between the mental states or actions of a rational agent.) And if my premise for this reasoning—my expectation that you will go there—was obtained by replicating your

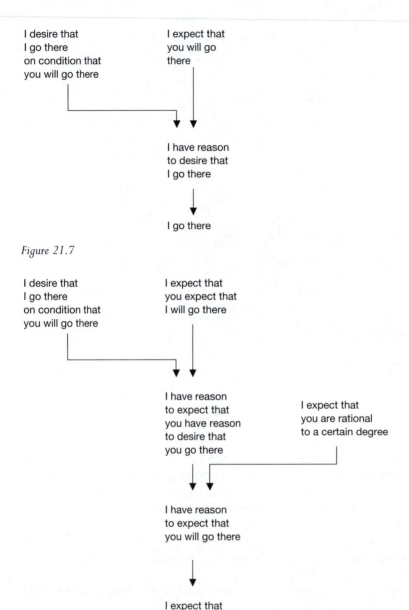

Figure 21.7

Figure 21.8

reasoning, my replication is shown in Figure 21.8. And if my premise for this replication—my expectation that you will expect me to go there—was obtained by replicating your replication of my reasoning, my replication of your replication is shown in Figure 21.9. And so on. The whole of my reasoning (simplified by disregarding the rationality premises) may be represented as in Figure 21.10 for whatever finite number of stages it may take for me to use whatever higher-order expectations may be available to me regarding our actions and our conditional preferences. Replications are nested to some finite depth: my reasoning (outer boundary)

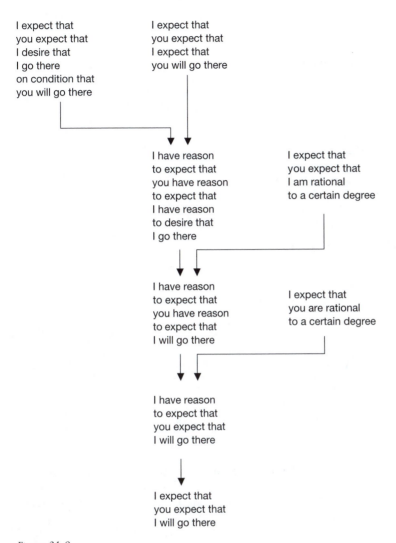

I expect that
you expect that
I desire that
I go there
on condition that
you will go there

I expect that
you expect that
I expect that
you will go there

I have reason
to expect that
you have reason
to expect that
I have reason
to desire that
I go there

I expect that
you expect that
I am rational
to a certain degree

I have reason
to expect that
you have reason
to expect that
I will go there

I expect that
you are rational
to a certain degree

I have reason
to expect that
you expect that
I will go there

I expect that
you expect that
I will go there

Figure 21.9

contains a replication of yours (next boundary), which contains a replication of your replication of mine (next boundary), and so on.

So if I somehow happen to have an *n*th-order expectation about action in this two-person coordination problem, I may work outward through the nested replications to lower- and lower-order expectations about action. Provided I go on long enough, and provided all the needed higher-order expectations about preferences and rationality are available, I eventually come out with a first-order expectation about your action—which is what I need in order to know how I should act.

Clearly a similar process of replication is possible in coordination problems among more than two agents. In general, my higher-order expectations about something are my expectations about x_1's expectations about x_2's expectations . . . about it. (The sequence $x_1, x_2 \ldots$ may repeat, but x_1 cannot be myself and no one can occur twice in immediate succession.) So when *m* agents are involved, I can have as many as $(m - 1)^n$ different *n*th-order expectations about

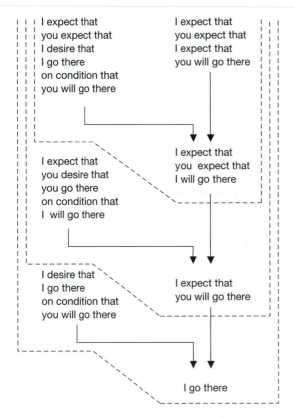

Figure 21.10

anything, corresponding to the $(m - 1)^n$ different admissible sequences of length n. Replication in general is ramified: it is built from stages in which $m - 1$ of my various $(n + 1)$th-order expectations about action, plus ancillary premises, yield one of my nth-order expectations about action. I suppressed the ramification by setting $m = 2$, but the general case is the same in principle.

Note that replication is *not* an interaction back and forth between people. It is a process in which *one* person works out the consequences of his beliefs about the world—a world he believes to include other people who are working out the consequences of their beliefs, including their belief in other people who . . . By our interaction in the world we acquire various high-order expectations that can serve us as premises. In our subsequent reasoning we are windowless monads doing our best to mirror each other, mirror each other mirroring each other, and so on.

Of course I do not imagine that anyone will solve a coordination problem by first acquiring a seventeenth-order expectation from somewhere and then sitting down to do his replications. For one thing, we rarely do have expectations of higher order than, say, fourth. For another thing, any ordinary situation that could justify a high-order expectation would also justify low-order expectations directly, without recourse to nested replications.

All the same, given the needed ancillary premises, an expectation of arbitrarily high order about action does give an agent *one* good reason for a choice of action. The one may, and normally will, be one reason among the many which jointly suffice to justify his choice. Suppose the agent is originally justified somehow in having expectations of several orders about his own and his partners' actions. And suppose the ancillary premises are available. Then each of his original expectations independently gives him a reason to act one way or another. If he is lucky, all these independent reasons will be reasons for the same action.[2] Then that action is strongly, because redundantly, justified; he has more reason to do it than could have been provided by any one of his original expectations by itself.

I said earlier that coordination might be rationally achieved with the aid of concordant mutual expectations about action. We have seen that these may be derived from first- and higher-order expectations about action, preferences, and rationality. So we generalize: coordination may be rationally achieved with the aid of a system of concordant mutual expectations, of first or higher orders, about the agents' actions, preferences, and rationality.

The more orders of expectation about action contribute to an agent's decision, the more independent justifications the agent will have; and insofar as he is aware of those justifications, the more firmly his choice will be determined. Circumstances that will help to solve a coordination problem, therefore, are circumstances in which the agents become justified in forming mutual expectations belonging to a concordant system. And the more orders, the better.

In considering how to solve coordination problems, I have postponed the answer that first comes to mind: by agreement. If the agents can communicate (without excessive cost), they can ensure a common understanding of their problem by discussing it. They can choose a coordination equilibrium—an arbitrary one, or one especially good for some or all of them, or one they can reach without too much mutual confidence. And each can assure the rest that he will do his part of the chosen equilibrium. Coordination by means of an agreement is not, of course, an alternative to coordination by means of concordant mutual expectations. Rather, agreement is one means of producing those expectations. It is an especially effective means, since it produces strong concordant expectations of several orders.

Suppose you and I want to meet tomorrow; today we happen to meet, and we make an appointment. Each thereby gives evidence of his interest in going where the other goes and of his intention to go to a certain place. By observing this evidence, we form concordant first-order expectations about each other's preferences and action. By observing each other observing it, we may also form concordant second-order expectations. By observing each other observing each other observing it, we may even form concordant third-order expectations. And so on; not forever, of course, but limited by the amount of reasoning we do and the amount we ascribe to each other—perhaps one or two steps more. The result is a system of concordant mutual expectations of several orders, conducive to coordination by means of replication.

The agents' agreement might be an exchange of formal or tacit promises. But it need not be. Even a man whose word is his bond can remove the promissory force by explicit disavowal, if not otherwise. An exchange of declarations of present intention will be good enough, even if each explicitly retains his right to change his plans later. No one need bind himself to act against his own interest. Rather, it will be in the interest of each to do just what he has led the others to expect him to do, since that action will be best for him if the others act on their expectations.

If one does consider himself bound by a promise, he has a second, independent incentive. His payoffs are modified, since he has attached the onus of promise breaking to all but one choice. Indeed, he may modify his payoffs so much by promising that the situation is no longer a coordination problem at all. For instance, the agent's promised action might become his dominant choice: he might wish to keep his promise no matter what, coordination or no coordination. If such a strong promise is made publicly, the others will know that they must go along with the one who has promised, for they know what he will do. Such forceful promising is a way of getting rid of coordination problems, not a way of solving them.

Explicit agreement is an especially good and common means to coordination—so much so that we are tempted to speak of coordination otherwise produced as *tacit* agreement. But agreement (literally understood) is not the only source of concordant expectations to help us solve our coordination problems. We do without agreement by choice if we find ourselves already satisfied with the content and strength of our mutual expectations. We do without it by necessity if we have no way to communicate, or if we can communicate only at a cost that outweighs our improved chance of coordination (say, if we are conspirators being shadowed).

Schelling has experimented with coordination problems in which the agents cannot communicate. His subjects know only that they share a common understanding of their problem—for instance, they may get instructions describing their problem and stating that everyone gets the same instructions. It turns out that sophisticated subjects in an experimental setting can often do very well—much better than chance—at solving novel coordination problems without communicating. They try for a coordination equilibrium that is somehow *salient*: one that stands out from the rest by its uniqueness in some conspicuous respect. It does not have to be uniquely *good*; indeed, it could be uniquely bad. It merely has to be unique in some way the subjects will notice, expect each other to notice, and so on. If different coordination equilibria are unique in different conspicuous ways, the subjects will need to be alike in the relative importance they attach to different respects of comparison; but often they are enough alike to solve the problem.

How can we explain coordination by salience? The subjects might all tend to pick the salient as a last resort, when they have no stronger ground for choice. Or they might expect each other to have that tendency, and act accordingly; or they might expect each other to expect each other to have that tendency and act accordingly, and act accordingly; and so on. Or—more likely—there might be a mixture of these. Their first- and higher-order expectations of a tendency to pick the salient as a last resort would be a system of concordant expectations capable of producing coordination at the salient equilibrium.

If their expectations did produce coordination, it would not matter whether anyone really would have picked the salient as a last resort. For each would have had a good reason for his choice, so his choice would not have been a last resort.

Thus even in a novel coordination problem—which is an extreme case—the agents can sometimes obtain the concordant expectations they need without communicating. An easier, and more common, case is that of a *familiar* coordination problem without communication. Here the agents' source of mutual expectations is precedent: acquaintance with past solved instances of their present coordination problem.

4. Convention

Let us start with the simplest case of coordination by precedent and generalize in various ways. In this way we shall meet the phenomenon I call *convention*, the subject of this book.

Suppose we have been given a coordination problem, and we have reached some fairly good coordination equilibrium. Given exactly the same problem again, perhaps each of us will repeat what he did before. If so, we will reach the same solution. If you and I met yesterday—by luck, by agreement, by salience, or however—and today we find we must meet again, we might both go back to yesterday's meeting place, each hoping to find the other there. If we were cut off on the telephone and you happened to call back as I waited, then if we are cut off again in the same call, I will wait again.

We can explain the force of precedent just as we explained the force of salience. Indeed, precedent is merely the source of one important kind of salience: conspicuous uniqueness of an equilibrium because we reached it last time. We may tend to repeat the action that succeeded before if we have no strong reason to do otherwise. Whether or not any of us really has this tendency, we may somewhat expect each other to have it, or expect each other to expect each other to have it, and so on—that is, we may each have first- and higher-order expectations that the others will do their parts of the old coordination equilibrium, unless they have reason to act otherwise. Each one's expectation that the others will do their parts, strengthened perhaps by replication using his higher-order expectations, gives him some reason to do his own part. And if his original expectations of some order or other were strong enough, he will have a decisive reason to do his part. So he will do it.

I have been supposing that we are given a coordination problem, and then given the same problem again. But, of course, we could never be given exactly the same problem twice. There must be this difference at least: the second time, we can draw on our experience with the first. More generally, the two problems will differ in several independent respects. We cannot do exactly what we did before. Nothing we could do this time is exactly like what we did before—like it in every respect—because the situations are not exactly alike.

So suppose not that we are given the original problem again, but rather that we are given a new coordination problem analogous somehow to the original one. Guided by whatever analogy we notice, we tend to follow precedent by trying for a coordination equilibrium in the new problem which uniquely corresponds to the one we reached before.

There might be alternative analogies. If so, there is room for ambiguity about what would be following precedent and doing what we did before. Suppose that yesterday I called you on the telephone and I called back when we were cut off. Today you call me and we are cut off. We have a precedent in which I called back and a precedent—the same one—in which the original caller called back. But this time you are the original caller. No matter what I do this time, I do something analogous to what we did before. Our ambiguous precedent does not help us.

In fact, there are always innumerable alternative analogies. Were it not that we happen uniformly to notice some analogies and ignore others—those we call "natural" or "artificial," respectively—precedents would always be completely ambiguous and worthless. *Every* coordination equilibrium in our new problem (every other combination, too) corresponds uniquely to what we did before under *some* analogy, shares *some* distinctive description with it alone. Fortunately, most of the analogies are artificial. We ignore them; we do not tend to let them guide our choice, nor do we expect each other to have any such tendency, nor do we expect each other to expect each other to, and so on. And fortunately we have learned that all of us will mostly notice the same analogies. That is why precedents can be unambiguous in practice, and often are. If we notice only one of the analogies between our problem and the precedent, or if one of those we notice seems far more conspicuous than the others, or even if several are conspicuous but they all happen to agree in indicating the same choice, then the other analogies do not matter. We are not in trouble unless conflicting analogies force themselves on our attention.

The more respects of similarity between the new problem and the precedent, the more likely it is that different analogies will turn out to agree, the less room there will be for ambiguity, and the easier it will be to follow precedent. A precedent in which I, the original caller, called back is ambiguous given a new problem in which you are the original caller—but not given a new problem in which I am again the original caller. That is why I began by pretending that the new problem was like the precedent in all respects.

Salience in general is uniqueness of a coordination equilibrium in a preeminently conspicuous respect. The salience due to precedent is no exception: it is uniqueness of a coordination equilibrium in virtue of its preeminently conspicuous analogy to what was done successfully before.

So far I have been supposing that the agents who set the precedent are the ones who follow it. This made sure that the agents given the second problem were acquainted with the circumstances and outcome of the first, and expected each other to be, expected each other to expect each other to be, and so on. But it is not an infallible way and not the only way. For instance, if yesterday I told you a story about people who got separated in the subway and happened to meet again at Charles Street, and today we get separated in the same way, we might independently decide to go and wait at Charles Street. It makes no difference whether the story I told you was true, or whether you thought it was, or whether I thought it was, or even whether I claimed it was. A fictive precedent would be as effective as an actual one in suggesting a course of action for us, and therefore as good a source of concordant mutual expectations enabling us to meet. So let us just stipulate that somehow the agents in the new problem are acquainted with the precedent, expect each other to be acquainted with it, and so on.

So far I have been supposing that we have a single precedent to follow. But we might have several. We might all be acquainted with a class of previous coordination problems, naturally analogous to our present problem and to each other, in which analogous coordination equilibria were reached. This is to say that the agents' actions conformed to some noticeable regularity. Since our present problem is suitably analogous to the precedents, we can reach a coordination equilibrium by all conforming to this same regularity. Each of us wants to conform to it if the others do; he has a *conditional preference* for conformity. If we do conform, the explanation has the familiar pattern: we tend to follow precedent, given no particular reason to do anything else; we expect that tendency in each other; we expect each other to expect it; and so on. We have our concordant first-and higher-order expectations, and they enable us to reach a coordination equilibrium.

It does not matter *why* coordination was achieved at analogous equilibria in the previous cases. Even if it had happened by luck, we could still follow the precedent set. One likely course of events would be this: the first case, or the first few, acted as precedent for the next, those for the next, and so on. Similarly, no matter how our precedents came about, by following them this time we add this case to the stock of precedents available henceforth.

Several precedents are better than one, not only because we learn by repetition but also because differences between the precedents help to resolve ambiguity. Even if our present situation bears conflicting natural analogies to any one precedent, maybe only one of these analogies will hold between the precedents; so we will pay attention only to that one. Suppose we know of many cases in which a cut-off telephone call was restored, and in every case it was the original caller who called back. In some cases I was the original caller, in some you were, in some neither of us was. Now we are cut off and I was the original caller. For you to call back would be to do something analogous—under one analogy—to what succeeded in some of the previous cases. But we can ignore that analogy, for under it the precedents disagree.

Once there are many precedents available, without substantial disagreement or ambiguity, it is no longer necessary for all of us to be acquainted with precisely the same ones. It is enough if each of us is acquainted with some agreeing precedents, each expects everyone else to be acquainted with some that agree with his, each expects everyone else to expect everyone else to be acquainted with some precedents that agree with his, etc. It is easy to see how that might happen: if one has often encountered cases in which coordination was achieved in a certain problem by conforming to a certain regularity, and rarely or never encountered cases in which it was not, he is entitled to expect his neighbors to have had much the same experience. If I have driven all around the United States and seen many people driving on the right and never one on the left, I may reasonably infer that almost everyone in the United States drives on the right, and hence that this man driving toward me also has mostly seen people driving on the right—even if he and I have not seen any of the *same* people driving on the right.

Our acquaintance with a precedent need not be very detailed. It is enough to know that one has learned of many cases in which coordination was achieved in a certain problem by conforming to a certain regularity. There is no need to be able to specify the time and place, the agents involved, or any other particulars; no need to be able to recall the cases one by one. I cannot cite precedents one by one in which people drove on the right in the United States; I am not sure I can cite even one case; nonetheless, I know very well that I have often seen cars driven in the United States, and almost always they were on the right. And since I have no reason to think I encountered an abnormal sample, I infer that drivers in the United States do almost always drive on the right; so anyone I meet driving in the United States will believe this just as I do, will expect me to believe it, and so on.

Coordination by precedent, at its simplest, is this: achievement of coordination by means of shared acquaintance with the achievement of coordination in a single past case exactly like our present coordination problem. By removing inessential restrictions, we have come to this: achievement of coordination by means of shared acquaintance with a *regularity* governing the achievement of coordination in a class of past cases which bear some conspicuous analogy to one another and to our present coordination problem. Our acquaintance with this regularity comes from our experience with some of its instances, not necessarily the same ones for everybody.

Given a regularity in past cases, we may reasonably extrapolate it into the (near) future. For we are entitled to expect that when agents acquainted with the past regularity are confronted by an analogous new coordination problem, they will succeed in achieving coordination by following precedent and continuing to conform to the same regularity. We come to expect conforming actions not only in past cases but in future ones as well. We acquire a general belief, unrestricted as to time, that members of a certain population conform to a certain regularity in a certain kind of recurring coordination problem for the sake of coordination.

Each new action in conformity to the regularity adds to our experience of general conformity. Our experience of general conformity in the past leads us, by force of precedent, to expect a like conformity in the future. And our expectation of future conformity is a reason to go on conforming, since to conform if others do is to achieve a coordination equilibrium and to satisfy one's own preferences. And so it goes—we're here because we're here because we're here because we're here. Once the process gets started, we have a metastable self-perpetuating system of preferences, expectations, and actions capable of persisting indefinitely. As long as uniform conformity is a coordination equilibrium, so that each wants to conform conditionally upon conformity by the others, conforming action produces expectation of conforming action and expectation of conforming action produces conforming action.

This is the phenomenon I call convention. Our first, rough, definition is:

A regularity R in the behavior of members of a population P when they are agents in a recurrent situation S is a *convention* if and only if, in any instance of S among members of P,

(1) everyone conforms to R;
(2) everyone expects everyone else to conform to R;
(3) everyone prefers to conform to R on condition that the others do, since S is a coordination problem and uniform conformity to R is a proper coordination equilibrium in S.

Notes

1   My account will demand no great sophistication about these numerical measures of desirability. If a foundation is required, it could be provided by decision theory as developed, for instance, by Richard Jeffrey in *The Logic of Decision* (New York: McGraw-Hill, 1965). I take it that decision theory applies in some approximate way to ordinary rational agents with imperfectly coherent preferences; our payoffs need never be more than rough indications of strength of preference.

2   Michael Scriven, in "An Essential Unpredictability in Human Behavior," *Scientific Psychology: Principles and Approaches*, ed. B. B. Wolman (New York: Basic Books, 1965), has discussed mutual replication of practical reasoning between agents in a game of conflict who want *not* to conform to each other's expectations. There is a cyclic alternation: from my $(n + 4)$th-order expectation that I will go to Minsk to my $(n + 3)$th-order expectation that you will go to Pinsk to my $(n + 2)$th-order expectation that I will go to Pinsk to my $(n + 1)$th-order expectation that you will go to Minsk to my nth-order expectation that I will go to Minsk . . . Scriven notices that we cannot both act on complete and accurate replications of each other's reasoning. He takes this to prove human unpredictability. But perhaps it simply proves that the agents cannot both have enough time to finish their replications, since the time either needs increases with the time the other uses. See David Lewis and Jane Richardson, "Scriven on Human Unpredictability," *Philosophical Studies*, 17 (1966), pp. 69–74.

Chapter 22

MARGARET GILBERT

SOCIAL CONVENTION REVISITED

1 Introduction

WHAT IS A SOCIAL CONVENTION? This question arises in many fields, among them law, economics, and other social sciences. It received a detailed treatment in David Lewis's book *Convention: A Philosophical Study*. Since its publication in 1969, Lewis's account of social convention has been influential. Many theorists have endorsed accounts that retain one or more of its central elements.[1] Most have also retained one particular aspect of Lewis's account: its individualism. An account that is *individualistic* in the sense I have in mind makes reference only to the personal inclinations, expectations, commitments, and so on of individual human beings.[2] A non-individualistic or *holistic* account is not limited in this way.

The account I have developed is holistic in that it crucially appeals to a concept of joint commitment that is not reducible to facts about what the individuals in question are personally committed to. The present discussion compares and contrasts my account of social convention with Lewis's.[3]

It may be observed that Lewis describes himself as seeking an account of "our common, established concept of convention".[4] Neither here nor elsewhere, as far as I know, does he write of "social" convention. Moreover, he aimed to contribute to our understanding of the conventionality of language—of the fact, in one description, that "[w]ords might be used to mean anything".[5] On the face of it, this is not a specifically social matter.[6] Be all that as it may, the sample conventions Lewis presents, and much else besides, suggests that his quarry is indeed a common, established concept of *social* convention.[7] I shall myself often write here of "convention" rather than "social convention", for brevity's sake.

Lewis sees himself as having described "an important phenomenon" whether or not any established concept applies to it.[8] He doubtless thinks that conventions in his sense *are ubiquitous phenomena that play an important role in human life*. He would also presumably say that they are *apt to play such a role, however ubiquitous they actually are*. The latter type of importance is evidently the easiest to gauge prior to empirical investigation.

Not unreasonably, Lewis sees exploration of "our common, established concept" as one way to arrive at the description of an important phenomenon. Perhaps, though, "not all of us do share any one clear general concept of convention".[9] What then? Even if a theorist does not capture a universally shared pretheoretical concept, he (or she) may articulate *a central* one. This too may well pick out something of importance.[10]

In what follows I first offer some starting points about social conventions in what I take to be a—if not the—central everyday sense.[11] They derive from the way people think and talk about convention in the course of their everyday lives. An adequate account of convention in the sense in question will explain these points. I argue that my account of convention does better than Lewis's in relation to this particular explanatory project. I conclude by discussing the relationship of the phenomenon described by my account to that described by Lewis's.

2 Starting points on social convention

2.1 Social conventions are "our" conventions

In everyday speech people say such things as: "The convention in this department is that we dress formally for department meetings"; "Our convention is more complex"; "Jane and I often eat out together. We need a convention as to how we split the tab". Conventions in the sense at issue, then—for short, now, "conventions"—may be said to be "in" groups such as academic departments, which may be said to "have" them, and whose several members may refer to them as "ours".

Conventions may also be ascribed to two or more particular individuals considered together—to "Jane and I", and so on. Such individuals, also, may refer to their conventions as "ours". I refer to the group members or the individuals in these cases as the "parties" to the convention.

2.2 They may be instigated by agreement—or not

Two or more people may adopt a convention by means of an agreement. Thus Julia may say "I suggest we adopt the convention that . . ." and her friends respond "Agreed." At this point, Julia may truly say: "Our convention is that . . ." One of Lewis's main aims in developing his account of convention was to show how people could come to have a convention *without* having adopted it in this way—as they surely can.

2.3 They may or may not offer specific protections

Consider Lewis's drivers who: ". . . are driving on the same winding two-lane roads . . . if some drive in the left lane and some in the right, everyone is in danger of collision".[12] One can imagine one of these drivers truthfully saying, of himself and the others, "Our convention is that we drive on the right" (This is most likely, I think, in the absence of a *law* to the same effect.).[13] The convention he speaks of presumably serves to prevent many crashes, injuries and deaths.

Other conventions do not offer the parties such obvious, specific protections or benefits.[14] Consider a department's convention that people dress formally for department meetings. It may be hard to argue that there needs to be any particular dress code for these meetings, or that anyone thinks this is so. Perhaps one member suggested the convention as a matter of caprice, and others, feeling concessive, agreed to adopt it. Perhaps, prior to that, no one cared how anyone dressed. They simply had no interest in the matter. As I now explain, the violation of even such a convention can have significant consequences for the violator.

2.4 One party's non-conformity offends against the others: the offense criterion

Suppose Molly is a member of the department just imagined. I take it that if Joe, another department member, turns up for a meeting in a tee-shirt and shabby jeans, Molly may well react negatively to his behavior. I have a particular negative reaction in mind, whose specifics will play an important role in the argument of this paper. Molly may well judge that Joe has *offended against* her in her capacity as a party to the convention. As a result, she may give Joe a look of rebuke or speak to him in a rebuking tone.

I take it that whether or not Molly does this, or is justified in doing so, all things considered, she is *in a position* to do so, since, as she judges, Joe has indeed offended against her.[15] If she does rebuke him, she may appropriately cite the fact that the department has this convention as a complete justification for the rebuke—which is not to say that it justifies it all things considered.

Generalizing: if one party fails to conform to a given convention, this offends against the other parties, as such. They are then in a position to rebuke him for this failure, and may appropriately cite the fact that their group has the convention as a complete justification for their rebukes. Conventions, then, are clearly forces to be reckoned with at least because they lay each party open to the rebukes of the other parties if he fails to conform.

If all this is granted, we have a fairly demanding criterion of adequacy for an account of convention: the account must explain how, for any convention, the non-conforming action of one party offends against the other parties, as such, who are for this reason in a position to rebuke him, their having the convention being a complete justification for the rebuke. I shall call this *the offense criterion*.[16]

[. . .]

4 Critique of Lewis

What, then, is the relationship between Lewisian conventions and conventions according to the everyday concept of convention now in question?

4.1 None of Lewis's conditions are necessary

Must any of Lewis's conditions (1) through (3) be fulfilled with respect to a regularity R in the behavior of a population P in order for R to be P's convention? For present purposes, the following example may suffice to cast doubt on the necessity of any one of them.[17]

I imagined earlier that at a meeting of Molly's department someone suggested the department adopt the convention that members dress formally for department meetings, and everyone explicitly concurred with the suggestion. As noted earlier, Molly could at once appropriately say: "our convention is that we dress formally for department meetings". This would seem to be so irrespective of whether anyone has yet conformed to it, and irrespective of whether it is in some sense true that whenever there is a department meeting the department's members conform to it.

Further, it may not be true that whenever a department meeting is upcoming, everyone expects that everyone conform to the convention. Knowing her colleagues well, Molly predicts that few will dress formally at the next meeting. Jack will want to upset people by dressing very informally, contrary to the convention. That's the way he is. Joe has nothing but shabby jeans in his wardrobe and will probably not get round to buying something special for some time, if he ever does. He will apologize, perhaps, but still not conform to the convention. Kate will probably forget to conform to the convention, though she will be disappointed to have done so when she realizes what has happened. Dave may forget—or he may intentionally conform to the convention; it is a toss-up what he will do. He tends to have his mind on other matters. Most others either have no particular expectations about who will conform to the convention and who won't, or their expectations are in line with Molly's, who will herself conform because she wishes to respect the fact that the department has, indeed, adopted this convention.

As to condition (3) [. . .] [i]n my first description of situation in which Molly's department had a convention—a description that did not seem to be self-contradictory—this condition was not satisfied. It seems, then, that it is not a necessary condition on convention.

It is true that the sample convention on which I am focusing has a special origin which is not necessary to conventions in general: its existence depends on its adoption by means of an agreement.[18] Nonetheless, there can certainly be such conventions, and it is possible that none of Lewis's conditions are satisfied with respect to them. It cannot be said that Lewis himself had no interest in this type of case. He was expressly concerned to give an account of convention "in its full generality".[19]

Possibly the convention envisaged here will not last long in the imagined circumstances. Nonetheless it is hard to doubt that it exists, and that it can exist without any of Lewis's conditions (1), (2), and (3), being satisfied.

4.2 Lewis's conditions are not sufficient

Given that none of Lewis's conditions are necessary, are they jointly sufficient? In discussion elsewhere I focused on two reasons for thinking they are not.[20] These reasons constitute, in effect, two further criteria of adequacy for an account of convention. I review them briefly before turning to the offense criterion, on which I focus here.

4.2.1 THE APPROPRIATE-"OUGHT" CRITERION

Intuitively, if something is our convention, then for that reason, all equal, I ought to conform to it, and this will be apparent to me and the other parties.[21] I take it that to say that I "ought" to conform, all equal, is to say that I have reason sufficient to mandate action in the absence of overriding considerations to the contrary. In short, I have *sufficient reason* to conform.[22] What mandates action here is *rationality* in a broad intuitive sense such that it is a matter of responding appropriately to relevant considerations. For short, it is a matter of *reason-responsiveness*.[23]

Now, one can infer that something ought to be done on a variety of bases. When the considerations in question are moral ones, the "ought" is sometimes said to be the "moral ought", and so on. An adequate account of convention will positively and convincingly characterize what we may pretheoretically dub the "ought" of convention. In other terms, it will explain the normativity of convention. Call this the *appropriate-"ought" criterion*.

Lewis says that "according to our common opinions" one who is party to a convention in his sense ought to conform to it, all equal: for it answers both to his own preferences and to those of the others involved.[24] Let us allow that this is so. This may, then, be an "ought" associated with some conventions and appreciated by at least some parties to some such conventions.

It is hard to see, however, how it can be *the* "ought" of convention, given that a convention can exist in the absence of an underlying coordination problem structure of inclinations or Lewisian preferences. This leaves open, of course, the precise nature of the "ought" of convention, something of which I say more in due course.

4.2.2 THE COLLECTIVITY CRITERION

Intuitively, if the members of a population, P, have a convention, they thereby constitute a collectivity or social group in a central, relatively narrow, intuitive sense—the sense represented in many of the lists of social groups offered by social scientists and others, where a typical list might include families, discussion groups, and sports teams. They might of course have constituted a collectivity on other grounds, before developing the convention. If this were not the case, they constitute one now. One feature of the collectivity so constituted—perhaps its most salient feature—is that it has the convention.

One might think this point was already implicit in the starting point listed earlier to the effect that social conventions are "our" conventions.[25] In any case I take the point about collectivity to be fleshing that starting point out in acceptable way.

I take it, then, that an adequate account of convention should be such that its proposed conditions on convention are sufficient for collectivity-hood in the relevant sense. Call this the *collectivity criterion*. I have argued elsewhere that it is not satisfied by Lewis's conditions on convention.[26]

The point that conventions are essentially collectivity-constituting has been questioned by Andrei Marmor.[27] He argues that many conventions "cut across societies and cultures". There surely is a sense in which many conventions do cut across societies and cultures. It is less clear that this militates against the idea in question. Suppose that many societies have the convention that men wear trousers and women wear skirts, where "trousers" and "skirts" are defined by some rough and ready physical parameters. In that sense, then, this convention "cuts across" all the pertinent societies. This supposition allows that there is more than one society, however, and that each society has the convention. There is nothing here, as yet, that refutes the proposed collectivity criterion.

With respect to his own example of a "cross-cutting" convention, Marmor asks: "Does it make sense to suggest that by complying with this convention, all of us become a collectivity?" This question is not clearly to the point. One may understand *compliance with a given convention* as a matter of generally conforming to a particular regularity in Lewis's "pair of properties" sense.[28] In proposing the collectivity criterion I did not mean that those who generally comply with a given convention in this sense thereby constitute a collectivity. Rather, members of a population that *has* a convention thereby constitute a collectivity. That is not, of course, to say what it is for a population to have a convention.

4.2.3 THE OFFENSE CRITERION

There are still other problems with Lewis's account with respect to the sufficiency of its conditions, some of which will be mentioned later.[29] I focus here on the offense criterion.

Suppose that in June's department Lewis's conditions on convention are fulfilled with respect to the regularity of dressing formally for department meetings. Now suppose that June fails to dress formally for today's meeting. Will Bob, another department member, appropriately feel offended against, and does he consequently have the standing to rebuke her? I suggest that he will not, given only the situation as described so far.

He may reasonably be surprised, even disappointed. After all, June acted contrary to his personal preferences. He may have reason to judge her to have acted badly. After all, she acted contrary to most people's preferences. Nonetheless, she has not offended against him in such a way that he now has the standing to rebuke her for doing so.

When, one might ask, has one person offended against another, in this way? I propose that X has in the relevant sense *offended against* Y by failing to *j* on some occasion only if X owed Y his *j*-ing on that occasion, where one who is owed an action is in a position to demand it as in some sense *his*.[30] One who was owed an action that has not been performed on the pertinent occasion is therefore in a position to rebuke the one who failed to perform it, a rebuke being the after-the-fact counterpart to a demand.

There is reason to think that the standing to *demand* an action is quite generally the standing to demand it as (in the pertinent sense) one's own. In that case one way of specifying the kind of *owing* at issue is simply to say that one who is owed an action is in a position to demand it.[31]

One might wonder under what circumstances, precisely, such owing occurs. For now the question to be addressed is whether it occurs, in the right way, when Lewis's conditions on convention are satisfied. I should explain why I have just said "in the right way".

Some philosophers argue or simply judge that if one person is about to violate a moral norm or principle, all others have the standing to demand that he does not violate it; they also have the standing to rebuke him if he violates it.[32] I am doubtful of the truth of this.[33] Even if it were true, however, that would not help Lewis's account of convention.

Suppose for a moment that the point about moral norms is right. Suppose, further, that failing to conform to a Lewisian convention is failing to conform to a moral norm (however that might be argued). Then non-conformity offends against everyone, not just the parties to the convention. Suppose that it does. That does not speak to the intuitive point that drives the offense criterion: non-conformity offends against the parties to the convention *as such*. If you like, they have been offended against in a special way. In other terms, there is a particular, *special right* here, a right of each party to the convention, as such, against every other party as such. I propose that Lewis's conditions on convention do not have the resources to explain this: in the example Bob is not in a position to demand *as his* June's dressing formally.

5 A radically different account of social convention

I turn now to the radically different account of convention first presented in *On Social Facts* and more fully elaborated here. It does well according to the various criteria of adequacy mentioned so far, and more also. It is worth listing several of its significant features at the outset.

First, it is a holist or non-individualist account in the sense introduced earlier. In particular, it crucially appeals to a concept of joint commitment that is not reducible to facts about what the individuals in question are personally committed to. Perhaps I should add, in order to defuse immediate concerns about the philosophical acceptability of this crucial concept, that it does concern what the individuals in question do in relation to one another, and how that affects them. In short, there is nothing "supraindividual" in a metaphysically questionable sense about this idea. Second, the account eschews the austere conceptual palette of game theory.[34] Third, it includes none of Lewis's three central conditions, positing neither conformity, nor expectations, nor a coordination problem structure at the level of personal inclinations or Lewisian preferences. Fourth, it concerns commitments of the kind I have elsewhere labeled "commitments of the will".[35] A familiar example is the commitment made when one makes a personal decision.

I turn now to the details of my account. I originally proposed that a social convention was a *jointly accepted fiat*.[36] I am ready still to phrase the account in terms of joint acceptance, as long as that is understood in terms of joint commitment as follows:

> Members of a population, P, *jointly accept* a given fiat if and only if (by definition) they are jointly committed to accept as a body that fiat.

Some immediate explanation of the technical terms in the *definiens* are in order.

What is joint commitment? I have written extensively on this topic elsewhere, and cannot attempt a full exposition here.[37] I hope that the following points will be helpful. They concern in particular the founding of a basic case of joint commitment.[38]

A joint commitment is to be contrasted with both a single, personal commitment, and a conjunction of personal commitments. A *personal* commitment, such as that created by a personal decision, is created by one person who is in a position unilaterally to rescind or cancel it. In contrast, a *joint* commitment is created by two or more people, neither of whom is in a position unilaterally to rescind or cancel it. One's participation in a given joint commitment commits him to promote its fulfillment in conjunction with the others, but this commitment of his is not personal in the sense just noted.

Two or more people are needed in order to create a conjunction of two personal commitments: each must commit himself. In the case of a joint commitment, all commit all. In order that this happen, each must express to the others, in conditions of common knowledge, his readiness to participate with the others in committing them all—perhaps under some general description such as "person driving on this island". All need to participate, likewise, in rescinding or otherwise concluding the commitment.

The expressions of readiness may be verbal or not, clear as the day or quite subtle. They may take place in a one-shot face-to-face interaction or, rather, over a longish period of time.[39] The latter process is most likely in a large population.[40] As I understand it, an everyday verbal agreement is one way to create a joint commitment. I say more about this later.

Moving on to the content of the joint commitment in question here: what is it to accept some fiat *as a body*? Briefly, the parties must emulate, as far as possible, a single body or person who accepts the fiat in question—call it "F". Conformity to F, except in special exculpating circumstances, is understood to be a major part of what it is incumbent upon each to do in order to conform to this joint commitment.

Having explained how the joint commitment construal of joint acceptance is to be understood, I now offer an account formulated somewhat to echo Lewis's:

A population P has a *convention* of conformity to some regularity in behavior R in situations of type S if and only if the members of P jointly accept, with respect to themselves, the fiat: *R is to be conformed to*.

I add the clause "with respect to themselves" to indicate that the fiat is understood to apply to members of P as such. It is not held to be universally applicable. The expanded version (in terms of joint commitment) runs:

A population P has a convention of conformity to some regularity in behavior R in situations of type S if and only if the members of P are jointly committed to accept as a body, with respect to themselves, the fiat: *R is to be conformed to*.

This representation of the fiat in question is supposed to show that it is *simple* in the following sense: *no particular rationale for it is presupposed.*[41]

According to my understanding of *social rules*, conventions on this account are a type of social rule: all such rules involve the joint acceptance of a fiat of some kind.[42] If the account is right, what distinguishes conventions from other types of rule is the simplicity—in the above sense—of the involved fiat.

Here is a fiat whose form is not simple in the relevant sense: *R is to be conformed to because morality requires this*. One would naturally refer to this as a moral principle, as opposed to a (mere) convention.[43] Here is another example: *R is to be conformed to on account of our generally conforming to it*. Those who jointly accept a fiat of this form may be said to have a "custom", as opposed to a convention. And another case: *R is to be conformed to because it has been conformed to in the past. It has been handed down.* Those who jointly accepted this fiat may be said to have a "tradition" as opposed to a convention.

In the case of a convention, on the account proposed, it is of course possible that R is generally conformed to in P, and it may have been conformed to for a long time. Members of P may be morally required to conform to R, irrespective of the convention, and so on. Whether or not any of these things is true, the parties to a convention, by definition, conceive of it as a simple fiat.

In so conceiving it, there is a sense in which they conceive it as *arbitrary*. Thus this account offers an explanation for the intuitive idea that conventions, as such, are in some sense arbitrary—an explanation different from that suggested by Lewis and, I suggest, a more plausible one. If that is correct then the present account may be considered better to have satisfied a further criterion of adequacy for an account of convention: that it offers a plausible explanation of the intuitive idea noted.[44]

Though simple in the sense just defined, the fiat in convention may *not* be simple in another way: it may involve some kind of qualification. For example, it might run: *R is to be conformed to, unless one lacks the financial means to conform.* Or: *R is to be conformed to—if one wishes to mark the fact that it is Christmas by one's color scheme.*[45]

I now turn to the assessment of my joint acceptance account of convention. Regarding the first three starting points mentioned earlier, I have suggested that the point about conventions being "ours" can be elided with the collectivity criterion. I turn to that shortly. Clearly the point that conventions may or may not be particularly beneficial to the parties is covered by the present account. It neither requires that the convention is beneficial nor precludes this. What of the points about conventions and agreements?

There is reason to see the making an agreement as a matter of jointly committing to uphold as a body a certain decision.[46] Supposing this is so, we can see how a convention on the present account can be initiated by agreement. If you and I jointly commit to upholding as a body the decision to accept (as a body) a certain fiat, we are thereby jointly committed to accepting as a body that fiat. In other words, we have the convention in question at once. This is the intuitive result.

Lewis's account does not do well in this respect. He notes that those who agree to conform to a given regularity may initially so conform out of respect for the agreement, without concern for the actions of the others or their impact on him. In this situation, as Lewis allows, there would not yet be a convention on his account.[47]

On neither of our accounts are agreements *necessary* to convention. As already indicated, in relation to my account, the necessary expressions of readiness for joint commitment need not be such that one would properly describe the parties as making an agreement. Both accounts, then, accord with pretheoretical judgement here.

I turn now to the collectivity criterion. My account does well according to this: it is plausible to argue when the members of a particular population, P, have a convention according to the joint acceptance account, they constitute a collectivity or social group in the relatively narrow, intuitive sense in question. Indeed, a central argument of *On Social Facts* is that *any* joint commitment founds a group in this sense.[48]

This may be a good place to note that my account accords well with something Lewis says prior to the development of his own. He writes: "somehow, gradually and informally, we have come to an understanding that this is what we shall use them [i.e. particular words] to mean".[49] It is then plausible to see him as proposing to offer an account of *how, quite generally, people come to an understanding that, as they would put it "this is what we are to do".*[50] In effect, the joint acceptance account of convention offers an account of what it is for us to come to an understanding about what we are to do, where no particular rationale for doing what we are to do is presupposed.

It is not clear, meanwhile, that any of the individual parties to a Lewisian convention are *in a position* to have an understanding about what *we* are to do. Even if each one individually comes to some understanding, and this is common knowledge, that is not enough, intuitively, for any one of them to say "*we* have come to an understanding that . . ." as opposed to "each one understands that . . .".[51]

Next I address the offense criterion. It can be argued that on the proposed account those with a convention will indeed offend against one another in their capacity as parties to the convention, should they fail to conform to it. The argument I have in mind, outlined below, focuses on the underlying joint commitment.

A background assumption concerns all commitments of the will. I take it that these are such that one is rationally required, all equal, to conform to them. I take this to be a matter of what a commitment of the will is.[52] I take this to be neither a moral nor a prudential matter. Evidently the notion of morality invoked here—as elsewhere in this paper—is such that moral considerations do not comprise all of those that generate requirements of rationality. Such a notion is quite standard, though broader notions, including residual notions, are also current.

Those who create a joint commitment, then, *together impose a constraint* on each of the parties with respect to what it is open to him to do, rationally speaking, in the future. For each is now committed, through the joint commitment, to conform to it. In the specific case of convention, each party is now committed at least to conform to the pertinent jointly accepted fiat.

It is therefore appropriate to say, in the vernacular, that the parties have together and as one *put their dibs* on those actions of each that will result in fulfillment of the joint commitment. Though to speak this way is to speak metaphorically, the metaphor *fits well*. This is another way of saying that there is an intuitive sense in which those who create a joint commitment, as co-creators of that commitment, come jointly to *own* the conforming actions of each of those subject to that commitment.

One can then say that before conforming actions occur they are *owed* to the other parties in the sense of "owe" here in question. Should one party threaten not to conform, any other can demand conformity of him saying, in effect, "I demand that you give me what is mine—in my capacity as one of us!" Again, the others can rebuke him if he fails to conform.

One who fails to conform to a joint commitment, then, offends against the other parties in the requisite sense: he did not give them what was theirs jointly and severally as co-creators of the joint commitment—what, consequently, he owed them. They have the standing to demand his conformity if non-conformity is threatened, and to rebuke him for non-conformity.

Note that this argument appeals essentially only to the normativity of any commitment—including personal decisions—and the jointness of the commitment in question. It does not constitute a moral argument except in some very broad or residual sense. Nor is it a prudential argument that appeals to the self-interest of the parties. I shall now assume that the conclusion of the argument has been made out, and that the offense criterion is satisfied by the joint acceptance account of convention.[53]

What of the appropriate "ought" criterion? On the joint acceptance account: is there an "ought" of convention and what is the argument for it? In short, how—if at all—does the account explain the normativity of conventions?

There is indeed an "ought" of convention on the joint acceptance account. According to this account, the normativity of convention, at its core, is the normativity of joint commitment. At this point a few words on that may suffice.

First, each party to a joint commitment is subject to a commitment of the will, and therefore has sufficient reason to conform to it. All equal, then, he ought to conform. Perhaps, too, his subjection to a commitment of the will "trumps" his contrary personal inclinations and welfare as such, in terms of what he has reason to do. Be that as it may, since the commitment here is joint, we need to consider the normative implications of that fact.

Here, centrally, each party owes every other his conformity to the commitment. Intuitively your owing me an action constitutes sufficient reason for you to perform the action. That does not mean that you must perform it whatever else is true. All else being equal, however, you ought to perform it. Thus there is an "ought" of owing, as there is an "ought" of commitments of the will generally. The former goes beyond the latter in its grounds. It too, however, is not the "ought" of morality or of prudence, for neither moral nor prudential considerations are involved either in arguing that you owe me the action, or in the derivation of the "ought".[54]

Intuitively, again, your owing me an action "trumps" your contrary inclinations, as such, in terms of what rationality requires you to do. If you owe me this action, how can you plausibly argue that your personal inclinations or, indeed, your personal benefit, as such, permit you not to perform it? As noted above personal commitments may also trump the agent's contrary inclinations and welfare as such. This will then be for a different reason though these reasons will have some connection with each other. And it will be of less moment since the personal commitment can be rescinded unilaterally. Be all this as it may, there is a consideration over and above one's being committed that can be brought into play in the case of joint commitment—one owes the action in question to another. And this is something that cannot be changed by a change of one's own mind.

Of course your owing me an action does more than give you sufficient reason to perform that action, where your inclinations and welfare as such take second place in terms of what rationality requires. It also gives me the standing to demand the action and to rebuke you if it is not performed. And this is something both of us have sufficient reason to acknowledge.

Not only do I have the standing to demand the action as mine, but I surely have some justification for doing so. After all, you owe me that action. This, too, you have sufficient reason to acknowledge. I may of course forebear from making the demand, and be justified in doing so all things considered.

It may be that if you owe me an action, then you ought morally to perform that action, all equal. In other words, you may be not only rationally but also morally required, all equal, to perform those actions that you owe. Be that as it may, there is on the joint commitment account a non-moral, non-prudential "ought" of convention. That there is such an "ought" is all to the good for convention, since the moral perspicacity of its followers may fluctuate, as may their personal inclinations and rankings of the outcomes.[55] This way, convention has a separate, and relatively stable normative leg to stand on.[56]

Given what has been said about the normativity of convention according to the present account, one can see how such conventions are apt to prompt the parties to conform to them. Assuming that they are reason-responsive, they will so conform in the absence of countervailing considerations that override those the convention provides. Given common knowledge among the parties of their reason-responsiveness, they will expect each other to conform to the convention absent countervailing considerations that override it.

I take it that sometimes moral considerations will override the convention from the point of view of what rationality requires. And if one decides a particular convention is itself immoral— a convention that excludes certain classes of persons from important opportunities, for instance—one may well judge that one ought not to conform to it, all equal. Widespread willful non-conformity in such circumstances—and a general abstention from responsive rebukes—may serve to terminate the convention as the parties gradually manifest their readiness to do so.

I conclude that the joint acceptance account of convention does well with respect to all of the intuitive tests I have proposed in relation to social convention according to a particular central everyday concept. Clearly it fares far better than Lewis's account in that regard. In the next section I discuss further the relationship between these accounts.

6 The two accounts related

Lewis's is an individualistic account. The joint acceptance account is holistic as a result of its appeal to joint commitment. Though this may seem to be a cost to some, it may be necessary if the pertinent everyday concept is to be properly articulated. It may also be necessary to capture what is a consequential and ubiquitous social phenomenon, whatever its name.

Some may wonder about the possibility of joint commitment. I see no reason to deny that people can jointly commit one another by virtue of their readiness to do so, expressed in conditions of common knowledge. In order to do this they need the concept of joint commitment. That does not mean that they need to have a word for it. Nor need it be easy to extract it from the way in which they explicitly think, talk, and act. Nor need it be easy to explain. It may still inform their thoughts, talk, actions, and interactions. Indeed, as I have argued elsewhere, it is plausible to see it as a fundamental everyday concept, embedded in many of the central concepts with which human beings approach one another.[57]

I propose, then, that with respect to the possibility of their instantiation in the world the concepts described by Lewis's and by my proposed accounts are on a par. In other terms, both are realistic and equally so.

According to the version of Lewis's account I presented earlier, all of the parties to a convention conform to it, and everyone expects almost everyone to conform. Call these the *conformity* and *expectation* conditions. The joint acceptance account incorporates neither of these conditions. Nonetheless, its relationship to them is close. As I have just argued, on my account, reason-responsive parties to a convention will conform to it, all equal. If the reason-responsiveness of the parties is common knowledge, they will also expect each other to conform, all equal.

Further, reason-responsive parties are likely to find conventions on the present account extremely useful if and when their inclinations constitute, in effect, a coordination problem. For suppose that one way or another they jointly commit to accept as a body a fiat that dictates actions for each such that each is inclined to act accordingly provided the others do. This will resolve the coordination problem, because a standing joint commitment "trumps" inclinations with respect to what one is rationally required to do. It will therefore set the course of the parties to the convention.[58]

7 Summary and conclusion

I have focused here on two accounts of social convention, David Lewis's, as set out in 1969 in his influential book *Convention*, and my joint acceptance account, further elaborated since its first presentation. Mine is neither a minor nor a major variant of his. One radical difference between our accounts is the individualism of his account versus the holism of mine. In the main body of the paper I have argued that my account answers better to what is at least *a* central everyday concept of social convention, emphasizing a particular criterion of adequacy— the offense criterion.

Social scientists do well to arrive at an articulated understanding of central everyday concepts such as that, or those, corresponding to everyday talk of "convention". One reason is the relevance of such concepts to *Verstehen* in something like the sociologist Max Weber's sense: social scientists do well to understand the terms in which people understand their own lives— the terms in which they act. If my account does capture a central everyday concept, therefore, it is worth the social scientist's attention. The same goes, of course, for Lewis's account. These accounts clearly latch on to different concepts. Though I have my doubts about Lewis's in this respect, both could in principle be central everyday ones.

An account of convention need not be judged in terms of its representation of a particular everyday concept, however central. It may usefully latch on to an important phenomenon, actual or possible, whether or not some everyday concept does so as well. Looked at in that way, also, the two very different accounts discussed here could both be successful. In that case neither should be ignored by those wishing accurately to describe the human condition.

Notes

1 See, e.g., Schiffer (1972), Burge (1975), Miller (1992), Marmor (1996), Millikan (1998). Lewis tells us that the game-theoretical side of his own account was inspired by Schelling (1960). Indeed, Schelling came close to a Lewisian account of social convention, associating "institutions and traditions" with "coordination games" (1960, p. 91).

2 In Gilbert (1989a) I used the technical label "singularist" instead of "individualistic" as I am construing that here.

3 I have previously published several discussions of Lewis's work, including criticisms of several of his game-theoretical points. See, e.g., Gilbert (1974, 1981, 1983a, b, 1984, 1989a: Chap. 6), (1989b, 1990). The present article draws on some of this material but makes no attempt to encompass it all. My own account of convention was first presented in Gilbert (1989a, Chap. 6). It is more finely articulated here.

4 Lewis (1969, p. 3).

5 Lewis (1969, p. 1).

6 Such conventionality can be seen as a matter of the sound-sense links or conventions incorporated in a given language considered as an abstract system of rules. On the face of it, a single individual can adopt such a convention for his private use, as in a diary, including his use on a single occasion. See Gilbert (1983a). Also Gilbert (1989a, pp. 385–390).

7 The sample conventions are at Lewis (1969, pp. 42–51).

8 Lewis (1969, p. 3).

9 Both of the preceding quotations are from Lewis (1969, p. 3).

10 As Lewis indicates, even one person's idiosyncratic concept may do this. (1969, p. 3). He has larger hopes. Thus Lewis (1975) argues that some putative counterexamples to his account fail because we may say the phenomenon in question is a "convention" by virtue of the more or less close relationship in which it stands to conventions in his sense—it is apt to become such a convention, for instance. Evidently he is not only interested in what *I* may say.

11 Cf. Gilbert (1989a, Chap. 5). Here I emphasize an important point not mentioned there.

12 Lewis (1969, p. 6).

13 Precisely what a law amounts to is a matter of great debate within jurisprudence. For some brief remarks on the topic that relate it to my account of convention see Gilbert (1989a, 405–407). See also Gilbert (2006a, Chap. 9).

14 By "specific" protections, etc., I mean those that are provided by a particular convention rather those that would be provided by any convention whatsoever. I say this mindful of the proposal in Durkheim (1951) to the effect that a certain critical mass of social conventions and the like is necessary to the human individual's wellbeing.

15 Clearly I do not think that everyone is in a position to rebuke any given person as and when they have reason to respond negatively to what that person has done. People may sometimes speak of "rebukes" when what is at issue is only purportedly a rebuke in the sense I have in mind. The terms "order", "command" and "punish" are similar in this respect. Cf. Gilbert (2006a, pp. 4–5).

16 I say more about what I take *offending against* to be when discussing how Lewis's account fares in light of this criterion.

17 These points hold, mutatis mutandis, for the version of Lewis's account in which the universal quantifications within conditions (1) through (3) are relaxed. For further discussion see Gilbert (1989a, Chap. 6) and elsewhere. Other critics of one or more of Lewis's conditions include Schiffer (1972), Jamieson (1975), Robins (1984), Miller (1992), Marmor (1996), Millikan (1998).

18 That is, an agreement proper as opposed to something akin to one.

19 Lewis (1969, p. 3). Lewis's discussion of the relation of conventions to agreements comes after and presupposes his account of convention. See the text, below.

20 Gilbert (1989a).

21 See Gilbert (1989a, pp. 349–351).

22 Care is needed to distinguish one's having sufficient *reason* for acting a certain way from one's having *reasons* for such action. See Gilbert (2006a, Chap. 2).

23 I deliberately avoid saying "reasons-responsiveness". See the previous note.

24 Lewis (1969, p. 97).

25 See Gilbert (1989a, Chap. 4).

26 Gilbert (1989a, pp. 355–361).

27 Marmor (1996, p. 360). Unless otherwise noted my quotations from Marmor come from this page. He raises other questions about my 1989a discussion of convention. I cannot attempt a full response here: some of the points made may nonetheless be pertinent. The same goes for some other critical discussions e.g. Latsis (2005).

28 Marmor may not mean this; but it is a natural way to construe what he says.

29 These problems include the intuitive relation of convention to agreements, rules, and arbitrariness.

30 Another way of saying that X owes Y his *j*-ing is to say that *Y has a right against X to X's j-ing*. For further discussion see Gilbert (2004), which critiques the account of promissory obligation in Scanlon (1998) as not explaining why the promisee has a right against the promisor to performance. Since a right can be waived, I do not say that X has offended against Y *if* X owed Y his *j*-ing, etc.

31 I write of "the kind of owing that is at issue here" to make it clear that people including philosophers use the words "owe", etc., in a variety of senses. For what appears to be a different use to that at issue here see the title of (and elsewhere in) Scanlon (1998).

32 Cf. Darwall (2006) who cites others with similar views.

33 See Gilbert (2005) for some discussion.

34 As indicated earlier, there is reason to understand Lewis's account in such reductive terms.

35 See e.g. Gilbert (2006a).

36 Gilbert (1989a, p. 377f).

37 Some relatively detailed sources are Gilbert (2003) and Gilbert (2006a, Chap. 7). This is not to say that I have covered all aspects of the matter or that those I have covered cannot be further clarified.

38 The non-basic case depends on a basic joint commitment authorizing a given person or body to create new joint commitments for the parties. See Gilbert (2006a, Chap. 7).

39 For an example of the generation of a jointly accepted fiat that involves a number of stages see Gilbert (1989a, p. 398). On the role of initiatory expressions of "we" in the process of generating joint commitments generally see Gilbert (1989a, Chap. 4).

40 On joint commitments in large populations, see Gilbert (2006a, Chap. 8). Both Lewis's and my account can cope with this kind of situation, and in similar ways.

41 Cf. Gilbert (1989a, pp. 373–374).

42 For a discussion of social rules starting from Hart (1961) and leading to a new proposal see Gilbert (1999a). See also Gilbert (1989a, p. 405). I might have proposed as a further criterion of adequacy for an account of social convention in the sense I have in mind that it imply that conceptions are rules. For some concordant discussion see Marmor (1996, p. 352f), and various dictionary entries. See also the quotation from Lewis about words, in the text below. I take it that my account does better than Lewis's on this "conventions are rules" criterion.

43 Morality itself need not be referred to in order for us to consider this a moral principle. An appeal to justice, or charity, would have the same effect.

44 Luca Tummolini emphasized this point, personal communication (2008).

45 This is one way of bringing an example in Millikan (1998) within the purview of my account.

46 See e.g. Gilbert (1989a, pp. 380–382) and, most recently, Gilbert (2006a, Chap. 10).

47 See Lewis (1969, pp. 45, 83–88).

48 Gilbert (1989a, esp. Chap. 4); see also Gilbert (2006a, Chap. 8). My technical term for a population of people who are jointly committed in some way with one another is "plural subject".

49   Lewis (1969, p. 1).
50   Lewis writes of "what we shall use them to mean". I take this to be imperatival in force: it is not a mere prediction. My point, in any case, relates to that interpretation of Lewis.
51   For an argument along these lines relating to Hart's conditions on social rules, see Gilbert (1999a).
52   I take the point to be intuitive: precisely why it is rationally required to conform to one's commitments, as such, all equal, is a good question I set aside here. For some discussion see Gilbert (1999b).
53   For further discussion see, e.g. Gilbert (1999b; repr. 2000) and Gilbert (2006a, Chap. 7).
54   It is implausible to suggest that my owing someone an action is, in and of itself, a matter of *moral requirement*. This latter is worth pointing out in light of a great tendency in the literature on rights to interpret "owing" in terms of moral requirements of a certain sort. Cf. Gilbert (2004).
55   Robins (1984) emphasizes the latter point.
56   Clearly, then, the parties to conventions in the sense of the joint acceptance account need not be "moralisers" in any but a very broad sense. Nor need their participation in the convention be a matter of deliberation or "voluntaristic" in any strong sense. On the latter point see e.g. Gilbert (2006a, pp. 223–234). The quoted terms are from Latsis (2005, p. 720).
57   See Gilbert (1989a, Chap. 7) and elsewhere.
58   For further discussion along these lines, with allusion to other "problems of collective action" including the prisoner's dilemma, see Gilbert (2006b).

References

Burge T (1975) On knowledge and convention. Philos Rev 84: 249–255

Durkheim E (1951) Suicide: a study in sociology (trans: Spaulding JA, Simpson G), Free Press, New York

Gilbert M (1974) About conventions. Second-Order 3:71–89

Gilbert M (1981) Game theory and convention. Synthese 44:41–93. Reprinted in Gilbert (1996)

Gilbert M (1983a) Agreements, conventions, and language. Synthese 54:375–407. Reprinted with some revisions in Gilbert (1996)

Gilbert M (1983b) Notes on the concept of a social convention. New Lit Hist 14:225–251. Reprinted in Gilbert (1996)

Gilbert M (1984) Coordination problems and the evolution of behavior. Behav Brain Sci 7:106–107

Gilbert M (1989a) On social facts. Routledge and Kegan Paul, London (Reprinted 1992, Princeton University Press, Princeton)

Gilbert M (1989b) Rationality and salience. Philos Stud 55:223–239. Reprinted in Gilbert (1996)

Gilbert M (1990) Rationality, coordination, and convention. Synthese 84:1–21. Reprinted in Gilbert (1996)

Gilbert M (1999a) Social rules: some problems with Hart's account, and an alternative proposal. Law Philos 18:141–171. Reprinted in Gilbert (2000)

Gilbert M (1999b) Obligation and joint commitment. Utilitas 11: 143–64. Reprinted in Gilbert (1996)

Gilbert M (2000) Sociality and responsibility: new essays in plural subject theory. Roman and Littlefield, Lanham, MD

Gilbert M (2004) Scanlon on promissory obligation: the problem of promisees rights'. J Philos 101:83–109

Gilbert M (2005) Shared values, social unity, and liberty. Public Aff Q 19:25–49

Gilbert M (2006a) A theory of political obligation: membership, commitment, and the bonds of society. Clarendon Press, Oxford

Gilbert M (2006b) Rationality in collective action. Philos Soc Sci 36:3–17

Jamieson D (1975) David Lewis on convention. Can J Philos 5:73–81

Latsis JS (2005) Is there redemption for conventions? Cambridge J Econ 29:709–727

Lewis D (1969) Convention: a philosophical study. Harvard University Press, Cambridge, MA (Reissued 2002, Blackwell Publishers Ltd, Oxford)

Lewis D (1975) Languages and language. In Gunderson K (ed) Language, mind and knowledge. Minnesota Studies in the Philosophy of Science 7:3–35, University of Minnesota Press, Minneapolis

Marmor A (1996) On convention. Synthese 107:349–371

Miller S (1992) On conventions. Australas J Philos 70:435–445

Millikan R (1998) Language conventions made simple. J Philos 95:161–180

Robins M (1984) Promising, intending, and moral autonomy. Cambridge University Press, Cambridge

Schelling T (1960) The strategy of conflict. Harvard University Press, Cambridge, MA

Schiffer S (1972) Meaning. Oxford University Press, Oxford

Chapter 23

JOHN R. SEARLE

WHAT IS AN INSTITUTION?

[. . .]

IN THE TWENTIETH CENTURY, philosophers learned to be very cautious about asking questions of the form, 'What is . . .?', as in, for example, 'What is truth?', 'What is a number?', 'What is justice?'. The lessons of the twentieth century (though these lessons are rapidly being forgotten in the twenty-first century) suggest that the best way to approach such problems is to sneak up on them. Do not ask, 'What is truth?', but ask, 'Under what conditions do we say of a proposition that it is true?'. Do not ask, 'What is a number?', but ask, 'How do numerical expressions function in actual mathematical practice?'. I propose to adopt this method in addressing the question, 'What is an institution?'. Instead of coming right out and saying at the beginning, 'An institution is . . .', I propose to start with statements reporting institutional facts. If we could analyze the nature of institutional facts and how they differ from other sorts of facts, then it seems to me we would be well on the way to answering our question, 'What is an institution?'.

In some intuitively natural sense, the fact that I am an American citizen, the fact that the piece of paper in my hand is a 20 dollar bill, and the fact that I own stock in AT&T, are all institutional facts. They are institutional facts in the sense that they can only exist given certain human institutions. Such facts differ from the fact, for example, that at sea level I weigh 160 pounds, or that the Earth is 93 million miles from the sun, or that hydrogen atoms have one electron. Of course, in order to *state* the fact that the earth is 93 million miles from the sun, we need the institution of language, including the convention of measuring distances in miles, but we need to distinguish the *statement* of this fact (which is institutional) from the *fact stated* (which is not institutional). Now, what is it about institutional facts that makes them *institutional*, and what sorts of things do they require in order to be the sorts of facts they are?

2. Observer independence, observer dependence and the objective/subjective distinction

I want to begin the investigation by making certain general distinctions. First, it is essential to distinguish between those features of the world that are totally independent of human feelings and attitudes, observer independent features, and those features of the world that exist only relative to human attitudes. Observer independent features of the world include force, mass, gravitational attraction, photosynthesis, the chemical bond, and tectonic plates. Observer relative features of the world include money, government, property, marriage, social clubs, and presidential elections. It is important to see that one and the same entity can have both observer independent features and observer dependent features, where the observer dependent features depend on the attitudes of the people involved. For example, a set of movements by a group of people constitutes a football game, not just in virtue of the physical trajectories of the bodies involved, but also in virtue of the attitudes, intentions, and so on of the participants and the set of rules within which they are operating. Football games are observer relative; the trajectories of human bodies are observer independent. I hope it is obvious that most of the phenomena we discuss in economics, such as money, financial institutions, corporations, business transactions, and public offerings of stock are all observer relative. One can say that, in general, the natural sciences are concerned with observer independent phenomena and the social sciences with observer relative phenomena.

A rough test for whether or not a phenomenon is observer independent or observer relative is: could the phenomenon have existed if there had never been any conscious human beings with any intentional states? On this test, tectonic plates, gravitational attraction, and the solar system are observer independent and money, property, and government are observer relative. The test is only rough-and-ready, because, of course, the consciousness and intentionality that serve to create observer relative phenomena are themselves observer independent phenomena. For example, the fact that a certain object is money is observer relative; money is created as such by the attitudes of observers and participants in the institution of money. But those attitudes are not themselves observer relative; they are observer independent. I think this thing in front of me is a 20 dollar bill, and, if somebody else thinks that I do not think that, he or she is just mistaken. My attitude is observer independent, but the reality created by a large number of people like me having such attitudes, depends on those attitudes and is therefore observer dependent. In investigating institutional reality, we are investigating observer dependent phenomena.

A second distinction we need is between different kinds of objectivity and subjectivity. Part of our puzzle is to explain how we create, out of subjective attitudes such as beliefs and intentions, a reality of corporations, money, and economic transactions, about which we can make objectively true statements. But there is an ambiguity in the objective-subjective distinction. Because objectivity and subjectivity loom so large in our intellectual culture, it is important to get clear about this distinction at the beginning of the investigation. We need to distinguish the *epistemic* sense of the objective-subjective distinction from the *ontological* sense. Thus, for example, if I say 'Van Gogh died in France', that statement can be established as true or false as a matter of objective fact. It is not just a matter of anybody's opinion. It is epistemically objective. But if I say, 'Van Gogh was a better painter than Manet', well that is, as they say, a matter of opinion or judgment. It is not a matter of epistemically objective fact, but is rather a matter of subjective opinion. Epistemically objective statements are those that can be established as true or false independently of the feelings and attitudes of the makers and interpreters of the statement. Those that are subjective depend on the feelings and attitudes of the participants in the discourse. Epistemic objectivity and subjectivity are features of *claims*. But in addition to this sense of the objective/subjective distinction, and in a way the foundation of that distinction, is an ontological difference. Some entities exist only insofar as they are experienced by human and animal subjects. Thus, for example, pains, tickles and itches, and human and animal mental events and processes generally, exist only insofar as they are experienced by human or animal subjects. Their mode of existence requires that they be experienced by a human or animal subject. Therefore, we may say they have a *subjective* ontology.

But, of course, most of the things in the universe do not require being experienced in order to exist. Mountains, molecules, and tectonic plates, for example, exist and would exist if there had never been any humans or animals. We can say that they have an *objective* ontology, because they do not need to be experienced by a conscious subject in order to exist.

It is important to emphasize that the ontological subjectivity of a *domain* of investigation does not preclude epistemic objectivity in the *results* of the investigation. We can have an objective science of a domain that is ontologically subjective. Without this possibility there would be no social sciences. In light of these two distinctions, we might say that one way to pose our problem for this discussion is to explain how there can be an epistemically objective institutional reality of money, government, property, and so on, given that this reality is in part constituted by subjective feelings and attitudes and, thus, has a subjective ontology.

With these two distinctions in mind, the distinction between observer relative and observer independent features of reality, and the distinction between the ontological sense of the objective/subjective distinction and the epistemic sense of that distinction, we can place our present discussion within the larger context of contemporary intellectual life. We now have a reasonably clear idea about how the universe works, and we even have some idea about how it works at the micro level. We have a pretty good account of basic atomic and subatomic physics, we think we have a good understanding of the chemical bond, we even have a pretty well-established science of cellular and molecular biology, and we are increasing our understanding of evolutionary processes. The picture that emerges from these domains of investigation is that the universe consists entirely of entities we find it convenient to call particles (even though, of course, the word 'particle' is not quite right). These exist in fields of force and are typically organized into systems, where the internal structure and the external boundaries of the system are set by causal relations. Examples of systems are water molecules, galaxies, and babies. Some of those systems are composed in large part of big carbon-based molecules and are the products of the evolution of our present plant and animal species. Now here is our general question, and here is its bearing on the social sciences. How can we accommodate a certain conception we have of ourselves as conscious, mindful, rational, speech act performing, social, political, economic, ethical, and free-will possessing animals in a universe constructed entirely of these mindless physical phenomena? It is not obvious that we can make all our self-conceptions consistent with what we know from physics, chemistry, and biology about how the world is anyhow. We might, for example, in the end, have to give up our belief in free will. But since our self-conception is pretty well established and is pretty well substantiated by thousands of years of human experience, we are reluctant to give up any central portions of it without some very powerful reasons for doing so. The investigation in this article is focused on one small part of that larger problem. How can there be a social and institutional reality, including economic reality, within a universe consisting entirely of physical particles in fields of force?

3. The special theory of the logical structure of institutional facts: *X* counts as *Y* in *C*

[. . .]

Though the structure of actual human societies is immensely complicated, the underlying principles, I believe, are rather simple. There are three primitive notions necessary to explain social and institutional reality. (There is a fourth, what I call the Background, that I will not go into here.)

Collective intentionality

The first notion we need is that of collective intentionality. In order to explain this notion, I have to say a little bit about intentionality in general. 'Intentionality' is a word that philosophers use to describe that feature of the mind by which it is directed at, or about, or of, or concerns, objects and states of affairs in the world. Thus, beliefs, hopes, fears, desires, and the emotions generally can in this technical sense be said to be intentional. It is important to emphasize that intentionality does not imply any special connection with intending, in the ordinary sense in which I intend to go to the movies tonight. Rather, intentionality is a very general notion having to do with the directedness of the mind. Intending in the ordinary sense is simply a special case of intentionality in this technical sense, along with belief, desire, hope, fear, love, hate, pride, shame, perception, disgust, and many others.

Now given that we all have intentional states in this sense – we all have hopes, beliefs, desires, fears, and so on – we need to discuss the role of intentionality in human social groups. It is a remarkable property that humans and many other animal species have that they can engage in cooperative behavior. Obvious examples are playing in an orchestra or playing team sports or simply engaging in a conversation. In such cases one does act individually, but one's individual actions – playing the violin part, for example, or passing the ball to another player – are done as part of the collective behavior. Sometimes there is even cooperative behavior across species as, for example, to take a simple case, when my dog and I go for a walk together. When I am engaged in collective action, *I* am doing what I am doing as part of *our* doing what we are doing. In all of these cases, an agent is acting, and doing what he or she does, only as part of a collective action. It is an extremely complicated question how exactly the intentionality of the individual relates to the collective intentionality in such cases, but I have discussed it elsewhere, and I will not go into it here (Searle, 1990).

Collective intentionality covers not only collective intentions but also such other forms of intentionality as collective beliefs and collective desires. One can have a belief that one shares with other people and one can have desires that are shared by a collectivity. People cooperating in a political campaign typically desire together that their candidate will win, and in a church, the people reciting the Nicene Creed are expressing their collective faith.

Collective intentionality is the basis of all society, human or animal. Humans share with many species of animals the capacity for collective intentionality and thus the capacity to form societies. Indeed, I will define a social fact as any fact involving the collective intentionality of two or more agents. Our problem, then, is to specify what is special about human collective intentionality that enables us to create special forms of social reality that go beyond the general animal forms. Both the Supreme Court making a decision and a pack of wolves hunting a sheep are engaged in collective intentionality and, thus, are manifesting social facts. Our question is, what is the difference between the general class of social facts and the special sub-class that constitute institutional facts?

The assignment of function

A second notion we need is that of the assignment of function. Again, human beings have a capacity that they share with some, though this time with not very many, other species of animals, the capacity to impose functions on objects where the object does not have the function, so to speak, intrinsically but only in virtue of the assignment of function. Tools are the obvious case. Humans are tool-using animals *par excellence*, but, of course, other animals have tools as well. Beaver dams and birds' nests are two obvious examples. And in some cases animals are even capable of discovering useful tools, when the use of the object as a tool is not already programmed into the animals as part of their genetic endowment. Think of Köhler's apes, for example. Assigned functions are observer relative.

If you combine these two, collective intentionality and the assignment of function, it is easy to see that there can be collective assignments of function. Just as an individual can use a stump as a stool, so a group can use a large log as a bench.

Status functions

The third item we need, to account for the move from social facts to institutional facts, is a special kind of assignment of function where the object or person to whom the function is assigned cannot perform the function just in virtue of its physical structure, but rather can perform the function only in virtue of the fact that there is a collective assignment of a certain *status*, and the object or person performs its function only in virtue of collective acceptance by the community that the object or person has the requisite status. These assignments typically take the form *X counts as Y*. For example, such and such a move in a football game counts as scoring a touchdown. Such and such a set of procedures counts as the election of a president of the United States. Such and such a position in chess counts as checkmate. These exhibit the general form of the assignment of status function, *X counts as Y*, or, more typically, *X counts as Y in context C*. In all of these cases, the *X* term identifies certain features of an object or person or state of affairs, and the *Y* term assigns a special status to that person, object, or state of affairs. Human beings have a capacity which, as far as I can tell, is not possessed by any other animal species, to assign functions to objects where the objects cannot perform the function in virtue of their physical structure alone, but only in virtue of the collective assignment or acceptance of the object or person as having a certain *status* and with that status a function. Obvious examples are money, private property, and positions of political leadership. In every case, the object or person acquires a function which can be performed only in virtue of the collective acceptance of the corresponding status.

I like to illustrate the distinction between status functions and other kinds of functions with a little parable. Imagine a tribe that builds a wall around its collection of huts, and imagine that the wall keeps members of the tribe in and intruders out, since it is difficult to get over the wall without the tolerance of the members of the tribe. But imagine that the wall decays to the point where it is nothing more than a line of stones, yet let us suppose that the people involved continue to – and watch this vocabulary closely – *recognize* the line of stones as a *boundary*. They recognize that they are not *supposed to* cross unless *authorized* to do so. Now, we are supposing that the wall, though it is no longer a large physical structure but simply a line of stones, continues to perform the same function that it did before, but this time not in virtue of its physical structure, but in virtue of the fact that the people involved continue to accept the line of stones as having a certain status. It has the status of a boundary, and people behave in a way that they regard as appropriate for something that they accept as a boundary. The line of stones has a function not in virtue of its physical structure, but in virtue of the collective assignment of a status, and with that status, a function which can only be performed in virtue of the collective acceptance of the object as having that status. I propose to call such functions *status functions*.

As this example is intended to make clear, the transition from physical function to status function can be gradual, and there may be no exact point at which we can say, the status function begins and the physical function ends. The vocabulary is revealing. 'You can't cross that' can mean either 'It is too high' or 'It is not allowed' (or both).

The general logical form of the imposition of status functions is, as I said, *X counts as Y in C*, though I will point out some exceptions later.

It might seem that this is a very feeble apparatus with which to construct institutional structures; surely the whole thing could come tumbling down at any moment. How can it do as much work as it apparently does? The answer, or at least part of the answer, is that this structure has certain purely formal properties that give it enormous scope. The first is that it iterates upward indefinitely. So, for example, when I make certain sounds through my mouth, making those sounds counts as uttering sentences of English; but uttering those sentences of English counts as making a promise; and, in that context, making a promise counts as undertaking a contract. Making that kind of contract in that context counts as getting married, and so on upward. Notice the logical form of this: X_1 *counts as* Y_1. But $Y_1 = X_2$ *counts as* Y_2. And $Y_2 = X_3$ *counts as* Y_3, and so on upward indefinitely.

Secondly, the whole system operates laterally as well as vertically. Thus, I do not just own property, but I own property as a citizen of the city of Berkeley in the country of Alameda in the State of California in the United States of America. Locked into this institutional structure I have all sorts of rights and obligations. For example I have to pay taxes to all four of those entities I just named, and all four are under obligations to provide me with all sorts of social services. I acquire various rights and duties as a property owner, and these interlock with other social institutions.

When the procedure or practice of counting *X* as *Y* becomes regularized it becomes a rule. And rules of the form *X counts as Y in C* are then constitutive of institutional structures. Such rules differ from regulative rules, which are typically of the form 'Do *X*', because regulative rules regulate activities which can exist independently of the rule. Constitutive rules not only regulate but rather constitute the very behavior they regulate, because acting in accordance with a sufficient number of the rules is constitutive of the behavior in question. An obvious contrast is between the regulative rules of driving, such as drive on the right-hand side of the road and the constitutive rules of chess. Driving can exist without the regulative rule requiring right or left; the rule regulates an antecedently existing activity. But chess cannot exist without the rules, because behaving in accordance with (at least a sufficient subset of) the rules is constitutive of playing chess.

Now I want to make a very strong claim. The institutional ontology of human civilization, the special ways in which human institutional reality differs from the social structures and behavior of other animals, is a matter of status functions imposed according to constitutive rules and procedures. Status functions are the glue that holds human societies together. Think not only of money, property, government, and marriage, but also of football games, national elections, cocktail parties, universities, corporations, friendships, tenure, summer vacations, legal actions, newspapers, and industrial strikes. Though these phenomena exhibit enormous variety, their underlying ontology reveals a common structure. The analogy with the natural world is obvious. Bonfires and rusting shovels look quite different, but the underlying mechanism that produces them is exactly the same: oxidization. Analogously, presidential elections, baseball games, and 20 dollar bills look different, but the underlying mechanism that produces them is the same: the assignment of status functions with their accompanying deontologies according to constitutive rules. (I will say more about deontology in a moment.)

We are now close to being able to give a provisional answer to the question which forms the title of this paper: 'What is an institution?' We have substituted for that question, the question: 'What is an institutional fact?' And I have claimed that these facts typically require structures in the form of constitutive rules *X counts as Y in C* and that institutional facts only exist in virtue of collective acceptance of something having a certain status, where that status carries functions that cannot be performed without the collective acceptance of the status. This I am claiming is the glue that holds society together. There is a gradual transition from informal but accepted assignments of status functions to full-blown established institutions with codified constitutive rules, but in both cases the crucial element of deontology is present, as we will see. Furthermore, the notion of 'collective acceptance' is intended to be vague, because I need to mark a continuum that goes from grudgingly going along with some social practice to enthusiastic endorsement of it.

As a preliminary formulation, we can state our conclusions so far as follows: an institutional fact is any fact that has the logical structure X *counts as* Y *in* C, where the Y term assigns a status function and (with few exceptions) the status function carries a deontology. An institution is any system of constitutive rules of the form X *counts as* Y *in* C. Once an institution becomes established, it then provides a structure within which one can create institutional facts.

Our original aim was to explain how the ontology of institutions fits into the more basic ontology of physics and chemistry and we have now done that: one and the same phenomenon (object, organism, event, etc.) can satisfy descriptions under which it is non-institutional (a piece of paper, a human being, a series of movements) and descriptions under which it is institutional (a 20 dollar bill, the president of the United States, a football game). An object or other phenomenon is part of an institutional fact, *under a certain description of that object or phenomenon.*

I am leaving out an enormous number of complexities for the sake of giving a simple statement of the bare bones of the ontology in question.

4. Status functions and deontic powers

How does it work, how does a set of status functions, deriving from systems of constitutive rules, function in the operation of society? The essential role of human institutions and the purpose of having institutions is not to constrain people as such, but, rather, to create new sorts of power relationships. Human institutions are, above all, *enabling*, because they create power, but it is a special kind of power. It is the power that is marked by such terms as: rights, duties, obligations, authorizations, permissions, empowerments, requirements, and certifications. I call all of these *deontic powers*. What distinguishes human societies from other animal societies, as far as I can tell, is that human beings are capable of a deontology which no other animal is capable of. Not all deontic power is institutional, but just about all institutional structures are matters of deontic power. Think of anything you would care to mention – private property, government, contractual relationships, as well as such informal relationships as friendship, family, and social clubs. All of these are matters of rights, duties, obligations, etc. They are structures of power relationships. Often the institutional facts evolve out of the natural facts. Thus, there is a biological family consisting of parents and their biological offspring. But humans have imposed on this underlying biology a rather elaborate formal and informal institutional structure, involving the respective statuses of the mother, the father, and the children. In so-called 'extended families' authority relationships and other status functions may include not only the parents and children but sundry other relatives. Furthermore, given the institutional structures, one may have families with parents and children where no one is biologically related to anyone else.

But that only forces the question back a bit: how exactly do these power relations function? The answer, which again is essential to understanding society, is that institutional structures create desire-independent reasons for action. To recognize something as a duty, an obligation, or a requirement is already to recognize that you have a reason for doing it which is independent of your inclinations at the moment.

It might seem paradoxical that I talk about institutional reasons for action as 'desire-independent reasons for action', because, of course, many of these are precisely the foci of very powerful human desires. What is more a field for human desire than money? Or political power? I think this question raises a deep issue: By creating institutional reality, we increase human power enormously. By creating private property, governments, marriages, stock markets, and universities, we increase the human capacity for action. But the possibility of having desires and satisfying them within these institutional structures – for example, the desire to get rich, to become president, to get a Ph.D., to get tenure – all presuppose that there is a recognition of the deontic relationships. Without the recognition, acknowledgment, and acceptance of the deontic relationships, your power is not worth a damn. It is only worthwhile to have money or a university degree or to be president of the United States if other people recognize you as having this status, and recognize that status as giving desire-independent reasons for behaving in certain ways. The general point is clear: the creation of the general field of desire-based reasons for action presupposes the acceptance of a system of desire-independent reasons for action. This is true both of the immediate beneficiaries of the power relationships (for example, the person with the money or the person who has won the election) and of the other participants in the institution.

[. . .]

6. Steps toward a general theory of social ontology. We accept (*S* has power (*S* does *A*))

I want now to discuss some of the further developments in the theory of institutional reality since the publication of *The Construction of Social Reality*. I want to mention two such developments. First, in the original statement of the theory, I pointed out that, in order for status functions to be recognized, there typically have to be some sorts of *status indicators*, because there is nothing in the person or the object itself that will indicate its status, since the status is only there by collective acceptance or recognition. Thus, we have policemen's uniforms, wedding rings, marriage certificates, drivers' licenses, and passports, all of which are status indicators. Many societies find that they cannot exist without status indicators, as, for example, the proliferation of identity cards and driver's licenses will attest. However, Hernando De Soto (2000) pointed out an interesting fact. Sometimes the status indicators, as issued by an official agency (where the agency is itself a higher-level set of status functions), acquire a kind of life of their own. How is this so? He points out that in several underdeveloped countries, many people own land, but because there are no property deeds, because the owners of the property do not have title deeds to the property, they are, in effect, what we would call squatters; they do not have status indicators. This has two consequences of enormous social importance. First, they cannot be taxed by the governing authorities because they are not legally the holders of the property, but, secondly and just as importantly, they cannot use the property as capital. Normally, in order for a society to develop, the owners of property have to be able to go to the bank and get loans against their property in order to use the money to make investments. But in countries such as, for example, Egypt, it is impossible for the vast amount of private property to be used as collateral for investments because so much of this property is held without the benefit of a property deed. The owners of the property are in effect squatters, in the sense that they do not legally own the property, though they live in a society where their status function is acknowledged and generally recognized and hence, on my account, continues to exist and generate deontic powers. But the deontic powers stop at the point where the larger society requires some official proof of the status functions. Thus, without official documentation, they lack full deontic powers. Collective recognition is not enough. There has to be official recognition by some agency, itself supported by collective recognition, and there have to be status indicators issued by the official agency.

A second and equally important development was pointed out to me by Barry Smith. He pointed out that there are some institutions that have what he calls 'free-standing Y terms', where you can have a status function, but without any physical object on which the status function is imposed. A fascinating case is corporations. The laws of incorporation in a state such as California enable a status function to be constructed, so to speak, out of thin air. Thus, by a kind of performative declaration, the corporation comes into existence, but there need be no physical object which is the corporation. The corporation has to have a mailing address and a list of officers and stock holders and so on, but it does not have to be a physical object. This is a case where following the appropriate procedures counts as the creation of a corporation and where the corporation, once created, continues to exist, but there is no person or physical object which becomes the corporation. New status functions are created among people – as officers of the corporation, stockholders, and so on. There is indeed a corporation as Y, but there is no person or physical object X that counts as Y.

An equally striking example is money. The paradox of my account is that money was my favorite example of the 'X counts as Y' formula, but I was operating on the assumption that currency was somehow or other essential to the existence of money. Further reflection makes it clear to me that it is not. You can easily imagine a society that has money without having any currency at all. And, indeed, we seem to be evolving in something like this direction with the use of debit cards. All you need to have money is a system of recorded numerical values whereby each person (or corporation, organization, etc.) has assigned to him or her or it a numerical figure which shows at any given point the amount of money they have. They can then use this money to buy things by altering their numerical value in favor of the seller, whereby they lower their numerical value, and the seller acquires a higher numerical value. Money is typically redeemable in cash, in the form of currency, but currency is not essential to the existence or functioning of money.

How can such things function if there is no physical object on which the status function is imposed? The answer is that status functions are, in general, matters of deontic power, and, in these cases, the deontic power goes directly to the individuals in question. So my possession of a queen in the game of chess is not a matter of my having my hands on a physical object, it is rather a matter of my having certain powers of movement within a formal system (and the formal system is 'the board', though it need not be a physical board) relative to other pieces. Similarly, my having a thousand dollars is not a matter of my having a wad of bills in my hand but my having certain deontic powers. I now have the right, i.e. the *power*, to buy things, which I would not have if I did not have the money. In such cases, the real bearer of the deontology is the participant in the economic transactions and the player in the game. The physical objects, such as chess pieces and dollar bills, are just markers for the amount of deontic power that the players have.

In the early part of *The Construction of Social Reality* I said that the basic form of the institutional fact was X *counts as* Y *in* C and that this was a form of the constitutive rule that enables us to create institutional facts. But my later formulation in the book gives us a much more general account. I said that the basic power creation operator in society is *We accept (S has power (S does A))*; and that we could think of the various forms of power as essentially Boolean operations on this basic structure, so, for example, to have an obligation is to have a negative power. What then, exactly, is the relationship between the two formulae X *counts as* Y *in* C and *We accept (S has power (S does A))*? The answer is that, of course, we do not just accept that somebody has power, but we accept that they have power in virtue of their institutional status. For example, satisfying certain conditions makes someone president of the United States. This is an example of the *X counts as Y in C* formula. But, once we accept that someone is president of the United States, then we accept that he has the power to do certain things. He has the positive power to command the armed forces, and he has the negative power, i.e. the obligation, to deliver a state of the union address. He has the *right* to command the armed forces, and he has the *duty* to deliver the address. In this case we accept that *S* has power (*S does A*) because *S* = *X*, and we have already accepted that *X* counts as *Y*, and the *Y* status function carries with it the acknowledged deontic powers.

Continuing with the example of the corporation, we can say that so and so counts as the president of the corporation and such and such people count as the stockholders. This is an example of the *X counts as Y in C* formulation, but, of course, the whole point of doing that is to give them powers, duties, rights, responsibilities, etc. They then instantiate the *we accept (S has power (S does A))* formula. But to repeat a point made earlier, the corporation itself is not identical with any physical object or any person or set of persons. The corporation is, so to speak, created out of nothing. The president is president *of* the corporation, but he is not identical with the corporation. The reasons for doing this are famous. By creating a so-called 'fictitious person' we can create an entity that is capable of entering into contractual relationships and capable of buying and selling, making a profit, and incurring debts, for which it is liable. But the officers and stockholders, are not personally liable for the debts of the corporation. This is an important breakthrough in human thought. So, what amounts to the corporation when we set it up? It is not that there is an *X* that counts as the corporation, but, rather, that there is a group of people involved in legal relationships, thus so and so counts as the president of the corporation, so and so counts as a stockholder in the corporation, etc., but there is nothing that need count as the corporation itself, because one of the points of setting up the corporation was to create a set of power relationships without having to have the accompanying liabilities that typically go with those power relationships when they are assigned to actual human individuals.

I regard the invention of the limited liability corporation, like the invention of double-entry bookkeeping, universities, museums, and money, as one of the truly great advances in human civilization. But the greatest advance of all is the invention of status functions, of which these are but instances. It is not at all necessary that there should exist status functions. Non-human animals do not appear to have them. But without them, human civilization, as we think of it, would be impossible.

7. Different kinds of 'institutions'

I have not been attempting to analyze the ordinary use of the word 'institution'. I do not much care if my account of institutional reality and institutional facts matches that ordinary usage. I am much more interested in getting at the underlying glue that holds human societies together. But let us consider some other sorts of things that might be thought of as institutions.

I have said that the fact that I am an American citizen is an institutional fact, but how about the fact that today is the 24 September 2004? Is that an institutional fact? What does the question ask? At least this much. Does identifying something as 24 September 2004 collectively assign a status function that carries with it a deontology? So construed the answer is no. In my culture there is no deontology carried by the fact that today is 24 September. In that respect, '24 September 2004' differs from 'Christmas Day', 'Thanksgiving', or, in France, '14 July'. Each of these carries a deontology. If it is Christmas Day, for example, I am *entitled* to a day off, and collective intentionality in my community supports me in this entitlement.

Since every day is some Saint's Day, there is presumably a subgroup for which 24 September is an important Saint's Day that carries an institutional deontology, but I am not in that subgroup.

I think there is a sense of the word 'institution' in which the Christian calendar or the Mayan calendar are a kind of institution (both of them were, after all, *instituted*), but it is not the kind of institution that I am attempting to analyze. A calendar is rather a verbal system for naming units of time – days, months, and years – and indicating their relationships. Similarly with other verbal systems. Different societies have different color vocabularies, but that does not make the fact that the cloth in front me is magenta into an institutional fact. Similar remarks could be made about systems of weights and measures. The fact that I weigh 160 pounds is the same fact as the fact that I weigh 72 kilos, even though this same fact can be stated using different systems of measuring weights.

More interesting to me are those cases where the facts in question are on the margin of being institutional. I think that the fact that someone is my friend is an institutional fact because friendship carries *collectively recognized* obligations, rights, and responsibilities. But how about the fact that someone is a drunk, a nerd, an intellectual, or an underachiever? Are these institutional concepts and are the corresponding terms institutional facts? Not as I am using these expressions, because there is no collectively recognized deontology that goes with these. Of course, if the law or custom establishes criteria under which somebody is a recognized drunk and imposes penalties as well as entitlements for this status, then being a drunk becomes a status function. *X* counts as *Y*. And, again, I might personally feel that, as an intellectual, I have certain sorts of obligations, but this is not yet an institutional phenomenon unless there is some collective recognition of my status and of these obligations. When I pointed out in a lecture that being a nerd was not a status function, one of my students told me that in his high school it definitely was, because as the class nerd he was expected to help other students with their homework. He was under certain sorts of collectively recognized obligations.

Another sort of 'institution' that I am not attempting to describe is massive forms of human practices around certain subject matters that do not *as such* carry a deontology, even though there are lots of deontologies within the practices. So, for example, there are series of practices that go with what we call 'science' or 'religion' or 'education'. Does that make science, religion, and education into institutions? Well, we are using institution as a technical term anyway, and it is open to us if we want to call these institutions, but I think it is very important that we not confuse science, education, and religion with such things as money, property, government, and marriage. Within such gross human practices as science, religion, and education there are, indeed, institutions and plenty of institutional facts. Thus, for example, the National Science Foundation is an institution, as is the University of California or the Roman Catholic Church. And the fact that Jones is a scientist, Smith a professor, and Brown a priest again are all institutional facts. Why then are not science, religion, and education institutions? To ask of any word *W*, Does *W* name an institution? is to ask at least the following:

1. Is *W* defined by a set of constitutive rules?
2. Do those rules determine status functions, which are in fact collectively recognized and accepted?
3. Are those status functions only performable in virtue of the collective recognition and acceptance, and not in virtue of the observer-independent features of the situation alone?
4. Do the status functions carry recognized and accepted deontic powers?

So construed, 'The National Science Foundation' names an institution. 'Science' does not. The rules of scientific method, if there are such, are regulative and not constitutive. They are designed to maximize the probability of discovering the truth, not to create status functions with deontic powers. All of that is consistent with the fact that in my subculture to say that someone is a 'scientist' is to state an institutional fact, because it assigns a *Y* status, on the basis of meeting certain *X* criteria, that carries certain rights and responsibilities, a more or less specific deontology.

As I said before, I do not much care whether or not we want to use the word 'institution' for both those practices whose names specify an institutional deontology and those which do not, but it is crucial to emphasize the important underlying idea: we need to mark those facts that carry a deontology because they are the glue that holds society together.

[. . .]

Methodological individualism

It seems to me that there is a certain amount of confusion surrounding the notion of 'methodological individualism'. Without going into too many details, I want to state the precise sense in which the views advocated in this article are consistent with methodological individualism. The sense in which my views are methodological individualist is that all observer-independent mental reality must exist in the minds of individual human beings. There is no such thing as a group mind or an Oversoul or a Hegelian Absolute of which our particular minds are but fragments. Another way to put this point, in light of the distinctions made in this article, is to say that all observer independent intentionality is in the minds of individual human beings. I want this sense of 'methodological individualism' to seem quite uncontroversial. It is perfectly consistent with the idea that there are predicates true of social collectives which are not in any obvious way true of individuals. So, for example, if I say that the United States government has a huge annual deficit, that statement has implications about the behavior of individuals, but it is not the individuals that have the 'huge annual deficit'. A second issue that this definition of methodological individualism enables me to sidestep is that concerning 'externalism' in the philosophy of mind. I do in fact think that mental states are entirely in the head, but many contemporary philosophers think that the contents of mental states are not in the head but include, for example, causal relations to the real world and to the surrounding society. I do not think these views are true, but I do not need to refute them for the purpose of this investigation. I simply insist that all mental reality is in the minds of individuals. This is consistent with the theory that says mental contents and hence minds are not in heads, although I happen to think that theory is false.

9. Conclusion

I have now offered at least preliminary answers to the questions posed at the beginning of this article. At the risk of repetition I will state them:

What is an institution? An institution is any collectively accepted system of rules (procedures, practices) that enable us to create institutional facts. These rules typically have the form of *X counts as Y in C*, where an object, person, or state of affairs *X* is assigned a special status, the *Y* status, such that the new status enables the person or object to perform functions that it could not perform solely in virtue of its physical structure, but requires as a necessary condition the assignment of the status. The creation of an institutional fact is, thus, the collective assignment of a status function. The typical point of the creation of institutional facts by assigning status functions is to create deontic powers. So typically when we assign a status function *Y* to some object or person *X* we have created a situation in which we accept that a person *S* who stands in the appropriate relation to X is such that (S has power (S does A)). The whole analysis then gives us a systematic set of relationships between collective intentionality, the assignment of function, the assignment of status functions, constitutive rules, institutional facts, and deontic powers.

The theory of institutions in this article is very much work in progress, as was the earlier work on which it is based. I see the theory of institutions as still in its childhood. (Maybe not in its infancy any more, but still its childhood.) Two methodological lessons for anyone wishing to pursue it further: First, because the institutional ontology is subjective, it must always be examined from the first person point of view. Institutional facts only exist from the point of view of the participants and for that reason no external functionalist or behaviorist analysis will be adequate to account for them. You have to be able to think yourself into the institution to understand it. Second, a consequence of this analysis is that society has a logical structure. Other parts of nature – the planetary system, mitosis, and the replication of DNA, for example – do not have logical structures. Theories about such parts of nature have logical structures but not the nature itself. But society consists in part of representations and those representations have logical structures. Any adequate theory about such phenomena must contain a logical analysis of their structures.

References

De Soto, Hernando (2000), *The Mystery of Capital: Why Capitalism Triumphs in the West and Fails Everywhere Else*, New York: Basic Books.

Searle, John R. (1995), *The Construction of Social Reality*, London: Allen Lane.

Searle, John R. (1990), 'Collective Intentions and Actions', in P. Cohen, J. Morgan, and M. E. Pollack (eds.), *Intentions in Communication*, Cambridge, MA: MIT Press; reprinted in Searle, John R. (2002), *Consciousness and Language*, Cambridge: Cambridge University Press, pp. 80–105.

Chapter 24

CRISTINA BICCHIERI

THE RULES WE LIVE BY

Introduction

DESPITE THE UBIQUITOUS reference to the concept of social norms in the social sciences, there is no consensus about the power of social norms to direct human action. For some, norms have a central and regular influence on human behavior, while for others, the concept is too vague, and the evidence we have about norm compliance is too contradictory to support the claim that they appreciably affect behavior. Those who doubt that norms have a behavior-guiding force argue that human behavior only occasionally conforms with the dominant social norms. If the same norms are in place when behavior is norm-consistent as when it is norm inconsistent, why should we believe that norms mediated any of it?

Much of the discussion about the power norms have to affect behavior arises from a confusion about what is meant by 'norm.' A norm can be formal or informal, personal or collective, descriptive of what most people do, or prescriptive of behavior. In the same social setting, conformity to these different kinds of norms stems from a variety of motivations and produces distinct, sometimes even opposing, behavioral patterns. Take for example a culture in which many individuals have strong personal norms that prohibit corrupt practices and in which there are legal norms against bribing public officers, yet bribing is widespread and tolerated. Suppose we were able to independently assess whether an individual has a personal norm against corruption. Can we predict whether a person, who we know condemns corruption, will bribe a public officer when given a chance? Probably not, but we could come closer to a good prediction if we knew certain factors and cues are present in this situation and have an influence on the decision. The theories of norms we have inherited, mainly from sociology, offer little help, because they did not develop an understanding of the conditions under which individuals are likely to follow a norm or, when several norms may apply, what makes one of them focal.

A first step in the direction of a deeper understanding of what motivates us to follow a norm is to clarify what we mean by a social norm. 'Norm' is a term used to refer to a variety of behaviors, and accompanying expectations. These should not be lumped together, on pain of missing some important features that are of great help in understanding phenomena such as variance in norm compliance. Inconsistent conformity, for example, is to be expected with certain types of norms, but not with others. In this chapter I put forth a 'constructivist' theory of norms, one that explains norms in terms of the expectations and preferences of those who follow them. My view is that the very existence of a social norm depends on a sufficient number of people believing that it exists and pertains to a given type of situation, and expecting that enough other people are following it in those kinds of situations. Given the right kind of expectations, people will have conditional preferences for obeying a norm, meaning that preferences will be conditional on having expectations about other people's conformity. Such expectations and preferences will result in collective behaviors that further confirm the existence of the norm in the eyes of its followers.

Expectations and conditional preferences are the building blocks of several social constructs, though, not just social norms. *Descriptive norms* such as fashions and fads are also based on expectations of conformity and conditional preferences, and so are *conventions*, such as signaling systems, rules of etiquette, and traffic rules. In both cases, the preference for conformity does not clash with self-interest, especially if we define it in purely material terms.[1] One can model descriptive norms and conventions as solutions to coordination games. Such games capture the structure of situations where there exist several possible equilibria and, although we might like one of them best, what we most want is to coordinate with others on *any* equilibrium; hence we act in conformity to what we expect others to do. Descriptive norms and conventions are thus representable as equilibria of original coordination games. *Social norms*, on the contrary, often go against narrow self-interest, as when we are required to cooperate, reciprocate, act fairly, or do anything that may involve some material cost or the forgoing of some benefit. The kinds of problems that social norms are meant to solve differ from the coordination problems that conventions and descriptive norms 'solve.' We need social norms in all those situations in which there is conflict of interest but also a potential for joint gain. The games that social norms solve are called mixed-motive games.[2] Such mixed-motive games are not games of coordination to start with, but social norms, as I shall argue, *transform* mixed-motive games into coordination ones. This transformation, however, hinges on each individual expecting enough other people to follow the norm, too. If this expectation is violated, an individual will revert to playing the original game and to behaving 'selfishly.' This chapter thus starts with a precise definition of social norms and only later considers what differentiates such norms from descriptive norms and conventions. Because all three are based on expectations and conditional preferences, I pay special attention to the nature of expectations (empirical and/or normative) that support each construct.

The definition of social norm I am proposing should be taken as a *rational reconstruction* of what a social norm is, not a faithful descriptive account of the real beliefs and preferences people have or of the way in which they in fact deliberate. Such a reconstruction, however, will have to be reliable in that it must be possible to extract meaningful, testable predictions from it. This is one of the tasks I undertake in Chapters 3 and 4. An important claim I make in this chapter is that the belief/desire model of choice that is the core of my rational reconstruction of social norms does not commit us to avow that we always engage in conscious deliberation to decide whether to follow a norm. We may follow a norm automatically and thoughtlessly and yet still be able to explain our action in terms of beliefs and desires.

The simplistic, common view that we conform to norms either because of external sanctions or because they have been internalized flies in the face of much evidence that people sometimes obey norms even in the absence of any obvious incentive structure or personal commitment to what the norm stands for (Cialdini et al. 1990). Many who postulate internal or external incentives as the sole reasons for compliance also maintain compliance is the result of a conscious process of balancing costs and benefits, culminating in a decision to conform or to transgress. Yet personal experience tells us that compliance is often automatic and unreflective: Even important social norms like those that regulate fair exchanges and reciprocation are often acted on without much thought to (or awareness of) their personal or social consequences. Whereas the literature on social norms has traditionally stressed the deliberational side of conformity, in this book I want to emphasize its automatic component. Both aspects are important, but too much emphasis on conscious deliberation may miss crucial links between decision heuristics and norms, as I explain in this chapter and the next [cf. Bicchieri 2006, ch. 2].

Whenever we enter any environment; we have to decide how to behave. There are two ways to reach a decision. One is somewhat ideally depicted by the traditional rational choice model: We may systematically assess the situation, gather information, list and evaluate the possible consequences of different actions, assess the probability of each consequence occurring, and then calculate the expected utility of the alternative courses of action and choose one that maximizes our expected utility. I dub this the *deliberational* route to behavior. The process of rational deliberation ending in the choice of a course of action is likely to be costly in time, resources, and effort and to require considerable skill. The deliberational way to behavior is likely to be chosen when one is held accountable for one's choice; when the consequences may be particularly important and long-lasting; or when one has the time, knowledge, and disposition to ponder over alternative choices. But even in these cases deliberation may fall short of the ideal. Behavioral decision theorists have gathered compelling evidence that actors systematically violate the assumptions of rational choice theory (Camerer 2003). Thus the deliberational way need not assume perfect rationality. It only requires conscious deliberation and balancing of what one perceives (or misperceives) as the costs and benefits of alternative courses of action. On occasion we do engage in conscious deliberation, even if the process is marred by mistakes of judgment and calculation.

A second way to reach a decision relies on following behavioral rules that prescribe a particular course of action for the situation (or a class of similar situations). These guides to behavior include habits, roles, and, of course, norms. Once one adopts a behavioral rule, one follows it without the conscious and systematic assessment of the situation performed in deliberation. The question of how a particular behavioral rule is primed is of great interest. The answer is likely to lie in the interplay of (external) situational cues and (internal) categorization processes. These processes lie beyond awareness and probably occur in split seconds. Models of mental processes (Lamberts and Shanks 1997) suggest that, when faced with a new situation, we immediately search for cues about how to interpret it or what is appropriate behavior for that situation. It is conjectured that we compare the situation we face with others we remember that possess similar characteristics, and that this comparison activates behavior that is considered most "normal" for this type of situation. The comparison process is one of 'categorization,' of finding relevant similarities between the current context and other ones we have experienced in the past. To efficiently search our memory and group a new event with previously encountered ones, we use cognitive shortcuts. Cognitive shortcuts play a crucial role in categorization and the subsequent activation of scripts and schemata.[3] Consequently, they are responsible for some norms rather than others being activated in different situations. Let us call this route to behavior the *heuristic* route. In the heuristic route, behavior is guided by *default rules* stored in memory that are cued by contextual stimuli. Norms are one class of default rules. According to the heuristic route, norm compliance is an automatic response to situational cues that focus our attention on a particular norm, rather than a conscious decision to give priority to normative considerations. On the heuristic view, norms are context-dependent, meaning that different social norms will be activated or appear appropriate, depending on how a situation is understood. In turn, our understanding of a situation is influenced by which previous contexts we view as similar to the present one, and this process of assessing similarities and 'fitting' a situation into a pre-existing category will make specific norms salient.

The distinction between deliberational and heuristic routes to behavior is a useful simpli-fication, and it should be taken as such. The truth is that we often combine the two routes, and what is a staple of the heuristic process can also be an object of deliberation. Conformity to a norm, for example, is not always an automatic, nondeliberational affair. Especially when we are tempted to shirk an obligation, the thought of the personal and social consequences of alternative courses of action is often present and important in determining our choice. I want to stress, again, that deliberation is not synonymous with 'rational deliberation', in part because the list of possible mistakes and cognitive impairments with which our decision processes are fraught is potentially very long. *Rational deliberation* is better conceived of as an ideal type, against which we measure the amplitude of our deviations. What is important in deliberation is the *conscious* processing of information and evaluation of options. Whether ideally or less than ideally rational, deliberation refers to beliefs and desires of which we are *aware*. Deliberation is the process of consciously choosing what we most desire according to our beliefs. In the deliberational view, beliefs and desires (preferences) are treated as mental states of which we are conscious, at least in the course of deciding which action to take.

The problem with taking beliefs and desires to be conscious mental states is that they can then play no role in the heuristic route to behavior. There is, however, a long and reputable philosophical tradition that takes beliefs and desires to be *dispositions* to act in a certain way in the appropriate circumstance. According to the dispositional account, to say that someone has a belief or a preference implies that we expect such motives to manifest themselves in the relevant circumstances. Thus, for example, one might automatically obey a norm of truth-telling without thinking of the beliefs and preferences that underlie one's behavior. These beliefs and preferences might become manifest only when they happen to be unfulfilled. To assess the nature of such beliefs and desires, all we need is a simple counterfactual exercise. Suppose we ask someone if he would keep telling the truth (as he normally and almost auto-matically does) in a world where he came to realize that people systematically lie. Our subject may answer in a variety of ways, but whatever course of action he claims he would choose, it is likely that he never thought of it before. *He did not know*, for example, that he would be ready to become a liar until he was put in the condition to reflect on it. Our subject may reason that it would be stupid on his part to keep telling the truth, as it would put him at an obvious disadvantage. Evidently his preference for sincerity is conditional on expecting reciprocity. If these expectations were not met, his preference would be different. Note that dispositions need not be stable: Preferences, for example, can be context-dependent, in the sense that even a small change of context may elicit different, even opposite, preferences. The research on framing effects shows just that (Tversky and Kahneman 1981). The heuristic way to behavior seems perfectly compatible with a dispositional account of beliefs and desires. Namely, the default rules that we tend to automatically follow are accompanied and supported by beliefs and desires that we become aware of only when they are challenged. Surprise in this case breeds awareness of our underlying motives. Moreover, whenever a norm is 'cued' or made salient in a particular environment, the mechanism that primes it elicits the beliefs and preferences that support that particular norm. The remainder of this chapter presents a taxonomy of norms that relies on preferences and beliefs as 'building blocks.'

The idea that social norms may be cued, and hence manipulated, is attractive. It suggests that we may be able to induce pro-social behavior and maintain social order at low cost. Norms differ in different cultures, and what cues a Westerner into cooperation will probably differ from what cues a Mapuche Indian (Henrich 2000). In both cases, however, it may be possible to structure the environment in a way that produces desirable behavior. If you sail along the Italian coast, you will notice large beach posters that invite sailors not to litter and pollute "your" sea. In Sweden, instead, environmentalist appeals always refer to "our" environment. The individualistic Italians are seemingly thought to be more responsive to an invitation to protect a "private" good, whereas Swedes are expected to be sensitive to pleas for the common good. Knowing what makes people focus on the environment in a positive way can be a powerful tool in the hands of shrewd policymakers. Still, developing successful policies that rely on social norms presents several difficulties. To successfully manipulate social settings, we need to predict how people will interpret a given context, which cues will 'stand out' as salient, and how particular cues relate to certain norms. When multiple conflicting norms could apply, we should be able to tell which cues will favor one of them. Many norms are not socially beneficial, and once established they are difficult to eliminate. If we know what induces people to conform to "anti-social" norms, we may have a chance to curb destructive behavior. Without a better understanding of the mechanisms through which norms control our actions, however, there is little hope of predicting and thus influencing behavior. The mechanisms that induce conformity are very different for different kinds of norms. Consequently, a good understanding of their diversity will prevent us from focusing on the wrong type of norm in our efforts to induce pro-social behavior.

In the remainder of this chapter I will introduce the reader to my definition of social norms, descriptive norms, conventions, and the conditions under which one might see individuals following any of these. I shall especially focus on the four (individually) necessary and (jointly) sufficient conditions for a social norm to exist that I develop in the following pages: contingency, empirical expectations, normative expectations, and conditional preferences.

Social norms

Social norms are frequently confused with codified rules, normative expectations, or recurrent, observable behavior. However, there are significant problems with such definitions of social norms. By the term *social norm*, I shall always refer to informal norms, as opposed to formal, condified norms such as legal rules. Social norms are, like legal ones, public and shared, but, unlike legal rules, which are supported by formal sanctions, social norms may not be enforced at all. When they are enforced, the sanctions are informal, as when the violation of a group norm brings about responses that range from gossip to open censure, ostracism, or dishonor for the transgressor. Some such norms may become part of our system of values, and we may feel a strong obligation to obey them. Guilt and remorse will accompany transgression, as much as the breach of a moral rule elicits painfully negative feelings in the offender. Social norms should also be distinguished from moral rules: As I shall argue in the following, expectations are crucial in sustaining the former but not necessarily the latter. In particular, conformity to a social norm is conditional on expectations about other people's behavior and/or beliefs. The feelings of shame and guilt that may accompany a transgression merely reinforce one's tendency to conform, but they are never the sole or the ultimate determinants of conformity. I will come back to this point later.

A norm cannot be simply identified with a recurrent, collective behavioral pattern. For one, norms can be either prescriptive or proscriptive: In the latter case, we usually do not observe the proscribed behavior. As anyone who has lived in a foreign country knows, learning proscriptive norms can be difficult and the learning process slow and fraught with misunderstandings and false steps. Often the legal system helps, in that many proscriptive norms are made explicit and supported by laws, but a host of socially relevant proscriptions such as "do not stare at someone you pass by" or "do not touch people you are not intimate with when you talk to them" are not codified and can only be learned by trial and error. In most cases in which a proscriptive norm is in place, we *do not* observe the behavior proscribed by the norm, and it is impossible to determine whether the absence of certain behaviors is due to a proscription or to something else, unless we assess people's beliefs and expectations. Furthermore, if we were to adopt a purely behavioral account of norms, nothing would distinguish shared fairness criteria from, say, the collective morning habit of brushing one's teeth. It would also be difficult to deal with those cases in which people pay lip service to the norm in public and deviate in private. Avoiding a purely behavioral account means focusing on the role expectations play in supporting those kinds of collective behaviors that we take to be norm-driven. After all, I brush my teeth whether or not I expect others to do the same, but I would not even try to ask for a salary proportionate to my education if I expected my co-workers to go by the rule of giving to each in proportion to seniority. There are also behaviors that can be explained only by the existence of norms, even if the behavior prescribed by the norm in question is never observed. In his study of the Ik, Turnbull (1972) reports that these starved hunter-gatherers tried hard to elude situations where their compliance with norms of reciprocity was expected. Thus they would go out of their way to avoid being in the role of gift-taker. A leaking roof would be repaired at night, so as to ward off offers to help and future obligations to repay the favor. Hunting was a solitary and furtive activity, so as to escape the obligation to share one's bounty with anyone encountered along the way. Much of the Ik's behavior can be explained as a successful attempt at *eluding* existing reciprocity norms. The Ik seemed to have collective beliefs about what sort of behavior was prescribed/proscribed in a given social context but acted in ways that prevented the underlying norms from being activated. Their practices demonstrate that it is not necessary to observe compliance to argue that a norm exists and affects behavior.

As Turnbull's example shows, having normative beliefs and expecting others to conform to a norm do not always result in a norm being activated. Nobody is violating the norm, but everybody is trying to avoid situations where they would have to follow it. Thus, simply focusing on norms as clusters of expectations might be as misleading as focusing only on the behavioral dimension, because there are many examples of discrepancies between normative expectations and behavior. Take the widely acknowledged norm of self-interest (Miller and Ratner 1998): It is remarkable to observe how often people (especially in the United States) expect others to act selfishly, even when they are prepared to act altruistically themselves. Studies show that people's willingness to give blood is not altered by monetary incentives, but typically those very people who are willing to donate blood for free expect others to donate blood only in the presence of a sufficient monetary reward (Wuthnow 1991). Similarly, when asked whether they would rent an apartment to an unmarried couple, all landlords interviewed in Oregon in the early 1970s answered positively, but they estimated that only 50% of other landlords would accept an unmarried couple as tenants (Dawes 1972). Such cases are rather common; what is puzzling is that people may expect a given norm to be upheld in the absence of information about other people's conforming behavior and in the face of personal evidence to the contrary. Thus, simply focusing on people's expectations may tell us very little about collective behavior.

If a purely behavioral definition of norms is deficient, and one solely based on expectations is questionable, what are we left with? Norms refer to behavior, to actions over which people have control, and are supported by shared expectations about what should/should not be done in different types of social situations. Norms, however, cannot just be identified with observable behavior, nor can they be equated with normative beliefs, as normative beliefs may or may not result in appropriate actions. In what follows I introduce a definition of social norms that will be helpful in shedding light on the conceptual differences between different types of social rules. My definition coincides with ordinary usage in some respects but departs from that usage in others. Given the fact that the term has been put to multiple uses, it would be unrealistic to expect a single definition to agree with what each person using the term means. The goal of giving a specific definition is to single out what is fundamental to social norms, what differentiates them from other types of social constructs.

[. . .]

Conditions for a social norm to exist

Let R be a *behavioral rule* for situations of type S, where S can be represented as a mixed-motive game. We say that R is a social norm in a population P if there exists a sufficiently large subset $P_{cf} \subseteq P$ such that, for each individual $i \in P_{cf}$:

1. *Contingency:* i knows that a rule R exists and applies to situations of type S;
2. *Conditional preference:* i prefers to conform to R in situations of type S on the condition that:
   (a) *Empirical expectations:* i believes that a sufficiently large subset of P conforms to R in situations of type S;
   and either
   (b) *Normative expectations:* i believes that a sufficiently large subset of P expects i to conform to R in situations of type S;
   or
   (b$'$) *Normative expectations with sanctions:* i believes that a sufficiently large subset of P expects i to conform to R in situations of type S, prefers i to conform, and may sanction behavior.

A social norm R is *followed* by population P if there exists a sufficiently large subset $P_f \subseteq P_{cf}$ such that, for each individual $i \in P_f$, conditions 2(a) and either 2(b) or 2(b$'$) are met for i and, as a result, i prefers to conform to R in situations of type S.

There are several features of the above definition that need explanation. First, note that a rule R can be a social norm for a population P even if it is not currently being followed by P. I defined P_{cf} as the set of 'conditional followers' of R, those individuals who know about R and have a conditional preference for conforming to R. I defined P_f as the set of 'followers' of R, those individuals who know about R and have a preference for conforming to R (because they believe that the conditions for their conditional preference are fulfilled). A behavioral rule R is a social norm if the set of its conditional followers is sufficiently large; a social norm is followed if the set of its followers is sufficiently large. Second, note that a social norm is defined relative to a population: A behavioral rule R can be a social norm for one population P and not for another population P'. Finally, the 'sufficiently large subset P_{cf} of P' clause reflects the fact that social norms need not be universally conditionally preferred or even universally known about in order to exist. A certain amount of opportunistic transgression is to be expected whenever a norm conflicts with individuals' self-interest. The 'sufficiently large subset P_f of P_{cf}' clause reflects the fact that, even among conditional followers of a norm, some individuals may not follow the norm because their empirical and normative expectations have not been fulfilled. Moreover, even among the members of P_f, occasional deviance due to mistakes is to be expected. How much deviance is tolerable is an empirical matter and may vary with different norms. For example, we would expect P_{cf} (the proportion of conditional followers) to be equal to P in the case of group norms, especially when the group is fairly small, whereas P_{cf} will be close to P in the case of well-entrenched social norms. For new norms, or norms that are not deemed to be socially important, the subset P_{cf} could be significantly smaller than P. I will discuss deviance and its effects in later chapters, when I address the issue of norm dynamics. It should also be noted that I do not assume P_f (the proportion of actual followers) to be common knowledge. Different individuals will have different beliefs about the size of P_f and thus have different empirical expectations. If so, they will have different thresholds for what 'sufficiently large' means. What matters to actual conformity is that each individual in P_{cf} believes that her threshold has been reached or surpassed.

Condition 1, the *contingency condition*, says that actors are aware that a certain behavioral rule exists and applies to situations of type S. This collective awareness is constitutive of its very existence as a norm. Note that norms are understood to apply to classes or families of situations, not to every possible situation or context. A norm of revenge, for example, usually applies to members of a kinship group and is suspended in case of proven accidental death. A norm of reciprocity may not be expected to apply if the gift was a bribe, and the rules that govern fair allocation of bodily organs differ from those that regulate the fair allocation of university Ph.D. slots. Situational contingency explains why people sometimes try to manipulate norms by avoiding those situations to which the norm applies (as the Ik did with food sharing and gift reciprocation) or by negotiating the meaning of a particular situation.

Condition 2(a), the *empirical expectations condition*, says that expectations of conformity matter. I take them to be *empirical expectations*, in the sense that one expects people to follow R in situations of type S because one has observed them to do just that over a long period of time. If the present situation is of type S, one can reasonably infer that, *ceteris paribus*, people will conform to R as they always did in the past. Notice that the fulfillment of Condition 2(a) entails that a social norm is *practiced* (or is *believed to be practiced*) in a given population (which may be as small as a group comprising a few members or as large as a nation); otherwise there would not be empirical expectations. Sometimes expectations are formed not by directly observing conforming behavior, but rather its consequences. This would happen, for example, with norms regulating private behavior. In this case, public support might be voiced for a norm that is seldom adhered to in private. If conformity to such a norm is believed to produce observable consequences, then observing such consequences will validate the norm. But if these consequences are the effect of other causes, people will draw the wrong inference and continue to believe that the norm is widely followed even when support is dwindling. Consider a norm of private behavior such as avoiding premarital sex; what we observe are the consequences of such behavior (teen pregnancy, etc.) or the lack thereof. If people take adequate precautions, there might be greater deviance than expected, but people might still believe that the norm is widely practiced in the population. Norms regulating private behavior may thus present us with cases in which Conditions 2(a) and 2(b) are satisfied. However, as I shall make clear in discussing Conditions 2(b) and 2(b'), there are many individuals for whom 2(b'), the possibility of sanctions, is a *necessary* condition for compliance. Such individuals will believe they are expected to follow the norm but will not expect to be sanctioned for transgressing it [Condition 2(b')], because deviance can be concealed. In this case, public endorsement of the norm may coexist with considerable private deviance.

The expectations mentioned in Condition 2(a) could, besides being empirical, also be *normative*, in the sense that people might think that everyone 'ought to' conform to R in situations of type S. The 'ought' implicit in a normative belief does not necessarily state an obligation. Take, for instance, a well-known convention such as the rule of driving on the right side of the road. We believe that people ought to follow that rule simply because, if they do not, they risk killing or being killed. If a person does not want to jeopardize her life, nor does she have an interest in causing harm to others, then we believe she 'ought to' follow the driving rule. The 'ought' in this case expresses prudential reasons and is akin to saying that, if you have goal x and the best available means to attain x is a course of action y, then you ought to adopt y. Consider, on the other hand, a rule of equal division. In this case, we may believe that others ought to 'divide the cake in equal parts' because this is the fair thing to do. We think they have an obligation to follow the rule, a duty to be fair. I do not ask for the moment what grounds this obligation, though I shall come back to this question later. At this point it is only important to make a distinction between a prudential 'ought' and the statement of an obligation. From now on, when I mention 'normative expectations' I will always refer to the latter meaning.

[. . .]

Conditions 2(b) and 2(b′) tell us that people may have different reasons for conditionally preferring to follow a norm. Condition 2(b), the *normative expectations condition*, says that expectations are *believed to be reciprocal*. That is, not only do I expect others to conform, but I also believe they expect me to conform. What sort of belief is this? On the one hand, it might just be an empirical belief. If I have consistently followed R in situations of type S in the past, people may reasonably infer that, *ceteris paribus*, I will do the same in the future, and that is what I believe. On the other hand, it might be a normative belief: I believe a sufficiently large number of people think that I have an obligation to conform to R in the appropriate circumstances. For some individuals, the fulfillment of Conditions 2(a) and 2(b) is sufficient to induce a preference for conformity. That is, such individuals recognize the legitimacy of others' expectations and feel an obligation to fulfill them. For others, the possibility of sanctions is crucial to induce a preference for conformity. Condition 2(b′) says that I believe that those who expect me to conform also *prefer* me to conform, and might be prepared to sanction my behavior when they can observe it. Sanctions may be positive or negative. The possibility of sanctions may motivate some individuals to follow a norm, either out of fear of punishment or because of a desire to please and thus be rewarded. For others, sanctions are irrelevant, and a normative expectation is all they need. Condition 2(b′) does not say that transgressions *will* be punished and compliance rewarded. It only states that a sufficiently large subset of P *may* be capable and willing to sanction others. As we shall see in a moment, normative expectations are essential for the enforcement of social norms.

Now suppose Conditions 1, 2(a), and either 2(b) or 2(b′) hold. Each of them is a necessary condition for conformity to R, but *contingency*, *empirical*, and *normative expectations* are not jointly sufficient to produce conformity to rule R in situations of type S. I might expect others to follow a rule of equal division, and believe that I am expected to follow that rule too, but when it is my turn to 'cut the cake,' I may be tempted to get a larger share, especially if nobody is observing my action. If I do not, it must be that I *prefer* to conform to the rule. However, this is no simple, unconditional preference for conformity. Condition 2, the *conditional preference condition*, says this preference is *conditional* on expecting others to conform to R and either believing that one is expected to conform to R or believing that those who expect one to conform also have a preference for collective conformity and are prepared to punish or reward. If so, the counterfactual "If I were to believe that others do not follow R or do not expect me to follow R, then I would not want to conform to R" must be true. What I am saying suggests that following a social norm may be contrary to self-interest, especially if we define it in purely material terms. Thus it may be the case that, in the presence of monetary or otherwise 'material' rewards, I have a tendency to prefer more to less but will prefer to 'share' if I believe that I am in a situation in which some form of generosity is the norm, if I expect others to be generous, and if I believe them to think I 'ought to' be generous in the circumstances. In this case, I might prefer to behave generously. Note that the generous behavior induced by adherence to a norm should not be confused with other motives, such as altruism or benevolence.

Before we continue our discussion of Condition 2, let us look at an example that will hopefully clarify what I mean by saying that the motive to follow a norm should be distinguished from other motives. Consider playing a one-shot prisoner's dilemma, where C stands for Cooperate and D stands for Defect.

If the payoffs in Figure 24.1 represent sums of money, just by looking at them it is not obvious what a player will choose. Suppose Self, the row player, only cares about his 'material' self-interest and thus prefers DC to CC, CC to DD, and DD to CD. If B stands for best, S for second best, T for third best, and W for worst, the preference ranking of a narrowly self-interested Self would look like that shown in Figure 24.2.

The narrowly self-interested person will always choose D, her dominant strategy. Self-interest, however, should not be confused with the desire for material incentives. A self-interested person is one whose ultimate desires are self-regarding, but these desires can involve 'immaterial' goods such as power and recognition, or the experience of 'benevolent' emotions. A self-interested person may want to 'feel good' (or reap social rewards like status and love) by reciprocating expected cooperation and in this case her preferences would look like those in Figure 24.3.

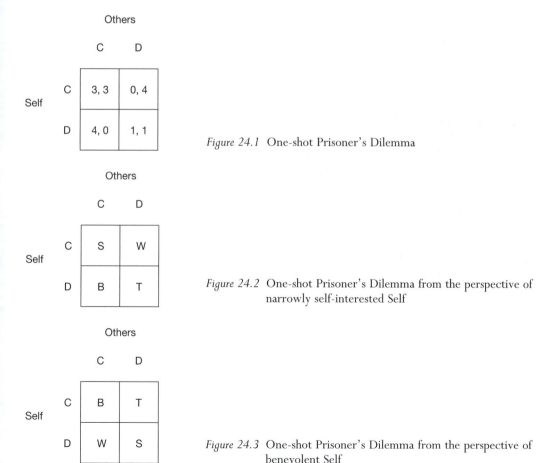

Figure 24.1 One-shot Prisoner's Dilemma

Figure 24.2 One-shot Prisoner's Dilemma from the perspective of narrowly self-interested Self

Figure 24.3 One-shot Prisoner's Dilemma from the perspective of benevolent Self

Note that a benevolent person would prefer CD to DC; that is, she would prefer, *ceteris paribus*, to be the righteous sucker rather than the spiteful cheat. This preference would probably be cost-sensitive, but if the costs are not too high, it makes sense to prefer to 'feel good about oneself' and be the loser rather than penalizing another to get some small benefit.

Benevolent motives are different from those of a pure altruist, whom I take to be a person whose ultimate desires are completely other-regarding. A pure altruist wants, first and foremost, the satisfaction of another's desires, at whatever cost to the self.[4] If the altruist believes his partner to be a narrowly self-interested type, the altruist's preference ranking would look like the one in Figure 24.4.

The person who instead follows a norm of generosity or cooperation need not have a desire to 'feel good': If the established norm is a cooperative one, provided Conditions 2(a) and either 2(b) or 2(b') are met, the preference ranking of the norm follower will look like the one in Figure 24.5.

The norm follower's preferences are similar to those of the self-interested, benevolent person, with a crucial difference: For the benevolent person, it is better to be the 'sucker' than the 'crook' (CD is preferred to DG); but for the norm follower, the reverse may be true.[5] This distinction should not be interpreted as denying that individuals can be both benevolent and norm followers. Benevolence, however, is usually directed to people with whom we habitually interact and know well. As social distance increases, benevolence tends to decrease. If most people were benevolent toward strangers, we would need no pro-social norms of fairness, reciprocity, or cooperation. In particular, we would have no need for those norms that 'internalize' externalities created by behavior that imposes costs on other people. Thus it is plausible that one is guided by benevolence (or even altruism) in interacting with family and friends, but when interacting with strangers, be guided by social norms. Moreover, whereas benevolence toward those who are close to us should be a relatively stable disposition, generosity or cooperativeness with strangers will vary according to our expectations, as defined in Conditions 2(a) and 2(b) or 2(b').

It may be objected that motivational distinctions are futile, because often observation cannot discriminate among them. If in a one-shot social dilemma experiment we observe consistent

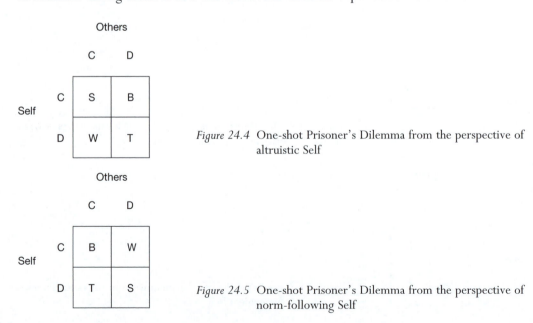

Figure 24.4 One-shot Prisoner's Dilemma from the perspective of altruistic Self

Figure 24.5 One-shot Prisoner's Dilemma from the perspective of norm-following Self

cooperative behavior, what can we say about the underlying preferences? If, as economists do, we take preferences to describe behavior and not motivation, what we observe is a 'revealed preference' for taking into account other people's welfare. *Why* we do that does not matter. Still, I believe motivations carry some weight. Up to now, most experiments have been geared to show that human behavior consistently deviates from the narrow, self-interested paradigm postulated by traditional economic models. Experiments have been very successful in this respect, yet they do not tell us why actors have other-regarding preferences. Is it altruism, benevolence, or are we priming norms of fairness and reciprocity? The answer is clearly important, and not just for the policymaker. What we now need is to test more sophisticated hypotheses about what goes on in the black box. To do so it is important to pay attention to the meanings of the concepts we use (and test). To tell altruism and benevolence apart is not very difficult: If an altruist is informed that the other defected, the altruist should keep cooperating. Never mind there are very few such people around: If they exist, that is the way altruists will behave. The benevolent individual and the norm follower are more difficult to set apart. For one, a norm follower may also be motivated by benevolence. If, however, some norm followers are not benevolent, the distinction would be most clear in all those situations in which people are forced to choose between CD and DC. Suppose we identify a subset of people who 'conditionally cooperate' in one-shot Prisoner's Dilemmas. That is, controlling for their expectations, they cooperate whenever they expect others to cooperate, too. It should be possible to perform another experiment on the same individuals in which the only choice is one between being the sucker or the crook: The subject might be told that the other player will choose next, and will have to choose the opposite of what she does. Provided the personal cost is not too high, the benevolent person should prefer being the sucker. A person who instead followed a cooperative norm for reasons other than benevolence would see no reason to be the sucker (possibly provided the cost to the other person is not too great).

Condition 2 (the *conditional preference condition*) marks an important distinction between social and personal norms, whether they are habits or have moral force. Take the habit of brushing my teeth every morning. I find it sanitary, and I like the taste of mint toothpaste. Even if I came to realize that most people stopped brushing their teeth, I would continue to do so, because I have independent reasons for doing it. It is likewise with moral norms: I have good, independent reasons to avoid killing people I deeply dislike. Even if I were to find myself in a Hobbesian state of nature, without rules or rights, I would still feel repugnance and anguish at the idea of taking a life. With this I do not mean to suggest that moral norms are a world apart from other rules. Instead, by their very nature, moral norms demand (at least in principle) an unconditional commitment.[6] Commitments of course may falter, and we may run afoul of even the most cherished obligations. The point is that, under normal conditions, expectations of other people's conformity to a moral rule are not a good *reason* to obey it. Nor is it a good reason that others expect me to follow a moral rule. If I find their expectation reasonable, it is because I find the moral norm reasonable; so the reason to obey it must reside in the norm itself. What I am saying goes against the well-known Humean interpretation of our moral obligation to follow the requirements of justice (Hume 1751). This moral obligation is, according to Hume, *conditional* on the expectation that others are following the norms of justice too. In my interpretation, Hume's requirements of justice are social norms, because they fulfill my conditions for a social norm to exist. What distinguishes norms of justice from other social norms is that many of us would have a conditional preference for abiding by such norms because we acknowledge that the normative expectations expressed by Condition 2(b) are *legitimate* and should therefore be satisfied. Their legitimacy may stem from recognizing how important it is for the good functioning of our society to have such norms, but of course their ongoing value depends on widespread conformity. There is nothing inherently good in our fairness norms, above and beyond their role in regulating our ways of allocating and distributing goods and privileges according to the basic structure of our society.[7] However, many of us would feel there is something inherently bad in taking a life, especially when the victim is a close kin. All known societies have developed similar rules against killing one's kin or mating with one's parents. The *unconditional* preference most of us have for not committing such acts may have an evolutionary origin, and typically contemplating killing or incest elicits a strong, negative emotional response of repugnance. What needs to be stressed here is that what makes something a social or a moral norm is our attitude toward it.[8] How we *justify* our conditional or unconditional allegiance has no bearing on the reality of the distinction, and the latter is all that matters to my definition of social norms.

Notes

1   What one most prefers in these cases is to 'do as others do,' or to coordinate with others' choices.
2   Well-known examples of mixed-motive games that can be 'solved' (or better, 'transformed') by norms of fairness, reciprocity, promise-keeping, etc., are the Prisoner's Dilemma, the Trust game, and Ultimatum games.
3   Schemata are cognitive structures that contain knowledge about people, events, roles, etc, Schemata, for events (e.g., a lecture, going to a restaurant, playing a chess game) are also called scripts. Chapter 2 further elaborates on the roles of scripts and schemata.
4   The choice to donate part of one's liver to an anonymous recipient is an example of altruism, because the risk of complications and even death from the procedure is sizable.
5   Again, I am assuming for simplicity that the norm follower is not also benevolent. If this were the case, Figures 24.3 and 24.5 would coincide, at least in all those situations to which benevolence applies. In large, anonymous groups, where the effects of one's actions are insignificant, we may expect less cooperation (or not at all) from the benevolent person, whereas the norm follower would not be affected.
6   It might be argued that even what we usually understand as moral norms are conditional. One may be thoroughly committed to respect the sanctity of human life, but there are circumstances in which one's commitment would waver. Imagine finding oneself in a community where violence and murder are daily occurrences, expected and condoned by most. One would probably at first resist violence, then react to it, and finally act it out oneself. Guilt and remorse would in time be replaced by complacency, as one might come to feel the act of murder to be entirely necessary and justified. The testimonies of survivors of concentration camps, as well as the personal recollections of SS officers, are frightening examples of how fragile our most valued principles can be.
7   The fact that 'fair' allocations reflect the structure of society is well known to anthropologists. In traditional, authoritarian societies, for example, the allocation of goods is based on rank. Such allocations are accepted by all the involved parties as just (Fiske 1992).
8   Our attitudes are also shaped in part by the norms that we internalize, which results in a positive feedback loop between attitudes and adherence to norms.

References

Allport, E.H. 1924. *Social Psychology*. Boston, Houghton Mifflin.
Camerer, C. 2003. *Behavioral Game Theory*. Princeton, Princeton University Press.
Cialdini, R. Kallgren, C., and Reno, R. 1990. "A Focus Theory of Normative Conduct: A Theoretical Refinement and Reevaluation of the Role of Norms in Human Behavior". *Advances in Experimental Social Psychology* 24: 201–34.
Dawes, R.J. 1972. *Fundamentals of Attitude Measurement*. New York, Wiley.
Fiske, S.T. 1992. "The Four Elementary Forms of Sociality: Framework for a Unified Theory of Social Relations", *Psychological Review* 99: 689–723.
Henrich, J. 2000. "Does Culture Matter in Economic Behavior? Ultimatum Game Bargaining Among the Machiguenga", *American Economic Review* 90: 973–79.

Hume, D. (1966). *An Enquiry Concerning the Principles of Morals* (1751). London: Free Press.

Lamberts, K. and Shanks, D. Eds. 1997. *Knowledge, Concepts, and Categories*. Hove, Psychology Press.

Miller, D. and McFarland, C. 1991. "When Social Comparison Goes Awry: The Case of Pluralistic Ignorance". In *Social Comparison: Contemporary Theory and Research*. J. Suls and T.A. Wills, Eds. Hillsdale, NJ, Erlbaum, pp. 115–33.

Miller, D. and Ratner, R. 1998. "The Disparity between the Actual and Assumed Power of Self-Interest." *Journal of Personality and Social Psychology* 74, 53–62.

Turnbull C. 1972. *The Mountain People*. New York, Simon & Schuster.

Tversky, A. and Kahneman, D. 1981. "The Framing of Decision and the Psychology of Choice", *Science* 211: 453–58.

Ullmann-Margalit, E. 1977. *The Emergence of Norms*. Oxford, Clarendon Press.

Wuthnow, R. 1991. *Acts of Compassion: Caring for Others and Helping Ourselves*. Princeton, Princeton University Press.

PART VII

Cultural evolution

E VOLUTIONARY SOCIAL SCIENTISTS borrow tools from biology to study, explain, and predict social and cultural phenomena. Although its origins can be traced back to the human ethology of the 1960s (see Griffiths 2008), the evolutionary approach came to prominence in the 1970s when so-called "sociobiologists" launched a provocative attack against traditional social science methods. This body of work (especially Wilson 1975) sparked a heated controversy in the academia and the media, which left sociobiology stained with accusations of biological determinism, political conservatism, and even sexism and racism. Partly for this reason, and partly as a consequence of internal developments, sociobiology re-emerged in the 1990s under the guise of evolutionary psychology (Tooby and Cosmides 1992), a programme aimed at the biological explanation of psychological mechanisms or "modules" – instead of behaviours as in the old sociobiology of the 1970s (Sterelny 1992).

Evolutionary psychology was also received with suspicion by social scientists. The latter's opposition to evolutionary theory is often motivated by worries of imperialism – the prospect that social science may be taken over by an allegedly "more fundamental" or "more scientific" approach to the study of human behaviour. These worries, however, are probably exaggerated and based on conceptual confusions that philosophers have contributed to dispel. The classic distinction between *proximate* and *ultimate* causes (Mayr 1961), to begin with, can be used to argue that standard and evolutionary social science trade with different kinds of explanations. While proximate causes are responsible for the behaviour of an organism, ultimate mechanisms explain why and how a certain organism became what it is. Evolutionary theory is chiefly concerned with the latter, historical issue, and is thus largely compatible with theoretical approaches that focus on (proximate) social explanations of social phenomena.

The epistemic credentials of evolutionary science are also controversial. Sociobiology and evolutionary psychology have been harshly criticized for using ad hoc explanations and "soft" data (e.g. Kitcher 1985, Dupré 2001). Among other things, the critics point out that we often know more – and, crucially, we can collect more data – about the proximate causes than about the evolutionary history of a social phenomenon. The appeal of biological accounts of morally and politically sensitive phenomena, amplified by uncritical media coverage, adds further concerns in the eyes of the sceptics.

Many of these concerns, however, do not apply to the variety of evolutionary social science reviewed in this section. While evolutionary psychology and sociobiology provide *genetic* explanations of social behaviour (or its underlying capacities), another influential genre of evolutionary social science focuses on purely cultural evolutionary processes and social units of selection. This programme asserts the existence of powerful analogies between the selection and transmission of genes and the mechanisms governing the diffusion of ideas, institutions, and cultural artefacts in human societies. Although philosophers have been precursors in this area (e.g. Popper 1971, Campbell 1980), the study of cultural evolution has made significant progress only after the introduction, three decades ago, of a new set of conceptual and technical tools which have unified the vocabulary and methodology of anthropology, game theory, and cognitive science.

The ethologist-turned-popular science writer Richard Dawkins has proposed one of the most fortunate and popular models of cultural evolution. His influential book *The Selfish Gene* (1976) includes a powerful defence of "genetic individualism," the thesis that natural selection operates primarily at the level of genes – rather than organisms, groups, or species as previously suggested by prominent evolutionary theorists (including, arguably, Darwin himself). During the so-called "levels of selection" controversy, Dawkins and other individualists argued that apparently puzzling phenomena such as the existence of "altruistic" traits in humans and other animals (behaviours that lead to a net reduction in the chances of survival of an organism, while helping the survival of conspecifics) can be satisfactorily explained as cunning strategies adopted by "selfish genes" that maximize their inclusive fitness under evolutionary pressure.

Although the attribution of egoism to genes was proposed as no more than a useful metaphor, Dawkins' book was full of provocative claims that fostered a huge secondary literature. In the excerpt reprinted in this anthology Dawkins extends the "selfish replicator" model to phenomena of cultural dissemination. While acknowledging that cultural phenomena are governed by mechanisms that cannot be explained directly in terms of genetic inheritance and selection, Dawkins suggests that their historical development follows a logic that is *formally* similar to that of genetic evolution. The key move is to replace the biological unit of selection (the gene) with a social/cultural counterpart (the "meme") which propagates or goes extinct depending on the evolutionary pressure/competition it faces in the socio-cultural arena.

Like other sociobiological ideas, memes have attracted fans and critics in great numbers. With hindsight, Dawkins' supporters have come to admit that "memetics" has failed to produce great scientific insights (Edmonds 2005). The heuristic power of Dawkins' proposal, therefore, can be best appreciated through the work of those critics who have investigated the *dis*-analogies between biological and cultural evolution, and who have been able to devise convincing empirical applications of their models. Dan Sperber's "epidemiological model" of cultural evolution is a prominent example. The starting point of the epidemiological model is that *mutation* is the norm and exact replication the exception in the propagation of cultural ideas and artefacts. From this respect, then, cultural evolution works in the opposite way to genetic evolution. Sperber (1996) uses as an example the transmission of fables and cultural myths from one generation to the next: it is unlikely that all narrators use exactly the same words or even the same plot when telling a tale. Nevertheless, some plots are more resilient than others, in the sense that their content and structure facilitate their preservation and diffusion in spite of the human tendency to introduce variations. Evolutionary explanations thus must pay attention to the factors that increase (or decrease) such resilience. According to Sperber, we must focus in particular on the capacities and limitations of our cognitive apparatus, which for contingent reasons (our brain did not evolve primarily for cultural transmission) has the tendency to retain and transfer certain cultural entities at the expense of others. Emotional factors, for example, make some elements of a tale (say, the "evil queen-mother") more salient than others; cognitive factors make some formulae easier to recall (Homeric verses may be a case in point), and so forth.

The epidemiological approach has encouraged a fruitful collaboration between evolutionary theory, cognitive science, anthropology, and the social sciences more generally. It has generated, moreover, a body of empirical work in areas as diverse as folk biological classification, the transmission of religious beliefs, and the evolution of norms of etiquette (Boyer 1994, Atran 1990, Nichols 2004). This is an important accomplishment in a field dominated by theoretical speculation at the expense of empirical data.

An important virtue of evolutionary theory is its unifying power, and one of the attractions of Dawkins' selfish gene (or meme) theory was its resonance with rational choice in social science. *Evolutionary game theory* resulted from the contamination between evolutionary biology and economics in the 1970s (Maynard Smith 1982). Abandoning the assumption of perfect rationality of standard game theory, evolutionary game theorists model "dumb" agents with a tendency to play mechanically the same strategies regardless of their own incentives and those of their opponents. Instead of being future-oriented (like rational strategic players) such agents are backwards looking: they learn by imitating the strategies that have been most successful in previous rounds. Via this process of adjustment, successful strategies replicate faster than less successful ones, which as a consequence tend to go extinct.

The third chapter reprinted in this section, Alexander and Skyrms' "Bargaining with Neighbours", applies evolutionary game theory to the evolution of social norms. The target of Alexander and Skyrms is the egalitarian norm prescribing that every member of a group should get an equal share of some available resource, other things being equal (they assume, for example, that there are no property rights). They model the sharing process as a two-person *Nash Demand game*, where each player indicates her own share and gets it if and only if the sum of proposed shares does not exceed the size of the cake. A well-known problem with this game is that every efficient allocation (i.e. every pair of demands adding up to 100 percent of the cake) is also a Nash equilibrium of standard game theory. This particularly severe problem of equilibrium selection has challenged game theorists to identify the strategy that will be more frequently played by real-life (as opposed to perfectly rational) agents.

When the Nash bargaining game is played in the laboratory, real players spontaneously coordinate on the 50-50 percent division. The intuitive explanation is that the egalitarian allocation stands out as *fair*, and is thus normatively compelling for socialized human beings as we are. Naturalistically-minded philosophers, however, will not be satisfied with this answer, for it only shifts the problem one step further: What is it that makes the egalitarian solution normatively compelling? Why do we intuitively judge it "fair"? Evolutionary game theorists claim that we consider fair those equilibria which have survived a process of selection over many repetitions of the bargaining game. They are – in game-theoretic jargon – "evolutionarily stable strategies" in the game of life.

As Alexander and Skyrms show, demonstrating that the egalitarian split is the unique evolutionarily stable strategy of the Nash Demand game is far from trivial (see also Skyrms 1996, Young 1998, Binmore 2005). One approach is to impose some structure on the range of possible interactions available to the players, for example by postulating that they bargain more frequently with their neighbours than with agents that are located further away in the game's (abstract) geographic space.

Evolutionary game theory has become increasingly popular in philosophy and in economics over the last two decades (Axelrod 1984, Sugden 1986, Skyrms 1996, 2004, Binmore 1998, 2005, Alexander 2007). Its "mainstream" version retains two characteristic elements of the sociobiological approach from which it originates, namely, *individualism* and *adaptationism*. Individualism, as we have seen, is the claim that selection takes place primarily at the level of genes (or memes, strategies) and that group selection is either ineffective or can be explained away in terms of lower-level (individualistic) selection processes. Adaptationism is the thesis that Darwinian selection dominates all other mechanisms and is the main determinant of evolutionary trajectories. As a consequence, the traits (or strategies, norms) that we currently observe must be optimal or nearly optimal given the organism's initial conditions, the available resources, and the competition it has faced in the past.

Both principles have been questioned and there exists a considerable literature in the philosophy of biology concerning whether they should be interpreted as empirical, heuristic, or purely definitional (analytic) claims (cf. e.g. Sober 1984, Okasha 2007). Their application in the social sciences raises extra problems because of the difficulty of identifying the unit of selection/transmission of cultural entities, and the interaction between biological and cultural evolutionary processes. Over the last three decades *gene-culture coevolution* has established itself as a plausible middle ground position granting a central explanatory role to both biological and cultural factors in the history of homo sapiens. Already in the 1970s population geneticists had convincingly argued that cultural traits could give rise to *genetically maladaptive* behaviours that are able to trump the force of genetic selection: birth control practices and technology, for example, can propagate quickly in spite of the fact that those who practice birth control leave fewer genetic offspring than those who do not (Cavalli-Sforza and Feldman 1981). The reason is that cultural transmission follows different pathways than genetic inheritance (it disseminates "horizontally" rather than "vertically", for example) and is influenced by various biases that make it particularly powerful even when it has fitness-reducing effects.

Peter Richerson and Robert Boyd outline some key properties of cultural transmission, and make a strong case for the use of Darwinian models in anthropology and social science. In *Not by Genes Alone* (2005), a recent summary of their life-long research programme, they argue that the use of such models is not hindered by the standard objections raised by critics. Although there are well-known dis-analogies between cultural and biological evolution (such as inexact replication, non-random mutation, and the holistic character of cultural entities), none of these is incompatible with *population thinking* – the use of quantitative models to keep track of the distribution of biological/cultural traits and their patterns of variation through time. This style of modelling, according to Boyd and Richerson, is the true hallmark of the Darwinian approach and what distinguishes it from alternative methods in social science and history.

Further reading

There is an old tradition of evolutionary modelling in economics, largely independent of the developments described above, which is reviewed and discussed philosophically by Hodgson (1993) and Vromen (1995). The interaction between economists and evolutionary theorists takes place nowadays mainly in the areas of evolutionary game theory and experimental economics (on the latter, see e.g. Gintis et al. 2005). Evolutionary game theory has attracted substantial criticism, but see in particular D'Arms et al. (1998), Sugden (2001). The emergence of proto-sociality in other primates and in our ancestors is currently a topic of intense research, see e.g. De Waal (2006), Boehm (1999). Useful philosophical discussions of gene-culture co-evolution can be found in Sober (1991), Wimsatt (1999), Sterelny (2006). An important spin-off of the sociobiology debate has been the proliferation of evolutionary accounts of morality, to which philosophers have contributed substantially – see e.g. Sober and Wilson (1998), Gibbard (1990), Joyce (2006).

References

Alexander, J.M. (2007) *The Structural Evolution of Morality*. Cambridge: Cambridge University Press.

Axelrod, R. (1984) *The Evolution of Cooperation*. London: Penguin.

Atran, S. (1990) *Cognitive Foundations of Natural History*. Cambridge: Cambridge University Press.

Binmore, K. (1998) *Game Theory and the Social Contract II: Just Playing*. Cambridge, MA: MIT Press.

Binmore, K. (2005) *Natural Justice*. Oxford: Oxford University Press.

Boehm, C. (1999) *Hierarchy in the Forest: The Evolution of Egalitarian Behavior*. Cambridge, MA: Harvard University Press.

Boyer, P. (1994) *The Naturalness of Religious Ideas*. Berkeley, CA: University of California Press.

Campbell, D. (1980) "Evolutionary Epistemology," in Schlipp, P.A. (ed.), *The Philosophy of Karl Popper*. La Salle: Open Court.

Cavalli-Sforza, L. and Feldman, M. (1981) *Cultural Transmission and Evolution: A Quantitative Approach*. Princeton, NJ: Princeton University Press.

D'Arms, J., Batterman, R., and Gorny, K. (1998) "Game Theoretic Explanations and the Evolution of Justice," *Philosophy of Science* 65: 76–102.

Dawkins, S. (1976) *The Selfish Gene*. London: Penguin.

De Waal, F. (2006) *Primates and Philosophers*. Princeton, NJ: Princeton University Press.

Dupré, J. (2001) *Human Nature and the Limits of Science*. Oxford: Oxford University Press.

Edmonds, B. (2005). "The Revealed Poverty of the Gene-meme Analogy – Why Memetics Per Se Has Failed to Produce Substantive Results," *Journal of Memetics* 9. http://cfpm.org/jom-emit/2005/vol9/edmonds_b.html

Gibbard, A. (1990) *Wise Choices, Apt Feelings*. Oxford: Oxford University Press.

Gintis, H., Boyd, R., Bowles, S., and Fehr, E. (eds. 2005) *Moral Sentiments and Material Interests*. Cambridge, MA: MIT Press.

Griffiths, P.E. (2008) "Ethology, Sociobiology, Evolutionary Psychology," in Sarkar, S. and Plutyinski, A. *Blackwell's Companion to Philosophy of Biology*. Oxford: Blackwell.

Hodgson, G. (1993) *Economics and Evolution*. Cambridge: Polity Press.

Joyce, R. (2006) *The Evolution of Morality*. Cambridge MA: MIT Press.

Kitcher, P. (1985) *Vaulting Ambition: Sociobiology and the Quest for Human Nature*. Cambridge, MA: MIT Press.

Maynard Smith, J. (1982) *Evolution and the Theory of Games*. Cambridge: Cambridge University Press.

Mayr, E. (1961) "Cause and Effect in Biology." *Science* 131: 1501–06.

Nichols, S. (2004) *Sentimental Rules*. Oxford: Oxford University Press.

Okasha, S. (2007) *Evolution and the Levels of Selection*. Oxford: Oxford University Press.

Popper, K.R. (1971) *Objective Knowledge: An Evolutionary Approach*. Oxford: Oxford University Press.

Richerson, P.J. and Boyd, R. (2005) *Not By Genes Alone*. Chicago, IL: University of Chicago Press.

Skyrms, B. (1996) *Evolution of the Social Contract*. Cambridge: Cambridge University Press.

Skyrms, B. (2004) *The Stag Hunt and the Evolution of Social Structure*. Cambridge: Cambridge University Press.

Sober, E. (1984) *The Nature of Selection*. Cambridge, MA: MIT Press.

Sober, E. (1991) "Models of Cultural Evolution," in P. Griffiths (ed.) *Trees of Life*. Dordrecht: Kluwer.

Sober, E. and Wilson, D.S. (1998) *Unto Others: The Evolution and Psychology of Unselfish Behavior*. Cambridge, MA: Harvard University Press.

Sperber, D. (1996) *Explaining Culture: A Naturalistic Approach*. Oxford: Blackwell.

Sterelny, K. (1992) "Evolutionary Explanations of Human Behavior," *Australasian Journal of Philosophy* 70: 156–73.

Sterelny, K. (2006) "The Evolution and Evolvability of Culture," *Mind and Language* 21: 137–65.

Sugden, R. (1986) *The Economics of Rights, Cooperation and Welfare*. London: Macmillan, 2nd edition (2004).

Sugden, R. (2001) "The Evolutionary Turn in Game Theory," *Journal of Economic Methodology* 8: 113–30.
Tooby, J.H. and Cosmides, L. (1992) "Cognitive Adaptations for Social Exchange," in J.H. Barkow, L. Cosmides, and J.H. Tooby (eds.) *The Adapted Mind.* Oxford: Oxford University Press, pp. 163–228.
Vromen, J. (1995) *Economic Evolution.* London: Routledge.
Young, P. (1998) *Individual Strategy and Social Structure: An Evolutionary Theory of Institutions.* Princeton, NJ: Princeton University Press.
Wilson, E.O. (1975) *Sociobiology: The New Synthesis.* Cambridge, MA: Harvard University Press.
Wimsatt, W.C. (1999) "Genes, Memes and Cultural Heredity," *Biology and Philosophy* 14: 279–310.

Chapter 25

RICHARD DAWKINS

MEMES
The new replicators

[. . .]

MOST OF WHAT IS UNUSUAL about man can be summed up in one word 'culture'. I use the word not in its snobbish sense, but as a scientist uses it. Cultural transmission is analogous to genetic transmission in that, although basically conservative, it can give rise to a form of evolution. Geoffrey Chaucer could not hold a conversation with a modern Englishman, even though they are linked to each other by an unbroken chain of some twenty generations of Englishmen, each of whom could speak to his immediate neighbours in the chain as a son speaks to his father. Language seems to 'evolve' by non-genetic means, and at a rate which is orders of magnitude faster than genetic evolution.

Cultural transmission is not unique to man. The best non-human example that I know has recently been described by P. F. Jenkins in the song of a bird called the saddleback which lives on islands off New Zealand. On the island where he worked there was a total repertoire of about nine distinct songs. Any given male sang only one or a few of these songs. The males could be classified into dialect groups. For example, one group of eight males with neighbouring territories sang a particular song called the CC song. Other dialect groups sang different songs. Sometimes the members of a dialect group shared more than one distinct song. By comparing the songs of fathers and sons, Jenkins showed that song patterns were not inherited genetically. Each young male was likely to adopt songs from his territorial neighbours by imitation, in an analogous way to human language. During most of the time Jenkins was there, there was a fixed number of songs on the island, a kind of 'song pool' from which each young male drew his own small repertoire. But occasionally Jenkins was privileged to witness the 'invention' of a new song, which occurred by a mistake in the imitation of an old one. He writes: 'New song forms have been shown to arise variously by change of pitch of a note, repetition of a note, the elision of notes and the combination of parts of other existing songs . . . The appearance of the new form was an abrupt event and the product was quite stable over a period of years. Further, in a number of cases the variant was transmitted accurately in its new form to younger recruits so that a recognizably coherent group of like singers developed.' Jenkins refers to the origins of new songs as 'cultural mutations'.

Song in the saddleback truly evolves by non-genetic means. There are other examples of cultural evolution in birds and monkeys, but these are just interesting oddities. It is our own species that really shows what cultural evolution can do. Language is only one example out of many. Fashions in dress and diet, ceremonies and customs, art and architecture, engineering and technology, all evolve in historical time in a way that looks like highly speeded up genetic evolution, but has really nothing to do with genetic evolution. As in genetic evolution though, the change may be progressive. There is a sense in which modern science is actually better than ancient science. Not only does our understanding of the universe change as the centuries go by: it improves. Admittedly the current burst of improvement dates back only to the Renaissance, which was preceded by a dismal period of stagnation, in which European scientific culture was frozen at the level achieved by the Greeks. But, as we saw in [Dawkins 1976] Chapter 5, genetic evolution too may proceed as a series of brief spurts between stable plateaux.

The analogy between cultural and genetic evolution has frequently been pointed out, sometimes in the context of quite unnecessary mystical overtones. The analogy between scientific progress and genetic evolution by natural selection has been illuminated especially by Sir Karl Popper. I want to go even further into directions which are also being explored by, for example, the geneticist L. L. Cavalli-Sforza, the anthropologist F. T. Cloak, and the ethologist J. M. Cullen.

As an enthusiastic Darwinian, I have been dissatisfied with explanations which my fellow-enthusiasts have offered for human behaviour. They have tried to look for 'biological advantages' in various attributes of human civilization. For instance, tribal religion has been seen as a mechanism for solidifying group identity, valuable for a pack-hunting species whose individuals rely on cooperation to catch large and fast prey. Frequently the evolutionary preconception in terms of which such theories are framed is implicitly group-selectionist, but it is possible to rephrase the theories in terms of orthodox gene selection. Man may well have spent large portions of the last several million years living in small kin groups. Kin selection and selection in favour of reciprocal altruism may have acted on human genes to produce many of our basic psychological attributes and tendencies. These ideas are plausible as far as they go, but I find that they do not begin to square up to the formidable challenge of explaining culture, cultural evolution, and the immense differences between human cultures around the world, from the utter selfishness of the Ik of Uganda, as described by Colin Turnbull, to the gentle altruism of Margaret Mead's Arapesh. I think we have got to start again and go right back to first principles. The argument I shall advance, surprising as it may seem coming from the author of the earlier chapters, is that, for an understanding of the evolution of modern man, we must begin by throwing out the gene as the sole basis of our ideas on evolution. I am an enthusiastic Darwinian, but I think Darwinism is too big a theory to be confined to the narrow context of the gene. The gene will enter my thesis as an analogy, nothing more.

What, after all, is so special about genes? The answer is that they are replicators. The laws of physics are supposed to be true all over the accessible universe. Are there any principles of biology which are likely to have similar universal validity? When astronauts voyage to distant planets and look for life, they can expect to find creatures too strange and unearthly for us to imagine. But is there anything which must be true of all life, wherever it is found, and whatever the basis of its chemistry? If forms of life exist whose chemistry is based on silicon rather than carbon, or ammonia rather than water, if creatures are discovered which boil to death at -100 degrees centigrade, if a form of life is found which is not based on chemistry at all but on electronic reverberating circuits, will there still be any general principle which is true of all life? Obviously I do not know but, if I had to bet, I would put my money on one fundamental principle. This is the law that all life evolves by the differential survival of replicating entities. The gene, the DNA molecule, happens to be the replicating entity which prevails on our own planet. There may be others. If there are, provided certain other conditions are met, they will almost inevitably tend to become the basis for an evolutionary process.

But do we have to go to distant worlds to find other kinds of replicator and other, consequent, kinds of evolution? I think that a new kind of replicator has recently emerged on this very planet. It is staring us in the face. It is still in its infancy, still drifting clumsily about in its primeval soup, but already it is achieving evolutionary change at a rate which leaves the old gene panting far behind.

The new soup is the soup of human culture. We need a name for the new replicator, a noun which conveys the idea of a unit of cultural transmission, or a unit of *imitation*. 'Mimeme' comes from a suitable Greek root, but I want a monosyllable that sounds a bit like 'gene'. I hope my classicist friends will forgive me if I abbreviate mimeme to *meme*. If it is any consolation, it could alternatively be thought of as being related to 'memory', or to the French word *même*. It should be pronounced to rhyme with 'cream'.

Examples of memes are tunes, ideas, catch-phrases, clothes fashions, ways of making pots or of building arches. Just as genes propagate themselves in the gene pool by leaping from body to body via sperms or eggs, so memes propagate themselves in the meme pool by leaping from brain to brain via a process which, in the broad sense, can be called imitation. If a scientist hears, or reads about, a good idea, he passes it on to his colleagues and students. He mentions it in his articles and his lectures. If the idea catches on, it can be said to propagate itself, spreading from brain to brain. As my colleague N. K. Humphrey neatly summed up an earlier draft of this chapter: '. . . memes should be regarded as living structures, not just metaphorically but technically. When you plant a fertile meme in my mind you literally parasitize my brain, turning it into a vehicle for the meme's propagation in just the way that a virus may parasitize the genetic mechanism of a host cell. And this isn't just a way of talking—the meme for, say, 'belief in life after death' is actually realized physically, millions of times over, as a structure in the nervous systems of individual men the world over.'

Consider the idea of God. We do not know how it arose in the meme pool. Probably it originated many times by independent 'mutation'. In any case, it is very old indeed. How does it replicate itself? By the spoken and written word, aided by great music and great art. Why does it have such high survival value? Remember that 'survival value' here does not mean value for a gene in a gene pool, but value for a meme in a meme pool. The question really means: What is it about the idea of a god which gives it its stability and penetrance in the cultural environment? The survival value of the god meme in the meme pool results from its great psychological appeal. It provides a superficially plausible answer to deep and troubling questions about existence. It suggests that injustices in this world may be rectified in the next. The 'everlasting arms' hold out a cushion against our own inadequacies which, like a doctor's placebo, is none the less effective for being imaginary. These are some of the reasons why the idea of God is copied so readily by successive generations of individual brains. God exists, if only in the form of a meme with high survival value, or infective power, in the environment provided by human culture.

Some of my colleagues have suggested to me that this account of the survival value of the god meme begs the question. In the last analysis they wish always to go back to 'biological advantage'. To them it is not good enough to say that the idea of a god has 'great psychological appeal'. They want to know *why* it has great psychological appeal. Psychological appeal means appeal to brains, and brains are shaped by natural selection of genes in gene pools. They want to find some way in which having a brain like that improves gene survival.

I have a lot of sympathy with this attitude, and I do not doubt that there are genetic advantages in our having brains of the kind which we have. But nevertheless I think that these colleagues, if they look carefully at the fundamentals of their own assumptions, will find that they are begging just as many questions as I am. Fundamentally, the reason why it is good policy for us to try to explain biological phenomena in terms of gene advantage is that genes are replicators. As soon as the primeval soup provided conditions in which molecules could make copies of themselves, the replicators themselves took over. For more than three thousand million years, DNA has been the only replicator worth talking about in the world. But it does not necessarily hold these monopoly rights for all time. Whenever conditions arise in which a new kind of replicator *can* make copies of itself, the new replicators *will* tend to take over, and start a new kind of evolution of their own. Once this new evolution begins, it will in no necessary sense be subservient to the old. The old gene-selected evolution, by making brains, provided the 'soup' in which the first memes arose. Once self-copying memes had arisen, their own, much faster, kind of evolution took off. We biologists have assimilated the idea of genetic evolution so deeply that we tend to forget that it is only one of many possible kinds of evolution.

Imitation, in the broad sense, is how memes *can* replicate. But just as not all genes which can replicate do so successfully, so some memes are more successful in the meme-pool than others. This is the analogue of natural selection. I have mentioned particular examples of qualities which make for high survival value among memes. But in general they must be the same as those discussed for the replicators of [Dawkins 1976] Chapter 2: longevity, fecundity, and copying-fidelity. The longevity of any one copy of a meme is probably relatively unimportant, as it is for any one copy of a gene. The copy of the tune 'Auld Lang Syne' which exists in my brain will last only for the rest of my life. The copy of the same tune which is printed in my volume of *The Scottish Student's Song Book* is unlikely to last much longer. But I expect there will be copies of the same tune on paper and in peoples' brains for centuries to come. As in the case of genes, fecundity is much more important than longevity of particular copies. If the meme is a 'scientific idea, its spread will depend on how acceptable it is to the population of individual scientists; a rough measure of its survival value could be obtained by counting the number of times it is referred to in successive years in scientific journals. If it is a popular tune, its spread through the meme pool may be gauged by the number of people heard whistling it in the streets. If it is a style of women's shoe, the population memeticist may use sales statistics from shoe shops. Some memes, like some genes, achieve brilliant short-term success in spreading rapidly, but do not last long in the meme pool. Popular songs and stiletto heels are examples. Others, such as the Jewish religious laws, may continue to propagate themselves for thousands of years, usually because of the great potential permanence of written records.

This brings me to the third general quality of successful replicators: copying-fidelity. Here I must admit that I am on shaky ground. At first sight it looks as if memes are not high-fidelity replicators at all. Every time a scientist hears an idea and passes it on to somebody else, he is likely to change it somewhat. I have made no secret of my debt in this book to the ideas of R. L. Trivers. Yet I have not repeated them in his own words. I have twisted them round for my own purposes, changing the emphasis, blending them with ideas of my own and of other people. The memes are being passed on to you in altered form. This looks quite unlike the particulate, all-or-none quality of gene transmission. It looks as though meme transmission is subject to continuous mutation, and also to blending.

It is possible that this appearance of non-particulateness is illusory, and that the analogy with genes does not break down. After all, if we look at the inheritance of many genetic characters such as human height or skin-colouring, it does not look like the work of indivisible and unblendable genes. If a black and a white person mate, their children do not come out either black or white: they are intermediate. This does not mean the genes concerned are not particulate. It is just that there are so many of them concerned with skin colour, each one having such a small effect, that they *seem* to blend. So far I have talked of memes as though it was obvious what a single unit-meme consisted of. But of course it is far from obvious. I have said a tune is one meme, but what about a symphony: how many memes is that? Is each movement one meme, each recognizable phrase of melody, each bar, each chord, or what?

I appeal to the same verbal trick as I used in [Dawkins 1976] Chapter 3. There I divided the 'gene complex' into large and small genetic units, and units within units. The 'gene' was defined, not in a rigid all-or-none way, but as a unit of convenience, a length of chromosome with just sufficient copying-fidelity to serve as a viable unit of natural selection. If a single phrase of Beethoven's ninth symphony is sufficiently distinctive and memorable to be abstracted from the context of the whole symphony, and used as the call-sign of a maddeningly intrusive European broadcasting station, then to that extent it deserves to be called one meme. It has, incidentally, materially diminished my capacity to enjoy the original symphony.

Similarly, when we say that all biologists nowadays believe in Darwin's theory, we do not mean that every biologist has, graven in his brain, an identical copy of the exact words of Charles Darwin himself. Each individual has his own way of interpreting Darwin's ideas. He probably learned them not from Darwin's own writings, but from more recent authors. Much of what Darwin said is, in detail, wrong. Darwin if he read this book would scarcely recognize his own original theory in it, though I hope he would like the way I put it. Yet, in spite of all this, there is something, some essence of Darwinism, which is present in the head of every individual who understands the theory. If this were not so, then almost any statement about two people agreeing with each other would be meaningless. An 'idea-meme' might be defined as an entity which is capable of being transmitted from one brain to another. The meme of Darwin's theory is therefore that essential basis of the idea which is held in common by all brains who understand the theory. The *differences* in the ways that people represent the theory are then, by definition, not part of the meme. If Darwin's theory can be subdivided into components, such that some people believe component *A* but not component *B*, while others believe *B* but not *A*, then *A* and *B* should be regarded as separate memes. If almost everybody who believes in *A* also believes in *B*—if the memes are closely 'linked' to use the genetic term—then it is convenient to lump them together as one meme.

Let us pursue the analogy between memes and genes further. Throughout [Dawkins 1976], I have emphasized that we must not think of genes as conscious, purposeful agents. Blind natural selection, however, makes them behave rather as if they were purposeful, and it has been convenient, as a shorthand, to refer to genes in the language of purpose. For example, when we say 'genes are trying to increase their numbers in future gene pools', what we really mean is 'those genes which behave in such a way as to increase their numbers in future gene pools tend to be the genes whose effects we see in the world'. Just as we have found it convenient to think of genes as active agents, working purposefully for their own survival, perhaps it might be convenient to think of memes in the same way. In neither case must we get mystical about it. In both cases the idea of purpose is only a metaphor, but we have already seen what a fruitful metaphor it is in the case of genes. We have even used words like 'selfish' and 'ruthless' of genes, knowing full well it is only a figure of speech. Can we, in exactly the same spirit, look for selfish or ruthless memes?

There is a problem here concerning the nature of competition. Where there is sexual reproduction, each gene is competing particularly with its own alleles—rivals for the same chromosomal slot. Memes seem to have nothing equivalent to chromosomes, and nothing equivalent to alleles. I suppose there is a trivial sense in which many ideas can be said to have 'opposites'. But in general memes resemble the early replicating molecules, floating chaotically free in the primeval soup, rather than modern genes in their neatly paired, chromosomal regiments. In what sense then are memes competing with each other? Should we expect them to be 'selfish' or 'ruthless', if they have no alleles? The answer is that we might, because there is a sense in which they must indulge in a kind of competition with each other.

Any user of a digital computer knows how precious computer time and memory storage space are. At many large computer centres they are literally costed in money; or each user may be allotted a ration of time, measured in seconds, and a ration of space, measured in 'words'. The computers in which memes live are human brains. Time is possibly a more important limiting factor than storage space, and it is the subject of heavy competition. The human brain, and the body which it controls, cannot do more than one or a few things at once. If a meme is to dominate the attention of a human brain, it must do so at the expense of 'rival' memes. Other commodities for which memes compete are radio and television time, billboard space, newspaper column-inches, and library shelf-space.

In the case of genes, we saw in Chapter 3 [of Dawkins 1976] that co-adapted gene complexes may arise in the gene pool. A large set of genes concerned with mimicry in butterflies became tightly linked together on the same chromosome, so tightly that they can be treated as one gene. In Chapter 5 [of Dawkins 1976] we met the more sophisticated idea of the evolutionarily stable set of genes. Mutually suitable teeth, claws, guts, and sense organs evolved in carnivore gene pools, while a different stable set of characteristics emerged from herbivore gene pools. Does anything analogous occur in meme pools? Has the god meme, say, become associated with any other particular memes, and does this association assist the survival of each of the participating memes? Perhaps we could regard an organized church, with its architecture, rituals, laws, music, art, and written tradition, as a co-adapted stable set of mutually-assisting memes.

To take a particular example, an aspect of doctrine which has been very effective in enforcing religious observance is the threat of hell fire. Many children and even some adults believe that they will suffer ghastly torments after death if they do not obey the priestly rules. This is a peculiarly nasty technique of persuasion, causing great psychological anguish throughout the middle ages and even today. But it is highly effective. It might almost have been planned deliberately by a machiavellian priesthood trained in deep psychological indoctrination techniques. However, I doubt if the priests were that clever. Much more probably, unconscious memes have ensured their own survival by virtue of those same qualities of pseudo-ruthlessness which successful genes display. The idea of hell fire is, quite simply, *self perpetuating*, because of its own deep psychological impact. It has become linked with the god meme because the two reinforce each other, and assist each other's survival in the meme pool.

Another member of the religious meme complex is called faith. It means blind trust, in the absence of evidence, even in the teeth of evidence. The story of Doubting Thomas is told, not so that we shall admire Thomas, but so that we can admire the other apostles in comparison. Thomas demanded evidence. Nothing is more lethal for certain kinds of meme than a tendency to look for evidence. The other apostles, whose faith was so strong that they did not need evidence, are held up to us as worthy of imitation. The meme for blind faith secures its own perpetuation by the simple unconscious expedient of discouraging rational inquiry.

Blind faith can justify anything. If a man believes in a different god, or even if he uses a different ritual for worshipping the same god, blind faith can decree that he should die—on the cross, at the stake, skewered on a Crusader's sword, shot in a Beirut street, or blown up in a bar in Belfast. Memes for blind faith have their own ruthless ways of propagating themselves. This is true of patriotic and political as well as religious blind faith.

Memes and genes may often reinforce each other, but they sometimes come into opposition. For example, the habit of celibacy is presumably not inherited genetically. A gene for celibacy is doomed to failure in the gene pool, except under very special circumstances such as we find in the social insects. But still, a *meme* for celibacy can be successful in the meme pool. For example, suppose the success of a meme depends critically on how much time people spend in actively transmitting it to other people. Any time spent in doing other things than attempting to transmit the meme may be regarded as time wasted from the meme's point of view. The meme for celibacy is transmitted by priests to young boys who have not yet decided what they want to do with their lives. The medium of transmission is human influence of various kinds, the spoken and written word, personal example and so on. Suppose, for the sake of argument, it happened to be the case that marriage weakened the power of a priest to influence his flock, say because it occupied a large proportion of his time and attention. This has, indeed, been advanced as an official reason for the enforcement of celibacy among priests. If this were the case, it would follow that the meme for celibacy could have greater survival value than the meme for marriage. Of course, exactly the opposite would be true for a *gene* for celibacy. If a priest is a survival machine for memes, celibacy is a useful attribute to build into him. Celibacy is just a minor partner in a large complex of mutually-assisting religious memes.

I conjecture that co-adapted meme-complexes evolve in the same kind of way as co-adapted gene-complexes. Selection favours memes which exploit their cultural environment to their own advantage. This cultural environment consists of other memes which are also being selected. The meme pool therefore comes to have the attributes of an evolutionarily stable set, which new memes find it hard to invade.

I have been a bit negative about memes, but they have their cheerful side as well. When we die there are two things we can leave behind us: genes and memes. We were built as gene machines, created to pass on our genes. But that aspect of us will be forgotten in three generations. Your child, even your grandchild, may bear a resemblance to you, perhaps in facial features, in a talent for music, in the colour of her hair. But as each generation passes, the contribution of your genes is halved. It does not take long to reach negligible proportions. Our genes may be immortal but the *collection* of genes which is in any one of us is bound to crumble away. Elizabeth II is a direct descendant of William the Conqueror. Yet it is quite probable that she bears not a single one of the old king's genes. We should not seek immortality in reproduction.

But if you contribute to the world's culture, if you have a good idea, compose a tune, invent a sparking plug, write a poem, it may live on, intact, long after your genes have dissolved in the common pool. Socrates may or may not have a gene or two alive in the world today, as G. C. Williams has remarked, but who cares? The meme-complexes of Socrates, Leonardo, Copernicus, and Marconi are still going strong.

However speculative my development of the theory of memes may be, there is one serious point which I would like to emphasize once again. This is that when we look at the evolution of cultural traits and at their survival value, we must be clear *whose* survival we are talking about. Biologists, as we have seen, are accustomed to looking for advantages at the gene level (or the individual, the group, or the species level according to taste). What we have not previously considered is that a cultural trait may have evolved in the way that it has, simply because it is *advantageous to itself*.

We do not have to look for conventional biological survival values of traits like religion, music, and ritual dancing, though these may also be present. Once the genes have provided their survival machines with brains which are capable of rapid imitation, the memes will automatically take over. We do not even have to posit a genetic advantage in imitation, though that would certainly help. All that is necessary is that the brain should be *capable* of imitation: memes will then evolve which exploit the capability to the full.

I now close the topic of the new replicators, and end on a note of qualified hope. One unique feature of man, which may or may not have evolved memically, is his capacity for conscious foresight. Selfish genes (and, if you allow the speculation of this chapter, memes too) have no foresight. They are unconscious, blind, replicators. The fact that they replicate, together with certain further conditions means, willy nilly, that they will tend towards the evolution of qualities which, in the special sense of this book, can be called selfish. A simple replicator, whether gene or meme, cannot be expected to forgo short-term selfish advantage even if it would really pay it, in the long term, to do so. We saw this in the chapter on aggression [of Dawkins 1976]. Even though a 'conspiracy of doves' would be better for *every single individual* than the evolutionarily stable strategy, natural selection is bound to favour the ESS.

It is possible that yet another unique quality of man is a capacity for genuine, disinterested, true altruism. I hope so, but I am not going to argue the case one way or the other, nor to speculate over its possible memic evolution. The point I am making now is that, even if we look on the dark side and assume that individual man is fundamentally selfish, our conscious foresight—our capacity to simulate the future in imagination—could save us from the worst selfish excesses of the blind replicators. We have at least the mental equipment to foster our long-term selfish interests rather than merely our short-term selfish interests. We can see the long-term benefits of participating in a 'conspiracy of doves', and we can sit down together to discuss ways of making the conspiracy work. We have the power to defy the selfish genes of our birth and, if necessary, the selfish memes of our indoctrination. We can even discuss ways of deliberately cultivating and nurturing pure, disinterested altruism—something that has no place in nature, something that has never existed before in the whole history of the world. We are built as gene machines and cultured as meme machines, but we have the power to turn against our creators. We, alone on earth, can rebel against the tyranny of the selfish replicators.

Chapter 26

DAN SPERBER

SELECTION AND ATTRACTION IN CULTURAL EVOLUTION

S UPPOSE WE SET OURSELVES the goal of developing mechanistic and naturalistic causal explanations of cultural phenomena. (I don't believe, by the way, that causal explanations are the only ones worth having; interpretive explanations, which are standard in anthropology, are better at answering some of our questions.) A causal explanation is mechanistic when it analyses a complex causal relationship as an articulation of more elementary causal relationships. It is naturalistic to the extent that there is good ground to assume that these more elementary relationships could themselves be further analysed mechanistically down to some level of description at which their natural character would be wholly unproblematic.

The kind of naturalism I have in mind aims at bridging gaps between the sciences, not at universal reduction. Some important generalizations are likely to be missed when causal relationships are not accounted for in terms of lower-level mechanisms. Other valuable generalizations would be lost if we paid attention to lower-level mechanisms only. If we want bridges, it is so as to be able to move both ways.

Social sciences explanations are sometimes mechanistic, but they are hardly ever naturalistic (with a few exceptions in demography and in historical linguistics). They fail to be naturalistic if only because they freely attribute causal powers to entities such as institutions or ideologies the material mode of existence of which is left wholly mysterious. If we want to develop a naturalistic programme in the social sciences, we must exert some ontological restraint and invoke only entities the causal powers of which can be understood in naturalistic terms.

Here is a proposal: let us recognize only human organisms in their material environment (whether natural or artificial), and focus on these organisms' individual mental states and processes and on the physical-environmental causes and effects of these mental things. Here is how, having so restricted our ontology, we might approach the social. A human population is inhabited by a much wider population of mental representations: that is, objects in the mind/brain of individuals such as beliefs, fantasies, desires, fears, intentions and so on. The common physical environment of a population is furnished with the public productions of its members. By 'public production' I mean any perceptible modification of the environment brought about by human behaviour. Productions include bodily movements and the outcomes of such movements. Some productions are long-lasting, like clothes or buildings; other are ephemeral, like a grin or the sounds of speech.

Typically, public productions have mental representations among their causes and among their effects. Mental representations caused by public productions can in turn cause further public productions, that can cause further mental representations, and so forth. There are thus complex causal chains where mental representations and public productions alternate. Public productions are likely to have many mental representations among their causes, and, conversely, every link in a causal chain may be attached to many others, both up and down the causal path.

Of particular interest are causal chains from mental representations to public productions to mental representations and so on, where the causal descendants of a representation resemble it in content. The smallest ordinary such causal chain is an act of successful communication. Typically, the public productions that are involved in communication are *public representations* such as linguistic utterances. Public representations are artefacts the function of which is to ensure a similarity of content between one of their mental causes in the communicator and one of their mental effects in the audience.

Communication is one of the two main mechanisms of transmission, imitation being the other. Transmission is a process that may be intentional or unintentional, co-operative or non-co-operative, and which brings about a similarity of content between a mental representation in one individual and its causal descendant in another individual. Most mental representations are never transmitted. Most transmissions are a one-time local affair. However, it may happen that the recipient of an act of transmission becomes a transmitter in turn, and the next recipient also, and so on, thus producing a long chain of transmission and a strain of mental representations (together with public representations in cases of communication) linked both causally and by similarity of content. Fast-moving rumours and slow-moving traditions are paradigmatic examples of such cultural causal chains.

The selection model

When you have a strain of representations similar enough in content to be seen as versions of one another, it is possible and often useful to produce yet another public version in order to represent in a prototypical manner their partly common content. Thus we talk of *the* belief in metempsychosis, *the* recipe for Yorkshire pudding, *the* story of King Arthur, each identified by a content. These are, of course, abstractions, at least as much so as *the* zebra, *the* Doric order, or *the* Russian peasant. It is tempting to see all the concrete representations that can be identified by means of a prototypical version as having the same content, with only negligible variations, thus as imperfect replicas of one another, but replicas nevertheless. Once this is done, it is but a step to seeing all tokens of the 'same' representation as forming a distinct class of objects in the world, just as all zebras are commonly seen as forming a natural kind. Granting such unity to strains of representations makes it possible to use, in order to develop a causal explanation of culture, one of intellectual history's most powerful tools: the Darwinian idea of selection.

On this approach, cultural representations are self-replicating representations. They replicate by causing those who hold them to produce public behaviours that cause others to hold them too. Occasionally representations 'mutate', possibly starting a new strain. The task of explaining the contents and evolution of a given culture can be seen, then, as one of finding out which representations are most successful at replicating, under what conditions, and why. Versions of this idea have been defended by, among others, Karl Popper, Donald Campbell, Jacques Monod, Cavalli-Sforza and Feldman, Boyd and Richerson, William Durham, and by Richard Dawkins who coined the name 'memes' for cultural replicators.[1] The success of the word 'meme' is such that it could be seen as confirming, or at least illustrating, the very idea of a meme. I will focus this discussion on Dawkins's memes, espoused in philosophy by Daniel

Dennett (1991, 1995) and developed in anthropology by William Durham (1991). My argument extends unproblematically (*mutatis mutandis*, of course) to all the other proposals mentioned.[2]

I have long argued that there is a severe flaw in attempting to develop a naturalistic explanation of cultural evolution on the basis of the Darwinian model of selection. I am not moved by any reservation concerning Darwinism. Quite the opposite, I believe that Darwinian considerations have a central role to play in the explanation of human culture by helping us to answer the fundamental question: what biological and, in particular, what brain mechanisms make humans cultural animals with the kinds of culture they have? In other words, to characterize 'human' in the phrase 'human culture', we must draw on biology, hence on evolutionary theory, hence on the Darwinian model of selection. It is 'culture' in the phrase 'human culture' that calls for some different and, I believe, novel thinking, albeit remaining, as we will see, within the broad Darwinian approach.

My two basic points over the years have been (1) that representations don't in general replicate in the process of transmission, they transform; and (2) that they transform as a result of a constructive cognitive process. Replication, when it truly occurs, is best seen as a limiting case of zero transformation. These remarks of mine have been taken as an emphatic way of making a correct, but unimportant, point to the effect that replication is not perfect.[3] But after all, hasn't Dawkins himself pointed out that 'no copying process is infallible', and that 'it is no part of the definition of a replicator that its copies must all be perfect' (Dawkins 1982: 85)?

Dawkins, however, is aware of the problem that looms. He writes:

> The copying process is probably much less precise than in the case of genes: there may be a certain 'mutational' element in every copying event. . . . Memes may partially blend with each other in a way that genes do not. New 'mutations' may be 'directed' rather than random with respect to evolutionary trends. . . . These differences may prove sufficient to render the analogy with genetic natural selection worthless or even positively misleading.
>
> (Dawkins 1982: 112)

Dawkins's main interest and most relevant contribution are to point out that the mechanism of Darwinian selection is by no means limited to biological material, but may apply to replicators of any substance and any kind.[4] Computer viruses are successful replicators (alas!) of a non-biological kind. Here is an example of an unquestionable cultural replicator. Every now and then, I receive in the mail a chain-letter saying something like:

> Make ten copies of this letter and send them to ten different people. This chain has been started at Santiago de Compostela. Don't break it! Mrs Jones sent ten copies of this letter the very day she received it, and that same week, she won a large prize at the National Lottery. Mr Smith threw away this letter without copying it, and the next day he lost his job.

Here is a text that causes enough of the individuals who receive copies of it to make and send further copies for the process of its distribution to be an enduring one.

Provided that certain conditions obtain, replicators will undergo a process of Darwinian selection. The two main conditions are that there should be variations among replicators, and that different types of replicators should differ in their chances of being replicated. In the case of the selection of genes, the source of variation is random mutation, which is, actually, failure to replicate properly. For selection to operate on replicators capable of mutating, a further condition has to be fulfilled. It has to do with the rate of mutation. Obviously, if genes mutated not just occasionally, but all the time, they wouldn't be replicators any more, and selection would be ineffective. How much mutation is compatible with effective selection? Here is George Williams's answer:

> The essence of the genetical theory of natural selection is a statistical bias in the relative rates of survival of alternatives (genes, individuals, etc.). The effectiveness of such bias in producing adaptation is contingent on the maintenance of certain quantitative relationships among the operative factors. One necessary condition is that the selected entity must have a high degree of permanence and a low rate of endogenous change, relative to the degree of bias.
>
> (Williams 1966: 22–3)

In fact, interesting replicators – genes in the biological case – can be characterized as entities replicating well enough to undergo effective selection.

In the case of genes, a typical rate of mutation might be one mutation per million replications. With such low rates of mutation, even a very small selection bias is enough to have, with time, major cumulative effects.[5] If, on the other hand, in the case of culture there may be, as Dawkins acknowledges, 'a certain "mutational" element in every copying event', then the very possibility of cumulative effects of selection is open to question.

There are, of course, bits of culture that do replicate. Some people copy chain-letters. Medieval monks copied manuscripts. Many traditional artefacts are replicas. Thus a pot may be copied by a potter, and some of her pots may be copied by other potters, and so on for many generations of pots and potters. This slow manual reproduction process has been superseded in modern times by more and more sophisticated technologies, such as printing, broadcasting, or e-mail forwarding, which allow massive replication. However, the number of artefactual replicas of a would-be cultural item is only a poor, indirect indicator of its genuine cultural success. Waste-paper baskets and their electronic counterparts are filled with massively replicated but unread junk, while some scientific articles read by only a few specialists have changed our cultural world. The cultural importance of a public production is to be measured not by the number of copies in the environment but by their impact on people's minds.

The most blatant cases of replication are provided by public productions, rather than by mental representations. However, when a public replica is produced by an individual rather than by a machine, this production is caused by an intention or plan of the individual – that is, a mental representation. Mental representations causing the production of public replicas can themselves be seen as mental replicas of mental representations. Jane's mental representation of a pot caused her to make a pot in conformity with this representation. This pot was seen by John, and caused in him the construction of a mental representation identical to Jane's. John's representation caused him to produce a pot identical to Jane's pot, and so on.

The question then arises as to whether the true memes are public productions – pots, texts, songs and so on – that are both effects and causes of mental representations or, as Dawkins (1982) argues, mental representations that are both causes and effects of public productions. With both options, however, there are similar problems. To begin with, most cultural items, be they mental or public, have a large and variable number of mental or public immediate ascendants.

Leaving aside mechanical and electronic reproduction, cases of new items produced by actually copying one given old item are rare. When you sing 'Yankee Doodle', you are not trying to reproduce any one past performance of the song, and the chances are that your mental version of the song was the child of the mental versions of several people. Most potters producing quantities of near-identical pots are not actually copying any one pot in particular, and their skill is typically derived from more than a single teacher (although there may be one teacher more important than the others, which complicates matters further still).

In general, if you are serious in describing bits of culture – individual texts, pots, songs or individual abilities to produce them – as replications of earlier bits, then you should be willing to ask about any given token cultural item: of which previous token is it a direct replica? In most cases, however, you will be forced to conclude that each token is a replica not of one parent token, nor (as in sexual reproduction) of two parent tokens, nor of any fixed number of parent tokens, but of an indefinite number of tokens some of which have played a much greater 'parental' role than others.

You might want, then, to envisage that this process of synthetic replication of a variable number of models is carried out by a natural equivalent of a morphing programme (i.e. a programme that takes, say, the image of a cat and that of a man as input, and produces the image of a creature somewhere between the cat and the man as output). Just as in a morphing programme, different inputs can be given different weights: you can have your cat-man more like a cat or more like a man, and Jill's skill and her pots may be more like Joan's than like Jane's, though still owing to both Joan's and Jane's skills and pots.

The model that comes to mind now is less immediately reminiscent of the Darwinian notion of selection than of the notion of 'influence' much used in the history of ideas and in social psychology. In the case of selection, genes either succeed or fail to replicate, and sexual organisms either succeed or fail to contribute half the genes of a new organism. Thus relationships of descent strictly determine genic similarity (ignoring mutations). Influence, by contrast, is a matter of degree. Two pottery teachers may have shared the same pupils, and therefore have the same cultural descendants, but their common cultural descendants may be much more influenced by one teacher than by the other. The resulting pots, too, may be descendants of both teachers' pots, but more like the pots of the one than those of the other.

There are, nevertheless, commonalities between the meme model and the influence model. Both involve an idea of competition. Both define a measure of success, in terms of the number of descendants in the one case, in terms of the degree and spread of influence in the other case. Both predict that the most successful items will dominate the culture, and that the culture will evolve as a result of differences in success among competing items. The meme model might be seen as a limiting case of the influence model: the case where influence is either 100 per cent or 0 per cent – that is, where descendants are replicas. Actually, formal models of influence in social psychology tend to concentrate on this limiting case (e.g. Nowak et al. 1990).

Both the meme model and the influence model see human organisms as agents of replication or synthesis, with little or no individual contribution to the process of which they are the locus. At most, the replicating agent may, to some extent, choose what to replicate, and the synthesizing agent may choose not only what inputs to synthesize, but also the weights to give to the different inputs. Among the factors in either reproductive or influential success, then, is the attraction that various possible inputs hold for the agents. However, once inputs (and weights in the case of synthesis) have been chosen, the outcome of a successful process of replication or synthesis is wholly determined. Moreover, on these two views, mental representations involved in cultural transmission never contain more information than the inputs they are supposed to represent or synthesize.

The attraction model

The influence model is right, as against the meme model, in treating replication in cultural transmission not as the norm but as a limiting case (of 100 per cent influence). Both are wrong, however, in assuming that, in general, the output of a process of transmission is wholly determined by the inputs (and weights, in the case of influence) accepted or chosen by the receiving organism. The stimulus-drivenness of both models is not the norm of cultural transmission; it too is a limiting case. Not much of culture is transmitted by means of simple imitation or averaging. Medieval monks copying manuscripts – apparently perfect examples of cultural replication – understood what they copied, and, on occasion, corrected what they took to be a mistake in earlier copying on the basis of what they understood. In general, human brains use all the information they are presented with not to copy or synthesize it, but as more or less relevant evidence with which to construct representations of their own.

Let me give three brief illustrations. First, consider your views on President Clinton. They are likely to be very similar to the views of many, and to have been influenced by the views of some. However, it is unlikely that you formed your own views simply by copying, or by averaging other people's views. Rather, you used your own background knowledge and preferences to put into perspective information you were given about Clinton, and to arrive by a mixture of affective reactions and inferences at your present views. The fact that your views are similar to many other people's may be explained not at all by a copying process, and only partly by an influence process; it may crucially involve the convergence of your affective and cognitive processes with those of many people towards some psychologically attractive type of views in the vast range of possible views on Clinton.

Take languages as a second illustration (see also Boyer 1993: 281). Languages are, at first blush, superb examples of memes: complex skills transmitted from generation to generation and similar enough across individuals to allow communication. However, as Noam Chomsky argued long ago (1972, 1975, 1986), a language such as 'English' is an abstraction to which correspond, in speaker's minds, mental grammars, and, in the environment, linguistic utterances. Individuals never encounter other people's grammar or representations of other people's grammar. Individual learners develop their own grammar on the basis of a large but limited set of linguistic utterances. Different individuals encounter very different sets of utterances. Acquiring a language does not consist in imitating these utterances. In fact, most utterances are never repeated. New utterances are not derived either by averaging or recombining old ones.

Clearly, what happens in language acquisition is that utterances are used as evidence for the construction of a mental grammar. How constraining is this evidence? Chomsky argued – quite convincingly – that the linguistic evidence available to the child vastly underdetermines the grammar. Moreover, many utterances, being grammatically defective, are bad evidence for the grammar to be constructed. Given this underdetermination, and given the differences in the inputs available to different children, the fact that children do each develop a grammar and, moreover, that within the same community these grammars converge, raises a deep problem. Again we owe to Chomsky at least the general form of the solution: there is a domain-specific, genetically specified language acquisition device in every child's mind. In the vast space of possible uses of the stimulation provided by linguistic utterances, children are attracted towards their use as evidence for grammar construction. In the vast space of logically possible grammars, they choose among just a few psychological possibilities, and end up converging on the one grammar psychologically available in the vicinity of the evidence they have been given. Just as it does not matter on which side of the trough you drop the ball, it will roll to the bottom, so it does not matter which French utterances a French child hears, she will construct a French grammar.

As a third example, take 'Little Red Riding Hood', as good an example of a meme as you will ever get. Here, there is no question but that many individuals who hear the tale do aim at retelling it, if not verbatim, at least in a manner faithful to its content. Of course, they don't always succeed, and many of the public versions produced by one teller for the sake of one or a few hearers differ from the several standard versions.

For instance, suppose an incompetent teller has the hunters extract Little Red Riding Hood from the Big Bad Wolf's belly, but forgets the grandmother. Meme theorists might want to argue – and I would agree with them – that such a version is less likely to be replicated than the standard one. The meme theorists' explanation would be that this version is less likely to have descendants. This is indeed plausible. There is another explanation, however, which is also plausible: that hearers whose knowledge of the story derives from this defective version are likely to consciously or unconsciously correct the story when they retell it, and, in their narrative, to bring the grandmother back to life too. In the logical space of possible versions of a tale, some versions have a better form: that is, a form seen as being without either missing or superfluous parts, easier to remember, and more attractive. The factors that make for a good form may be rooted in part in universal human psychology and in part in a local cultural context. In remembering and verbalizing the story, tellers are attracted towards the better forms. Both explanations, in terms of selection and in terms of attraction, may be simultaneously true, then; the reason why defective versions have fewer replicas may be both that they have fewer descendants and that the descendants they have are particularly unlikely to be replicas.

I hope the general idea is now clear: there is much greater slack between descent and similarity in the case of cultural transmission than there is in the biological case. Most cultural descendants are transformations, not replicas. Transformation implies resemblance: the smaller the degree of transformation, the greater the degree of resemblance. But resemblance among cultural items is greater than one would be led to expect by observing actual degrees of transformation in cultural transmission. Resemblance among cultural items is to be explained to some important extent by the fact that transformations tend to be biased in the direction of attractor positions in the space of possibilities.

How, then, should cultural transmission be modelled? Isn't a Darwinian selection model still the best approximation – to be corrected maybe, but not discarded? To try and answer, let me review the case by means of simple, sketchy formal considerations.

Imagine a population of items that are individually capable of begetting descendants, and that have a limited life-span. Let us imagine that these items come in 100 types, with relationships of similarity among the types such that we may represent the space of possibilities by means of a 10 by 10 matrix (see fig. 26.1). Imagine some initial stage (which might, e.g., have been experimentally contrived) at which we have a random distribution of, say, 10,000 items among the 100 types. Suppose we examine our population after a number of generations, and observe a different distribution. While the overall size of the population is roughly the same, and there is still a scatter of items across the space of possibilities, some types are now much better represented than others. More specifically, we observe that items tend to be concentrated at and around two types. Imagine that repeated observations show this distribution to be roughly stable.

A well-known kind of explanation of such a state of affairs would be that some of the types were better at replicating initially, and increased in numbers until a kind of ecological equilibrium was reached, at which the more successful types can keep up a higher representation than the others. Suppose, however, that we investigate the manner in which items in this population actually beget descendants, and discover that an offspring is *never* of the same type as its parent!

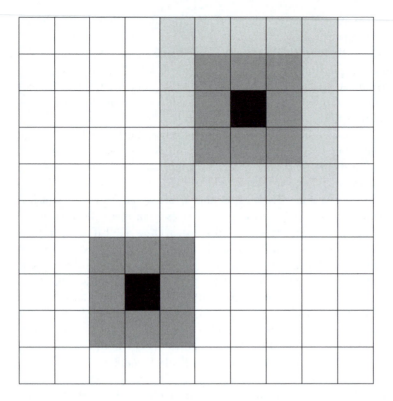

Figure 26.1 The space of possibilities. After a few generations, density is
greater in the two shaded areas

Rather, the offspring is always of one of the eight types adjacent in the matrix to that of its parent
(see fig. 26.2). Ecological equilibrium among differently endowed replicators cannot then be
the explanation since this is a transformative, rather than a reproductive, descent system.

An alternative explanation would start from the assumption that the eight possibilities for
the offspring of a parent of a given type are not equiprobable. A parent is more likely to beget
a transform that differs from it in a given direction. Suppose that the differences in transformation
probabilities are such that the matrix has two attractor points. If we trace the descent line of a
given item, it will not look like a true random walk in the space of possibilities, but will seem,
rather, to be attracted towards one or the other of these attractors (fig. 26.3) If the departure
point of a descent line is far from the attractors, then it is likely that the arrival point will be near
one of them. If the departure point is near an attractor, then it is likely that the whole line will
stay in its vicinity.

If items begot replicas, then differences in initial reproductive success and ecological
equilibrium would explain the observed distribution. Since items beget transforms, however,
differences in transformation probabilities provide a better explanation.

Transformation and replication can combine. For instance, all the types might have at all
times an equal probability of, say, 1 in 9 of replicating instead of transforming. In this case,
although some replication would occur, the difference in distribution between the types would
be entirely explained by differences in the probabilities of given transformations. Or the
probability of an item replicating rather than transforming might differ according to its type.
We could, then, in principle, have a dual explanation invoking both reproductive success and

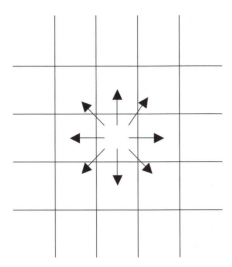

Figure 26.2 An item begets descendants of neighbouring types

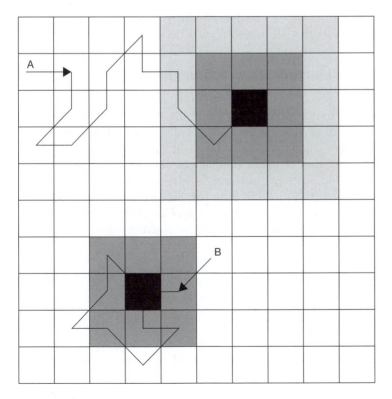

Figure 26.3 Descent lines tend to move towards an attractor (line A) or
to stay in its vicinity (line B)

attraction. However, in such a case, for the sake of generality and simplicity, reproductive success in a given region is better considered as defining, or contributing to the definition of, that region as an attractor.

The multiplicity and varying number of 'parents', or sources, for the same item, which is, as we noted, a typical aspect of cultural evolution, is also more naturally handled in terms of attraction. The generation of new items in a space of possibilities with attractor regions is to be expected somewhere between existing items and nearby attractors. A simple distance metric is not to be expected, however. The actual mechanisms of generation determine both which items will be transformed and in what manner.

The attraction model easily incorporates the influence model as a special case: the case in which the space of possibility does not include a nearby attractor, and where a simple metric will predict where new items will emerge.

Note that an attractor, as I have characterized it, is an abstract, statistical construct, like a mutation rate or a transformation probability. To say that there is an attractor is just to say that, in a given space of possibilities, transformation probabilities form a certain pattern: they tend to be biased so as to favour transformations in the direction of some specific point, and therefore cluster at and around that point. An attractor is not a material thing; it does not physically 'attract' anything. To say that there is an attractor is not to give a causal explanation; it is to put in a certain light what is to be causally explained: namely, a distribution of items and its evolution, and to suggest the kind of causal explanation to be sought: namely, the identification of genuine causal factors that bias micro-transformations.

Ecological and psychological factors of attraction

The existence of attractors is to be explained by two kinds of factors: psychological and ecological. The environment determines the survival and composition of the culture-bearing population; it contains all the inputs to the cognitive systems of the members of the population; it determines when, where and by what medium transmission may occur; it imposes constraints on the formation and stability of different types of public productions. The mental organization of individuals determines which available inputs are processed, how they are processed, and which information guides behaviours that, in turn, modify the environment.

Psychological factors interact with ecological factors at several levels, corresponding to different time-scales: that of biological evolution, that of social and cultural history, that of the cognitive and affective development of individuals, and that of micro-processes of transmission.

It is within the time-scale of biological evolution that a species emerges endowed with mental capacities that make cultural transmission possible. The role of biology is not just to make cultures possible, without any effect on their character and content. The picture of the human mind/brain as a blank slate on which different cultures freely inscribe their own world-view, the picture of world-views as integrated systems wholly determined by socio-cultural history – these pictures, which many social scientists still hold, are incompatible with our current understanding of biology and psychology.

The brain is a complex organ. Its evolution has been determined by the environmental conditions that could enhance or hamper the chances of our ancestors to have offspring throughout phylogeny. There are good reasons to believe that the brain contains many sub-mechanisms, or 'modules', which evolved as adaptations to these environmental opportunities and challenges (Cosmides and Tooby 1987, 1994; Tooby and Cosmides 1989, 1992). Mental modules – that is, adaptations to an ancestral environment – are crucial factors in cultural attraction. They tend to fix a lot of cultural content in and around the cognitive domain the processing of which they specialize in.

Evolutionary pressures are likely to have favoured not only the emergence of specialized mental mechanisms, but also some degree of cognitive efficiency within each of these mechanisms and in their mutual articulation. At any given time, humans perceive more phenomena than they are able to pay attention to, and they have more information stored in memory than they can exploit. Cognitive efficiency involves making the right choices in selecting which available new information to attend to and which available past information to process it with. The right choices in this respect consist in bringing together input and memory information, the joint processing of which will provide as much cognitive effect as possible for as little mental effort as possible.

Deirdre Wilson and I have argued that the effect–effort balance in the processing of any given piece of information determines its degree of relevance (Sperber and Wilson 1986/1995). We claim that human cognitive processes are geared to the maximization of relevance. Most factors of relevance are highly idiosyncratic, and have to do with the individual's unique location in time and space. Some factors of relevance, however, are rooted in genetically determined aspects of human psychology. Thus, the processing of stimuli for which there exists a specialized module requires comparatively less effort and is potentially more relevant. For instance, from birth onwards, humans expect relevance from the sounds of speech (an expectation often disappointed, but hardly ever given up).

It is plausible that individuals should be equipped so as to tend to optimize the effect–effort balance not just on the input side, but also on the output side. Public productions, from bodily movements, to speech, to buildings, even when they are modelled on some previous productions, are likely to move towards forms where the intended effect can be achieved at minimal cost.

Human culture has been around long enough for biological evolution to have been affected by it, in turn. Gene-culture 'co-evolution' (Boyd and Richerson 1985; Durham 1991; Lumsden and Wilson 1981) helps explain in particular the existence in humans of abilities that are specifically geared to cultural interaction, such as the language faculty (Pinker and Bloom 1990; Pinker 1994). Gene-culture co-evolution is, however, too slow a process to explain cultural changes in historical time.

Generation after generation, humans are born with essentially the same mental potential. They realize this potential in very diverse ways. This is due to the different environments, and in particular to the different cultural environments, into which they are born. However, from day one, an individual's psychology is enriched and made more specific by cultural inputs. Each individual quickly becomes one of the many loci among which is distributed the pool of cultural representations inhabiting the population. The cultural history of a population is both that of its pool of cultural representations and that of its cultural environment. These macro-ensembles – the pool of representations and the environment – evolve as an effect of micro-processes, where the causes belong to the environment and the effect to the pool, or conversely.

In general, the phrase 'cultural environment' is used very loosely, and refers to a collection of meanings, values, techniques and so forth. So understood, it has little to do with the physical environment. Its ontological status is, at best, very vague; its causal powers are mysterious. By 'cultural environment', I mean an ensemble of material items: all the public productions in the environments that are causes and effects of mental representations. The cultural environment thus understood blends seamlessly with the physical environment of which it is a part. The causal powers it exerts on human minds are unproblematic: public productions affect sense-organs in the usual, material way. They trigger the construction of mental representations the contents of which are partly determined by the properties of the triggering stimuli, and partly by pre-existing mental resources.

Cultural attractors emerge, wane, or move, some rapidly, others slowly, some suddenly, over historical time. Some of these changes have ordinary ecological causes: over-exploited ecological niches lose their economic attraction; rarely walked paths become overgrown; some practices tend to increase, and others to decrease, the size of the populations that might be attracted to them, and so on.

Most historical changes in attractors, however, are to be explained in terms of interactions between ecological and psychological factors of attraction of a kind specific to cultural evolution. The cultural environment causes at every instant the formation of mental representations, some of which themselves cause public productions, and so on. This process modifies the relative density of mental representations, as well as that of public productions, in different areas of the space of possibilities. In particular, density tends to increase in the vicinity of attractors. An increase in the density of public productions in the vicinity of an attractor tends to reinforce the attractor, if only because of the increase in probability that attention will be paid to these more numerous productions. On the other hand, an increase in the density of mental representations in the vicinity of an attractor may weaken the attractor. The repetition of representations having the same tenor may decrease their relevance and bring individuals either to lose interest in them or to reinterpret them differently.

Established practices (in matters of dress, food, etiquette, etc.) act as strong attractors. At the same time, because of their expectability, established practices are often low on relevance, while manifest departures from established practices are often an easy way to attract attention and achieve high relevance. Once public productions massively converge towards some cultural attractor, they may foster the emergence of nearby competing attractors. This is illustrated in a dramatic way by the rapid turnover of fashions, which quickly lose their power because of their very success.

When, on the contrary, one encounters practices that remain stable for generations, one may suppose that they somehow maintain a sufficient level of relevance in spite of repetition, and try to see whether such is indeed the case, and why. A repetitive practice may remain relevant because its effects are. This is the case, for instance, with technological practices, the economic effects of which are important to people's welfare, or even survival. A repetitive practice may remain relevant because it is in competition with other practices, and the choice of one rather than the others by a given individual at a given time may be quite consequential. This is the case with practices used to assert one's belonging to some minority. A repetitive practice may remain relevant because different individuals are in competition for the right to engage in it, and because success in this competition is consequential. This is the case with ritual practices marking promotion to some desired status. A repetitive practice may remain relevant because, without perceptibly modifying its public form, it lends itself to different interpretations according to the agent, the circumstances, and the stage in the life cycle. This possibility of reinterpretation is typical of religious practices (see Sperber 1975).

On the time-scale of individual life cycles, ecological and psychological factors also interact in a specific manner. At different stages of their psychological development, individuals are attracted in different directions. Initially, the main psychological factors of attraction are genetically determined; but experience – that is, the cognitive effects of past interactions with the environment – becomes an increasingly important factor in attraction.

For much of childhood, information that allows the child to develop competencies for which she has an innate disposition is attended to and used for this purpose. The child becomes a competent speaker, a competent climber, thrower, catcher, eater, drinker, a competent manipulator of objects, a competent recognizer of animals, a competent predictor of other people's behaviour, and so on. In all these domains, new information achieves relevance easily, because it meets the not yet satisfied needs of specialized modules. As basic competencies are acquired, however, attraction shifts to new information relevant in the context of the already acquired basic knowledge. It shifts in particular to cultural information – for instance, religious representations – that seems to challenge basic competencies. It shifts also to information relevant to the various goals that the individual has acquired the ability to conceive and pursue.

The contribution of individuals to cultural transmission varies throughout the life cycle. Not only do individuals transmit different amounts and different contents, they also transform what they transmit in different directions, and transmit to different audiences according to their stage in life. The amplitude of transformations also varies with the age and social role of the communicator and with those of the audience. In some configurations, a relatively conservative communication appears more relevant. In other configurations, the search for relevance demands innovation. From the point of view of individuals, cultural attractors seem to move along a path that in fact combines historical changes with the individuals' own movement in their life cycle and in their social relationships.

It is the micro-processes of cultural transmission that make possible gene-culture co-evolution, and that bring about the historical evolution of culture and the cultural development of individuals. My argument has been that these micro-processes are not, in general, processes of replication. I am not denying that replications occur and play a role in cultural evolution. I am arguing that replications are better seen as limiting cases of transformations. Constructive cognitive processes are involved both in representing cultural inputs and in producing public outputs. All outputs of individual mental processes are influenced by past inputs. Few outputs are mere copies of past inputs. The neo-Darwinian model of culture is based on an idealization, which is good scientific practice. However, this idealization is itself based on a serious distortion of the relevant facts, and this is where the problem lies.

The neo-Darwinian model and the ideas of replication and selection seemed to offer an explanation of the existence and evolution of relatively stable cultural contents. How come, if replication is not the norm, that among all the mental representations and public productions that inhabit a human population and its common environment, it is so easy to discern stable cultural types, such as common views on Bill Clinton, tellings of 'Little Red Riding Hood', English utterances, and also handshakes, funerals and pick-up trucks? For two reasons: first, because, through interpretative mechanisms the mastery of which is part of our social competence, we tend to exaggerate the similarity of cultural tokens and the distinctiveness of types; and second, because, in forming mental representations and public productions, to some extent all humans, and to a greater extent all members of the same population at any one time, are attracted in the same directions.

Even if it contrasts with the neo-Darwinian models of culture put forward by Dawkins and others, the model of cultural attraction that I have outlined is, quite obviously, of Darwinian inspiration in the way it explains large-scale regularities as the cumulative effect of micro-processes. The culture of a given population is described as a distribution of mental representations and public productions. Cultural evolution is explained as the cumulative effect of differences in frequency between different possible transformations of representations and of productions in the process of transmission. In the study of cultural evolution, borrowing Darwin's selection model is not the only way, and may not be the best way, to take advantage of Darwin's most fundamental insight.

Notes

1 See Sober (1991).
2 On the other hand, the view of cultural evolution put forward by Pascal Boyer (1993: ch. 9) and my own are very close. Boyer's arguments and mine are in part similar, in part complementary. Boyer offers a detailed discussion of the models of Lumsden and Wilson (1981), Boyd and Richerson (1985), and Durham (1991). There is also a good deal of convergence with Tooby and Cosmides (1992). Two other original and important approaches, that of the cognitive anthropologist Ed Hutchins (1994), and that of the philosopher Ruth Millikan (1984, 1993) would deserve a separate discussion.
3 This is how I seem to be interpreted by Dennett (1995: 357–9).
4 A theme developed in detail by Millikan (1984).
5 See Wilson and Bossert (1971: 61–2); Maynard Smith (1989: 20–4).

References

Boyd, R. and Richerson, P.J. 1985. *Culture and the Evolutionary Process*. University of Chicago Press.
Boyer, P. 1993. *The Naturalness of Religious Ideas*. University of California Press.
Chomsky, N. 1972. *Language and Mind*. Harcourt Brace Jovanovic.
Chomsky, N. 1975. *Reflections on Language*. Pantheon.
Chomsky, N. 1986. *Knowledge of Language*. Praeger.
Cosmides, L. and Tooby, J. 1987. "From Evolution to Behaviour: Evolutionary Psychology and the Missing Link". In J. Dupré (ed.) *The Latest on the Best: Essays on Evolution and Optimality*. MIT Press, pp. 277–306.
Cosmides, L. and Tooby, J. 1994. "Origins of Domain-Specificity: The Evolution of Functional Organization". In L.A. Hirschfeld and S.A. Gelman (eds.) *Mapping the Mind: Domain Specificity in Cognition and Culture*. Cambridge University Press, 85–116.
Dawkins, R. 1982. *The Extended Phenotype*. Oxford University Press.
Dennett, D. 1991. *Consciousness Explained*. Little, Brown.
Dennett, D. 1995. *Darwin's Dangerous Idea: Evolution and the Meaning of Life*. Simon and Schuster.
Durham, W. H. 1991. *Coevolution: Genes, Culture and Human Diversity*. Stanford, CA: Stanford University Press.
Hutchins, E. 1994. *Cognition in the Wild*. MIT Press.
Lumsden, C.J. and Wilson, E.O. 1981. *Genes, Mind and Culture*. Harvard University Press.
Maynard Smith, J. 1989. *Evolutionary Genetics*. Oxford University Press.
Millikan, R.G. 1984. *Language, Thought, and Other Biological Categories*. MIT Press.
Millikan, R.G. 1993. *White Queen Psychology and Other Essays for Alice*. MIT Press.
Nowak, A., Szamerei, J. and Latané, B. 1990. "From Private Attitude to Public Opinion: A Dynamic Theory of Social Impact". *Psychological Review* 97: 362–76.
Pinker, S. 1994. *The Language Instinct*. New York: Morrow.
Pinker, S. and Bloom, P. 1990. "Natural Language and Natural Selection". *Behavioral and Brain Sciences*, 13(4), 756–58.
Sober, E. 1991. "Models of Cultural Evolution". In P. Griffiths (ed.) *Trees of Life: Essays in the Philosophy of Biology*. Kluwer, 17–38.
Sperber, D. 1975. *Rethinking Symbolism*. Cambridge University Press.
Sperber, D. and Wilson, D. 1986. *Relevance: Communication and Cognition*. Blackwell, 2nd ed. 1995.
Tooby, J. and Cosmides, L. 1989. "Evolutionary Psychology and the Generation of Culture, Part I: Theoretical Considerations". *Ethology and Sociobiology*. 10: 29–49.
Tooby, J. and Cosmides, L. 1992. "The Psychological Foundations of Culture". In J. Barkow, L. Cosmides and J. Tooby (eds), *The Adapted Mind: Evolutionary Psychology anhd the Generation of Culture*. Oxford University Press, 19–136.
Williams, G.C. 1966. *Adaptation and Natural Selection*. Princeton University Press.
Wilson, E.O. and Bossert, W. 1971. *A Primer for Population Biology*. Sinauer.

Chapter 27

JASON MCKENZIE ALEXANDER AND BRIAN SKYRMS

BARGAINING WITH NEIGHBORS
Is justice contagious?

WHAT IS JUSTICE? The question is harder to answer in some cases than in others. We focus on the easiest case of distributive justice. Two individuals are to decide how to distribute a windfall of a certain amount of money. Neither is especially entitled, or especially needy, or especially anything—their positions are entirely symmetric. Their utilities derived from the distribution may be taken, for all intents and purposes, simply as the amount of money received. If they cannot decide, the money remains undistributed and neither gets any. The essence of the situation is captured in the simplest version of a bargaining game devised by John Nash.[1] Each person decides on a bottom-line demand. If those demands do not jointly exceed the windfall, then each person gets his demand; if not, no one gets anything. This game is often simply called *divide-the-dollar*.

In the ideal simple case, the question of distributive justice can be decided by two principles:

Optimality: a distribution is not just if, under an alternative distribution, all recipients would be better off.

Equity: if the position of the recipients is symmetric, then the distribution should be symmetric. That is to say, it does not vary when we switch the recipients.

Since we stipulate that the position of the two individuals is symmetric, equity requires that the just distribution must give them the same amount of money. Optimality then rules out such unlikely schemes as giving each one dime and throwing the rest away—each must get half the money.

There is nothing new about our two principles. Equity is the simplest consequence of the theory of distributive justice in Aristotle's *Politics*. It is a consequence of Immanuel Kant's categorical imperative. Utilitarians tend to stress optimality, but are not completely insensitive to equity. Optimality and equity are the two most uncontroversial requirements in Nash's axiomatic treatment of bargaining. If you ask people to judge the just distribution, their answers show that optimality and equity are powerful operative principles.[2] So, although nothing much hangs on it, we shall feel free to use moral language and to call the equal split *fair division* in divide-the-dollar.

I. Rationality, behavior, evolution

Two rational agents play the divide-the-dollar game. Their rationality is common knowledge. What do they do? The answer that game theory gives us is that *any* combination of demands is compatible with these assumptions. For example, Jack may demand ninety percent thinking that Jill will only demand ten percent on the assumption that Jill thinks that Jack will demand ninety percent and so forth, while Jill demands seventy-five percent thinking that Jack will demand twenty-five percent on the assumption that Jack thinks that Jill will demand seventy-five percent and so forth. *Any* pair of demands is *rationalizable*, in that it can be supported by a hierarchy of conjectures for each player, compatible with common knowledge of rationality. In the example given, these conjectures are quite mistaken.

Suppose we add the assumption that each agent somehow knows what the other will demand. Then any combination of demands that total the whole sum to be divided is still possible. For example, suppose that Jack demands ninety percent knowing that Jill will demand ten percent and Jill demands ten percent knowing that Jack will demand ninety percent. Then each player is maximizing payoff given the demand of the other. That is to say that this is a Nash equilibrium of divide-the-dollar. If the dollar is infinitely divisible, then there are an infinite number of such equilibria.

If experimental game theorists have people actually play divide-the-dollar, they *always* split equally.[3] This is not always true in more complicated bargaining experiments where there are salient asymmetries, but it is true in divide-the-dollar. Rational-choice theory has no explanation of this phenomenon. It appears that the experimental subjects are using norms of justice to select a particular Nash equilibrium of the game. But what account can we give for the existence of these norms?

Evolutionary game theory (reading 'evolution' as cultural evolution) promises an explanation, but the promise is only partially fulfilled. Demand-half is the only evolutionarily stable strategy in divide-the-dollar.[4] It is the only strategy such that, if the whole population played that strategy, no small group of innovators, or "mutants," playing a different strategy could achieve an average payoff at least as great as the natives. If we could be sure that this unique evolutionarily stable strategy would always take over the population, the problem would be solved.

But we cannot be sure that this will happen. There are states of the population which are evolutionarily stable where some fraction of the population makes one demand and some fraction makes another. The state where half the population demands one third and half the population demands two thirds is such an evolutionarily stable polymorphism of the population. So is the state where two thirds of the population demands forty percent and one third of the population demands sixty percent We can think of these as pitfalls along the evolutionary road to justice.

How important are these polymorphisms? To what extent do they compromise the evolutionary explanation of the egalitarian norm? We cannot begin to answer these questions without explicitly modeling the evolutionary dynamics and investigating the size of their basins of attraction.

II. Bargaining with strangers

The most widely studied dynamic evolutionary model is a model of interactions with strangers. Suppose that individuals are paired at random from a very large population to play the bargaining game. We assume that the probability of meeting a strategy can be taken as the proportion of the population that has that strategy. The population proportions evolve according to the replicator dynamics. The proportion of the population using a strategy in the next generation is the proportion playing that strategy in the current generation mutiplied by a *fitness factor*. This fitness factor is just the ratio of the average payoff to this strategy to the average payoff in the whole population.[5] Strategies that do better than average grow; those which do worse than average shrink. This dynamic arose in biology as a model of asexual reproduction, but more to the point here, it also has a cultural evolutionary interpretation where strategies are imitated in proportion to their success.[6]

The basins of attraction of these polymorphic pitfalls are not negligible. A realistic version of divide-the-dollar will have some finite number of strategies instead of the infinite number that we get from the idealization of infinite divisibility. For a finite number of strategies, the size of a basin of attraction of a population state makes straightforward sense. It can be estimated by computer simulations. We can consider coarse-grained or fine-grained versions of divide-the-dollar; we can divide a stack of quarters, or of dimes, or of pennies. Some results of simulations persist across a range of different granularities. Equal division always has the largest basin of attraction and it is always greater than the basins of attractions of all the polymorphic pitfalls combined. If you choose an initial population state at random, it is more probable than not that the replicator dynamics will converge to a state of fixation of demand-half. Simulation results range between fifty-seven and sixty-three percent of the initial points going to fair division. The next largest basin of attraction is always that closest to the equal split: for example, the four-six polymorphism in the case of dividing a stack of ten dimes and the forty-nine/fifty-one polymorphism in the case of dividing a stack of one-hundred pennies. The rest of the polymorphic equilibria follow the general rule—the closer to fair division, the larger the basin of attraction.

For example, the results running the discrete replicator dynamics to convergence and repeating the process 100,000 times on the game of dividing ten dimes are given in table 27.1.

The projected evolutionary explanation seems to fall somewhat short. The best we might say on the basis of pure replicator dynamics is that fixation of fair division is more likely than not, and that polymorphisms far from fair division are quite unlikely.

We can say something more if we inject a little bit of probability into the model. Suppose that every once and a while a member of the population just picks a strategy at random and tries it out—perhaps as an experiment, perhaps just as a mistake. Suppose we are at a polymorphic equilibrium—for instance, the four-six equilibrium in the problem of dividing ten dimes. If there is some fixed probability of an experiment (or mistake), and if experiments are independent, and if we wait long enough, there will be enough experiments of the right kind to kick the population out of the basin of attraction of the four-six polymorphism and into the basin of attraction of fair division and the evolutionary dynamics will carry fair division to fixation. Eventually, experiments or mistakes will kick the population out of the basin of attraction of fair division, but we should expect to wait much longer for this to happen. In the long run, the system will spend most of its time in the fair-division equilibrium. Peyton Young[7] showed that, if we take the limit as the probability of someone experimenting gets

Table 27.1 Convergence results for replicator dynamics – 100,000 trials

Fair Division	62,209
4–6 Polymorphism	27,469
3–7 Polymorphism	8,801
2–7 Polymorphism	1,483
1–9 Polymorphism	38
0–10 Polymorphism	0

smaller and smaller, the ratio of time spent in fair division approaches one. In his terminology, fair division is the *stochastically stable equilibrium* of this bargaining game.

This explanation gets us a probability arbitrarily close to one of finding a fair-division equilibrium if we are willing to wait an arbitrarily long time. But one may well be dissatisfied with an explanation that lives at infinity. (Putting the limiting analysis to one side, pick some plausible probability of experimentation or mistake and ask yourself how long you would expect it to take in a population of 10,000, for 1,334 demand-six types simultaneously to try out being demand-five types and thus kick the population out of the basin of attraction of the four-six polymorphism and into the basin of attraction of fair division.[8]) The evolutionary explanation still seems less than compelling.

III. Bargaining with neighbors

The model of random encounters in an infinite population that motivates the replicator dynamics may not be the right model. Suppose interactions are with neighbors. Some investigations of cellular automaton models of prisoner's dilemma and a few other games show that interactions with neighbors may produce dynamical behavior quite different from that generated by interactions with strangers.[9] Bargaining games with neighbors have not, to the best of our knowledge, previously been studied.

Here, we investigate a population of 10,000 arranged on a one hundred by one hundred square lattice. As the neighbors of an individual in the interior of the lattice, we take the eight individuals to the N, NE, E, SE, S, SW, W, NW. This is called the Moore (8) neighborhood in the cellular automaton literature.[10] The dynamics is driven by imitation. Individuals imitate the most successful person in the neighborhood. A generation—an iteration of the discrete dynamics—has two stages. First, each individual plays the divide-ten-dimes game with each of her neighbors using her current strategy. Summing the payoffs gives her current success level. Then each player looks around her neighborhood and changes her current strategy by imitating her most successful neighbor, providing that her most successful neighbor is more successful than she is; otherwise, she does not switch strategies. (Ties are broken by a coin flip.)

In initial trials of this model, fair division *always* went to fixation. This cannot be a universal law, since you can design "rigged" configurations where a few demand-one-half players are, for example, placed in a population of demand-four and demand-six players with the latter so arranged that there is a demand-six type who is the most successful player in the neighborhood of every demand-one-half player. Start enough simulations at random starting points and sooner or later you will start at one of these.

We ran a large simulation starting repeatedly at randomly chosen starting points. Fair division went to fixation in more than ninety-nine point five percent of the trials. The cases where it did not were all cases where the initial population of 10,000 contained fewer than seventeen demand-one-half players. Furthermore, convergence was remarkably quick. Mean time to fixation of fair division was about sixteen generations. This may be compared with a mean time to convergence[11] in discrete replicator dynamics of forty-six generations, and with the ultra-long-run character of stochastically stable equilibrium.

It is possible to exclude fair division from the possible initial strategies in the divide-ten-dimes game and start at random starting points that include the rest. If we do this, all strategies other than demand-four dimes and demand-six dimes are eliminated and the four-six polymorphic population falls into a "blinking" cycle of period two. If we then turn on a little bit of random experimentation or "mutation" allowing the possibility of demand-five, we find that as soon as a very small clump of demand-five players arises, it systematically grows until it takes over the whole population—as illustrated in figure 27.1. *Justice is contagious.*[12]

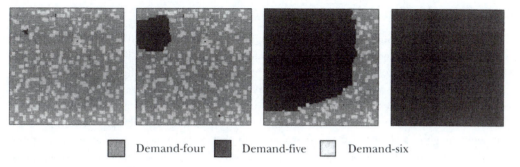

Demand-four ■ Demand-five □ Demand-six

Figure 27.1 The steady advance of fair division

IV. Robustness

The bargaining-with-neighbors model of the last section differs from the bargaining with strangers model in more than one way. Might the difference in behavior that we have just described be due to the imitate-the-most-successful dynamics rather than the neighbor effect? To answer this question, we ran simulations varying these factors independently.

 We consider both fixed and random neighborhoods. The models using fixed neighborhoods use the Moore (8) neighborhood described above. In the alternative random-neighborhood model, each generation a new set of "neighbors" is chosen at random from the population for each individual. That is to say, these are neighborhoods of *strangers*.

 We investigated two alternative dynamics. One imitates the most successful neighbor as in our bargaining-with-neighbors model. The other tempers the all-or-nothing character of imitate-the-best. Under it, an individual imitates one of the strategies in its neighborhood that is more successful than it (if there are any) with relative probability proportional to their success in the neighborhood. This is a move in the direction of the replicator dynamics.

 In table 27.2, A and B are bargaining with neighbors, with imitate-the-best-neighbor and imitate-with-probability-proportional-to-success dynamics, respectively. The results are barely distinguishable. C and D are the random-neighborhood models corresponding to A and B, respectively. These results are much closer to those given for the replicator dynamics in table 27.1. The dramatic difference in convergence to fair division between our two models is due to the structure of interaction with neighbors.

Table 27.2 Convergence results for five series of 10,000 trials.

| | Bargaining with Neighbors | Bargaining with Strangers | | |
	A	B	C	D
0–10	0	0	0	0
1–9	0	0	0	0
2–8	0	0	54	57
3–7	0	0	550	556
4–6	26	26	2560	2418
fair	9972	9973	6833	6964

V. Analysis

Why is justice contagious? A strategy is contagious if an initial "patch" of that strategy will extend to larger and larger patches. The key to contagion of a strategy is interaction along the edges of the patch, since in the interior the strategy can only imitate itself.[13]

Consider an edge with demand-five players on one side, and players playing the complementary strategies of one of the polymorphisms on the other. Since the second rank of demand-five players always meet their own kind, they each get a total payoff of forty from their eight neighbors. Players in the first rank will therefore imitate them unless a neighbor from the polymorphism gets a higher payoff. The low strategy in a polymorphic pair cannot get a higher payoff. So if demand-five is to be replaced at all, it must be by the high strategy of one of the polymorphic pairs.

In the four-six polymorphism—the polymorphism with the greatest basin of attraction in the replicator dynamics—this simply cannot happen, even in the most favorable circumstances. Suppose that we have someone playing demand-six in the first rank of the polymorphism, surrounded on his own side by compatible demand-four players to boost his payoff to the maximum possible.[14] Since he is in the first rank, he faces three incompatible demand-five neighbors. He has a total payoff of thirty while his demand-five neighbors have a total payoff of thirty-five. Demand-five begins an inexorable march forward as illustrated in figure 27.2. (The pattern is assumed to extend in all directions for the computation of payoffs of players at the periphery of what is shown in the figure.)

If we choose a polymorphism that is more extreme, however, it is possible for the high strategy to replace some demand-five players for a while. Consider the one-nine polymorphism, with a front line demand-nine player backed by compatible demand-one neighbors. The demand-nine player gets a total payoff of forty-five—more than anyone else—and thus is imitated by all his neighbors. This is shown in the first transition in figure 27.3.

But the success of the demand-nine strategy is its own undoing. In a cluster of demand-nine strategies, it meets itself too often and does not do so well. In the second transition, demand-five has more than regained its lost territory, and in the third transition it has solidly advanced into one-nine territory.

Analysis of the interaction along an edge between demand-five and other polymorphisms is similar to one of the cases analyzed here.[15] Either the polymorphism cannot advance at all, or the advance creates the conditions for its immediate reversal. A complete analysis of this complex system is something that we cannot offer. But the foregoing does offer some analytic insight into the contagious dynamics of equal division in "bargaining with neighbors."

Initial		Iteration 1
5544		5554
5544		5554
5564	⇒	5554
5544		5554
5544		5554

Figure 27.2 Fair division versus four-six polymorphism

Initial		Iteration 1		Iteration 2		Iteration 3
55*111*		555*11*		5555*1*		55555
55*111*		555*11*		5555*9*		55559
55*111*		5*9991*		555*99*		555*99*
55*911*	⇒	5*9991*	⇒	555*99*	⇒	555*99*
55*111*		55*111*		555*99*		555*99*
55*111*		555*11*		5555*9*		55559
55*111*		555*11*		5555*1*		55555

Figure 27.3 Fair division versus one-nine polymorphism

VI. Conclusion

Sometimes we bargain with neighbors, sometimes with strangers. The dynamics of the two sorts of interaction are quite different. In the bargaining game considered here, bargaining with strangers—modeled by the replicator dynamics—leads to fair division from a randomly chosen starting point about sixty percent of the time. Fair division becomes the unique answer in bargaining with strangers if we change the question to that of stochastic stability in the ultra-long-run. But long expected waiting times call the explanatory significance of the stochastic stability result into question.

Bargaining with neighbors almost always converges to fair division and convergence is remarkably rapid. In bargaining with neighbors, the local interaction generates clusters of those strategies which are locally successful. Clustering and local interaction together produce positive correlation between like strategies. As noted elsewhere,[16] positive correlation favors fair division over the polymorphisms. In bargaining with neighbors, this positive correlation is not something externally imposed but rather an unavoidable consequence of the dynamics of local interaction. As a consequence, once a small group demand-half players is formed, justice becomes contagious and rapidly takes over the entire population.

Both bargaining with strangers and bargaining with neighbors are artificial abstractions. In initial phases of human cultural evolution, bargaining with neighbors may be a closer approximation to the actual situation than bargaining with strangers. The dynamics of bargaining with neighbors strengthens the evolutionary explanation of the norm of fair division.

Notes

1 "The Bargaining Problem," *Econometrica*, XVIII (1950): 155–62.
2 Menachem Yaari and Maya Bar-Hillel, "On Dividing Justly," *Social Choice and Welfare*, I (1981): 1–24.
3 Rudy V. Nydegger and Guillermo Owen, "Two-Person Bargaining: An Experimental Test of the Nash Axioms," *International Journal of Game Theory*, III (1974): 239–50; Alvin Roth and Michael Malouf, "Game Theoretic Models and the Role of Information in Bargaining," *Psychological Review*, LXXXVI (1979): 574–94; John Van Huyck, Raymond Batallio, Sondip Mathur, Patsy Van Huyck, and Andreas Ortmann, "On the Origin of Convention: Evidence From Symmetric Bargaining Games," *International Journal of Game Theory*, XXIV (1995): 187–212.
4 Robert Sugden, *The Economics of Rights, Cooperation, and Welfare* (New York: Blackwell, 1986).
5 This is the discrete time version of the replicator dynamics, which is most relevant in comparison to the alternative *bargaining-with-neighbors* dynamics considered here. There is also a continuous time version. As comprehensive references, see Josef Hofbauer and Karl Sigmund, *The Theory of Evolution and Dynamical Systems* (New York: Cambridge, 1988); Jorgen W. Weibull, *Evolutionary Game Theory* (Cambridge: MIT, 1995); Larry Samuelson, *Evolutionary Games and Equilibrium Selection* (Cambridge: MIT, 1997).

6   Jonas Björnerstedt and Jörgen Weibull, "Nash Equilibrium and Evolution by Imitation," in Kenneth J. Arrow et al., eds., *The Rational Foundations of Economic Behavior* (New York: Macmillan, 1996), pp. 155–71; Karl Schlag, "Why Imitate, and If So How?" Discussion Paper B-361 (University of Bonn, Germany, 1996).

7   "An Evolutionary Model of Bargaining," *Journal of Economic Theory*, LIX (1993): 145–68, and "The Evolution of Conventions," *Econometrica*, LXI (1993): 57–94; and Dean Foster and Young, "Stochastic Evolutionary Game Dynamics," *Theoretical Population Biology*, XXXVIII (1990): 219–32.

8   For discussion of expected waiting times, see Glenn Ellison, "Learning, Local Interaction and Coordination," *Econometrica*, LXI (1993): 1047–71; and Robert Axtell, Joshua M. Epstein, and H. Peyton Young, "The Emergence of Economic Classes in an Agent-Based Bargaining Model," preprint (Brookings Institution, 1999).

9   Gregory B. Pollack, "Evolutionary Stability on a Viscous Lattice," *Social Networks*, XI (1989): 175–212; Martin A. Nowak and Robert M. May, "Evolutionary Games and Spatial Chaos," *Nature*, CCCLIX (1992): 826–29; Kristian Lindgren and Mats Nordahl, "Evolutionary Dynamics in Spatial Games," *Physica D*, LXXV (1994): 292–309; Luca Anderlini and Antonella Ianni, "Learning on a Torus," in Cristina Bicchieri, Richard Jeffrey, and Brian Skryms, eds., *The Dynamics of Norms* (New York: Cambridge, 1997), pp. 87–107.

10   We find that behavior is not much different if we use the von Neumann neighborhood: N, S, E, W, or a larger Moore neighborhood.

11   At .9999 level to keep things comparable.

12   Ellison (*op. cit.*) found such contagion effects in local interaction of players arranged on a circle and playing pure coordination games.

13   For this reason, "frontier advantage" is used to define an unbeatable strategy in Illan Eshel, Emilia Sansone, and Avner Shaked, "Evolutionary Dynamics of Populations with a Local Interaction Structure," working paper (University of Bonn, 1996).

14   In situating the high strategy of the polymorphic pair in a sea of low-strategy players, we are creating the best-case scenario for the advancement of the polymorphism into the patch of demand-five players.

15   With some minor complications involving ties.

16   Skyrms, "Sex and Justice," *Journal of Philosophy*, XCI, 6 (June 1994): 305–20 and *Evolution of the Social Contract* (New York: Cambridge, 1996).

Chapter 28

PETER J. RICHERSON AND
ROBERT BOYD

CULTURE EVOLVES

"**WHEN A DOG BITES A MAN**, that is not news," goes the journalistic aphorism, "but when a man bites a dog, that is news." To many anthropologists, the claim that culture evolves will seem more like "Dog bites man" than "Man bites dog"—it may or may not be true, but it certainly is not news. In fact, the idea that culture evolves is as old as the discipline of anthropology itself. The nineteenth-century founders of anthropology, Lewis Henry Morgan and Edward Tylor,[1] thought that all societies evolved from less complex to more complex through the (in)-famous stages of savagery, barbarism, and civilization. Such progressive evolutionary theories continued to be important throughout most of the twentieth century in the work of noted anthropologists like Leslie White, Marshall Sahlins, Julian Steward, and Marvin Harris. During this period, evolutionary theories became less ethnocentric and more realistic. Evolutionary stages were given less-loaded terms such as *bands, tribes, chiefdoms*, and *states*,[2] and models were developed that allowed for the effect of local ecology on the trajectories of cultural evolution.[3] Though evolutionary theories no longer dominate contemporary anthropology, they continue to have important defenders like Robert Carneiro, Allen Johnson, and Timothy Earle.[4] The attraction of such progressive evolutionary theories is plain to see. The archaeological and historical records leave no doubt that the average human society has become larger, more productive, and more complex over the last ten thousand years. Although unilineal theories of human progress have fallen out of favor, the general trend toward greater complexity is not in doubt.[5]

However, we mean something quite different when we say culture evolves. Remember that the essential feature of Darwin's theory of evolution is population thinking. Species are populations of individuals that carry a pool of genetically acquired information through time. All of the large-scale features of life—its beautiful adaptations and its intricate historical patterns—can be explained by the events in individual lives that cause some genetic variants to spread and others to diminish. The progressive evolutionary theories debated by generations of anthropologists have almost nothing in common with this Darwinian notion of evolution. Very little of this work focuses on the processes that shape cultural variation; it is mainly descriptive. Those accounts of cultural evolution that do provide mechanisms typically focus on external causes of change. People's choices change their environment, and these changes lead to different choices. For example, a common argument is that the evolution of political and social complexity is driven by population growth—denser populations require economic intensification and facilitate political complexity, division of labor, and so on.[6] Such processes are more akin to ecological succession than evolution. In the same way that lichen colonizing a glacial moraine change the environment, making the soil suitable for grasses which in turn further change the soil, making way for shrubs, simpler societies change their environments in ways that make more-complex societies necessary.

There is little doubt that such successional processes have played a role in human history. However, they are far from the whole story;[7] culture evolves. Human populations carry a pool of culturally acquired information, and in order to explain why particular cultures are as they are, we need to keep track of the processes that cause some cultural variants to spread and persist while others disappear. The key is to focus on the details of individual lives. Kids imitate one another, their parents, and other adults, and both children and adults are taught by others. As children grow up they acquire cultural influences, skills, beliefs, and values, which affect the way that they lead their lives, and the extent to which others imitate them in turn. Some people may marry and raise many children, while others may remain childless but achieve prestigious social positions. As these events go on year after year and generation after generation, some cultural variants thrive while others do not. Some ideas are easier to learn or remember, some values are more likely to lead to influential social roles. The Darwinian theory of cultural evolution is an account of how such processes cause populations to come to have the culture they have.

The Darwinian theory of culture presented here emphasizes the generic properties of different types of processes. For example, some cultural variants may be easier to learn and remember than others, and this will, all other things being equal, cause such variants to spread, a process we call biased transmission. The basic kinds of processes are the *forces* of cultural evolution, analogous to the forces of genetic evolution, selection, mutation, and drift. In any particular situation, the concrete events in the lives of real people are what really goes on. However, by collecting similar processes together, and working out their generic properties, we build a handy conceptual tool kit that makes it easier to compare and generalize across cases. While we make no pretense that our scheme is a finished and final account, we do think that the tools in hand are useful for understanding how culture evolves.

A Darwinian account of culture does not imply that culture must be divisible into tiny, independent genelike bits that are faithfully replicated. Rather, the best evidence suggests that cultural variants are only loosely analogous to genes. Cultural transmission often does not involve high-fidelity replication; nor are cultural variants always tiny snippets of information. Nonetheless, cultural evolution is fundamentally Darwinian in its basic structure. Analogies to ordinary biological evolution are useful, but only because they provide us with a handy, ready-made tool kit to use in building a theory rooted in the best social science.

Skeptics who distrust Darwinism are common, particularly in the social sciences. But Darwinism is not inherently an individualist, adaptationist footpad sneaking into the social sciences to explain everything by genetic reductionism. Nor does it signal a return to the progressive, Eurocentric ideas of the past. A great variety of substantive theories arise when the all-important details are specified. Some models end up looking a lot like rational choice; and in others, arbitrary cultural differences can arise from the dynamics of interacting cultural elements. Some models lead to long-term directional change in which artifacts or institutions become more efficient, while others lack such trends.

[. . .]

The forces of cultural evolution

We call the processes that cause the culture to change *forces* of cultural evolution. We divide the evolving system into two parts. One is the "inertial" part—the processes that tend to keep the population the same from one time period to the next. In this model cultural inertia comes from unbiased sampling and faithful copying of models. The other part consists of the forces— the processes that cause changes in the numbers of different types of cultural variants in the population. These processes overcome the inertia and generate evolutionary change.

[. . .] Transmission biases are forces that arise because people's psychology makes them more likely to adopt some beliefs rather than others. Natural selection is a force that results from what happens to people who hold different cultural variants. We focus on biased transmission and natural selection here as a device to introduce the logic underlying our models of cultural evolution, and in subsequent chapters we extend our analysis to include the other forces introduced in table 28.1.

Biased transmission

Biased cultural transmission occurs when people preferentially adopt some cultural variants rather than others. Think of it as comparison shopping. People are exposed to alternative ideas or values and then choose among them (although the choice may not be a conscious one).[8]

Table 28.1 A list of cultural evolutionary forces

Random forces
Cultural mutation. Effects due to random individual-level processes, such as misremembering an item of culture.
Cultural drift. Effects caused by statistical anomalies in small populations. For example, in simple societies some skills, such as boat-building, may be practiced by a few specialists. If all the specialists in a particular generation happen, by chance, to die young or to have personalities that discourage apprentices, boat-building will die out.

Decision-making forces
Guided variation. Nonrandom changes in cultural variants by individuals that are subsequently transmitted. This force results from transformations during social learning, or the learning, invention, or adaptive modification of cultural variants.
Biased transmission
Content-based (or direct) bias. Individuals are more likely to learn or remember some cultural variants based on the their content. Content-based bias can result from calculation of costs and benefits associated with alternative variants, or because the structure of cognition makes some variants easier to learn or remember.
Frequency-based bias. The use of the commonness or rarity of a cultural variant as a basis for choice. For example, the most advantageous variant is often likely to be the commonest. If so, a conformity bias is an easy way to acquire the correct variant.
Model-based bias. Choice of trait based on the observable attributes of the individuals who exhibit the trait. Plausible model-based biases include a predisposition to imitate successful or prestigious individuals, and a predisposition to imitate individuals similar to oneself.

Natural selection
Changes in the cultural composition of a population caused by the effects of holding one cultural variant rather than others. The natural selection of cultural variants can occur at individual or group levels.

The diffusion of innovations provides a fund of well-studied examples of how biased transmission works. This body of work was pioneered by a landmark study by sociologists Bryce Ryan and Neal Gross of the spread of hybrid corn (maize) in two Iowa farm communities in the early 1940s. Following their lead, thousands of case studies of the diffusion of innovations have been published.[9] These studies indicate that in both traditional and contemporary societies, innovations often spread as the result of personal contact. People adopt an innovation like hybrid maize after observing the behavior of friends and neighbors who have already adopted the innovation. Once they have observed the innovation firsthand, their decision about whether to adopt the innovation is strongly affected by the perceived utilitarian advantage of the new crop. Is the hybrid seed more resistant to disease? Is there a ready market for the new crop? If so, people will tend to adopt the new crop and the innovation will spread.[10] The decision to adopt a new idea, crop, or any other cultural variant may also be affected by the number or prestige of the people who have already adopted it, leading to varieties of biased transmission that we will consider in detail in [Richerson and Boyd 2005] chapter 4.

Because biased transmission results from the (not necessarily conscious) comparison of alternative variants, the resulting rate of cultural change depends on the variability in the population. Initially, innovations spread slowly because few people practice them, and so few other people are in a position to observe the innovation and compare it with their existing behavior. As the innovation becomes more common, more people are exposed to it and can compare it with other behaviors, and the rate of adoption of the innovation accelerates. As the old behavior becomes rare, there are fewer people still practicing it and fewer opportunities to make the comparison, so the rate of spread of the new behavior slows. This process, which has been documented in many different cases, generates a characteristic S-shaped trajectory.

The rate at which a population changes by biased transmission also depends on how hard it is to evaluate alternative behaviors. If a new crop variety has substantially higher yields than existing crops, then farmers will easily detect the difference. Hybrid corn had about a 20% yield advantage over traditional varieties, so its use spread rapidly. Similarly, after sweet potatoes were introduced to coastal New Guinea from the New World sometime in the 1700s, they swiftly replaced other crops in the cool highlands because they performed much better than typical tropical plants. This happened even though the Europeans who brought the sweet potatoes to New Guinea went no further than the coast and didn't even know that people lived in the highlands until the 1930s.[11] However, the benefits of many other desirable traits may be much harder to detect. The practice of boiling drinking water substantially reduces infant mortality from diarrhea. Nonetheless, the practice may fail to spread, because the effects of boiling water are difficult to discern. There are other ways of getting diarrhea, and people can't see the microbes in the water. People who believe that disease is caused by magic may find it hard to believe that boiling drinking water is useful. Figuring out which variant is best is often hard even if they have very different payoffs. Traits whose beneficial effects only become apparent over time are especially difficult to evaluate.

Biased transmission doesn't always result from an attempt to evaluate alternative cultural variants according to cultural standards or rules. Biases are often caused by universal characteristics of human cognition or perception. For instance, many linguists believe that some linguistic features are "marked," meaning that they are harder to produce and perceive than alternative unmarked features. Languages that denote the subject and object of sentences with word order are less marked that languages accomplishing this function by changing the form of the noun. Such unmarked features are simpler, and accordingly appear earlier in first language acquisition. Many linguists also believe that "internal" language change (as opposed to change that results from contact between languages) typically proceeds from marked to unmarked.

Such changes tend to make the language easier to produce and understand. Thus, language learners confronted with two slightly different grammatical variants will tend to adopt the less marked of the two, and in this way biased transmission can drive language change.[12] This hypothesis is somewhat controversial, but if it turns out to be true, it will provide a good example of how biases may arise from the workings of human psychology.

    [. . .]

Natural selection of cultural variations

The logic of natural selection applies to culturally transmitted variation every bit as much as it applies to genetic variation. For natural selection on culture to occur,

- people must vary because they have acquired different beliefs or values through social learning,
- this variation must affect people's behavior in ways that affect the probability that they transmit their beliefs to others, and
- the total number of cultural variants that can exist in the population must be limited in some way.

Or, in other words, cultural variants must compete.

    You can substitute the appropriate genetic terms in this list to recover the standard textbook account of how genes evolve by natural selection. The basic logic is identical. All other things being equal, beliefs that cause people to behave in ways that make their beliefs more likely to be transmitted will increase in frequency. If the behaviors that are shaped by the beliefs acquired by imitation are important ones, they may affect many aspects of individuals' lives: who they meet, how long they live, how many children they have, or whether they earn tenure. All of these factors could affect the probability that an individual becomes available as a model for others to imitate or a teacher with the opportunity to instruct the naive.

    To the extent that people acquire beliefs from their parents, natural selection acts on culture in almost exactly the same way it does on genes. For example, religious beliefs affect both the survival and the reproduction of people who practice them. Sociologists Susan Janssen and Robert Hauser compared the fertility of a large sample of people living in Wisconsin. Catholics (both men and women) had 20% more children, on average, than did non-Catholics. Similarly, epidemiologists L. McEvoy and G. Land report that members of the Reformed Latter-Day Saints Church of Missouri have age-adjusted mortalities about 20% lower than control populations belonging to other religions. Behavior genetic studies indicate that religious affiliation (whether you are a Mormon or a Catholic) is culturally transmitted. In Janssen and Hauser's case, people's religious beliefs are strongly correlated with the beliefs of their parents. Thus, beliefs that lead to high fertility and low mortality will increase, because people holding such beliefs are more likely to survive to adulthood and have larger families if they do, and because the children in these families will tend to have the same beliefs as their parents.

    Whenever individuals are culturally influenced by teachers, peers, celebrities, and so on, natural selection acting on cultural variation can favor the increase of behaviors that increase the chance of attaining such non-parental roles. In this same scenario, when the traits that maximize success in becoming a parent are different from those that maximize success as a teacher, priest, or celebrity, natural selection acting on cultural variation can cause genetically maladaptive traits to spread.

Consider one of the most bizarre traditions in the whole ethnographic record: the existence of a subculture of people who devote more time to, and are prouder of, the length of their publication list than the number of their children. The phenomenon is potentially explicable by the effect of selection on cultural variation. We, of course, are members of this odd group and can testify to the evolutionary pressures from firsthand experience. Some of our readers will have observed university faculty at close range and may well share our experiences. To see how the selection valuing long CVs can overwhelm the complex, powerful mixture of primary and secondary urges favoring having children, consider the young assistant professor just beginning her career. Entering a new university, she needs to acquire many new beliefs or modify old ones acquired as a graduate student. She needs to know how hard to work on teaching, what the standards are by which committee work is judged, and how much time should be devoted to graduate students. And, most critical of all, how much effort should she devote to her research? Is career advancement possible if time is also devoted to family and recreation?

In making their choices, many assistant professors decide to follow the example of older and more-experienced faculty. These senior faculty represent a biased sample of the original population of assistant professors hired, because those who did not work hard and publish lots of papers were not promoted to tenure and hence aren't available to pass on their experience. Imitating tenured faculty will cause our new assistant professor to aspire to high standards in research and likely enough to postpone starting a family and limit the number of her children. This force operating on many assistant professors over several generations has produced a population that puts very high value on publications and substantially curtails child-bearing. Note that we have simplified the whole story here. Throughout the educational career of our aspiring professor, she has been exposed to teachers who have faced similar career/family dilemmas, and the most successful and most influential will have been mainly those who favored career. She is liable to have fallen in love with one of her ambitious graduate school peers who shares the same background socialization and career ambitions. A successful midcareer anthropologist of our acquaintance describes the sympathetic concern of her African friends. So proud of their big families, they could not comprehend that a healthy woman would "freely" choose to have but one child.

Selection for successful research faculty is driving behavior in a quite different direction from what we would predict if it were acting on genes. The role of tenured faculty member is a kind of cultural parent and social selection agent rolled into one. Potentially, natural selection on cultural variation can select for success in any role that is active in cultural transmission—biological parent, friend, leader, teacher, grandparent, and so on. The biological system is much simpler in this regard, as long as we stick with conventional organisms. There are only two roles, male and female, to worry about, and both parents make equal contributions of genes to the offspring. There are many patterns of genetic transmission that lead to the same general sorts of complexities as culture, such as Y chromosomes (transmitted from fathers to sons) and mitochondrial DNA (transmitted only by mothers),[13] but nothing quite like human culture.

Of course our young assistant professor will also take her own preferences into account as she makes decisions. If she is ambivalent about having children, she may readily adopt the publish-or-perish mentality of her most ambitious colleagues. If she is very eager to have children, she will hope that her tenure committee is more impressed by quality than quantity, and think about starting a family soon. The effect of preferences that bias decision making will lead to biased transmission. If the bias is strong, the effect of selection on the pool of models will have little effect. Plausibly, however, the bias will be weak in this case. In deciding how much time to devote to their families, young professionals must estimate not only the immediate effect on their careers and home lives but also the long-run effects on the development of their children. Biological urges to have children may be satisfied by having one or two, and the urge to achieve professional success seems to tap deeply felt biases as well. In such cases the information available to individuals may be very poor, and sentiments conflicted. Plausibly, aspiring academics will rely almost entirely on traditional beliefs, and if they do, the selective process that winnows tenured faculty will have an important effect on how faculty behave.

Why distinguish selection and biased transmission?

Biased transmission occurs because people preferentially adopt some cultural variants rather than others, while selection occurs because some cultural variants affect the lives of their bearers in ways that make those bearers more likely to be imitated. Almost every other author who has written about this topic, including biologists Luigi Cavalli-Sforza, Marcus Feldman, and Richard Dawkins, and anthropologist William Durham,[14] describes biased transmission as a form of selection, often using the term *cultural selection*. This is not unreasonable—biased transmission is a process of selective retention. Human populations are culturally variable. Some variants are more likely to be imitated than others, and thus some variants have higher relative "cultural fitness."

Nonetheless, we think that distinguishing between biased transmission and *natural* selection is very important. Biased transmission depends on what is going on in the brains of imitators, but in most forms of natural selection, the fitness of different genes depends on their effect on survival and reproduction, independent of human desires, choices, and preferences. We can understand the evolution of beak morphology in birds by asking how beaks of different size and shape affect the bird's ability to acquire food. True, we need to know something about other aspects of the bird's phenotype, so the fitness of genes affecting beak size does depend on other genes, but the dependence is much weaker than for biased transmission. Biased transmission is more like a genetic evolutionary process called meiotic drive, in which "driver" genes cause the chromosomes carrying them to be disproportionately likely to be incorporated in eggs and sperm. Meiotic drive is clearly a form of selection, but most biologists think that it is useful to distinguish it from plain vanilla natural selection.

We think that the same kind of distinction should be made in the case of cultural transmission. Consider something such as acquiring an aversion to addictive drugs. If this bias is common, it will tend to suppress the spread of addiction. But even people with biases against drugs may sometimes be tempted and succumb to an addiction that could land them behind bars, or otherwise remove them from the pool of people who exercise strong cultural influence on others. Both effects may be quite important in keeping rates of drug addiction down. The aversion to addictive substances is an example of biased transmission, while the processes that influence the number of addicts available as models exemplify selection. Although distinguishing the effects of biased transmission and selection in specific empirical cases is not always easy, the distinction is important, because these processes often lead to very different evolutionary outcomes.

In our experience, most people's intuition is that psychological forces like biased transmission are much more important than natural selection in cultural evolution. They feel in control of their culture and believe they came by most of it by choice. But the truth is, we often have much less choice than we think. As Mark Twain put it,

> We know why Catholics are Catholics; why Presbyterians are Presbyterians; why Baptists are Baptists; why Mormons are Mormons; why thieves are thieves; why monarchists are monarchists; why Republicans are Republicans and Democrats,

Democrats. We know that it is a matter of association and sympathy, not reasoning and examination; that hardly a man in the world has an opinion on morals, politics, and religion that he got otherwise than through his associations and sympathies.[15]

Crucial questions hang on the relative importance of biased transmission and natural selection. If the psychological forces are much more important, then the causes of cultural evolution will ultimately trace back to innate primary values—all complex, adaptive behavior will ultimately be explained in terms of how natural selection shaped the innate aspects of psychology—and culture will have only a proximate role. However, if natural selection acting on cultural variation is important, then it is also an ultimate cause. Perhaps Durham's culturally transmitted secondary values are not always secondary at all. And so we will argue!

Population thinking is useful even if cultural variants aren't much like genes

Adopting a Darwinian approach to culture does not mean that you have to also believe that culture is made of miniscule, genelike particles that are faithfully replicated during cultural transmission. The evidence suggests that sometimes cultural variants *are* somewhat genelike, while at other times they are decidedly not. But—and this is a big but—in either case, the Darwinian approach remains useful.

You are forgiven if you find this assertion surprising. Over the last decade or so, a lot of ink has been spilled in discussions of whether cultural variants are genelike particles. On one side of this debate are "universal Darwinists" like evolutionary biologist Richard Dawkins, philosopher Daniel Dennett, and psychologist Susan Blackmore. These authors sometimes seem to be arguing that genelike replicators are necessary for adaptive evolution, and they also think that cultural variants, which they refer to as memes, are discrete, faithfully replicating genelike particles. Because cultural variants are genelike, Darwinian theory can be applied to cultural evolution, more or less unchanged.[16] On the other side are a diverse group of critics like the anthropologists Dan Sperber and Christopher Hallpike, who argue that cultural variants are not particulate and are not faithfully replicated, so Darwinian ideas of variation and selective retention cannot be used to understand cultural evolution.

We don't agree with either side in this argument. We heartily endorse the argument that cultural evolution will proceed according to Darwinian principles, but at the same time we think that cultural evolution may be based on "units" that are quite unlike genes. We encourage you not to think of cultural variants as close analogs to genes but as different entities entirely, about which we know distressingly little. They must be genelike to the extent that they carry the cultural information necessary to create cultural continuity. But, as you will see, this can be accomplished in most un-genelike ways.

The modest requirements for the properties of cultural variants are a potent rejoinder to those who believe that we can't theorize about cultural evolution until we understand exactly what cultural variants are like. If it were true that adaptive evolution depended critically on the units of transmission, Darwin and all his followers would still be marking time, waiting for the developmental work definitively showing how genes give rise to the properties of organisms. Understanding how complexes of genes interact in development to create the traits upon which selection falls is a current hot topic in biology, if not *the* hot topic. Darwin had a very un-genelike picture of how organic inheritance worked, complete with the inheritance of acquired variation. He nonetheless did remarkably well, because the essential Darwinian processes are tolerant of how heritable variation is maintained. For the same reason, we can black-box the problem of how culture is stored in brains by using plausible models based on observable features that we do understand, and forge ahead.

[. . .]

Replicators are not necessary for cumulative evolution

Dan Sperber and his colleagues cognitive anthropologists Pascal Boyer and Scott Atran have argued that because cultural variants do not replicate, cumulative cultural evolution is unlikely to result from the selective retention of cultural variants. They believe that the transformations that arise during cultural transmission are usually so large as to swamp the relatively weak evolutionary forces like biased transmission and natural selection.

This argument comes in two different flavors: Sometimes, Sperber and his colleagues maintain, social learning leads to systematic transformation, so that people observing a variety of different behaviors tend to infer the same underlying cultural variant. Sperber refers to such preferred variants as "attractors," because systematic transformations create a new nonselective force that moves the population toward nearby attractors. He thinks that this process is usually so strong that selective processes can be ignored.[17] In other situations, Sperber argues that the transformations that occur during social learning are unsystematic, so that people observing the same behavior infer very different cultural variants; consequently, cultural replication is so noisy and inaccurate that weak selective forces would be swamped.[18] Let's consider each of these arguments in turn.

Weak bias and selection can be important even when guided variation is strong

In many parts of the world, agricultural landowners receive a share of the crops raised on their land in lieu of rent, a practice called sharecropping. Economic theory predicts that the landowner's share will depend on the quality of the land. Owners of high-quality land should get a larger share, because they provide a more-valuable input. Since land quality varies continuously, there should be all kinds of sharecrop contracts—62.3% for the landowner, 36.8% for the landowner, and so on and so on. However, typically sharecrop contracts fall into a few simple ratios. In Illinois, for example, the vast majority of contracts are of two types: 1:1 and 2:1 for the farmer.[19] Now suppose that there is a cultural variant that is the farmer's mental representation of the optimal sharecrop contract. This could take on any share between zero and one. However, further suppose that there are attractors at simple integer ratios, perhaps because such shares are easier to learn and remember. In a particular county, the optimal share might be 1.16:1. Farmers who used this contract might be more attractive as models because they make more money, and thus biased transmission would favor a 1.16:1 contract. However, the attractor would tend to increase the frequency of 1:1 contracts, and if this force were strong compared to bias, most farmers would end up believing that the 1:1 contract is best, even though they could make more money by demanding the larger share.

This example also shows that if there are multiple attractors, weak selective forces can be important even if attractors are overwhelmingly strong. Suppose that there are two equally strong attractors for sharecrop contracts, 1:1 and 2:1, and that a population of farmers starts out with a range of contracts. After a short while, everybody will think one of the two simple ratios is the best contract—some 1:1 and others 2:1. Because these are strong attractors, they will be transmitted extremely faithfully. People who observe somebody using a 1:1 contract will correctly infer that that person thinks even shares are the best contract. Similarly, people observing a 2:1 contract in action will correctly infer the underlying belief. If the 2:1 contract is a little more profitable for landlords, 2:1 contracts will gradually replace the 1:1 contract, because other landlords are more likely to imitate the successful. In effect, *multiple* strong attractors lead to discrete, genelike cultural variants. Only if one attractor is stronger than the sum of all the other forces acting on other attractors will they completely determine the evolutionary outcome.

Adaptive evolution can occur even when transmission is very noisy

When cultural transmission is noisy, it cannot produce cultural inertia for exactly the same reasons that genetic transmission does. To see this, suppose there are only two cultural variants in some domain, labeled A and B. Each generates different but overlapping distributions of observable behavior. When cultural learning occurs, naive individuals, perhaps children, observe a sample of individuals from these distributions, make inferences, and then adopt their own mental representation. This process is very sloppy—a naive individual who observes an A infers that the individual is an A 80% of the time and a B 20% of the time. Similarly, a naive individual who observes a B infers B 80% of the time and A 20% of the time. It is clear that this kind of social learning will not lead to replication at the population level. Suppose that 100% of the people initially have cultural variant A. After one generation 80% will be A, after two generations it will be 68%, and by generation 5 or so, the population will have converged to a random distribution of cultural variants. Only very strong selection or bias could generate cumulative adaptation.

However, just because cultural transmission is inaccurate, it does not necessarily follow that there can be no cultural inertia or cumulative evolution of adaptations. Transmission processes can lead to accurate replication at the level of the population even when individual social learning is loaded with errors. As before, suppose that every naive individual observes the behavior of a number of models and makes inferences about the beliefs that gave rise to each person's behavior, and that people make the wrong inference 20% of the time. Now, suppose that individuals adopt the cultural variant that they believe is *most common* among their models. This is a form of biased transmission, because some variants are more likely to be adopted than others. However, unlike the biases discussed above, the nature of the bias is independent of content. It depends only on which variant is more common, and represents a "conformist" bias in social learning. In the next chapter you will see that there is good evidence that people do have a conformist bias, and that there are good evolutionary reasons why this should be the case. A conformist bias at the individual level leads to reasonably accurate replication at the population level even when individual inference about underlying mental representations is inaccurate. For example, if everyone is A, 20% of the As are mistaken for Bs, but the chances are that most naive individuals will observe samples in which A is the most common variant as long as these samples are large. Conformist bias corrects for the effect of errors because it increases the chance that individuals will acquire the more common of the two variants.

Yet the combination of high error rates and a conformist bias does not result in the same kind of "frictionless" adaptation as genetic replication. Highly accurate, unbiased genetic replication allows minute selective forces to generate and preserve adaptations over millions of years. Error-prone cultural replication, even when corrected by a conformist bias, imposes modest, but still significant forces on the cultural composition of the population. This means that only selective forces of similar magnitude will lead to cumulative adaptation. We do not think this is a problem: the forces of bias and natural selection acting on cultural variation are probably much stronger than those that shape genetic variation because they work on shorter timescales, and are often driven by psychological processes, not demographic events. The empirical record supports this somewhat, providing examples of innovations that spread over decades, not millennia.

Cultural replication can be quite accurate

Cultural transmission does not *have* to be biased and inaccurate. In fact, sometimes arbitrary cultural variants are transmitted with considerable fidelity. Take word learning, for example. The average high school graduate has mastered about sixty thousand words—an astounding feat. Learning words is a difficult inferential problem for the reasons already mentioned. The child on the nursery floor hears the word *ball* and surveys the scene. Perhaps the adult is referring to the red ball rolling across the floor, but many other inferences are possible. It could be that the adult is referring to moving red objects, the fact that it is warm, or the fact that the ball is rolling north. Despite seemingly endless opportunities for confusion, children acquire about ten new associations between a range of sounds and a meaning every day.

According to developmental linguist Paul Bloom, children use a variety of strategies to acquire their immense vocabularies.[20] They behave as if they start with the assumption that words refer to objects, and even very young children have innate presumptions about what objects are. Our hypothetical child will interpret the red ball as an object because it is connected, bounded, and moves as a unit unless some further evidence proves otherwise.[21] "Joint attention" provides another important mechanism for learning language.[22] Children follow the gaze of adults, who can often be induced to pay attention to what a child is paying attention to. In the course of these games, the adult often names the object of joint attention, usually as a part of a more-complex utterance: "A red ball! I'll roll you the red ball!" To extract *ball* and *red* out of such a language stream as names of a certain kind of round object and a color that applies to many objects is quite a feat, but the potential ambiguity is sharply limited by the assumption that the utterance is only relevant to the object of joint attention, the red ball. Another strategy children use is what psychologists call "fast mapping." Suppose a three-year-old is presented with two balls, one red and one turquoise. An experimenter asks, "Toss me the chromium ball, not the red one, the chromium one!" The child knows the color term *red* very well but not *chromium* or *turquoise*. Typically the child simply assumes that *chromium* means "turquoise" and many retain this false hypothesis for at least a week. In many cases, further experience confirms hypotheses formed by fast mapping and they go on to become a durable part of the vocabulary. Grammatical cues also play a role in language learning. For example, the child knows that *red ball* is not an action from its role in the sentence. These are only a few of the mechanisms that allow kids to accurately acquire a huge vocabulary without any innate predispositions about what words mean.

Historical linguistics suggests that these mechanisms can maintain detectable similarities in languages over hundreds of generations. Sir William Jones, the Chief Justice of India, launched the discipline of historical linguistics at the end of the eighteenth century by demonstrating that Sanskrit has certain remarkable resemblances to European languages such as Greek and Latin, resemblances too numerous to be explained by chance. Instead, these languages and a variety of others belonging to the Indo-European language family are all descendants of a single language known as Proto-Indo-European. As the people speaking this language spread out across Eurasia, linguistic communities became isolated and the languages gradually diverged. Exactly how long ago this occurred is controversial. Some think that the speakers of Proto-Indo-European were the earliest farmers who dispersed from their agrarian homeland in southwestern Asia beginning about ten thousand years ago. Others think that they were horse-mounted nomadic herders who emerged from Central Asia or southeastern Europe about six thousand years ago.[23] To be conservative, let's suppose that Proto-Indo-European was spoken six thousand years ago, or roughly 240 human generations in the past. Contemporary Indo-European languages are connected to the speakers of Proto-Indo-European by a chain of cultural transmission 240 generations long. Each generation, children learned the sound-meaning associations from adults, and then served as models for the next generation. Thus the similarities that historical linguists use to link these languages have survived 480 generations of cultural transmission, indicating that cultural transmission can be quite accurate indeed.

Cultural variants need not be particulate

Many people believe that cultural inheritance must be particulate if it is to undergo Darwinian evolution because, the story goes, only particulate inheritance conserves the variation necessary for the action of natural selection. Biology textbooks often illustrate this idea by explaining how the discovery of Mendelian genetics rescued Darwin from the problem posed by a British engineer named Fleeming Jenkin. Jenkin was nobody's fool—a longtime associate of the great but antievolutionist physicist Lord Kelvin, he played a key role in the design and construction of the first transatlantic cable and made important contributions to economics, including inventing the supply and demand curve. Nowadays, however, he is mainly known for pointing out that if inheritance works by taking the average of the parental genetic contributions, as Darwin proposed, then the amount of variation would be reduced by half each generation. Therefore, the variation necessary for natural selection to be effective would rapidly disappear. This critique vexed Darwin greatly, but it wasn't resolved until geneticists like R. A. Fisher showed that variation persists because genes don't mix; each parent's genes remain separate particles in offspring.

This story is true but misleading. Because mutation rates are very low, the particulate nature of genetic inheritance is crucial for maintaining genetic variation. However, perhaps the analog of mutation in cultural transmission is not so low.[24] We can even imagine that cultural transmission is sufficiently noisy and error prone that blending inheritance would be an *advantage* in keeping cultural variation from growing disastrously large. In a noisy world, taking the average of many models may be necessary to uncover a reasonable approximation of the true value of a particular trait. For example, when you speak, the sounds that come out of your mouth depend on the geometry of your vocal tract. For example, the consonant *p* in *spit* is created by momentarily bringing your lips together with the glottis open. Narrowing the glottis converts this consonant to *b*, as in *bib*. Leaving the glottis open and slightly opening the lips produces *pf*, as in the German word *apfel*. Linguists have shown that even within a single speech community, individuals vary in the exact geometry of the vocal tract used to produce any given word. Thus, quite plausibly, individuals vary in the culturally acquired rule about how to arrange the inside of the mouth when they are saying any particular word. Languages vary in the sounds used, and this variation can be very long lived. For example, in dialects spoken in the northwest of Germany, *p* is substituted for *pf* in *apfel* and many similar words. This difference arose about AD 500 and has persisted ever since.[25]

Now suppose that children are exposed to the speech of a number of adults who vary in the way that they pronounce *pf*. Each child unconsciously computes the average of all the pronunciations that she hears and adopts the tongue position that produces approximately the average. There is no doubt that this act of averaging would tend to decrease the amount of variation in the population each generation. However, phenotypic performances also will vary as a result of age, social context, vocal tract anatomy, and so on. Moreover, learners will often misperceive a performance. These sorts of errors in transmission will keep pumping variation into a population as blending bleeds it away. Further note that the errors one makes will affect one's performance and will thus affect what learners use as the basis for constructing their own way of saying *pf*. Some variation will always remain if any heritable errors occur in the cultural transmission process, as surely they do.

With this sort of averaging mechanism, mental rules are not particulate, nor do they replicate. A child may well adopt a rule that is unlike any of the rules in the brains of its models. The phonological system can nonetheless evolve in a quite Darwinian way. More-attractive forms of pronunciation can increase if they have a disproportionate effect on the average. Rules affecting different aspects of pronunciation can recombine and thus lead to the cumulative evolution of complex phonological rules. In fact, this model faithfully mimics all the usual properties of ordinary genetic evolution. We are confident of this claim, because models exactly like it have been used in population genetics to represent the evolution of characters such as height that are affected by many genes, each with a small effect. They provide a good approximation to genetically more-realistic models and are much easier to analyze.[26]

Cultural variants need not be small, independent bits

Many people believe that a Darwinian approach to cultural evolution requires breaking culture into little, independent bits, an anathema to many anthropologists who believe that cultures are tightly integrated systems of shared meanings. Just as the syntax of a language is made up of a system of interdependent rules, so are the cultural meanings embedded in systems of kinship, cosmology, law, and ritual. Since Darwinian models require that cultures be decomposed into independent, atomistic traits, the argument runs, Darwinian models must be wrong. For example, Christopher Hallpike complains:

> The absence of any . . . structural concepts inevitably reduces the examples of memes and culturgens to ridiculous laundry lists of odds and ends—Dawkins's tunes, catch-phrases and ways of making pots, and Lumsden and Wilson's food items, colour classifications, 6000 attributes of camels among the Arabs, and the ten-second-slow-downs by which drivers cause traffic jams.
>
> In fact, such theories of basic units of culture do not rest on any evidence, or any sociological theory at all, but are simply proposed because if one is trying to explain culture on the basis of a neo-Darwinian theory of natural selection, it is highly inconvenient *not* to have a "unit" like a meme or culturgen, quantifications of which can be treated as continuously variable over time like the gene.[27]

This criticism misses the mark. Perhaps we (and others of our persuasion) have fostered this view by choosing very simple examples to illustrate our ideas, but there is absolutely nothing in the theory that requires that cultural variants be little bits of culture. People may choose between great, linked cultural complexes—between speaking Spanish or Guarani, or between remaining a Catholic or becoming a Seventh-Day Adventist; or they may choose between smaller, more loosely linked items of knowledge—between pronouncing *r* at the end of a word or not, or between different views about the morality of contraception. At a *formal* level, Darwinian methods will apply equally well in either case. We keep track of the different variants, independent little bits or big complexes as the case may be, present in a population, and try to understand what processes cause some variants to increase and others to decline. The same logic applies whether the variants are individual phonological rules or entire grammars.

Cultures are not tightly structured wholes

Whether cultures actually *are* tightly integrated wholes is an important empirical question. While there has been surprisingly little systematic attention paid to this problem, a great mass of observational data bear on it. We believe that these data suggest that culture is a complex mixture of structures. Some cultural variants are linked into coherent wholes, while others float promiscuously from culture to culture.

The data from linguistics suggest that even the tightly interlinked rules underlying language sometimes diffuse and recombine. Words, phonological rules, and syntax all can diffuse and recombine independently, and as a result, different components of a single language often have a different evolutionary history. You can see this in the history of English. Some words in the English lexicon are derived from French, while others come from German. In German, the object sometimes comes before the verb in a sentence, but in French the object always follows the verb. English adopts the French syntax, although the majority of spoken English vocabulary is derived from German. Most English phonology is descended from a Germanic language; but unlike German speakers, English speakers distinguish [v], as in *veal*, from [f], as in *feel*, apparently as a result of the influence of Norman "loan words." Linguists Sarah Thomason and Terrence Kaufman[28] provide many examples from other languages, including the Ma'a language spoken in northern Tanzania that has a basic lexicon related to Cushitic languages and a grammar related to Bantu languages. They summarize by saying that "any linguistic feature can be transferred from any language to any other language."[29] They go on to argue that it is the actual pattern of social, political, and cultural interaction that determines the extent and kinds of diffusion among languages.

While the linguistic data suggest that any linguistic feature can diffuse from one language to another, they also suggest that the rate at which different features diffuse depends on a number of linguistic and social factors. What linguists call "typological distance" seems to be the most important linguistic factor. Typological distance measures the extent to which two languages have similar structure. All other things being equal, the more similar two languages are the higher the rate of borrowing. In turn, more highly structured subsystems of language diffuse and recombine at a slower rate than less structured systems. Individual words are more or less independent of each other, and as a result, they are the first items to diffuse when two languages come into contact. Inflectional morphology (for example, different verb forms that depend on the person, timing, or type of action) is linked in a complex, multidimensional system and therefore will diffuse very slowly unless the inflectional morphology of neighboring languages shares a similar structure.[30] For example, Norse had a substantial impact on English grammar even though only a small number of Danes occupied a small part of England for a relatively short time, because the typological distance between Norse and Old English was small. The rate and direction of diffusion is also strongly influenced by many social factors, the extent of bilingualism, the context in which bilingual speakers use each language, and the relative prestige of groups speaking different languages.[31]

Good evidence also suggests that language is not a good predictor of material culture—anthropological jargon for the kinds of tools, containers, dwellings, and clothing that people use. One recent study compared the artifacts collected at a number of villages on the northern coast of New Guinea during the early 1900s with the languages now spoken in those villages.[32] There was no association between language spoken and the kinds of artifacts used when the distance between villages was held constant. This means that the material cultures of two villages thirty kilometers apart with closely related languages are no more similar than the material culture of two villages thirty kilometers apart in which completely unrelated languages are spoken. Studies in Africa and North America come to the same general conclusion.[33]

A vast amount of anecdotal data provides circumstantial evidence that other components of cultures are a mix of loosely and more tightly linked elements. There are obviously many examples of important cultural similarities and differences that do not map onto linguistic differences. For example, male and female genital mutilation are common customs throughout central and eastern Africa and are practiced by people who speak very distantly related languages. California acorn-salmon hunter-gatherers and maize farmers of the Southwest both encompassed diverse language groups. The spread of religious practices, including the Sun Dance on the Great Plains, Islam across central Asia, and millenarian movements in Melanesia, along with the contemporary spread of Protestantism in Latin America, provide additional examples of cultural practices diffusing across many different cultures/languages. On the other hand, that ritual practices and systems of religious belief can be identified as they diffuse among widely different cultures suggests that the many beliefs that make them up *are* reasonably tightly integrated and as a result *do* cohere. Some scholars, such as philologist Georges Dumézil,[34] argue that cultures have a set of core beliefs, and these core beliefs create cultural continuity over thousands of years.

[. . .]

Darwinian tools help get the right answer

We are advocating that social scientists change the way they do business, *supplementing* their usual tool kit with ideas imported from biology. Naturally enough, many of them resent unsolicited advice from outside their disciplines. The philosopher Elliot Sober has captured one common reaction in a paper in which he argues that population-based models of cultural change will be of little interest to social scientists, because cultural evolution depends on learning rules. As he puts it,

> My main reason for skepticism is that these models concern themselves with the *consequences* of transmission systems and fitness differences, not with their *sources* [his emphasis].

To understand why some ideas spread but others do not, you need to know people's learning rules, their transmission biases, and the like. Why did someone invent a given cultural variant in the first place? Why is it attractive to others? You have to know which ideas will be imitated and which will be ignored. This knowledge does not come from within the Darwinian model, Sober argues; rather, it has to come from some other theory. Given learning rules, Darwinian models can predict the trajectory of cultural change, but according to Sober, this is of much less interest to social scientists than people's preferences. In other words, Sober thinks that population-based theories take all the important stuff as given, and concentrate on the stuff that nobody really cares about. The hard parts of social science don't involve its population-level properties, and the population level, unlike the biological case, is trivial. This critique has in common with many others the idea that cultural evolution is somehow so different from organic evolution that population-level processes simply don't matter.

There are three things wrong with this argument. First, it assumes that content-driven biases are the only important process affecting cultural change, and this is simply false. Biases are important, but so are processes like natural selection, which can only be understood in terms of the population dynamics of alternative cultural variants. Second, it assumes that once you know people's learning rules, how they make choices about which culture to imitate and perform, it's easy predict the evolutionary outcome. Or, in other words, we are all good intuitive population thinkers. Much experience in the relatively simpler world of evolutionary biology suggests that this is not the case. Finally, the biases are themselves the result of interacting genetic and cultural evolutionary processes. Understanding the evolution of the rules requires a theory that can work out how rules influence the social environment, which in turn influences what social information is available.

Notes

1   Burrow 1966 provides a classic account. See also Richerson and Boyd 2001b.
2   White 1949; Sahlins, Harding, and Service 1960.
3   Steward 1955; Sahlins, Harding, and Service 1960; Harris 1979.
4   Johnson and Earle 2000; Carneiro 2003.
5   See Sahlins, Harding, and Service 1960 and Steward 1955 for two approaches to dealing simultaneously with the complexity of the evolution of particular traditions and the general trend. For an authoritative modern treatment of this kind of evolutionism, see Johnson and Earle 2000.
6   E.g., Cohen 1977 on the origin of agriculture. Harris 1977, 1979 and Johnson and Earle 2000 make population pressure the engine of cultural evolution.
7   Richerson, Boyd, and Bettinger 2001; Richerson and Boyd 2001a.
8   For a technical discussion see Boyd and Richerson 1985, chap. 5.
9   Ryan and Gross 1943. Rogers 1983 surveys this literature, counting 3,085 studies from 10 different disciplines as of that date.
10 Rogers with Shoemaker 1971 showed that perceived advantage was one of the commonest effects in studies of the diffusion of innovations. This book did a primitive meta-analysis of some fifteen hundred diffusion-of-innovation studies. Henrich 2001 shows how a quantitative analysis of such adoption data can be used to estimate the influence of the various forces of evolution.
11 Wiessner and Tumu 1998; Yen 1974. See Crosby 1972, 1986 for a discussion of the rapid spread of many New World crops in the Old World following the voyages of Columbus, and of Old World plants and animals in the New.
12 Labov 1994 discusses the principles internal to the structure of language that help drive linguistic evolution.
13 Hamilton 1967; Dawkins 1982; Jablonka and Lamb 1995; Rice 1996.
14 Cavalli-Sforza and Feldman 1981; Dawkins 1976; Durham 1991.
15 "Cornpone Opinions," Twain 1962, 24.
16 See Blackmore 1999 for a review of the work done using the meme concept. Richard Dawkins's foreword to Blackmore's book gives a particularly clear example of how important the high fidelity of transmission is taken to be by Dawkins at least. See Durham and Weingart 1997 for a discussion of alternative proposals for the unit of cultural inheritance. Dennett 1995 in *Darwin's Dangerous Idea* provides an extended argument in favor of the idea that replicators are necessary for cumulative adaptation.
17 Sperber 1996, chap. 5.
18 Sperber 1996; Boyer 1998, 1994; Atran 2001.
19 Burke and Young 2001. In addition to the 1:1 and 2:1 contracts, they also observed a small number of 3:2 contracts, and, even among the highly market-oriented farmers of Illinois, virtually no other shares. Burke and Young also show that farmers don't adjust shares by varying other inputs such as fertilizer or pesticides.
20 Bloom 2001.
21 Mallory 1989.
22 Spelke 1994.
23 Sperber 1996.
24 Tomasello 1999.
25 Bynon 1977.
26 Cavalli-Sforza and Feldman 1976, 1981; Karlin 1979; Lande 1976.
27 Hallpike 1986, 46.
28 Thomason and Kaufman 1988. See also Thomason 2001.
29 Thomason and Kaufman 1988.
30 Ibid.
31 Ibid.
32 Welsch, Terrell, and Nadolski 1992.

33 Jorgensen 1980; Hodder 1978.
34 Dumezil 1958; Hallpike 1986; Mallory 1989, chap. 5.

References

Atran, Scott. 2001. The trouble with memes—Inference versus imitation in cultural creation. *Human Nature— An Interdisciplinary Biosocial Perspective* 12: 351–81.

Blackmore, Susan. 1999. *The meme machine.* Oxford: Oxford Univ. Press.

Bloom, Paul. 2001. *How children learn the meanings of words.* Cambridge. MA: MIT Press.

Boyd, Robert, and Peter J. Richerson. 1985. *Culture and the evolutionary process.* Chicago: Univ. of Chicago Press.

Boyer, Pascal. 1994. *The naturalness of religious ideas: A cognitive theory of religion.* Berkeley, CA: University of California Press.

Boyer, Pascal. 1998. Cognitive tracks of cultural inheritance: How evolved intuitive ontology governs cultural transmission. *American Anthropologist* 100: 876–89.

Burke, Mary A., and Peyton Young. 2001. Competition and custom in economic contracts: A case study of Illinois agriculture. *American Economic Review* 91: 559–73.

Burrow, J. W. 1966. *Evolution and society: A study in Victorian social theory.* Cambridge: Cambridge Univ. Press.

Bynon, Theodora. 1977. *Historical linguistics.* Cambridge: Cambridge Univ. Press.

Carneiro, Robert. 2003. *Evolutionism in cultural anthropology.* Boulder, CO: Westview Press.

Cavalli-Sforza, Luigi L., and Marcus W. Feldman. 1976. Evolution of continuous variation: Direct approach through joint distribution of genotypes and phenotypes. *Proc. Natl. Acad Sci. USA.* 73: 1689–92.

Cavalli-Sforza, Luigi L., and Marcus W. Feldman, 1981. *Cultural transmission and evolution: A quantitative approach.* Monographs in Population Biology, vol. 16. Princeton, NJ: Princeton Univ. Press.

Cohen, Mark N. 1977. *The food crisis in prehistory: Overpopulation and the origins of agriculture.* New Haven, CT: Yale Univ. Press.

Crosby, Alfred W. 1972. *The Columbian exchange: Biological and cultural consequences of 1492.* Westport, CT: Greenwood.

Crosby, Alfred W. 1986. *Ecological imperialism: The biological expansion of Europe, 900–1900.* Studies in Environment and History. Cambridge: Cambridge Univ. Press.

Dawkins, Richard, 1976. *The selfish gene.* Oxford: Oxford Univ. Press.

Dawkins, Richard. 1982. *The extended phenotype: The gene as the unit of selection.* San Francisco: Freeman.

Dennett, Daniel C. 1995. *Darwin's dangerous idea: Evolution and the meanings of life.* New York: Simon & Schuster.

Dumezil, G. G. 1958. *L'Ideologie Tripartie des Indo-Europeens.* Brussels: Collection Latomus, vol. XXXI. *Latomus— Revue d'etudes Latines.*

Durham, William H. 1991. *Coevolution: Genes, culture, and human diversity.* Stanford, CA: Stanford Univ. Press.

Durham, William H. and Peter Weingart. 1997. Units of culture. In *Human by nature: Between biology and the social sciences,* ed. P. Weingart, S. D. Mitchell. P. J. Richerson and S. Maasen, 300–13. Mahwah, NJ: Lawrence Erlbaum Associates.

Hallpike, C. R. 1986. *The principles of social evolution.* New York: Oxford Univ. Press.

Hamilton, William D. 1967. Extraordinary sex ratios. *Science* 156: 477–88.

Harris, Marvin. 1977. *Cannibals and kings: The origins of cultures.* New York: Random House.

Harris, Marvin. 1979. *Cultural materialism: The struggle for a science of culture.* New York: Random House.

Henrich, Joseph. 2001. Cultural transmission and the diffusion of innovations: Adoption dynamics indicate that biased cultural transmission is the predominate force in behavioral change. *American Anthropologist* 103: 992–1013.

Hodder, Ian. 1978. *The spatial organisation of culture, new approaches in archaeology.* Pittsburgh: Univ. of Pittsburgh Press.

Jablonka, Eva, and Marion J. Lamb. 1995. *Epigenetic inheritance and evolution. The Lamarckian dimension.* Oxford: Oxford Univ. Press.

Johnson, Allen W. and Timothy K. Earle. 2000. *The evolution of human societies: From foraging group to agrarian state.* 2nd ed. Stanford, CA: Stanford Univ. Press.

Jorgensen, Joseph G. 1980. *Western Indians: Comparative environments, languages, and cultures of 172 western American Indian tribes.* San Francisco: W. H. Freeman.

Karlin, Samuel. 1979. Models of multifactorial inheritance. 1. Multivariate formulations and basic convergence results. *Theoretical Population Biology* 15: 308–55.

Labov, William.1994. *Principles of linguistic change: Internal factors*. Oxford: Blackwell.

Lande, Russell. 1976. The maintenance of genetic variability by mutation in a polygenic character with linked loci. *Genetic Research* 26: 221–35.

Mallory, J. P. 1989. *In search of the Indo-Europeans: Language, archaeology, and myth*. New York: Thames & Hudson.

Rice, W. R. 1996. Sexually antagonistic male adaptation triggered by experimental arrest of female evolution. *Nature* 381: 232–34.

Richerson, Peter J., and Robert Boyd. 2001a. Institutional evolution in the Holocene: The rise of complex societies. In *The origin of human social Institutions*, ed. W. G. Runciman, 197–234. Oxford: Oxford Univ. Press.

Richerson, Peter J., and Robert Boyd. 2001b. Built for speed, not for comfort: Darwinian theory and human culture. *History and Philosophy of the Life Sciences* 23: 423–63.

Richerson, Peter J., Robert Boyd, and Robert L. Bettinger. 2001. Was agriculture impossible during the Pleistocene but mandatory during the Holocene? A climate change hypothesis. *American Antiquity* 66: 387–411.

Rogers, Everett M. 1983. *Diffusion of Innovations*. 3rd ed., New York: Free Press.

Rogers, Everett M., and F. Floyd Shoemaker. 1971. *Communication of innovations: A cross-cultural approach*. 2nd ed., New York: Free Press.

Ryan, Bryce, and Neal C. Gross. 1943. The diffusion of hybrid seed corn in two Iowa communities. *Rural Sociology* 8: 15-24.

Sahlins, Marshall David, Thomas G. Harding, and Elman Rogers Service. 1960. *Evolution and culture*. Ann Arbor: Univ. of Michigan Press.

Spelke, Elizabeth. 1994. Initial knowledge: Six suggestions. *Cognition* 50: 431–45.

Sperber, Dan. 1996. *Explaining culture: A naturalistic approach*. Oxford: Blackwell.

Steward, Julian II. 1955. *Theory of culture change: The methodology of multilinear evolution*. Urbana: Univ. of Illinois Press.

Thomason, Sarah Grey. 2001. *Language contact: An introduction*. Washington, DC: Georgetown Univ. Press.

Thomason, Sarah Grey, and Terrence Kaufman. 1988. *Language contact, civilization, and genetic linguistics*. Berkeley and Los Angeles: Univ. of California Press.

Tomasello, Michael. 1999. *The cultural origins of human cognition*. Cambridge, MA: Harvard Univ. Press.

Twain, Mark. 1962. *Mark Twain on the damned human race*. Ed. and with an introduction by Janet Smith. 1st ed., New York: Hill & Wang.

Welsch, R. L. J. Terrell, and J. A. Nadolski. 1992. Language and culture on the North Coast of New Guinea. *American Anthropologist* 94: 568–600.

White, Leslie A. 1949. *The science of culture, a study of man and civilization*. New York: Farrar Straus.

Wiessner, Polly, and Akii Tumu. 1998. *Historical vines: Enga networks of exchange, ritual, and warfare in Papua New Guinea*. Smithsonian Series in Ethnographic Inquiry. Washington, DC: Smithsonian Institution Press.

Yen, D. E. 1974. *The sweet potato and Oceania: An essay in ethnobotany*. Honolulu: Bishop Museum Press.

Index